The
HOUSEHOLDERS'
ENCYCLOPEDIA

THE HOUSEHOLDERS' ENCYCLOPEDIA

**Stanley Schuler and
Elizabeth Meriwether Schuler**

SATURDAY REVIEW PRESS

New York

Published simultaneously in Canada by Doubleday Canada Ltd., Toronto.

Library of Congress Catalog Card Number: 74-154281

ISBN 0-8415-0214-5

Saturday Review Press
380 Madison Avenue
New York, New York 10017

Printed in the United States of America

Design by Tere LoPrete

Preface

Many books have been published in past years that instruct and inform the reader on home repair and do-it-yourself projects. *The Householders' Encyclopedia,* however, goes beyond the occasional need to mend or build and offers the reader a complete manual of home care. This helpful, all-inclusive encyclopedia for the house and apartment will assist even the most inexperienced handyman or woman—and both men and women will find this book extremely useful. The range of topics is unlimited: the reader can learn how to arrange storage space in an attic or how to burglarproof the house. There are sections here dealing with maintenance of air conditioners and barbecues, with concrete-mixing and electric motors, and with fixing broken pottery and cleaning brass.

Many jobs are fully illustrated with clear, step-by-step diagrams that explain exactly what each process entails. Laying linoleum is no more complicated than splicing electrical wiring, as the illustrations clearly indicate. Explanations for papering a wall, tying unusual knots, and repairing a roof are also accompanied by helpful drawings.

This book provides important information about the products every householder uses daily, and will serve as a guide to ensure prevention of common accidents. The reader will find invaluable safety advice in this manual about faulty electrical wiring, heating equipment, cooking equipment, and dangerous chemicals.

This encyclopedia will be a welcome member of every household. Regardless of the problem, the careful instructions and detailed diagrams will make every home owner, renter, or apartment dweller an expert around the house.

The
HOUSEHOLDERS' ENCYCLOPEDIA

Abaca Fiber. A tough Philippine vegetable fiber used to make manila rope and also occasionally woven into table mats, etc. Clean by wiping with mild detergent solution. If one of the fibers in a mat is broken, cut it out or try to glue it together with white glue.

Abrasives. There is no need to stock up on a lot of different abrasives, because you can never be sure what your next project will require. But there are some you should keep on hand at all times.

Sandpaper is the workhorse abrasive. You use it for all kinds of work—from removing old, scarred paint to achieving the finest satin finish in varnish.

When you buy sandpaper, the basic choice is between ordinary flint paper and production paper. The latter is almost three times as expensive, but because it is made with an exceptionally tough grit, it sands about ten times faster and lasts about ten times longer.

While most sandpaper of both the standard and production types is designed for dry work only, some sandpaper can be used also for wet sanding of paint and other finishes. When used wet, a little soapy water is sprinkled on the surface to be sanded, or the paper is dipped in water. The water acts as a lubricant which keeps the paper from scratching and helps prevent it from clogging with particles of paint.

Sandpaper is available in grades from extra-coarse—No. 16—to exceptionally fine—No. 600. Most handymen rarely need anything finer than No. 150.

Large sheets of sandpaper are a better buy than packets of small sheets, because the latter contain an assortment of grades, many of which are too fine to be used very often. Large sheets are easy to tear or cut into usable pieces of any size.

The cardinal rule in sanding—as in using all other abrasives—is to work with the grain. Another rule when giving a piece of painted, varnished, or otherwise finished wood its final finish is never to sand too long or too hard in one spot, because the friction creates heat which destroys the finish and clogs the sandpaper.

For rough work—as in sanding siding on a house—sandpaper is held in your hand and pressed against the wood with your fingers. But when doing fine sanding—as on a piece of furniture—you should wrap the paper around a block of wood to assure even pressure on the sanded surface. Wrap it around a broomstick when sanding a concave surface; inside a curved piece of linoleum when sanding a convex surface.

When you sand a flat surface, such as a table top, be careful not to apply more pressure at the edges than in the middle.

Emery cloth is similar to sandpaper except that the grit, derived from a granular mineral substance called emery, is applied to fabric. This makes it much more flexible and easier to use on rounded and irregular surfaces. It is used on metal as well as on wood.

The cloth comes in fine, medium, and coarse grades.

Steel wool, although available in coarse grades, is not so coarse as the coarsest sandpaper and is therefore used mainly for final finishing of wood surfaces. It is also excellent for cleaning metal, smooth masonry materials, and other materials on which sandpaper would be almost useless. It can be used dry or with any kind of nonflammable solvent.

Grades range from No. 0000 (finest) to No. 3.

Wear gloves when working with steel wool, especially the coarse grades: the particles are needle sharp and form nasty splinters. To protect your eyes, do not blow the particles off a surface; wipe them off slowly instead. On furniture and other fine work, it is advisable to use a rag slightly moistened with turpentine or water to remove every vestige of the wool. You must do this if you intend to apply latex paint to a surface, because the water in the paint will cause any steel threads that are left to rust

Bronze wool is similar to steel wool but made of bronze. It should be used in place of steel wool when you are working on a boat or other article which will be in frequent contact with water, since the small particles left in the wood will not rust and cause stains.

Spun glass blocks, which resemble a very soft pumice stone, are sometimes used in cabinet work to smooth and shape wood. They cut very rapidly, but in the process they are worn out very rapidly, leaving a fine black dust over everything.

Pumice stone is a very fine powder used to bring furniture wood to a high luster or to soften the luster on varnish or similar glossy finishes. Apply the powder with a piece of dense cloth, such as felt, dipped in salad oil or water. Do not use a great deal of pressure, and clean the surface frequently to see how the work is going. When you finally achieve the desired effect, remove all traces of the stone with a damp cloth; otherwise the final finish will be cloudy.

Rottenstone is a powder similar to pumice stone but less scratchy. It is used in the same way to achieve the finest possible polish on finished furniture. It is also used to polish metal.

Liquid sandpaper is an extremely toxic liquid used to wash and remove the gloss on paint so a new coat of paint will adhere tightly. Thus it performs one of the minor functions of an abrasive, though it cannot properly be called an abrasive.

ABS Plastics. ABS stands for acrylonitrile-butadiene-styrene. These strong, tough plastics are used in pipe and pipe fittings, tool handles, utensil handles, radio cabinets, etc. They can be cleaned with detergent solution. If broken, mend them with plastic-mending adhesive.

Acetate. Cellulose acetate (the proper name) is a plastic which is used in such solid articles as lampshades, playing cards, and spectacle frames. It is also woven into a fabric much like rayon. The material withstands moderate heat and freezing temperatures, oil, gasoline, and most household chemicals. But it is dissolved or damaged by alcohol, alkalis, acetone, and acetic acid.

Solid articles can be cleaned with a mild detergent in warm water or with a cleaning fluid, but should not be scrubbed with anything abrasive. If broken, articles can be reglued with a plastic-mending adhesive.

Acetate fabrics can be machine-washed in warm water and rinsed in cold. Dry in a dryer at low heat for about 15 minutes or hang on a line without clothespins. Iron at low heat, as for rayon—preferably before the fabric is completely dry. The fabric can also be dry-cleaned.

Acetone. A solvent most commonly found in the home in the form of fingernail polish remover. It dissolves a number of materials, including acetate, rayon, and acrylic, and must therefore be used with care. It is also highly flammable.

Acoustical Tile. Acoustical tiles are porous surfacing materials designed to absorb noise and thus make the rooms in which they are used quieter. They do not stop the transmission of noise from one room to another.

Although the tiles are made of various materials, in various sizes, and with various surface finishes, all are effective in controlling noise to some degree. When buying tiles, however, you should be sure to ask about their "noise-reduction coefficient." In rooms that are noisy—kitchens and family rooms, for example—use tiles with a coefficient of .60 to .70. Elsewhere you need a coefficient of only .40 to .50.

Acoustical tiles are usually installed only on the ceiling; but if this fails to reduce the noise in a room sufficiently, you can also install them on one or more walls or in a frieze on all walls. Thick carpets, heavy draperies, and upholstered furniture also help to absorb noise.

In an existing house, the tiles are cemented directly to the ceilings. And it's a good idea to install them in the same way in a new house because the base material—usually gypsum board—helps to reduce sound transmission between rooms. The ceiling base must, of course, be sound, dry, and level. Use the adhesive recommended by the tile manufacturer. Just dab a little of this on the back of each tile near the four corners and press the tile in place.

In a new house, or if old ceilings are in poor condition, tiles can be nailed or stapled to 1-by-3-inch wood furring strips which are themselves nailed to the joists or old ceiling. Or in a room with a very high ceiling, you can slip the tiles into a grid of metal channels hung at any height.

Whatever the installation method, it is very important to install the tiles from the center of the ceiling toward the sides as described under *Floors, Resilient* (page 106). Otherwise the border tiles at opposite ends and opposite sides of the room will not be of uniform width.

Tiles that are loose or badly stained can easily be cut out of a ceiling and replaced. Interlocking flanges on the new tile will have to be cut off, as a rule. The tile is then installed with nails or adhesive.

If tiles are permanently soiled or stained, or if you want to change their color, you can paint them with any kind of paint. Even repeated painting should not reduce their sound-absorbing ability. The paint should, however, be thinned more than usual; and ideally it should be applied with a spray gun.

Most tiles can be washed with a detergent solution and rinsed. Nonwashable tiles must be cleaned with a dough cleaner like that used on nonwashable wallpaper.

Acrilan. Trade name for Monsanto's acrylic fiber.

Acrylic. The acrylics rank high as versatile and useful plastics. In solid forms, they are strong and rigid, resist blows and staining. But they are easily scratched, and over a long period may yellow slightly from exposure to light.

In fibers, acrylics resemble wool. They are resilient, resistant to abrasion, mildew, and moths, nonallergenic, slow to soil, and easy to clean.

Both the solids and the fibers are resistant to common household chemicals and oil, but are damaged by cleaning fluids, gasoline, perfume, and acetone. They cannot withstand temperatures over 180 degrees.

To clean solid acrylic articles, dust with a soft, damp cloth; wash with a nonabrasive detergent and water—don't put them in a dishwasher. Waxing with an automobile paste wax maintains a soft luster and also helps to conceal shallow scratches. Broken articles can be glued with plastic-mending adhesive.

Acrylic fabrics are washed in warm water and rinsed in cool. They should be removed from the washer as soon as they are rinsed to keep wrinkles from setting. They can then be hung on a line to dry, or they can be dried in a dryer at low heat for about 15 minutes, followed by 10 minutes of tumbling without heat. Iron with a cool iron.

For how to clean acrylic carpets, see *Rugs.*

Aerosols. Over 300 different products are presently packaged in aerosol cans or bottles, and the number continues to grow. This is not because the products are better than those packaged in other ways but because they are usually more convenient to use. They save time, make little mess, do not spill if turned over, deteriorate very little, and can in some cases be used in otherwise hard-to-get-at places.

Aerosols contain a liquid or gas propellant. When you press the actuator button on top of the container, the propellant ejects the product in the container from the nozzle. Although we generally think of aerosols as spraying devices, some put out a mist, stream, foam, or droplets.

Most aerosols are continuous-dispensing devices; that is, the product comes out of them as long as your finger is on the actuator button. But other types of aerosols have been introduced in recent years. One of the most useful is called Preval. It consists of a container of propellant and a separate bottle. All you do is fill the bottle with paint, insecticide, or whatever you want to apply as a spray, screw it to the container of propellant, and press the valve. As a paint sprayer, the Preval is valuable because it allows you to spray any kind of paint. (The paints put up in conventional aerosol cans are special formulations.) For instance, you can paint the front surfaces of a radiator with a brush; then paint the inner surfaces by spraying.

How to use aerosols. There is certainly nothing very mysterious about using aerosols; nevertheless, many people do not use them properly. Several rules should be followed:

1. Read the directions on the container.

2. Hold the container as directed. If you don't, the aerosol may not work or may work improperly. It may also run out of propellant before you have used all the product.

3. Use the aerosol well away from your face. The propellant is normally not hazardous; but if you should breathe in a lot of it, it might be.

4. Don't inhale the spray mist. Some of the products put up in aerosols are poisonous.

5. Keep aerosols away from children.

6. Separate aerosols containing foods from those containing other products.

7. Never expose aerosol cans or bottles to the heat of a range, radiator, or furnace or to full sunlight. Don't keep them in a closed-up parked car in the summer.

8. Do not puncture or break an aerosol container.

9. When you are about to throw out an aerosol, make sure it is empty by depressing the actuator button and holding it until nothing more comes out. Then place the container in a garbage can. Do not put it in an incinerator, compactor, or fire.

Air Cleaners. Less than 10 percent of the dust, smoke, gas, smog, pollen, and other particles that fill the air inside your house are visible. Yet it has been determined that a city home accumulates an average of 2 pounds of dust every week. The big, visible particles settle rapidly out of the air on horizontal surfaces. The invisible particles settle much more slowly on vertical and underside surfaces as well as on top of horizontal surfaces.

Coping with the debris that pollutes the air is a much more difficult task today than it was in the past. Cleaning the house with a dust cloth, dust mop, and vacuum cleaner hardly scratches the surface. That's why we are hearing more and more about a new mechanism called an air cleaner that is supposed to snatch particles out of the air before they have a chance to settle and cling to the many surfaces in the home.

There are several types of air cleaner. Their efficiency, which varies widely, is measured by two methods—the weight method and the National Bureau of Standards' dust-spot method. Only the latter gives an accurate picture because it evaluates the air cleaner's efficiency in removing both visible and invisible particles from the air. By contrast, the weight method is concerned only with the visible particles.

Most of the air cleaners made for residential use are designed for installation in the return duct of a forced warm-air heating system or central air-conditioning system. The simplest of these—a standard feature on all modern warm-air heating plants—is known as a viscous-impingement-type filter. It is a flat frame containing a fibrous material such as fiberglass which is coated on one side with a viscous film. It has a dust-spot efficiency of 5 to 10 percent.

Self-charging electrostatic filters resemble the viscous filters but are filled with shredded polystyrene, a material which, like a nylon carpet, holds a static charge and therefore attracts and captures small dust particles. These filters have an efficiency of 15 to 20 percent; but the efficiency decreases as the humidity in the house rises.

Charged-media filters are fibrous or metal plates that are given a high-voltage charge that attracts the particles passing over them. They have an efficiency of 20 to 40 percent.

Best of all the air cleaners are the two-stage electronic, or electrostatic, devices. They remove large particles with a screen. Smaller particles going through the screen enter a treatment chamber, where they are given a strong electrical charge. They then enter a collecting chamber where they are trapped by a series of charged metal plates. These air cleaners are so efficient that they have a dust-spot rating of 70 to 95 percent.

Portable two-stage electronic air cleaners are made for use in homes that do not have a ducted heating or air-conditioning system. The largest can clean the air in a room measuring about 20 by 30 feet.

All air cleaners must be cleaned periodically to remove the accumulated dirt. In some cases, this is done by washing; in other cases, the filters are replaced. Deluxe models of two-stage electronic filters wash and dry themselves. The wash cycle is controlled by either a manual dial or an automatic timer.

Operating an air cleaner. No air cleaner, whether it's an inexpensive filter or an expensive two-stage device, can snatch dirt and other particles from the air in the house once they have settled on a surface. The dirt must be in the air stream passing through the cleaner. It is obvious, therefore, that the best way to remove the greatest possible amount of dirt from your house is to keep the furnace blower operating all the time. By thus changing the air throughout the house the dirt is given less time to settle.

The other obvious way to eliminate as much dirt as possible in the house is to keep your doors and windows shut.

Air Conditioners, Central. A central air conditioner is a large electrical refrigerating mechanism that cools, dehumidifies, filters, and circulates the air within a house in summer. The conditioner is usually installed in connection with a forced warm-air heating system burning gas or oil, and uses the same ductwork. But in homes with hot water or steam heat, the air conditioner is installed by itself and has its own system of ducts.

A central air conditioner is purchased when you want to cool your entire house. You could, of course, cool the house by putting several room air conditioners into strategically located rooms; but these would not perform as efficiently and economically as a central unit. Furthermore, they add nothing to the beauty of the house indoors or out.

Families living in centrally air-conditioned houses cite several principal benefits: They sleep better. They have fewer allergies. Their general health is improved. They spend less money on vacations and recreation outside the home. And because the doors and windows are kept shut, all housecleaning chores are substantially reduced.

How an air conditioner works. An air conditioner is a heat-transfer device; that is, it takes heat from one place and transfers it to another. The principle of heat transfer can be seen in many commonplace phenomena. For example, when a block of ice is placed in a picnic food container, heat from the air in the container is absorbed by the ice and the air in the container becomes cold. As the ice continues to absorb heat, it begins to melt. The water dripping out of the container's drain is actually carrying heat away—in effect, transferring it to the ground.

An air conditioner does the same thing, but more effectively. Made in two parts, it consists of an indoor section which absorbs heat from the home and transfers it to an outdoor section, where it is dissipated into the atmosphere.

The way an air conditioner works is quite simple: A refrigerant which circulates continuously through the system cools the indoor evaporator coils. The cold coils (like the block of ice) absorb heat from the indoor air, which is drawn into the air conditioner through ducts by a large fan. The cooled, dehumidified air is then returned to the house through the supply ducts.

Having absorbed heat from the room air through the cold coils, the refrigerant proceeds to boil and changes to a gaseous state. It is then drawn into a compressor, where the gas is put under greater pressure with a resultant increase in temperature.

From the compressor the gas enters the condenser coils facing outdoors. Because the gas is much hotter than the outdoor air being circulated over the coils by a fan, the heat dissipates into the air. This, in turn, lowers the temperature and pressure of the gas, and it condenses back into a liquid state.

As the liquid passes through a capillary tube, the pressure and temperature drop still lower, and finally the cold liquid passes into the evaporator coils once again.

Because the process is continuous, the evaporator coils are cold at all times.

Types of air conditioner. Basically, central air-conditioning equipment falls into two general categories: the single-package system and the split system. Both systems provide exactly the same kind of cooling. The decision to use one system rather than the other is generally based on the technical and economic requirements of the particular installation.

In the single-package unit, all components of the air conditioner—the evaporator, compressor, condenser, fan, and blower—are contained in one cabinet. If the cabinet is placed deep inside the house, heat from the condenser coils is carried outdoors through ducts. However, if the system is installed through an exterior wall, no venting is required. The adaptability of the single-package system also allows it to be mounted completely outdoors on a slab next to the house or even on the roof. In this case, a short length of ductwork connects the equipment to the duct distribution system inside the house.

Single-package units that incorporate gas-fired heating furnaces with the cooling equipment are available. These devices are generally mounted on the roof or on a ground-level slab.

In the split system, the two parts of the air conditioner are separated: the evaporator with blower is located completely indoors, while the condenser section and compressor are outdoors. For many years, split systems were put in place and charged with refrigerant at the site. This was a time-consuming and costly operation. Today, while on-site charging is sometimes used, most air conditioners are charged at the factory. This has cut installation costs markedly.

The split system can be installed in a variety of ways and its versatility has made it popular over the years. Generally, the outdoor section is mounted on a slab or placed through the foundation wall. The indoor section is installed in the attic, suspended from the basement ceiling, set on the basement floor, or tucked into a closet.

Heat pumps. A heat pump is also called a reverse-cycle air conditioner. In summer, it cools the house. In winter, it automatically reverses itself and heats the house. In the latter case, instead of taking heat from the house and dissipating it outdoors, it takes heat from the outdoor air (or sometimes from water in a well) and discharges it into the house.

In milder climates, where winter temperatures rarely dip much below the freezing mark, a heat pump is quite economical to operate because it is able to extract all the heat it generates from the outdoor air. The only thing you must pay for is the electricity to run the pump. In colder climates, however, supplementary resistance heaters are built into the heat pump to augment the supply of heat extracted from the outdoor air. These raise the operating cost considerably. Even so, heat pumps are being installed in many northern areas where electric rates are low.

How large an air conditioner do you need? This must be figured carefully because it's obvious that if your air conditioner is too small, it won't cool your house adequately. On the other hand, if it is too large, it will be inefficient and expensive to run. Furthermore, it will not be able to reduce humidity in the house as fast as it can lower the temperature; as a result, the house may feel cold and clammy.

The size of an air conditioner is stated in terms of its cooling capacity. This is measured in British thermal units per hour according to standards established by the Air Conditioning & Refrigeration Institute. More than 90 percent of the central air conditioners and heat pumps on the market today carry the ARI seal indicating that the stated capacity of the units is certified by this organization.

To determine whether you need a central air conditioner with a capacity of 40,000 Btu/hr or 60,000 Btu/hr is a complicated business which you should not undertake yourself. If you plan to air condition an existing house or a new custom-built house, ask two or three reputable, reliable air-conditioning contractors to inspect the house (or plans) and then to submit details and estimates of the work to be done.

In making his survey of the house, each contractor must determine how much "heat gain" can be expected in the entire house as well as in each room. To arrive at this answer, he must take into consideration such things as the size of the entire house; the size of each room; the size, number, and orientation of the windows; the construction of the exterior walls and roof; the planting around the house; the number of persons in the family; how many guests you have frequently; etc.

Once these facts are established, the contractor—with the aid of a load-estimating form developed by the Air Conditioning & Refrigeration Institute—can determine what size and type of air conditioner you need. It should be pointed out that if you invite three contractors to give you estimates and one of them comes up with a recommendation for a unit that is substantially smaller or larger than the others, you should not make a move to proceed with the project until you learn the reason for the discrepancy.

Ductwork. An air-conditioning system is only as good as the installation.

The ductwork and registers for each room should be sized in accordance with the heat-gain calculation for the room. The registers should be located where the greatest heat gain occurs—near a picture window, for example.

A return air grille and duct for each level of the house must be provided to carry the air in the living and sleeping areas back to the air conditioner where it is cooled, dehumidified, and filtered again.

If the cooling system being installed will be independent of the heating system, the contractor should install the registers high on the walls or in the ceiling. This is because cool air tends to flow downward.

On the other hand, if the cooling system is being combined with a warm-air heating system, the location of the registers depends on where you live. For example, if you live in a warm climate where cooling is more important than heating, the registers should be placed high on the walls or in the ceiling. But if you live in a cold climate where heating is of top importance, the registers should be placed in the walls just above the floors. In this case, however, you should install double-deflection registers that can be adjusted to deflect cool air upward and warm air downward.

In speaking to your contractor about the ductwork installation, you should find out whether he ordinarily uses wire or straps to suspend the ducts from the ceilings. The latter are better because they are stronger. The contractor should also use a flexible connection, such as canvas, between the main duct and the air conditioner in order to deaden the noise made by the air conditioner and blower.

Another thing to ask the contractor is if he uses ductwork that is stamped with a long X pattern. This pattern tends to reinforce the ducts and to eliminate vibratory noises which may occur otherwise.

Wiring. All central air conditioners require their own 240-volt circuits. Generally, if your house has a 100-amp main service, there is adequate capacity to operate a conventional air conditioner. But if you install a heat pump, a larger service is usually required.

Central air conditioner features. One of the few unusual central air conditioner features is a two-stage system employing a split evaporator connected to two separate condensing units. Under normal heat-load conditions, one condenser and one-half the evaporator are sufficient to control humidity and hold indoor temperatures at comfortable levels. As the heat load increases, the second condenser turns on to maintain the temperature called for by the thermostat. The system reduces current consumption. Of greater importance, it reduces the possibility of the contractor's installing an air conditioner that is too small or too large for the house.

Other features touted by air-conditioner manufacturers are to be found in most units made. Consequently, the things you should look for in an air conditioner are not its features but its overall quality. Is it sturdily constructed? Is the condensing unit well protected against the weather? Does it operate quietly? Can you get at the filters readily?

Operating a central air conditioner. Start the air conditioner at a rather high-temperature setting to give it time to warm up and also to bring down the temperature and humidity in the house. Let it continue at this setting for about 24 hours; then gradually lower the thermostat one degree at a time until you hit the right level of comfort. Keep it at this point from then on except: (1) when you are going to give a big party, reduce the temperature about three degrees several hours before your guests arrive; (2) when the weather is cloudy and humid, reduce the temperature one or two degrees in order to keep indoor humidity from building up.

Run your air conditioner continuously when the weather is hot. You may save a few pennies if you turn it off; but since starting and stopping wear out an electric motor faster than continuous operation, the latter should help to prolong the life of your air conditioner. And it will also keep your house more comfortable.

Set the blower to operate steadily so that you have continuous air circulation throughout the house even when the thermostat is not calling for cooling.

Keep the house closed up tight. An open window not only wastes money and comfort but may also upset the operation of the air conditioner. In hot climates, it even pays to install insulating glass in windows to reduce loss of cooled air. In the north, if you have combination screens and storm windows, close the storm sash.

Shade windows exposed to the hot sun with blinds, shades, or awnings.

Don't block the supply registers or returns.

How to take care of a central air-conditioning system. Check the filter once a month and replace or clean it whenever it is dirty—probably three or four times during the cooling season.

In the spring and fall, lubricate the blower and motor which circulate the air in the house and the fan and motor in the condensing unit. Use SAE No. 30 oil. Wipe dust from the blower blades. Clean the

condensing unit thoroughly every spring and inspect it monthly thereafter. Dirt, leaves, and grass clippings will reduce the condenser's efficiency. If rust spots appear on the housing, sand them well and apply a rust inhibitor and final coat of paint.

If blower and duct dampers are adjustable, they should be set at high-speed, or summer, settings in the spring and at low-speed, or winter, settings before the heating season.

Because of the cost and complexity of a central air conditioner, it is advisable to have it serviced every spring by a heating-cooling contractor. The heating system should be serviced in the fall.

If something goes wrong. Check whether the thermostat and other controls are properly set; whether the filters are clogged; whether the house current is on.

If ice forms on the cooling coil, turn the air conditioner off for a couple of hours to let it melt. If ice forms again after you restart the unit, call a serviceman.

If the compressor starts to cycle rapidly, turn it off at once and call for help.

Air Conditioners, Room. Like a central air conditioner, a room air conditioner lowers the temperature and humidity and filters the air. Depending on the model, it may also recirculate room air without cooling it, exhaust stale air, and bring in fresh air.

Small room units are effective only in the room in which they are installed; hence their name. But many large units will cool three or four rooms or even an entire small house.

The great majority of room air conditioners are air-cooled units which must be installed partly inside and partly outside the house. Ordinarily they are placed on the sill of a double-hung or casement window; but this location interferes with the view and reduces the amount of light admitted. In new houses and apartments, therefore, air conditioners are now usually mounted in a hole cut through an outside wall. This may be below or above a window, above a door—anyplace you like.

Room air conditioners are generally designed for cooling only. Heat-pump models, however, cool the house in summer and heat it in winter. For more about how they work, see *Air Conditioners, Central—Heat Pumps* (page 8).

As with central air conditioners, the cooling capacity of room conditioners is expressed in Btu/hr, but the organization that establishes the standards for rating room air conditioners is the Association of Home Appliance Manufacturers (AHAM). Room units are available with capacities of about 4000 Btu/hr up to 32,000 Btu/hr. The size you need should be determined by an appliance dealer after he makes an inspection of the room or rooms you want to cool.

The dealer will also tell you whether you can plug the air conditioner into an existing wiring circuit or whether you must install a new circuit. This depends on the voltage and amperage of the model recommended.

Room air conditioners operate on 120 or 240 volts alternating current. If you buy a 120-volt unit which operates at less than 7.5 amps, you can plug it into an existing 120-volt, 15-amp circuit. If it is rated above 7.5 amps, however, it requires a separate circuit of its own.

All 240-volt air conditioners need a separate circuit with special wiring. In an old house, the cost of installing this is fairly high. On the other hand, the cost of operating a 240-volt air conditioner is usually lower than the cost of operating a 120-volt model of comparable size. The initial cost of the conditioner may be lower, too.

Air conditioner features. These do not vary greatly between makes. But the following features which are not found in all models are desirable if you are not trying to economize: an automatic thermostat; a fan with two or three speeds; and a fresh-air intake and stale-air exhaust. In addition, you should consider how quiet an air conditioner is when operating at top fan speed and how easy it is to clean the filter.

Operating a room air conditioner. Since air conditioners are heavy and bulky, let the dealer install a large unit for you. If you put in a small window unit, follow the manufacturer's installation instructions carefully.

If a conditioner is exposed for long hours to the sun, erect some kind of shade over it; otherwise its efficiency will drop.

For fastest cooling and greatest air movement, select the highest fan speed. Low speed is best for normal use, however—especially at night.

Remove and clean the filter every month during the cooling season. Made of metal or plastic, it can be washed under a stream of water. If you live in a dirty city, you should also have the entire unit steam-cleaned every couple of years.

Oil the fan motor at the start of every cooling season.

If the air conditioner freezes up, turn it off for a few hours and then restart it. When a heat-pump model that you are using for heating begins to cool down, the outside coils are frozen. You can correct matters by switching the unit to cooling for a few minutes. Then turn back to heating.

If something goes wrong. Check the following points before calling a serviceman:

Is the conditioner plugged in?

Has the fuse blown?

Is the filter clean? (The conditioner will labor if it is not.)

Has the air conditioner frozen up? (See above.)

If the air conditioner is noisy, check whether the grille is loose and whether the conditioner is sitting securely on the windowsill.

Alabaster. A white, smooth, fine-grained stone from which decorative objects are made. Clean with mild detergent solution. Treat like marble if badly stained. If an object is broken, clean and dry the broken edges, apply epoxy glue, and press together.

Alcohol. A solvent for shellac and alcohol-based paints, stains from carbon paper, iodine, grass stains, etc. For painting purposes, denatured alcohol is usually used. Rubbing alcohol, which is milder and safer, is used otherwise (and may be used in painting as well).

Alpaca. Alpaca is the lustrous, wool-like hair of a South American animal closely related to the llama. It is woven into a fabric which is also called alpaca and is sometimes used in rugs. Clean it like wool.

Aluminum. Aluminum is used in and around the house for siding, roofing, gutters and leaders, wiring, windows, sliding glass doors, screens, ladders, cooking utensils, and many other things. The material has an excellent strength-to-weight ratio, does not rust and is relatively low in cost. But it is not without a few problems.

For one thing, while it does not rust, it does corrode—develop pits, holes, and an unsightly crustiness—when exposed to salt air and polluted industrial atmospheres. Some alloys, it is true, are more resistant to corrosion than others; and for this reason, it is a good idea to buy the more expensive aluminum products rather than the cheap articles made of lightweight alloys. But an even better way to keep aluminum outdoors from disintegrating is to buy products that are coated at the factory with a tough, baked-on finish.

A second problem with aluminum is that it is difficult to join by soldering. Consequently, broken articles are difficult to repair; and gutters are difficult to make completely watertight.

Because aluminum is fairly soft, it scratches and bends rather easily.

Finally—a minor problem—aluminum is corroded rapidly by concrete and therefore should not come into direct contact with it. (You can, however, insert it in concrete if it is coated with asphalt roofing cement.)

How to repair aluminum. Holes. Dab plastic metal on small holes. On larger holes, apply an aluminum patch with epoxy glue.

Dents. Try to work these out with your fingers. If this can't be done, hold a block of wood against the concave side and tap the metal with another block of wood or hard rubber mallet. Don't work from the center out but from the edges in.

Metal, torn. Overlap the edges (or apply a patch if overlapping is impossible) and rivet the pieces together with aluminum rivets, or screw together with aluminum self-tapping screws. If the joint must be watertight, coat the overlapped edges with epoxy glue or silicone or polysulfide rubber caulking compound. For instructions on soldering aluminum, see *Soldering.*

Heavy metal, broken. Glue with epoxy.

Metal, corroded. If it is not corroded badly, you can smooth the surface to some extent with steel wool or emery cloth. Otherwise use a file.

How to clean aluminum. Metal with a baked-on finish is cleaned with a detergent solution. Add a chlorine bleach if the surface is mildewed. Use naphtha or cleaning fluid to remove grease, tar, or oil-based caulking compound; and rinse well afterwards.

Aluminum with a natural finish is cleaned in the same way; but if dirt is stubborn, scrub with naval jelly. You can also use very fine steel wool on aluminum that is not anodized. (To test whether aluminum is anodized, rub a clean, lacquer-free spot with a pencil eraser. If a bright spot appears, an anodized finish has been applied.)

To protect aluminum. If a natural finish is desired, an application of any good wax—such as a white cleaning wax—will protect aluminum indoors. Outdoors, apply two coats of methacrylate lacquer.

If a colored finish is desired, clean the metal well and brush on a primer coat of zinc chromate. Follow this with one or two coats of any good exterior trim paint.

Aluminum Foil. This indispensable wrapping material is commonly available in supermarkets in standard and heavy-duty grades and in several widths. The finish is generally smooth. Lightly embossed foils are also available but have no particular advantages.

For the use of foil as a food wrap, see *Food Wraps.* The material has a number of additional uses. You can, for example, use it as a smooth disposable surface on which to mix epoxy glue. Or you can spread it in a drip pan under an automobile to catch grease and oil.

Use it also to line the bottoms of roasting pans and electric ovens, and the reflector pans under electric range surface units. You can even cover the entire top of a range, except for the burners, when you're cooking something that splatters badly.

If aluminum or wood gutters leak, coat the troughs with asphalt roofing cement or rubber caulking compound and smooth a piece of foil into it.

Damaged aluminum flashing can be repaired temporarily in the same way.

Tack or staple foil over mouse holes (aluminum flashing is better, however).

Wrap foil tightly around paintbrush bristles to protect them. If you must put off cleaning brushes for a few hours, you can keep the paint from hardening by wrapping them in foil.

Angora. A wool-like material made from the lustrous hair of the Angora goat. It is also called mohair. Launder like wool.

Anidex. Anidex is a new elastic fiber that can be blended with many other fibers without changing their natural appearance. It also has high resistance to sunlight, heat, and many household chemicals. Its principal uses are in clothing and upholstery fabrics which are meant to conform to the contours of the furniture.

Anidex can be machine-washed and dried at normal settings. Unlike spandex, it is unaffected by chlorine bleaches. The recommended ironing temperature is below 320 degrees.

Antique Satin. A fabric woven from several fibers and with a slubbed texture (rough, prominent, irregular horizontal lines). It is used for draperies, bedspreads, and upholstery. It should be dry-cleaned.

Ants. See *Pest Control.*

Armetale (arm-met-*tale*). A heavy alloy of ten metals used in tableware and ornaments. The pieces are hand-cast, and have a pewter-like finish and a slightly undulating and imperfect surface which adds to their beauty. They can be used for baking and surface cooking.

Armetale is washed with a mild detergent solution or in a dishwasher. If stained, clean it with brass polish.

Armoire. A tall, deep, heavy but movable cabinet for hanging clothes. It was yesterday's clothes closet. Today it is commonly called a wardrobe. Take care of it as you would any piece of wood furniture.

Arnel. Celanese Corporation's trade name for its triacetate fiber.

Asbestos Cement. See *Roofs, Asbestos-Cement,* and *Walls, Asbestos-Cement.*

Ash Trays. An ash tray is supposed to keep smokers from scattering ashes all around the house and to protect the furniture. But it is an obvious fact that many ash trays fail to do their job because they are poorly designed.

To be effective, ash trays should meet the following requirements: The base should be wide and flat so that the ash tray cannot be tipped easily. The rim should be narrow and devoid of cigarette and pipe holders (thus forcing smokers to put cigarettes all the way into the tray so they cannot fall out). The bowl should be deep enough—preferably ¾ inch or more—to contain the cigarettes.

It is also desirable that ash trays be made of material that is not damaged or stained by burning matches and tobacco, and that they be dishwasher-proof.

Note that one of the best-designed and handsomest ash trays meeting most of the above requirements is a ceramic bowl set in a partial metal sheath. But these trays must never be put in a dishwasher or allowed to soak in a sink because water gets between the bowl and the sheath and slowly drips out on the table even when you think you have dried them perfectly.

Asphalt Tile. See *Floors, Asphalt-Tile.*

Attic Storage. Some people go to great lengths to arrange special storage facilities in the attic; others do not. One approach is as good as the other. If there are any rules for storing things in the attic, they are the following:

1. Because attics generally reach furnace-like temperatures in the summer, do not store in them anything that will melt—candles, for example.

2. Because attic temperatures may also drop below freezing in winter, don't store in them anything that may be damaged by freezing.

3. If large attic louvers face the prevailing wind, they should be covered in winter to keep out snow, which may melt on stored articles.

4. If you store anything in which mice may nest, keep it in tight chests or boxes—preferably chests that are lined with aluminum sheet.

5. Beware of moths.

6. Whether you build special storage facilities or not, try to group stored articles logically so that you will know where

to look for them. If you keep an inventory of what is in the attic and where, so much the better.

7. Install enough lights so that you can see what you are looking for.

8. Make sure attic stairs are sturdy (disappearing stairs frequently are not).

Awls. See *Tools, Workshop—Brad awl.*

Awnings. Awnings are made of cotton duck, drill, or canvas; painted aluminum or fiberglass. The last two are by far the most durable and easy to maintain because you can hose them off when dirty; but they are permanently installed and hideous.

Fabric awnings are usually put up in the spring and taken down in the fall—a simple but fussy little job. Before installing them, dust thoroughly and, if necessary, scrub with a heavy-duty detergent and rinse well.

Fabric awnings that become very dirty and stained can be made somewhat more presentable by brushing on one or two coats of paint made for application to canvas.

If fabric is torn, glue a patch of the same material to the underside with fabric-mending adhesive. If the patch is very large, stitch it on a sewing machine as well.

If an awning leaks through the pores, spray or brush on a waterproofing compound made for use on tents and sold by sporting goods stores.

When storing awnings, let them hang open if possible. Otherwise, roll or fold them loosely. Don't crease.

Axes. See *Tools, Workshop.*

Axminster. A well-known type of woven rug named for an English town. See *Rugs.*

Bacon Cooker. A toaster-sized and -shaped electrical appliance which cooks up to eight slices of bacon on a vertical cooking surface, then turns itself off and keeps the bacon warm.

Bamboo. As used in the home—primarily in furniture and sometimes in knife handles—bamboo is usually varnished. If this is scratched, sand it well and touch up with well-thinned varnish.

If bamboo is broken, coat the edges with white wood glue and clamp them together for 24 hours. A wood dowel inserted in the bamboo can be used to reinforce the mend.

Clean bamboo with detergent solution.

Barbecues, Indoor. The idea of building a barbecue into the kitchen or family room so you can have charcoal-broiled steaks the year round is appealing. But there is a major problem that must be overcome.

The barbecue itself is of minor concern. It is usually nothing more than a heavy metal box with grids. A motorized rotisserie available as an extra may be installed above it. Some barbecues burn charcoal; others burn gas which heats ceramic coals; still others use electricity.

Most barbecues are installed in a raised masonry hearth and are completely surrounded by masonry; but if the barbecue is encased in an insulated shell, it can be recessed in any counter alongside wood cabinets. Gas grills, of course, require a gas line. Electric grills require their own 240-volt circuit.

But the installation of the barbecue does not end here. You also need a first-class ventilating system. A kitchen exhaust fan—even the largest—just won't do. It is not powerful enough to carry off the great volume of smoke, grease, and heat. And don't forget that charcoal grills give off carbon monoxide, too: more than one person who has charcoal-grilled steaks indoors has been killed by this gas.

What you really need is one of the big commercial exhaust fans that are used in restaurants. It's a bit noisy and may cost more than the barbecue itself, but you have no choice.

The fan must be installed in a hood that extends beyond the sides of the grill. If the barbecue is installed against a wall or in a corner, the hood must be a minimum of 24 inches deep and must extend a minimum of 1 inch beyond both ends of the grill. If the barbecue is installed in a peninsula or island, the edges of the hood must extend 4 inches beyond all edges of the grill.

The height of the hood is important, too. It must be no more than 30 inches above the grill surface, and ideally it should be less—especially in a peninsula or island location.

The duct from the hood must lead outdoors. It should be as short and straight as possible, not only to carry off the products of combustion rapidly, but also to make it easy to clean out the grease that accumulates inside. This means that the ideal location for a barbecue is against an exterior wall. Never vent a grill into a fireplace or heating flue.

Unfortunately, even though you do a theoretically perfect job of ventilating a barbecue, there is no guarantee that you will get satisfactory ventilating performance on all occasions. That is why one Midwest range manufacturer has introduced a radically new type of barbecue. This is a counter-top unit with an exhaust fan in the bottom of the grill itself. The electric heating element is rated at 2800 watts to assure fast broiling of any steak.

As meat is being broiled, the grease drips down past the electric element onto a bed of hot marble chips. The smoke rising from the chips gives the meat its charcoal flavor. The grease vapors are carried into the exhaust fan by a stream of cool air flowing across the chips. At the same time, smoke from the meat is sucked into the fan through a surface-level vent. From the fan, both the grease vapors and the smoke are ducted outdoors. Excess grease drips into a closed jar under the grill.

When using any indoor barbecue grill you should make sure that the room is well ventilated but not drafty. Clean the exhaust fan frequently, the duct occasionally.

Barbecues, Outdoor.

Grills. There are three things to bear in mind when choosing a grill:

1. Simple, open grills with nothing more than a grid and a fire underneath are good only for broiling and limited roasting. If you add a motor-operated spit, or rotisserie, roasting is greatly improved. If a grill has a tight cover, it can also be used for smoking.

2. That typical charcoal flavor you love is given to meat not by some secret ingredient in charcoal, but by the smoke rising from grease dripping on red-hot fuel. It follows that gas and electric grills are as good for "charcoal" broiling as conventional charcoal grills. They are also easier to start.

3. If you intend to keep a grill clean and store it properly, buy an expensive one made of heavy, rigid metal. Cheap grills are an abomination because they break, wobble, and topple over easily when you move them. But, of course, if you don't take care of a grill, a cheap one is the only sensible kind to buy.

How to take care of a grill. Store it under cover in a dry place. Avoid blazing fires which burn off the paint on the grill. If the paint film is damaged, clean the metal and apply a rust-inhibiting primer and then a finish coat.

Tighten screws and bolts holding the grill together regularly, and grease the wheels; then you will be able to move the grill over rough or uneven ground without shaking it apart or turning it over.

Wash the grid and spit after use with detergent solution. Wash grease spatters from hood or lid also.

Charcoal. You have a choice between pure lump charcoal, hardwood briquets made of a blend of hardwoods held together usually with a filler, lignite briquets made of lignite coal, and fruit-pit briquets made of charred, pulverized fruit pits and nutshells. The first two are the fastest to reach cooking temperature; the last two continue burning for the longest time.

All charcoal soaks up moisture if exposed to the air. This makes it slow to ignite, and it burns less efficiently. It should therefore be kept in a dry place indoors or in a tight container such as a large potato chip can or drum in which chlorine for the swimming pool is delivered.

If your grill has a grate, the fire is built directly on this. If the grill is a bowl-type brazier, first fill the bowl partially with gravel or vermiculite and build the fire on this. The filling improves the draft, makes a level firebed, protects the metal, and absorbs drippings.

Use an electric starter to start a fire: it is fast and safe. Another fast but more hazardous way to start a fire is to soak six briquets with starter fluid, spread six dry briquets on top, and toss a match onto the pile.

If you want to save partially burned charcoal after you are through cooking, don't douse the coals with water. Bury them in the firebed instead, or close the top of the grill tightly.

Caution: Carbon monoxide in large amounts is given off by burning charcoal. So do not use your portable grill indoors.

Barkcloth. A cotton fabric with an irregular weave and nubby texture. It may be used for slipcovers and draperies. Launder like other cottons but use warm water only.

Basement Bulkheads. A basement bulkhead, or hatchway, is the low, slanting structure that covers the outside stairs into a basement. It is usually a constant source of leaks.

In old houses, bulkheads were made of wood raised several inches off the ground on masonry walls. As long as the wood does not rot, the bulkheads are perfectly satisfactory, although the doors are heavy and hard to open. Leaks that develop around the bottom edges and between the top of the bulkhead and the house wall can be sealed with silicone or polysulfide rubber caulking compound. But the only way to control leaks around the edges of the doors (and not very well at that) is to tack strips of rubber or heavy polyethylene film to the doors over the cracks.

In new houses, bulkheads are generally prefabricated steel units resting on masonry walls. They are lighter and generally more watertight than wood, though not perfect. Leaks around the door edges cannot be stopped (but fortunately they are not common). Use caulking to seal gaps under and at the back of the bulkhead.

How to replace an old wood bulkhead with a steel unit. Tear off the old structure. If the walls on which it rested are level and flat, assemble the steel unit, set it in place, and draw lines around the edges on the house wall. Then remove the bulkhead and cut out the siding along the pencil lines. Reset the bulkhead and slip the flange at the top between the siding and the sheathing. Assemble the doors on the bulkhead frame and move the frame slightly from side to side until the bottom and top door edges form straight lines. Then drill through the bottom flanges of the frame into the masonry walls. Insert lead or plastic anchors in the masonry and secure the bulkhead to these with screws. Finish the job by caulking the bottom and back edges of the bulkhead. Then apply a couple of coats of exterior enamel.

If the masonry walls on which the old bulkhead rested are not level or sound, you must first chip off the tops. Then fit the bulkhead to the house wall and set it in place in the manner described. Raise the bulkhead off the masonry walls on chunks of brick and level it carefully. Then build a frame of greased boards around the top of the masonry walls and pour in concrete to the bottom of the bulkhead. While the concrete is soft, push screws or bolts into it through the bulkhead flanges.

(Note that if the house wall is of brick, stone, or concrete, the bulkhead frame must be screwed directly to it. Before tightening the screws, run a fat ribbon of caulking compound around the back edges of the bulkhead.)

Basements. The first thing everyone asks about a basement is, "Is it dry?" Basements have other problems—some of them stemming from moisture—but there is no question but that a dry basement is of prime concern.

In the past, basements were usually built of solid poured concrete, and whatever leaks occurred were caused by the settling and cracking of the walls. Today, basement walls are almost always made of hollow concrete block, and leaks are generally attributable to badly made mortar joints and inadequate external waterproofing measures.

How to keep water out of an existing basement. One of the first things to check whenever leaks develop in a basement is whether the ground around the house slopes toward the foundation walls. If it does, you should regrade so the ground slopes away from the walls for about 10 feet.

If the house is on a hillside, the hill should be cut back so there is a level space at least 10 feet wide behind the house. A ditch or drain at the base of the hill should then be constructed to carry the water away around the sides of the house.

In addition to correcting the grade, you should also make sure that water from the gutters is carried away from the house as far as possible. Ideally, the downspouts should empty into underground drains which lead into the community storm drains or into dry wells. If this is impossible, you should at least put concrete basins under the downspouts to divert the water a few feet away from the house. An alternative is to attach to each spout a flexible tube that automatically rolls up into a bundle when dry and rolls out away from the house when full of water.

If water oozes through the walls. This is a fairly common problem, especially with concrete-block walls. Unless the pressure on the outside of the walls is heavy, you can probably stop the slow leaking by applying one to three coats of a cement waterproofing paint. First remove any paint or other finish that is already on the walls, and brush off encrusted salts. Then scrub the waterproofing cement, which is like a thick paint, into the pores according to the manufacturer's directions.

If water enters through cracks. Chip the crack open with a hammer and cold chisel. Try to shape it in an inverted V—so that it is wider in back than at the surface. Blow out the crumbs. Then fill with latex cement or, if the wall is damp, with a mixture of 1 part Portland cement and 2 parts sand.

Cracks and holes that admit a stream of water must be filled with hydraulic cement. This is a special material that will set up even in water. To use it, mix with water and hold it in your hand until it heats up; then cram it into the crack and hold it under pressure for 3 to 5 minutes. See *Concrete—Hydraulic Cement* (page 52).

If water enters through an open joint between a wall and floor. Open the joint with a cold chisel and clean it thoroughly. Allow it to dry. If necessary, play a propane torch on it until the moisture disappears. Then fill it with asphalt roofing cement or with silicone or polysulfide rubber caulking compound.

If you are unable to dry out the joint, fill it with Portland cement mortar or hydraulic cement, depending on how much moisture is present.

Cracks in the floor. These are filled like cracks in walls. If the entire floor is cracked and wet, cover it with a 2-inch reinforced topping of concrete. See *Floors, Concrete.*

If serious leaking persists despite the preceding measures. You are in for a major job that should be done by a masonry contractor: you must dig out the ground around the basement walls and waterproof them on the outside. Two important steps are involved: First, you must lay 4-inch drains around the entire house at the level of the footings. The drains are made of composition pipe perforated along one side. The pipes, which form a continuous loop, are laid in crushed stone. At the lowest point they empty into a drain which carries the water from the house to a storm sewer or dry well. Second, you must cover the walls from the footings up to ground level with a waterproof membrane consisting of layers of roofing felt embedded in asphalt and then cover that with concrete.

An alternate solution for a serious basement leakage problem is to install a sump pump at the lowest point in the floor. As long as the sump (pit) is free of trash, the pump is in working order, and the electricity is on, a sump pump is an efficient and useful device which automatically gets rid of water when it reaches a predetermined level in the sump. Before having one installed, however, you should note that it does not stop water from entering the basement. And it does not keep water from standing in puddles on the basement floor unless the entire floor is pitched slightly toward the sump.

If water enters the basement through windows in the areaways. This happens only during or after heavy storms when surface water floods over the tops of areaway walls. The best way to stop this (besides sloping the ground away from the areaways) is to build up the areaway walls a couple of inches above ground level. Just add a course of bricks or topping of concrete; or if you have steel areaway walls, pull them up slightly. If there are footing drains around the house, it is also wise to install a 2-inch vertical pipe between the drains and each areaway. The top of the pipe should be about 1 inch below the bottom of the areaway window. Cover it with a strainer.

How to get rid of mustiness. This results from dampness in the basement, so the control is obvious: stop leaks. Insulate sweating water pipes with strips of fiberglass wrapped spirally and covered with tape. Insulate a sweating water tank with a fiberglass jacket made for the purpose. Open the windows.

Should the mustiness persist, turn on the furnace occasionally to help dry the basement out. In an extreme situation, you may have to install a dehumidifier.

How to finish basement walls. You can make concrete-block walls attractive by painting them with latex, Portland cement, or epoxy paint (see *Concrete—How to paint concrete*). If you prefer smooth walls, or paneling, you must first apply 1-by-3-inch wood strips (in this case known as furring strips). The strips are usually installed vertically on 16-inch centers, but if you use solid wood paneling, they are installed horizontally. The fastest way to attach them to the walls is with a power-actuated stud driver; see *Wall Anchors—Studs.*

For the exact method of covering the walls, see *Walls, Gypsum-Board; Walls, Plywood;* etc.

How to build a basement ceiling. If you use gypsum board, see *Walls, Gypsum-Board.* If you use acoustical tile, see *Acoustical Tile.*

How to finish a basement floor. You can paint it, of course, but you won't be happy with the results because the paint will soon wear off. It is much better to put in a resilient floor. See *Floors, Resilient.*

How to clean and repair a basement floor and stop dusting. See *Floors, Concrete.*

Basement Storage. The main thing to consider when storing anything in the basement is that the basement is dry and that there is enough circulation of air and heat to prevent mildew (see *Basements*). But even when these conditions prevail, it is advisable not to store anything directly on the floor. Raise it a couple of inches on wood blocks. And don't store anything that will soak up moisture: awnings and rug cushions, for instance.

Actual storage arrangements depend on what you are storing. Here are a few suggestions:

Tools. Hang all that can be hung on the wall above the workbench. Put small items—especially if they have cutting edges—in compartmented drawers. Keep planes and power tools in boxes or on shelves.

Paints. Buy inexpensive steel utility shelf units which come knocked down and are easily assembled with a few nuts and bolts. The units usually have four or five shelves up to 6 feet long and 1 foot deep. Anchor each shelf unit to a wall to prevent it from falling forward.

Door and window screens. Store them flat in parallel pairs of wide, U-shaped wood racks suspended from the ceiling joists.

Lumber. Store long boards in the same kind of suspended racks. Store short pieces upright in boxes or barrels. Panels of plywood, hardboard, and gypsum board should be stored on one of their long edges and cinched tight against a wall to prevent warping.

Bath Linens. Most bath linens are made of cotton terry, but a few are a terry-like blend of cotton and rayon. Hand towels and fingertip towels are sometimes made of linen as well as cotton.

Top-quality terry towels are much thicker, tighter, and softer than cheap towels and will last much longer. In fact, you can reasonably expect a top-quality towel to last for about three years even when used regularly.

Bath linens include the following articles:

	Approximate size (inches)
Bath towel	24 x 46
Jumbo bath towel	36 x 72
Hand towel	16 x 30
Fingertip towel	11 x 18 (some linen towels are much smaller)
Washcloth	12 x 12
Bath mat	20 x 36

Of the above articles, bath towels get the most use by every member of the family. It is therefore well to have at least two or three for each person. You should also provide about two hand towels and three washcloths for each family member who uses them (all don't). The other articles you need are two bath mats per bathroom and about three fingertip towels for guests.

Bath rugs, toilet seat covers, and tank covers complete the list of bath linens. They are today generally made of a synthetic which is easy to wash (provided you can cram the pieces into your washer and dryer). Rug sizes and shapes are variable; and if you don't like what is on the market, you can have a wall-to-wall carpet made to fit the bathroom (or you can cut it to fit yourself).

How to launder bath linens. Wash in hot water with a heavy-duty detergent. Use normal agitation and spin speeds. Rinse in warm water. Dry at high heat in a dryer. Towels and washcloths dried in this way are much softer and fluffier than those dried on a line.

Towel bars. Soggy bath linens are neither pleasant to use nor attractive to smell. Ergo: You should be sure to install in every bathroom enough towel bars of large enough size to permit the linens to be spread out after they have been used.

Unfortunately, if your bathrooms are like most, they do not provide sufficient towel-hanging space. But the problem may not be difficult to solve.

It is possible that you can install a second bar about 2 feet above the one you now have. Other usually open spaces on which you may be able to install bars are the back of the door, the wall above the head of the tub, the wall above the toilet tank, the side or sides of a vanity or washbasin.

Several useful devices for increasing towel space are ladder bars, swinging bars, extendable bars, and freestanding towel racks.

Bathroom Cabinets. Also called medicine cabinets, bathroom cabinets are designed either to be recessed in a wall—usually over the washbasin—or to be mounted on the surface.

Recessed units are preferable. They come in a wider range of sizes, and don't stick out at you. If you want to install one, you should first determine how much space there is between the studs. As a rule,

in order to do this, you must cut an opening in the wall. The cabinet should be the exact size of the stud space or the next size smaller. (It's possible to cut out a stud to install a larger cabinet, but this involves a fair amount of carpentry and also presents wall-finishing problems.) The height of the cabinet depends on what is available.

To cut an opening in a plaster wall, use a sharp cold chisel. Don't try to drive this all the way through the plaster at one time because you will succeed only in making a larger and more jagged hole than you want. Instead, just nibble away at it.

In any other type of wall, draw an outline of the cabinet and bore 1-inch holes at the corners of the outline. Then cut from hole to hole with a keyhole saw.

When you install the cabinet, make sure it is level, and screw it directly to the studs. If the cabinet is smaller than the stud opening, you must, of course, insert wood shims between it and the studs.

Surface-mounted cabinets are used when there are pipes or electric cables in the wall or when the stud space is less than 3½ inches deep. To install, check the level of the cabinet and attach with screws. The screws should be driven into at least one stud.

The height at which a bathroom cabinet is hung depends on its size and on the height of the adults using the bathroom. As a general rule, the middle of the cabinet should be about 60 inches above the floor.

How to clean cabinets. Because medicines and toiletries spill and drip, the shelves in bathroom cabinets are rarely very clean. If they are made of glass or plastic, however, it is a simple matter to wash them with warm water or detergent solution. Painted shelves, on the other hand, eventually get badly stained and eroded. To avoid the nuisance of repainting them every few years, cover them with an adhesive-backed vinyl.

If a cabinet has sliding doors, clean out the tracks every six months with a sponge and old toothbrush. Hinged doors need to be oiled occasionally with a spray-on silicone lubricant.

If you wallpaper the bathroom. Don't struggle to paper around the cabinet.

Remove it from the wall instead and hang the paper right over the opening. When it is dry, cut it out with a razor blade and replace the cabinet.

Bathroom Cleaning. A fresh and sparkling-clean bathroom can be a permanent feature of your home if you give it routine daily care plus a few periodic extras.

Bathroom fixtures, when new, can simply be washed with a sponge or soft cloth, using a solution of detergent and water. For older fixtures, scrub worn surfaces, stubborn spots, and rings with a cloth and mild cleanser. (Avoid using abrasive cleansers. If used regularly, they will etch enamel surfaces and destroy their sheen.)

Remove any scummy "bathtub ring" caused by soap residue and hard-water minerals with a nonprecipitating water conditioner on a damp sponge. (To prevent this stubborn build-up and to make bathing more enjoyable, add a little water conditioner or a special bath product to the water when you bathe.)

Faucets, shower heads, and other chromium-plated fittings should be washed with a sponge or cloth and warm water to remove water spots; towel them dry to restore their gleam. Remove soap scum or hard-water spots by rubbing them with vinegar.

If you live in a hard-water area, minerals in the water often leave rusty-yellow, green, or blue stains, particularly around drains. If you have a dripping faucet, one of the commonest causes of such stains, having the faucet fixed is the best solution. To remove rust spots or mineral stains, use one of the following three procedures until the stain is gone. They are given here in progression for from mild to severe stains. The first procedure is safe for the finish on any washbasin or bathtub. The second two can damage a porcelain surface that is not acid-resistant. All of today's porcelain-on-steel fixtures and most porcelain-on-cast-iron fixtures are acid- and alkaline-resistant. If your fixtures are relatively new and come from a dependable manufacturer, they probably are acid- and alkaline-resistant.

1. Shave half a bar of naphtha-base soap into ½ gallon of hot water and add ¼ cup of paint thinner or cleaning solvent. Use a stiff brush or fine steel wool to scrub the stained area with this solution; then rinse.

2. Sponge the stains with vinegar or diluted lemon juice and let stand 3 or 4 minutes. Rinse; then use a mild cleanser.

3. Make a solution of 1 part oxalic or muriatic acid to 10 parts water. (The acids are available at most housewares and hardware stores.) Swab the stained area with the solution; then quickly and thoroughly rinse it away. If the stain is on a vertical surface, you can thicken the solution with cornmeal. (Caution: Oxalic and muriatic acids are very powerful and toxic. Take these precautions: Wear rubber gloves; inhale as little as possible of the fumes; don't let the solution touch chromium hardware; store acids out of reach of children.)

There are special rust removers that help remove mineral deposits as well. These are strong chemicals and should be used only when necessary to remove stains, not as a regular cleaning procedure.

For how to clean clogged or sluggish drains, see *Bathtubs; Lavatories;* or *Toilets.* Drain cleaners are not of much use in bathrooms because stoppages are not caused by grease.

Toilet bowl exteriors can be cleaned with a sudsy cloth in the same way as other fixtures. Unless you live in a hard-water area, a detergent solution is all that is needed for routine cleaning of the inside of the bowl. Another type of cleaner is automatic—a container holding a detergent solution hangs inside the water tank and releases detergent with each flushing.

For periodic, thorough cleaning, use a crystalline-powder toilet-bowl cleaner. (Follow the package instructions for the amount to use and the length of time it should stand in the bowl.) With a long-handled cleaning brush, scrub all interior surfaces thoroughly, particularly under the rim and in the trap. (Caution: Never use this type of bowl cleaner along with bleach or chlorinated cleaning products. The combination can form irritating, sometimes toxic gases.)

Bathroom walls should have a water-resistant covering, whether paint, tile, or paper, both for easy cleaning and for protection against the normal water-spattering and the high moisture levels they are exposed to. Most of the wall area will need only an occasional wiping with a damp or sudsy cloth.

Tile or other wall covering around the tub and shower often collects a film caused by soap and hard-water elements. You can remove light film by scrubbing the wall surface with a water conditioner or mild detergent solution. You also can use a spray-on tile and bathroom cleaner. To remove a heavier, stubborn accumulation, use an all-purpose liquid or spray cleaner and scrub with a stiff-bristled brush. Rinse the surface, then rub it dry with an old terry towel to make it sparkle.

If the grout (or cement) between tiles is discolored, scrub it with cleansing powder and a stiff-bristled brush. (Don't scrub so vigorously, though, that you remove or dislodge the grout.) There also are special tile cleaners for tough stains on both grout and tile.

Mirrors and windows, unless badly soiled, can be cleaned with clear water. Vinegar or ammonia added to the water will step up its cleaning power; they are particularly effective for cutting through greasy film. (Use a cotton swab to clean hard-to-reach corners.) You also can use specific products such as spray-on window cleaners or paper toweling squares that come saturated with a special cleaning solution. After washing, dry thoroughly with paper towels, a chamois, or a lint-free cloth.

Floors usually are of the same materials used in the kitchen, laundry, or utility areas in the home, and generally pose no unique cleaning problems.

Resilient flooring such as vinyl, vinyl-asbestos, and linoleum should be washed and waxed regularly. Mop with a detergent solution and polish with a water-based self-polishing or buffing wax. Or clean with a one-step wax that cleans as well as polishes.

Ceramic tile needn't be waxed. Scrub it as often as needed with detergent or an all-purpose cleaner and water. Use a stiff brush and scouring powder on stubborn spots.

Bathroom rugs and carpeting should be cared for according to the manufacturer's instructions. Vacuum regularly; wipe up stains or spills immediately. Many small carpets or rugs can be laundered in an automatic washer; others should be shampooed as needed.

Cleaning tips: Mildew thrives in damp climates and in dark, moist places, so spots such as a shower stall or laundry hamper are prime mildew targets. To get rid of existing mildew, scrub the affected areas with ammonia or a spray disinfectant. Rinse with water and then sponge with either hydrogen peroxide or chlorine bleach to remove any discoloration; then rinse thoroughly. Use a spray disinfectant regularly; it will help to prevent mildew.

Other precautions: Leave the shower door open when not in use, and be sure that all laundry is dry when it goes into the hamper.

Clean the medicine cabinet or other storage areas periodically and discard any old medicines, cosmetics, and out-of-date supplies. They are dust collectors—and some may be harmful to use in their antiquated state.

Dust lighting fixtures regularly both for cleanliness and to get full advantage of the light.

Use an old toothbrush as a handy aid for cleaning hard-to-reach corners and crevices.

If the bathroom is small and cleaning equipment is hard to maneuver, connect just one wand to your vacuum cleaner and use the dusting brush or crevice tool to reach into corners. If a long-handled mop is too unwieldy for crowded quarters, cut its handle in half.

If any hard-water problems—bathtub rings, water stains, scummy build-up—are a continual annoyance, you may want to consider installing a water-softening system. It would be an aid in the kitchen and laundry areas as well.

Bathtubs. Bathtubs are made of fiberglass-reinforced plastic, porcelain enamel on cast iron, and porcelain enamel on steel. You can also have a tub custom-made in your home out of ceramic tile laid on a concrete base.

Many of the new plastic tubs include the surrounding walls. Some are molded in one piece; others are made up of several large pieces that are joined together in the bathroom with a special sealant. In either case, elimination of the joints between the tub and the walls makes for much easier cleaning and prevents leaking.

Although tubs have been redesigned rather extensively in the past few years, most are still rectangular. From the housewife's standpoint, these are better than square or round tubs because they are narrower and therefore easier to reach across and clean. Tubs installed on the bathroom floor are also easier to clean than sunken tubs.

How to repair tubs. Cracks between the rim and walls. Clean out the cracks and let them dry thoroughly. Blow out crumbs of dirt and plaster that remain. Then fill with silicone caulking compound and smooth it with a knife or spatula while it is still plastic.

Most silicone caulks are not paintable. If you wish to conceal the caulked joint, quarter-round ceramic tiles especially made for use around tub rims are available. They can be set in silicone caulking or the mastic supplied by the tile maker.

Faucet leaks. See *Lavatories.*

Drain clogged. If the tub has a pop-up stopper, lift the stopper out and clean it. This may do the trick, but probably won't.

If the tub has a stopper that is controlled by a handle in the end wall of the tub (the stopper may or may not be a pop-up), remove the screws holding the handle assembly in place and lift out the entire assembly. At the end of the control rod is a wire coil. Clean this: it is undoubtedly choked with hair and scum. Then replace the handle assembly.

In old-fashioned tubs that have rubber stoppers, try to remove the stoppage by fishing down the drain with a stiff wire with a hook at the end.

If the above measures fail, run a little water into the tub. Then place the rubber cup of a plunger over the drain opening and work the handle up and down to create in the drain line a suction which loosens the stoppage.

Shower head clogged. See *Shower Heads.*

How to clean tubs. See *Bathroom Cleaning.*

Batik (buh-*teek*). Batik is a Javanese dyeing process used to produce brightly colored fabrics that are also called batik. Wall hangings, curtains, bedspreads, and many other things can be treated in this way. Linen and rayon are the fabrics most often used.

The process is similar to sarasa; but instead of paste, hot wax is used to cover areas that are not to be dyed.

The dyed fabrics should be dry-cleaned when they become soiled.

Batiste. A fine, sheer, or semi-sheer fabric made of cotton, silk, or polyester. It is best to hand-wash in warm water, dry over a line, and iron with a cool or warm iron.

Bats. See *Pest Control.*

Battery-Operated Appliances. Appliances that are run by batteries rather than off the household electrical system include drills, carving knives, mixers, toothbrushes, hedge trimmers, lawn mowers, clocks, TV sets, radios, and toys. Their great value is that you can take and use them anywhere. They are also safe because they operate at low voltage.

In some appliances, the batteries used are ordinary dry cells like those in flashlights. After a while, they begin to wear out, go dead, and must be replaced. If you don't let them get too exhausted, however, you can revive them with a special type of dry-cell charger.

Other appliances come with rechargeable batteries which are usually made of nickel-cadmium. These last a long, long time if you do not allow them to become completely discharged. They can be recharged time and time again simply by connecting the appliance into an electrical outlet. If you forget to unplug the appliance after the batteries are charged, no harm is done.

Except for the fact that they are powered by batteries and have direct-current rather than alternating-current motors, cordless appliances are no different from conventional appliances and should be cared for in the same way.

Bedbugs. See *Pest Control.*

Bedding. Also see *Mattresses* and *Pillows.*

Sheets. Some sheets are made of nylon satin or linen. The great majority, however, are made of percale or muslin. Both of these materials are woven out of either cotton or a permanent-press blend of cotton and polyester. Of the two, percale sheets are finer, softer, and lighter in weight.

The durability, comfort, and beauty of sheets and pillowcases are a direct reflection of the thread count of the fabric. The higher the count, the better. Percale sheets are woven with 180 or 200 threads per square inch. Muslin sheets are woven with 112, 128, or 140 threads per square inch.

For flat sheet sizes, see *Beds*. Fitted top sheets designed to fit around the foot of a mattress are roughly the same size. Fitted bottom sheets which fit around all four corners of a mattress are the size of the mattress plus about 6 inches on all sides.

The main advantage in buying flat sheets is that you can use them as either top or bottom sheets. Therefore, if you follow the habit of washing the bottom sheet twice a week and substituting the top sheet for it each time, you need only three sheets per bed. This reduces your initial investment and saves a little storage space; but the sheets wear out faster, of course.

The advantage of fitted sheets is that they simplify bed-making. This is especially true if the sheets have elasticized corners. But regardless of the frequency with which you change beds, you need two bottom sheets and two top sheets per bed. (You also need four flat sheets if you normally change both sheets on each bed once a week.)

Pillowcases. The materials used for pillowcases are identical with those for sheets.

Cases for standard-size pillows measure 42 by 34, 36, or 38 inches. (The first figure, representing the width of a case, is actually double the width of the case laid flat.) Queen-size cases are 42 by 40 inches; king-size, 42 by 46 inches. For very plump pillows use cases 45 inches wide.

You should have two pillowcases for each pillow that is in regular use.

For how to launder pillowcases and sheets, see *Laundering*. Cases that are badly stained by perspiration and grease

should be soaked in an enzyme presoaker before washing.

Blankets. Wool is the standard blanket fiber by which all others are judged. There is nothing warmer or more resilient.

Wool blankets vary considerably, however. There are heavy, unattractive utility blankets, weighty Hudson Bay blankets, and much lighter blankets with an unequalled luster and feel of luxury. Most of the wool blankets made today are mothproofed. The lighter blankets can be machine-washed, but the heavier weights should be dry-cleaned.

Blankets of acrylic, polyester, or blends of synthetic fibers weigh less than wool, are nonallergenic, mothproof, and quite warm. They are easily washed and dried and you don't have to worry about shrinkage. But they lack the resiliency and luxury of wool; and they have a tendency to shred or pill even though the best blankets are treated to minimize this.

Cotton flannelette and blends of cotton and polyester are used in very lightweight summer blankets. Some people also use these blankets in the winter as sheets.

So-called thermal, or cellular, blankets are made of cotton and synthetics. They have become very popular because they are usable in summer and winter. In summer, they let body heat escape and cooling breezes enter. In winter, if you toss a sheet over them, they retain warmth as well as several conventional blankets but weigh less.

Another new type of lightweight blanket with good thermal qualities is made of urethane foam with nylon flocking.

Standard blanket sizes are as follows:

	Approximate Size (inches)
Twin	66 x 90
Double	80 x 90
Queen	90 x 90
King	108 x 90
Long twin	66 x 100
Long double	80 x 100
Extra-long twin	66 x 108
Extra-long double	80 x 108
Bunk	54 x 80

There are also blankets measuring 72 by 90 inches which are designed for use on either twin or double beds. They are not, however, particularly desirable for double beds unless used with a full-size double-bed blanket because they don't stay tucked in.

A few blankets have fitted corners at the foot.

Depending on where you live and how warm you keep your house, you may need one to three blankets for each bed.

Electric blankets. These have soared in popularity because they are light in weight, yet you need only one blanket per bed even in the coldest weather. The least expensive blankets automatically maintain the heat you select throughout the night; but if you need more or less heat, you must readjust the control. By contrast, the best blankets automatically adjust to the room temperature.

Because the warmth provided by an electric blanket comes from the small, insulated wire that is laced through it, the blanket fabric is usually nothing more than a synthetic of medium quality. As a result, electric blankets cost very little more than conventional blankets. Operating cost comes to about 50 cents a month.

Electric blankets are made in twin, double, queen, and king sizes. All are usually a few inches shorter or narrower than conventional blankets of the same size. Twin blankets have a single control; doubles have either single or dual control; queen and king sizes always have dual controls. With dual controls, a man can adjust his side of the blanket to one temperature while his wife adjusts her side to another temperature.

For how to launder electric blankets, see *Laundering* (page 185). Dry-cleaning should not be attempted because the cleaning fluid may damage the insulation on the wiring.

Comforters. Comforters, or quilts, are most commonly made with cotton covers and polyester lining so they can be machine-washed and dried at medium temperature. But many other more luxurious fabrics, such as silk and velvet, are also used for covers. These must be dry-cleaned. Since comforters are usually

not tucked in, they may be slightly smaller than conventional blankets.

Blanket covers. Blanket covers are thin, light throws which serve one useful purpose: they help to keep the blankets clean when someone is sick in bed or has breakfast in bed or throws back the bedspread to take a nap. Covers used for this purpose are 90 inches long and come in 72-, 90-, and 108-inch widths.

Another type of blanket cover, called a night spread, is sometimes used as a summer bedspread or substitute bedspread when the regular spread is being cleaned. It is 108 inches long so it can be pulled up over the pillows.

Bedspreads. It is very possible that bedspreads have been made out of every fabric ever woven. The selection available today in any large store is almost overwhelming. Several styles are offered. Sizes even for beds of the same size are varied.

Questions you may want to ask when you are shopping for a bedspread are: Does it suit the room decoratively? Will it resist wrinkling when people lie on it? Will it resist soiling or at least showing soil? Can it be laundered or must it be dry-cleaned? (In the latter case you may need to buy an extra bedspread.) Will it be easy to handle when you make the bed? If it does not reach the floor on all sides, will it hang down far enough to cover blankets and sheets that are not tucked in?

Mattress pads. Mattress pads used to protect mattresses are covered on both sides with cotton, or on the top with cotton and on the bottom with moisture-proof vinyl, or on the top with latex foam and on the bottom with urethane foam. The filling may be polyester, nylon, or a mixture of cotton and polyester. The pads are held flat by elastic bands that loop around the corners of the mattress, or they are entirely edged with elastic that fits over all top edges of the mattress. Some pads completely envelope the mattresses like slipcovers.

All pads are machine-washable with heavy-duty detergent in warm water. Dry in a dryer at medium heat. Shrinkage is very difficult to prevent.

Beds. The following are today's mattress sizes. Actual bed sizes may be a few inches wider, longer, or both.

Type of bed	Size (inches)	Flat sheet Size (inches)
Twin	39 x 75	72 x 104
Twin long	39 x 80	72 x 115
Double	54 x 75	81 x 104
Double long	54 x 80	81 x 115
Queen	60 x 80	90 x 115
King	76 x 80	108 x 115
Bunk	30 x 75	63 x 104
	39 x 75	72 x 104
Folding cot	30 x 75	63 x 104
	39 x 75	72 x 104
	48 x 75	72 x 104
Studio cot	30 x 75	63 x 104
	33 x 75	63 x 104
	39 x 75	72 x 104
Youth bed	33 x 66	63 x 99
Crib	24 x 42	
	27 x 52	

Sofa beds vary in size, but they are similar to standard beds and take the same bedding.

Sheet sizes shown are averages. In buying sheets, be sure to get flat bottom sheets large enough to tuck under all four mattress edges at least 6 inches. The same size can be used as top sheets.

Making beds. Almost all homemakers make beds every day and the great majority change the linens once a week. A majority make all the beds in the house even though there may be other people who could make at least their own.

The fastest and least tiring way to make a bed is to do one side, then the other. Starting on one side, toss the top sheet and blanket back and straighten and tuck in one-half of the bottom sheet. Then pull up the top sheet, smooth it out, and tuck in the bottom. Then do the blankets one by one. Tuck in the sides all together. Plump up the pillow lightly and put it in place.

Move to the other side of the bed and repeat the process. Then put on the bedspread halfway from that side; smooth it out, and tuck it in under the pillow. Finally move back to the first side of the bed and finish with the spread.

Use of fitted, or contoured, sheets speeds bed-making considerably. You can also help yourself to a certain extent if you put a few stitches in the top of all sheets, blankets, and spreads to indicate the edges of the mattress. This makes it easier to center the bedding exactly so that you don't wind up with more hanging down one side than the other.

As indicated, most women prefer to change both sheets on a bed once a week on the same day. Some, however, follow the practice of taking off and washing the bottom sheet twice a week and replacing it each time with the top sheet. Thus they have a fresh top sheet more or less all the time.

Mattresses on regularly occupied beds should be turned from side to side at least once a month and from end to end every two months. They should be covered at all times with mattress pads. You may, in addition, cover them with zippered mattress covers.

How to clean beds. When turning mattresses from side to side, vacuum around the sides of the spring and along the bedrails. Vacuum both sides of the spring every two months. Vacuum under beds every couple of weeks. (A dust ruffle does not prevent dust from accumulating under a bed—it merely hides it.)

If mattresses develop an odor, take them outdoors and air them in bright, hot sunshine for a half-day on each side.

Pillows may have to be laundered or dry-cleaned every couple of years depending on how stained they become. Air them outdoors once a year. Pillow covers are available to help keep them clean.

For how to take care of a wood bed frame, see *Furniture, Wood.* For a metal frame, see the entry for the appropriate metal.

How to repair bed frames. If a slat is broken, it is easy to cut a new one—preferably out of maple or yellow pine. (Each bed should have three slats at least. Four or five give added security.)

If the cleat on which the slats rest comes loose from a wood bed rail, reattach it with plenty of screws. Set some of them in new holes. For extra strength, use glue plus screws.

If a bed frame wobbles badly, it may be possible to do something about the hardware attaching the rails to the headboard and footboard. If not, reinforce the joints with angle irons.

If a bed squeaks, make sure all joints are well glued. Shorten the slats slightly if they fit tight between the rails, and rub the ends with paraffin. Rub the ends of the rails with paraffin also. If squeaking continues, you might try replacing the slats (which usually are the noise-makers) with short, L-shaped steel supports that hang on the rails.

Bees. See *Pest Control.*

Bemberg. A form of rayon fabric with fine filaments and a low luster. It is used in clothing. Dry-clean or launder like rayon.

Benzine. See *Naphtha.*

Beta Fabric. Beta fabric is a fiberglass which goes into fireproof draperies and curtains as well as other articles not used in the home. The material has the basic characteristics of conventional fiberglass fabrics but is made of ultra-fine fibers with exceptional softness, strength, pliability, and durability. For how to wash and repair beta, see *Fiberglass Fabric.*

Birds. See *Pest Control.*

Bird's-eye. Any plain fabric with small diamonds woven in. The way it is laundered depends on the fiber used.

Blankets. See *Bedding.*

Bleaches. For the types of laundry bleach and how to use them, see *Laundering* (page 178). For how to use a wood bleach, see *Floors, Wood* (page 114).

Chlorine and wood bleaches are very potent chemicals and must be handled with care. Follow the directions on the bottle carefully.

The sun is also a strong bleaching agent, but its action is not so rapid or so extreme.

Blenders. The sharp, high-speed, whirling blades at the bottom of a blender make short work of many jobs that can be tedious and time-consuming. But frequently the blender just sits on the kitchen counter neglected except for mixing milk shakes, various cocktails, or fruit juices.

Depending on its design, a blender can stir, puree, whip, grate, mix, chop, grind, blend, and liquefy—and it can replace the kitchen utensils that usually do these jobs, such as the grater, grinder, and chopper. (There are some jobs blenders cannot do satisfactorily such as whipping cream, beating eggs, and mashing potatoes. These are best left to mixers.)

A blender can have as few as two operating speeds to as many as a dozen. On the simpler models, speeds often are labeled "low," "medium," and "high." On more complex blenders, various speeds are indicated by the job each does best, such as "grate," "chop," or "blend."

Blender containers are made either of glass or durable plastic. Although plastic containers can become stained and scratched and sometimes are not recommended for the dishwasher, they have the advantage of being lighter in weight and not easily breakable.

Most blender containers have pouring spouts and are marked both in cup and ounce measures. The removable cap of the container lid, also with measure markings, makes it easy to add ingredients during blender operation or to insert a spatula to guide the contents.

The cutting assembly is removable in many blenders, so you can empty thick or sticky contents easily and clean the blender blades thoroughly.

One of the newest ideas in blenders is a unit that has a built-in electric heating element with settings up to 375 degrees. You can use it to cook soups and sauces, for instance, while it stirs them to a fine consistency.

How to use a blender. Be careful not to overblend foods. You can have frozen orange juice bubbling and ready for the table in a matter of seconds, but if you overdo, you'll have to serve orange foam. Many blenders feature a built-in timer to stop the blender in the nick of time.

When preparing a complete recipe in the blender, put in the liquid ingredients first, then the dry ones. Cut any solid foods, such as cooked meats and vegetables, into 1-inch-square pieces before adding them to the blender. Large, bulky chunks of food slow down the motor and don't blend smoothly. If the motor seems to be laboring, try a faster speed; or turn the motor on and off repeatedly to guard against motor overloading.

Measure ingredients as you add them by using the markings on the side of the blender container. Pour liquids and thin batters from the container; but remove heavy, thick mixtures from the bottom if it is removable.

Many container lids feature a removable center making it easy to add ingredients while the blender is running.

In many blending operations, food must be kept moving toward the blades. This is usually done through the lid with a rubber spatula—never a metal instrument. Some makes have spatulas built in. However, if food becomes clogged in the bottom of the container, you must stop the motor before going to work with a spatula.

How to care for blenders. Wash the container thoroughly after every use. Be sure to get all food particles out from around the blades. If this proves difficult, remove the blades. Use detergent solution, rinse well, and dry well. The water should not be very hot for most plastic containers. Never plunge a container that has been used to mix icy cold foods into hot water.

Keep the base clean with a damp sponge.

Follow manufacturer's directions about oiling the power unit.

Ice cubes cannot be crushed in a blender unless you use a special attachment. However, you can add one ice cube at a time to a two-cup or larger mixture.

If the blades become bent, try straightening them with pliers; but if you don't get them pitched properly, blender operation will probably be affected.

Bobèche. See *Candlesticks.*

Boilers. See *Heating Systems.*

Bolts. See *Metal Fasteners.*

Bone. Bone is used to a limited extent to make handles for knives and forks. Since these are stuck to the metal with cement, you should wash them by hand in mild detergent solution. Do not put them in a dishwasher.

If bone is broken, glue the pieces together with cellulose or epoxy glue.

Bone China. An expensive, unusually white, translucent type of china. See *China.*

Bookcases. There is no basic difference between freestanding and built-in bookshelves except that you can take the former with you when you move and the latter will not tip over on their fronts. For how to build bookcases, see *Shelves.*

Books.

How to handle books. Don't crack a new book wide open when you first look at it: you will break the backbone. Lay it on a table and open the front and back covers and smooth them down lightly. Then starting at either the front or back, open a few pages and run your finger down the center crease. Turn over a few more pages and smooth down the crease. Continue in this way all the way through the book.

Even when a book is old and pliable, you should not open it more than 180 degrees. And never carry a book by one cover with the pages and other cover dangling.

How to store books. Books should stand upright or lic flat. Don't let them slant. And don't cram them together too tightly because you may damage the covers. You will also damage the backbone because you won't be able to pull out a book without tugging on the top of the binding.

Although many people dislike their looks, leaving the jackets on books protects the bindings.

Bookshelves should, of course, be high enough so that you don't scrape the top edge of a book when you put it in or take it out.

How to clean books. You can do a quick once-over with a dust cloth, but the only way to get books really clean is to take them out of the shelves and snuff up the dust on the tops with a vacuum cleaner. Then vacuum the shelves and, if necessary, wipe them with a damp cloth. Let them dry thoroughly before replacing books.

If books are in frequent use, the paint on shelves will get nicked and worn, requiring repainting.

Leather-bound books should be treated every year with a leather conditioner, such as neat's-foot oil.

In damp summer weather, watch out for mildew and brush it off covers. Spread mildewed pages open.

How to repair books. Torn pages. Don't use cellulose tape: it darkens with age and picks up dirt along the edges. Place a sheet of wax paper under the torn edge, butt the edges of the tear, and spread a thin film of white library paste over them. Then apply a scrap of white tissue paper and smooth it down. When the paste is dry, tear off the unpasted edges of tissue paper.

Loose pages. Spread a very narrow line of white paste down the torn edge and glue the page to one of the adjacent pages.

Bottled Gas. See *LP Gas.*

Bottles. If you can't get bottles clean inside with a bottle brush and detergent, soak them overnight in hot water and baking soda. For very stubborn soil, place bottles in a strong solution of baking soda, bring to a boil, and simmer for a while.

Bouclé (boo-*klay*). A nubby fabric used for draperies, slipcovers, bedspreads, and clothing, bouclé is distinguished by small loops on the surface. Made of many different fibers, it is washed or dry-cleaned accordingly.

Brace and Bit. See *Tools, Workshop.*

Brass. You can usually tell the difference between solid brass objects and those that are plated with brass by their weight. The former are much heavier.

To clean solid brass and give it a lustrous finish requires a good brass polish and lots of elbow grease. Just dampen a soft rag with the polish and rub the metal hard. You can use an old toothbrush to get into deeply carved areas. Continue polishing until no trace of dirt shows on a clean rag.

If the article is very badly stained and dirty, you will save a great deal of time and energy if you scrub it first with household ammonia and fine steel wool. You will be amazed how quickly the soil disappears. But unfortunately, the shine does not last very well unless you follow up the treatment with an application of brass polish.

Brass polish is used on plated brass also but should never be applied to any type of brass with a lacquered finish. To clean the latter, just wash with a mild detergent solution and dry well.

If lacquer on brass wears off, don't try to touch up the bare spots. Strip off all the lacquer with lacquer thinner instead. Clean the metal well and then spray on one or two coats of fresh lacquer.

If plated brass wears thin, take the article to a silversmith or plating shop.

To keep brass from tarnishing, wrap it in tarnish-resistant paper or, less effective, in anything that will more or less keep out the air.

When brass is broken or torn, or two pieces are separated, it is best to solder or weld the pieces together (see *Soldering*). But they can also be stuck together with epoxy glue.

To remove dents, hold a block of wood against the concave side and tap the other side with a hard rubber mallet or stick of wood. Always work from the outer edges of the dent toward the center.

Breakfront. A tall, handsome cabinet with a vertical center section that projects out beyond the narrower sections on either side; often used for storing and displaying china. For how to take care of a breakfront, see *Furniture, Wood.*

Bric-a-Brac. A collection (it need not be large) of small articles used for ornament. Since these may be made of many different materials, they must be fixed in different ways if damaged. Refer to the entry for the material you have trouble with.

Most pieces of bric-a-brac can be cleaned with a damp cloth or a little detergent solution.

Brick. There are bricks that look like the things we have long known as bricks; and there are also bricks made in squares, hexagons, octagons, and even fleur-de-lis. All are handled in the same way.

Working with bricks. When bricks are used for paving in the garden, it is generally desirable to lay them without mortar on a bed of gravel and sand, or stone dust. (The technique is described under *Walks.*)

For brick walls and other vertical structures, mortar is essential. Use a ready-made mix or a homemade mix of 1 part masonry cement and 3 parts sand. Add enough water to make a stiff but workable mortar.

If bricks are dry (and particularly if they are of very coarse, porous texture), hose them down with water before laying them or, better, soak them for about an hour. This keeps them from drawing moisture out of the mortar before it sets.

For horizontal joints, spread an even ribbon of mortar across the tops of no more than three bricks that were previously laid; then with the point of your trowel, make a slight furrow down the center of the ribbon.

MAKING HORIZONTAL MORTAR JOINTS

Vertical mortar joints are made by buttering mortar on one end of the brick being laid.

Place the new brick squarely in position against the end of the adjacent brick and on the ribbon of cement on top of the bricks below. Do not twist it. Tap firmly into place so that the mortar joints are ½ inch thick. Then remove the excess mortar. Finish the joints, when the mortar has set a bit, with the point of your trowel, a grooving tool, or length of pipe. Mortar stains remaining on the wall can be scrubbed off about two weeks later with a weak solution of muriatic acid. Get as little of this into the joints as possible.

Two points to be noted are: (1) Never make exposed vertical joints by slushing mortar down between two bricks. These joints are rarely strong and watertight. (2) If you are unable to lay bricks on a fresh mortar bed within several minutes, or

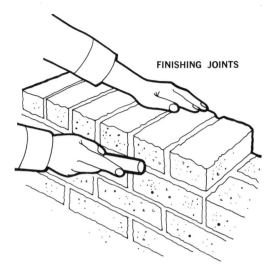

FINISHING JOINTS

if you must change the position of a brick already laid, throw the mortar back into the mortar box (and mix it in well) and apply new mortar. The old mortar has lost some of the moisture and resultant strength.

To build a straight wall of bricks, establish the ends, or corners, first and work to a line stretched between them. Keep laying up the end bricks one or two courses ahead of those in between. Use a carpenter's level or plumb line to check the vertical.

BUILDING A STRAIGHT BRICK WALL

To cut a brick, score it on both sides with a cold chisel and rap it sharply on either line with the chisel.

How to repair brick structures. If mortar joints are crumbling. Scrape the joints as clean as possible and blow out crumbs. Then pack in latex cement and strike off.

An alternative is to clean the joint and wet it with water; then pack in 1 part masonry cement and 2 to 3 parts sand.

Slight cracks in joints can be filled by brushing in a pea-soup-like grout of cement and water.

If a brick is broken. Chip it out completely with a cold chisel; then chip out the mortar slightly. Spread a thin layer of latex, vinyl, or epoxy cement on the old mortar or on the sides of the replacement brick, and tap the brick into place. Fill the joints with additional cement.

If you must salvage a brick that is cracked in two, stick the pieces together with silicone rubber adhesive and keep them under pressure for 24 hours.

Salvaged brick. Used bricks are often extremely attractive, but unfortunately they tend to spall and crack and should not be used in structures which must be strong and weathertight. But there is no reason why you shouldn't use them in walks, terraces, and barbecues.

The easiest way to remove mortar from old bricks is to chip it off with an old hand ax or mason's trowel. Then scrub with a wire brush.

How to clean brick. Dirt. Scrub with a strong detergent solution and rinse well. In air-polluted cities, it is sometimes necessary to have brick buildings steam-cleaned by professionals.

Efflorescence. This is a white, powdery deposit that occurs when moisture dissolves the salts in masonry. To remove the deposit, scrub with a stiff bristle or wire brush; wash with 1 part muriatic acid in 3 parts water; and rinse thoroughly. If the efflorescence continues to return, inspect the brick structure to determine how and where moisture is getting in.

Vanadium stains. These are green or brown stains that generally appear after a brick structure has been given an acid wash. To obliterate them, dissolve a 12-ounce can of Drano in 1 quart water and apply the solution liberally with a paintbrush. Don't bother to scrub. After three days, wash off the white salt that appears on the bricks with water.

Manganese stains. These are brown, oily stains that appear on the mortar joints between certain gray or brown bricks. Brush on 1 part Brick Klenz (made by Economic Laboratory, Garwood, New Jersey) in 3 parts water. Do not rinse.

Paint stains. Apply paint remover.

Rust stains. Mix 1 pound oxalic acid in 1 gallon water and apply with a brush or sprayer.

Smoke. Scrub with an abrasive cleanser.

Oil and grease. Scrub with Big Red (Texas Refinery Corp., P.O. Box 711, Fort Worth, Texas) or Clix (National Chemsearch Corp., P.O. Box 10087, Dallas, Texas). For small stains, you can make a poultice of benzene or trichlorethylene mixed with talc or whiting to form a thick paste. Trowel this on the stain; allow it to dry; then brush off. If the stain persists, repeat the treatment.

Moss. Scrub with a strong solution of chlorine bleach and rinse well. This may not work but at least it won't kill any surrounding vegetation. Should the treatment fail, your only resort is to brush or spray the moss with a solution of Ammate (sold in gardening stores).

How to paint brick. Use latex or Portland cement paint, as for concrete.

Broadcloth. This is a fine, smooth, closely woven material used primarily for clothing. The way it is washed or dry-cleaned depends on whether it is made of wool, cotton, or polyester.

Brocade. Brocade is a rich, elaborately decorated, heavily textured fabric made of satin, silk, or velvet. It frequently incorporates metallic threads. When soiled, it should be dry-cleaned. To iron, turn right side down, cover with a pressing cloth, and switch your iron to a low-heat setting.

Brocatelle (brah-ca-*tell*). A stiff, brocade-like fabric with a design in high relief. It is used mainly in upholstery and draperies. Although made of several washable fabrics, it should be dry-cleaned.

Broilers, Electric. Counter-top broilers and broiler combinations often are more convenient to use than a range broiler, and since they are portable, you can cook barbecue-style in the dining room, living room, porch, or patio.

You can choose a unit that broils only, broils and spit-roasts, broils and bakes, or performs all three tasks.

Broilers usually are of open, uncovered design (similar to a simple barbecue grill), with a grill or rack above the heating element and a drip pan or tray below. It is easier to cook foods to the desired degree of doneness if the height of the grill can be adjusted. One unusual type of broiler is a vertical design. The food is held in a hinged, two-sided rack that is adjustable to foods as varied as thin bacon strips and thick steaks. The rack slips into a slot with heating elements on both sides.

Broiler-rotisseries have a motor-driven spit suspended above the heating element. On most models, the height of the spit can be adjusted for the size and type of food being cooked. One model is hinged to fold to a thickness of only 4 inches for compact storage. When folded, all accessories such as the spit and motor can be stored inside.

Broiler-ovens are enclosed in cabinets. Small, simple models have one heating element and can be converted from broiling to baking merely by turning the appliance over. The larger units usually have heating elements in both top and bottom. Most are equipped to spit-roast. A few have griddles on the cabinet top. Both large and small models are thermostatically controlled.

Clean a broiler after every use. Wash removable parts in the sink and the broiler itself with paper towels followed by a sponge dipped in detergent solution. Avoid using abrasive cleansers.

Wipe off the outside of the broiler with detergent solution. If food and grease are baked on, see *Chromium Plate* for how to clean.

Bronze. Bronze is an alloy of copper and tin. It is usually found in the home in the form of rather thick, heavy articles such as sundials and medallions. Clean it like brass with brass polish. If an article is broken, you can repair it with epoxy glue; but it is better to have it welded.

Bronze Wool. See *Abrasives.*

Brooms. When you buy a broom, buy the best. It doesn't cost that much more than a cheap broom, but it lasts much longer and isn't a constant source of irritation.

The best brooms are made of yellow straw. Anything else is a waste of time. Organizations of the blind make some of the best brooms you can buy.

For general purposes, buy a big broom measuring about 10 inches wide and 14 inches long. You can also make good use of a whisk broom for little jobs. Children's brooms made of straw make splendid hearth brooms.

There is no crying need for a push broom when you have a large straw broom; but there is no doubt that it is useful for cleaning large expanses, such as terraces and basements. Push brooms for household use are 14, 18, and 24 inches wide. You can get brooms with soft or stiff bristles. The former are good on slick floors; but the latter are more generally useful and almost essential on concrete, brick, and other semi-rough floors. The best bristles are made from the palmyra palm. They stay stiff when wet and are not damaged by oil or grease. A street broom with very stiff, long bristles is useful for outdoor work. A new indoor broom which might also be useful has a rubber squeegee blade inserted between the rows of bristles.

Push brooms have screw-in wood handles, and the broom heads have two sockets so you can reverse them when the bristles become worn. This is a worthy idea but it doesn't work because the handles have an annoying tendency to come loose. You can prevent this to some extent by wrapping the handle threads in a strip of friction tape before screwing into the head. A better idea is to drive a round-headed steel screw through the broom head into the handle after the latter has been screwed in tight.

Store brooms by clamping the handles in U-shaped spring wall clamps. If a broom gets very dirty, wash it out under a hard stream of water and shake it as dry as possible. To lengthen the life of a straw broom, do not use it as a scrubbing brush. Buy a long-handled scrubbing brush instead: it is cheaper and does a better job.

Brushed Chrome. This is actually stainless steel with a dull matte finish. It is used on major appliances. When it is very dirty or greasy, it must be washed with a detergent solution; but this treatment ordinarily leaves streaks, so you should finish the job by rubbing with a cloth dampened with rubbing alcohol or with a solution of 2 tablespoons water softener in 1 quart warm water.

To remove stubborn stains, clean with detergent and then apply a strong grease and carbon remover and allow it to stand for 30 minutes or longer. Then agitate the remover and rinse it off.

If the steel is scratched, leave well enough alone.

Brushes. There are household brushes made for general scrubbing and floor scrubbing (the latter have long handles); dusting; and also for cleaning sinks, dishes, vegetables, bottles, coffee-makers, and so on.

Brushes with natural bristles clean better than those with nylon because the bristles are stiffer; but the nylon bristles look and stay cleaner. Those with long wood handles are much sturdier and less likely to break than those with plastic handles.

Old toothbrushes are very useful for cleaning silverware and other articles with deeply embossed or carved surfaces.

Also see *Paintbrushes.*

Buckram. A stiff, cotton fabric used for clothing linings and bookcovers. Wash in hot water and dry at high heat.

Built-ins. Since World War II, interest in building furniture and equipment into the house has burgeoned. There have been three principal reasons for the trend: (1) Theoretically, built-ins are more attractive than freestanding pieces simply because they blend into their surroundings and eliminate dark cracks and crannies. (2) Theoretically, they help to organize the space in a room better. (3) They simplify housecleaning because dirt cannot get behind or under them.

The last is a completely valid point. For example, when an oven is built into a large cabinet or wall, you never have to worry about cleaning around the sides, top, or bottom. Similarly, a built-in bathroom vanity simplifies floor mopping because dirt does not collect under or behind it and you don't have to mop around legs.

However, there are no grounds for the blanket contention that built-ins are more attractive than freestanding pieces. They may be; and then again, they may not be. And while it may be true that built-ins sometimes do make for better organization and utilization of space in the house, it is equally true that they sometimes make a room difficult to use well—and what's more, you are stuck with these difficulties.

One other point against some built-ins is that while they simplify cleaning, they may add to your work or discomfort in other ways. For example, a built-in bed is a miserable thing to make. A built-in seat is, as a rule, wretched to sit on.

In short, building built-ins just because they have enjoyed some vogue doesn't make any sense. You should first make sure that they are the most logical answer to your needs. You should then design them with care to make certain they are both functional and decorative.

Bureau. A chest used in the bedroom. See *Drawers* and *Furniture, Wood.*

Burglarproofing the House. This is a matter of growing concern to people all over the United States. As a result, new gadgets and elaborate systems for foiling intruders are being rushed to the market by many business firms. Many of these are of little value; many have not been tested adequately; many are being sold by high-pressure tactics. If you are interested in protecting your home against burglars, take plenty of time to investigate how well such devices work, what they cost, who has used them, what your police department thinks of them.

One thing you should remember about burglarproofing your house is that if a burglar is determined to get in, he probably will no matter what you do. But generally he is interested only in jobs that he can do quickly, easily, and safely. Therefore the main aim in burglarproofing most homes is to scare the burglar away and, failing that, to slow him down.

Here are a number of things you can or should do to discourage intruders:

Equip all exterior doors with top-quality locks—not the cheap things that most builders install. The man who can best advise you as to what you need is a locksmith—not a hardware dealer. Chances are he will recommend cylinder locks (which are also recommended by the International Association of Chiefs of Police) and perhaps deadbolts in addition.

Since burglars tend to prefer back, side, and garage doors to front doors, it is just as important that you put good locks on them as on front doors.

French doors should be protected by locks and also by bolts that catch in the floor and top doorjamb.

Sliding doors are usually pretty difficult to jimmy, and if you live in a built-up area, no sensible burglar will give serious thought to rousing the neighborhood by breaking the glass. However, you can make the doors even harder to open simply by laying a metal rod in the inside track.

Windows should have locks, too. They won't stop a burglar from breaking the glass and entering. But they will slow him down.

Floodlight your yard. Inasmuch as about half of all burglaries take place during the day, lights may be only 50 percent effective. But they are inexpensive to install and operate. For most homes you need only four to six to illuminate the area all around the house.

Get a dog. It doesn't have to be a German shepherd or Doberman. And it certainly doesn't have to be a big dog of any description, because many of them are very lethargic watchdogs. All you need is a dog that is alert and makes noise; and if he happens to be suspicious of strangers and mildly frightening (but not frightening enough to scare off deliverymen), so much the better.

Improve the shrubbery at the rear of the house. If it is tall and not too dense, it is easy for a burglar to hide in. You should either trim it back or replant with dense, thorny plants which no one would dare

climb into (and which might even catch a man).

Install an alarm system. There are plenty of good ones and plenty of poor ones. They cost from a few dollars to $500 and more. The main thing is to make sure that they work, and that they do not interfere with your own movements unnecessarily, and that the alarm they sound is loud.

Don't be careless yourself. Don't leave your house unlocked even when you are working out back in the garden, up in the attic, or have stepped next door for a cup of coffee.

Don't pin notes on your door when you go out.

Don't hide the door key where the burglar knows everyone hides the key—under the mat, over the door, in a flower pot, behind a post.

Stop mail, newspapers, milk, and other deliveries when you go out of town for more than a couple of days, and notify the police.

Don't carry on in public about your possessions, vacation plans—anything that may invite the interest of a burglar.

Don't open your house to the public on house or garden tours.

Burlap. This rough-textured material made of jute or sometimes hemp is often used for draperies and bedspreads, as a background for needlework and appliqués, and as a wall covering. It is a strong, durable fabric but ravels easily and fades badly. It must be dry-cleaned. Iron with a hot iron.

Burlap is applied as a wall covering in the same way as wallpaper, but there are several points of difference: Use cellulose paste and apply it to two or three strips ahead of your work so it will have time to soak into the fibers. After the burlap is on the wall, smooth lightly from the center toward the edges. Be careful not to stretch or warp the fibers. To avoid raveling or distorting the fibers at the top and bottom of each strip, trim with scissors rather than a razor blade. Butt the joints.

There is no satisfactory way to clean burlap wall coverings. Just do the best you can with cleaning fluid. When a wall becomes very dirty or faded, the only way to restore its appearance is to paint it. At least three coats will be required to produce a fairly even finish.

Calico. A simple, inexpensive cotton fabric used mainly in clothing. Wash like cotton.

Cambric. This is a soft, smooth, lightweight fabric sometimes made of linen but usually made of cotton. Launder like these materials.

Camel's Hair. The hair of the two-humped camel. It is woven (sometimes with wool) into a soft, beautiful clothing fabric and is also used in throws. Articles made of it should be dry-cleaned.

Candles. Candles wilt in hot weather; and once that happens, it is difficult to make them look decent again. So if you live in a climate where the temperature soars, remove candles from their holders and store them in a box. Some people even put them in the freezer.

If the surface of a colored candle is chipped, lay the candle flat and hold the chip in tweezers over the break. Then melt it with a match into the break. You won't achieve a perfect surface, but at least the chipped area will be covered.

If the chip is missing, melt a little paraffin in a pan and tint it with a crayon. Then drip it into the break.

Candlesticks. To keep candles from dripping onto candlesticks and the furniture, use bobèches. These are slightly cupped flattish rings—usually of glass—which are slid down over the candles and rest on the candlestick holders.

Candlewick. A cotton fabric with small, button-like tufts of threads on the front side. The tufts are spaced and arranged to form a decorative design. The material is used mostly for bedspreads. Wash it like cotton. Dry in a dryer on low heat to avoid shrinkage, or dry on a line on a windy day.

Can Openers. Many people scoffed at electric can openers when they were introduced; but they soon discovered what they thought to be an unnecessary luxury was, in fact, a tremendous convenience. Today, few other appliances are as popular.

The hand-operated Miracle can opener which nips a can rim like a pair of pliers does an excellent cutting job and leaves a smooth, safe rim—just as an electric can opener does. But using it seems like frightful drudgery once you have operated an electric opener.

Electric can openers are available in counter-top or hanging models. They often are combined with other small appliances, particularly a knife sharpener or an ice crusher. Jar and bottle openers and juicers are also teamed with can openers.

Most can openers have a magnet to hold the top suspended when it's free of the can (so it won't fall into the contents) and are able to hold securely and cut open even the largest fruit-juice can. (Some also have a special supporter foot to pull out for an extra-large can.) Some can openers stop automatically when the top has been cut off; others stop only when you turn them off.

Some can openers have a cutting assembly that pops out when you pull it or push a button. The magnet comes with it. In other can openers, the magnet lifts off, and the cutting wheel must be unscrewed. Obviously, the pop-out type is a time-saver; and because you wash it more often, it operates more efficiently. A dirty cutting assembly looks nasty and does not hold a can well or cut well.

Wash the assembly in a strong detergent solution. Take care not to lose any of the parts. Wipe off the body of the can opener with detergent solution, too.

Canvas. Canvas is a strong, heavy, closely woven utility fabric—usually of cotton—which is not much used around the home except for chair seats and backs, awnings, and as a covering for decks (which see). It fades and soils readily and is difficult to clean except by hard scrubbing in a very hot detergent solution. For white canvas, use a strong bleach.

Holes and tears can be mended with needle and heavy thread; but an easier solution is to glue on a patch with pinked edges. Use fabric-mending adhesive.

Carbon Tetrachloride. A cleaning fluid and solvent; but because it is extremely toxic, you should never use it. See *Cleaning Fluids.*

Carpet Beetles. See *Pest Control.*

Carpet, Indoor-Outdoor. Developed for outdoor use on terraces, decks, entry walks, pool decks, etc., this revolutionary carpet is today used indoors more than out. The reasons: It's low in cost; also durable and easy to maintain. But it does not by any stretch of the imagination measure up to regular indoor carpet in beauty and luxurious comfort.

Because good indoor-outdoor carpets are made of synthetic materials, they do not rot, mildew, or shrink, and are extremely resistant to fading, heat, and stains. But they have a low melting point and will burn readily if you drop cigarettes or burning charcoal on them.

The original indoor-outdoor carpet was made of polypropylene. This is still widely used because of its extra-low cost. Acrylic and nylon carpets, however, are considerably more attractive and durable.

Whatever the material, indoor-outdoor carpet must be laid on a smooth surface if you expect it to look well for a long time. Carpet laid on a rough or uneven surface wears out more rapidly at the high spots.

Most home owners make their own installations since the carpet is easy to cut with scissors or a sharp knife, and does not ravel. Anchoring with adhesive or with double-faced adhesive tape is not necessary except where the carpet may be scuffed.

Whether installed outdoors or in, indoor-outdoor carpet should be given the same care as ordinary rugs. Vacuum it regularly, and when it becomes dirty all over, clean it with a hose and a broom. Wipe up spills promptly, and don't give stains any more time to set than you can help. See *Rugs.*

If possible, change the position of the carpet or give it a quarter turn if it begins to show heavy wear from traffic. Some carpet looks the same on the topside and underside and can be flipped over.

If a carpet is burned in spots or develops a hole, you can cut out the damaged sections and set in patches.

Carpets. See *Rugs.* Although carpets and rugs are actually the same thing, carpets are usually considered to cover a floor from wall to wall. Hall and stair runners are also called carpets. By contrast, rugs cover only part of the floor in a room.

Carpet Sweepers. A carpet sweeper is a lightweight tool with a long handle and wide, flat cleaning head containing one or two round brushes and a dustpan. As you push the sweeper back and forth on the floor, the revolving brushes pick up dirt which is then removed by built-in combs and dropped into the dustpan.

The best carpet sweepers can be adjusted to clean either carpets or bare floors. They are surprisingly effective but they cannot be compared with a vacuum cleaner—even a lightweight upright vacuum cleaner. On the other hand, they are considerably lighter than vacuums, and since you don't have to plug them in, they are less of a nuisance to operate.

In short, a carpet sweeper should not be used for thorough cleaning; but it's a useful tool for tidying up the house.

There is little to go wrong in a carpet sweeper. Just keep the brushes free of threads and strings that wrap around them. Clean the combs, too. The brushes need to be replaced when the bristles are worn down.

Carpet Tiles. Carpet tiles with adhesive backing resemble indoor-outdoor carpet and are made of the same materials (usually polypropylene) but are designed for indoor service only. They are available in 9-, 12-, and 18-inch squares and also in special shapes of roughly the same size.

The tiles can be laid on any smooth, clean, dry, dust-free floor on or below grade. There is no need to remove wax or to take up resilient flooring. They are installed, like resilient floor tiles, from the center of the room (see *Floors, Resilient,* page 106). Arrows on the back show the direction in which they should be laid.

There is nothing to peel from the back of the tiles. You just stick them to the floor. They will hold securely once installed but can be removed and placed elsewhere at any time.

Although the tiles are resistant to stains and moisture, spills should be cleaned up promptly. Vacuum regularly to take up dust and grit.

Cashmere. Made from the undercoat hairs of Kashmir goats, this fabric is one of the softest, most luxurious, and expensive materials used for clothing. There are also imitation cashmere fabrics made from sheep's wool. In either case, garments should be dry-cleaned.

Casters. If a caster falls out of a leg every time the furniture piece is lifted, wrap the shank with adhesive or friction tape and force it into the socket.

Clean casters once a year to remove dust, dirt, and threads that may keep them from turning. Add a drop of oil or spray with silicone lubricant, and be sure to remove the excess that might drip on the floor.

Cast Iron. Cast iron is used in cooking utensils, barbecue grills, hot plates, small cooking stoves, outdoor furniture, etc. It is heavy, thick, rather brittle, and has a slightly coarse, dull-gray surface. It rusts rapidly when wet.

Most cast-iron articles are painted—usually black—to keep them from rusting. New iron can be coated with two coats of enamel; but it is better to apply a rust-inhibiting primer and then enamel. Once finished, the paint film should not be allowed to crack or chip so that water can reach the metal. For this reason, any article exposed to the weather should be painted every spring.

If a thick paint coating becomes scarred or broken and the iron shows rust marks, chip off the paint with a cold chisel. To remove rust, use sandpaper, steel wool, a wire brush, a scraper—anything that seems to make an impression. After the worst of the rust is gone, apply naval jelly or any other type of rust remover. Then rinse with naphtha or turpentine, dry, apply a primer and new enamel.

Cast-iron utensils are not finished; but some such as frying pans gradually acquire a film of grease that protects them to considerable extent against rusting. These utensils should never be washed with soap or detergent or put into a dishwasher, because that would cut the grease film. Just wipe with paper towels, wash under the faucet, and dry well.

Utensils without a grease film can be washed with soap or detergent.

Cast iron that breaks can be permanently repaired only by welding. Articles that do not get heavy use or are not exposed to heat can be mended with epoxy glue. The broken edges must be well cleaned before the glue is applied.

Caulking. Caulking compound is a mastic used outside and inside the house to seal joints that might otherwise admit water or air.

Joints that are most commonly caulked include those around door and window frames, at the juncture of different materials (metal flashing and masonry, for example), between exterior steps and landing platforms, between lengths of aluminum gutter, and around the rims of tubs and shower-stall receptors. You should make a point of examining and repairing all caulked joints every six months.

Many joints are caulked at the time a house is built. But because of the settling and shrinkage of the structure, many other cracks and joints open up which must later be caulked by the home owner. In addition, the original caulking often gives way and must be replaced.

Caulking compounds are much alike in appearance but quite unlike in performance. Do not use old-style compounds with an oil base. The best materials available today are made either with silicone or polysulfide rubber. These cost considerably more than other compounds. But they are much more durable and flexible, dry out slowly, and resist cracking. As a result, when you apply them to a joint, you can be pretty certain that the joint will remain tight and sound for years.

Furthermore, both of these compounds have great strength even when immersed in water, and they stick with remarkable tenacity.

Caulking comes in squeeze tubes, which are good for small jobs. It is also available in rigid cartridges, which are used in a caulking gun. Use the latter if you have a lot of caulking to do.

When caulking a joint, make sure that it is clean and dry. Squeeze the compound into it evenly and slowly, making sure that the joint is well filled. Outside the house, leave the bead as is. Inside, smooth it down with a small spatula, knife blade, or round pencil with eraser removed. Wipe up the excess at once.

C Clamps. See *Tools, Workshop.*

Cedar Closets. The value of cedar closets is that they repel moths, that is, discourage them from entering. They do not kill moths; consequently, you should make sure that clothes are clean and uninfested when they are stored.

Cedar boards used to build a closet are 3/8 inch thick, 2 to 4 inches wide, and 2 to 8 feet long. They usually come in bundles which cover approximately 30 square feet. The boards are tongue-and-grooved along the edges and also at the ends. This helps further to keep out moths and other insects; makes for fast construction once the first boards have been installed; and because of the interlocking end joints, it is not necessary to make all vertical joints over studs, where they can be nailed.

You can line an existing closet with cedar boards. But before doing so, remove shelves, shelf supports, and baseboards.

In an attic or basement, erect a framework of 2-by-4s for the closet. These should be spaced 16 inches apart on centers. The cedar boards are applied to the inside surfaces of the studs and joists.

In a basement, to protect clothing against mildew, cover the concrete slab with heavy polyethylene film, and erect the floor on 2-by-4s laid on top.

Install the cedar boards horizontally, one wall at a time. Work from the bottom up. Scribe the first board to the floor so that the top edge is perfectly level. All succeeding boards should then fall into place. You need only one finishing nail per stud to hold them.

For the best appearance, the boards should be scribed to the end walls carefully so that they meet in the corners without cracks. The alternative is to make the corner joints as well as you can and then to close them with quarter-rounds.

For maximum effectiveness in repelling moths, the floor and ceiling of the closet should be made with cedar boards; the back of the closet door should be lined with cedar; and the shelves and baseboards should be of cedar, too (1-inch-thick cedar boards for shelves are available).

Weatherstrip the door at the sides and top to seal the cracks around it. Underneath, install an aluminum threshold with a vinyl strip that presses against the bottom of the door.

Do not apply any finish to the cedar because it will seal off the boards' aroma. If in time the boards seem to lose their aroma, you can restore them to normal by sanding with fine sandpaper or steel wool.

Ceilings. Cracks and holes in ceilings are repaired as in walls of the same material.

In most rooms, ceilings need to be cleaned only when there are cobwebs and dust festoons. Use a small vacuum cleaner brush and avoid touching it directly to the ceiling, since it may make smears.

To wash grease from kitchen ceilings—a job that you may have to do about once a year—get up on a ladder with a sponge and bucket of detergent solution. Use wide semi-circular strokes. Change the solution frequently. Unless the room is a small one that you can cover in short order, don't try to wash the entire ceiling at once. Go over a relatively small area and rinse well while the surface is still wet.

Smoke stains on ceilings are washed off in the same way. Unfortunately, even though a stain may be confined to a fairly small area, the area when cleaned may stand out as boldly as when it was dirty; so you may wind up washing the entire ceiling.

How to build a ceiling. The easiest material to apply is acoustical tile or non-acoustical ceiling tile. See *Acoustical Tile.*

The basic technique for applying gypsum board is described under *Walls, Gypsum-Board.* Use ½-inch boards if there is a room overhead; 3/8-inch otherwise (the former make a slightly better sound barrier).

If you are also installing gypsum board on the walls in the room, put up the ceiling first. You will need a helper to raise, hold, and secure the heavy panels. In addition, you will probably find it helpful to support each panel with a T-shaped brace. Use a 2-by-2 or 2-by-4 for the upright; any board about 2 feet long for the crossbar. The brace should be about 1 inch longer than the distance from the floor to the bottom of the gypsum panels.

BRACE FOR BUILDING A GYPSUM-BOARD CEILING

Ceiling Tile. This is another name for acoustical tile, but it refers also to tiles that lack acoustical characteristics. It should be noted that ceiling tiles are not limited to use on ceilings. See *Acoustical Tile.*

Cellophane. Cellophane is a plastic film made of viscose. Closely related to rayon, it is widely used as a packaging material. Two layers of cellophane can be sealed tight shut by placing them together and pressing them briefly with a warm iron.

Cellulose Cement. See *Gluing.*

Cement. See *Concrete.*

Centipedes. See *Pest Control.*

Ceramics. Ceramics, made from clay by shaping and firing at high temperatures, include bricks and tiles and other mundane articles as well as beautiful china, earthenware, pottery, porcelains, and the like. For how to use and/or take care of a specific ceramic article, see the entry for that article or material.

Chairs. For how to take care of chairs, refinish, and reupholster them, see various entries under *Furniture.*

How to repair wood chairs. Loose joints. All are fixed in the same way, but for simplicity we shall talk only about rungs.

If the rung is loose but cannot be pulled completely from the mortise, dribble white glue around the joint and work the rung back and forth in order to flow the glue further down. If the looseness persists, drive a small finishing nail through the leg into the concealed side of the rung, cut the nail off flush with the leg, countersink, and fill the hole with plastic wood.

If the rung is completely loose, scrape the old glue from the end and from inside the mortise. Test whether the rung can be driven all the way into the mortise. If it cannot be, reduce the diameter very slightly with a file. Coat the rung and inside of the mortise with a little white wood glue, reset the rung, and wipe off excess glue. Then tie a strong cord around the leg and the leg at the other end of the rung. Slip pieces of cardboard or folded newspaper between the cord and the legs. Insert a short stick of wood between the parallel strands and turn it around and around to pull the legs together as tightly as possible. Do not remove the tourniquet for 24 hours.

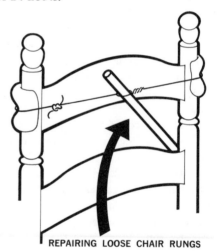

REPAIRING LOOSE CHAIR RUNGS

If the end of a rung is too small to hold in the mortise, coat it with glue and wrap it solidly with thread. When the glue dries, thus cementing the thread to the wood, apply additional glue and reset the rung in the way just described. An alternate solution is to coat the rung with glue and set it into the leg. Then tap toothpicks around it into the joint.

Wobbly chair legs. If it is impossible to force glue into the joints, try to figure out some way of reinforcing them with angle irons. The only other solution is to tie the four legs together with a metal stretcher like that shown. Unfortunately, this is an ugly device and should therefore be used only if it can be concealed by the chair frame.

REPAIRING WOBBLY CHAIR LEGS USING METAL STRETCHER

Set screw eyes in legs above rungs. Loosen turnbuckle, attach it to screw eyes with equal lengths of galvanized wire, and then retighten turnbuckle.

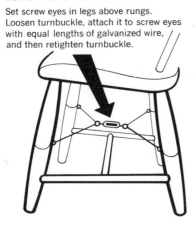

Leg, rung, or slat broken. If it is a longitudinal break, coat the broken edges with white wood glue and clamp them together for 24 hours with C clamps. A sharp break, however, cannot be glued successfully, even with epoxy. The pieces must be doweled together by a professional.

If a leg or other piece breaks sharply close to the mortise, the only way to remove what is left from the mortise is to saw off the protruding stump; then drill out the hole. A new leg will then have to be set in.

Wood seat broken. Apply white wood glue to the broken edges or dribble glue into the crack. Then reinforce the seat underneath by screwing flat steel mending plates across the break. Better still, cut out of 1/8-inch tempered hardboard a square slightly smaller than the chair bottom, and glue and screw this to the bottom.

Chair legs of different length. Stand the chair on a piece of plywood. Lay a saw flat on the plywood and cut off the end of the longest leg. Repeat this process as necessary, sawing off only the thickness of the saw blade each time.

Veneered chair back cracked. Thin, cut-out backs of chairs are often cracked or shattered by some one leaning back too hard. Brush or dribble glue into the broken

wood. Wipe off the excess. Sandwich the back between sheets of wax paper and two boards. Clamp the boards tight with C clamps.

Springs in Danish chair weak. These are commonly made of rubber strap webbing or plastic-covered coil springs. If replacements are not available, you can buy flat, S-type steel springs from mail-order houses. Cut to the proper length and attach to the frame with the clips that come with the springs. Space the springs 1 to 1½ inches apart.

Challis (*shall*-lee). A fabric, once made of wool but now of rayon or cotton. It looks like soft, extremely lightweight wool; is used for blanket covers and clothing. Launder it like rayon or cotton.

Chambray (*sham*-bray). A fine, lustrous cotton, silk, or linen fabric used in clothing. The color effect is changeable. Launder cotton and linen chambray like cotton; silk chambray like silk.

Chamois. A soft, pliable, light-colored, oil-tanned leather which is indispensable for drying windows, automobiles, etc., after washing. It is very absorbent, and does not leave lint on the dried surface.

Before using a chamois, soak it in water till it is wet through; then squeeze dry. It will now take up the water on the windows rapidly. Whenever it becomes sodden, squeeze it dry again.

Some chamois are stronger than others, but even the best eventually start to disintegrate if wrung out too hard. Squeezing is better.

When you are through using a chamois, wash it out in soapy water if dirty; rinse well; squeeze dry; and hang it spread out over a line.

Chest of Drawers. For how to take care of a chest of drawers or refinish it, see *Furniture, Wood,* and *Knobs and Pulls.*

Tops of chests that receive hard wear—in the bedroom and dining room, particularly—should be covered with scarves or plate glass.

Chests. Chests are nothing more than boxes with hinged lids. They are used for storing jewelry, silver, toys, tools, linens, cushions, firewood—just about anything.

Some chests are beautiful and should be treated like the fine furniture they are. Others are simple utility storage units which you may or may not bother to paint or stain.

To build a utility chest, use 1-inch boards or 5/8-inch plywood or both. Make the bottom out of plywood. Fit the sides around the edges of the bottom. For strength, glue the joints in addition to nailing or screwing them. Cut the top to cover the sides and attach it to one side with T hinges (see *Hinges*) screwed inside the side and to the bottom of the top. To keep the top from being thrown open and eventually coming loose, connect it to one end of the box with a lightweight chain or arm like that used on storm windows. Use a hasp to keep the lid closed and, if you want, locked.

Chevron Fasteners. See *Wood Fasteners.*

Chiffon. Chiffon is a soft, loose, lightweight fabric made of silk, rayon, or nylon and used in clothing. It must be dry-cleaned. Iron with a cool iron.

Fabrics that are called chiffon velvet, chiffon taffeta, etc., are not usually chiffon. In their case, the word "chiffon" is used as an adjective to describe a material resembling chiffon in sheerness and softness.

Chiffonier. A tall chest of drawers generally used for storing clothes; but some types of chiffoniers have been used for storing books or china. See *Drawers* and *Furniture, Wood.*

Chifforobe. A tall chest of drawers with an adjoining cabinet for hanging clothes. See *Drawers* and *Furniture, Wood* for how to take care of one.

China. Of the several types of dinnerware and other ceramic articles you can buy, china (also called chinaware or sometimes Chinese porcelain) is the finest. Made of a carefully concocted mixture of clay and stone and fired at high temperatures, it is lovely to look at and touch, translucent, non-water-absorptive, and resistant to damage. Bone china is exceptionally white as a result of the addition of bone ash.

Almost all china today is glazed after it is decorated. This is called underglazing.

As a result, it can be safely washed in the dishwasher. Gold paint, however, is applied after glazing and gold-decorated china should be washed by hand. Most old china is also decorated after it is glazed (this is called overglazing) and should not go into a dishwasher.

If a piece of china of any type is broken, wash and dry it well. Then glue it together with cellulose cement or epoxy glue. The latter is better if the piece is used and washed frequently. Cellulose cement, however, makes a neater mend because it is colorless.

One of the small problems in repairing china—as well as other kinds of dinnerware and glass—is to hold the pieces together while the glue is setting. Just paste a strip or two of cellulose tape or masking tape across the break after gluing.

For a discussion of what china a family should buy, see *Dinnerware.*

Chintz. A colorful cotton fabric available with and without a glazed finish. It is used in clothing, slipcovers, and curtains. Launder in luke-warm water to preserve the finish. The more expensive the fabric, the more permanent the glaze. Press while damp with a moderately hot iron.

Chisels. See *Tools, Workshop—Carpenter's chisel; Cold chisel.*

Christmas-Tree Lights. If Christmas-tree lights are not kept in good condition, they have great potential for starting fires.

Before hanging lights on a tree, inspect the wires to see that they are not broken or pulled out of the sockets and that the insulation is intact. If broken, splice the wires and solder them, if possible (see *Electric Cords*). If the insulation is cut, overwrap the area tightly with cellulose electrical tape. Rather than trying to fix a defective socket (a pretty hopeless job), cut it out and splice the wires.

Check the bulbs and replace any that are defective. A bulb that works but that has slightly loosened from its base is not safe.

Because there is some danger of starting a blaze if you plug a light string into an outlet under the tree, plug it permanently into an extension cord that is plugged into an outlet removed from the tree. Plug the latter in and out to turn the lights on and off.

Never use lights on an aluminum tree; and if a fir or pine tree dries out badly, discontinue using lights on it.

When storing lights, remember that mice sometimes gnaw on the insulation. To prevent this, wrap the strings—whether you keep them in their original boxes or not—in heavy aluminum foil.

Lighting outdoor trees. Use bulbs and strings made for outdoor service. They are not damaged by moisture. Use heavy-duty outdoor extension cords, too.

To keep water out of connections between extension cords and between an extension cord and a light string, wrap the connection with electrical tape and drape it on a stake off the ground.

To keep moisture out of sockets and to hold bulbs tight, slip rubber washers over the bases of all 6-watt and larger bulbs. A strip of cellulose electrical tape wrapped around the socket opening does equally well.

Check insulation and bulbs as for indoor strings.

To protect the trees, do not use the metal spring clips on the light sockets to hang the lights. They shred the bark badly. Hang the lights instead with Christmas-tree ornament hooks. (You should do the same thing on live indoor trees).

Christmas-Tree Ornaments. It is almost impossible to keep from breaking a certain number of these fragile articles every December when you put up and take down your tree. But there is no excuse for breaking them when you are taking them out of their boxes, putting them back in, or storing them away.

To remove an ornament from a box, try to grasp the entire thing in your fingers. If you can't do that, put a finger under the neck and pull it upright; then lift it out by the hanger. Ornament necks are rather easily broken if you pull the wire hanger sideways against the neck.

Before lifting the ornament completely free from its niche in the box, make sure it is secure on the hanger. If a hanger tends to pull loose, remove it entirely and bend the legs open a little; then replace it in the ornament. If it still pulls loose, replace it with a new hanger. (You should salvage those from broken ornaments.)

When packing ornaments in a box, don't try to force a large one into a small niche. Make sure, also, that the box is deep enough for the ornament.

Wad tissue paper lightly around ornaments you particularly value.

If you lose the dividers for a box, don't just jumble a lot of ornaments together—especially large ornaments. Wrap each one individually in tissue paper or nest them in wadded tissue paper.

When a box tears at the corners, reinforce it with brown wrapping tape. It does not give adequate protection to ornaments otherwise. Boxes that are beyond hope should be discarded. Shoe boxes make good replacements.

If you have a special closet or cabinet just for Christmas ornaments and similar fragile objects, you can stow the small boxes away individually. But if the ornaments go into a closet with a lot of other things, pack the boxes into large cartons. In either case, don't wedge the ornament boxes in too tight a space.

Christmas Trees. A Christmas tree is not a joy if it sprinkles the house with needles, making extra work for the housewife, and if you worry that it may go up in smoke at any time.

One species of conifer is about as good as another when it comes to holding and losing needles. The critical question is the freshness of the tree. If it is cut just about a week before you put it up, it should go through the Christmas season with all its needles intact. Danger from fire is minimal. If it is cut earlier than this, it will not perform as well, but you can improve its needle-holding ability and make it less flammable if you stand it in a bucket of water in a cool but not freezing place for as many days as possible. (Some tree stands have a reservoir so the trunks can stand in water throughout the holiday.)

A live tree is safer than any cut tree, of course. If you buy one, dig the planting hole before the ground freezes and keep the soil from the hole in the basement. If you delay digging, however, you can get the frost out of the ground by building a fire on top of it.

Keep the tree indoors for no more than a week, and water its roots regularly. When you plant it outdoors, water it well, let the ground freeze, then apply a heavy mulch of hay or leaves.

Aluminum and plastic trees are safer than conifers and cleaner as well. The aluminum needles may cut tender skin, however. And you must *never* hang lights on aluminum.

To keep trees of all types from toppling and making a first-class mess, use a heavy stand with wide-spreading legs that do not come loose. Shape the end of the trunk to fit as far down in the holder as possible, and anchor it with the bolts provided.

As a further safeguard, tie several strands of fine wire to the trunk of tall trees and fasten them, guy-wire fashion, to nails driven in the top edges of nearby window and door frames.

Chromium Plate. Chromium plate, also called chrome-plated steel, can usually be cleaned with water alone; but use a detergent solution for grease. If the surface feels slightly gritty and is lightly speckled, apply brass polish.

When food and carbon become baked on, as often happens with waffle irons, wash with detergent; then brush on a strong grease and carbon remover. Allow this to stand for 30 minutes or longer. Then swirl it around with a brush and rinse with water.

Slight scratches in chromium can be concealed to some extent by applying a chrome cleaner and protector. Products of this kind are sold by auto supply stores.

If chromium plate is chipped or scratched from the base metal, clean the area well, apply a red-lead primer, and then a chrome-finish aluminum paint.

Cinder Blocks. A type of concrete block with a very rough texture.

Cleaning Closets. Ideally, the cleaning closet should be in a central location in the house. Also ideally, it should not be more than 16 inches deep, because much space is wasted otherwise. Shelves should be no more than 12 inches deep so you can see and easily get at what is on them. Cover them with vinyl flooring or wall covering so you can clean up spills readily.

The door should be hinged so you can hang things on the back. Leave a gap of 1 inch between the bottom and the floor to admit air and help to prevent spontaneous combustion of oily cloths. It is also a good idea to drill three or four 1-inch holes near the top of the door to promote even better air circulation.

If the closet walls are made of pegboard, you can hang everything that is to be hung exactly where you want it; and later you can rearrange things as necessary. In a new house, the pegboard should be nailed directly to the studs. In an existing house, nail it to 1-inch-thick furring strips which are, in turn, nailed to the old walls.

Use U-shaped spring clips to hold the broom, mops, and other long-handled tools. These should not be used for a vacuum-cleaner hose, however, because they will in time damage the hose. A better way to hang the hose (which has an irritating tendency to fall to the floor if simply tossed over a coat hook) is to screw a spiral door spring to the wall in a horizontal position. Then nail a staple across the middle. This should be loose enough so the spring can move. To store the hose, slip one end up through the spring. Other cleaning tools can also be held in the spring. See *Basement Storage.*

Cleaning Equipment and Supplies. When you have a good, general-purpose vacuum cleaner, you are off to an excellent start in the housecleaning department (see *Vacuum Cleaners*). But it is only a start. You need a lot of other things, too, and you may have use for still others.

The necessities follow:

Broom. A big one made of straw. Small brooms with synthetic bristles are a farce.

Whisk broom. Use it for little jobs, such as whisking off upholstery, draperies, stair runners.

Dustpan. The plastic pans may not last as long as metal, but the lip stays straight and smooth.

Wet mop. If you use a cotton mop—a very simple but good kind—think about investing in a wringer pail. It eliminates much mess and saves your hands. But it is not a necessity. Only the mop is.

Pail. You can get by with one, but you can well use more. The 12-quart size is ample. Make sure it is metal.

Scrubbing brush. You don't need it often, but you can't live without it. Get a big one. When the bristles wear down, replace it.

Toilet brush. Preferably one per bathroom. The old-fashioned kind with a wood handle is a great deal better than the new kind with a plastic handle. The same can be said for brushes with bristles as opposed to those made with rubber heads.

Sponges. Lots of them. The cellulose rectangles are good, expendable, and cheap.

Chamois.

Squeegees. Ideally, you should have the exact-size squeegee for each different small pane size.

Household detergent.

Cleansing powder. You need a general-purpose cleanser and also a tough one for use on rust spots.

Drain solvent.

Toilet bowl cleaner.

Scouring pads.

Single-edged razor blades for cleaning up paint splatters, etc.

Paper toweling.

Treated dust cloths.

Clean rags.

Furniture polish.

White appliance wax.

Floor waxes. Water-based for use on resilient floors; solvent-based for use on wood floors.

Wax applicator.

Upholstery shampooer and shampoo.

Scratch cover-up.

Spot removers of various types.

Brass polish.

Silver polish.

Oven cleaner.

The following cleaning items are necessities in some homes, useful in others:

Untreated dust mop. A definite necessity if you have large expanses of wood, quarry tile, flagstone, or brick floors. But in homes with only a small amount of bare floor, the vacuum cleaner can be used for dusting.

Lightweight upright vacuum cleaner or carpet sweeper.

Electric floor polisher and rug shampooer.

Dust brush. The type that resembles a hairbrush, with long, soft bristles.

Furniture wax.

Ceramic-tile cleaner. You must have it if the type of water in your home stains the grout between tiles.

Disinfectant.

Steel wool. Of course you can always steal it from the workshop.

Rottenstone or powdered pumice stone for removing certain stains from wood.

Several household staples that do not necessarily belong in the cleaning closet but that must be stored someplace (so why not here?) are:

Light bulbs.

Insecticides.

Yardstick.

For more about many of these cleaning tools and supplies, see specific entries such as *Brooms* and *Pails*.

Cleaning Fluids. If you are going to keep things clean around your house, it's essential that you have on hand a cleaning fluid to use on grease, tar, oil, adhesive-tape, and chewing-gum stains. But whatever the liquid, it must be treated with respect. It may be highly flammable; or the fumes may be toxic.

The most dangerous cleaning fluid from the standpoint of health is carbon tetrachloride. It is nonflammable; but if you breath in the fumes to any extent, you may die. It also is harmful to the skin. *Don't ever buy this fluid.*

The other nonflammable cleaning fluids that are most often used for home cleaning contain trichloroethylene, perchloroethylene, or trichloroethane. These are less toxic than carbon tet; nevertheless, when you use them, you must work outdoors or in a well-ventilated room. Since the fumes tend to fall, don't let a child or pet play under your feet.

The flammable cleaning fluids contain a petroleum distillate. They are far less toxic than the foregoing fluids, but you should not take chances with them anyway. Work in a ventilated place. And stay well away from the kitchen range and all other sources of fire.

Whatever cleaning fluid you buy, read the directions carefully before using it. Store it out of reach of children. Never use it in the washing machine. And never place articles you have cleaned in a dryer until after they have been thoroughly washed in water.

Cleansers. Cleansers remove soil that other cleaning agents cannot touch. Although the powders made today are much less abrasive than old-fashioned cleansers (in fact, they are commonly called non-abrasive cleansers), if you tested them on some of the softer plastics or on silverware you would find that they are still capable of dulling the surface. For this reason, they should generally be used only on metals, porcelain enamel, tile, and concrete. There are times, however, when you may need them to remove stubborn spots on softer materials, such as resilient flooring.

Two kinds of cleanser are needed in the home: a general-purpose type and one for removing stains and rust on plumbing fixtures.

Many good general-purpose cleansers are on the market, and all are being improved almost constantly. The type that currently appears most effective contains trisodium phosphate—a potent cleanser in its own right—and chlorine.

For rust stains, use a cleanser containing oxalic acid. Zud is an example.

Clocks. There is very little that most of us can or should do about the clocks in our homes except to keep them going. Dust them regularly and wipe off the face and case (if made of anything other than wood) occasionally with a damp cloth. On a wood case, use furniture polish.

In handling clocks that do not have glass or plastic over the faces, take care not to bend the hands.

If a plastic clock case is cracked, reglue it with plastic-mending adhesive.

To adjust the speed of a pendulum clock, raise the weight on the pendulum to make it go faster; lower it to make it go slower. To raise the weight, turn the knob under it clockwise; to lower, turn the knob counterclockwise.

To hang a wall clock with a pendulum, use a carpenter's level to make sure it is straight up and down from front to back; otherwise the pendulum will not swing straight. You can wedge the clock out from the wall by sticking thumb tacks into the back at bottom or top.

An electric wall clock is best hung on a special clock hanger-outlet—a rectangular box with the outlet recessed inside. You can cut off the excess cord on the clock, or open the clock and wrap the cord loosely around the works.

Cloisonné (kloy-zon-*ay*). Cloisonné is a lovely, intricate type of enamel in which thin strips of metal separate the colored areas. If damaged in any way, cloisonné should be repaired by a craftsman specializing in enameling. To clean cloisonné, wash with detergent solution. Use the appropriate metal polish on the back of the piece.

Closets. Adding closets to a house does not require a great deal of skill or work.

The very easiest thing you can do is to put in a prefabricated, preassembled closet made of particle board. Units measuring 30 inches deep, 94 inches high, and 3 or 4 feet wide are available. They incorporate bi-fold doors, two shelves, and a clothes rod.

To install one of the closets, cut out a section of baseboard of the same width, slide the closet out of its carton, and stand it upright against the wall, which forms the back of the closet. Secure the sides to the wall by toenailing them from the inside or fastening them with angle irons. To close the space between the top of the closet and the ceiling, push the adjustable valance attached to the closet upward. It can be used for ceilings up to 8 feet 2 inches high. If a ceiling is higher, remove the valance and close the space with ½-inch plywood of the proper height. Then insert the closet shelves and rod.

Building a conventional closet is only slightly more difficult.

If the closet is to be installed in a corner (the normal location), draw lines on the floor and ceiling to mark the front and side of the closet. Then cut a 2-by-4 into two short lengths equal to the inside depth of the closet plus 3 5/8 inches. Nail these to the floor and ceiling ½ inch back from the side lines and parallel with them. Cut a 2-by-4 the width of the closet and nail it to the ceiling ½ inch back from the front line. Cut 2-by-4s to fit on either side of the door opening and nail them to the floor ½ inch back from the front line.

The studs for the walls should be cut from 2-by-4s. You will need one stud at the back of the side wall, one for the midpoint of the side wall, two where the side and front walls join, one on either side of the door, and one at the end of the front wall. If any space between two studs is more than 16 inches wide, another stud should be installed between them. Toenail the studs between the floor and ceiling timbers.

Apply ½-inch gypsum board inside and outside the closet. You can, of course, apply any other type of sheet material, such as plywood or hardboard, on the outside; and you can install cedar boards inside. For how to apply these materials, see the appropriate entry.

Install the door casing and trim and hang the door (see *Doors*). Install a steel closet shelf that is adjustable in length (see *Shelves,* page 268).

Closet dimensions. These are variable in the extreme. Some suggestions about the most desirable dimensions are given under *Clothes Closets, Cleaning Closets,* and *Linen Closets.*

How to repair sagging closet shelves and rods. To bolster a shelf, simply screw a large L-shaped shelf bracket to the wall (into a stud) under the middle of the shelf, and then screw it to the shelf.

If a rod sags, loop a wire around it and tie it to a screw eye driven into the bottom of the shelf above the rod. But if the shelf is sagging, too, you must brace it with a shelf bracket.

How to light a closet. Install permanent wiring and center a simple porcelain lampholder with a pull-chain on the wall above the door or on the ceiling forward from the closet shelf. Screw in a 25-watt bulb.

The light can also be controlled by a special switch which is installed in the hinge jamb. The switch automatically turns the light on when the door is opened; off when the door is closed.

If you prefer not to install a permanent light and wiring, a closet light with an extension cord that plugs into any nearby outlet is available. Mounted on the door-jamb inside the door on the latch side, it turns on and off automatically as the door is opened and closed.

A cordless closet light that operates on flashlight batteries works in the same way.

How to control mildew in closets. See *Mildew.*

Clothes Closets. You may never have occasion to build or remodel clothes closets, but if you do there are several dimensions you should think about: (1) Unless it is a big, walk-in closet, a clothes closet should be 24 to 27 inches deep. Anything deeper is a waste of space. (2) The rod should be no less than 5 and no more than 6 feet above the floor. (3) The shelf is 2 inches above the rod and should be at least 8 inches below the closet ceiling.

The wider a closet is, the better. But in order to get at all the clothes on the rod, the door must be almost as wide as the closet. This means that on large closets you may have to use a bi-fold, folding, or sliding door (see *Doors*). Unfortunately, nothing can be hung on the backs of these.

To make maximum use of the space in a desirably shallow closet, many people substitute an 8-foot, ceiling-high door for the conventional 6-foot-8-inch door. This permits installation of two deep shelves rather than one shallow shelf. To be sure, the deep shelves are not an unmixed blessing because the top one is fairly inaccessible and it is easy to lose things in the back of both. On the other hand, they do increase storage space appreciably.

How to make use of a deep, narrow clothes closet. You will never be happy with this kind of a closet but you can improve matters by installing a clothing carrier from the front to the back of the closet. This device incorporates a sliding rod on which clothes hangers are hung. To get at a suit or dress, you just pull the handle on the front of the rod and the rod slides straight out through the closet door opening.

The carrier is screwed to a cleat or under a shelf at the back of the closet and under the top doorjamb at the front. Use a 24-inch carrier for closets 24 to 30 inches deep; 30-inch for closets 30 to 36 inches deep; 36-inch for closets 36 to 42 inches deep; 42-inch for closets 42 to 48 inches deep; 48-inch for closets 48 to 54 inches deep. Ten-, 12-, 16-, and 20-inch carriers are also made for installation in shallow closets.

Another way to improve a deep, narrow closet is to buy a rolling garment rack with a rod for hanging garments, a bottom shelf for shoes, and a top shelf for hats, etc. Some racks can be adjusted in length. For example, a 30-inch rack can be expanded to 48 inches.

Shoe racks. The only reason for storing shoes at the bottom of a closet is to make use of that otherwise useless space. Actually the shoes are not so easy to see and reach as they should be. To keep them from getting kicked around the bottom of the closet, build a 12-inch-deep shelf across the back of the closet 3 to 4 inches above the floor. Close in the space under the shelf so that it does not become clogged with dust and dirt.

A more convenient type of shoe rack is a metal unit with loops over which shoes are slipped toes up. The rack is hung on a wall or back of the door.

Other useful clothes closet accessories. Trouser and skirt hangers with swinging clamp arms. These are usually screwed to a closet wall.

Hanger made of a one-piece steel rod constructed in spiral form holds four trousers or skirts in a tight grip. Mounted on a closet door, it takes up little space.

Coat hooks of various designs. The best are made of heavy cast metal.

Garment brackets to hold coat hangers. They are slightly L-shaped and up to 10 inches long. Mount them on doors in closets which are slightly deeper than necessary.

Hat racks.

Tie racks.

Suspension clothes rods, trouser racks, and skirt racks are hooked over the closet rod and hang about 3 feet below it. They make use of the storage space below men's jackets, skirts, sweaters, and other short articles hung on the top rod.

Zippered garment bags. Those with see-through vinyl fronts are most useful. Small bags are much easier to manage and last longer than large bags.

Zippered storage bags with shelves hang from the closet rod.

Hanging handbag file made of see-through vinyl also hangs from the closet rod. A shoe file of similar design is available but is useful only for women's shoes.

Shelf boxes for dustless storage of hats, shoes, handbags, accessories, etc. They have see-through fronts which are closed with zippers.

Clothes Dryers. The automatic dryer has lagged behind the automatic washer in popularity. Main reason: A feeling on the part of many homemakers that clothes cannot be dried as well in an appliance as on a line exposed to sun and breeze. The exact opposite is the truth.

Clothes dried in a dryer come out softer, fluffier, and with fewer wrinkles than clothes dried on a line. There is no difference in the way they smell (anyone who questions this can buy a dryer in which the circulating air is exposed to an ozone lamp).

What's more, a dryer saves an enormous amount of wearisome work and makes your laundering operations independent of the weather.

Dryers operate on a 240-volt electrical circuit (and some can also be used on 120 volts, although they take twice as long to dry a load of clothes) or on natural or LP gas (these require a 120-volt circuit to rotate the dryer drum). But despite the difference in the fuel used, there is no difference in the operation or performance of the machines.

The most common type of dryer—electric or gas—is a twin of the automatic washer. It has no definite name; but for ease of identification, we shall call it simply an automatic dryer. It has a large rotating drum, accessible through a door in the front of the cabinet, which tumbles the clothes through a stream of warm air.

The most expensive dryers provide a selection of cycles for heavy fabrics, delicate fabrics, permanent press, etc.; a choice of heats; and a choice between fully automatic drying and timed drying. In automatic drying, you simply press a button and the dryer automatically provides the proper temperature and drying time. Some models have an electronic sensor that measures the amount of moisture in the load and turns off the machine when the right degree of dryness is reached. In timed drying, you select the temperature and turn a dial to the desired drying time. Clothes can be dried for a few minutes up to about 2 hours. An average mixed load of cottons, linens, and heavy rayons takes about 40 minutes.

An extremely important feature in all top-model dryers and many medium-priced units as well is a 10-minute cool-down period at the end of the drying period. In this cool-down, the drum continues to rotate but the heat is turned off. This helps to prevent permanent-press fabrics and polyester knits from setting wrinkles as they would if they were allowed to cool off in a heap in the bottom of the dryer drum. Some dryers also sound a signal to warn that the clothes should be removed.

Automatic dryer capacities are similar to automatic washer capacities.

A second type of dryer is the combination washer-dryer. This is the same in size and appearance as a conventional automatic dryer, and does the same drying job. The only difference is that it also washes your clothes. The two kinds of combination washer-dryers are described more fully under *Washing Machines.*

A third type of dryer is a 120-volt electric dryer of compact size. The dimensions vary considerably between makes. One unit looks like a half-size conventional automatic dryer on casters. Others are smaller—no larger than a portable typewriter—and hold about 2 pounds of wet clothes. Whatever the design, compacts have the same tumble-drying action as full-size dryers.

Operating an automatic dryer. For convenience, the dryer is usually installed next to or near the washer. An electric dryer is permanently wired in. A gas dryer must be connected to a gas inlet but the electric cord is plugged into any outlet.

Unless your dryer is installed in a large basement or on a porch, some means should be provided to get rid of the hot, moist air it gives off. (If you don't do this, you will get severe condensation on windows and walls.) The best solution is to vent the dryer directly to the outdoors via a 4-inch metal flue pipe or a flexible plastic hose sold by appliance dealers. The vent line is connected to the back, bottom, or either side of the dryer and can be run through the stud or joist spaces or across the floor. It should be as straight as possible and no more than 20 feet long if it has one elbow; 15 feet with two elbows.

If direct venting is impossible, install a powerful exhaust fan in the laundry.

As a rule, clothes that have been washed together can be dried together. Avoid overloading the dryer. Toss the articles into the dryer drum in any order. It is not necessary to untangle them unless they are literally tied in knots. But make sure they do not contain nails, bobby pins, or other sharp metal objects. Close the door, set the controls, and push the start button.

You can stop the dryer at any time by opening the door. This is a safety feature. Press the start button to restart it.

The dryer shuts off automatically at the end of the cycle. Remove permanent-press articles, polyester knits, laminated fabrics, and any other items that readily set wrinkles as soon as possible. Clean out the lint trap and replace it securely. The dryer is now ready for another load.

If for any reason the dryer drum becomes dirty, you can clean it when it is cool with a mild detergent solution. Wipe it out monthly with a dry cloth to remove lint. Clean the cabinet exterior occasionally with detergent solution or white appliance wax. If the dryer is vented directly to the outdoors, pull it out from the wall twice a year and vacuum the exposed mechanism and floor. Put your vacuum hose into the vent line and clean it also. If the dryer is not vented, you should vacuum behind it at least every two months.

In addition to drying clothes, some dryers can be used to sprinkle clothes before ironing; to take wrinkles out of dry clothes; or to dry such things as newspapers and shoes without tumbling.

Articles that should never be dried in a dryer because of the fire hazard include padded bras and other articles made of foam rubber, galoshes, and rubber-coated tennis shoes, cleaning cloths, mops impregnated with wax, and garments labeled "dry away from heat." Articles that have been home dry-cleaned must also be kept out of the dryer until they have been thoroughly washed and rinsed to remove all traces of flammable fluid.

Fine woolen knits, fiberglass, and permanently pleated articles should also be kept out of the dryer to protect their shape.

If something goes wrong. Scratches in the enamel surface can be repaired with touch-up enamel.

Replace a burned-out light in the control panel or dryer drum or a burned-out ozone lamp in accordance with the manufacturer's instructions.

If anything else goes wrong with your dryer, call a serviceman. Before doing so, however, make sure that:

The fuse has not blown.

The gas pilot light is on.

No metal object has fallen into the dryer drum and caused a short circuit.

The lint trap is clean.

The vent line is not obstructed.

Clothes Hangers. The best hangers for women's dresses, blouses, coats, and jackets are covered with fabric to keep the garments from sliding off. Plastic and wood hangers with notches for straps are not so effective.

The most expensive hangers for men's coats and jackets are made of thick, polished wood with a contoured back. There is no evidence, however, that these actually keep garments in better shape than simple triangular wood hangers with a crossbar; and they take up more room.

The best trouser hangers are folding, clamp-type gadgets that hang on the closet rod. Larger hangers of the same type are used for skirts. They are easier to use than finger-like hangers into which trousers are slid from front to back. (The latter, however, are useful in fairly deep closets with wasted wall space.)

Tiered blouse, skirt, and slacks hangers that hold up to six garments, one immediately above the other, are useful space savers but awkward to use.

How to repair clothes hangers. If trousers and skirts are not held tight in folding trouser hangers, glue thick strips of felt to the clamping edges with white wood glue.

If the hook in the top of a wood hanger is loose, push it down through its hole as far as possible, coat the end with epoxy cement, and then pull the hook up. Let the glue set for 24 hours.

Cockroaches. See *Pest Control.*

Coffee-Grinders. Electric coffee-grinders are important to anyone who appreciates the superior taste of freshly ground coffee. On some grinders you can preset the size of the grind, from coarse to very fine. Others are controlled by eye and hand: you stop the grinder when the coffee has achieved the desired grind. Grinders are available as separate appliances and also as mixer attachments. (You can also grind coffee beans in a blender.)

A few old-fashioned, hand-cranked grinders are available, too, but these don't hold a candle to the electric models.

Wash out the coffee-bean container with detergent solution occasionally so that it doesn't build up off-flavors.

Coffee-Makers. Most homemakers switch coffee-makers a number of times during their homemaking careers. The reason is obvious: After making coffee in the same way for a long time, you get tired of the way it tastes; and since there are many kinds of coffee-makers and innumerable brands of coffee, it just seems like a good idea to try making coffee another way.

Coffee-makers are generally made of stainless steel, aluminum, porcelain-enameled steel or aluminum, glass or glass-ceramic. One is as good as the other, although glass will, of course, break.

Nonelectric coffee-makers. In percolators, rather coarsely ground coffee is placed in a perforated metal basket atop a hollow tube. When the water underneath begins to boil, it jets up through the tube and out onto the coffee. The longer you perk the coffee, the stronger it becomes.

The standard percolator holds 8 cups, although other sizes are available.

In drip pots, which are generally smaller, finely ground coffee is placed in a basket or compartment in the top of the coffee-maker. This may or may not be lined with filter paper to slow the flow of water and clarify the coffee. Boiling water is then poured directly on the coffee or into a peforated compartment above it, and it slowly drips through into the bottom of the coffee-maker. The strength of the brew depends on the amount of coffee used and the speed with which the water flows.

Espresso coffee-makers are essentially drip pots.

Electric coffee-makers. These range in shape from short and rounded to tall and tapered. They come in sizes from 2- to 4-cup units for small families to urns holding 30 or more cups for a party. Regardless of shape or size, all coffee-makers should be sturdy and well balanced, with a comfortable, heat-resistant handle that keeps your hand well away from the pot. They should be easy to clean so there will be no oily coffee residue that produces bitter brew from even the best coffee grounds. An immersible coffee-maker with a fairly short, wide spout makes washing easy. Stainless steel and aluminum are the materials most often used for percolators; glass and glass-ceramic containers are available also. Water-level markings for the number of cups should be easy to see, whether marked on the inside or outside of the container. Some coffee-makers have a clear tube on the outside indicating the water level inside.

Other useful features shared by most well-designed electric coffee-makers include a control to adjust the strength of the brew from mild to strong; an indicator light to signal when the perking is complete (particularly useful if the pot doesn't have a glass knob on top); and better-designed thermostats that prevent the water from boiling during brewing and keep the coffee at serving temperature.

How to care for a coffee-maker. Needless to say, you should not take a glass coffee-maker from the range and plunge it into cold water. Neither should you take an icy cold pot and fill it with boiling water.

Rinse all coffee-makers thoroughly after every use; and to prevent a build-up of coffee oils and odors on the inside surfaces, wash them weekly with detergent solution. If the surfaces become stained, use a cleanser. In any case, rinse and rinse again.

An easier and even more thorough way to clean nonelectric pots is to put them in the dishwasher once a week. The pots must, of course, have large enough openings so that the hot detergent solution can get into them: hour-glass-shaped pots are impossible to wash in a machine.

Comforters. See *Bedding.*

Compactors. A compactor is a new electrical appliance designed to facilitate disposal of all types of refuse—food wastes, paper, fabrics, metals, glass, etc.

The unit fits under the kitchen counter in a space about 15 inches wide. It incorporates a drawer in which the user places a large plastic-lined paper bag. Trash is tossed into the bag as it accumulates. When the door is closed and a start button is pushed, a powerful metal ram descends on the trash and compacts it to approximately one-quarter of its original size. At the same time, an automatic dispenser sprays a measured amount of deodorant on the trash. When the bag is full (it holds roughly 20 to 30 pounds), it is folded shut and put outdoors for collection.

A family of four which accumulates an average amount of trash uses about one bag a week.

Compactors can be installed on a 120-volt, 15-amp lighting circuit or a 20-amp small-appliance circuit. The ram cover is easily removed for cleaning with detergent solution and the entire collection drawer can, if necessary, be removed for washing.

Concrete. Concrete is not an attractive material as it is most often used. It is not a material the average home owner has any great interest in. It is just a material—basic, strong, durable, utilitarian. Yet anyone concerned with home upkeep and improvement must inevitably use it, and contend with the problems that arise in handling it.

Working with poured concrete. If you need only a small quantity of concrete, you can save work—but not money—by buying bags of mixes to which you simply add water. For very large jobs, have ready-mixed, ready-to-pour concrete delivered by truck.

If mixing your own concrete, you should first make a five-sided wooden measuring box with inside dimensions of 12 by 12 by 12 inches (1 cubic foot). You also need a smooth mixing platform with low sides measuring about 6 by 8 feet.

The four ingredients of concrete are:

(1) Portland cement. Ordinary Portland cement is used for most jobs; but if you live in a cold climate or if you are constructing a walk or driveway on which you may use salt to remove snow and ice, use Type 1A Portland cement. This incor-

porates an air-entraining agent that produces a concrete that is more resistant to scaling and alternate freezing and thawing. Whichever cement you use, it is usually most convenient to buy 94-pound bags comprising 1 cubic foot.

(2) Sand. Buy builder's sand; do not use sea sand. Builder's sand is a coarse mixture of grains of different size—some tiny, some fairly large. It must be free of dirt and vegetable matter.

(3) Coarse aggregate. This consists of clean pebbles or crushed stones between ¼- and 1-inch diameter.

(4) Water. Use clean water from the tap.

The table gives the proportions recommended by the Portland Cement Association for three standard concrete mixes. Although you may increase or decrease the total size of a batch of concrete, do not deviate from these proportions unless the concrete proves too stiff or too wet. In these cases—and in these cases only—you may add sand and aggregate to a wet mix or withhold sand and aggregate from a stiff mix. But do not change the amount of water.

To mix concrete, spread the desired amount of sand on your mixing platform. Spread the cement on top. Turn the materials over with a shovel until the mix-

CORRECT PROPORTION OF MATERIALS FOR DIFFERENT PURPOSES

Kind of Work	Gallons of Water for Each 1-Sack Batch			Trial Mixture for First Batch			Maximum Aggregate Size
	Damp Sand and Pebbles	Wet Sand and Pebbles	Very Wet Sand and Pebbles	Cement	Sand	Pebbles	
Garden walls, Retaining walls, Nonwatertight foundations, Foundation footings	6¼	5½	4¾	Sacks 1	Cu. Ft. 2¾	Cu. Ft. 4	Inches 1½
Watertight basement walls and floors, Lawn rollers, Cold frames, Hotbeds, Well platforms, Septic tanks, Sidewalks, Flagstone walks, Driveways, Play courts, Barbecue base and walls, Porch floors, Garden pools, Steps, Gate posts	5½	5	4¼	1	2¼	3	1½
Fence posts, Mailbox posts, Flower boxes, Benches, Birdbaths, Sundials	4½	4	3¾	1	1¾	2	¾

ture is uniform in color. Then add coarse aggregate and continue turning until the entire mass is of uniform consistency.

Make a hollow in the middle; pour in some of the water and keep on mixing. Continue thus, adding water gradually and mixing, until the entire batch is evenly damp. It is now ready to use—and should be used within the next 30 minutes.

If pouring concrete in forms, as for a walk, coat the forms each time they are used with crankcase oil. The forms must be braced at frequent intervals to keep them from bulging outward. If steel reinforcement is required, secure it so that it will be more or less centered in the concrete. Rust does not destroy the steel's effectiveness.

As you pour concrete (whether in forms or not), spade it well to fill any voids. This also settles the coarse aggregate, leaving a more evenly textured surface.

If making a walk or other flat surface, your next step is to strike off the concrete with a straight board resting on the edges of the forms. Draw the board from one end of the paving to the other while sawing it back and forth across the paving. Then, when the moisture on top of the concrete begins to disappear, smooth the concrete lightly with a wood float (a short length of board with a handle on one side). This leaves an excellent nonskid surface; but for added protection, you can brush the surface lightly with a stiff broom. If, on the other hand, you want a smooth surface (which is less durable than a nonskid surface), let the wood-float surface set until quite stiff; then smooth it with a mason's steel finishing trowel.

To achieve an exposed-aggregate finish, place ordinary concrete in the usual way and smooth it. Then scatter ½-inch to ¾-inch aggregate (pebbles, marble chips, etc.) evenly on the concrete and pat it in until it is completely embedded. As soon as the concrete starts to harden, carefully brush the cement away from the upper part of the aggregate. Use a fine spray of water—but not too much water—to help loosen the cement. Then let the concrete cure. Concrete that sticks to the pebbles can be removed when dry by scrubbing with 1 part muriatic acid in 9 parts water.

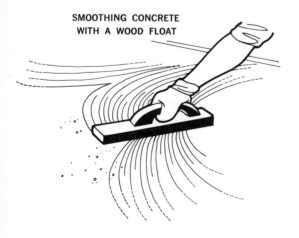

STRIKING OFF CONCRETE WITH A STRAIGHT BOARD

SMOOTHING CONCRETE
WITH A WOOD FLOAT

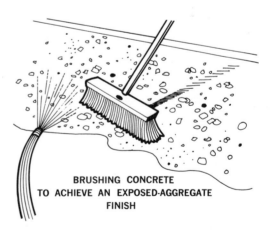

BRUSHING CONCRETE
TO ACHIEVE AN EXPOSED-AGGREGATE
FINISH

Concrete can be colored in several ways but the simplest is to mix a pure mineral oxide made for use in concrete with *white* Portland cement. The pigment should never exceed 10 percent of the weight of the cement. To produce a vivid color, mix 7 pounds pigment with 1 bag of cement; for a pastel, use 1½ pounds pigment. The dry pigment and cement must be mixed very thoroughly to assure a uniform color.

To cure concrete—no matter how it is finished—allow it to set until it no longer shows fingerprints when pressed lightly. Then sprinkle with water and cover with damp burlap. Keep this in place and damp for six days.

Concrete for masonry construction. Mortar for a stone wall is made of 1 part Portland cement and 3 parts sand. When building with brick, concrete block, cinder block, or tile, use 1 part masonry cement (which contains lime) and 2½ to 3 parts sand. In either case, mix the dry ingredients in a box, bucket, or metal wheelbarrow; then add water to make a heavy, plastic mix. It should not be so dry that it looks crumbly. Neither should it ooze water.

Before building a masonry structure, porous materials—especially bricks—should be hosed down or soaked in water. This keeps them from drawing water out of the mortar.

Mortar joints should be at least ½ inch thick. Building with stone, they may be much, much thicker; but generally a good maximum is ¾ inch. Apply the mortar in heavy dollops just before you embed masonry blocks in it. When you are working with bricks, you can apply enough mortar for about three bricks; but with heavier building blocks, apply only enough mortar for about two units. If bricks (or whatever building material you are using) are not soon embedded in fresh mortar, the mortar loses some of the moisture and strength. However, it can be thrown back into the mortar box, mixed in well, and reused.

Latex cement. Latex cement is made by mixing a dry powder with liquid latex. The resulting concrete is very strong even when applied in layers only 1/16 inch thick. (By contrast, Portland cement cannot be used in thicknesses of less than ½ inch.) It is used for resurfacing rough and uneven concrete slabs and steps; for filling shallow cracks; and for resetting bricks, stones, etc., without chipping out all the old mortar. It can even be used to resurface wood floors and floors covered with paint.

A similar material which is used for the same purposes is a cement containing vinyl. It is mixed with water.

A third material of the same type is epoxy cement made by mixing a bottle of emulsion with a bottle of hardener and then stirring in dry cement. It is the toughest of the special cements.

Hydraulic cement. This cement is used to stop active leaks in masonry walls. To use it, mix with tepid water to form a cake with putty-like consistency. Hold in your hands for about 2 minutes, until it is warm; then force it into the leaking hole and keep pressure on it for 3 to 5 minutes until it sets and the leak stops.

How to repair concrete. Cracks. Cut the crack open with a cold chisel. It should be at least ¼ inch wide and the same depth. Blow out loose crumbs. Allow the concrete to dry thoroughly if damp. Then fill with latex cement; press it in firmly; and trowel smooth.

If a concrete slab resting on uneven ground is broken in two, a wide strip of concrete should be broken out with a sledge; or one whole side of the slab should be removed. Then dampen the broken edges with water and brush on a creamy mixture of cement and water. Fill the break with the third mixture (for Fence posts, etc.) listed in the table on page 50. Cure for six days under damp burlap.

Holes. If the hole is very large, follow the directions immediately above. Holes about 1 to 6 inches across are filled with 1 part Portland cement and 2½ parts sand. First dampen the edges of the hole with water and brush on a mixture of cement and water. Small holes are most easily filled with latex cement.

Breaks in concrete objects such as birdbaths. Brush the broken edges clean. If necessary, use water, but allow to dry completely. Then coat one edge with silicone rubber adhesive and press the two pieces together firmly. Clamp or weight them together for 24 hours.

Roughness and unevenness. Clean the surface and allow it to dry. Then trowel on latex cement. If the topping is thin, the cement should be rather damp. For a thick topping, make a heavier mixture. A thick topping can be built up in two layers applied about 2½ hours apart.

How to clean concrete. Dirt. Scrub hard with warm water or a strong detergent solution.

Paint. Soften with paint remover and scrape off.

Oil and grease. If the stains are new, apply a garage floor cleaner available from an auto supply store or brush ordinary cat litter back and forth over them. Old stains are treated with one of the special heavy-duty cleaners used in gas stations.

Rust stains. Scrub with a bristle brush and a phosphoric acid cleaner (for example, Rust-Oleum Surfa-Etch). Rinse thoroughly.

Smoke stains. Scrub with an abrasive cleanser.

How to paint concrete. If the concrete is dirty or covered with mildew, efflorescence, or moss, scrub it first with 1 part muriatic acid in 3 parts water. Rinse well. Then apply a latex primer followed by one or two finish coats of latex paint.

Another excellent finish for concrete—particularly exterior walls—is Portland cement paint. After cleaning the surface, dampen it uniformly with a hose; then apply a coat of paint with a stiff bristle brush. After it has set for a couple of hours, sprinkle it with water every few hours. A second coat is applied in the same way 24 hours later. This should be kept damp for 48 hours.

For an exceptionally durable, glossy finish, use epoxy paint. This is particularly recommended for concrete floors.

How to store Portland cement. If cement absorbs moisture, it deteriorates and loses strength. It must therefore be kept in a completely dry place, preferably in a sealed bag. Even under ideal storage conditions, however, a bag of cement may become hard. Usually it can be made soft and usable again by rolling the bag on the floor. If small lumps remain, screen them out. The cement can be used for unimportant jobs. But since the lumps are an indication that the cement has absorbed moisture, it is a better idea to throw the bag away.

Concrete Blocks. Unless you need the greater strength, weight, and water resistance of poured concrete, concrete blocks are preferred for vertical surfaces because they are more attractive and easier to handle. Most blocks are roughly 8 by 8 by 16 inches, but other sizes and designs are available.

Concrete blocks are cleaned and painted like concrete (which see). For how to build with concrete blocks, see *Walls, Concrete-Block.*

Condensation Control. In winter, the invisible water vapor that is present in all houses tries to escape outdoors. When it strikes a cold surface, such as a windowpane or an exterior wall, it condenses into visible moisture which can damage paint, blister wallpaper, and cause wood to rot.

In short, condensation is a menace to all homes in cold climates. This is especially true of houses built since World War II, because they are so heavily insulated and tightly weatherstripped that there is no easy way for water vapor to escape.

Fortunately, however, condensation is not difficult to control.

Stop it before it starts. This actually is easier said than done because most of us are not about to cut down on our use of water. Nevertheless, you should remember that a number of the things you do in the house produce water vapor in large quantities; so it makes sense at least to try to do these things in a way that produces somewhat less water vapor.

For example, cooking obviously produces much steam if the pots are not covered; less if they are.

Mopping floors with a damp mop instead of a wet one reduces water vapor.

Washing clothes and dishes in automatic machines which are closed during operation eliminates much of the water vapor generated by hand-washing.

Shower bathing creates more water vapor than tub bathing; and bathing in scalding water creates more water vapor than bathing in warm water.

One other thing you most certainly should do to reduce the water vapor in your house is to make sure that your basement and any crawl spaces under the house are dry. For ways to cope with basement dampness, see *Basements*.

In crawl spaces—the partially excavated areas under a house—you should cover the soil with some sort of membrane that will keep moisture in the soil. Large sheets of heavy polyethylene film do the job well if the edges are overlapped about a foot. Or you can cover the soil with a 2-inch layer of unreinforced concrete.

Provide ventilation. This is the best way to get rid of excess water vapor rapidly.

In the kitchen, you need a ventilating fan that exhausts directly outdoors or into a duct leading to the outdoors. Small fans of the same type are desirable in bathrooms. See *Fans, Ventilating.*

In the laundry, the automatic dryer should be equipped with a duct to the outdoors. Lacking this, you should install a ducted ventilating fan in the room. See *Clothes Dryers—Operating an automatic dryer.*

Fixed screened ventilators should be installed in all crawl spaces. They should be placed as high as possible in the foundation walls. Leave them open the year round.

Screened ventilators may also be required in attics or closed roof spaces and in exterior walls if it proves impossible to keep water vapor out of these spaces by other means.

Insulate the outside walls, roof, and floors over unheated spaces. You should also insulate windows and doors with storm sash or insulating glass. Thus you keep the inner surfaces of all exterior walls warm enough to prevent water vapor from condensing on them.

Install vapor barriers. As their name implies, vapor barriers are materials that stop water vapor from passing through to the other side.

In the house, vapor barriers are required on the inside (sometimes called the warm side) of all exterior walls, the roof (or top-story ceilings), and floors over unheated spaces. Thus they keep water vapor from passing through these surfaces into the stud and joist spaces where it will condense.

Vapor barriers and insulation work together hand in glove to keep water vapor under control. One is no good without the other. If you have insulation but not vapor barriers, the water vapor can go right into and through the insulation and condense on the first cold surfaces with which it comes into contact. On the other hand, if you have vapor barriers but not insulation, the inner surfaces of the house may become so cold that water vapor condenses on them.

In new houses, vapor barriers are usually integral parts of the insulating batts and blankets that are installed in the walls, roof, and floor. They are made of tough, specially coated paper which is stapled to the face of the studs and joists in order to keep the insulation in place. The flanges of the vapor barriers on each strip of insulation must overlap so that there is no opening through which water vapor can escape.

Another type of vapor barrier used in new houses is a continuous sheet of polyethylene film which is stretched over the entire outside wall or ceiling of a room and then stapled to the structural timbers.

In existing houses, where it is impossible to install a vapor barrier inside the walls and ceilings, a barrier is applied directly to these surfaces in the form of oil or latex paint, varnish, shellac, or lacquer. While one coat may be enough, two are better to assure that a continuous film is applied to all surfaces.

Walls that are covered with wallpaper or vinyl should be painted, too. But whereas you need two coats under ordinary papers, only one is required under fully washable paper and vinyl.

On wood floors over crawl spaces, varnish or some other hard clear finish is generally adequate; but since there is no way to prevent many of the cracks from opening, it is well to install some sort of sheet material between the underside of the floor and the insulation between the joists.

Resilient, seemless, and ceramic-tile flooring form good vapor barriers. Brick, flagstone, and quarry tile floors, however, are effective only if laid in concrete.

Copper. In the raw state, copper is not a terribly attractive metal; but as it tarnishes, it turns a warm brown. And if exposed to the weather, it gets covered with an attractive green oxide.

How you clean copper depends on the color you want. If you like the green oxide, don't touch the metal with anything except a little water. To retain the warm brown, simply wash the metal with a mild detergent solution.

To get rid of the green oxide requires hard scrubbing. Start with household ammonia and fine steel wool; scrub hard; and rinse thoroughly. When the metal is bright, apply brass polish and rub with clean rags until no vestige of dirt comes off on them.

To go from brown back to the original bright copper color, apply brass polish and rub. To retain a bright copper color, spray the metal with a couple of coats of clear lacquer.

Because it is an excellent conductor of heat and is usually used in rather thin sheets, copper is easy to solder when it develops a hole or is torn. See *Soldering*. Holes are filled with plastic metal which can be given a copper color by rubbing with a penny.

If copper roofing or flashing is torn and you are hesitant about soldering it for fear of igniting the wood substructure, cover it with a patch of copper or aluminum foil embedded in asphalt roofing cement.

To remove scratches in copper, rub with fine steel wool or emery cloth.

Dents are obliterated by holding a block of wood against the concave side and tapping with a hard rubber mallet or stick of wood. Work from the edges in.

Corduroy. Corduroy is a sturdy cotton fabric with closely spaced, soft pile cords. Good garments made of it should be dry-cleaned. Lesser articles can be washed like cotton. Then tumble-dry in a dryer to remove the wrinkles. Corduroy should not be ironed.

Cork. Cork is generally used in the home in rather thin sheets to cover floors or walls or to make bulletin boards and mats. The material fades rapidly in the sun; and it is readily stained and damaged.

Cork is most easily cleaned and its stain resistance is improved if it is covered with some kind of protective coating—varnish, lacquer, shellac, or simply a paste floor wax. But whether finished or not, the only way to remove soil is by washing with a detergent solution. Rinse well. Stains that penetrate into the pores can be removed only by sanding. Burn marks are removed in the same way.

If cork is badly dented or develops holes, grate a bottle cork into tiny slivers on a kitchen grater. Make a thick putty of these with clear lacquer or white shellac and smooth into the dent or hole with a spatula. When dry, sand smooth.

Cork can be bonded to another material with linoleum paste or rubber cement. Pieces of cork are glued together with rubber cement.

Cornices. A cornice is a prominent, long, narrow, horizontal structure projecting out from a wall at or near the top. Indoors, cornices are most commonly used over windows to conceal the tops of draperies. They are also often used to conceal fluorescent tubes (see *Lighting*, page 191).

Window cornices are easily built of 1-inch-thick white pine boards. The boards are generally of 6-inch nominal width, but 8-inch boards may be used. The cornice should be long enough to project at least a few inches beyond both sides of the window; and sometimes they extend much further.

Cut the face board and then the two end pieces. The latter should be 6 inches long. If the cornice is to be painted or stained, miter the ends of the face board and one end of each end piece at 45-degree angles; apply white wood glue to the cut surfaces; and nail the end pieces to the face board with 3-inch finishing nails.

If the cornice is to be covered with fabric, make the end pieces 5¼ inches long and butt them to the back of the face board at the corners. Fasten with glue and nails.

Cornices generally have tops, although there is no law that they must. One drawback of tops is that they are dust-catchers. In any case, to make a top, simply cut a board to fit inside the face board and the end pieces, and nail it in with finishing nails.

The easiest way to hang a cornice over a window is to drive two strong nails into the top edge of the top casing, about 6 inches from each end. Let the nails stick out about 1 inch. Center the cornice over the window, press it against the wall and mark the location of the nails. Drill small holes in the cornice at these points and slip them over the nails. The cornice can be removed at any time so you can more easily get at the drapery hardware, roller shade, etc.

If you want to hang the cornice above the casing, screw two or three 3-inch iron angles to the underside of the top and then to the wall.

Cornices often have elaborately cut lower edges or are decorated with small moldings. If they are to be covered with fabric, they are normally padded with cotton upholstery filling or urethane foam. Fold the fabric around the bottom edges of the boards and staple to the inside. The top edges are stapled to the top of the cornice.

A lighted cornice is built in the same way. The fluorescent fixture may be mounted on the wall; but in that case the cornice should be at least 8 inches high so you cannot see the light except from almost directly underneath. In a 6-inch-high cornice, the light should be mounted under the top as close as possible to the back of the face board. Be sure the cornice is very securely fastened to the wall, because otherwise the weight of the fixture may pull it down.

The inside surfaces of a lighted cornice should be painted white. If they are left natural or painted any other color, the light reflected on the wall in back of and below the cornice will also be colored.

Corrosion. Corrosion—the eating away of metal that occurs when it is exposed to moisture and oxygen—respects no man, no metal. Once started it is often hard to stop. But it can be prevented.

The best method in those cases where you have an opportunity to choose between two or more different metals or materials is to select the one which is most

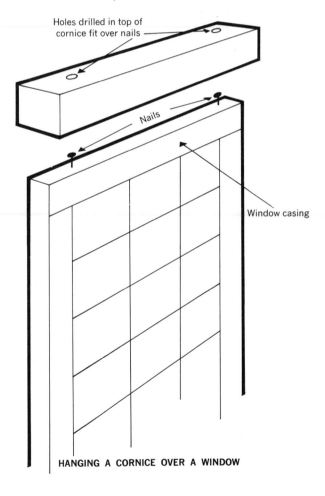

Holes drilled in top of cornice fit over nails

Nails

Window casing

HANGING A CORNICE OVER A WINDOW

naturally resistant to corrosion. Usually your own or somebody else's experience tells you which this is. But when a plumbing system is to be hooked up to a well, it may be advisable to have a chemical analysis made of the water before deciding which pipe and water tank to use.

If you don't have a choice of materials, you must usually protect against corrosion by the use of paint, chemical inhibitors, or common sense.

Following are the simple measures you can take to prevent corrosion:

Pipes. Install pipe most resistant to corrosion: plastic, copper, red brass. In cases where water is extremely corrosive, it is also advisable to install a water conditioner or neutralizer of the appropriate type. Consult a manufacturer of water-conditioning equipment.

To prevent accelerated corrosion, do not join together pipes or fittings of dissimilar metal. Install a special insulating joint between the pipe and water heater if they are not of the same metal.

Do not install pipes of dissimilar metal in the same trench in the ground or close to each other. Don't use cinders as fill around steel pipe.

Wrap cold-water lines with fiberglass tape to prevent external corrosion resulting from sweating.

Water heaters. Install a water heater with a solid copper, copper-on-steel, or glass-lined steel tank.

Do not heat water above 140 degrees in an indirect heater with copper coils if the water has been softened.

Faucets. Install top-grade faucets (and other sink and bathroom fittings). The cheap grades so often used—especially in development houses—are eaten out by corrosive waters.

Replace brass screws on compression faucet spindles with Monel.

Toilets. Replace brass linkages with Monel. Use plastic instead of metal floats.

Boilers. When water is heated repeatedly in a heating system, it loses its oxygen and becomes noncorrosive. It is therefore essential to prevent leaks which necessitate the addition of fresh water. Drain the boiler infrequently and then only enough to draw off sediment.

Nails. Use galvanized steel or aluminum nails in all exterior construction. If ordinary steel nails are used, countersink the heads and cover with putty at once.

Flashing. Install copper or aluminum flashing. But be sure to separate aluminum from concrete with a thick coating of asphalt roofing cement.

Metal roofs. Prime galvanized steel with zinc dust paint and cover with exterior oil paint. Paint terne with acrylic exterior paint.

Gutters and leaders. Prime galvanized steel with zinc dust paint and apply exterior oil paint. Paint aluminum with zinc chromate primer and oil paint.

Screens. Use fiberglass screen cloth; or keep metal cloth varnished or painted.

Metal doors and windows. If aluminum, install only those that bear the quality seal of the Aluminum Architectural Manufacturers' Association. This is especially important if you live near the ocean or in the vicinity of chemical plants or the like. If windows are steel, maintain tight putty joints and keep the metal painted.

Outdoor electric outlets, switches, etc. Install only the weatherproof type. For extra protection of boxes installed in the open, paint them with liquid neoprene.

Play equipment. Prime clean, bare metal with rust inhibitor and cover with trim and shutter enamel.

Ornamental iron. Clean as much as possible; then prime with a rust inhibitor and cover with trim and shutter enamel.

Charcoal grills. Store under cover. Clean and oil joint between brazier and center post frequently. Clean and oil inside of center post. Lay fire on vermiculite, sand, or pebbles to prevent paint from peeling off bottom of brazier.

Cooking utensils. Do not use alkalies such as baking soda or sal soda on aluminum. Avoid letting highly seasoned food stand for a long time in aluminum utensils. Rinse utensils well to remove particles of steel wool pads that may be used to scour them.

Don't scrub cast iron with steel wool, abrasive cleansers, or strong detergents. They remove the protective grease film.

Garbage cans. Use rubber or plastic cans or line metal cans with paper or plastic bags. The bottom of steel cans can also be painted inside and out with asphalt roofing cement.

Garden tools. Clean and dry thoroughly after every use. Store in a dry place or rub after use with an oily rag.

Wash out fertilizer spreaders after every use and dry well. Rinse sprayers thoroughly after every use; leave open and hang upside down.

Garden power tools. When storing for the off-season, clean thoroughly, rub bare metal with an oily rag, touch up chipped paint. To prevent rusting of cylinders, pistons, and valves in engines, remove spark plug and squirt oil into the hole; then turn engine over two or three times with the starter cord.

Workshop tools. Dry thoroughly if exposed to moisture. Store in a dry place. Rub occasionally with an oily rag.

Silverplate. Do not wash in a dishwasher or clean with urea dip cleaners.

Corrugated Fasteners. See *Wood Fasteners— Wiggle nails.*

Cotter Pins. See *Metal Fasteners.*

Cotton. Cotton is the basis of more textiles than any other fiber. It is strong and versatile; but fabrics made of it attract dirt, sometimes wrinkle readily, and deteriorate when exposed to the sun.

Unless otherwise specified, cottons should be washed often in hot water and rinsed in warm. Dry in a dryer at high heat for about 40 minutes, but avoid overdrying because this makes the fabric feel harsh and stiff. Press with a hot iron.

Since cotton fibers are naturally cream-colored, white materials tend to revert to this color unless they are bleached occasionally.

Use starch if you want cottons to feel smooth and crisp.

Counter Tops. Counters in the kitchen and bathroom must be watertight, easy to clean, and resistant to scratching and staining by myriad acids, alkalies, etc.

The best all-around counter-top material is 1/16-inch laminated plastic. It meets all the requirements just stated. In addition, because it comes in large sheets which are butted tight together, tops made of it have no seams that can leak or catch dirt. It withstands considerable heat (although it will be damaged if you put a hot iron or cast-iron frying pan on it). And you can set glasses down on it without making too much noise and without damage to them.

Solid-colored plastic can be used in bathrooms. But in the kitchen, choose a patterned material because small scratches made by cutting directly on the counter do not show up so clearly.

Ceramic tile is more durable, scratch- and heat-resistant; but greasy dirt lodges in the many joints, making cleaning a great deal more difficult. It is also easy to chip glasses on tile.

A new glass-ceramic material which is available in tiles 12 3/8 inches square and also in a few larger sizes up to about 25 by 48 inches shows considerable promise although it has not been widely used. It has essentially the same characteristics as ceramic tile; but counters made of it have fewer joints and are consequently somewhat easier to clean. On the other hand, the material is presently available in very few colors.

Maple blocks made of thick strips of wood glued together are used in small sections, usually near the range or sink, as cutting blocks. Stainless steel, once popular for counters, is now rarely used because it never looks clean.

Counter-top design and construction. Kitchen counters are 25 inches deep and usually have a 4-inch-high backsplash to protect the walls and keep liquids from dripping down behind the counters. The backsplash may be built to any height, however; and it may also be eliminated in areas used primarily for storage.

Tile counters are edged with tile, and glass-ceramic with stainless-steel strips. Plastic counters may also be edged with steel but look better and are easier to clean if self-edged (that is, edged with the same plastic used on the top itself). Edges can also be formed by molding.

You can build your own ceramic-tile counters (see *Tile, Ceramic*); but the other types should be constructed by professionals. Plastic tops are normally built in shops, but are sometimes constructed on the job with contact adhesive. The former are better because the plastic is bonded to the base of chipboard or plywood under pressure.

Basin counters in bathrooms are normally 21 inches deep, but may be deeper.

How to clean and repair counter tops. See *Plastic Laminates* or *Tile, Ceramic.* Glass-ceramic is treated like ceramic tile. To clean a wood counter area, wipe it dry promptly when wet. Remove water stains with mineral oil. Other dirty and stained patches can be sanded with very fine sandpaper and rubbed with mineral oil. Use sandpaper followed by mineral oil to obliterate scratches.

Crepe. Crepe is a soft fabric with a crinkled surface. It is made of silk, wool, cotton, or a number of synthetics, and the method of laundering varies accordingly. Some crepes should be dry-cleaned, however.

Crepe-Backed Satin. A silk, rayon, or nylon fabric resembling a satin crepe and used in clothing. It is reversible. Dry-clean.

Crepe de Chine. A silk crepe which should be dry-cleaned.

Cribs. For how to take care of and refinish cribs, see *Furniture, Children's,* and *Furniture, Wood.*

The standard-size crib is 53 by 30½ inches, but smaller sizes which can be carried through doorways are available. The top rails on most modern cribs are covered with tough white plastic to protect them against biting. It should be noted, however, that the plastic is not indestructible, and if broken, it might injure a child.

Crockery. Earthenware containers. For how to clean and repair them, see *Earthenware.*

Crown Derby. An English china. See *China.*

Crystal. An especially beautiful type of glass. See *Glass.*

Curtain Rods. See *Drapery Hardware.*

Curtains. Curtains and draperies not only improve the looks of most windows, but also add beauty to rooms and to the entire house when you look at it outdoors, increase privacy, and filter or screen out the rays of the sun. Because of their prominent positions in the house, they require more than passing attention from the housewife.

The exact difference between curtains and draperies is not clear. If the two are used together on a window, the curtains always hang inside the draperies (sometimes the curtains are referred to as underdraperies). But while curtains are used by themselves more often than draperies, there is no rule that draperies cannot be used by themselves. And while curtains are generally made of lighter fabrics than draperies, there is no rule that they must be.

The accepted lengths for both curtains and draperies are to the sill, to the bottom of the apron under the sill, and to within 1 inch or a little less of the floor. Curtains start at the top of the window frame; draperies start at that point, a little above the frame, or at the ceiling.

Café curtains are curtains that cover only part of a window. The most common arrangement is a double café with one curtain extending from the top of the frame to just below the center of the window; and the other curtain extending from the center of the window to the sill. A single café covers either the bottom half or bottom three-quarters of a window. It may also go all the way to the floor. A triple café divides the window into three equal parts. A quadruple café also divides a window into three equal parts and a fourth part equal to the other three in length hangs between the sill and the floor.

Curtain and drapery materials. In selecting curtain and drapery material, your first consideration is the beauty of the material and its appropriateness to your decorating scheme. But you must also think about its resistance to soiling and the deteriorating effects of the sun, and the ease of cleaning.

In the stores today, the emphasis—very sensibly—is on permanent-press fabrics and fiberglass for both curtains and draperies because they are easy to wash and require no ironing. In addition, fiberglass is not affected by the sun and therefore does not need lining. It is also flameproof. Permanent press, because it usually contains polyester, also has good resistance to sunlight though it is not the equal of fiberglass in this respect.

Old-fashioned cotton organdy is not to be overlooked for curtains, however, because it wears well and launders easily—but requires ironing and occasional starching. It does better for shaded rather than sunny windows.

For sheer glass curtains, ninon is unbeatable.

In addition to fiberglass and permanent press, the choice of fabrics for draperies is almost unlimited. Whatever you use, it is well to remember that fabrics with a shiny finish have greater resistance to the sun than those with a dull finish.

Lining draperies. Fiberglass draperies, as noted, do not need to be lined. And light-to medium-weight fabrics with an open weave are generally not lined because you want the sunlight to filter through: the draperies are supposed to look airy and informal.

It is not essential to line heavy fabrics either; but as a rule, they are. The lining gives the draperies a more finished look from outside, especially when they are drawn. It may improve the hang of the draperies. It protects against fading and sun damage. And it may help to keep out cold and keep in warmth.

Favorite lining materials are sateen and cotton twill. Acrylic foam and metallized fabrics are used for insulating purposes.

How to measure for curtains and draperies. Use a 6-foot folding rule or steel tape, not a dressmaker's tape measure.

Install the rod in its proper position. Since the top of the drapery will be slightly above the top of the rod, measure from ½ inch above the top edge of the rod to what will be the bottom of the drapery. If you are making your own draperies, add 7 inches for hems.

The width of the drapery equals the length of the rod plus the returns. Double the figure to allow for pleats or folds when straight, tailored draperies are drawn. If the material you use is very light, you might even triple the figure. For draw draperies on traverse rods, add 3 inches to permit overlapping when they are drawn.

In the case of sheer, ruffled curtains, each panel should equal the length of the rod. And if curtains crisscross, each panel should be twice the length of the rod.

Rods and draperies for sliding glass doors and picture windows should be wide enough so that when the draperies are open, they come just to the edges of the door or window frames.

Rod-to-rod curtains that are stretched tight over wood-framed glass doors and casement windows should extend 1 inch beyond each side of the glass, and should extend about 2 inches beyond the top and bottom of the glass. (The rods are centered horizontally ¾ inch above and below the glass.) To allow for fullness, the curtain should be twice the width of the glass.

Hooks. Use slip-on hooks for all fiberglass and unlined draperies and curtains. The same hooks are also used for all other draperies and curtains, but the less expensive pin-type is more common. Round rings up to 1½-inch diameter are available for use on round rods. Curtains with casings are run directly onto round or flat rods.

Pleater hooks are of the slip-on type. If you use them, permanent pleats in draperies and curtains are unnecessary; consequently the draperies and curtains can be washed and ironed flat. This is an obvious advantage if you don't use no-iron materials. On the other hand, the hooks are rather exasperating to install.

Cleaning curtains and draperies. Frequent dusting with a soft brush or simply giving the curtains a shake will delay the need for thorough cleaning. You can use a smooth metal or plastic vacuum cleaner tool, too; but be sure to use minimum suction. Even then, you will have to hold lightweight curtains at the bottom to keep them from disappearing into the vacuum.

More and more curtains and draperies made today can be laundered. Fiberglass must be hand-washed and drip-dried; other new materials can go into the washer and dryer. In all cases, remove pin-type and slip-on hooks. Sewed-on rings should also be removed if curtains are machine-washed.

For how to launder curtains and draperies, see *Laundering* (page 185).

Some drapery fabrics should be dry-cleaned rather than laundered; and you will save yourself a lot of work if you also dry-clean all very large draperies, whether washable or not.

To extend the life of curtains and draperies. 1. Keep them clean.

2. If possible, alternate panels between windows with different exposures. This will help to prevent those on south and west windows from wearing out faster than those on east and north windows.

3. Try not to let curtains get soaked by rain. This is especially important if there is a roof directly below a window, because rain striking the roof may bounce up through an open window carrying hard-to-cope-with staining materials from the roof surface.

Cushions. See *Pillows* and *Furniture, Upholstered.*

Cutlery. See *Kitchen Tools* and *Tableware.*

Dacron. A polyester made by DuPont.

Damask. Damask is a handsome fabric with a design woven in. It is made from a number of different fibers and is used, among other things, for upholstering, draperies, bedspreads, and table linens. Some damasks are washable; others should be dry-cleaned.

Decks. In modern parlance, a deck is a raised wood structure with a wood floor which serves as an outdoor living space. A porch is a deck; but unlike porches, many decks are built at some distance from the house.

In yesterday's language, a deck was—and often still means—a roof deck. This is an open, flat roof area which is also used for outdoor living.

How to maintain and repair a roof deck. This is a chore that cannot be taken lightly because of all the roofs on a house, a roof deck is the most likely to spring a leak. This means you must keep an eye on it constantly and inspect it carefully at least once a year. Keep it swept free of debris which might be ground into the surface or which would interfere with the rapid runoff of water. Shovel off snow in winter.

Make sure that furniture used on the deck has smooth feet that will not cut through the surface.

If the deck is covered with tar and gravel, the surface should be protected against wear of feet and indentation by furniture by covering it with sections of wood grating. These are most easily made of 4- or 6-inch boards spaced ½ inch apart and nailed crosswise to 4-inch boards spaced 16 inches on centers. If the roofing underneath becomes worn or cracked despite the gratings, it can be repaired by scraping the gravel aside and applying roofing cement. Then replace the gravel.

Canvas decks must be kept covered with oil-based deck paint. They may need to be repainted every year.

If canvas becomes torn, raise it slightly and clean the wood under it as best you can with a small spatula and vacuum cleaner. Try not to enlarge the tear. Then spread paste white lead in a thin layer on the wood. Out of new canvas, cut a patch about 1 inch longer and wider than the tear; insert it through the tear and spread it down smoothly. Over it spread additional white lead. Then smooth down the torn canvas and drive closely spaced copper tacks around the edges. Apply one or two coats of deck paint when the lead dries.

New roof decks are frequently covered with silicone rubber roofing compound or seamless flooring much like that used in kitchens. These are more durable than canvas and considerably easier to keep clean and to maintain. In time, however, seamless flooring will have to be reglazed or resurfaced—both jobs for a professional installer. You can repair silicone roofing, when worn or damaged, simply by brushing on additional silicone roofing.

How to build a modern deck. Because it is very important that you use timbers of the right size, you really should have an architect design the deck you have in mind. The following suggestions and drawings must be used only as a guide.

For lumber, use decay-resistant redwood or cypress, or Douglas fir, yellow pine, or other good structural woods which have been pressure-treated with wood preservative. See *Wood.*

The deck should be built up from concrete piers that extend below the frost line. Piers 10 inches in diameter are adequate. They should rest on footings twice as wide and 1 foot deep. The piers should rise 1 foot above grade level, although they can go higher if the deck is to be fairly close to the ground and if the girders are laid directly on the piers.

Wood columns extending up from the piers must be bolted firmly to them. Use 6-by-6-inch timbers and space them 7 feet apart on centers along the two long sides of the deck. Across the tops of the columns in each row lay wood girders 6 inches wide and 8 inches high. The girders should be spiked securely to the columns.

The girders support the floor joists, which are installed at right angles to them. If the joists are made of good-grade 2-by-8-inch redwood timbers spaced 12 inches on centers, they can be used in a 12-foot span (meaning that the deck is 12 feet wide). The same size joists of Douglas fir or yellow pine can span 14 feet.

Lay the joists on edge on top of the girders or frame them into the side of the girders. In the latter case, you should hang them in U-shaped steel hangers. The alternative is to nail a 2-by-2-inch wood strip (in this case known as a ledger strip) to the side of each girder, flush with the bottom. Notch the joists to rest on this. The ledger strips must be nailed to the girders at each

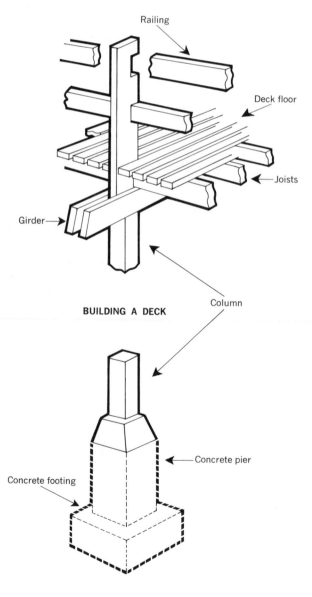

BUILDING A DECK

joist with three 16d nails; and the joists must be toenailed to the girder with three 10d nails.

The deck floor is normally made of 2-by-4 or 2-by-6 timbers spaced ½ inch apart. If the joists are closely spaced, however, you can use 1¼-inch boards just as well.

If the deck is high above ground, install diagonal braces at the four corners between the columns and the girders and end joists.

If the deck is attached to the side of the house, support the joists at the house end on a 2-by-8 ledger spiked into the joists in the wall. For added safety, the ledger should be supported from below by 2-by-6-inch timbers which are also spiked to the wall.

The National Safety Council recommends that a railing should be built around any deck or porch that is more than 10 inches off the ground.

Deep-Fry Cookers. These electrical appliances are designed for deep-frying such foods as potatoes, shrimp, chicken, and doughnuts. A deep basket fits inside to hold the food being cooked. Without the basket, a deep-fry cooker also can be used as a saucepan or Dutch oven for preparing stews, roasts, soups, and gravies.

The cookers have a thermostatic control to provide the proper temperature for various jobs. This makes them considerably easier and more reliable to use than deep fryers which are heated on the top of a range.

Some deep-fry cookers are immersible for easier washing. But don't let the slight difficulties of washing a nonimmersible cooker keep you from cleaning it well after every use with detergent solution.

Wipe off the outside of the cooker with detergent solution as necessary. If food becomes baked on, clean like chromium plate.

Dehumidifiers. High humidity in a house causes condensation in winter (see *Condensation Control*) and in summer not only makes life miserably sticky but also causes rusting, warping, and mildewing.

If you have an air conditioner, it automatically reduces humidity as it pulls down the temperature. If you don't have an air conditioner, the easiest way to improve matters in both summer and winter is to buy a dehumidifier.

Most dehumidifiers now in use are moderately small, roll-around electrical appliances that can be plugged into any 120-volt outlet. But you can also buy bags of a chemical—called a dessicant—which absorbs moisture until it is soaking wet. In some cases, it is then discarded; in others, it can be baked and used again and again.

The electrical dehumidifiers incorporate a fan that sucks in humid air and passes it over refrigerated coils. There the water vapor is condensed and drips off into a collection bucket or a hose connected into a house drain. The dehumidified air is returned to the room.

Many dehumidifiers have thermostats that turn the appliances on and off when the humidity reaches the selected level. Some automatically shut off when the collection bucket is almost full. Others flash a light.

Dehumidifiers are rated according to the number of pints of water they will extract from the air in 24 hours. The ratings are based on standards set by the Association of Home Appliance Manufacturers (AHAM). Sizes range from about 14 to 28 pints.

Generally, a 14-pint unit will serve an area up to 1500 square feet; a 28-pint unit will serve an area of about 2500 square feet.

Dehumidifiers are most efficient when the doors and windows are closed. Clean the air intake and outlet grilles and the condenser coils regularly with a damp cloth.

Delft. A lovely type of earthenware which has a white glaze and is usually decorated in blue. It should be washed by hand in detergent solution. Repair broken pieces with cellulose cement.

Denim. Traditionally, denim was a tough, heavy cotton twill fabric used for work clothing. But it has been greatly refined and is now made in lighter weights and many colors out of blends of cotton and synthetics. Stretch denim is also available.

Cotton denim is washed in warm water and dried at moderate heat, since high temperatures cause considerable shrinkage. Denim made of a blend is laundered like permanent-press fabrics.

Desks. A desk can be a fine piece of furniture which is useful for writing checks and long-hand notes, or it can be a utilitarian work table on which you can spread out and use modern office equipment. It is a rare desk that is both handsome and really useful.

The fine furniture pieces are made of wood and sometimes have inlaid leather tops. Workaday desks are made entirely of wood, of wood with a laminated plastic top, or of steel with a laminated plastic or linoleum top.

When working at a wood desk, make sure the top is covered with a desk pad. On desks with drop-leaf tops, be sure also that the tops are fully supported on pull-out slides. For care of a wood desk, see *Furniture, Wood.*

Clean steel, plastic, and linoleum desk surfaces with a damp cloth or cloth dipped in detergent solution. Cleaning fluid may also be needed to get up some ink and carbon paper stains. When writing with a hard pencil or ballpoint pen on a linoleum top, use a desk pad.

For repairing desk drawers, see *Drawers.*

Detergents. Detergents are made for dishwashing, general household cleaning, and laundering. (For a discussion of laundry detergents, see *Laundering.*)

Detergents for hand dishwashing are much milder than those for machine dishwashing. The latter contain a rather high percentage of chlorine and are quite caustic. For this reason, they are much more effective in killing bacteria on dishes, glassware, and flatware than hand-dishwashing detergents.

Household detergents, whether sold in powder or liquid form, have done much to make housecleaning easier. They cut through dirt, grease, and many other types of soil rapidly. Some contain a high concentration of ammonia. Spray-on detergents tend to be more powerful cleansers than those that are diluted in water.

Although some detergent manufacturers say that it is unnecessary to rinse after using their compounds, rinsing is always advisable—especially if you plan to paint or wax the cleaned surface.

Water pollution. Detergents have been widely blamed as water polluters in the past few years; and although there is no agreement about why they cause trouble, it is generally conceded that some of them do. The worst offenders are machine-dishwashing and heavy-duty laundry detergents. Hand-dishwashing detergents, light-duty detergents, and household detergents are thought to do little, if any, damage.

The situation is confusing; but while it may alarm died-in-the-wool ecologists, there seems to be little reason to become unduly upset. The detergent industry, prodded by the government, is working hard to develop safe, nonpolluting detergents, and almost certainly will in the near future.

In the meantime, you can do three things:

1. If you have a septic system, make sure that it is properly sized to your home and is clean and in good working order.

2. Find out whether your water is soft. If it is, use soap for laundering rather than detergent.

3. If your water is hard, use a phosphate detergent.

Dimity. A sheer, crisp cotton fabric with a corded effect, dimity is used for clothing. Launder it like cotton.

Dinnerware. The word "dinnerware" is usually restricted to dishes that are made of china, stoneware, earthenware, pottery, or melamine and that are used to eat on or serve from at breakfast, lunch, dinner, etc. The word should, however, be broadened to cover two other categories: (1) Dishes made of glass, pewter, stainless steel, special alloys, and silver. (2) Articles that are not dishes but are more or less equally essential to serving and eating meals.

Using this broad definition, we list here the pieces of dinnerware that the average, modern American family can make best use of. (Glasses and flatware are omitted because they are covered under *Glassware* and *Tableware,* respectively.)

	Approximate size (inches)
Dinner plates	10–11
Dessert and salad plates (also used for luncheon and breakfast)	7–8
Bread-and-butter plates	5–6
Cereal dishes (also used for soup)	6–7
Soup bowls	8–9
Fruit dishes	5–6
Teacups	3½–4
Tea saucers	6
Demitasse cups	variable
Demitasse saucers	4½–5
Platters	variable
Vegetable dishes	variable
Salad bowl	variable
Sugar bowl	variable
Cream pitcher	variable
Gravy boat	variable
Coffeepot	variable
Teapot	variable
Water pitcher	variable
Salt and pepper shakers	variable
Hot mats	variable
Coasters	3

How many of these articles your family needs depends on the size of the family, the way you live, how you entertain, your budget, and other factors. It is worth noting, however, that manufacturers and retailers of dinnerware sell services for 8 or 12 persons. Such services include 8 or 12 table settings, most consisting of a dinner plate, dessert-salad plate, bread-and-butter plate, teacup and saucer. They may, in addition, include a variety of serving pieces—usually a sugar bowl and creamer, platter, and vegetable dish. Many dinnerware designs are also sold from open stock, which enables you to buy just the number of place settings or individual pieces you need.

Many families buying dinnerware try to acquire a best set and an everyday set. The best set is usually china; the everyday set something less expensive. This thinking is logical and reasonable, but it is also somewhat fallacious, because while everyday dinnerware gets much harder wear than the best set, expensive dinnerware is more durable than inexpensive earthenware and pottery and even melamine. In the long run, therefore, you might save money if you bought china—not necessarily the best—or stoneware for everyday use.

How to store dinnerware. Everyday dinnerware is best stored near the dishwasher. Cup racks of several types are on the market. They permit you to store a dozen or so cups in small shelf space. But unfortunately, they offer more opportunity for chipping your cups than if you hang them on cup hooks under shelves.

Where you store your best service is immaterial. It is, however, a very good idea to keep it in quilted, zippered storage cases. The plate cases are available in several sizes and hold 12 plates each with felt separators between plates. Cup cases hold a dozen cups. Individual cases of different sizes are available for other pieces.

If you don't have storage cases, wrap your best dinnerware in plastic bags. They offer no protection against chipping, but do at least keep off dust and grease.

How to care for dinnerware. See *China; Earthenware; Pottery; Stoneware;* or *Melamine.*

Dishwashers. Although a dishwasher is not, as some homemakers contend, an essential appliance, there is no doubt that it simplifies and shortens a tiresome chore; turns out cleaner, brighter dishes and glasses; helps to protect dishes against breakage; and destroys most bacteria and thus contributes to improved family health.

Dishwashers are effective in these ways for the following reasons:

1. Dishes do not need to be thoroughly rinsed off. True, you should remove large and hard food particles before putting dishes in the racks; and you must loosen cooked-on particles. But softer, smaller particles are readily removed in the dishwasher and either filtered out or ground up and then flushed down the drain.

2. Most utensils can be washed as easily as dishes and glasses. The obvious exceptions are pieces so large that they cannot

fit into the dishwasher (but there are very few of these) and those that are encrusted with burned food.

3. Dishwashers are so large that the average family does not have to run them more than once or at most twice a day. Some manufacturers state dishwasher capacity in terms of table settings; but because there is not general agreement about what goes into a table setting, others do not. In any event, a quick glance into any dishwasher will convince even the most skeptical housewife that it will hold a lot of things.

4. Dishwashing action is thorough yet gentle. Water is cascaded on the dishes from every direction by revolving spray arms, jets, and impellers. The driving spray is hard enough to dislodge almost all soil, yet not hard enough to move articles that have been properly placed in the plastic-covered racks.

5. Whereas the temperature of the water used for dishwashing in a sink is about 110 degrees, that in a dishwasher runs from 130 to 160 degrees. It is usually raised to and maintained at these temperatures by electric heaters built into the dishwasher. In several makes, the temperature may be boosted briefly to 180 degrees. During the long drying period that follows, even higher temperatures are reached. Most bacteria exposed to such high heat are killed.

6. The detergents used in dishwashers assist in killing bacteria as well as in removing soil. In addition to containing chlorine, which is not put into hand-washing compounds, they are far more alkaline and caustic than handwashing compounds.

Types of dishwasher. Both built-in and portable dishwashers are on the market. The built-ins are front-opening appliances that are installed under a standard kitchen counter—usually adjacent to the sink. All units are 24 inches wide.

Portable dishwashers are about the same size. All roll around on casters; and when in use are hitched to the sink faucets and drain into the sink. One kind of portable is top-opening; two others are front-opening. One of the front-opening portables is sometimes called a convertible dishwasher because it can be built into a standard 24-inch opening under the counter if and when you decide you don't like rolling it around.

A wood cutting-board top is incorporated in some portable dishwashers.

A compact dishwasher is also available if you don't have room for a full-size machine. It is a small, round counter-top model that holds about four place settings at one time.

Dishwasher features. In addition to those already alluded to, you should consider the following features when shopping for a dishwasher.

Cycles. A full, so-called normal dishwashing cycle lasts for about 50 to 60 minutes. It includes one or two wash periods, as many as four rinses, and a drying period. Short cycles take 30 to 40 minutes.

Except for the least expensive models, which provide only a normal cycle, most dishwashers today offer several cycles. In fact, some have as many as six. These include such special cycles as "short-wash"; "china-crystal" for fragile articles; "pots-and-pans" for very heavily soiled utensils. "Rinse-and-dry," for dusty pieces, does nothing but rinse in hot water and dry. "Rinse-and-hold" is used to rinse the worst of the soil off breakfast or luncheon dishes. You can then hold them, without washing, until you put in dinner dishes and have a full load. "Plate-warming" allows you to take the chill off dishes before bringing them to the table. No water is used.

How often you would use all four or six cycles on a deluxe dishwasher is problematical. Most people never use more than one or two cycles.

Arrangement of interior. Actually, until you have used a dishwasher for a while, you can't be sure whether you will like the way the racks are arranged or not. But the more adjustable and movable the racks, the better: it makes it much easier to use the dishwasher to wash such outsize things as 12-inch plates, turkey platters, and large roasters.

The flatware basket should be capacious. A special basket which may prove useful is a covered small-items basket in which you put little things that might be bounced about if placed in the dish or glass racks.

Ease of loading. This is important with any dishwasher but especially so with top-opening portables. In most machines, the arrangement and flexibility of the racks are the controlling factors. But several manufacturers have introduced top-opening portables with tub rims that slant toward the front so you can more easily reach the bottom of the tub (the tops are flat, however).

Positive water fill assures that the dishwasher will fill to capacity with hot water before it starts washing and rinsing. It protects against inadequate washing if your water pressure is low.

How to operate a dishwasher. Built-ins must be installed by a plumber. The hot- and cold-water supply lines are usually extensions of the supply lines to the sink. The drain connects into the sink drain above the trap or into a garbage disposer.

On portable dishwashers, the hoses have a snap-on adapter permitting quick connection to the sink faucet. A built-in valve relieves pressure so the hose can be disconnected without splashing. A special valve lets you use the faucet while the dishwasher is in operation. When not in use, hoses are stored in a recess in the back of the dishwasher.

Although dishwashers have built-in heaters to raise or maintain the temperature of the incoming water, you should set the thermostat on your water heater at 140 to 160 degrees. This is because the temperature drops as the water passes from the heater through the pipes to the kitchen. So if you start with a high water-heater temperature, the heaters in the dishwasher will have ample time to bring the water up to the desired washing temperature.

Both portable and built-in dishwashers must be connected into their own 120-volt, 20-amp electrical circuit. If you have a disposer, however, both appliances can share this circuit. Portable dishwashers have a retractable cord with a grounded plug that is plugged into a wall outlet. Built-ins are permanently wired in. In some communities, the code requires that the electrical circuit be controlled by a wall switch in addition to the dishwasher switch.

To use a compact dishwasher, you connect the fill hose to the sink faucet and position the dishwasher so it will drain into the sink. It does not run by electricity; the spray arm is turned by water pressure. Its size naturally limits what can go into it (you'll need to wash pots, pans, mixing bowls, etc., by hand), and loading it can be a little tricky until you get used to it. But properly loaded, it washes well and can be a boon in the dishwashing department.

Read the dishwasher manufacturer's suggestions for loading the racks. You don't have to follow them slavishly: modern dishwasher racks are, in fact, designed for random loading. But generally the suggestions are sound.

In loading the flatware basket, be careful to place pieces wide end down. Otherwise, ice tea spoons with long, thin handles and two-tined forks, for example, may drop through the holes in the bottom of the basket and impede or even break the revolving spray arm.

If your water is hard, fill the wetting agent dispenser when empty (about every one or two months). The dispenser automatically adds a rinse-aid liquid to the final rinse so that glasses and dishes will dry with less spotting.

When starting out with a new dishwasher, try different brands of dishwasher detergent to see which gives the best results. And don't use too much, because if your water is soft, an overdose of detergent may etch glassware. Begin by filling the detergent cup halfway. Then increase the amount as seems necessary to get your dishes really clean. If you happen to run out of dishwasher detergent, do not substitute laundry detergent or hand-dishwashing detergent. They will clog the machine with suds.

If your dishwasher offers a choice of cycles, select the one that best suits each load. It may save water and it may also do a better job than the normal cycle. As noted earlier, however, most dishwasher users find it easier just to use the normal cycle for almost all loads. This does no harm.

Check frequently whether food particles are left in the bottom of the tub, and remove any you find. Some dishwashers, especially older models, have filter screens that must be cleaned every few days.

The dishwasher tub cleans itself, but in hard-water areas a white film may develop. If this cannot be removed with a damp cloth and cleanser, fill two small bowls with 1 cup white vinegar each. Place these on the lower rack and run the dishwasher through its full cycle.

Clean cabinet exterior with detergent solution or white appliance wax. Clean brushed-chrome panels with rubbing alcohol.

Wood tops on portable dishwashers should be wiped dry promptly when they are wet. Remove water stains with mineral oil. Other dirty and stained areas can be sanded with very fine sandpaper and rubbed with mineral oil. Use sandpaper followed by mineral oil to obliterate scratches.

If something goes wrong. First check whether the fuse has blown, the dishwasher is plugged in and turned on, the water is on, the controls have been properly set, and the door closed tight. If you still don't get action, call a serviceman.

Dishwashing. If you wash all dishes and utensils by hand, you will need the following equipment:

Dishwashing brush. A round brush made in Holland and named Swish is one of the few dishwashing brushes now made that combines desirable stiffness with durability. Most are of woeful quality.

Metal scouring pads.

Hand-dishwashing detergent.

Cleanser.

Dish rack.

Spray hose if you have a double-bowl sink.

Double-bowl sink, or a sink with a built-in drainboard, or a molded rubber drainboard.

Dish towels.

Scrape food scraps from cooking utensils immediately after serving food, and rinse quickly under running water or fill with water to soak. Greasy utensils, however, should simply be wiped clean with a paper towel.

Scrape plates as soon as possible after they come from the table and run them under a stream of water if there is time. Plates with egg particles should always be rinsed in cold water since hot water will tend to make the egg adhere to the plates.

When you start washing dishes, run a couple of inches of hot water into the sink and add detergent in the amount recommended by the maker. Place your dish rack in one of the sink bowls or on the drainboard. Unless a built-in drainboard is on the wrong side of the sink, the rack should be on your left side if you scrub dishes with your right hand; on your right side, if you scrub with your left hand.

Wash the cleanest articles first (usually glasses and silverware) and progress to the dirtiest. Don't overload the sink at any time—particularly when you are washing glasses and cups, which bob around in the water. And don't let table knives with hollow handles, woodenware, or kitchen tools with wood handles soak in the dishwater. When washing fine china or crystal, place a rubber mat in the bottom of the sink to help guard against chipping.

Scrub each piece in soapy water. If your dish rack is in a sink bowl, you can place the washed piece directly in the rack. When the rack is full, spray the pieces with hot water to rinse off the detergent.

If your dish rack is on a drainboard, however, the spray is of no value. So after washing dishes and utensils in soap, rinse them briefly under a stream of hot water and stand them in the rack.

Change the dishwater when it gets very dirty or begins to cool.

If food stubbornly clings to utensils, do not wear out your brush trying to get it off. Attack it with cleanser, and if this doesn't work, with a scouring pad. If you still can't make progress, fill the utensil with a little hot water and add baking soda. Soak overnight. If necessary, bring the solution to a boil and then simmer for a while.

If your water is reasonably soft, dishes rinsed in very hot water will air-dry with little spotting. But if your water is hard, use a clean, absorbent dish towel. On utensils that were greasy, use paper towels.

Silverware should always be hand-dried.

Disinfectants. Disinfectants are used in the home to kill bacteria and fungus growths in bathrooms, kitchens, a sick room, baby's room, and on all kinds of articles ranging from garbage pails to telephone receivers. They should also be used in your laundry when someone in the family is ill or has an infection.

The most effective disinfectant for home use is a phenolic material identified on the label by the word "phenol." Depending on the formulation, it can be mixed with water and applied with a sponge, or it can be applied by aerosol spray.

Other disinfectants which rank just a shade behind the phenolics are pine-oil disinfectants, quaternary disinfectants, and liquid chlorine disinfectants. The last are the same as chlorine laundry bleaches. When using them, you must take care not to get them on fabrics; and you must never use them with ammonia or toilet-bowl cleaners.

Pine-oil disinfectants have a pleasant pine scent. At least one product contains phenol.

Quaternary disinfectants are identified on the label by the words "benzalkonium chloride" and/or "n-alkyl dimethyl benzyl ammonium chloride."

When buying a disinfectant, read the label to make sure the product will do what you need it for. By federal law, the label must provide an accurate description of the product. You will find that some products can be used for many more purposes than others.

Doeskin. An expensive, soft, woolen fabric used in clothing. It must be dry-cleaned.

Doeskin gloves are made of animal hide. Wash them carefully in lukewarm water with mild soap. Rinse well. Hang up to dry. Before they are completely dry, work them with your fingers to soften the leather; then slip them on your hands to shape them.

Door Bells. Modern door bells and chimes operate at low voltage provided by a small transformer connected to a 120-volt wiring circuit at an outlet box in the basement or utility room. The bell system is wired with small, lightly insulated wire which can be tucked behind moldings, under floor boards, etc.

The door button has two wires. If you are installing a bell at only one door, one wire runs to the bell (which is usually installed in the kitchen) and the other wire runs to either one of the terminals on the transformer. Another wire is then run from the other transformer terminal to the bell. In a two-door system, one wire runs from each door button to the same terminal on the transformer; the second wire from each button runs to the bell. Another wire runs from the transformer to the bell.

Chimes are wired in essentially the same way, but for best service, use a transformer made especially for use with chimes.

How to repair a door bell. If the bell doesn't ring, the odds are that the door button is corroded and needs to be removed and cleaned with a knife and emery cloth. Make sure wires are attached securely. If you still don't get a ring—and everything else seems all right—replace the button. A new one costs little.

Sometimes a bell fails to ring because the low-voltage connections at the transformer are loose. You can tighten these without turning off the current. But if you want to check and perhaps tighten the high-voltage connections, the current must be cut off.

Door Closers. For screen doors, a coiled steel spring is as good as any more expensive pneumatic closer. For how to adjust it, see *Screen Doors.*

But a pneumatic closer is needed on storm doors, because it can be adjusted to close slowly and thus cushions the doors against slamming, which might break the glass.

Pneumatic closers (actually the cushioning is done by a liquid) like those used on large doors in public buildings are the most reliable but far more costly than the average home owner will appreciate. So the chances are that if you buy a closer, you will get one of the long cylindrical types. Instructions for attaching these come in the box. Like the best closers, they can generally be adjusted to close at various speeds.

Clean door closers regularly so they operate smoothly. If a closer is used on a combination storm and screen door, the speed should be adjusted whenever you replace the screen inset with the glass inset and vice versa.

An annoying problem with many closers is their tendency to come loose from the doorjamb. The screw holes become enlarged; and frequently the screws themselves are bent. You can prevent this from happening only by not using the hold-open washer on the closer to hold a heavy door open while you are bringing in packages.

To refasten a closer that is loose, force wooden pegs coated with glue into the screw holes and let the glue set for 24 hours before drilling new holes and resetting the screws.

Door Hardware. The hardware used on or in connection with doors includes locks, latches, hinges, knobs, catches, pulls, stops, and tracks for several types of door. **Locks and latches** made today are classified as cylindrical, tubular, or mortise-type. The first is the most common, easy to install, and difficult for intruders to open. The second is quite similar. The last is the oldest type and consists of a slim rectangular box that is recessed in the edge of the door.

Although all locks and latches look pretty much alike, there is considerable difference in their quality. Don't buy the cheap, lightweight, or builder's grade. They are calculated to fall apart in short order. The so-called medium-grade items are much better; the commercial grade is the best of all (in fact, these are really better than you need).

Since many hardware and building supplies stores do not carry the better grades of hardware, you may save time if you go directly to a locksmith or what is known as a builder's hardware supplier.

Instructions for installing locks and latches are enclosed in the boxes in which they come.

Sliding door tracks with rollers of 1-inch diameter or larger are preferred because the rollers are less likely to jump out of the tracks than smaller rollers.

Tracks for lightweight cabinet doors are simple U-shaped aluminum channels that hold the doors in place at top and bottom. The best tracks have a slight recess or a slight bulge in the center of the U to reduce friction as the doors are shoved from side to side.

Hinges. See *Hinges.*

Stops to keep doors from banging into walls are generally screwed into the baseboard or into the floor. In situations where these cannot be used, you can install a hinge-pin stop on one of the door hinges.

Knobs and pulls. See *Knobs and Pulls.*

How to take care of door hardware. Once a year, put a drop of oil on latch and lock tongues and at the base of knobs.

When painting doors, remove knobs and escutcheons. Even though this little job takes time, it saves painting time and you don't have to figure out how to get paint splatters off the hardware.

If a lock or latch breaks, don't waste time trying to fix it. Remove it from the door and let a locksmith worry about it.

Clean door tracks once or twice a year with a vacuum cleaner and damp rag.

If magnetic door catches make too much noise when the door closes, paste a bit of cellulose tape over the strike plates.

Doormats. Although there is nothing very pretty about doormats, you can't do without them if you want to preserve the appearance of your floors and rugs, prolong their life, and avoid unnecessary housework.

The best exterior mat is made of dense cocoa fiber. It removes the maximum amount of dirt and moisture from shoes, is heavy enough to stay put in front of the door, and resists wear (even a puppy has a hard time tearing it apart). Its one drawback is that it isn't very easy to clean.

Link rubber mats last longer than cocoa and clean better, but don't do the all important dirt- and water-removing job well. Nylon fiber mats, by contrast, remove dirt but not moisture, are easy to clean, but not so durable as cocoa.

Vinyl and sheet-rubber mats are the least serviceable.

The best indoor mats are nylon carpet-toppers. These are the same mats that are used inside office buildings and churches. They are extremely absorbent—they sop up dirt and water like a sponge.

Clean all mats frequently, depending on the construction either by hosing off or by beating.

Doors. We don't usually think of doors as part of the operating equipment in the home, but they really are. If they don't work well and if they don't efficiently close off what they are supposed to close off, they are a constant irritant.

Some differences between doors. Exterior doors are 1¾ inches thick; interior doors, 1 3/8. Because they are heavier, exterior doors should be hung with three hinges rather than two.

Interior doors are usually made of wood. Exterior doors are, too. But many exterior doors are also made of glass (it should be tempered if in large sheets) or factory-finished steel. The newest material for both exterior and interior doors is urethane.

Flush doors have a smooth slab surface. Recessed-panel doors have flat recessed panels. Raised-panel doors have recessed panels with slightly raised centers. Louvered doors are made with overlapping horizontal slats.

To a certain extent, these differences affect the way you take care of doors. But the most important difference in doors is in the way they are installed and operate.
Hinged doors. This is the most familiar kind of door because it is the most generally useful. In the house, it is almost always hung with butt hinges.

How to hang a hinged door. Lay the door over a pair of sawhorses and cut off the lugs, if any, at the top of the door. Sand the cut surfaces. Then measure the height and width of the framed door opening, and check whether the corners are square.

A well-fitted door is the same shape as the door opening. There should be 1/16-inch clearance at the sides of the door and the top; and if there is a threshold, 1/16-inch clearance at the bottom. If there is no threshold, the door should be cut off at the bottom just high enough to clear the rug in the room into which it swings.

Cut off the bottom of the door as necessary. If the door has been ordered properly and if the frame is of standard size, it should not be necessary to saw down the sides of the door to remove a lot of wood. Just measure the desired width of the door, and draw a straight line from top to bottom along the edge in which the latch will be installed. Plane the door to this line.

Because of their size, doors set on edge tend to wobble and this makes it very difficult to plane an edge square. You should, therefore, build a door jig. Place a 5- or 6-foot length of 2-by-4 flat on the floor; find the center, and nail a 27-inch board to this, vertically, at right angles and just to the left of the center mark. Nail a similar board on the other side of the center mark. The space between the uprights should be 1½ inches if you are working on an interior door; 1 7/8 inches if it's an exterior door. Brace each upright by nailing a board diagonally from the top to the end of the 2-by-4. Now set the door into the slot and get on with your planing.

Before removing all the wood down to the pencil line, set the door in the door opening hard against the hinge jamb; and draw a pencil line down the latch side of the door against the latch jamb. This will show you where the door will need a little more or less planing to fit into the opening perfectly.

Finish planing the edge and round off the sharp corners very slightly.

Interior doors up to 32 inches wide are hung with 3½-inch hinges. For wider doors, use 4-inch hinges. Exterior doors require 4½- and 5-inch hinges. The hinges should be the same distance from the top and bottom of the door as they are on other doors in the house.

First place the door in the opening and insert a wedge on the latch side to force it hard against the hinge jamb. Then place a 4d finishing nail on top of the door; stick a large wedge under the door; and force the door against the top jamb. Mark the hinge locations on the door and the jamb with a sharp pencil.

Place the door in the jig, and with a try square and sharp pencil outline the position of the hinges. The open edge of each hinge should be set about ¼ inch from the back edge of the door. That is, the

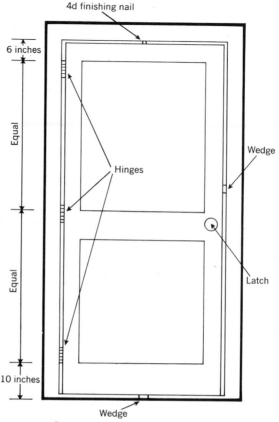

6 inches

Equal

Equal

10 inches

4d finishing nail

Hinges

Wedge

Latch

Wedge

**HANGING A HINGED DOOR:
ESTABLISHING POSITIONS OF HINGES**

hinge leaf should actually overlap a 1 3/8-inch door 1 1/8 inches.

Mark the hinge locations on the jamb in the same way. The leaves overlap the jamb for the same distance—1 1/8 inches.

Indicate the thickness of the hinge leaves on the door and jamb also.

Cut along the pencil lines on the edge of the door with a sharp chisel. Then starting at the top of one hinge mortise, make a series of closely spaced, slanting, shallow cuts across the mortise. Rake out the wood with the chisel and then, working from the side, chisel the mortise flat and set in the hinge to see whether the mortise is deep enough. If not, chisel out a little more wood until the face of the hinge leaf lies parallel with the door edge.

Make the other hinge mortises in the same way.

Screw the two hinges to the door. Be sure the head of the loose pin is facing up. Then pull out the pins and screw the other

half of the hinges to the jamb. Until you become experienced at hanging doors, use only one screw in each leaf at this point and do not drill holes for the others. Then set the door in the opening. If the hinge leaves fit together neatly, install the missing screws in the jamb. If one of the hinges doesn't quite fit together, you can usually adjust matters by loosening the single screw in the jamb leaf slightly so that the leaf can be moved up or down.

When inserting the pins in the hinge, note that they usually have a little ridge on one side directly under the head. This is supposed to fit into a notch in the hinge leaf. Turn the pin until it does.

Most latches and locks used today have cylindrical bodies. They are usually installed so the knob is 38 inches above the floor. Follow the directions that come with the set. Generally all you have to do is to drill a large hole through the door from front to back. Drill a smaller hole

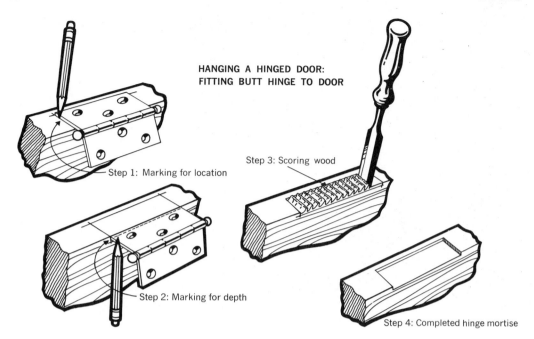

HANGING A HINGED DOOR:
FITTING BUTT HINGE TO DOOR

Step 1: Marking for location

Step 2: Marking for depth

Step 3: Scoring wood

Step 4: Completed hinge mortise

from the edge of the door into the large hole and, with a chisel, mortise the edge to receive the latch front. Assemble the latch and secure it in the door. Then on the jamb locate the strike to receive the latch. Cut the mortise with your chisel and cut out a deeper hole for the latch tongue.

How to finish doors. Use semi-gloss alkyd paint or spar or urethane varnish indoors. Use trim enamel or urethane varnish on the outer surfaces of exterior doors. Steel and urethane doors do not need painting, of course. When painting, prime the doors first and follow with one or two finish coats.

On paneled doors, paint the edges of each panel and then the centers of the panels. Complete all the top panels and then do the raised surfaces surrounding. Then do the bottom panels and the surrounding raised surfaces.

On louvered doors, paint the louvers first and then the raised surfaces. On flush doors, just start at the top and work down. If you brush the paint on horizontally and smooth it out with light up-and-down strokes, you will get a smoother finish.

How to weatherstrip doors. See *Weatherstripping.*

How to correct problems with hinged doors. If a door won't close because it

binds against the hinge jamb, loosen the hinges and insert narrow strips of cardboard, called shims, under the pin-side edges of the hinges. This forces the door away from the hinge jamb. If the door strikes the latch jamb, insert shims under the mortise-side edges of the hinges, thus pulling the door away from the latch jamb. Never plane down the edges of a door until you have exhausted all other possibilities of making it work properly. If planing becomes unavoidable, always plane the hinge edge and then make the mortises for the hinges deeper.

If a door strikes the jamb at the top or the threshold underneath, it is usually easiest to take the door off and plane down the top or bottom edge. However, if there is a wide gap under a door that strikes the top jamb, or if there is a wide gap above a door that strikes the threshold, it is a better idea to unscrew the hinges from the jamb and move the door and hinges down or up a fraction of an inch. This will necessitate extending the mortises in the jamb. The old screw holes must be plugged tight, preferably with wood pegs, before the screws are reset.

If a door latch doesn't catch or hold in the strike plate, remove the plate and shim it out with cardboard or thin strips of

(a) Door won't close because it binds against hinge jamb

(b) Door won't close because it strikes latch jamb

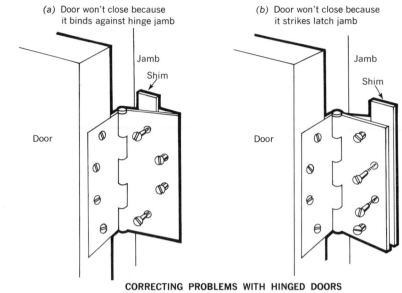

CORRECTING PROBLEMS WITH HINGED DOORS

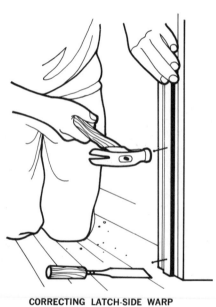

CORRECTING LATCH-SIDE WARP
ON HINGED DOORS

wood. The alternative is to insert shims the size of the hinge leaves in the mortises in the hinge jamb.

If a door rattles when closed, the strike plate must be set further back from the front edge of the jamb. Unscrew the plate and with a chisel extend the mortise back just far enough to hold the door tight.

If a door hangs on a slant, you can true it up by placing shims the size of the hinge leaves in the jamb under the top or bottom hinge.

If a door is warped and cannot be latched except by pushing hard against it, pry the stops from the latch and top jambs. Close the door and latch it; then draw a pencil line around the back edges of the jambs. Renail the stops along the pencil lines.

If a door is warped on the hinge side, a third hinge should be installed midway between the top and bottom hinges.

Swinging doors. These are always used indoors, usually between the kitchen and dining room. The doors are generally pivoted so they can swing in either direction; but double-acting hinges may also be used.

If a swinging door strikes any of the jambs or the threshold, the easiest way to correct matters is to take it down and plane the offending edge.

The main trouble with swinging doors, however, is sluggish action. Remove the cover and clean the spring at the bottom of pivoted doors at least once a year. Then apply a little oil, graphite, or grease. Lubricate hinges on hinged doors regularly.

Bi-fold doors. These are, in effect, split down the middle and hinged at the split. One leaf is pivoted next to one of the side jambs; the upper outside corner of the other leaf fits into a track on the top jamb. When the door is opened, the jamb leaf swings out like an ordinary hinged door, and the other leaf folds back against it.

Bi-fold doors are usually used on closets, either singly or in pairs. They do not have a latch and do not close tight at what would be the latch jamb. But they give full access to the closet, and when open take up less space than a hinged door.

If a door slips out of plumb, you can straighten it by loosening and adjusting the pivot at the bottom of the door or the pivot socket at the top of the door.

Sliding doors. The best sliding door—which is rarely installed because of its cost—glides into a pocket in the wall to one side of the door opening. You can hang a single door of this type or a pair that meet in the middle of the opening.

Bypass sliding doors are always installed in pairs or, sometimes, trios. Wooden doors of this type are suspended from parallel tracks screwed to the top jamb. Both slide either to right or left within the door opening. This means that the door opening can never be more than 50 percent open.

In the house, bypass sliding doors are generally used on closets. They require little attention, although they sometimes jump the track if pushed too hard. If a door hangs on a slant, it can be plumbed by adjusting the hanger arms on the back.

Heavy glass sliding doors are frequently installed in exterior walls to separate rooms from the terrace. These doors slide in floor tracks and are also held in place by ceiling tracks. Weatherstripping keeps out air, water, and dirt.

Because many people have been seriously injured when they walked into sliding glass doors, almost all doors built today are made of shatterproof tempered glass or plastic- or wire-reinforced glass. Fixed glass panels adjacent to glass doors should also be shatterproof. If you have older doors of breakable glass, you should have the glass replaced or paint some design on them to make them more visible.

Bottom tracks of sliding glass doors must be vacuumed frequently to clean out dust and grit. Wash tracks occasionally and rub them with paraffin or floor wax. If water seeps in under the tracks, apply silicone or polysulfide rubber caulking compound.

Folding doors. These are made of narrow strips of wood hinged together at the sides. When closed, the doors look like a piece of corrugated roofing. When open, they compress into a tight bundle at one side of the door opening.

The doors, which can be installed in small as well as very wide openings, are hung from tracks that are screwed to the top jamb of a door opening or to the ceiling. Since the doors cannot be used while paint is drying on them, they should be taken down for painting if the opening cannot be blocked.

Accordion doors. Like folding doors, these can be used in small and large openings. They are made with a metal frame which is covered on both sides with tough vinyl. Hung in tracks, they collapse accordion-fashion into a bundle when they are opened.

How to make a door opening. The rough opening for a door should equal the height of the door plus 1¾ inches to allow for the top jamb plus ½ to 1 inch for clearance at the floor line. The width of the opening equals the width of the door plus 2½ inches to allow for the side jambs.

Find the stud that will form one side of the door opening and measure 4 feet to the left or right. This should bring you to another stud. Cut the wall open between these studs to a height equal to the rough opening plus 3¼ inches. Cut off the two center studs at this height and remove them from the opening.

Cut three 2-by-4s the height of the rough opening less 1 5/8 inches. Stand one of them on the soleplate and nail it to the first stud.

Measure off the width of the rough opening and mark it on the soleplate. Then nail the other 2-by-4s together, stand them on the soleplate at this mark, and toenail them to the plate.

Cut out the soleplate within the rough opening.

Cut two pieces of 2-by-4 to fit snugly between the two studs and nail them together to form a double header. Lay this across the top of the 2-by-4s previously cut and toenail it to them. Then drive spikes up through the header into what remains of the two center studs.

The rough door opening is now completed.

Kits of lumber to frame doors are available at lumber yards. Buy a kit for the

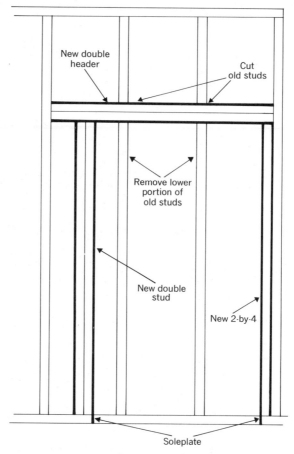

New double header

Cut old studs

Remove lower portion of old studs

New double stud

New 2-by-4

Soleplate

MAKING A DOOR OPENING

width of door you are installing. The jambs should be 1/16 inch wider than the thickness of the wall. Cut the side jambs to the height of the door plus clearance underneath. Then fit the top jamb into the side jambs and nail them together.

Set the jambs in the center of the rough opening and check the top with a carpenter's level to make sure it is level. Then drive two shingles between each side jamb and the studs at the top of the opening. One shingle should be driven from one side of the jamb; the other from the opposite side. The thin edges should overlap, thus forming a flat wedge.

Cut a rough board to fit exactly between the side jambs at the top. Place this on the floor between the side jambs, and then drive shingle wedges between the side jambs and the studs at the bottom of the opening.

Hang a plumb line down along one of the side jambs to make sure it is straight up and down. If it isn't, adjust the bottom

wedges. Then drive casing nails through the jamb and wedges into the studs. Let the heads protrude a bit until the other jamb is plumbed.

Check the other side jamb for straightness, and nail it in the same way. Then insert three additional double wedges behind each side jamb. On the latch side of the door they should be evenly spaced. On the hinge side, one wedge should be at the level of the top hinge; a second wedge at the level of the bottom hinge; and the third wedge midway between. Before driving nails through these wedges, check the jamb with your plumb line once more.

Trim the door opening with casings similar to those used on older doors in the house. Apply them in the same way. Position the stops on the jambs so that when the door is closed, its face will be flush with the edges of the jambs.

How to close an old door opening. Remove the trim and jambs. Cut a 2-by-4 the width of the opening and nail it to the

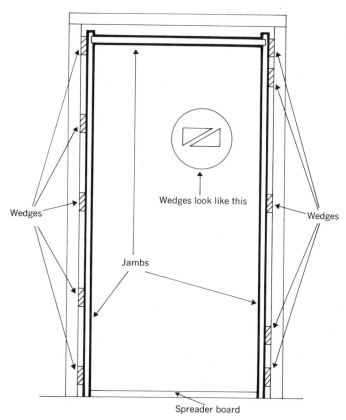

Wedges

Wedges look like this

Wedges

Jambs

Spreader board

INSTALLING DOOR JAMBS

floor to form a soleplate. Then cut another 2-by-4 to form a stud for the center of the opening. Toenail this to the soleplate and to the header at the top of the opening. Then, unless the surrounding walls are made of special material, close the opening with gypsum board. It may be necessary to fur this out from the studs slightly to make it level with the surrounding walls.

Dotted Swiss. A sheer fabric with thick woven dots on the front surface. If made of cotton, it should be hand-washed. If made of a blend of cotton and synthetic fibers, it can be machine-washed in warm water and dried at low heat in a dryer.

Drafts. Most cold drafts are caused by air stealing in around the edges of windows and exterior doors and interior doors at the head of unheated basement stairs or the foot of attic stairs. For how to stop these, see *Weatherstripping.*

For how to stop cold air from seeping through walls, windows, and floors over crawl spaces, see *Insulation.*

On windy days, drafts are sometimes caused by wind blowing through the kitchen ventilating fan. This is a problem especially with fans that exhaust to the outdoors through metal ducts. The entrance of air can be minimized, though not stopped, by installing a weatherhood on the end of the duct.

In homes with warm-air heating, rather violent drafts may result when the furnace blower comes on as the thermostat calls for heat. The drafts can be stopped and conditions in the house made far more comfortable if you have the system redesigned to give continuous air circulation. See *Heating Systems.*

Drains. A house should have two systems of drains. One carries off the waste water and wastes from bathrooms, kitchen, and laundry (see *Plumbing System, Household*). The other—which many houses lack—carries off storm water through gutters, leaders, and footing drains into dry wells or the community's storm sewer. Floor drains in basements, garages, and areaways are part of the storm drain system (see *Basements*).

The two systems should never be interconnected. However, in houses with septic systems, laundry water is sometimes drained into a dry well rather than the septic tank. This helps to prevent over-loading of the septic system.

Draperies. See *Curtains.*

Drapery Hardware. The drapery hardware you use depends on the style of the curtain or drapery to be hung; on whether you want to draw the curtains and how; on whether the curtain is to be hung inside the window casing, on the window casing, above the casing, or from the ceiling; and on how much money you want to spend. The choice is wide and confusing.

Simple curtain rods. *Flat steel rods* are the simplest available. They are curved at the ends and hook over flat brackets that are mounted on the casings or the wall. You can get single or double rods. Standard rods will support lightweight curtains only. They extend to only about 4 feet, although a straight extender rod can be inserted for a somewhat greater span. For draperies, you need reinforced heavy-duty rods. Largest sizes will extend to as much as 10 feet. Simple screw-in supports with a U-shaped bend in the end can be used to hold up rods that sag.

One thing to remember about these flat rods is that you must tilt them upward several inches in order to hook them over the brackets. This means that if the top of a window is directly below the ceiling, you should use some other kind of rod.

Round steel rods are often called brass rods because many have a brass finish. But they sometimes have an enamel finish. The rods are held in small brackets by screw-on barrel-like sleeves. Brackets are available for mounting inside the casing or on the outside of the casing. You can also get gooseneck brackets for outside-casing mounting if you want the curtains to project out from the window a bit.

Round steel rods can be cut to almost any length; if over 5 feet long, however, they are likely to need support at the center. Use the same supports as for flat steel rods.

You can bend round rods to go around corners or to fit into bow windows.

Large rods. These are usually ornamental rods up to about 1¼-inch diameter. They are made of wood or steel. Most rods are round but there are also squares. They are sometimes installed inside the casing in brackets like those used to support wooden closet rods; but they are generally hung in large U-shaped brackets projecting out from the wall or casing.

Spring-tension rods. These should be used only for light curtains because they are held in place inside casings only by a spring that presses the rubber end tips against the casings.

The rods are round or oval. An oval rod 1 inch across can be extended as much as 7 feet.

Traverse rods. The first thing to note when you are buying traverse rods is the ease and quietness with which they operate. The second thing is the strength and weight of the rods. The larger or heavier your draperies, the stronger the rods must be. Middle supports are made for all rods, but these do not offer as much assurance against sagging as rods that are built for strength in the first place.

Draperies hung on traverse rods are attached to slides, or carriers, that move back and forth when you pull the control cord. Most rods are designed to hold a drapery panel at both ends. When closed, the panels meet in the center of the rod; when open, they pull back to the ends. The majority of rods are straight, but there are a few right-angle rods designed for instal-lation in corners and a few curved rods for use in bow windows. There are also straight one-way rods designed to pull a single drapery either to the left or to the right.

All traverse rods are adjustable within certain limits. The shortest rod is 28 inches. The longest—a monster—extends to 26 feet. One-way rods extend to 13 feet.

The simplest rods hold a drapery only. Other rods hold a drapery and curtain or drapery and valance. And still other rods hold drapery, curtain, and valance. When the traverse rod is coupled with an ordi-nary curtain rod on which the curtains are adjusted by hand, it is called a combi-nation traverse and curtain rod. In a double traverse rod, both the draperies and curtains are cord-controlled.

Traverse rod brackets may be mounted on the face of the casing, on the wall beyond the casing, or on the ceiling. They are sometimes installed inside the casing. A window widener is a rod with brackets that are mounted on the casing, but the rod itself extends several inches beyond the casing.

How to install traverse rods. Rods should come complete with all brackets and screws. Installation directions are also enclosed. Follow these carefully.

In the average installation, all you have to do is screw the brackets and center support (if needed) to the window casing, extend the rod to the proper length, and install it in the brackets. The cords can be cut off to any length and weighted with plastic pulls. This arrangement does not, however, make the cords sufficiently taut to assure smooth movement of the draperies. The preferred practice is to loop the cord through a tension pulley which comes with the rod. The pulley is screwed to the floor, baseboard, or wall.

Final step in installing a rod is to work the slides back and forth to make sure they are operating smoothly and meet in the center. If they do not meet in the center, you will find in the back of one of the center slides a sort of hook. The cord is looped around this—or should be. Pull the control cords to draw the other slides all the way to the end of the rod. Release the cord from the slide with the hook and push that slide back to its end of the rod. Tighten the cord and then loop it around the hook. The slides should now meet in the exact center of the rod.

When traverse rod brackets are mounted on the window casing, the screws supplied by the manufacturer will hold them secure. But if the brackets are mounted on a wall, the screws alone should be counted on only if the wall is paneled in wood. If the wall is plaster, the screws should be driven into plastic or lead anchors (see *Wall Anchors*). In any other kind of wall, use very long screws and drive them through the board into the studs. If this is impossible, the brackets must be put up with split-wing toggle bolts or hollow-wall anchors.

How to repair traverse rods. There isn't too much that is likely to go wrong.

If for some reason the curtains do not meet at the center of the rod, follow the directions above.

If a cord looped through a tension pulley becomes slack, untie one end from one of the center slides, pull the cord taut, and retie to the center slide. If the cord ends dangle, put heavier weights on them.

If the pulleys and carriers are unusually noisy, spray them lightly with silicone lubricant.

Café curtain hardware. Many of the rods described above can be used for café curtains as well as for full-length draperies.

Decorative accessories. Such things as tiebacks, holdbacks, and festoon rings are widely available in a variety of designs. They are easily installed with screws.

Drawers.

How to repair drawers. Drawer sticks. If this trouble occurs only in humid weather, remove the drawer and let it dry thoroughly for several days next to the furnace or under an electric heater or heat lamp. If you can't remove it, turn the heat on in the room for several days to shrink the wood. Then cover all surfaces with shellac or varnish to seal out moisture. If the drawer is still stuck so badly that you can't even get it out of its pocket, set a 75-watt incandescent bulb inside on top of a trivet to dry it out.

If the drawer sticks in dry weather, remove it, turn it upside down, and plane, scrape, or sand down the runners a fraction of an inch. Then rub the runners and the sides of the drawer with paraffin. Sometimes you must also scrape down the sides.

Joints loose. Scrape off old glue and apply new. Then place boards at either end of the drawer, tie them together with cords, and twist the cords together in tourniquet fashion.

REPAIRING LOOSE DRAWER JOINTS
Tie heavy cord loosely around drawer. Pass stick or other rigid object under, then over cord to form loop. Twist until tight. Allow to rest against side.

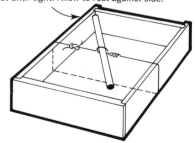

Bottom split. Cut a piece of tempered hardboard to fit snugly in the drawer and glue this on top of the old bottom.

Drawer wobbles from side to side as it slides in and out. The drawer runners glide on narrow boards attached to the sides of the chest. Glue small strips of wood on top of these boards close to the sides of the drawer. Make sure the strips are parallel.

Available types of drawer. Anyone can knock together a simple drawer, but it takes skill and usually special tools to make a good one. In other words, if you need to build a drawer into a cabinet or under a counter, for instance, it is better to buy one.

Wood, steel, and plastic drawers are available. They come in all sizes—either the drawers alone or the drawers in frames. You can, for instance, buy small plastic drawers that can be hung in steel racks supplied by the manufacturer or built into a wood frame; other plastic drawers that slide out from simple plastic frames for kitchen cabinets; wood drawers in individual frames that can be stacked one on top of another; steel drawers in a frame that is open on the sides, top, and back for building into a closet or under a workbench; and so on.

Dresden. A beautiful china which was once produced at Meissen, Germany, near Dresden. See *China.*

Dresser. A bedroom chest of drawers. See *Furniture, Wood,* and *Drawers.*

Drill. Drill is a strong, close-woven cotton twill fabric much like denim. It is used in clothing and awnings. Launder like cotton.

Drills. See *Tools, Workshop—Electric drill.*

Dry Wells. Dry wells are large covered wells into which water from the roof, footing drains, and sometimes the washing machine is drained. Their purpose is to collect and dispose of this water underground, away from the house. When used to dispose of roof water—their most common task—they help to prevent wet basements and erosion of the ground at the foot of downspouts.

Dry wells are, in short, substitutes for a storm sewer; and like most substitutes, they are not as good as the first-stringer, because in time they are very likely to become clogged, and even when new, they may not absorb all the water that pours into them. But if you don't have a storm sewer running by your house, dry wells should prove useful.

Dry wells should be located at least 8 feet from the house so that they do not build up water pressure against the foundation walls. They should be dug deep enough so that the top is at least 1 foot below the ground level. If they are higher than this, grass over them will grow poorly in dry weather.

The size a dry well should be is impossible to figure exactly. But if the roof area of your house measures under 2000 square feet, you ought to get by with a single well. If the soil is very porous, the well should be 3 feet in diameter and 4 feet deep; for loam, 4 by 5 feet; for clay, 5 by 6 feet. For a larger house, put in two or more dry wells. And if the soil is extremely dense clay, you should put in two or more wells for a small house.

After the hole for a dry well is dug, it should be lined with reasonable care to keep it from collapsing and to allow water to leach out into the surrounding ground. An excellent lining can be made with cesspool blocks, if available. Or you can use rough, more or less rectangular rocks. You can also use a large steel drum or wood barrel with the ends cut off, holes bored in the sides, and coated inside and out with asphalt roofing cement; but because of their size, you will need two dry wells where one would do otherwise.

When the hole is lined, an opening is made just below the top rim for the drain leading from the downspouts. Make the drain of long, 4-inch plastic or composition pipes. These should be pitched toward the dry well at a rate of about 1 inch per foot.

Fill the well with rough stones, bricks, or chunks of concrete. Don't pack them in tightly; the larger the interstices, the more water the well will hold. Then cover the well with coarse aluminum mesh and cover this with a layer of old 1-inch boards. Finally shovel back the soil.

To keep dry wells from clogging, put strainers in all gutter openings or cover the gutters with mesh.

Duck. Duck is a sturdy cotton fabric much like canvas but considerably lighter. It is used in clothing and also in awnings. Wash like cotton.

Rips in duck can be mended with needle and thread. In the case of awnings, however, a better solution is to cut out a patch with pinking shears and apply it with fabric-mending adhesive.

Dust Cloths. You can make a perfectly good dust cloth out of an old cotton knit undershirt sprayed with silicone to make it pick up and hold dust better. But treated flannel cloths that can be washed and rewashed without further treatment are available and excellent.

Whatever dust cloth you use, wash it when it becomes so impregnated with dust that you cannot shake it clean. When dry, spray untreated cloths again with silicone. This can be applied between washings, although it should not be necessary.

Dusting. The aim of dusting is to pick up the dust, not just to move it around. So move your dust cloth across the surface being dusted slowly. Don't flick the cloth at the surface. And don't use a feather duster.

If dust is heavy, use a vacuum-cleaner dusting tool rather than a dust cloth to pick it up.

Lift and dust under objects on tables, chests, and other surfaces.

When doing a thorough dusting job, work from the high points in the room down. For instance, do the tops of pictures and mirrors; then the bottoms. Do the finials of lamps and then the base and then the table top.

Shake your dust cloth outdoors when it is dirty. And don't forget to close the door behind you so the dust won't drift back inside.

Dynel. Union Carbide's trade name for its modacrylic fiber.

Earthenware. Earthenware is a relatively inexpensive type of dinnerware and other ceramic objects. Made of fairly coarse clays, it is semi-vitreous; and if the glaze is cracked, water will stain the body clay. It is also quite easy to chip.

Modern earthenware is underglazed and can be washed in the dishwasher without fear of obliterating the decorations. But older, overglazed earthenware should be hand-washed.

Repair broken pieces with cellulose cement.

For a discussion of what pieces of earthenware a family should buy, see *Dinnerware.*

Efflorescence. A white, powdery deposit that sometimes appears on brick and other masonry walls. For how to remove it, see *Brick.*

Electric Cords. Too many fires are started every year by defective electric cords; so don't take chances with them. If the insulation is cracked or cut in only one or two spots, the cord can be made safe by wrapping the cut area with black plastic electrical tape. But if a cord is cracked or frayed in many places or stiff with age, throw it out.

Cords are repaired in different ways, depending on their size. The small cords used on lamps and for extensions are most easily fixed with clamp-on splicers. Since these vary somewhat, follow the directions on the package. Generally, all you have to do is to cut cleanly through the cord with a pair of pliers, scissors, or pruning shears; insert the end or ends in the clamp-on device; and clamp it in place. You will find clamp-on plugs, outlets, and splicers in hardware and variety stores.

Large cords used in heavy-duty extensions, on power tools, and motors will not fit into the clamp-on devices; furthermore, many of them contain ground wires. Repairs are therefore somewhat more complicated.

The plugs and outlets used are attached to the cords with screws. If you are repairing a two-wire cord (ungrounded type), cut the end off cleanly; strip back the outer insulation for about 2 inches; remove about ¾ inch of the inner insulation from the ends of the two wires; and if the wires are made up of many tiny strands, twist them tight. Then insert the two wires through the back of the plug or outlet.

At this point, if you are replacing a plug, you should tie the wires together just where they emerge from the outer insulating sheath in what is known as an underwriters' knot. This is supposed to keep you from yanking the cord out of the plug. You then wrap one of the wires around one of the prongs, wrap it clockwise around the adjoining screw, and screw it down tight. Wrap the other wire around the other prong and screw. It makes no difference which wire is attached to which screw. Finally, slip the fiber cover that conceals the inside of the plug over the prongs. The cord is now ready for service.

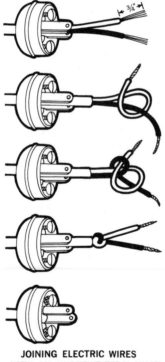

**JOINING ELECTRIC WIRES
WITH AN UNDERWRITERS' KNOT**

The procedure for attaching a grounded plug or outlet is essentially the same. In this case, however, you must attach the black wire to the gold screw; the white wire to the silver screw; and the colored ground wire to the screw adjacent to the U-shaped prong.

If a heavy-duty cord—whether two- or three-wire—is cut in two, it can be spliced by neatly cutting out the broken section. Then remove about 4 inches of the outer insulation from the two cords, and 2 inches of insulation from the ends of all the wires. Bend the wires opposite each other together and twist them tightly around each other. (In a three-wire cord, be sure wires of the same color are joined together.) Ideally, you should solder each joint so that it will never pull apart. Then wrap each joint separately with black plastic tape. Bundle the wires together, and overwrap the entire mend with tape.

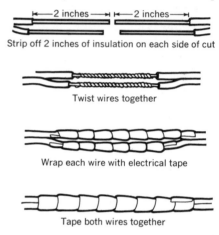

Strip off 2 inches of insulation on each side of cut

Twist wires together

Wrap each wire with electrical tape

Tape both wires together

SPLICING ELECTRIC WIRES

Cords used on heating appliances (irons, toasters, portable heaters, for example) can be fixed in the same way as the heavy-duty cords just described. But it is a much better idea to replace them entirely.

Adapter plugs. Since about 1960, there has been a concerted drive by the electrical industry to ground all circuits to make them safer. As a result, almost all outlets installed in houses today are of the grounded type—with three rather than two holes. And the plugs on most appliances and power tools are also of the grounded type—with three rather than two prongs.

However, there are still many ungrounded cords, plugs, and outlets in use.

You can plug an ungrounded two-prong plug into any grounded three-hole outlet. But it is impossible to plug a grounded three-prong plug into an ungrounded two-hole outlet unless you use an adapter. This inexpensive little device has three holes in one end, two prongs in the other, and a small pigtail wire near the prongs.

If you want to connect an appliance with a grounded plug to an ungrounded extension cord, just insert the plug into the adapter's three holes, and then plug the adapter's two prongs into the extension cord's outlet. Ignore the pigtail. However, if you are connecting a grounded appliance into an ungrounded wall outlet, insert the adapter in the outlet and connect the pigtail in one of the three following ways: (1) If the wires connecting the outlet into the electrical system run through BX cable or rigid metal conduit, connect the pigtail to one of the two screws holding the outlet in the metal outlet box. (2) If the outlet is connected with nonmetallic cable containing a ground wire, connect the pigtail to the ground wire. (3) If the outlet is connected with nonmetallic cable without a ground wire, connect the pigtail to a water pipe.

After the adapter is connected, plug the appliance cord into it. The appliance is now safely grounded.

Electric Motors. Electric motors are the most reliable mechanisms in your home. They run on and on with little or no attention. Nevertheless, you should know several things about them:

1. Continuous operation does less harm than repeated stopping and starting. Starting puts a load on a motor and this causes it eventually to wear out. But once a motor is running, it can purr along happily for days on end.

2. Motors need extra power to start; then they settle down and use relatively little power. But sometimes this initial surge causes a temporary overload on the electrical circuit into which the motor is connected and thus may cause a fuse to blow. This is most likely to happen if, at the time the motor starts, the circuit is already loaded close to capacity.

One way to prevent blowing of fuses for this reason is to install time-delay fuses which absorb a temporary overload.

3. In recent years, the demand for electricity has been so great that American utility systems have at times been seriously overloaded and have experienced sharp voltage drops. These are apparent in the home when lights suddenly dim and motors run slow.

There is nothing to worry about if the voltage drop is momentary. But if it persists for any length of time, you should immediately disconnect or turn off all large motor-driven devices: refrigerator, freezer, washer, dryer, oil burner, water pump, swimming pool pump, etc. Do not turn them on again until the voltage drop is corrected. The reason for this is that if the motors happen to be running at the time full power is restored, the sudden surge may knock them out completely.

4. If a motor is covered by water as a result of flooding, it will stop running. Do not try to start it when the water recedes. Call in the appropriate serviceman or a motor repair expert; or take the motor to the latter. It is more than likely that it must be baked out for a couple of days before it will run again.

5. Modern motors are permanently lubricated and should never be oiled unless the manufacturer advises it. In that case, follow directions. If you have any old motors with oil cups or oiling points, put a few drops of oil in them about every three months. Use SAE No. 10 oil for large motors, thin household oil for small motors.

6. Try not to let motors become clogged with dirt, dust, and lint. Blow them clean after you use them or dust them with a paintbrush. But don't take them apart.

What to do if a motor doesn't run. Make sure that it is plugged in, that the fuse hasn't blown, and that the outlet is not defective.

Turn the motor on and then check whether there is a break in the cord. To do this, hold the cord in two hands, bend a short section into a U, and flex it up and down. Repeat this procedure for the entire length of the cord. Wiggle the cord hard where it enters the motor and the plug. If the motor suddenly starts, you have found the break.

Some motors contain carbon brushes which are concealed beneath rather obvious screw caps. Remove each cap and slide out the spring inside. Attached to the end of the spring is a hard black carbon "brush." If this is worn down, replace with a new brush of the same size available from hardware stores.

If a motor hums but doesn't start, the device it is driving may be stuck. Turn the motor off at once, before it burns out, and try to loosen the device by hand and then with a wrench. Use oil to help free it.

Electric Outlets. It is not uncommon for outlets to become defective. When this happens, they should be replaced with a new outlet of the same kind.

First, shut off the current by flipping the circuit breaker or removing the fuse. Then take off the outlet plate; remove the two screws holding the outlet in the box; pull the outlet out of the box; and unscrew the wires connected to it. Attach the new outlet in the same way the old outlet was connected. The bare ends of the wires should be wrapped clockwise around the screws. In some outlets, however, you can simply insert the ends of the wires in holes in the back of the outlet and then clamp them by tightening the screws.

Push the outlet back into the box. Make sure the outlet is centered and that neither terminals nor bare wires touch the sides of the box. Then screw the outlet to the box, replace the cover, and reset the circuit breaker.

An important thing to remember in making this simple repair is that the black wire (which is the hot wire) must always be connected to the gold screw and the white wire must always be connected to the silver screw. If there is a colored ground wire, it is connected to the colored grounding screw.

Electric Switches. To replace a defective switch, turn off the current at the circuit breaker or fuse box. Unscrew the switch plate, remove the switch from the box, disconnect the wires, and reconnect them to the new switch exactly as before.

In a single-pole switch with two terminals, the black wire goes to the gold screw; the white wire to the silver screw. In a three-way switch with three terminals, the black wire goes to the single gold screw; the other wires to either of the side-by-side silver screws. If you are confused about wiring a four-way switch with four terminals, call an electrician.

Although the switch you are replacing may be an old-fashioned kind with two buttons, you can substitute a modern toggle switch for it.

Electrical System, Household. We do not recommend that you wire your own home or that you even make extensive changes and additions to an existing system. These

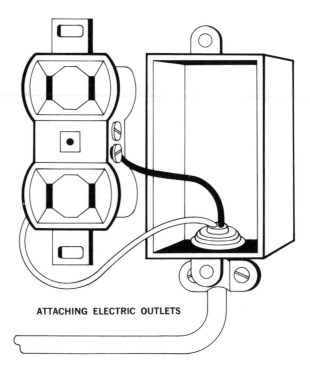

ATTACHING ELECTRIC OUTLETS

are jobs that should properly be left to experts. For your comfort and convenience, however, you should have a good understanding of what goes into an adequate wiring system and how it is laid out.

Four points should be remembered: (1) If the wires and service entrance equipment are too small, you will not be able to use all the electrical appliances you may eventually want; the appliances and lights you do have will operate at partial efficiency; you will be plagued with blown fuses; and you run the risk of fire. (2) If you don't have enough outlets correctly placed, your room arrangements may be upset and you will forever be using your appliances and lamps at inconvenient spots. (3) If you don't have enough switches, you will bark your shins while stumbling around a dark house trying to turn on the lights. (4) It's better and cheaper to overwire a house in the beginning than to try to add wiring later. The use of electrical equipment is growing so fast that even though a minimum wiring system may be adequate today, it will have to be expanded later.

Fortunately, it is not difficult to make sure your wiring is adequate for your present as well as your future needs. If you follow the rules below, you can rest assured that from the electrical standpoint your house is as livable as it can be.

The service drop is the wires running from the light pole to the house. It is the utility's job to install these. Three wires are needed to provide the 240-volt service required to run a range, water heater, dryer, central cooling system, or electric heating system.

If you want the wires run underground instead of overhead, you must pay extra; but of course the installation is invisible and therefore more attractive.

The service entrance is the cable running from the end of the service drop to the meter, then to the main disconnect switch (or master switch), and finally to the circuit-breaker panel or fuse box. The cable should consist of three No. 2 wires rated for 100-amp service, thus giving your home an electrical capacity of 24,000 watts. If you are going to heat your home

electrically, however, you need 200-amp service.

The circuit-breaker panel should also be rated at 100 or 200 amp. One breaker is provided for each branch circuit, and there should be space to add several more breakers in case your electrical needs increase. (Circuit breakers have almost completely replaced fuse boxes in new homes today. But fuse boxes are still common in older homes.)

The circuit-breaker panel is commonly installed in the garage, utility room, or basement; but if you put it in the kitchen, where the electrical load is usually heaviest, you should cut the cost of wiring and save steps and time in resetting a circuit breaker that trips off. In larger houses—and especially in houses where it is not feasible to bring the service entrance cable directly to the kitchen—it's a good idea to install the main circuit-breaker panel in the garage and a branch panel in the kitchen. In very large houses, several branch panels are advisable from the convenience standpoint.

The branch circuits carry electricity from the circuit-breaker panel to the points at which it is needed. Use No. 12 wire for all 120-volt circuits; No. 6 wire for 240-volt circuits.

The type of cable used is determined largely by your local electrical code. In a few cities, the wires must go through metal conduit. In other areas, BX cable—a flexible metal-armored cable—is used. But most houses are now wired with nonmetallic sheathed cable (a plastic-covered cable).

The following branch circuits are required:

One 15-amp, 120-volt lighting circuit for each 500 square feet of floor area. These circuits supply electricity to the lights and to all convenience outlets except those used for cooking and laundry appliances.

Two two-wire, 20-amp, 120-volt appliance circuits for the convenience outlets in the kitchen, laundry, and dining room. These take care of all your small appliances such as an iron and toaster, and also a small refrigerator, gas range, gas dryer, and ice-maker. A more modern alternative is to provide one three-wire, 20-amp circuit for operation of small appliances.

One 20-amp, 120-volt circuit for an automatic washer.

One 20-amp, 120-volt circuit for a dishwasher and garbage disposer.

One 20-amp, 120-volt circuit for a food freezer.

One 20-amp, 120-volt circuit for a no-frost refrigerator.

One 15-amp, 120-volt circuit for the heating plant.

One 20-amp, 120- or 240-volt circuit for each room air conditioner.

One 20-amp, 120- or 240-volt circuit for a water pump.

One 20-amp, 120- or 240-volt circuit for each bathroom heater. One of these circuits will also serve an attic fan.

One 20-amp, 120-volt circuit for a workshop.

One 40-amp, 240-volt circuit for a central air conditioner.

One 50-amp, 240-volt circuit for an electric range.

One 30-amp, 240-volt circuit for an electric clothes dryer.

One 240-volt circuit for an electric water heater (check your utility for the required amperage).

If electric radiant heating is used, it requires one or more separate 240-volt circuits.

Having provided the necessary number of circuits and installed the proper size wires, you can be sure that a full supply of electricity is delivered to every outlet. Your lights and appliances will operate at full efficiency. You will rarely, if ever, trip a circuit breaker because of an overload caused by running too many lights and appliances at one time.

Your next problem is to bring electricity to the points at which you need it, and to provide the switching to control it easily.

Convenience outlets that are used primarily for the connection of lamps should be provided in the main rooms on the basis of one outlet per 150 square feet of floor space. Location of the outlets depends on the most logical placement of the furniture. In other words, decide where your furniture will be and where you are likely to need lamps and to use appliances before you make your wiring plan. But in any case, outlets are usually installed 12 inches above the floor and should be spaced so that no point along the floor line is more than 6 feet from an outlet. In front of long walls of floor-to-ceiling windows, where wall outlets cannot be used, use floor outlets.

In halls, locate outlets where lamps (if any) are to be used and where they will be most useful for plugging in the vacuum cleaner. In long halls, outlets are needed every 15 feet. In large, wide halls, space the outlets so that no point along the floor line is more than 10 feet from one.

In the dining room, if the table is to be placed against the wall or if there is a built-in counter of any kind, install one outlet (connected to the appliance circuit) just above the table or counter.

In the bathroom, provide one outlet near the mirror 3 to 5 feet above the floor. (Many bathroom lighting fixtures incorporate outlets). Other outlets may be needed if the bathroom is large or compartmentalized.

In the kitchen, outlets (connected to the appliance circuits) should be 44 inches above the floor. Provide one outlet per 4 feet of work surface and make sure that every work surface has at least one outlet. Separate outlets are also needed at a breakfast table or bar and at a planning desk.

In the laundry, provide at least one outlet (connected to an appliance circuit) 3 to 4 feet above the floor.

In basements, provide at least two convenience outlets—one to be located at the workbench.

In attics, one outlet is recommended so you can light your way into dark corners and also so you can use a vacuum cleaner.

In the garage or carport, provide one outlet. On porches, terraces, and patios adjoining the house, provide one weatherproof outlet per 15 feet of solid wall. Install them 18 inches above the paving (higher in the far North).

At the front door, provide one weatherproof outlet at least 18 inches above grade for Christmas lighting. Additional exterior outlets are recommended for garden lighting and use of garden power tools.

Install special clock-hanger outlets wherever electric wall clocks are to be used.

Install outlets for all heavy-duty plug-in appliances such as washers and room air conditioners at least 12 inches above the floor and as close to the appliances as possible.

Many types of convenience outlet are available. Most commonly used is the double, or duplex, outlet. But because we are using so much electrical equipment these days, you should consider triple outlets at least at those places (the bedside, for example) where you are likely to plug in three things at once. Another type of outlet with even greater flexibility is the plug-in strip, which provides outlets every 18 to 24 inches. These are especially good in the kitchen and workshop. There are also such special outlets as a safety outlet for use in children's rooms; a sealed floor outlet; a combination electric power and TV outlet; and a fan hanger outlet. Regardless of design, all outlets should be of the grounded type—with three rather than two holes per receptacle. These are needed for modern appliances; but can still be used for cords (such as lamp cords) with two-prong plugs.

Wall switches must be provided to control all built-in lighting fixtures; and it is desirable to provide switch control for at least one convenience outlet in the living room and each bedroom. (In the latter case, the switch should control only one side of the outlet; thus the other side will stay "hot" all the time and the operation of a clock or radio will not be interrupted.)

Switches should usually be located 4 feet above the floor on the latch side of doors or the traffic side of arches. They should be placed within the room in which the light is located except in the following cases: control exterior and porch lights from indoors; control lights on stairs that are closed off by doors from the adjoining hall or room; control lights in large storage rooms from the adjoining room.

Caution: Do not install any switch—or outlet—within arm's reach of a plumbing fixture.

For convenience and safety, it is important that at least one built-in lighting fixture in each room, hall, stairway, or other enclosed area be controlled from switches located at every regularly used entrance into that area. (The exception to this rule is when two entrances are within a few feet of each other. In that case, one switch can be eliminated.) The need for this multiple switching is obvious: no matter through what door you enter a room, you can turn on a light to see what you are doing.

The best general-purpose switches are of the silent type—especially the so-called mercury switches.

Identifying electrical circuits. If you know exactly which outlets, lights, and switches in your house are controlled by each circuit breaker or fuse, you will save yourself a good deal of time when you someday want to make a change or repair in your electrical system.

The easiest way to identify outlets is to turn on all the lights in the house, then open the circuit breakers one by one and make a list of the lights that are out and the outlets that are not working. To check unused outlets, plug in a lamp.

Number the circuit breakers with a grease pencil. Then print a legible list of the lights and outlets each breaker controls. Paste this inside the cover of the circuit-breaker panel.

Cutting off the current. This is the first thing you should do when making a repair on the household electrical system. All you have to do if you have a circuit-breaker panel is to flip the toggle switch controlling the circuit you are working on. If you have fuses, you either unscrew the fuse if it is the plug type, or pull it out if it is the cartridge type. Note, however, that fuses are safe to remove only if the wires and terminals in the fuse box are completely hidden. If they are exposed, don't take chances: pull the master switch at the service entrance panel before removing and replacing the fuses.

The master switch is also pulled off when major alterations are being made to the electrical system and in emergencies. such as fire and flood.

Replacing fuses. Two basic types of fuses are encountered in homes: the plug fuse, which screws in, and the long cartridge fuse, which looks like a firecracker and is held in metal clips. Plug fuses are available in 10-, 15-, 20-, 25-, and 30-amp sizes and are used for lighting and appliance circuits. Cartridge fuses are available in 10- to 60-amp sizes and are used in large appliance circuits (for ranges and dryers, for example).

Standard fuses of both types blow when a short circuit occurs and when a circuit is overloaded because you are using too many lights and appliances at one time. Time-delay fuses of both types absorb a momentary overload without blowing. They are used mainly in circuits that serve electric motors over about ¼ horsepower.

When a plug fuse is blown, a metal strip visible through the window in the back of the fuse is burned through; and the window itself usually becomes cloudy. But there is no way of telling whether a cartridge fuse is blown except by removing it from the fuse box and testing it; consequently, if a circuit protected by two cartridge fuses goes dead, you should replace them both even though one of them may still be good.

Before replacing any fuse (or resetting a circuit breaker), however, you should try to determine what caused it to blow. The usual answer is that you tried to operate too many appliances at the same time. When this is the case, disconnect one of the appliances and you will not have any more trouble.

Sometimes, however, the source of the trouble is a short circuit. A momentary flash of light in some part of the electrical system is one indication of a short. Burn marks on wires, sockets, etc., are another. But many shorts occur without leaving visible evidence. It follows that when a fuse blows, if you are positive it was not caused by overloading the circuit, a short circuit must have occurred. In this case, your first step should be to disconnect all lamps, appliances, and extension cords on the circuit. Then replace the fuse. If the new fuse blows, the trouble is somewhere in the wiring system and you should call in an electrical contractor. Do not use the circuit until he has checked it out. If the new fuse does not blow, on the other hand, the short probably occurred in one of the plug-in items you disconnected.

Selecting fuses of the proper size. Actually, you have no choice in this matter. Each wiring circuit in a house is designed for a fuse of a certain size; and while it is perfectly safe to use a fuse of smaller size, you must never use a larger size.

For example, if a circuit is made with No. 14 wire, it should be fused at 15 amps, no more. If No. 12 wire, 20 amps. If No. 10 wire, 30 amps.

If you should overfuse a circuit, you make it possible for the wires in the circuit to overheat and start a fire. Similarly, if you substitute a penny for a fuse—as some foolish people have done to their sorrow—you make it possible for the wires to overheat.

Generally, the best rule to follow in replacing fuses is to put in a fuse exactly like the one that has blown. But if you move into a house that was occupied by someone else, you can't be sure that he always followed this rule. So if you find in the fuse box a variety of fuses of 25 amps or more that are not protecting circuits to large appliances, you should ask an electrical contractor to check the situation. Most circuits in the average house are fused at 15 or 20 amps.

Miniature circuit breakers. These resemble plug fuses and may be substituted for them. When they blow, instead of replacing them, you simply press a button in the back. This makes it unnecessary to keep a supply of fuses available in anticipation of need. On the other hand, the miniature breakers cost almost ten times as much as fuses.

Emery Cloth. See *Abrasives.*

Enamels. Enamels are small decorative objects and pieces of jewelry made by bonding colorful enamels to metal and sometimes glass at high heat. To clean enamels, wash with a soft cloth dipped in detergent solution. Apply an appropriate metal polish to the metal back of the enamel. Repairs should be made professionally.

Enamelware. Strictly speaking, bathtubs and washbasins are enamelware. But as a rule, the name is applied only to utensils made by bonding porcelain enamel to metal. Utensils made this way are often very colorful and remarkably durable. But the enamel may chip if struck a sharp blow; and the enamel on less expensive utensils will craze if they are placed, when empty, directly on a gas burner or electric unit.

The most durable enamelware (and also the heaviest to handle) has a cast-iron base. Steel and aluminum are also used. Whichever you buy, read the manufacturer's directions for using.

One of the advantages of enamelware is that it is easily cleaned with soap, water, and a bristle brush. Avoid metal scouring pads. If food particles stick stubbornly, soak the utensil in a solution of ammonia or baking soda; or apply a strong grease and carbon remover and let it stand for at least 30 minutes.

If stains on enamel do not respond to the above treatment, rub them with a cleanser containing oxalic acid.

Chipped areas should be cleaned and dried thoroughly. Then apply a porcelain or epoxy touch-up enamel.

English Worcester. An English china. See *China.*

Epoxy Cement. See *Concrete* (page 52).

Epoxy Glue. See *Gluing.*

Étagère (ay-tazh-*air*). A tall, shallow, free-standing piece of furniture used for display and storage of ornaments, books, etc. It resembles a bookcase but is open on all four sides. You can place it against a wall or use it as a room divider.

Construction may be of wood or of metal with glass shelves. For care of an étagère, see *Furniture, Wood,* or *Furniture, Metal.*

Evaporative Coolers. An evaporative cooler is an electrical appliance which is not very popular but which is useful to cool the house in areas with low humidity. All it does is blow dry air through a wet pad. Under the right circumstances, it can lower room temperatures about 10 degrees.

Evaporative coolers come in various sizes. The largest are installed outside the house. Somewhat smaller units are placed in windows. Portable units are set on a table or rolled around on casters.

Extractors.

Juice extractors. About the size and shape of an ice bucket, this electrical appliance extracts the juice from almost any vegetable or fruit. Unlike a juicer, which squeezes the juice out of citrus fruits, an extractor removes the juice from fruits or vegetables by throwing them against a rotating disk. The juice is separated from the pulp, skin, and seeds and is drained out through a spout. These are useful appliances in preparing special liquid diets.

Remove the juicing disk and basket after use and wash in detergent solution. Then rinse well and dry.

Laundry extractors. These are large, obsolete appliances occasionally found in apartment house laundries. They are used to extract excess water remaining in clothes after washing in a washer.

Fabric Finishes. Special finishes have been given to many fabrics for generations. The process of mercerization, for example, was developed in 1850 to give luster to cotton. But never in the past did finishes play the role in fabric use, performance, and laundering that they do today.

Of the various new finishes that we hear more and more about, the following are the most important:

Permanent press. Unheard of just a few years ago, permanent press today is a common household term and has caused a revolution in what can be expected in both the use and care of fabrics. Permanent-press garments have the ability to return to their original shape after proper laundering—unwanted wrinkles go out, creases and pleats stay in. Permanent press is available in a wide and increasing variety of men's, women's, and children's ready-to-wear clothes, yard goods, linens, and home furnishings. The most popular fabric since the early days of permanent-press finishing has been a blend of polyester and cotton. Although this is still used extensively, virtually any blend of man-made or natural fibers can be produced in a permanent-press fabric.

For how to launder permanent press, see *Permanent Press.*

Soil-release finishes. Oily stains have been a problem with permanent press fabrics for two reasons: the polyester fiber used so often clings tenaciously to oily soil, and some of the resins used on permanent-press fabrics also tend to hold oily soil. The newest breakthrough in permanent-press fabrics is the development of finishes with anti-soiling and soil-releasing qualities. The finishes either prevent problem soil from becoming embedded in the fabric or make it easy to remove with normal laundering. Brand names include Come Clean, Dan Clean, Fybrite, Soilex, Visa, and X-It. Hang tags may not mention a soil-release finish by name, but will state that "stains will not be a problem."

These finishes make stain removal much easier, but special attention still may be required at times. Removing the stain as soon as possible remains important. Pre-spotting the stain with liquid laundry detergent or, for really bad oily stains, dry-cleaning fluid will aid in stain removal.

Soil and oil repellents. These are fluorine-based finishes called fluorochemicals. They are colorless, odorless liquids that are commonly applied to clothing and upholstery fabrics to repel water and resist staining by oil and watery substances. Instead of being absorbed by the fabric, spills remain on the surface until they are blotted away or shaken off.

Major textile manufacturers are skeptical of the repellents' ability to help keep treated fabrics clean. But furniture manufacturers and retailers appear to feel otherwise, because many make much of the fact that their upholstery materials are treated with Scotchgard or Zepel. The merits of the argument are difficult to determine.

However, this much is certain: Soil and oil repellents attain maximum effectiveness only when they are applied at the factory or by trained applicators. They are much less effective when you apply them yourself with an aerosol. Furthermore, despite claims that they do not change the appearance of a fabric when applied by aerosol, they often do.

One other thing to note about these repellents is that when they are used to waterproof so-called washable rainwear, extra pains must be taken to rinse out all detergent, for if any is left in the fabric, water repellency is reduced or lost.

Shrinkage-control finishes. These are used primarily on cotton, wool, and some types of rayon, since most man-made fibers have built-in shrink resistance. Before purchasing a fabric that might shrink, read the label—not only to see if a shrinkage-control finish has been applied but also what level of shrinkage might be expected. A 5 percent shrinkage can cause considerable difference in overall size and length. Even with shrinkage control, care must be used in washing and drying. Water that is too hot or overdrying in the dryer will cause unnecessary shrinkage.

Wash-and-wear, minimum-care, and other wrinkle-resistant fabrics. As compared with fabrics with permanent-press finishes, these fabrics have the ability to shed wrinkles but do not have total shape retention: they may shed pleats and creases, too. Their wrinkle-shedding ability may be achieved either by built-in qualities of the fabric or by a finish. Many fabrics composed entirely of man-made fibers—particularly the polyesters, acrylics, and nylons—provide such excellent wash-and-wear performance that a finish is not required.

Wash-and-wear cottons and rayons are gradually disappearing as permanent-press fabrics take their place. Cottons and rayons with wash-and-wear finishes have much better wrinkle resistance than untreated fabrics. They are seldom truly wash-and-wear, however, and usually require steam pressing.

Hygienic finishes. These are designed to retard the growth of bacteria and fungi and thus to help prevent the spread of diseases, reduce perspiration odor, and arrest mildew attack. They are used primarily on such things as sleeping bags, blankets, socks, and diapers. If you live in a humid climate, where mildew is a problem, it is a good idea to make sure that all cotton, linen, and rayon fabrics have been given a hygienic finish.

Flame-retardant finishes. As a result of a 1954 federal law, it is illegal to use dangerously flammable fabrics in clothing unless they have been given a flame-retardant finish. Unfortunately, however, not all such finishes are durable after laundering or dry-cleaning.

Faience (fay-*aunts*). A high-quality glazed earthenware. Wash it with detergent solution, but not in a dishwasher. If broken, glue the pieces with cellulose cement or epoxy glue.

Faille (file). A soft fabric with definite crosswise ribs, faille is made of silk, rayon, or acetate and should be cleaned like them.

Fans, Attic. The usual attic fan is a large, powerful fan designed to improve conditions in the home by exhausting hot air through an attic vent, bringing in cool air, and creating air currents throughout the house. The fan can be turned on at any time to suck the hot air out of the living and sleeping areas, but is most effective when used in the evening to get rid of the hot air and replace it with cooler air from outdoors.

Fans of two types are used. One is installed in the attic (or sometimes in a penthouse above a flat roof) in a horizontal position directly over a shuttered opening in a hall ceiling. The other is installed in a vertical position behind a louvered opening in the end of the attic or in a suction box over the ceiling opening. But despite these differences, both fans work in the same way.

In modern installations, when you flick the switch controlling the fan, the shutters in the ceiling opening automatically open. You can then feel the hot air surging upward into the attic and out the exhaust louvers. When the fan is turned off, the shutters automatically close.

Since air conditioners became fully accepted by the public, attic fans have declined in popularity; but they are still installed in new houses in northern areas where summer cooling is an off-again-on-again thing. In these areas, you need a fan that can change the air in the house once every minute and a half. To figure exactly what size fan is needed, multiply the floor area of all rooms by the ceiling height. (Do not include closets and other dead-space areas.) Then divide the answer by 1½. This gives the cubic-foot-per-minute (CFM) rating of the fan you need.

The size of the shuttered ceiling opening and of the louvered exhaust opening depends on the size of the fan. They must have a large enough unobstructed opening (called net free area) to handle the volume of air moved by the fan. Since the ceiling grille is usually sold with the fan, you are safe in assuming that it is of the proper size. To make sure that the carpenter who installs the louvered exhaust opening gives you the right size, ask the fan manufacturer for its recommendation.

The ceiling opening is generally made in a central hall on the top floor of a house. If this cannot be arranged, it should be cut in the inside corner of the room nearest the center of the house.

The exhaust opening should face away from the prevailing wind; and if possible, you should install two openings to different points of the compass.

An attic fan is served by its own 120-volt, 20-amp circuit; but the same circuit can be used for a built-in bathroom heater.

How to use an attic fan. Because the outdoor temperature usually drops after sundown, operation of an attic fan should begin at that time and continue until the house is comfortable. On very hot nights, run the fan at high speed during the early evening and switch to low speed later. If you have a one-speed fan, you can control its operation with an automatic timer that turns on and off at a preset time during the night.

Fan operation need not be limited to nights, however. By turning it on for brief intervals during a hot day, you can exhaust the supercharged attic air and thus better maintain comfortable conditions in the living areas. Always draw the outside air in from the shady side of the house and preferably through hall and bathroom windows so the cool air of the other rooms is disturbed as little as possible.

One point to bear in mind when using an attic fan is that air always follows the path of least resistance, which means that the greatest volume of air comes through those windows and doors nearest the fan. Therefore, when cooling the house, the windows farthest from the fan should be opened wide while the others should be completely or partly closed.

If instead of cooling the entire house you wish to cool only certain rooms, open the windows in the occupied rooms and close the hall doors to the other rooms.

When it comes time for the family to retire, the best practice is to open the windows throughout the house so that the temperature of every room will be reduced. Then, in the morning, the windows and doors on the sunny side of the house should be closed and the shades lowered. Only those windows needed for fresh air should be left open.

Two precautions should be taken in using an attic fan: (1) Never operate it when there is a fire in the fireplace. (2) Close fireplace dampers before turning the fan on. Such is the strength of the fan that it will pull soot into the rooms.

How to maintain an attic fan. In the spring, before using the fan, you should do the following things:

1. Turn the fan over by hand and lubricate the bearings and motor according to the maker's directions. SAE No. 10 oil is used.

2. Clean and check all moving parts.

3. Tighten all bolts, nuts, set-screws, etc., which may have worked loose. Tighten fan and pulley screws particularly.

4. Lubricate shutters in ceiling opening.

5. Clean exhaust opening to get rid of insect nests built there the year before.

If things go wrong. Check whether the fuse has blown; if this is not the case, call a serviceman.

Attic exhaust fans. These are a special type of 16-inch exhaust fan designed for the sole purpose of exhausting hot air from a closed attic or roof space before it can penetrate into the rooms below. The fans have a thermostat which turns them on automatically when the attic temperature reaches a preset point, then turns them off when the temperature drops.

An attic exhaust fan costs less than a standard attic fan and is also simpler to install since you need an exhaust opening only. But it is of more limited value than a standard fan since the role it plays is entirely negative. Nevertheless, when used in an air-conditioned house, it does help to reduce the load on the conditioner, thus increasing its cooling efficiency as well as slightly reducing its operating cost.

Fans, Portable. Fans do not lower the temperature. They give you an impression of coolness by keeping the air moving. Some models, particularly those which are mounted in windows, also bring cool air in from outdoors and exhaust hot air from indoors.

There are stationary and oscillating table fans, floor fans, hassock fans, pedestal fans, roll-around fans, and window fans. Some are tiny; others have blades 20 inches across.

The volume of air that fans will move is measured in cubic feet per minute. Unfortunately, while this CFM rating is known to the manufacturer, it is not always indicated on the carton in which the fan is packaged. But when you are buying a fan, look for it and ask about it.

A CFM rating depends on such things as the fan's speed, blade shape and size, and the design of the case. The higher the CFM rating, the more air the fan moves. This may not, however, mean that the air moves at high speed or penetrates deep into a room.

A quiet fan may be the result of good design. But it may be that the fan doesn't move very much air. If you want a quiet fan that really stirs up the air, the only way to find out which is best is to turn them on, listen, and feel the breeze.

One other point to consider in buying fans is the design of the grille. If you have children, you want to make sure that they cannot poke their fingers through the grille and touch the revolving blades.

How to care for fans. Oil according to the maker's directions. Most modern fans need no attention; but older models—especially the oscillating type—usually do.

Clean fans thoroughly at the end of the summer. Remove as much dust, lint, and grease as you can with a dry cloth or paper towels; then sponge with detergent and dry. Wrap fans in plastic dry-cleaner's bags before storing them.

How to repair fans. If a fan doesn't run, be sure it is plugged in. Check the cord and plug for a break.

If blades are bent, you may be able to straighten them with your fingers. If not, remove the grille and the blades and shape them with a rubber mallet.

Fans, Ventilating. A ventilating fan is essential to a pleasant kitchen. It is also required in a bathroom that has no window and in a laundry that includes a dryer that is not vented directly to the outdoors. It is desirable in bathrooms with windows, especially those which are heated electrically.

Three kinds of ventilating fan are available. The oldest is installed in an outside wall or ceiling. It sucks in air from the room and blows it directly outdoors or, in the case of ceiling fans, through a duct to the outdoors.

The second kind of fan is a ducted hood fan that is mounted in a hood, or canopy, directly over the kitchen range. It also sucks in the room air and vents it to the outdoors, usually through a duct.

The third ventilating fan is a nonducted hood fan that hangs over the range. All it does is suck in air from the kitchen, filter out the smoke, grease, and odors, and return the clean air to the kitchen through an opening in the top.

Kitchen ventilation. The range is, of course, the source of smoke, odors, and grease. Along with the sink, it is also the source of water vapor which condenses on windows and walls. Consequently, the ventilating fan should be placed as close as possible to it.

Because a hood hangs over a range (or built-in cook top) much of the smoke, odors, and grease given off in cooking rises into it naturally. It follows that a hood fan is somewhat more efficient than an ordinary wall or ceiling fan.

Note, however, that a nonducted hood fan does not carry off water vapor. This may seem like a minor failing but actually it is not. Water vapor is troublesome because when it condenses on windows, it streaks the glass and damages the finish on the frame and sill. If it gets inside the wall, it may also cause wood to rot and outside paint to peel.

In other words, the best way to ventilate a kitchen is with a ducted hood fan. If for some reason you can't or don't want to install one of these, the second choice is a fan mounted in an exterior wall directly behind the range. Third choice is a ceiling fan directly above the range, provided that the duct leading from it is not more than 10 feet long. Last choice is a nonducted hood fan. This should be used only in a two-story house when the range is located more than 10 feet from an outside wall. (If the expense does not worry you, it would be a good idea to install a wall fan in the kitchen along with a nonducted hood fan.)

Whatever fan you use in a kitchen, it is advisable to install the model that has the highest CFM capacity. This assures that it will clear the air in a kitchen in a hurry.

Installation. Installation should be made by the dealer. Hood fans should be just high enough above the cooking surface so that you can see into pots at the back of the range without stooping. They should never be hung more than 30 inches above the surface. The hood should cover all or most of the surface. Beware of hoods with sharp edges and teeth.

Wall fans are centered behind the range, preferably 18 to 24—but no more than 30—inches above the cooking surface.

In all cases, ducts must contain as few bends as possible. As noted, they should be under 10 feet in length. Wall fans have an exterior door that opens and closes when the fan is turned on and off. With ducted fans, however, it is necessary to install at the end of the duct a weather-hood which swings shut and keeps out wind and rain when the fan is not in use.

In a one-story house, it may be easier to run a duct through the roof than through an outside wall.

All ventilating fans can be connected into a 120-volt, 15-amp lighting circuit.

Bathroom ventilation. Most people use a ceiling fan—perhaps one that also incorporates a light and heater. In a bathroom that has a window, you can also use a wall fan. Generally, a 100-CFM capacity is considered adequate, but it doesn't hurt to put in something a little larger.

If an attic has louvered openings at the end, a ceiling fan can exhaust directly into it. No duct is required.

Laundry ventilation. This is not necessary if your dryer is vented into a 4-inch pipe or tube leading to the outdoors. Otherwise you should have a fan to get rid of the great amount of water vapor given off by the dryer. Use the largest available wall or ceiling fan. Ducts for a ceiling fan should be as straight as possible and no more than 10 feet long.

Ventilating fan maintenance. Bathroom fans need to be cleaned about once a year to remove dust and lint. A laundry fan needs twice-a-year cleaning at least.

The frequency with which a kitchen fan is cleaned depends on how much frying you do and how close the fan is to the range. Monthly cleaning is advisable.

Wall and ceiling fans rarely have filters. All you do is unscrew the grille and wash it in detergent solution at the sink. Clean the fan blades and as much of the housing and duct as you can reach with a cloth dipped in detergent solution.

Remove the bottom filter (made of metal) from a hood fan and soak it in detergent solution at the sink. Scrubbing with a soft brush will speed the process. Fiberglass filters can sometimes be cleaned in the same way, but without brushing. Charcoal filters should be replaced whenever they cease to remove odors efficiently.

Follow the maker's directions about oiling the fan.

Faucets. The simplest, least expensive faucets are compression faucets. Until World War II, they were used throughout homes, but today they are generally limited to the laundry, basement, garage, and outdoors. New faucets used in bathrooms and kitchens are of various designs which are easier to use—often with one hand—and less likely to drip.

For how to repair faucets, see *Lavatories.*

Felt. Felt is a nonwoven fabric made by bonding together wool fibers (which are often mixed with rayon or cotton). The resulting material is dense and usually rather thick, but has little strength. It must be dry-cleaned.

If felt is torn or worn out, it can be repaired only by pasting on a patch with fabric-mending adhesive. Bevel the edges of the patch before application with a razor blade.

Felt is often bonded to the base of lamps, bookends, and other accessories to keep them from scratching the tables on which they are placed. If felt used for this purpose is separated from wood, reglue with white wood glue. If separated from glass, pottery, etc., use rubber cement.

Felt used for covering walls has a special backing material. It is hung with wheat paste.

Fiberboard. See *Walls, Fiberboard.*

Fiberglass Fabric. This material is widely used for curtains and draperies because of its unique characteristics. It is fireproof and not damaged by heat when hung in front of radiators. It is not damaged by the sun and resists fading and therefore does not need to be lined. It hangs straight and retains its shape. It attracts soil but does not absorb it.

Fiberglass fabrics should be handwashed. Use a warm detergent solution and simply dunk the fabric up and down repeatedly. Never rub, scrub, or twist. Rinse twice in the same way in warm water. Then drip-dry. Do not iron.

Most stains on fiberglass can be removed by sponging with warm detergent solution. For grease stains, lay the fabric over a blotter and drip cleaning fluid through. Rust stains are impossible to remove, so make sure that drapery hooks are rustproof. Avoid pin hooks; use slip-in hooks instead.

Tears in fiberglass should be sewn with fiberglass yarn.

Fiberglass-Reinforced Plastics. These colorful, translucent sheet materials are used in terrace roofs, fences, porch enclosures, decorative panels, movable screens, shower doors, garage doors, skylights, modern furniture, and so on. They are strong, durable, and resistant to weather, mild acids, salt air, corrosion, mildew, and fire. They will not rot or warp.

Sheets are flat or corrugated, and come in various sizes. Special moldings, flashing strips, and other parts that may be needed with corrugated sheets are sold by the plastics dealer.

Reinforced plastics are easy to work and build with. You can cut them with an ordinary handsaw, metal-cutting saw, or circular saw with an MX (abrasive) blade. To mark the sheets, use a grease pencil or crayon.

Fasten the sheets with ordinary nails, round-headed screws, or bolts. When the sheets are installed outdoors, however, use aluminum screw nails with neoprene washers under the heads. The sheets should be drilled before nails are driven; otherwise they will craze.

To make waterproof joints in a terrace roof, lap the panels approximately 2 inches. Special mastic strips are laid between the sheets for a positive seal.

How to repair reinforced plastics. Scratches can be removed by careful sanding with fine paper. Very small holes and fine breaks can be filled with polyester resin available from boat dealers. But bad breaks are hopeless.

If panels in a roof leak, remove the nails, separate the panels, and remove the old mastic strip. Replace it with a new strip and renail.

How to clean reinforced plastics. Just washing or hosing with water normally does the trick. If not, scrub with a heavy-duty detergent. Although the panels have good resistance to scratching, it is best not to use abrasives on them.

Figurines. These small ornamental objects may be made of earthenware, glass, metal, wood, plaster, or other material. For how to clean and repair them, see the entry for the appropriate material.

Files. See *Tools, Workshop.*

Fire-Alarm Systems. A fire-alarm system will not put out a fire, but it should warn you if a fire gets started.

A good system—costing several hundred dollars—consists of heat detectors installed on the ceiling in all danger areas throughout the house; a smoke detector in the bedroom area and a second in the living room; and a loud alarm. Such a system should also bear the label of either the Underwriters' Laboratories (UL) or the Factory Mutual Laboratories (FM). It should be served by its own 120-volt, 15-amp electrical circuit and also by batteries in case the power fails. And it should provide a means by which you can test it once a week without setting a fire or damaging the sensors.

If this sounds like a large order, it is. That's why you should make very certain when installing such a system that the man doing the work is qualified and honest. Check him out with the Better Business Bureau. Beware of door-to-door salesmen and their gimmicks.

While there is no real substitute for a complete fire-alarm system that is properly designed and installed, there are single-station fire alarms that you can install yourself in areas that you consider particularly vulnerable. Some of these are good enough to have won UL or FM approval.

One effective unit is an aerosol can connected to a horn by a fusible link. If the link is melted by a sudden rise of the air temperature, the horn gives off a blast.

Another unit that needs no electricity is a spring-wound alarm. The spring is sensitive to heat and unwinds and sets off a buzzer when the room temperature rises.

Fire Extinguishers. Fire extinguishers are your first defense against tragedy. If you can lay your hands on an extinguisher and use it when a fire is just beginning, you have a good chance of putting it out. If you're a little slow, an extinguisher will still help to discourage a fire until the fire department can answer your alarm.

Fires are categorized in three ways:

Class A fires are fires in wood, paper, and fabric.

Class B fires are in grease, oil, gasoline, paint, flammable liquids.

Class C fires are fires in electric wires and equipment. They are caused by short circuits and overloads.

Class A fires are relatively easy to fight because they are extinguished by water; and one of the best extinguishers is nothing more than a flexible hose that is permanently connected to an indoor faucet. The faucet can be installed under a bathroom washbasin or kitchen sink, or in the laundry, utility room, or basement.

A substitute for a hose is a tank extinguisher that contains water under pressure. Unfortunately, even the smallest of these is a bit heavy for a woman to hustle around the house. Furthermore, you must check the pressure every six months (if it needs air, take it to a gas station and attach the air hose).

Class B and C fires are more difficult to fight because they shrug off water. In the past, a variety of extinguishers was used. These generally contained carbon tetrachloride or carbon dioxide. None, however, is so effective or safe as a newer unit called a dry-chemical extinguisher.

The chemical in this extinguisher can snuff out Class B and C fires in short order. A pressure gauge on the extinguisher indicates whether it is ready for use. If for some reason it is not, it can be recharged by a fire-extinguisher dealer.

Since the introduction of the first dry-chemical extinguisher, a new multi-purpose dry-chemical extinguisher has appeared. As the name implies, it is effective against Class A fires as well as B and C; so it is obviously the best extinguisher for the home. It should be remembered, however, that it does not completely take the place of a hose in case of a Class A fire because it is effective over a distance of only 12 feet and because the small portable units will completely discharge their contents in less than 30 seconds. Therefore, with only a dry-chemical extinguisher, you might well have trouble getting a big Class A blaze under control.

In fighting any kind of fire, whether with dry chemicals, water, or other means, remember always to direct the extinguisher at the base of the flames.

Where to locate extinguishers. You should have a dry-chemical extinguisher in the kitchen and garage, near the furnace, and in the workshop or wherever paints are stored. Since you can never tell where an electrical fire may start, you should also have a dry-chemical extinguisher in the bedroom area.

Hang the extinguishers on the wall near the door that is most often used to enter the protected room. Don't place it close to the most likely source of fire—say, the range—where you may not be able to reach it after a fire has started.

What to do with obsolete extinguishers. Replace them if you can with dry-chemical extinguishers bearing the Underwriters' Laboratories (UL) label. Remember, however, that if they are operable, they are still useful. So until you replace them, check them regularly and have them serviced as necessary.

Fireplace Equipment. This includes a poker, shovel, broom, and their holder; fender; wood basket; andirons or dogs; and grate. Except for the grate and dogs, which are cast iron, the pieces may be of cast iron, steel, or brass.

If any of them are broken, have them welded. Articles that are not exposed directly to heat may be mended with epoxy glue but the mend will lack strength.

Dust steel and cast iron frequently, and wash occasionally with water or detergent solution. If you dry thoroughly, there is no reason to worry about rusting.

For how to clean and polish brass articles, see *Brass*.

Also see *Fireplace Screens*.

Fireplaces.

How to build a fire. Good fires don't just happen. To begin with, they require well-seasoned logs that have been split if they are much over 4 inches in diameter. Beech, oak, ash, birch, and sycamore are among the best burning woods. For a quick, hot, but short-lived fire, use pine (and don't forget the pine cones).

There are numerous fire-starters, all of which have their faithful adherents; but it is still hard to beat newspaper and kindling. Crumple five or six sheets of paper lightly and lay them between the andirons toward the back of the firebox. For kindling, use an assortment of sticks of various sizes up to about 1 inch across. The softwoods are best. Chips, shavings, and pine cones are excellent, too. Lay the sticks lengthwise and front-to-back.

Place three to five logs on top of the kindling. The largest log should be near the back of the fireplace; but a small one should be behind it so that the large log will catch and burn on all sides. Don't place the logs—or kindling—so close together that air does not circulate between them freely. A fire needs plenty of air to burn well.

Open the damper all the way. Some are stiff and heavy and need a hard push. If the house is "tight," open a window or door to give the starting fire an extra dose of air. If the chimney is outside the house and the weather is cold, a fire may smoke excessively when started. You can often prevent this by crumpling a sheet of newspaper into a long, loose bundle, lighting it and holding it up the chimney to create a draft. Then light the newspapers under the logs in several places.

Burning trash in the fireplace. There is no reason why you shouldn't burn trash in the fireplace, provided you don't get carried away with the operation. Most people get into trouble by tossing too much trash on at one time. This is especially dangerous when they are disposing of excelsior and shredded paper. The roaring fire that results may start a chimney fire, burst right out of the fireplace into the room, or damage the fireplace equipment. Moral: Feed burnable trash into a fire very slowly and in small amounts.

When lighting a pile of trash, touch the match to the top of the pile, not the bottom. And make certain the damper is open.

Cleaning the hearth. There is no rule about how often this should be done. Remember, however, that if the ashes are allowed to get too deep, they interfere with the best placement of the kindling and logs and they are likely to affect combustion by reducing the air supply. So it's advisable to clean out ashes whenever you get an accumulation a couple of inches deep between the andirons.

If your house is in a very windy location, you may find it necessary to remove all ashes when the fireplace is not in use, because the wind coming down the chimney and past the damper can scatter them all over a room.

How to remove stains from the fireplace breast and hearth. Scrubbing with detergent solution usually does the trick. But for further details, see entry for the material involved.

How to correct a persistently smoky fireplace. 1. Check and clean the damper. It may not be opening all the way because of encrusted soot. If you can take it out of the fireplace, do so. In any case, clean it as well as you can with a wire brush. Free the pivots with a knife.

If the damper is broken, have it repaired or replaced by a fireplace expert.

2. Clean the smoke shelf. This is the ledge just behind the damper. It is an important part of a fireplace because it deflects air blowing down the chimney before it reaches the fire. If it isn't clean, however, it may work in the opposite way.

3. Clean the chimney. You can do this yourself—if you don't mind climbing on roofs—by putting a couple of weights in a burlap bag, stuffing it with leaves, and pulling it up and down inside the flue with a rope. (Make sure the fireplace opening is completely covered so the soot doesn't drift around the room.) But it's a lot easier and safer to hire a professional chimney sweep.

If you burn a fire every day, you should have the chimney cleaned at least once a year. If you burn a fire only occasionally, however, chimney cleaning should not be required more than once every three to five years.

In addition to removing soot, one of the things a chimney cleaner should look for in the flue is any unusual obstruction. This might be a fallen chunk of mortar or it might very well be a flock of chimney swifts. Whatever it is, it must be removed. To prevent further infestations of birds, cover the top of the chimney with 1-inch galvanized mesh.

(Various materials, such as common salt and old zinc dry cells, can be burned in fires to clean chimney flues, but the practice is dangerous because you actually set fire to the soot. Furthermore, the cleaning action is far from perfect.)

4. Cap the chimney. However, this should be considered only if the chimney does not extend 2 feet above the highest part of a pitched roof, 3 feet above a flat roof, or if it is surrounded by tall trees or buildings.

If any of these conditions prevail, there is a good chance that air is being forced down the chimney, thus preventing the escape of smoke.

To build a chimney cap, all you need to do—if you are as strong as an ox and have an equally strong helper—is to erect four little columns of bricks on top of the chimney at the four corners and lay on these a slab of thin flagstone. The columns should be built high enough so that the four openings under the flagstone cap are at least equal in area to the area of the flue opening. The mortar used to build the columns consists of 1 part Portland cement, 1 part hydrated lime, and 6 parts sand.

If a chimney that is capped has two or more flues, a solid wall of brick (called a withe) should be built across the chimney between each pair of flues.

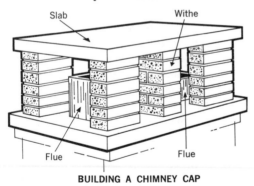

BUILDING A CHIMNEY CAP

5. Decrease the size of the fireplace opening. It may be too large in relation to the flue opening. To test whether this is the cause of smoking, start a fire in the fireplace. Then hold a wide board tight against the fireplace breast and lower it gradually from the top until the smoking stops. You can then have a metal hood built to cover the fireplace opening down to the same point. The alternative is to lay bricks in the bottom of the firebox up to a height that would be equal to the depth of the hood (that is, if you would need a

hood 4 inches deep, raise the hearth 4 inches). Or you can lay bricks up against the sides of the firebox to reduce the width of the opening.

If you choose to build up the bottom of a fireplace, you should first test the effect by setting any bricks you happen to have without mortar. But for a permanent alteration, use firebricks and lay them in fire clay.

6. Call in a fireplace expert if smoking persists.

How to correct a smoky fireplace with more than one opening. Fireplaces that open in two, three, and even all directions are becoming more and more common. To operate properly, all require more air in the room than a conventional fireplace. And even when this is provided, smoking is a frequent problem. Unfortunately, you may not be able to stop this, although you may improve matters by covering one or more of the openings with glass fire screens. Sometimes it is necessary to install a small ventilating fan in the flue.

You can experiment with closing the fireplace openings simply by covering them temporarily with gypsum board. But if you don't make progress, don't be surprised. Call in an expert—and don't be surprised if he, too, fails to come up with an answer.

How to repair fireplaces and chimneys. If mortar joints are cracked or eroded, scrape them clean and fill them with the cement-lime-sand mixture called for earlier.

If a leak develops in the chimney cap around the flue, remove the broken concrete or clean out the crack and fill with the cement-lime-sand mixture. The concrete around the flue should slope down toward the outside edges of the chimney top.

If cracks develop in the hearth or firebox, you can fill them with the same mixture, but it is better to use fire clay.

If a wall surrounding a chimney is so hot that you can't touch it, call in a fireplace expert at once. Don't use the fireplace.

How to install a prefabricated fireplace. Two types of prefabs are available. The oldest is the circulating fireplace—a steel shell which is set on a conventional hearth and surrounded with masonry. This type of unit, which forms a fireplace of conventional size, should be installed by a mason.

The other type of prefab is akin to the old Franklin stove. Although of various designs, this is essentially a small metal box which is usually raised off the floor and uses large metal pipes for flues. It is not permitted in all communities, but if it is in yours, you will find that installation is a simple matter of following the manufacturer's instructions.

All the small prefabs must be installed at least 4 inches from all walls. In addition, you should usually cover the walls with incombustible material. All require a hearth of brick, stone, concrete, etc., which extends at least 6 inches beyond the fireplace on all sides.

The flues, which are generally 8 inches in diameter, can be extended up through the roof or out through an exterior wall and then upward above the roof. A space of at least 2 inches is required between the flue and any surrounding combustible material. The best practice is to use a conventional flue pipe within the room, and from the ceiling or wall line use a special, insulated metal flue. (The same kind of flue is sometimes used for conventional fireplaces.)

Gas and electric fireplaces. These are generally small stove-like units, but traditional mantel fireplaces are sold as well. You can also install the heating elements in any wood-burning fireplace.

The gas fireplaces have ceramic logs which give off real flames. The fireplaces must be vented to the outdoors through 4-inch flues.

The electric fireplaces also have imitation logs which can be controlled either to give off heat alone or heat with a flickering flame effect. The units can be plugged into a 120-volt, 15-amp outlet. No venting is required.

Fireplace Screens. The safest firescreen is a flexible unit that is permanently installed inside the fireplace opening or on the fireplace breast. If properly fitted, there are no cracks around the edges or between the overlapping curtains through which sparks can escape.

Flexible screens are also available in freestanding frames. Other freestanding screens either have three folding panels or are made in one rigid piece somewhat resembling a huge, handleless coal shovel standing on its blade. Of these, the latter is the ugliest but probably the safest because it is harder to tip over and fits close enough to the fireplace breast to contain sparks.

All these screens are made of strong steel mesh and are held in a frame of steel or brass. The mesh should be vacuumed every month or two to remove ash, dust, and lint. If it is necessary to wash it with detergent solution, dry it as well as possible and place in front of a hot fire to dry completely.

For how to clean brass, see *Brass.* Note that on some screens the brass is lacquered and should not be cleaned with brass polish.

An unusual type of screen used mainly on fireplaces having more than one opening is made of tempered glass in a metal frame. The glass must be washed frequently outside and in with vinegar and water or ammonia and water to keep it clean and sparkling.

Fire Prevention. The following is excerpted from a booklet prepared by the engineering and safety department of the American Insurance Association:

Prevent disaster through good planning, good housekeeping, and safe habits. Over 1000 fires occur in the United States daily. Every year, thousands of lives are lost through fire. Obviously, fire prevention is of vital concern to all.

To protect your family and your property against fire, plan ahead, practice good housekeeping, and develop safe habits.

Plan ahead when building, making additions, and installing new equipment.

Good housekeeping includes a periodic check for fire hazards.

Carelessness causes most home fires. Acquire safe habits.

Matches and smoking. Matches and smoking cause about 25 percent of all fires of known origin. Tips for careful smokers:

Keep matches and lighters out of the reach of children. Have plenty of large noncombustible ash trays in every room (see *Ash Trays*).

Never toss a lighted match away. Make sure it's out, then put it into an ash tray. Don't drop it into a wastebasket.

Never, but never smoke in bed. You might fall asleep and drop your cigarette. A fire in the bedding can release toxic gases which could suffocate you before you awoke.

Electricity and TV. Fuses are "safety valves" for electric circuits. A blown fuse means the circuit is overloaded or defective. Be sure your fuses are the right size for your circuits—usually 15 amps for circuits for lights.

Choose UL-listed electrical appliances and cords.

Have a competent electrician make repairs and extend wiring when necessary.

Do not obstruct the ventilation required for the TV set. Don't install your TV in a tight cubicle unless it is especially designed for such installation. Leave TV repairs to qualified repairmen.

Heating equipment. A qualified professional should clean and inspect your heating system and chimneys annually. If repairs are needed, call in an expert.

Should the ceiling and walls near the furnace feel hot, you may need additional insulation to keep them from charring or catching fire.

If you have a fireplace, keep a sturdy metal screen in front. Provide metal cans for ashes.

Set portable heaters level and out of the way of traffic. Keep them away from anything that might catch fire.

Turn off portable heaters before you go to bed.

Cooking equipment. The kitchen contains many potential fire hazards.

If your stove uses fuel oil or kerosene, read and follow the manufacturer's instructions. Store the fuel outside. Refill removable reservoirs and small portable heaters outside. Any spillage must be wiped up at once.

Keep your stove in good repair and free of grease.

Make sure curtains cannot blow across the cooking surface. Combustibles should not be hung close to the stove.

If the pilot light or gas burner accidentally blows out, ventilate thoroughly. Read instructions before attempting to relight it.

Protect your children. About 20 percent of all fire fatalities are children under five years. Many more suffer burns. Special care should be taken to protect your children from fire.

Never leave young children alone, not even for a short time. Have a dependable baby-sitter stay with the children while you are away. Give the sitter specific instructions on what to do in case of fire.

Put matches or lighters away, out of the reach of children.

Don't use lighted candles for decorations at children's parties.

Turn pot handles so they don't stick out beyond the edge of the stove where children can reach them.

When buying or making children's clothing, avoid flimsy, fast-burning materials.

Important precautions. 1. Rubbish, paints, and rags should not be left near the furnace.

2. Paints should be stored in a cool place, in tightly covered cans.

3. Oily or paint-soaked rags should be discarded. If you want to keep some, store them in tightly covered metal containers.

4. Never use highly flammable liquids for any household purpose. The vapors could set off an explosion.

5. If you keep a small supply of gasoline in the garage, store it in an approved safety can.

6. Oil drippings in the garage should be cleaned up promptly.

What to do in case of fire. 1. Get everybody out of the house.

2. Call the fire department.

If you smell smoke, do not rush out into the hallway. First, place the palm of your hand against the door. If the door feels cool, open it slightly. Pass your hand across the opening. If the air seems cool, it should be safe to enter the hallway.

Close doors behind you as you leave the

house. After everyone is safely out of the house, call the fire department.

If the door feels hot, that hallway is already filled with deadly heated gases. Keep the door closed. Use another escape route, or wait at a window for rescue. Arouse people by shouting.

Now, before fire breaks out in your home: (1) Figure out two possible routes to the ground from every room in the house, especially the bedrooms. Hold actual fire drills until everyone knows exactly what to do. (2) Learn where the fire alarm box nearest your home is. Post the number of the fire department near your phone.

Fire protection. If you live in an area where you and your neighbors may have to fight your own fires until the fire apparatus arrives, keep the following supplies on hand:

1. Fire extinguishers. Get those bearing the UL label. Keep them handy. Inspect them every year, and refill (if necessary) according to the manufacturer's instructions.

2. Water supply. If you don't have a deep well or pond, consider providing one or the other. Be sure your water supply is accessible by road.

3. Ladders. Keep one or two ready for use on roof fires or in making rescues from upstairs when stairways are cut off from use.

4. Garden hose and buckets. Keep the buckets filled with water and the garden hose ready to be hooked up. (The latter should be completely empty of water. If water is in it, it may freeze and make the hose useless.)

5. Hand-operated pump tank.

Flagstone. Large, smooth, flat stones used for paving. See *Stone; Walks; Floors, Stone.*

Flannel. Flannel is a very soft, warm fabric usually made of wool but sometimes made in part of cotton. Used in clothing, it is best dry-cleaned.

Flannelette. A lightweight wool, wool-and-cotton, or cotton flannel with nap on one side only. It is used for pajamas, baby blankets, and shirts. Wash in tepid water and dry at low heat.

Flashing. Flashing is a flat strip of metal or asphalt roll roofing used to prevent leaks through exterior joints in the house. Unfortunately, it occasionally develops holes itself; so you should make a practice of inspecting it annually. Here is how to make repairs:

Small holes. If the flashing is metal, clean the area around the hole and seal it with solder or plastic metal. You can also apply a dab of asphalt roofing cement or silicone or rubber caulking compound, but these are less attractive.

Holes in asphalt flashing are plugged with roofing cement.

Small tears. These are sealed in the same way after the torn edges are nailed down. The alternative is to smear roofing cement on the metal and embed in it a patch of metal of the same kind.

Flashing loose from masonry. Chip out the broken and weak mortar and blow out the crumbs. Push the flashing metal into the crack if it has sprung loose. Then fill the crack with latex or epoxy cement.

Leaks in a closed valley. In a closed valley, the roof shingles come together in a tight joint. To stop a leak, cut aluminum flashing into a 12- or 15-inch square and bend it diagonally. Then insert one of the bent corners under the shingles, and push the metal up as far as it will go.

REPAIRING FLASHING: LEAKS IN A CLOSED VALLEY

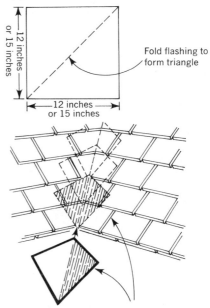

Push flashing squares up as far as they will go, starting with the lowest course of shingles

Leaks between a wall and shed roof. Cut 9-inch-wide strips of aluminum flashing. Bend it lengthwise and push the upper half up under the siding. Then bend the lower half down on the roof and secure it by smearing asphalt roofing cement underneath. It is easier to work with strips about 3 feet long than with one strip running the full length of the roof. The short strips should, of course, be overlapped about 3 inches or more at the ends.

Leaks over windows or doors. If the wall is masonry, fill the joint between it and the top of the window casing with caulking compound. If the wall is wood, however, it is better to insert a metal flashing strip. This should be 4 inches longer than the width of the casing; and wide enough to bend down over the casing about 1 inch and to extend up the wall to the next course of wood.

Pry the siding above the casing loose, and push the flashing up under it. Then hammer the siding back into position, thus bending the flashing at the bottom. Fold the flashing down over the drip cap and secure it to the top front edge with small aluminum nails.

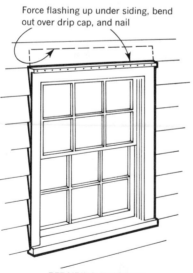

Force flashing up under siding, bend out over drip cap, and nail

REPAIRING FLASHING:
LEAKS OVER WINDOWS OR DOORS

Leak between a vent pipe and flashing. Seal with silicone or polysulfide rubber caulking or with asphalt roofing cement.

Valley flashing needs replacing. This is a big job since the roofing on both sides must be removed before new flashing can be installed. Call in a roofing contractor.

Flashlights. Although flashlights come in many shapes, all operate in the same way and should be cared for in the same way.

Three types of battery are used, but the various sizes are not available in all types. Zinc batteries are the oldest, cheapest, and shortest-lived. Alkaline batteries cost approximately three times as much as zinc and are supposed to last up to ten times as long, but it is questionable whether they do. Nickel-cadmium batteries are most expensive but last for many months.

Both zinc and alkaline batteries can be recharged—if they have not run down too far—in a special battery charger. Nickel-cadmium batteries can and must be recharged repeatedly by plugging them into a 120-volt electric outlet.

For a cylindrical flashlight to work, the batteries must be installed with all positive terminals (brass buttons) pointing in the same direction—toward the bulb. If a flashlight fails to light, it is usually because one of the batteries was inserted upside down. The second most likely cause is a dead battery or bulb. The third cause may be rust on the contact points. This can be removed with a knife or sandpaper. At the same time, make sure there is no rust on the bottom of the case or on the narrow metal strip connected with the switch. If the spring in the bottom of the case is compressed, stretch it slightly.

Flashlights with 6-volt rectangular batteries are cleaned in roughly the same way if they do not operate.

Despite the fact that most modern flashlights are reasonably watertight and some, made for use on boats, are extremely so, all should be taken apart and dried thoroughly after immersion.

Flatware. Flatware includes all silver or stainless steel pieces that are more or less flat; for example, trays, trivets, and cutlery.

Generally, pieces that are bent, broken, or scratched should be repaired by a jeweler. But you can make a few simple repairs yourself.

If the tines of a fork are bent, wrap a

piece of paper around them and bend them back into position with pliers. The bent tip of a spoon can often be straightened with the fingers; if not, with pliers.

Many knives and forks have hollow handles and are made in two pieces. If the blades or tines come loose from the handles, clean the tangs (the narrow piece that is inserted in the handle), coat with epoxy glue, and reset. If this doesn't do the job, take the pieces to a jewelry store.

Hollow-handled pieces should never be washed in a dishwasher or ultrasonic cleaner because the cement in the handles may be weakened.

For how to clean flatware, see entry for appropriate metal. For how to choose flatware, see *Tableware*.

Fleas. See *Pest Control*.

Flies. See *Pest Control*.

Floor Polishers. Don't expect any floor polisher made for household service to do the same job as the big polishers used by professional floor cleaners. Even so, they are almost essential for applying and maintaining buffable floor wax.

The best and most expensive floor polishers have one large single disk. These have enough power and weight to achieve a fairly even gloss and are not too large for a woman to maneuver.

Combination floor polishers and rug shampooers with two disks do a poorer polishing job but are excellent for cleaning carpets. Because of this, and also because they are fairly inexpensive, they far outsell the single-disk machines.

If you choose a combination appliance, it is well to invest in one with three, or at least two, speeds, because floor scrubbing and waxing are best done at a slower speed than polishing. Ideally, shampooing is done at an intermediate speed, but use low speed if you have a two-speed machine.

The better machines also have a larger liquid shampoo dispenser and weigh more than less expensive models.

Two-disk floor polishers that cannot be used for shampooing are worth nothing.

Before using a polisher-shampooer, vacuum the floor or carpet well; otherwise foreign particles ground into it by the revolving disks will damage it. Take care

not to run the appliance over the cord. After shampooing, drain the dispenser and dry the appliance all over. Wash waxing brushes and felt buffing pads in detergent solution occasionally. Keep all brushes free of lint, string, etc.

Floors, Asphalt-Tile. This is the least expensive permanently installed resilient flooring and also the least attractive. But it is excellent on below-grade concrete slabs because it is very resistant to alkalies. It can also be used on all other floors.

Asphalt tile is durable and resists traffic damage. But it is brittle, has very little resilience, indents badly, and is noisy. And because it is not very resistant to grease, you should think twice about installing it in kitchens and workshops. It also requires more frequent cleaning and waxing than other resilient materials because of its porosity.

Note that when you lay asphalt tile, you may have to warm the tiles in an oven to make them conform to an uneven surface. Warming also facilitates cutting along curved lines.

See *Floors, Resilient*.

Floors, Brick.

How to build. In the past, brick floors were almost always laid in concrete. Today, for reasons of economy, they are usually laid without mortar. The result is equally good.

Use any dense, low-absorption brick. If you are covering a concrete slab, make sure it is smooth and level, and cover it with two layers of 15-pound building felt. If the concrete is uneven, cover it with a ½-inch cushion of sand.

Bricks can also be laid on a subfloor of ¾-inch plywood. This need not be covered.

Place the bricks together as tightly as possible. Stagger the joints in adjacent rows or use a herringbone pattern for maximum resistance to movement. Sweep fine sand into the joints and let it work down for a week or so before taking up the excess. Then apply two coats of a colorless concrete masonry sealer to hold the sand in place and to prevent staining of the bricks. Finish with liquid wax.

How to maintain brick floors. Because of the open joints and slight roughness of the bricks, you can clean the floor better with a vacuum cleaner than with a broom or mop. If the floor becomes grimy, go over it with a mop slightly dampened in detergent solution. Wax or buff every two months.

Floors, Ceramic-Tile. In homes, ceramic-tile floors are found almost exclusively in the bathroom; consequently they are often damp and require frequent mopping—not to prevent leaks, because these occur only if the mortar joints are cracked, but to keep the tiles clean and skidproof (wet tiles, especially of the large size, are often very slippery). Water usually takes up most soil, but you will have to use a mild detergent solution occasionally. Dry well.

For more about maintenance and repair, see *Tile, Ceramic.*

Floors, Concrete.

How to clean. Most people are content simply to sweep a concrete floor; but you will do a better job of getting up dirt if you first scatter a sweeping compound over it. This acts like a sponge and soaks up particles that escape a dry broom. The compound can be reused time and again.

When a floor becomes very dirty, hose it down with water and scrub hard. For spotless results, scrub with a strong detergent solution and then rinse.

How to prevent dust. Clean the floor thoroughly; then treat it with a mixture of 20 percent zinc fluosilicate and 80 percent magnesium fluosilicate. Make at least two applications—the first with ½ pound fluosilicate dissolved in 1 gallon water; all others with 2 pounds fluosilicate in 1 gallon water. Swab the floor thoroughly. Let it dry between applications. After the last application, rinse with water to remove encrusted salts.

How to resurface a badly cracked and broken floor. Rough, pitted, and uneven floors can be resurfaced with latex cement; but don't use this on a floor that is in really bad shape. Clean the floor well and scarify smooth areas with a pick. Flood with water and allow it to stand overnight. Sop up the excess and let the floor dry for a couple of hours. Then brush on a creamy grout of water and cement. Since this should not dry, cover only a small area at a time.

Pave the floor—grouted area by grouted area—with 1 to 2 inches of concrete made of 1 part Portland cement, 1 part sand, and 1½ parts coarse aggregate graded from 1/8 to 3/8 inch. Use enough water to make a smooth mortar. Bring the concrete to the proper level by drawing a board across it, compact with a wood float, and trowel smooth. Keep covered with damp burlap for six days.

If you apply a 2-inch topping, it should be reinforced with heavy wire mesh.

For how to make other repairs and remove stains, see *Concrete.*

Floors, Cork. Cork tile is not widely used today on floors because, although it is quiet and comfortable underfoot, it is not very durable or easy to maintain, it dents under light loads, stains readily, and fades badly.

A newer kind of cork tile is a fusion of cork and vinyl. This is a little less quiet and resilient than solid cork, but in all other respects is an improvement. It also costs considerably more.

Both tiles can be installed only on suspended floors. They may also be pasted to walls.

For how to repair pure cork tile, see *Cork.* For repairs of vinyl-cork tile, see *Floors, Vinyl.* Also see *Floors, Resilient.*

Floors, Linoleum. The oldest of the resilient flooring materials, linoleum is still widely used because it is moderate in cost and lasts a long time. Available in sheet form, it can be installed only on suspended floors.

Linoleum has excellent grease resistance and is about as easy to maintain as any resilient material. It also has good fade resistance. In other respects it ranks about midway between the best and the worst.

Battleship linoleum is a heavy-gauge material in plain colors famed for its durability.

Small holes in linoleum can be fixed by scraping fine shavings from a remnant, mixing them with a colorless lacquer to make a putty, and spreading it into the holes. Allow the putty to dry, and smooth it with fine steel wool or sandpaper.

See *Floors, Resilient.*

Floors, Quarry-Tile.

How to lay tile. Quarry tiles can be laid

on sand, but it is better to stick them down permanently. Usually this is done by bedding them in mortar in the same way that flagstones are handled (see *Walks*). But note these differences: The tiles should first be soaked in water for 15 minutes or more. Space tiles ½ inch apart. The standard mortar is made with 1 part Portland cement and 6 parts sand. To keep from displacing tiles once set, work from a plank suspended above the floor, and do not walk on the tiles for 24 hours. Wipe up mortar stains with a wet rag at once.

An easier way to install tiles on floors is to lay them with an organic adhesive on an exterior-grade plywood base. Follow directions under *Tile, Ceramic*. Grout the joints with mortar made of 1 part Portland cement and 3 parts sand. If you make it thin enough to pour from a can, you will get the job done faster and also keep the face of the tiles cleaner.

To cut clay tiles, score a line with a cold chisel. Then, starting at the nearest edge, break off tiny bits of tile with a pair of pliers until you reach the line.

How to clean quarry tiles. You can wax quarry tile if you wish with a water-based wax. This gives it a warm glow but, of course, increases maintenance since you must rewax occasionally. Furthermore, there is little need to protect the tiles with wax since the material is so dense that it does not stain readily.

To care for unfinished tiles, sweep, dust, or vacuum as necessary. Wash with mild detergent solution. If joints are so dirty that scrubbing with detergent does not get them clean, use a liquid cleaner recommended for cleaning joints in ceramic tile. For how to remove stains, see *Tile, Ceramic*.

Floors, Resilient. A resilient floor is a floor covering made of linoleum, vinyl, vinyl-asbestos tile, asphalt tile, rubber tile, or cork. The materials come either in large sheets or tiles of several sizes and shapes. When choosing among these materials, several points must be considered.

1. What is the grade level of the subfloor? If it is below grade—in a basement, for instance—it is undoubtedly made of concrete and never completely dry. Conse-

quently, it can be covered only with those resilient materials that are resistant to moisture and alkalies.

An on-grade floor is one resting directly on the ground surface. It is also made of concrete, and you are therefore limited to the same resilient materials that are used below grade.

If a floor is suspended (this is sometimes referred to as an above-grade floor), it is not in contact with the ground; and even though it may be made of concrete (though more likely of wood), it contains little moisture. Consequently, you can cover it with any type of resilient material.

2. How much moisture is in the floor or may eventually enter the floor? Concrete that is excessively damp should never be covered with a resilient floor. Similarly, you should never lay a resilient floor on a wood subfloor that is built on sleepers over an on-grade or below-grade slab, for even though the subfloor is presently dry, it may not stay dry.

3. Will very much water be spilled on the floor or used to keep it clean? Floors in bathrooms, laundries, and kitchens, for instance, are exposed to considerable moisture. A floor in an entryway might be, too. In these cases, it is advisable to use sheet materials rather than tiles simply because there are fewer joints for water to enter.

4. Will the floor be exposed to a great deal of sunlight—as in a room with large picture windows? Sunlight fades resilient floors (as well as seamless and wood floors) in the same way it fades fabrics. True, some resilient materials are more fade-resistant than others, but all are affected. In choosing a floor, therefore, bear in mind that pastels and reds and yellows are especially subject to fading. Grays and browns are best.

5. Do you plan to lay the floor yourself? If so, you should use tiles because anyone with a little patience can lay them. Sheet materials should be put down only by professionals.

6. What are the characteristics of the flooring material? Here you must think about the relative durability, ease of maintenance, resilience, etc., of the available floors. These are covered in detail under *Floors, Asphalt-Tile; Floors, Cork;* etc.

How to lay a resilient tile floor. Preparing the subfloor. Any subfloor on which you intend to lay resilient tiles must be firm, clean, smooth, and level. First, remove all old flooring and adhesive, paint, varnish, and wax. Wipe up grease and oil spots thoroughly. Chip out and fill cracks and holes in concrete; and level and smooth the surface where necessary by troweling on a thin layer of latex cement. If concrete is exceptionally porous or dusty, apply a special primer recommended by the flooring dealer.

To determine whether a concrete floor is dry enough to be tiled, brush the same primer on several 3-by-3-foot areas and allow it to dry for 24 hours. If you then can scrape the primer off the floor easily, the concrete must be allowed to dry further.

If a wood subfloor is made of a single thickness of ½-inch plywood, or boards that are not tongued and grooved, or of tongue-and-groove boards over 3 inches wide, it must be covered with smooth ½-inch plywood. You can use ½-inch plywood or ¼-inch hardboard underlayment (this is not tempered hardboard) if the subfloor is a single thickness of tongue-and-groove boards less than 3 inches wide.

If a wood subfloor is of double thickness with faceboards more than 3 inches wide, it should be covered with ¼-inch plywood or hardboard. But if the faceboards are less than 3 inches wide, all you have to do is renail the loose boards, sand down irregularities, and cover the entire floor with lining felt.

Before installing felt or underlayment or before laying tiles, pry up the quarter-round shoe moldings along the baseboards.

Hardboard and plywood underlayments come in 3-by-4- and 4-by-4-foot panels and are applied with 1¼-inch ring-grooved underlayment nails spaced 6 inches apart throughout each panel. Start laying the panels from a corner of the room. The panels in adjoining rows should be staggered.

Lining felt is used only on strip wood floors. It does not conceal irregularities: these must be sanded down or filled. But it does help to bridge and hide the joints between the strips. The felt comes in long, 3-foot-wide rolls which are laid from wall to wall at right angles to the boards. Apply linoleum paste with a notched spreader in 3-foot strips; roll the felt into this, and smooth it down with your hands or an old wallpaper smoothing brush with bristles trimmed to 1 inch. Butt the edges of adjoining strips.

Ordering tiles. To figure how many tiles you need, measure the length of the room in inches and divide by 9 (if ordering 9-by-9-inch tiles) or 12 (if ordering 12-by-12-inch tiles). If the answer does not come out even, figure to the next highest whole or half-number. Repeat the process for the width of the room. Then multiply the two numbers. To allow for trimming and waste, order about 10 percent more tiles than the answer calls for.

If a room has offsets, figure each of these separately and add to the total.

When the tiles are delivered, store them in a warm room (about 70 degrees) for 24 hours or longer so that they will lose some of their stiffness. The room in which the tiles are laid should also be warm.

Planning the job. It's a real trick to lay resilient tiles so the rows are exactly parallel with the walls. If you are certain that the walls in the room are straight and at exact right angles to one another, you can save time and trouble by starting to lay tile in a corner, along the most conspicuous wall, and going straight across the room. To be sure, the tiles along the far wall and one of the side walls will probably have to be cut; but you will not notice them too much once the room is furnished.

On the other hand, if your walls are crooked, the only way to make sure the tiles will look straight is to start in the center of the room and lay them toward the four sides. This method also assures borders of equal width on opposite sides of the room.

To find the center, find the midpoints of the two end walls. (In an irregularly shaped room, ignore alcoves, pilasters,

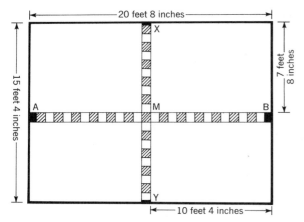

TILING FLOORS. Border tiles at walls A and B should be of equal size. Border tiles at X and Y should also be equal to each other and as nearly equal as possible to those at A and B.

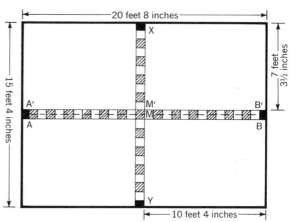

TILING FLOORS. If end tiles at walls X and Y are not nearly equal to end tiles at walls A and B, move center tile up half a tile. Establish new center line A'B' and new midpoint M'.

etc.) Stretch a chalked carpenter's line between these points and snap a chalk line on the floor. Then measure along the chalk line to its midpoint. With a large carpenter's square, draw a line at right angles to the midpoint. Then lay your chalked line over this and snap a line from side wall to side wall.

Starting at the midpoint on the lengthwise chalk line, lay a row of loose tiles along the line to the end walls. Then lay a row of loose tiles along the crosswise line to the side walls. If the border tiles along all walls are more or less equal in width, you are now ready to lay the tiles permanently. However, if the tiles along two of the walls are very narrow while the others are very wide (as in the sketch), you should try to improve matters.

To do this, draw another line parallel with A–B. This should be 4½ inches to one side of A–B if you are using 9-by-9-inch tiles; 6 inches if you are using 12-by-12-inch tiles. Now re-lay the loose tiles along the new line and the crosswise line. You will find that the border tiles are approximately equal in width, as in the second sketch.

Laying tile. Many tiles today come with an adhesive backing. To use them, you just pull off a paper covering and stick them down. If you prefer conventional tiles, use the adhesive recommended by your flooring dealer. Most are applied with a paint-

brush. Do not cover any more floor at one time than the directions specify.

Tiles are laid by setting one edge down into the adhesive, then snapping the whole tile into the paste. Don't try to slide them. When tiles are down, smooth them into the adhesive. You can walk on them immediately.

Tiles are made in perfect squares. To lay them in straight rows at perfect right angles to one another, simply butt the edges tight.

When using marbelized tiles or similar designs, the usual practice is to alternate the direction of the pattern. In other words, the first tile runs north and south; the next east and west; the next north and south; etc.

If any adhesive gets on the face of the tiles, wipe it off at once.

When you reach a wall, the last row of tiles will probably have to be cut to fit. Lay one tile (marked A in the sketch) over the adjacent tile in the next to last row. Lay a second tile (marked B in the sketch) on top and shove it against the baseboard. Draw a line along the edge of the overlapping tile (B). Cut on this line.

To fit tiles around pipes, measure from one side of the pipe to the edge of the tile, then from another side of the pipe to another edge of the tile. Measure the diameter of the pipe. Use dividers to make these measurements. Transfer measure-

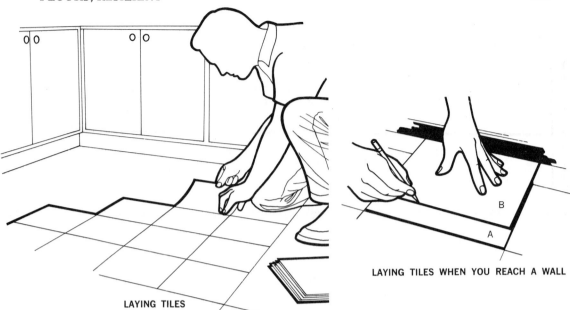

LAYING TILES

LAYING TILES WHEN YOU REACH A WALL

ments to a piece of paper cut to the size of a tile. Cut out a pattern in the paper and use this to help you cut the tile to fit. Be sure to cut a slit from the hole in the center of the tile to the nearest edge. The tile can then be fitted around the pipe.

Follow the same routine in fitting tiles around radiator legs. This is the preferred way of dealing with radiators. It's a great deal easier, however, to remove radiators before tiling a floor. Do not replace them until the tiles have been down for 24 hours.

When fitting tiles around other unusually shaped built-ins, such as bathtubs and toilet bowls, cut out a paper pattern first. If the tile which is then cut does not fit snugly against the built-in, you can cut a new tile. But if the tile is off only a fraction of an inch, the open joint can be filled with plastic filler sold by the flooring dealer or with silicone caulking compound.

Vinyl, vinyl-asbestos, and other flexible tiles can be cut with scissors or a sharp knife. A curved linoleum knife is especially useful. To cut asphalt tiles, which are very hard and brittle, score them with a knife and crack along this line. If an asphalt tile

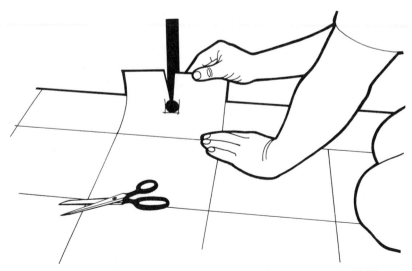

LAYING TILES AROUND PIPES OR OTHER OBSTRUCTIONS IN A ROOM

is to be cut along an irregular or curving line, however, you must first soften it slightly in a warm oven. Then cut it with a knife while it is still flexible.

After an entire room has been tiled, go over the floor foot by foot and smooth it down once again. It is best to use a roller rented from the flooring dealer (but do not roll asphalt tile).

If individual asphalt tiles are not completely stuck down, heat them very slightly with a propane torch and mold them to the subfloor.

Your last step is to replace the shoe moldings along the baseboards.

How to maintain resilient floors. After a newly laid floor is cleaned to remove all traces of adhesive, scuff marks, etc., it should be waxed. Cork and vinyl-cork floors are waxed with a solvent-based wax made especially for these types of floor. All other resilient floors must be waxed either with a water-based wax or with a self-polishing acrylic floor finish. If you prefer wax, use any of the three types available (see *Waxes*), and always apply it in very thin coats not more than once a month. Even with light-colored waxes, if you apply too much or too often, the floor will gradually take on a yellow cast. Acrylic finishes are applied like wax with a lamb's-wool applicator and give the same finish but usually last a little longer.

Another point to remember: After the first application, you should not wax under base cabinets or within 6 inches of the walls, because these areas get little wear.

Never apply lacquer or any other hard finish to a resilient floor: it will yellow and wear badly; you cannot patch it so that the patch is invisible; and if you try to remove it, you will damage the floor.

Here is the sensible way to maintain resilient floors throughout the year:

1. Dry-mop, sweep, or vacuum daily to take up grit that will abrade the surface. Wipe up spills as they occur. Remove heel marks with one of the many heavy-duty spray-on detergents on the market.

2. Damp-mop once or twice a week, as necessary, to remove soil.

3. Wash the floor with a mild detergent recommended for the purpose every three or four weeks. Don't use any more water than necessary, and rinse well—again, with as little water as possible.

Too much washing is not good for resilient floors. Professional floor cleaners, in fact, rarely wash them. They simply clean the surface with fine steel wool pads on the bottom of their floor polishers; and then go over the floor a second time with a cleaner-wax and their floor polishers.

4. After washing, apply a thin coat of wax.

5. When the wax build-up begins to yellow and looks uneven, the floor must be completely "stripped." If you have taken good care of your floor and have not applied too much wax, this job should be necessary no more than once a year.

If in doubt whether a floor needs stripping, try it first on a small, inconspicuous area. If this looks markedly brighter than the surrounding floor, the job is called for.

Use a one-step, packaged wax remover. It is much easier and less messy to work with than a homemade solution of ammonia and water.

First sweep the entire floor. Then mix the wax remover in water and apply it liberally to a 10-square-foot area. After about 3 minutes, scrub the area with an electric floor scrubber, a stiff fiber brush, or fine steel wool. (But never use steel wool on high-gloss vinyl floors.)

Sponge up the dirty water when all the wax is off and proceed to another area.

When the entire floor has been stripped, rinse it well. If any wax remains, repeat the stripping operation and rinse. Then let the floor dry and apply a new coat of wax.

To remove stains. If you work too hard on a stain, you will wind up by removing the wax on the floor and making a clean spot that stands out about as prominently as the stain did in the first place.

Try water or a mild detergent solution as a starter. If this doesn't work, apply a white appliance wax—which should take care of heel marks, food stains, shoe polish, grease, tar, and crayon. If the stain still remains, dip a damp rag or fine steel wool in a mild abrasive cleanser and rub.

Chewing gum and paint should be scraped off as completely as possible with a dull knife. Then touch up the spot with a little cleaning fluid.

Blot up solvents, such as nail-polish remover, immediately. If they harden, scrape with a dull knife. Then smooth the spot with an abrasive cleanser and fine steel wool.

Burns should also be obliterated with cleanser and steel wool.

How to repair resilient floors. If a tile is broken, cracked, or develops a large hole, replace it with a new tile. Do not try to pry up the old tile around the edges because you will succeed only in damaging the adjacent tiles. Cut or break the tile across the middle and work from that point toward the edges.

Scrape out as much of the adhesive as possible and use a vacuum cleaner to get up the crumbs. Then fit a new tile in the hole. If it is a fraction too large, scrape the edges lightly and evenly with a sharp knife blade held perpendicular to them. Then apply adhesive to the back of the tile and smooth it down.

If a sheet floor has a large hole, place a matching scrap over it, hold it down firmly and cut around the hole in a rectangle. Use a sharp knife and plenty of pressure so that you cut through both layers at once. Then remove the damaged material by working from the center of the rectangle toward the edges, scrape out the adhesive, and glue in the patch.

Bulges in sheet floors can be collapsed, as a rule, by making a slit through the center and spreading adhesive underneath.

If fairly deep scratches appear in any type of resilient floor, try to conceal them with wax. If this doesn't work, proceed as follows: In the case of vinyl-asbestos and asphalt tiles, sand the scratch and apply wax. In the case of softer materials, run the blade of a screwdriver along the scratch to press down the edges. This reduces the crack to a thin line which may be almost unnoticeable. If you are unhappy with the results, sand the scratch away.

How to prevent dents in resilient floors. This is almost impossible to do, even though some resilient flooring materials dent less than others. The only solution is to use large, flat-bottomed floor protectors or furniture cups under furniture legs. These help to spread the weight of the furniture over a larger floor area.

Floors, Rubber. Rubber floor tiles should be installed only on suspended floors and on on-grade concrete slabs. Special adhesive is used. The tiles are very comfortable underfoot but their resistance to grease and abrasion is only fair.

Clean rubber-tile floors as necessary with a mild detergent solution. Keep your mop well wrung out. Never use abrasives or abrasive cleansers. Buff with very fine steel wool to remove stubborn stains. Apply self-polishing, water-based wax only.

Tiles that are damaged in any way should be replaced

See *Floors, Resilient.*

Floors, Seamless. Seamless floors are made by pouring plastic from a can and spreading it around the room in an unbroken layer with a trowel and roller. Result: The floor has no seams except where it meets the baseboards.

Actually, a seamless floor can also be made with 12-foot-wide rolls of vinyl sheet flooring if the room is less than 12 feet wide. So it is not quite fair for seamless flooring manufacturers to have usurped the name "seamless."

Be that as it may, since seamless flooring was introduced in the United States from Germany about 1960, it has made great progress and has been used in many homes—especially in kitchens. The flooring is durable, shows little wear under heavy traffic, and is resistant to most acids, alkalies, and solvents. And it's extremely easy to clean and should never be waxed. On the minus side, it has little resilience; is no more fade-resistant than resilient flooring materials; and some types tend to turn yellow. Furthermore, whether the flooring can be used on below-grade slabs is questionable.

Seamless floors are made with urethane, epoxy, or acrylic, or combinations of these plastics. To lay a floor, it is necessary first to prepare the base with extreme care. Then a coat of colored plastic is poured and spread out on the floor. Tiny chips of plastic are embedded evenly in this. After drying, the chips are smoothed by sanding and several coats of clear plastic are applied as a sealer.

Although seamless flooring materials are sold for do-it-yourself installation, we do not recommend that you undertake such a project. The work is exacting and precise. Even manufacturers have trouble training professional crews to make failure-proof installations. Many seamless floors have caused trouble—not because of material failure, but because of bad workmanship.

How to maintain seamless floors. Dry-mop, sweep, or vacuum daily. When soiled, wash with warm water and a mild detergent or ammonia. Do not wax.

Stains generally come off with detergent. For heavy grease, use a nonflammable grease solvent. If stains persist, treat as on resilient floors.

As soon as a floor becomes dull and cloudy, it should be reglazed (given a new top coat of clear plastic). An acrylic floor usually needs this treatment every six months; urethane floors may go three to five years. Acrylic floors should first be cleaned; urethane floors should be sanded as well. The glaze is applied with a roller and must dry for about 12 hours before you can walk on it.

Epoxy floors do not need reglazing but must be resurfaced in traffic areas now and then. This is a job for experts.

Floors, Slate. Lay and clean like stone floors. For how to repair, see *Stone*.

Floors, Stone. These are laid in mortar like stone walks or in an organic adhesive like quarry tile. If the edges are square and smooth, you can also lay the stones on plywood without mortar (see *Floors, Brick*). In this case, fill the joints with fine sand. The entire floor must then be covered with two coats of colorless masonry sealer to hold the sand in place. The sealer also helps to protect the stones against staining. Finish with a buffable water-based wax.

Because of the rough texture of most stones, they tend to collect and hold dust and lint; so vacuum them often. Damp-mop with a detergent solution as neces-

sary. Buff the floor every six to eight weeks; and rewax about every four months.

For how to remove stains, see *Brick* (page 30).

Floors, Vinyl. Although vinyl is the most expensive resilient flooring material, it is being used more and more because of its exceptional beauty and practical characteristics. It can be installed on suspended floors, on-grade floors, and below-grade floors, and is available in both sheets and tiles.

Several types of vinyl flooring are on the market:

Sheet vinyl made with a thin backing material is exceptionally durable and resistant to grease, alkalies, and stains. It can also support considerable weight without denting badly and withstands strong sunlight without excessive fading. It is very easy to maintain, but is only moderately quiet and resilient.

Sheet vinyl with a cushioned backing duplicates the advantages of ordinary sheet vinyl. In addition, it is the quietest of all resilient floors and the most comfortable to walk on.

Homogeneous vinyl tile differs from the sheet materials in that it has no backing and is usually of uniform composition throughout. It ranks very slightly below sheet vinyl in most respects. It will, however, bear heavier loads without denting than any other resilient material.

Rotovinyl is a sheet material in which the design is printed on the surface and then covered with a film of clear vinyl. (In the other vinyls, the design is inlaid, that is, extends all the way through the material.) The material has several kinds of backing, including a cushion which gives it resilience. Although rotovinyls have roughly the same characteristics as other vinyls, they are much lower in cost and durability; and some of them can be used only on suspended floors.

Another basic difference between vinyl flooring materials is that some require waxing while others do not. The latter have a softly glossy finish which is restored simply by washing: wax may either dull the finish or may not adhere.

How to repair inlaid vinyl floors. If small holes develop, grate a scrap of the material into a coarse powder; mix with a little acetone or methyl ethyl ketone to form a putty; spread into the holes; and smooth with steel wool when dry.

If vinyl is cut, cover the cut with a 1-inch strip of heavy aluminum foil. Hold the foil down at one end with a piece of masking tape or friction tape. Heat an iron to highest heat and draw it evenly along the foil several times. No pressure is necessary. The heat should seal the cut edges together. If the foil is stuck down, dampen it with a rag. Then clean the floor with an abrasive cleanser.

See *Floors, Resilient.*

Floors, Vinyl-Asbestos. Vinyl-asbestos flooring is available in tile form only. It is a favorite with home handymen because it is easy to install and fairly low in cost.

Vinyl-asbestos can be installed on suspended, on-grade, and below-grade floors. It is moderately durable, has excellent resistance to grease and alkalies, and is easy to maintain. But it lacks resilience, is fairly noisy underfoot, and resists indentation only moderately well.

See *Floors, Resilient.*

Floors, Wood. Oak is the most popular wood for flooring; maple comes next. Both are sold in several grades; and in both cases, the grades primarily reflect the appearance of the wood, not its wearing quality. So before you buy, inspect what is available.

Pine and fir may be used in vacation homes for flooring because they are inexpensive; but they do not wear well enough to be used in year-round homes.

How to lay a wood floor. Wood blocks, also called parquet, are easier to handle than strips (boards). Some blocks are solid; many more are laminated. Almost all are prefinished, and this is what you should use because even though you pay more for them, you are spared the difficult task of finishing the floor once it is laid.

If blocks are going over a concrete slab (they are used mainly for this purpose), the slab should be on-grade or suspended—not below-grade. It must, of course, be free of cracks and holes, clean, reasonably smooth, and level. To check whether it is dry enough, place several 2-foot-squares of rubber or heavy plastic on it. After 24 hours, if there is moisture on the slab or the bottom side of the squares, you must allow the floor to dry further.

Prime the floor with liquid asphalt and allow it to dry. The blocks are then laid in adhesive recommended by the flooring manufacturer. This is applied with a notched spreader.

Blocks are positioned like resilient floor tiles. Ideally, you should start laying them in the center of the room and work toward the sides; but if a room is square, you can also start in the most conspicuous corner and work across the room in two directions. The grain in adjacent blocks is alternated in direction. To allow for expansion, leave a space of at least ¼ inch between all sides of the floor and the baseboards.

Wood blocks can be laid over an existing wood floor if it is smooth and sound. Old finish should be removed. If the floor is in poor condition, however, it should be covered with ¼-inch plywood. In new construction, the subfloor should be of ¾-inch plywood laid directly on the joists.

When you lay strip flooring, you have a choice between prefinished and unfinished material. The former costs more but provides a very even, durable finish. You must, however, handle and install the strips with great care lest you mar the finish. You can be less careful with unfinished flooring.

If strip flooring is to be laid over an old strip floor, the existing boards should be nailed down securely to prevent squeaking; but no other preparation is required. The new boards must run at right angles to the old, which may mean that they are also at right angles to the floor boards in adjoining rooms. This is not a serious fault, but as a rule strip flooring is continued from room to room.

In new construction, strips are laid over a subfloor of ½-inch plywood.

To lay a strip floor over on-grade and below-grade concrete slabs, clean the slab thoroughly, apply an asphalt primer, and allow it to dry. Wood furring strips spaced

16 inches apart, center to center, are then laid across the floor. The strips should be 1-by-2s or 1-by-3s that have been pressure-treated with wood preservative. Stick them to the floor with roofing cement. Cover them with heavy polyethylene film, which serves as a moisture barrier. Use a continuous strip if possible; otherwise tape all joints. Continue the film up the walls on all sides of the floor a few inches—it will be concealed by the baseboards.

Nail a second layer of furring strips over the first. Then install the flooring strips at right angles to the furring strips.

Whatever the construction of the sub-floor, you should provide a ½-inch expansion space between the finish floor boards and the walls.

For standard 25/32-inch flooring use 2¼-inch, No. 5 spiral floor screw nails or 8d cut steel floor nails. The flooring strips at the sides of the room are face-nailed (the baseboards should cover the nail-heads). In all other boards, the nails are driven through the side tongue at an angle of 45 to 55 degrees. If you can rent the special nailing machine used by professionals, it automatically positions the nails and greatly speeds the installation. Otherwise drive the nails in fairly close to the boards with a hammer and then finish the job with a nailset.

Each bundle of strip flooring contains long and short pieces. Before you start nailing down the strips, lay out several rows so that you can achieve the most attractive arrangement of colors, grains, and end joints. The joints in adjacent rows should always be staggered at least 6 inches apart. Avoid clustering short pieces at the ends of the room.

All strips must be snugged up tight at the ends and along the sides. When tapping a strip home, lay a scrap of flooring against the side or end and hammer this, not the strip itself.

Wide-board, or plank, floors are laid like strip floors. However, the boards come in long lengths and are fastened down with flathead screws driven through the face of the boards in a random pattern. The screw heads are countersunk about ½ inch and are concealed by round wood plugs avail-able from the flooring dealer. Special drills which simultaneously bore the screw holes and holes for the plugs greatly simplify installation of the boards.

How to finish unfinished wood floors and refinish old floors. You will have to rent a large drum sander (which resembles an upright vacuum cleaner) to do the center of the floor, and an edger, or disk sander, to finish around the sides. You will also need a handscraper to get into corners and other tight spots.

Before sanding, go over the floor with hammer and nailset and drive in all protruding or high nails. Fasten loose boards. Close doors and open windows. Since no machine can sand right up to the shoe molding, remove the molding so you can get closer to the baseboards.

Three grades of sandpaper are usually required for refinishing, but you will get by with only two on a new floor. Start with No. 3½ paper; progress to No. 1½; and finish with No. 2/0. Never omit the final sanding with fine grit because a floor that is open-pored from semi-rough sanding soaks up finish and develops an uneven gloss which cannot be cured by additional coats of finish.

If possible, you should always run the drum sander with the grain. If old floor boards are badly cupped or uneven, however, your first cut may have to be made diagonally across the grain. The last cut is always with the grain. Whichever direction you are going in, remember to keep moving; otherwise the sander will dig a hole in the floor in no time. The best sanding procedure is to make a forward and backward trip over the same boards; then move over and do the adjacent boards in the same way.

When using the edger, make sure it is level; otherwise it will also cut unwanted holes in the floor. It makes no difference whether you move with the grain or across it here.   .

If either the drum sander or the edger does a poor job of sucking up the dust it creates, sweep the floor frequently as you work so you can see the condition of the boards. When all sanding is completed, sweep again and make a close inspection of the boards. You may have to start up the motors once more.

There will also be some spots that the sanders could not reach which you must scrape and sand by hand. Always work with the grain. To keep your scraper sharp so it cuts like a razor, touch up the blade frequently with a small file.

Now vacuum the floor thoroughly.

If there are stained areas in the floor, bleach them with ½ cup oxalic acid crystals in 1 quart water. Keep swabbing this on the stains until the wood returns to its proper color. Then apply a neutralizing agent made by mixing 1 cup borax in 1 quart hot water. After this, let the wood dry, sand it thoroughly, and vacuum once again. You are ready at last to apply a new finish.

To change the color of the wood, use an oil stain. For certain types of finish, however, water stains are recommended. You should therefore decide on your finish and read the directions before you buy stain.

When applying floor stain and finish, don't paint yourself into a corner. Do closets first. Then start at the wall or corner farthest from your escape door.

Apply stain with a wide brush, allow it to soak in for a few minutes, then go over it with rags to remove the excess and to even out what's left. If the color is not dark enough, let the stain stand on the wood a little longer. The stain must dry thoroughly—preferably for 24 hours or more—before the final finish is applied.

Innumerable clear finishes are used on wood floors. Probably the best—because it is easy to apply, quite durable, and can be touched up without showing lap marks—is penetrating floor sealer.

For an extra-tough, long-lasting, scratch-resistant finish, use urethane varnish or a product called Target.

Two coats are usually sufficient. Just brush the finish on evenly with the grain and let it dry. If the first coat raises the grain slightly, hand-sand the entire floor lightly with 2/0 paper. Vacuum up all dust and apply a second coat. After the final coat dries, put on a coat of wax.

How to maintain wood floors. Wax gives a soft glow to wood floors and also helps to protect the hard finish. Always use a solvent-based wax. You should never deliberately put water or water-based wax on wood because it may raise the grain or cause warping or swelling. Several kinds of waxes for wood floors are available. All clean as well as wax. See *Waxes.*

Sweep up grit and mop up spills promptly. Both can damage wood. In heavily traveled areas, it is wise to dry-mop or vacuum wood floors almost daily; but in less heavily traveled areas, clean the floors—probably with your vacuum—whenever you clean the rugs.

Floors that receive a lot of wear should be rewaxed or buffed about once a month. Go over others in the same way about every two or three months. If you build up too much wax or if waxed surfaces wear unevenly, remove the wax by machine- or hand-buffing with steel wool. Scrubbing with naphtha will also remove excess wax.

How to remove stains. Most stains on wood floors actually stain the wax coating only. You can remove many of them simply by rubbing with floor wax or white appliance wax. If this doesn't work, rub with naphtha or fine steel wool. Since these remove wax as well as stains, you must complete the job by applying new wax.

White appliance wax should also be used to remove heel marks, crayon, and lipstick.

If a shellacked floor is spotted by alcohol, rub lightly with steel wool and apply new shellac which is well thinned with denatured alcohol.

Water spots can usually be removed by rubbing with cigarette ashes and vegetable oil.

Scrape off paint with a sharp knife. If it gets into the pores of the wood, try rubbing with naphtha or cleaning fluid. If this doesn't work, leave well enough alone. More violent action will produce unhappy results.

Candle wax should also be scraped off with a knife. Then rub with naphtha.

How to repair wood floors. Floor squeaks. If the floor is over a basement or crawl space, drive thin wedges (wood shingles are good) between the offending board and the joists. If you cannot get at the underside of a floor, locate the joists

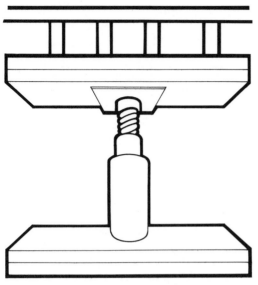

RAISING SAGGING FLOORS

Floor sags. You will need one or two adjustable steel jackposts. Set a pair of 2-by-4s, one on top of the other, flat on the floor directly under the sagging girder or joists. Place the jackpost on this base. The top of the post should touch the girder; or if there isn't a girder, put a pair of 2-by-4s on top of the post under the joists. Screw the post up tight; then continue screwing—not more than ½ inch every three days—until the floor is reasonably level. The jackpost can be left in place or replaced with a permanent wood post or lally column (a big steel pipe filled with concrete).

Floor vibrates when someone walks across it. There is no cure unless the space below the joists is open. In that case, if the joists look undersized (which they may well be), nail additional timbers of the same size to each one. If the joists appear to be of the proper size, then you need more bridging between the joists. Bridging is a simple X-shaped device of wood (and sometimes metal). Cut 1-by-2- or 1-by-3-inch boards to match the bridging that is already in place; and nail in one or two rows midway between the existing rows.

by tapping the floor until it gives off a solid sound. Drill small holes diagonally through the floor boards toward the joists. Then drive in 4- or 5-inch finishing nails. Countersink the heads and cover with plastic wood.

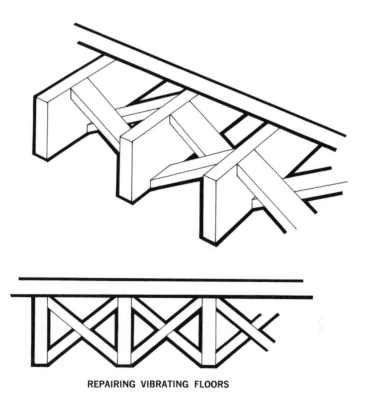

REPAIRING VIBRATING FLOORS

Burns. Scrape with a knife, then remove remaining charred wood with sandpaper. Clean with naphtha and refinish.

Scratches. If the scratch goes through to the wood, the only way to get rid of it is by heavy sanding followed by refinishing. But you can conceal it to some extent by applying a thin line of the floor finish with an artist's paintbrush.

If the scratch is in the finish only and the floor is finished with penetrating sealer, remove the wax and brush on new penetrating sealer, which will blend right in with the old. Similarly, if the floor is shellacked, rub with alcohol to soften the shellac and obliterate the scratch. For scratches in other finishes, just rub well with wax and look the other way.

Adjacent boards warped upward at the edges. This may happen if there is excess moisture in the space underneath. You can try to flatten the boards by driving long screws through them—hopefully into a joist—and tightening them bit by bit over a period of several weeks. But don't count on success, especially if the wood is oak. You are more likely to succeed if you saw along the joint with an electric circular saw. This severs the tongue on one of the two boards and makes it easier to flatten the boards either with screws or with finishing nails driven in diagonally.

In extreme cases, if the warped boards are under a rug and the bulge is very noticeable, or in an uncovered area where they may be dangerous, the only cure may be to cut out the boards entirely and replace them. The alternative (for a rug-covered area) is to cut out the bulging area with a circular saw and fill in with a pine board cut roughly to shape. Gaps around the fill-in board will be bridged satisfactorily by the rug cushion and rug.

Board in porch floor rotten, badly damaged, or warped in one spot. Porch floors are made of one thickness of pine boards nailed directly to joists. If the defective board is tongued-and-grooved, saw through the tongue in the defective area. Find the joists on both sides of the defective area and drill a 1-inch hole through the board next to both joists. Cut through the board along the joists with a

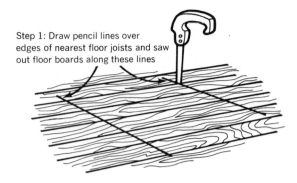

Step 1: Draw pencil lines over edges of nearest floor joists and saw out floor boards along these lines

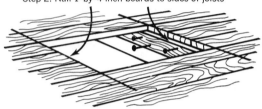

Step 2: Nail 1-by-4-inch boards to sides of joists

REPAIRING A ROTTEN SPOT IN A PORCH FLOOR

keyhole saw or saber saw and pry the board out. Nail 1-by-4-inch wood cleats to the joists under the hole. Cut a new floor board, set it into the hole, and nail it to the cleats.

Wide gaps between old floor boards. This is a common problem with very old pine floors. There is no filler that will hold in the gaps except possibly one of the new flexible caulking compounds, which are anything but attractive. Therefore the only good solution—and a difficult one—is to plane and whittle strips of clear pine to fit the gaps. Set them in place with white wood glue and brads.

Gap between floor and shoe molding or shoe molding and baseboard. This is caused by settling and shrinkage. The first problem occurs because the shoe molding is nailed to the baseboard; the second because the shoe molding is nailed to the floor. To correct matters, pry off the shoe molding and scrape off paint and floor finish encrustations on it. Then set the shoe molding in place and renail with long finishing nails. If possible, the nails should miss both the baseboard and the floor and be driven into the subfloor.

Foam. Urethane foam has largely replaced

latex foam in mattresses, cushions, pillows, upholstery, etc. The material, in addition to being resilient, is buoyant, nonallergenic, and long-lasting. It is available in varying degrees of resiliency.

The foam is commonly sold in ½-, 1-, 2-, 3-, 4-, and 5-inch thicknesses and in several widths and lengths. Special shapes are available. It is readily cut with a sharp knife. Small pieces can be joined together with plastic-mending adhesive, but the joint will be stiff and nonresilient.

Despite the rise of urethane, latex foam is still used in high-priced furniture and cushions. It bounces back faster after you sit on it and holds its shape better and longer. In addition, coverings have less tendency to slide on it than on urethane foam.

Food Grinders. A food grinder can grind all kinds of foods—meats, fish, cheese, breads, fruits, vegetables—and is indispensable for some dishes. Food is put in a hopper and fed with a wooden pusher to the grinding area. Usually two cutting disks—one for coarse and the other for fine grinding—come with the appliance.

Electric grinders cost about three times as much as hand-cranked units but are, of course, much easier to work. Grinders are also sold as accessories with some stand-type mixers.

Wash a grinder thoroughly in detergent solution after use, and dry it well.

If you have an old-fashioned food grinder that clamps to a table or counter top, protect the top if made of wood by covering it on both sides with pieces of thin plywood or hardboard. On a plastic counter top, use sheets of rubber cut from an old tire tube or gasket material to protect the surface and keep the grinder from slipping.

Food Preparation Centers. These are small, multi-purpose, counter-top appliances with a single power unit and a variety of interchangeable attachments. Depending on the make and model, they can be used for mixing, blending, kneading dough, grinding meat, shredding lettuce, opening cans, juicing oranges, crushing ice, and sharpening knives.

Electrical appliances. For two food pre-paration centers, a table mixer is the basic power unit. In one make, the mixer head is permanent and the attachments are connected into it. In the other make, after the mixing bowl and beaters are removed, the other appliances are attached to the stand.

In another type of preparation center, there is a basic power unit to which various appliances can be attached. The power unit either sits on a counter or is built into its own cabinet.

A fourth preparation center has a motor that is built in under the counter. The only thing visible is a flat metal plate with a recessed control knob and a recessed connection that holds and drives the interchangeable attachments.

Nonelectric food preparation centers. Originally nothing more than meat grinders, these appliances now do many of the things electric food preparation centers do. They stand on the counter and are driven by a crank. Obviously, they are slower than the electrical appliances and they are not as cheap as you might expect. But they last for years without giving trouble. One make, in fact, is guaranteed for five years.

Pros and cons. The principal advantage of all electrical food preparation centers is that you need only one motor to operate a number of appliances. This means you pay much less than you would if each appliance had its own motor. You also need somewhat less storage space. On the other hand, all combination appliances or tools are more prone to breakdowns than individual appliances. This is largely because the user has to handle them more as she plugs in one attachment, removes it, and plugs in another, ad infinitum. Furthermore, if the power unit breaks down, all the attachments are put out of commission. Finally, the simple business of switching attachments may, in time, seem like a nuisance.

These are advantages and disadvantages you ought to weigh when considering purchase of a food preparation center.

One point you should bear in mind is that you don't have to buy all the attachments just because they are available. Generally, you can start out with just the power unit and a single attachment and add on from there when you feel like it.

Food Warmers. The simplest way to keep food warm in the kitchen is to put it in the oven at the lowest temperature setting. But there are newer ideas for food warming.

One of these is a small infrared heater that fits neatly under a wall cabinet and provides a 12-by-15-inch band of gentle heat on the counter top below. The unit can be plugged into any outlet.

Another food warmer is primarily a large ventilating hood with two infrared bulbs built into the heater. Food is placed on a rack that folds down from the back of the heater.

A similar warmer can be built by a handyman. All you have to do is mount one or two inexpensive porcelain lampholders on the underside of a shelf, screw in infrared bulbs, and direct the light downward on food placed 18 inches or more below.

Electric food warmers are for the most part trays of various sizes. Large trays—up to 12 by 30 inches—have adjustable thermostats to maintain the desired temperature throughout plus a marked hot spot which is kept at a higher heat. Some models have a drawer or bin for rolls.

Most warming trays are designed for placement on a table or buffet, but some are incorporated into complete serving carts. There are also special bowl-shaped bread warmers.

Less efficient than the electric warmers and also more dangerous are those heated by canned heat (Sterno) and candles.

Food Wraps. Aluminum foil is the most versatile food wrap because you can wrap it around food packages of all shapes and completely seal out air; cover dishes; and use it for various other culinary and nonculinary purposes. (See *Aluminum Foil.*) For freezing foods and such jobs as stopping leaks in gutters, use heavy-duty foil. For most other purposes, the less expensive lightweight foil is more than adequate.

Plastic (polyethylene) bags are excellent for storing odd-shaped food packages in the refrigerator or freezer and for wrapping sandwiches. Larger bags are used for storing many other articles that need special protection as well as for collecting garbage and leaves. The plastic, however, is thin and easily punctured by anything pointed; so don't try to stretch a small bag over an irregularly shaped food item such as a chicken that is to be frozen.

Polyethylene also comes in rolls, and Saran is available in that form also. Both can be used like aluminum foil to cover dishes and wrap all kinds of food packages. Saran is especially good because it sticks tenaciously to other materials and to itself.

Wax paper has lost ground to the preceding wraps mainly because it does not stay in place unless secured in some fashion. But it gives good protection in the refrigerator (not the freezer) otherwise. And you need it also for lining cake pans, etc.

Freezer wrap, also called meat wrap, is a special paper used for long-term storage of odd-shaped food parcels. The best paper is covered with a layer of cellophane; cheaper grades are plastic-coated. Except for the very cheapest wrap, all cost more than heavy-duty aluminum foil and are not reusable as foil is.

Formica. Brand name for the laminated plastic made by the Formica Division of American Cyanamid.

Formite. Proprietary name for a sheer canvas interlining made of rayon and cotton blended. Wash in warm water and dry at low heat.

Fortrel. Polyester fiber made by the Celanese Corporation.

Freezers. Approximately 1,000,000 families each year buy food freezers. Some undoubtedly do this on the spur of the moment, without giving the matter enough thought, and wind up regretting their impulse. But most families that buy and operate freezers find they are a real convenience.

In 1965, when the U.S. Department of Agriculture made a survey of home freezer owners in the Fort Wayne, Indiana, area, it found that they believed the advantages of owning a freezer far outweighed the disadvantages. Here, specifically, are the advantages mentioned most frequently by city and suburban freezer owners:

	Percentage of families mentioning
Save time in shopping; don't shop so often	32
Freeze local, home-grown, in-season fruits and vegetables	29
Save money on food other than meat	23
Save money on meat	22
Have food other than meat on hand	21
Buy food in quantity	15
Buy sides and quarters of meat	13
Have meat on hand	13
Can cook and bake ahead	12
Freeze leftovers: there's no spoilage or waste	10

Farm homemakers generally agreed with these opinions. In addition, they told government researchers they were enthusiastic about their freezers because they were able to freeze their own home-grown meat and produce; because they had a greater variety of foods all year and were therefore able to serve better meals; and because freezing is easier than canning.

More than 80 percent of the homemakers said there were no disadvantages to owning a freezer. Of the minority who did express any dissatisfaction, most objected to the nuisance of defrosting. One other minor complaint was that frozen food could not be prepared as quickly as canned food.

A very few people also worried about power failures.

Types of freezer. Freezers are either upright and front-opening like refrigerators, or chests that open at the top. They perform equally well, but each type has its special advantages.

Upright freezers take up less floor space and foods are easier to find and reach on the shelves.

Chest freezers lose less cold air than uprights each time they are opened. Odd-shaped packages fit into them better; and you can lift out all packages without bringing the others tumbling down as in upright freezers. On the other hand, finding and retrieving the foods takes more effort.

What size freezer do you need? The capacities of uprights range from 6 to 31 cubic feet. The smallest models fit under a kitchen counter. Chest freezers range from 4 to 28 cubic feet. (Capacities are measured in accordance with standards set by the Association of Home Appliance Manufacturers [AHAM].) Each cubic foot holds approximately 35 pounds of frozen food.

It is impossible for anyone to determine precisely what size freezer he needs. Some home economists have suggested that 6 cubic feet should be allowed for each member of a family. But farm families and other families with vegetable gardens are usually the only ones that require this much capacity.

Actual studies show that the median-size freezer owned by urban families is 15 cubic feet; by farm families, 18 cubic feet. The USDA estimates the monthly cost of operating such freezers comes to about $4.90 and $5.30, respectively. (These figures allow for amortization of the freezer, repairs, electricity, and packaging of foods.)

Freezer features. No-frost performance is available in some freezers. Although desirable in combination refrigerator-freezers, this feature may not be worth its extra price and operation cost in a separate freezer. Freezers need defrosting only once or twice a year, and you can delay the defrosting by scraping off accumulated frost with a plastic or wooden scraper. Then, too, foods frozen for long periods will deteriorate somewhat from the slight temperature rise during each defrost cycle, and they will dehydrate gradually because of the forced dry-air circulation.

Look for well-designed shelves, baskets, or other dividers. Shelves in upright models seldom are adjustable because most of them (with the exception of no-frost models) have cooling coils built right into the shelves, giving you faster freezing action. Uprights often have a pull-out basket at the bottom. A few models have guard rails on shelf fronts that keep stored foods from falling out and that pull down as an aid in loading, unloading, and searching for foods.

Door shelves in uprights vary widely among the different models as to the number, spacing, and type of foods they can hold. Storage for canned foods is sometimes highly specialized, or there may be no provision at all. Check not only for efficient use of available space but also whether shelf supports will keep foods from falling out or tipping over when the door is opened or closed—a nuisance to be avoided.

Chest freezers, because of their design, are much less compartmented, but they may have vertical dividers or sliding baskets.

Special points to check include the following: Is the temperature control located where it will be easy to reach? If the freezer will be put in an out-of-the-way place, does it have an interior light located so that it won't be obscured by stored food? Can the freezer be locked?

Operating a freezer. Freezers are designed to operate wherever the temperature holds above 32 degrees. If you keep one outside or in an unheated garage, make sure the temperature does not go below that point; and protect it from moisture, which will cause unfinished or scratched metal surfaces to rust.

Plug the freezer into its own 20-amp circuit. Keep it level by adjusting the leveling screws underneath.

When starting a new freezer, set the control at a normal, or midpoint, setting. After 24 hours, adjust it up or down as necessary. The inside temperature should hold at zero or a bit lower.

If the power fails. Because of the heavy insulation in the walls, door, top, and bottom of a freezer, frozen foods should keep for about 48 hours during a power failure. This assumes, of course, that the door or lid is not opened and that the weather is not blistering.

If you have reason to think the power will be off longer than this, either move the contents of the freezer to a locker plant or scatter 25 pounds of dry ice through the freezer.

After a power failure, check the contents to determine whether they still contain ice crystals. If they do, they can be refrozen. If not, they should be used promptly or discarded if they show signs of spoilage.

How to care for a freezer. See *Refrigerators* (page 242).

Frieze. A heavy woolen fabric with a pile made of loops of varying height. It is scratchy, stiff, and durable; used in upholstery. It must be dry-cleaned.

Fryers. See *Deep-Fry Cookers.*

Frying Pans, Electric. As a supplement to or replacement for range units, the electric frying pan is probably the most popular small cooking appliance. One of its major advantages is its portability. It is not confined to the kitchen, but can be used to cook and serve food right at the dining room table.

The term "frying pan" or "skillet" is too limiting for most of today's models, which can also roast, broil, bake, or simmer. One change that makes this appliance especially versatile is a high-domed cover which allows larger quantities and varieties of food to be cooked. Many frying pans now have buffet-type handles on two sides rather than one long handle. These models are attractive and easy to carry and store. One unit has snap-off legs for easy storage.

Nonstick surfaces are popular and a definite advantage at clean-up time. Most skillets are square or rectangular, with rounded corners. A few are round. Most are immersible in water for cleaning.

A number of frying pans list suggested cooking temperatures on the handle or control—a real convenience. Most have a signal light that goes off when the selected temperature has been reached.

In those frying pans that can broil, a broiling element fits in the lid and foods go on a rack in the pan. Other models have a basket for deep frying. One has a warming tray beneath the pan.

Immediately after draining grease from an electric frying pan, wipe the sides and bottom with a paper towel; otherwise the bottom will be covered with a nasty brown mess which melts on the counter when the pan is hot. Wash the pan well, top and bottom, with detergent solution or cleanser.

To remove baked-on grease and carbon, apply a strong grease and carbon remover; let it stand for 30 minutes or more; then swirl it around with a brush and wash it off.

Fur. The only furs that most people own are pieces of clothing; but some have fur rugs and throws and stuffed animal heads.

Animal heads require frequent dusting with a vacuum, and it is a smart idea to spray them twice a year with a good moth repellent. If they become very dirty, let a taxidermist clean them.

Fur rugs and throws should be vacuumed frequently with a tank or canister machine—not one with beaters. Use minimum suction, even though this does not get out all the embedded dust and dirt. Just turning the rug over on the floor will shake out some of the dirt, but don't beat it or shake it violently. When soiling is excessive, send the piece to a fur cleaner for cleaning, general restoration, and mothproofing. Store in a cold-storage plant in summer.

Neither rugs nor throws should be exposed to too much sunlight or heat, because the leather may dry out, crack, and then disintegrate. The sun also may cause fading of the hairs. Fur clothing should be protected in the same way.

Other rules for taking care of fur clothing are:

1. Always hang garments on a contoured wood hanger in a cool, airy closet.

2. If garments become wet, dry them in a cool, airy place.

3. If soiled or stained, don't try to clean garments with anything except a cleaning powder. If this doesn't work, send the piece to a fur cleaner.

4. Have garments professionally cleaned and restored at least once a year—usually in the spring when you put them into cold storage.

Also see *Imitation Fur.*

Furnaces. See *Heating Systems.*

Furnishing the Home. Furnishing the home is fun. It is also rather frightening because it costs so much. Before you start shopping, therefore, you should do several things:

1. Make sure you know which style of furniture you like. You don't have to stick to just one, of course; but one should predominate.

2. Draw an accurate plan of each room to be furnished. Then, on tissue paper laid over the plan, sketch in the pieces of furniture you want. These must be drawn to the same scale used for the room plan. Keep making different arrangements on different pieces of tissue until you find the one that is right.

3. Work out a realistic furnishing budget. In the long run, you will be smart to buy a few very good things and fill in with odds and ends.

Following is a check list of commonly used furnishings. The sizes given are very rough averages. The first figure is the width; the second, depth.

	Size (inches)
*Living room furnishings**	
Sofa	72 x 33 and 84 x 33
Love seat	54 x 33 and 60 x 30
Wing chair	30 x 34
Lounge chair	33 x 33
Danish chair	26 x 28
Straight chair	20 x 18
Cocktail table	42 x 18
End table	18 x 30
Drum table	32 (diameter)
Card table	30 x 30
Spinet piano	52 x 25
Baby grand piano	57 x 57
Piano bench	30 x 14
Color TV set (console)	33 x 30
Seven-drawer desk	48 x 20
Bookcase	36 x 10
Carpet	
Draperies	
Floor lamps	
Table lamps	
Fireplace screen	
Fireplace tools	
Pictures	
Accessories	
Clock	

Family room furnishings are more or less identical.

Dining room furnishings

	Size (inches)
Table	42 x 60
Arm chair	20 x 20
Side chair	18 x 20
Buffet	48 x 18
Carpet	
Draperies	
Pictures	

Bedroom furnishings

Bed	see *Beds*
Four-drawer chest	32 x 18
Double dresser	48 x 18
Night table	20 x 16
Seven-drawer desk	48 x 20
Straight chair	20 x 18
Dressing table	34 x 18
Dressing table stool	15 (diameter)
Bookcase	36 x 10
Easy chair	27 x 30
Mirrors	
Carpet	
Floor lamps	
Table lamps	
Draperies	
Windowshades	
Pictures	

Hall furnishings

Chest or table	32 x 18
Straight chair	20 x 18
Carpet	
Mirror	
Accessories	

Kitchen furnishings

Breakfast table	36 (diameter)
Chair	16 x 16
Stool	14 x 14
Curtains	

For information about other kinds of home furnishings, see *Bath Linens; Bedding; Dinnerware; Glassware; Kitchen Tools; Kitchen Utensils; Table Linens; Tableware.*

Furniture, Children's. Most children's furniture is made of wood and is cared for and repaired like standard-size wood furniture. The same points should also be considered in its purchase. In addition, you must make sure that paint applied to the furniture is free of lead; otherwise a child chewing on the furniture will be poisoned, perhaps fatally.

Actually, it is doubtful whether any children's furniture made today in the United States is finished with lead paint. But this may not be true of second-hand or hand-me-down furniture; consequently, any such painted furniture that you acquire should be stripped down to the bare wood and refinished with nontoxic paint. (Varnish and other clear finishes applied to furniture are lead-free.)

Furniture, Metal. Chromium-plated steel, brass-plated steel, painted steel, aluminum (usually with a baked enamel finish), wrought iron, and cast iron are used to make various furniture pieces and parts. All can be cleaned quickly with detergent solution. Abrasives should not be used except to remove rust and corrosion.

For how to make repairs, see entry for the appropriate metal.

Furniture, Plastic. All-plastic furniture is rare today, although a very few, very modern pieces are made entirely of clear acrylic or of molded or sculptured urethane foam of various densities. But a great deal of furniture is made in part of plastics. The materials most often used are the following:

Laminated plastics—in table, desk, and chest tops.

Polyester—in chair frames and backs, arms and legs, cabinet doors, mirror frames, headboards, ornamental panels, rosettes, plaques, etc. Polyester is also reinforced with fiberglass to make chair seats and backs.

Styrene—in parts similar to those made of polyester.

Urethane—in chair and sofa cushions, upholstery fabric, and also in parts similar to those made out of polyester and styrene.

Vinyl—in upholstery materials; as a veneer on tables, chests, desks, cabinets, etc.; and for some molded parts.

In some cases, plastic furniture parts look like plastic. In other cases, they resemble wood and other materials, and are so cleverly textured and colored that you cannot identify them as plastics.

From the homemaker's standpoint, the great advantages of plastic in furniture are the ease with which it can be cleaned; its resistance to abrasion, staining, etc.; and the fact that it does not warp, contract, or expand. If soil marks cannot be wiped off with a damp sponge, they almost always can be removed with detergent solution. No polishing or waxing is necessary, although many women like the glow that white appliance wax or furniture polish gives.

For how to repair damage to plastic furniture, see the entry for the appropriate plastic.

Furniture Polishes. Furniture polishes and cleaners are designed for specific jobs related to the kinds of furniture you have and the results you want. Before buying a new or unfamiliar wax, read the label to find out the type of furniture or finishes for which it is recommended, whether it cleans and waxes, and what degree of luster it promises.

For furniture that doesn't need a protective wax and for quick dustings, use those products that simply remove grime and dust. Some aerosol products can be sprayed directly on furniture; others are sprayed on the dustcloth so it will attract and hold dirt. Either type is preferable to using a dry cloth, which simply scatters the dust and sometimes grinds it into surfaces. Special cloths and disposable towels pretreated to attract dust and dirt are also fast dusters.

If one-shot cleaning and polishing is what you want, there are products that pick up dust, fingerprints, and smudges and also deposit a layer of wax to protect the furniture. Aerosol spray products do this dual job in an instant. Those that you squirt or pour from a container require a little more time and effort to spread evenly—but cost less.

These instant products should never be used for certain types of furniture, however. Some antiques, for instance, have a mellow patina that's been achieved through years of rubbing with a paste wax. You should keep using this. You should also use paste wax on furniture surfaces such as table tops and fronts of bureau drawers that are exposed to hard wear and skin oils.

You should never use a product that produces a high or medium luster on furni-ture meant to have a dull finish, such as teak or oiled walnut. To keep such furniture dust-free and protected, you can use either a low-luster cream polish or an oily polish. For the sake of the furniture, choose one method and stick with it.

Special waxes or cleaners also are available for surfaces such as marble, laminated plastics, plastic furniture, and kitchen furnishings. Another special kind of polish contains a stain for covering up scratches in wood furniture.

Furniture, Reed. Reed furniture is like wicker but made with various strong marsh grasses. Clean and repair like willow (which see).

Furniture, Upholstered. Because you cannot see inside upholstered furniture, it is difficult to tell quality pieces from poor. Generally about all you can do is to shop at a store you trust and remember that the price tag, in this instance, is not often misleading.

Good upholstered furniture feels right and looks right. Springs (which you probably cannot see but may be able to feel) are of the coiled type, closely spaced and tied together. Flat, S-type springs produce a firmer cushion and are used in less expensive furniture (on the other hand, they stay put; they do not suddenly break loose and make bulges as coiled springs do).

Filling material must, by law, be described on the label attached to all upholstered pieces. Animal hair (no longer widely used) is less desirable than synthetic fibers and cotton. Urethane foam does not hold its shape as well as foam rubber. A mixture of down and feathers is excellent.

The best upholstery fabrics from a maintenance standpoint are closely woven (so they won't soak up dust so rapidly) and made of polypropylene or nylon (both of which have good abrasion resistance and can generally be cleaned with a damp cloth). Vinyl is even better but not so attractive.

How to take care of upholstered furniture. Vacuum the upholstery regularly to extract dust and gritty dirt. If possible, turn cushions now and then to distribute wear. Sponge soil from vinyl, polypropylene, and nylon occasionally with a cloth barely dampened in water. Yearly shampooing of fabrics that can withstand such treatment is advisable. Launder slipcovers on the same schedule or even more often.

Home treatment of upholstery fabrics with a soil- and oil-repellent finish is not recommended.

How to remove stains. Follow the directions under *Rugs;* but be sure to test the removal agent on an inconspicuous corner of the upholstery first.

How to re-cover a straight chair seat. Turn the chair upside down and remove the screws that hold the seat to the frame. Pull the tacks from around the edges of the old cover, and spread the cover smooth on top of your new material. Cut the latter to this pattern and place it under the chair seat. Then pull the edges up and over the edges of the seat and tack or staple them to the bottom.

If the padding in the old seat is in poor shape, it can most easily be replaced with a 1-inch thickness of urethane foam. Cut the foam ¼ inch larger on all sides than the base of the seat. Bevel the edges with scissors. Then place the foam—beveled edges down—on the base and glue it in place with the cement sold by the foam supplier. The upholstery fabric should then be cut 2 inches larger on all sides than the foam.

How to retie sagging chair or sofa springs. Turn the chair upside down and remove the fabric cover carefully. If it is in good condition, it can be reused. Then remove or loosen the heavy canvas webbing.

In a coiled spring chair, the springs are tied together at the top and bottom and to the chair frame. The chances are that you will find only a few of the strings broken and in need of replacement; but since you now have the chair open, you may feel moved to replace them all as a hedge against future trouble.

The top edges of the springs should be tied first. Working from the left side of the chair to the right, tie all the springs across the chair. Then tie them from front to back.

Tie a piece of stout twine to the left edge of the first spring. Leave about 10 inches of twine hanging. Then pull the twine across the spring and tie it securely to the right edge. Then tie to the left and right edges of the adjacent spring. And so on to the other side of the chair. The spaces between all springs should be even; their width depends on how many springs the chair contains.

When all the springs are tied at the top across the chair and front to back, tie knots in the loose ends of twine and drive large tacks through them into the chair frame. The outer edges of the springs should be bent downward toward the frame. This gives the seat its rounded contour.

The bottom edges of the springs are tied in the same way, but the outer edges of the outer springs should not be bent.

The canvas webbing should now be retacked to the frame or it may be replaced with new webbing. The strips are interwoven and spaced so that they cross directly under each spring. Double the end of the first strip and fasten it to the bottom edge of the frame with three or four large tacks; then pull it across the chair, tighten it, and drive one tack through it into the frame. Then double back the loose end about 2 inches and drive in about three more tacks. All succeeding strips are handled in the same way.

The webbing should be as taut as a drum. The best way to achieve this is to buy a webbing stretcher; but you can make a reasonably good substitute by driving about five large finishing nails all the way through a short 2-inch-wide board. Countersink the heads slightly. Shorten the points of the nails to about ½ inch and sharpen them with a file.

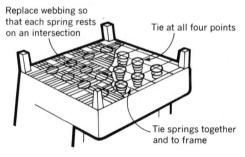

Replace webbing so that each spring rests on an intersection

Tie at all four points

Tie springs together and to frame

REWEBBING A CHAIR SEAT

To use the stretcher, tack a webbing strip down at one end, draw it across the bottom of the chair, and pull it tight. Place the nailhead edge of the stretcher against the side of the frame and pull the webbing over the teeth. By pulling down on the webbing, you force the stretcher to pull it taut across the bottom of the chair frame.

When the webbing is in place, sew the springs to the crossings. Then replace the fabric cover with small tacks.

How to smooth a lumpy seat. If you can easily remove the fabric covering the seat, this is not a difficult repair; otherwise you had better let a professional take over.

Remove the upholstery and muslin underneath. If the lumpiness is caused by bunching up of the cotton padding, remove the cotton and smooth out the stuffing underneath. Then replace the cotton or install new cotton. This is available in long, wide rolls. Taper the edges of the pieces used. Then replace the muslin and upholstery fabric.

If the springs in the seat have come loose or changed position, remove all the padding and take off the burlap covering the springs. Retie the springs in the manner described earlier. Then replace the burlap, padding, muslin, and upholstery.

How to stuff a loose seat or back cushion. Open the rear edge of the cushion cover by cutting the stitches at the cord line. You can now add padding similar to the original or you can replace it entirely with a cushion of urethane foam. In the latter case, the foam should be cut about ¾ inch longer and wider than the cover measurements from cord to cord. Double it up, push it into the cover, open it flat, and adjust its position. The cover should be snug. Then sew up the opening.

Furniture, Wood. This entry is concerned primarily with furniture that is made almost entirely of wood; but it applies to any furniture that incorporates wood.

Good wood furniture is well braced and sturdy. Chairs don't wobble when you sit on them, or other pieces when you try to push them from side to side. Drawers have dove-tailed joints and a center glide. They slide in and out easily and straight. On large surfaces, grains are well matched. The use of veneers is extremely common and should not be construed as a deficiency of the furniture. Veneers are actually less likely to split, warp, swell, or shrink than solid wood.

How to take care of wood furniture. Dust as necessary. Remove finger marks, grease, sticky dirt, etc., with a cloth dampened very slightly in mild detergent solution. Apply furniture polish about every half-year to surfaces that get little wear. Use sparingly and rub well. Table and desk tops, bureau fronts and chair arms that receive heavy wear should be polished monthly. If you use a good paste wax rather than a polish, you need to apply it only about once every four months; but buff it monthly between times. A polishing disk on an electric drill is useful.

If the finish becomes dull and hazy and does not respond to buffing, remove it with a paste cleaner like that used to clean automobiles.

How to remove stains. See *Wood.*

How to refinish wood furniture. Removing old finish. There is, of course, no need to remove the old finish if it is sound and smooth and you intend to apply enamel. But you should wash it thoroughly with naphtha to remove polish and wax. Then, if the surface is very glossy, go over it with steel wool to roughen it slightly so that the new finish will adhere well.

If you are applying a transparent finish, the old finish should be removed entirely. Sometimes when a finish is so old and brittle that it can be scratched off with your fingernail, all you have to do is scrape it off dry. More tenacious finishes, however, must be softened with a prepared paint-and-varnish remover. Use a paste-type remover on vertical surfaces; it sticks better than liquid removers. For how to use paint removers, see *Paint Removal.*

Preparing the bare wood. Make whatever repairs are necessary. (See *Wood* and the repair section below.) Then sand the wood thoroughly until it is as smooth as silk. Always work with the grain; otherwise you are bound to make scratches which are difficult to remove.

When working on a flat veneered surface, such as a table top, be careful not to sand more heavily near the edges than in the center. See *Veneer*.

Staining wood. Use oil stain, and before applying it to the exposed furniture surfaces, test it on a hidden area. Allow it to stand for only about 3 minutes, then wipe it off. If the color is not as deep as you want, make a second application and let it stand for about 3 minutes. Continue in this way until you achieve the desired tone.

When staining the exposed surfaces, allow the stain to stand for as long as it took to make your test, or a little less. If staining more than one piece of furniture, use the same timing for all pieces that are made of the same wood. But if one piece is made of, say, pine and another of maple, each piece must be tested separately and stained according to its own timetable.

Wipe off stain after it has penetrated sufficiently with clean rags. Discard the rags as soon as they are wet. Hard rubbing helps to even out the stain so it is uniform over the entire piece of furniture. Then let the stain dry for 48 hours. If the final finish is applied before then, it may streak the stain.

Filling wood. Paste wood fillers are used to fill the pores of coarse, open-grained woods such as oak. They are not essential, but they help to assure a smoother, more even finish.

Use a filler of the color selected for the final finish and dilute it 50-50 with turpentine. Brush it on evenly, first with the grain and then across it. When the liquid starts to evaporate and the paste turns dull, rub it off with coarse rags. Then let it dry overnight and sand or steel-wool the wood once more.

Applying varnish. Varnish should be applied in a warm (70 degrees or higher) room. Vacuum the room thoroughly the day before applying varnish so there will be less dust that might settle on the wet finish. Just before dipping into the varnish, remove dust from the furniture piece with a cloth dampened in turpentine.

The first coat of varnish should be thinned about 10 percent with turpentine. The second coat is applied as it comes from the can. Apply in light coats with the grain and do not brush it out too much, since this creates bubbles.

Let the first coat dry 24 hours and sand lightly. Remove the dust with your vacuum and a turpentine-dampened cloth. Let the second coat dry 24 hours, too. Then rub it down with very fine steel wool to remove the high gloss and brush marks and even out the finish. After applying one or two coats of paste wax and buffing them well, the finish will have a fine, satiny sheen.

For an even finer finish, rub down the varnish after it has been steel-wooled with powdered pumice stone or rottenstone mixed with a little linseed oil. Apply this with an old felt pad. Use firm but not heavy pressure and go over all surfaces evenly. The stone will remove any scratches left by the steel wool.

Applying other finishes. Shellac finish. This is not as durable as varnish but produces a handsome luster. Use white shellac and dilute it 50-50 with denatured alcohol. Apply five thin coats and sand or steel-wool each when dry. Since shellac dries very rapidly, you can put on two or three coats in a day. Finish with paste wax.

Oil finish. This is an excellent finish which tends to darken slightly with time. After the stain has dried thoroughly, mix 2 parts boiled linseed oil with 1 part turpentine; warm it slightly in a double boiler; then brush it on the surface and rub it in for several minutes with a cloth dipped in the mixture. Then remove the excess and rub vigorously for about 20 minutes until the wood actually feels warm. Allow the oil to dry for several days. Make two to four additional applications in the same way. Allow the last application to dry a week before applying paste wax.

Wax finish. This is a very easy way to finish furniture (as well as wood paneling), but does not protect the wood to the same extent as the foregoing finishes. Use a prepared stain-wax of the desired color. Follow directions on the can: Brush the finish on; let it stand briefly; then remove the excess with rags and allow the finish to dry. Although no further treatment is essential, it is a good idea to make an application of ordinary paste wax.

Bleached finish. To make an ordinary bleached finish, treat the wood with a commercial bleach rather than stain. Follow the maker's directions for applying the bleach, and take care not to get the stuff on your skin. When the wood dries, steelwool it thoroughly. If the wood is not bleached as light as you want it, make a second and third application. Then finish with varnish, shellac, or water-white lacquer.

Pickled pine finish. Bleach the wood; allow it to dry; smooth it with steel wool; and apply one coat of water-white lacquer thinned 1 to 10 with lacquer thinner. Steel-wool the surface again; brush on a silver-gray stain, making sure to get it into the wood pores; let it stand for a while, then remove it with coarse rags. When dry, go over the surface once more with steel wool, and apply several coats of water-white lacquer.

Limed oak finish. This is the same as a pickled pine finish except that the wood pores are filled with white oil paint.

Painting furniture. If the furniture is unfinished, apply one coat of enamel undercoater. Then mix the undercoater 50-50 with the enamel and apply a second priming coat. Finish with one coat of enamel from the can.

If the wood has open pores, these should be filled with paste filler before the undercoater is applied.

On furniture with a sound finish, apply one coat of undercoater mixed with enamel and a final coat of enamel.

For an antique finish, buy a kit containing undercoater and glazing liquid. Follow directions.

On flat surfaces, first brush with the grain, then go across it with a feathery stroke. On turned chair legs, etc., apply enamel around the leg and smooth off with a light up-and-down stroke. Keep your brush well saturated except when smoothing off.

In painting chairs, turn them upside down and work first on the legs; then set them upright and work on the back, then on the seat. Paint tables in the same way. Remove drawers and hardware from chests before painting. Set the drawers face up

and paint them. Then finish the top of the frame, then the front, then the sides and back. Take beds apart and lay the pieces flat when painting them.

Gabardine. Gabardine is a tight twill fabric used in clothing and made of wool, cotton, or rayon. It should generally be dry-cleaned; but cotton gabardine can be washed in lukewarm water.

Galvanized Iron. The common but improper name for galvanized steel. See *Steel.*

Garbage Bags. The latest trend in municipal garbage collection is to permit or require home owners to put out their garbage and other refuse in large paper or plastic bags rather than cans. Results: Fewer germs and flies, clean lawns and streets (without snarling dogs), noiseless, faster pickup.

The paper bags are preferred. They are made of strong weatherproof paper and hold 30 gallons (roughly 50 pounds) of assorted trash, including broken pieces of glass and jagged metal. Bags are made for dry storage only, or for wet and dry storage. Outdoors, they are generally hung in an open metal rack which screws to the wall of the house, off the ground. The rack has a top. A completely enclosed rack for extra protection against animals is available (however, animals are rarely attracted to the bags because the bags are thrown out with the garbage and never get dirty or smelly).

Although these bags are rather large to use indoors, there is no reason why they should not be, if you have room. Here they can be suspended in metal holders mounted on casters.

In some communities, the paper bags are supplied free to home owners. Elsewhere they can be bought for about 15 cents each. The simplest outdoor racks cost about $7.

Plastic bags can be used indoors or out in the same way, but they must be of .3-mil thickness. These, unfortunately, are not generally available. The lighter (.15-mil), cheaper bags which are now sold in every supermarket and hardware store can be used only to line garbage cans. They are, of course, helpful in keeping cans clean; and they can be collected quickly, quietly, and without a lot of mess. You will also find them useful for wrapping and storing all kinds of things. But they can be torn easily, and may break if loaded heavily. Furthermore, tests in California show that, unlike paper bags, they do not discourage flies unless you have refuse collection at least twice a week.

An especially irritating thing about plastic bags is that they are packaged in so many different ways (usually badly) and in so many sizes that it is very easy to bring home the wrong size.

Garbage Cans.

In the kitchen. From the standpoint of aesthetics and convenience, the best place to put a garbage can is under the sink. But unfortunately, because the space is limited and rather inaccessible, you can use only a small can which needs frequent emptying.

Larger cans, or baskets, which are placed in whatever open space happens to be available, have in recent years been designed so that in themselves they are not so offensive in appearance; but after you get through lining them with plastic liners and filling them with trash, the effect is something else again. Without question, the neatest can has a metal outer cover with a lid that pops open when you step on a foot pedal. Waste is stored inside in a durable polyethylene pail that lifts out when full.

Outside the house. Large garbage cans are made of galvanized steel, aluminum, and semi-rigid plastic. The traditional can is round; newest designs are rectangular to save space.

The steel can is sturdiest and heaviest; but although it is covered with a heavy coating of zinc, it will eventually rust and require replacement. Aluminum cans are more durable and also lighter. Many communities require metal cans because they are fireproof and rodent-resistant. Steel cans that give off a dull thump rather than a reverberating clang when they are handled have been developed.

Plastic cans make less noise, and are somewhat easier to clean because they are seamless. But they have a tendency to break when roughly handled—especially in cold weather. Buy the best quality only; they are guaranteed for three years.

Underground garbage cans are desirable because they are invisible. They consist of a heavy steel case with a step-on lid (which can trip up the unwary) and a galvanized steel insert. But they hold only 20 gallons—which is hardly adequate except for a tiny family that doesn't read newspapers or attract junk mail.

How to take care of garbage cans. This is a chore nobody likes, and for that reason, nobody does it very well. Use of plastic liners, of course, simplifies matters but does not obviate the need to wash cans at least once a week with hot detergent solution. Use a long-handled sink brush with a teardrop-shaped head. Drain thoroughly and dry in the sun.

When an old steel can shows signs of rusting, scrub the bottom well and dry it. Remove rust with a steel brush. Then brush on liquid asphalt roofing cement. Small holes in cans can be sealed with plastic metal.

Metal tops and the rims of metal cans should be tapped back into shape when bent in order to keep out rodents and as many flies as possible.

Garbage Compactors. See *Compactors*.

Garbage Disposers.
Housewives who have used disposers almost always rate them as indispensable. The reason: Disposers eliminate food waste in seconds—long before it can turn into disagreeable garbage; they save clean-up time and mess; and trips to the garbage can are cut down.

A garbage disposer is a compact electrical grinding mechanism which can be installed below the opening in almost any kitchen sink. When you fill it with food waste and turn on the electricity and water, it quickly chews the solids into tiny particles which are flushed down the drain into the sewer. Inside the drain lines, the food particles have a scouring action which actually helps to prevent clogging of the pipes.

Most new disposers can handle all kinds of food waste, although some may have difficulty with fruit pits, large bones, and fibrous materials such as cornhusks. They can also, as a rule, grind up soft paper and cigarettes if these are mixed with food wastes. Other materials should not be dropped into the grinding chamber.

Installation of disposers is prohibited in

a handful of cities; but their widespread acceptance is indicated by statistics which show that roughly a million and a half houses are equipped with disposers every year. In a number of communities, disposer installation in new and remodeled homes is mandatory.

The appliance can also be installed in homes with septic systems (but not cesspools). There are, however, no universal regulations about the size of the septic tank that must be used. The Federal Housing Administration's Minimum Property Standards stipulate that if you have a disposer, you need a 750-gallon tank for a two-bedroom house; a 900-gallon tank for three bedrooms; a 1000-gallon tank for four bedrooms. Beyond that, you need 250 gallons of extra capacity for each additional bedroom. In some communities, however, even larger tanks are required.

Types of disposer. There are two: Batch-feed disposers handle one load of waste at a time. You load the waste into the grinding chamber, turn on cold water, and set a special cover into the sink opening. The cover serves as an electrical switch. When turned on, it starts the grinding wheel. You turn the cover to "off" when the waste has disappeared down the drain. The cover also serves as the sink stopper and strainer.

Continuous-feed disposers are controlled by a wall switch. As long as the electricity and water are on, you can continue to drop waste into the grinding chamber.

Although continuous-feed disposers are certified safe for household use by Underwriters' Laboratories, accidents are possible. Batch-feed disposers are safer because you cannot add anything to or reach inside the grinding chamber while in operation.

The only other difference between the two disposers is that batch-feed units are generally high in price. Continuous-feed units are available in a wide range of prices, from very low to high.

In the long run, the best disposer to buy is a fairly expensive unit. It is built with tougher materials which wear longer and resist corrosion. Look also for a model that has pivoted cutters on the cutting

wheel, because these rarely are jammed by tough pieces of waste.

How to operate a disposer. If a sink has an opening of about 4 inches in diameter, a disposer can usually be installed in it. Smaller openings can be enlarged with a boring tool; larger openings can be reduced with adapters. Installation, in all cases, should be made by a licensed plumber.

Each disposer requires its own 120-volt, 20-amp circuit, but if you have a dishwasher, both appliances can be connected into the same circuit.

A disposer operates best when the grinding chamber is filled with waste of different types. Do not overload. Be careful not to drop cutlery into the chamber: it probably won't hurt the disposer, but good-bye cutlery.

Always turn on water when operating the disposer. Cold water should be used because it does not melt grease, which may clog the drain.

If the sink drain should become clogged—an unlikely situation—do not pour a caustic drain cleaner into the disposer because it is likely to damage metal parts. Call a plumber.

If something goes wrong. If your disposer won't work, you may need a serviceman. But it may be simply that the fuse has blown. Check this point.

The motor may also have been overloaded. To check this, let the disposer cool for several minutes; then press the overload reset button near the bottom of the disposer.

To unjam a disposer. As noted, disposers with pivoted cutters rarely jam. Other models have an automatic reversing action: if jammed, the cutting wheel automatically starts revolving in the other direction. In still other models, you must flick a switch to reverse the cutting wheel. In a few models, the cutting wheel can be reversed only by inserting a special wrench (which comes with the appliance) in the bottom of the disposer.

Very old disposers can be unjammed with a broom handle thrust against the cutting wheel. Always turn off the electricity when resorting to this operation.

Gas. Natural gas used in the home for heating, water heating, cooking, drying laundry, and incinerating trash is a colorless, nontoxic, lighter-than-air chemical to which an odorant has been added.

The following are general safety rules for using gas:

1. Report any odor of gas to the gas company at once.

2. If gas piping or an appliance develops a leak, turn off the gas valve immediately and ventilate the area well. Do not light matches or lighters or turn on electric switches or equipment. Report the leak at once to the gas company. In the unlikely event that the gas company will not help you, call a plumber.

3. Never try to find a gas leak with a lighted match or open flame.

4. If you notice an extremely strong smell of gas, such as might occur if a pipe were broken, evacuate the building and adjacent buildings at once. Call the gas company from a telephone outside the building.

5. If for any reason the main gas valve has been turned off, don't turn it on yourself. Call the gas company.

6. Notify the gas company before undertaking any excavating work near underground pipes. Should a gas leak ignite outdoors, don't try to extinguish it. Call the fire department and gas company.

7. Don't try to repair, adjust, or make changes in your gas piping and appliances. Always call a qualified serviceman.

8. Don't let young children turn on gas appliances without proper supervision.

9. Follow sensible safety practices when working near an open gas flame. Keep curtains, papers, flammable fluids, flammable clothing, etc., far away. Don't store combustible material such as paints in the vicinity.

The following rules for using gas appliances have been prepared by the American Gas Association:

1. Before lighting a heating appliance, such as a furnace or water heater, read the maker's lighting instructions on the nameplate.

2. Gas appliances should light readily from the pilot light or lighter. This is particularly important in cases where the burners are installed in confined spaces. If a burner does not ignite quickly, a flash may occur from the delayed ignition. Never light an appliance if an odor of gas is present.

In cases where a gas burner fails to light or has gone out, the combustion chamber and flue may become filled with unburned gas. The appliance gas valve should be turned off until the source of the trouble has been corrected.

Always give unburned gas time to clear away before attempting to light a burner. This is particularly important when you are trying to light an oven burner with a match and the match goes out before the burner lights. Don't leave the burner on while reaching for another match. The gas will build up an accumulation which might cause a flash when a lighted match is applied.

3. Keep the burning surface clean of dirt, match ends, grease, etc. They are a common cause of appliance malfunction. Regular inspection and maintenance by the dealer—particularly of gas-fired heating equipment—will assure clean, reliable, economical, safe operation of gas appliances.

4. Do not block off or obstruct the supply of fresh air to a gas appliance. Do not block vents, especially on range ovens. If the air supply to a burner is reduced in any way, improper combustion may result and carbon monoxide may be produced.

5. If a gas flame appears yellow-tipped and seems to jump off the burner, it may not be getting the proper mixture of air and gas. If you're in doubt about how to make the proper adjustment, call in a serviceman.

6. In order to carry the by-products of combustion out of the house, gas-fired water heaters, furnaces, boilers, and incinerators must have an approved flue connection to a Class A chimney. Flues, pipes, and chimneys should be inspected at least once a year.

To test whether a flue is working properly, hold a lighted match under the skirt of the draft hood after the appliance has been working 15 minutes. If the flue is clear, the flame will be drawn toward the draft hood. A blocked flue should be cleaned promptly, because it causes trouble.

If you buy gas equipment. Look for the Blue Star seal issued by the American Gas Association which certifies that the equipment design complies with national safety standards.

Gasoline. Mechanics often use gasoline for cleaning oil and grease off metal parts and floors; but this is an extremely bad practice because of the great danger of explosion. Use kerosene instead: it is nonexplosive and does a better cleaning job.

Germicides. See *Disinfectants.*

Georgette. A crepe fabric made of silk. It should be dry-cleaned. Iron with a cool iron.

Gingham. A crisp fabric used mainly in clothing. It is made entirely of cotton or a cotton-synthetic blend. Launder like permanent-press fabrics.

Glass. Glass differs in quality, in the way it is formulated, in the way it is made, and in the way it is decorated; but for practical purposes, the glass used in tableware, kitchen utensils, vases, bottles, decorative objects, and windows falls into one of three categories:

1. Plain glass made from soda lime. It may be clear, milky, colored, pressed, cut, engraved, etc.; but in the final analysis, it is glass. Period.

2. Crystal. The most beautiful glass because it is so brilliant. It rings like a bell. It is also quite fragile. Its unique characteristics stem from the fact that the glass is formulated with lead oxide. Lead crystal is the same as crystal.

3. Heat-resistant glass. A workhorse kind of glass made from borosilicate and used for cooking utensils and outdoor light bulbs.

Heat-resistant glass is much less likely to break than other glass when placed in cold or hot water after it has been in protracted contact with heat or cold. But don't rely on it 100 percent. If shifted directly from a hot stove into a sink of cold water, watch out.

Glass of all kinds is usually easy to get sparkling clean by washing in detergent solution and rinsing in hot water. If the water is fairly soft, the glass will air-dry without much spotting; but after contact with hard water, it should be hand-dried with a lint-free towel.

If stains persist on glass, fill or soak the glass in a detergent solution to which several tablespoons of vinegar have been added. Or soak in a solution of household ammonia.

Don't expect painted designs on glass to last very long if you wash the glass in a dishwasher. Even hand-washing may eventually remove the designs.

Special glass cleaners that are made for mirrors, crystal, and lighting fixtures are no better than a detergent solution but are popular because they are easy to use. The ingredients, or their proportions, differ from brand to brand. You may find that one type will be more effective than another for the particular kind of dirt that settles in your locality. Some products are made especially for cleaning fine glass— crystal chandeliers or other lighting fixtures. Besides the sprays, there are individual squares of paper toweling treated with glass cleaner. You dampen the towels before using them, and follow by wiping the surface dry with a clean paper towel.

To repair a broken piece of glass, wash and dry it thoroughly. Then apply cellulose cement or epoxy glue to both broken edges and press them together until the glue sets. Do not use the piece for 24 hours.

Rough edges on glass can be smoothed with silicon-carbide cloth.

Glass-Ceramics. Glass-ceramics are man-made materials invented by the Corning Glass Works. They are called glass-ceramics because they are neither glass nor ceramic but are closely related to both.

There is no single glass-ceramic composition. Rather, there are families. The material most familiar in the home belongs to the Pyroceram family. The type of Pyroceram used in cooking utensils has the smoothness and impermeability of glass but is stronger, more heat-resistant, and virtually impervious to sudden changes in temperature. By contrast, another type of Pyroceram used in tableware is stronger than the cookware but not as strong thermally.

All glass-ceramics may be washed in a dishwasher. If broken, they can be glued with epoxy or cellulose cement; but the mend will not hold if the piece is given normal use.

Glass, Flat. There are many types of flat glass, and you may on occasion have uses for most of them.

Sheet glass is ordinary window glass. It comes in three grades and three weights. The grade with the fewest imperfections is AA; that with the most, B. Single-weight glass is used in openings up to 2 feet square; double weight in larger openings.

Plate glass is used in mirrors and in windows where you want an undistorted view.

Heavy sheet glass is about the same thickness as plate but with more imperfections. However, since it scratches less than plate, it is excellent for shelving.

Picture glass, used to cover pictures, is very thin.

Tinted glass is plate. It absorbs heat and reduces glare, but the tint distorts the view.

Insulating glass is a sandwich made with two layers of glass on either side of an air space.

Textured glass diffuses light, and is used mainly for privacy.

Tempered glass is plate glass that has been specially treated. It is four to five times stronger than regular plate, and if it breaks, it breaks safely into fragments like rock salt. It is commonly used in modern sliding glass doors. (Laminated and wired glass are sometimes used for this purpose, too.)

How to cut glass. Confine your work to sheet glass. First, clean the glass well and remove stickers. Place it on a flat table covered with several layers of newspaper. Apply a drop of oil to the little wheel at the end of your glass cutter.

Use a yardstick as your cutting guide and wet the side pressed against the glass so it will not slip. Hold the cutter straight up and down between your first and second fingers. Your thumb should be under the handle. Starting just inside the far edge of the glass, press down on the cutter and pull it in a continuous straight line across the glass and off the near edge.

Break the glass immediately—before the cut gets "cold"—by holding it on opposite sides of the cut and bending sharply downward. If one strip is too narrow to grip, place a slot in the cutter head over the edge of the narrow strip and bend downward. Tapping the underside of the glass with the cutter may make it easier to break.

Glassware. The main function of glassware is to provide something to drink out of. Glass dessert plates, asparagus dishes, candy dishes, pitchers, teacups, salad bowls, cocktail shakers, decanters, etc., are also glassware but of secondary importance.

Glasses are kept in the kitchen or dining room or both places for use at meals, in a bar cupboard, and in the bathrooms. Because they are especially fragile, stem glasses are usually reserved for company, and tumblers are used for everyday living. Whatever the design of the glasses, those made of crystal are also usually reserved for company.

Types of glasses in common use today are:

Water glasses—called goblets when made with stems. Usually hold 8 ounces.

Juice glasses—usually stemless, but combination juice and wine glasses are sold. 4 ounces.

Beverage or ice-tea glasses—stemless. 12 ounces.

Cocktail glasses—with or without stems. 2 to 4 ounces.

Highball glasses—stemless. 8 ounces.

Old-fashioned glasses—stemless. 4 ounces.

Double old-fashioned glasses—stemless. 8 ounces.

Wine glasses—with stems. 5 to 9 ounces.

Sherbet-champagne glasses—with stems. 6 ounces.

Liqueur glasses—very variable in design and size.

Brandy snifters—with stems. 10 ounces up.

Glasses are commonly sold in sets of four of one kind. Although every family is its own doctor when it comes to buying glassware, a young family might well aim to acquire a dozen everyday water glasses, four juice glasses, and eight of each of the following: goblets, beverage, cocktail, old-fashioned, highball, and liqueur.

How to store glasses. Glasses that are not used very often should be stored bottoms up. They will collect just as much dust as if stored bottoms down, but only the outside needs cleaning.

Unless your storage space is cramped, do not stack glasses. They are more likely to break and sometimes they become stuck. If they are stuck, try filling the top glass with cold water and run warm water over the bottom glass.

How to care for glassware. See *Glass.*

Glazing Compound. See *Putty.*

Gluing. Because of several fairly new adhesives, you can today stick together just about everything that breaks. All you need are these easy-to-use glues:

Cellulose cement. This old, familiar product is still the best for mending glass and ceramics if they are not exposed to heat or very much moisture. Apply it to both surfaces; let dry; then apply a second coat and clamp the broken pieces together for a couple of hours. The glue is so transparent that even if you fail to wipe off the excess, it is hardly noticeable.

Epoxy glue. Epoxy is the strongest of all glues. But since it is expensive and a bit tricky to use, you may want to save it for the tough jobs that thwart other glues. For instance, epoxy is ideal for mending glass and ceramic ovenware because it is unaffected by water or oven heat. Because of its incredible strength, it can be used to repair chair legs that are broken across the grain (normally wood broken in this way must be doweled or splinted). And it is unique in its ability to bond dense materials such as metal to metal, wood, stone, and ceramics; and marble to marble.

Epoxy generally comes in two tubes. You squeeze equal amounts from each tube, mix together on a scrap of aluminum foil, apply to the broken surfaces, and press together for several hours. The makers say clamping is unnecessary, but it makes for a neater joint.

Fabric-mending adhesive. This adhesive is used for repairing and patching all fabrics from sheer silk to heavy canvas. Apply a thin coat to one surface and immediately smooth the other surface down on top. After 8 hours, when the glue is dry, it is resistant to both water and heat.

Plastic-mending adhesive. One of the newer glues, plastic-mending adhesive fills an old need. It fixes vinyl, phenolic, acrylic, and styrene plastics among others; fails only on polyethylene (unless specially treated), polypropylene, and nylon. It can also be used on china, wood, and leather. The glue is waterproof but deforms slightly under heat (as do many plastics). To use it, just apply to both broken surfaces and clamp them together overnight.

Plastic metal. This is a metallic (steel or aluminum) paste which is used primarily to seal holes in cooking utensils, pipes, water tanks, and auto bodies. But it is also useful for cementing metal to metal or to other materials. In either case, clean and roughen the surfaces to be mended and apply a coat of the thick plastic to one. Then, if the plastic is used as a filler, mold it to shape as much as possible; if used as an adhesive, clamp together the pieces under repair. Allow to dry for 2 hours (or longer if the temperature is below 70 degrees). The hardened plastic can be sanded or filed smooth.

Resorcinol glue. This strong, waterproof glue, the best for outdoor use on wood, comes in two parts. The powder is mixed into the liquid in the proportions specified. The glue is then applied to both surfaces and allowed to harden, under clamps, for 24 hours. It leaves a reddish stain.

Rubber cement. If a mended material is subject to repeated flexing, rubber cement should be used. It is excellent for paper, rubber, leather, cork, etc. Usually the ordinary desk-type cement is adequate, but stronger types are available (for example, a thick black mixture is used to stick pieces of rubber together and to fill small holes in rubber articles). For the best bond, apply rubber cement to both surfaces being glued; let dry; then apply a second coat to one surface and immediately press the surfaces together.

Silicone rubber adhesive. This is a thick, rubbery, waterproof glue with a vinegary odor. It is used to bond such things as glass, ceramics, metal, brick, stone, marble, and concrete. It is also used for setting ceramic tiles and hanging mirrors on walls. One of its advantages is that the surfaces to be glued do not have to fit together neatly; the adhesive can be used to span gaps of ¼ inch or more. Just apply it to one of the surfaces and press the second to it. Do not clamp too tightly.

The most familiar silicone adhesive is sold mainly for caulking cracks around the rims of bathtubs. It is white or more or less transparent. Miracle Adhesive is a brand name for a gray or black glue which is widely used in construction work.

White wood glue. There are no true all-purpose adhesives, but this polyvinyl resin glue which dries clear comes fairly close. You can use it on wood, paper, cloth, leather, and other porous materials. Application is very easy. Just spread the glue on one surface and clamp the broken pieces together.

How to glue. Although different glues are handled in different ways, several basic rules cover the use of all:

1. Make sure that the surfaces to be glued are dry and clean. Scrape off old glue.

2. Don't apply glue in thick coats. Thin coats do at least as well, and usually better.

3. Clamp the glued pieces together until the glue has dried completely. Use steel or wood C clamps if possible. Otherwise, bind round pieces together with thread or string; hold irregular pieces together with cellophane or adhesive tape; weight down large flat pieces; or use tourniquets (see *Furniture, Wood*).

4. Wipe off excess glue immediately. Place wax paper between the clamps and the piece being mended; it will prevent them from sticking together.

5. Give the glue plenty of time to dry. The larger the surface that is glued or the deeper the hole, the longer the drying time.

6. If gluing a patch over a hole or tear, round the corners of the patch. They will not come loose as easily as square corners.

7. When mending thin pieces of plastic or wood, reinforce the break with a glued-on splint of the same material.

Grasscloth. A fabric much like burlap made out of vegetable fibers. Used almost entirely as a wall covering, it generally comes laminated to a paper backing and is pasted to walls like wallpaper. Cleaning is next to impossible, though you can try a sponge barely dampened in soapy water or cleaning fluid. The material can be painted.

Grass Rugs. Grass rugs are made in various sizes and weaves out of several different grasses. They are remarkably durable, attractive, and can be used indoors and out. They are usually laid directly on the floor, but thinner rugs are sometimes cushioned with several layers of newspaper.

Vacuum a grass rug frequently to remove dirt and grit from the interstices (use suction only); and lift, and clean the floor underneath occasionally. When dirty, wash the rug with heavy-duty detergent solution, rinse well, and dry in the sun (if possible) as rapidly as possible.

If fibers are broken, they can be glued together with white wood glue.

To skid-proof a grass rug, brush a coat of neoprene rubber on the back. To change the color of a rug, apply oil stain of the type used on furniture and houses.

Griddles. Flat-surfaced, smooth, and usually rectangular, griddles can be used for grilling, frying, and pan-broiling. Many of them have nonstick surfaces to make cooking and cleaning easier.

The simplest griddles are made of heavy aluminum or cast iron. Though they are much easier to handle than iron, aluminum griddles have an unfortunate tendency to warp. On the other hand, when you place a large cast-iron griddle across two burners, there is danger that the high heat it stores up may damage the porcelain range surface between the burners.

Many ranges come with griddles. These are built into the tops of gas ranges and cooktops, and usually convert to an extra burner. On electric ranges, the griddle is sometimes built in but is usually a separate utensil which, in some cases, plugs into the convenience outlet on the range back-splash.

Portable electric griddles are more pre-dictable than others because they are thermostatically controlled. But there is no need for this appliance if you have a waffle iron that converts to a grill.

Aluminum griddles can be washed in the dishwasher if small enough to fit into the tub. Cast-iron griddles, however, must never go into a dishwasher because this will destroy the protective grease coating and bring on rust. In fact, you shouldn't use soap or detergent unless the griddle is so soiled that you can't get it clean in any other way.

Grilles. Grilles are, in effect, large, coarse screens which are designed to let some-thing through (such as air, heat, or light) while keeping something out (such as birds, rodents, or vision). Some are orna-mental.

Grilles are most commonly made of steel or aluminum but are also made of wood, plywood, hardboard, plastics—even con-crete. Whatever their construction, they are usually serious dirt catchers and very hard to clean. Smart practice calls for fre-quent vacuuming with a brush. When the grille finally gets really dirty—perhaps with grease—try to remove it from its perma-nent position and dunk it in a sink or bathtub full of strong detergent or ammonia solution. If this is impossible, then you are in for the tedious job of scrubbing it inch by inch with a brush. After washing, rinse well—preferably with a hose—and dry as well as possible—preferably outdoors in the sun on a windy day.

In selecting a grille through which air is supposed to pass in fairly large volume, remember that the cross-members restrict air passage; therefore you may need a very large grille in order to provide a free open-ing of adequate size.

Grills, Electric. See *Waffle Irons.*

Grinding Wheels. See *Tools, Workshop.*

Grosgrain (*grow*-grain). A fine, heavy fabric with definite rounded ribs which is used in ribbons, trimmings, and clothing. It is made of silk or a combination of rayon and cotton, and should be dry-cleaned.

Grospoint (*grow*-point). An embroidery stitch. See *Needlepoint.*

Gutters. Many speculative builders do not put gutters on their houses simply because they would add to the cost. They are right—if you want to talk in pennies. Many modern architects argue against gutters because they feel they often detract from the lines of the house. To a certain extent, this is true. Many people feel that gutters are a headache, especially if the house is overhung by trees, because they must be cleaned out a couple of times during the year. This, also, is true.

On the other side of the coin, it must be pointed out that gutters are extremely use-ful for several reasons: (1) They carry water falling on the roof into leaders (downspouts) which should carry it away from the foundations of the house. This helps to prevent leaks in basement and crawl spaces. (2) If an entrance is under an eave, gutters keep you from getting deluged when you walk in and out of the house during a storm. (3) Gutters protect the foundation planting which is otherwise beaten down by water pouring off the eaves. (4) Finally, gutters carry off quan-tities of water which would otherwise be driven against the windows and sides of the house during a windy storm.

How to hang gutters. Gutters are made of copper, aluminum (painted or un-painted), galvanized steel (painted or un-painted), vinyl, and wood. Copper gutters are best but so expensive they are rarely installed anymore; furthermore, installa-tion should be made by a sheet-metal worker, because the joints are soldered. Vinyl is excellent also, but the joints leak even when made by a professional. Wood is attractive and durable if you keep after it; but the long lengths are heavy, hard to handle, and hard to join. Galvanized steel is strong and inexpensive but short-lived.

This leaves aluminum gutters—and al-though they are far from perfect, they are most desirable for do-it-yourself installa-tion. Use the type that comes from the factory with a durable paint finish: they look better and will last longer, especially in corrosive atmospheres.

Aluminum gutter troughs and leader pipes come in 10-foot lengths. For installation you also need end caps for each complete gutter; slip-joint connectors to join gutter troughs to one another and to other sections of the gutter; gutter outlets measuring 12 inches in length; short corner troughs for inside and outside corners; hangers to support the gutter; leader elbows to connect the gutter to the leaders; and leader straps to support the leaders.

Gutter hangers are spaced 30 inches apart. Three styles are used for aluminum gutters. One is a T-bar hanger which is bolted to the front and back of the gutter and then nailed to the roof. Another is a sort of L-shaped hanger which is screwed to the fascia. The last is a metal tube which is placed inside the gutter and through which a spike is driven into the fascia. The last two are used when the fascia is set back from the edge of the eaves only an inch or two. Of the two, the L hanger is the better because it is much stronger. T-bar hangers are used otherwise.

Before installing gutters, it is highly advisable to install aluminum drip edges along the eaves in order to ensure that water drips straight into the gutters instead of curling back up under the eaves and dripping down behind the gutters. On most roofs, it is generally a simple matter to slip the wide flange of the drip edge up between the roofing and the sheathing. Nail down each strip at the ends.

Although aluminum gutters weigh little, their length makes them awkward to handle—especially if you are working on a ladder. You should therefore have someone help you by supporting one end while you are working at the other. All your helper needs is a long pole or board with some sort of V-shaped cradle at the upper end.

Gutters should be sloped 1/16 inch per foot. If a gutter is under 35 feet long, you need only one leader. This can be installed at either end or in the middle—just so long as the gutter slopes toward it. If a gutter is over 35 feet, you need two leaders—

usually at the two ends, which means that the gutter is sloped from the middle toward each end.

If using T-bar hangers, drill holes in the front and back of each length of gutter near the top, and bolt the crossbar of the T in place. The flexible strap is then bent more or less upright and nailed to the roof deck. If the roof is covered with asphalt shingles, lift the shingle butts carefully and nail the strap underneath. On other roofs, nail the strap on top of the roofing and cover the nails with asphalt roofing cement to prevent leaks.

L-shaped hangers are installed in two pieces. First the hanger bracket is nailed to the fascia. Then the hanger strap is inserted under the front lip of the gutter and hooked to the bracket. All the straps for each length of gutter should be inserted in the gutter before the gutter is hung.

To use spike hangers, drill holes in the front and back of the gutter near the top. Then insert the ferrule across the gutter and drive the spike through the holes and ferrule into the fascia.

In their literature, aluminum gutter manufacturers and retailers imply that it is as easy to slip a length of gutter into a slip-joint connector as it is to put a letter in an envelope. Actually, this is one of the most fiendish little jobs ever devised. For some reason, the gutters and connectors always just miss fitting together, so you wind up pushing and pulling and bending and twisting and wedging. For this reason, if the gutter is not too long and if you have a helper, it is a good idea to assemble the entire gutter on the ground. If this is impossible, you should at least install the connector to one length of gutter trough before hanging the gutter. Then you must connect only the other length of gutter trough when you are on the ladder.

After all sections of a gutter are joined together and hung, seal the joints at each connector with silicone caulking compound.

On houses that have very little roof overhang, the leaders can be connected directly to the gutter outlets; but generally it is necessary to insert 45-degree elbows between gutters and leaders. The first elbow, which points toward the house, slips up over the drop pipe in the gutter outlet. The second elbow, which is installed in reverse position, slips over the end of the first elbow. The straight leader pipe then slips up over the end of the second elbow. And at the ground, another elbow, pointing away from the house, slips over the end of the straight pipe. Unlike gutter joints, joints in the leader line are easily made, strong, and do not need sealing.

The leader line is secured to the house wall with aluminum straps. These are bent around the straight leader pipe at the top and bottom and nailed to the wall. On leaders less than about 15 feet in length, you need only two straps; on longer leaders, three.

How to carry water away from the foundation walls. Although the elbow at the bottom of a leader directs water away from the house, it doesn't carry it far enough. You can improve matters by placing on the ground under the pipe a slab of concrete shaped like a shallow trough or a trough made of wood. You can also connect to the pipe a large flexible hose that rolls out away from the house when full of water and rolls back up to the leader when dry.

A better solution is to omit the bottom elbow and connect the leader directly into a 4-inch plastic drain that carries the roof water underground into the footing drains (see *Basements*) or dry wells located some distance from the house (see *Dry Wells*). To keep leaves and debris out of the underground drain, fill the opening between the top of the drain and the leader with folded wire mesh or concrete.

How to maintain gutters. To keep leaves from clogging the gutter outlets and leaders, install wire strainers made for the purpose in each outlet. These should be cleaned every fall and spring.

If there are large trees near the house, a better way to prevent clogging of gutters is to cover them from end to end with gutter guards made of aluminum or vinyl mesh. These are 6 inches wide and come in rolls up to about 25 feet long. Theoretically,

they should stay in place if the upper edge is slipped under the shingles; but you may also have to tie them along the front edges to the gutter hangers. Don't try to install them permanently because they must be removed now and then to clean out the roofing granules, dirt, twigs, and small debris that filter through them.

Check all metal gutters annually to make sure they are hanging properly. If bent, they can usually be straightened with your hands, a mallet, and a pair of pliers to adjust the hangers. But if badly twisted, they may have to be taken down and straightened on the ground.

To keep galvanized steel gutters from rusting and wood gutters from splitting and decaying, coat the troughs every couple of years with asphalt roofing cement or asphalt roof coating.

To keep ice from freezing in gutters and backing up under the roofing and then dripping down through the ceilings and walls below, arrange electric heating cable in a zigzag pattern along the eaves. Special kits are made for the purpose. For a roof 30 feet long, you need a 100-foot cable. The cable is arranged in the manner illustrated. Plug it in to an interior or a weatherproof exterior outlet. For best results, it is also laid in the bottom of the

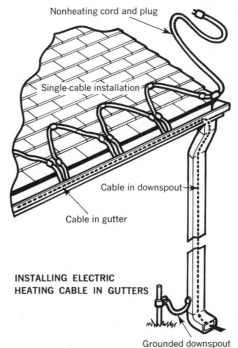

Nonheating cord and plug

Single-cable installation

Cable in downspout

Cable in gutter

INSTALLING ELECTRIC HEATING CABLE IN GUTTERS

Grounded downspout

gutter and run down through the leader. The gentle heat keeps the gutter and leader free and cuts open channels in the ice and snow on the roof so that, when melted, the water can flow off freely.

How to repair gutters and leaders. Holes in gutters. If holes are small, seal them with a dab of silicone caulking compound or with thick asphalt roofing cement. For a large hole, brush the trough clean and smear a thin layer of roofing cement in the bottom and to the sides. Smooth heavy-duty aluminum foil into this and cover it with a second layer of cement.

Holes in leaders. Try plugging small holes with plastic metal or silicone caulking. If the hole is large, however, you should replace that section of leader with a new section of the same metal. If for some reason it is necessary to use a different metal, coat the inside of the pipe at the upper end and the outside of the pipe at the lower end with asphalt roofing cement. This will insulate the metals and help to prevent rapid corrosion.

Hangers broken. Replace them. It is possible, however, to repair a T-hanger if the strap tears loose from the crossbar by making a hook in the end of the strap. Then loop a piece of strong wire through the hook and around the crossbar.

Hammers. See *Tools, Workshop—Claw hammer.*

Hardboard. A thin, dense, very hard building panel made of compressed wood fibers. It is used for numerous construction purposes, from lining the bottoms of bureau drawers to building walls. But in all cases, it is used and finished in the same way. See *Walls, Hardboard.*

Harris Tweed. Trademark for a handsome, rather rough wool fabric made in the Scottish Outer Hebrides and used in clothing. It should be dry-cleaned.

Heat Bulbs. In addition to being useful in loosening up tight muscles, infrared heat bulbs can be used to keep food warm (see *Food Warmers*), bake out wet motors, supply a spot of warmth in a basement work area, thaw out a frozen pipe, etc. The bulbs are rated at 250 watts. Screw them into a standard lamp socket.

Heaters, Portable.

Electric heaters. The simplest and best portable heaters are electric. They range from small bowl-shaped units that heat entirely by radiation to large fan-forced radiant heaters with automatic thermostats. The majority of heaters operate at 120 volts, and can be plugged into any outlet; however, if you operate a 1650-watt heater on a 15-amp circuit that is serving other appliances or lights, it will almost surely cause an overload. Very large portable heaters rated at up to about 5600 watts operate only at 240 volts.

A desirable safety feature found on many modern heaters is a tip-over switch which automatically turns the heater off if it is overturned. Some heaters also have a heat-limit switch which turns off the heater if the airflow is blocked.

Electric steam heaters work more slowly than the radiant units but retain their heat a little longer. Despite claims, they are not more efficient; on the contrary, they are somewhat less.

Heating elements on modern heaters should be replaced by a serviceman. But the cone in a bowl heater simply screws in and out like a light bulb. On some older heaters, if the coiled-wire heating element breaks near the terminals, it is generally a fairly simple matter to stretch the wire and reconnect it.

The efficiency of an electric heater depends to some extent on how clean the reflecting surface is. When the heater is not in use, therefore, it is a good idea to keep it in its carton or draped with plastic film to keep off dust. If dust does settle and stick to the surface, try dislodging it with a paintbrush or the blower end of your vacuum cleaner. If the surface is badly clogged and smudged, unscrew the grille and clean the reflector with a cloth dipped in detergent solution. Take care not to damage or dislodge the heating element.

Kerosene heaters. These put out a lot of heat but should be used only in a well-ventilated area, such as a garage, because they produce carbon monoxide. They are also a fire hazard.

Heating Systems. You may never do anything about your heating system except to turn it on in the fall and off in the spring, but in order to get full value out of it at reasonable cost, you should understand a little about how it works.

Fuel. This is the No. 1 heating concern of most home owners because it's what makes heating expensive. Today the fuels in widest use are gas, oil, and electricity. Coal has just about disappeared from homes and LP gas has hardly gotten a start except in rural areas because it is generally too costly.

Despite the grossly exaggerated claims made by the distributors of the three leading fuels, there is actually little to choose between them when it comes to dependability, safety, and cleanliness. Consequently, the only important question you have to settle when choosing a fuel is what it costs. The answer is different in every part of the country. In some areas, gas costs less; in others, oil; in others, electricity. True, electricity usually is the most expensive; but in a house that is under construction, you can compensate for this by putting in enough extra insulation to reduce power consumption to a point where it is quite competitive with the other fuels.

If you are building a new house or putting a new heating system in an old house, the only way to determine which fuel should cost least is to have representatives of the three industries calculate how much fuel you will use in an average year and then multiply the answer by the price you will pay for the fuel.

Forced warm-air heating systems. Warm-air heat, as it is commonly called, is the most popular system currently in use. This is mainly because it is inexpensive to install. In addition, the system gives fast heat and allows you to cool, clean, and humidify the air in the house. The principal disadvantage of the system is its occasional noisiness. And if the system is poorly designed and installed in the first place, it is difficult to correct.

Forced warm-air heating systems burning gas, oil, or electricity can be installed in houses of any size. The center of the system is a furnace that discharges heated air from the top, bottom, or one end. Whatever the furnace design, if you have occasion to buy a new one or replace an old one, you should make certain that it is guaranteed for at least 10 years. That is your best assurance that it is well designed and constructed.

When heated air leaves the furnace, it is circulated through the house by supply ducts installed under the floors and in the walls. The ducts are laid out in several ways depending on how the house is built. In colder climates, where a warm house in winter is more important than a cool house in summer, the supply registers are in the floor, baseboards, or just above the baseboards in exterior walls. Where possible, installation is made under windows, and the registers are designed to spread a blanket of warm air over the glass and the surrounding wall. Location of the registers in exterior walls also helps to warm the floor—a very important job in houses built on a concrete slab or over a crawl space.

In warm climates, where cooling in summer is more important than heating in winter, the supply registers are installed high in the walls and in the ceilings.

After the heated air cools down, it flows back to the furnace through return registers and ducts. At the furnace, it is again heated and filtered and it may also be humidified; then, once again, it enters the house.

The heating system is controlled by a thermostat. Usually, when the thermostat calls for heat, the burner in the furnace and the large blower that circulates the air turn on together, then, when the temperature in the house has risen to the selected point, they turn off together. However, heating experts now feel that continuous air circulation is desirable because it maintains more even conditions in the house at all times. Consequently, the usual practice in new forced warm-air systems is to set the blower to operate more or less continuously, independent of the thermostat. Old systems usually can easily be adjusted in the same way.

Several types of thermostat are used in

homes. All are efficient, but the clock-controlled type is recommended if you are in the habit of lowering temperatures at night. It automatically turns on the heat before you get up in the morning and turns it off at your usual bedtime. Another special control incorporates an outdoor as well as an indoor thermostat. The former measures outdoor temperature changes and raises or lowers the indoor temperature before the changes are felt inside.

Most houses have only one thermostat; but it is often smart—especially in sprawling houses—to install two or more, each controlling the heat within a separate zone. This permits you to keep one part of the house warmer than another, or you can reduce the heat input in rooms with a sunny southern exposure.

Thermostats should be located on an inside wall of a room responsive to outdoor temperature changes. The living or dining rooms are usually the best; bedrooms, bathrooms, and kitchens are not recommended except when they are individually or zone-controlled. A thermostat should never be placed on an outside wall; near a window or outside door; in closets or stairwells to unheated attics or basements; near a radiator or register, fireplace, TV set, or lamp; in the path of the sun's rays; or in a corner where there is no air circulation.

Operating a forced warm-air heating system. There is nothing very mysterious about operating this or any other heating system: you just set the thermostat and let it take over. Some people leave the thermostat at the same setting all the time. But studies have proved that if you lower the thermostat about 10 degrees between 10 P.M. and 7 A.M., you will reduce fuel consumption substantially—perhaps as much as 10 percent.

The filters must be checked and cleaned or replaced about once a month during the heating season. If they become clogged with dirt, the furnace must operate for longer periods to force enough air through the filters into the house. Some filters are cleaned by washing in detergent solution; others are replaced completely.

Take a look at the burner flame at least once a month. If you use gas, a yellow tip on the flame indicates the burner needs adjustment. If you use oil, burner adjustment is called for if the flame is too smoky, stringy, or noisy. In both cases, the adjustment should be made by a serviceman.

Ideally you should have the furnace serviced by a professional sometime during the summer or early fall. This is especially important with an oil burner, which has more moving parts than a gas burner. If you do your own servicing, the following steps should be taken: (1) Turn off the furnace and add about six drops of SAE No. 30 oil to the cups or tubes on the blower and motor. (2) Check the belt driving the blower for excessive wear and proper adjustment. Replace it if it is cracked or frayed. To check the adjustment, press down on the belt midway between the pulleys. It should have between ¾- and 1-inch deflection. If it bends more or less than this, adjust it by means of the bolt under the blower motor. (3) Clean the blower blades and compartment. (4) Remove and clean the registers and the ducts behind them with a vacuum. This should be done two or three times a year.

Gravity warm-air heating systems. Most of these systems have been replaced by forced warm-air systems, but they are still encountered in some old houses. The furnace is usually located in the center of the basement. Heated air rises naturally through large ducts which connect to registers in the floor or baseboards near the middle of the house. Cool air returns through registers and ducts near the outside walls or windows.

In compact houses, gravity systems are quite efficient. But they are also quite dirty. This is especially true of floor furnaces, which are installed in vacation homes.

Gas-fired wall heaters. These are sometimes used to heat very small homes, usually in mild climates. They are tall, slim furnaces that are installed on the first floor in the middle of the house. Heated air flows from the top of the furnace into the surrounding rooms through wall grilles or openings. Ducts are used to carry the air to more distant rooms.

Some wall heaters have blowers. Less efficient units heat by gravity alone.

Forced hot-water systems. This so-called wet system is particularly popular in the Northeast. It is easier to install properly than a warm-air system, takes up less space, and is very fast and reliable. In addition, the boiler can be equipped with an indirect water heater to heat the water used for bathing, dishwashing, and laundering. On the other hand, the system cannot be used for cooling, filtering, or dehumidifying the air in the house; it costs more to install; and it must be drained if you close up the house in winter.

Forced hot-water systems are built around a boiler that burns gas, oil, or electricity. The best boilers, made of cast iron, are guaranteed to last many years. Steel boilers are usually short-lived.

Water heated in the boiler is circulated to the radiators throughout the house by a small pump, which in old houses normally operates only when the thermostat calls for heat. In new houses, however, the pump is sometimes set for continuous operation to keep the radiators warm at all times. An expansion tank near the boiler allows the water to expand and contract as the temperature changes and protects the system against abnormal pressures. If pressure does become too high, a relief valve opens automatically.

In some forced hot-water systems, only one pipeline is used to supply the hot water and return the cooled water. This is a compact, economical arrangement especially adapted to small houses. For large houses, separate supply and return lines are recommended. In the newest type of system, called the "series loop," a single pipe runs from one heating outlet to the next—all around the house until it returns to the boiler. This is easy and inexpensive to install in small new houses as well as in old houses; but you cannot shut off individual radiators as in the other systems.

Radiators used with hot-water heating systems today are much smaller and slimmer than old-fashioned types. They may be freestanding or recessed in the wall. But in new houses, the usual practice is to install long, low baseboard units because they are more attractive, blanket the windows and walls with warm air, produce uniform room temperatures, keep the floor warm, and do not produce hot spots in the rooms.

An alternative way to heat a home with hot water is to circulate the water through long coils of pipe buried in the floors, ceilings, or walls. This is called radiant heating. The system was briefly popular a number of years ago because it was completely concealed and produced very even warmth. But it also created problems; and if the coils of pipe started to leak, it was a disaster.

Thermostats used in forced hot-water systems are identical to those used in warm-air systems and installed in the same way.

Operating a forced hot-water heating system. Lower the thermostat at night to reduce fuel consumption.

Check the burner flame monthly to make sure it is properly adjusted (see above).

Oil the circulating pump according to the maker's directions.

In the fall, vent all radiators to get rid of trapped air that prevents even heating.

Have an oil burner serviced annually by a professional. He should also check and drain the boiler as necessary. A gas burner generally needs to be serviced only every two or three years.

Gravity hot-water heating systems. Like gravity warm-air systems, these have been pretty well superseded by forced hot-water systems. They can be adapted only to small houses.

The boiler must be located in the basement, and the waterlines to the radiators are pitched upward. As the water is heated, it rises and circulates to the radiators. When it cools, it returns to the boiler through a separate pipeline. The drawback of this system is that when the thermostat calls for heat, there is a time lag until the water in the boiler is hot enough to start circulating.

Steam heating systems. These are also rare today although they are found in many old houses. The water in the boiler is heated to form steam, which then rises and circulates naturally to the radiators. There it gives off its heat, condenses, and the water returns to the boiler.

Radiators used with a steam system are upright, freestanding, or recessed units. Baseboard radiators are not recommended. The radiators are vented continuously. The system is quite fast but not the equal of a forced hot-water system. The heat is rather uneven; and the radiators become dangerously hot to touch.

Electric heating systems. Electric heating has become amazingly popular in the past few years because it is clean and efficient; and if you heat each room individually—as most home owners do—you don't have to heat the entire house to the same temperature. Some rooms can be hot; some cool; and some that are empty can be cut off entirely. Furthermore, since the room heaters have no moving parts, they require no service.

Despite these advantages, most people have a nagging doubt about electric heat: What does it cost to operate? The answer is that if your utility has an electric heating rate of under 1½ cents a kilowatt-hour and if your house is heavily insulated (see *Insulation*), the cost of the current used is approximately the same as the cost of gas or oil.

Room heaters of three basic types are used. Most popular are baseboard heaters and long, recessed floor heaters, both of which are usually installed along exterior walls under windows.

In small rooms, where there is not enough wall space for baseboard units, heaters shaped like a dress box are recessed in a wall or ceiling.

The third type of heater, which is invisible, is a large grid of wires concealed in the ceiling.

When room heaters of any type are installed in a house, each room and hall has its own thermostat.

Central electric heating systems are also available. Some are exactly like a forced hot-water heating system burning gas or oil; others are exactly like a forced warm-air system. There are also systems in which a circulator carries air or water to the rooms where it is heated by small heaters under control of a room thermostat.

Yet another type of central system is built around a heat pump that heats the air in winter and then reverses itself and cools the air in summer. The air is delivered to the rooms throughout the house via ducts. See *Air Conditioners, Central—Heat pumps.*

Operating an electric heating system. Central systems are operated like comparable gas- and oil-fired systems. The only difference is that since the "burner" is nothing more than an immobile strip of metal that glows red hot when current is passed through it, this particular part of the heating system does not require regular servicing.

To operate individual room heaters, all you have to do is adjust the thermostat up or down. Turning the thermostat down at night saves money.

How to heat an addition. If you decide to turn your attic into a bedroom or to make a completely new addition on the house, one of the first questions that should occur to you is: How am I going to heat it?

It is very possible that the answer will not be as simple as you might think. The reason is that when a person builds a house, he rarely puts in a larger furnace or boiler than is necessary. And since the furnace or boiler cannot be enlarged, you can't expect it to heat the addition without reducing comfort in the rest of the house. The only way to make sure of this, however, is to ask a heating contractor to inspect your heating system and plans for the addition. If he finds that the furnace or boiler is large enough to heat the addition, then all he has to do is to figure out a way to get the necessary new ducts or pipes into the addition. This may not be easy.

If you cannot expand an existing heating system, you have to install in the addition a separate heating system. Most people today choose one of the small, thermostatically controlled, built-in electric heaters of the type described above. This may require an increase in the size of the electrical service and the installation of extra-thick insulation in the addition; but the heaters themselves and the wiring are easy to put in. Furthermore, you do not require a chimney or flue as you do with most other kinds of small room heaters.

If something goes wrong with your heating system. Don't try to repair a heating system yourself. But before calling a serviceman, take the following steps:

Check whether the electrical fuse protecting the line serving the furnace has blown.

Are the filters in a forced warm-air system clogged? Is the belt that drives the blower broken or slipping?

If the circulating pump on a forced hot-water system has stopped, does it need oil? Put a few drops in the lubricating cups.

Is there water in the glass gauge on a steam boiler? If not, the water level may have dropped so low that the burner has shut off. Fill with water until the gauge is half full.

Is there oil in the tank?

If you burn oil, the burner may not be running because there was an overload on the electrical circuit which activated the overload switch. To restart the burner, just push the red button on the control box. You may not have any further trouble.

If the gas pilot light has gone out, relight it in accordance with directions on the furnace.

If your electric power fails. All modern heating systems are run by electricity; so if the power fails, the heat goes off. If you have electric heat or an oil burner, there is nothing you can do to protect yourself. But if you have a gas-fired forced warm-air system, you may be able to get some heat by switching the furnace to manual control. Ask your serviceman to show you how to do this next time he is in your house.

Heat Pumps. These are year-round electric air conditioners that cool in summer and heat in winter. Both central and room units are used. See *Air Conditioners, Central—Heat pumps.*

Hemp. Hemp is a tough vegetable fiber used in making rope and woven squares that are sewn together into rugs. The squares have a carpet-like look and are very durable.

Clean and repair like straw (which see). If a square is damaged, cut it from the rug and sew in a new one with strong linen thread or twine.

Hi-Fi Systems. High-fidelity systems are designed to reproduce music and speech with the greatest possible realism and faithfulness to the original performance. Most systems are custom-designed for the user; accordingly, they vary considerably in their components and performance. Every system, however, must include either a record player or tuner (radio receiver) or tape recorder or all three; a preamplifier, power amplifier, and speaker (or speakers: modern systems have two—or more—speakers for stereo sound reproduction). The usual practice is to install the record player, tuner, preamplifier, and amplifier together; the speakers may be installed at the same location or elsewhere in the room (or even in another room).

Although they can be and often are installed in a freestanding cabinet or piece of furniture, hi-fi components are very easily built into walls, bookcases, or "music walls" either in new or old houses. In every case, you must provide adequate ventilation in the enclosure for the tuner, preamplifier, and amplifier. Allow space between the units and surrounding walls, and provide breathing holes in the enclosure.

You can assemble your own speakers for a high-fidelity system or buy ones that are ready for use. If you are building or remodeling, you can achieve excellent results by building a speaker—or a whole series of speakers—into the wall. This saves money and produces hard-to-equal performance. In any case, the best location for a single speaker is in a corner, somewhat raised off the floor.

For how to care for a hi-fi system, see *Record Players.*

Hinges. There are many types of hinge. The following are those you are most likely to use:

Butt hinge. This is the most common type of hinge, appearing on almost all hinged doors. It is semi-concealed—when a door is closed, you can see only the pinned joint.

The largest butt hinges have a removable pin and are used on large or heavy doors so you can take out the doors without unscrewing the hinge leaves. The hinges are as wide as they are high when open.

Smaller butt hinges have a fixed pin. They are generally used on smaller and lighter doors. Some are square; others are narrower than high when open.

Both butt hinges are mortised—set into the wood so that the face of the hinge is level with the wood. The hinges should be large enough so that one of the leaves will extend almost all the way across the edge of the door on which they are mounted. (For example, on interior doors, which are 1 3/8 inches thick, it is customary to use a 3½-inch hinge. This is mortised into the edge of the door 1 1/8 inches.)

A nonmortised butt hinge has three flat fingers in place of each leaf. When the door is closed, the fingers on the two sides interlock. This kind of hinge is used on doors up to 1 3/8 inches thick.

Butt hinges are made of many metals. You should use noncorrosive hinges outdoors, and in damp locations indoors also. Don't be fooled by the finish. Those beautiful brass hinges are probably made of steel covered with a brass wash which will wear off in no time at all.

T hinge. This is a T-shaped hinge with a tapering upright and a rectangular crossbar like that on a butt hinge. The hinge is, of course, installed sideways—not up and down. The rectangular leaf is mortised into or screwed directly to the doorjamb; the tapering leaf is screwed to the face of the door. The hinge is used when the door is not of sufficient thickness to hold a butt hinge screwed into the edge. It is a type commonly used on gates.

T hinges are available in widths from 3 to 12 inches. All are made of galvanized or plated steel.

Strap hinge. This has two tapering leaves of galvanized or plated steel. Widths range from 3 to 10 inches. The hinge is used when the exposed face of the jamb is flush with the door and when the jamb does not have sufficient thickness to hold a T hinge—as on wood bulkheads.

H-L hinge is largely an ornamental hinge used on cabinets. Both leaves are screwed to the exposed surface of the jamb and door.

Loose-pin cabinet hinge is excellent for use on plywood and particle-board doors, because the door leaf screws into the edge and back of the door to hold it securely. The leaf is not visible on the front of the door.

For how to install hinges, see *Doors.*

If a hinge squeaks, spray it with silicone lubricant. If it is stiff, scrape the paint or rust from the joints at the pin.

Hollow-Wall Screw Anchors. See *Wall Anchors.*

Hollow Ware. Silver (or other metal) pieces that are scooped out to some extent are called hollow ware. Bowls, vegetable dishes, pitchers, sugar bowls, creamers, teapots, and coffeepots are typical pieces. Candlesticks are also hollow ware.

For how to clean hollow ware, see entry for appropriate metal. Do not soak weighted pieces, such as candlesticks, in water. Hollow ware that is damaged in any way should be repaired by a jeweler. Silver-plated pieces can be replated by a silversmith.

Homespun. A loosely woven, rather heavy fabric with a plain, coarse, usually crude weave. Any fiber can be used, but cotton and wool are most common. The way in which the material is cleaned depends on the fiber.

Hopsacking. A coarsely woven, rather bulky fabric made usually of cotton or rayon. It is used in clothing and draperies. Machine-wash in warm water and dry at low heat.

Horn. Animal horn is sometimes used in decorative objects and to make handles. Wash it as necessary with detergent solution, but avoid scrubbing it with abrasives or steel wool. If horn is broken, the pieces can be stuck together with cellulose cement or epoxy glue.

Hornets. See *Pest Control—Bees, hornets, wasps.*

Hotplates. One- and two-element electric hotplates are on the market. The best have fully enclosed heating elements like those on electric ranges. The cheapest use coiled-wire elements.

If spillovers occur, the elements will burn off the residue in short order. You can wipe enclosed elements with a damp cloth, but don't pick at coiled elements.

Housecleaning. Housecleaning falls into four categories: (1) tidying or picking up; (2) routine cleaning; (3) thorough cleaning; (4) special cleaning.

Tidying up is the process of going through all rooms that were occupied or used in the preceding 24 hours and making things neat. It involves emptying ash trays, straightening pictures, swishing out washbasins, etc.

Routine cleaning involves honest-to-goodness cleaning work such as sweeping, mopping, vacuuming, dusting, etc. Some jobs are done two or three times a day, for example, wiping up kitchen counters. Others are done daily, for example, sweeping the kitchen floor. And others are done only once a month, for example, dusting walls and ceilings.

Thorough cleaning is, for most women, a twice-a-year operation when they go through the entire house and tear it apart and put it back together again. Some home economists question how exhaustively modern homemakers need to thorough-clean their homes; and it may be true that they do not work as hard as homemakers of the past. But there seems to be little doubt that most women still feel it is necessary to do something that they think of as thorough cleaning.

The special cleaning category includes jobs that are unscheduled but not quite unexpected. Washing the kitchen ceiling, for example, or laundering a slipcover on which a guest spilled a plate of food.

Because of the diversity of cleaning jobs to be done in every home, it is impossible for anyone except a complete recluse to have a precise system of cleaning the house. In the course of time, however, every homemaker comes up with a sort of semi-system that works quite well until she moves, has a new baby, gets a job, or buys a revolutionary new kind of vacuum cleaner. Then the system is changed—hopefully for the better.

Developing a housecleaning system. Step 1. One thing that helps in developing some kind of housecleaning system is to make mental note of all the areas and items that need to be cleaned. They may include the following:

Walls and ceilings
Woodwork
Windows
Storm sash
Screens
Draperies and curtains
Venetian blinds
Shades
Awnings
Shelves
Radiators or registers
Inside drawers and cabinets
Bare floors
Rugs and carpets
Furniture
Mattresses
Pillows and cushions
Blankets
Comforters
Other bedding
Bathroom, kitchen, and table linens
Fireplaces and fireplace equipment
Lighting fixtures
Lamps
Pictures
Mirrors
Books
Silverware
Brass and other metal objects
Ornaments
Vases
Exterior walls
Gutters and leaders
Shutters

Step 2. The next step in developing a housecleaning system is to make some kind of decision about how much time you are willing to devote to the job. Obviously, until you have actually worked around a house for a while, you have no idea how much time each job demands.

Therefore, it may help to know what other homemakers do.

The figures in the table below are from a survey of working and nonworking wives made in the 1950s by the General Electric Company. Both groups were asked how often they did certain housecleaning chores and how much time they spent on each chore each time it was done. The frequency figures below represent the answers of the largest percentage of women, but not necessarily a majority. The time figures are approximate averages for all the women interviewed.

Chore	Working wives	Full-time housewives
Tidying up		
Frequency	Daily	Daily
Time spent	18 min.	20 min.
Cleaning rugs		
Frequency	Once a week	Daily or twice a week
Time spent	32 min.	28 min.
Mopping or sweeping floors		
Frequency	Once a week	Daily
Time spent	30 min.	30 min.
Waxing floors		
Frequency	Monthly	Monthly
Time spent	60 min.	65 min.
Washing kitchen and bathroom floors		
Frequency	Once a week	Once a week
Time spent	37 min.	41 min.
Dusting furniture		
Frequency	Twice a week	Daily
Time spent	29 min.	26 min.
Dusting walls and ceilings		
Frequency	Monthly	Monthly
Time spent	49 min.	48 min.
Washing bathroom fixtures		
Frequency	Daily	Daily
Time spent	19 min.	19 min.
Thoroughly cleaning house		
Frequency	Twice a year	Twice a year
Time spent	26 hours	17 hours
Washing blankets		
Frequency	Twice a year	Twice a year
Time spent	74 min.	79 min.
Shampooing or airing rugs		
Frequency	Twice a year	Twice a year
Time spent	3 hr. 6 min.	3 hr. 18 min.
Washing or airing draperies		
Frequency	Twice a year	Twice a year
Time spent	69 min.	71 min.
Polishing furniture		
Frequency	Monthly	Monthly
Time spent	3 hours	3 hours
Cleaning venetian blinds		
Frequency	Monthly	Monthly
Time spent	2 hr. 48 min.	4 hours
Washing windows		
Frequency	Monthly	Monthly
Time spent	2 hr. 36 min.	2 hr. 42 min.
Washing kitchen walls		
Frequency	Twice a year	Twice a year
Time spent	3 hr. 12 min.	3 hr. 24 min.

Chore	Working wives	Full-time housewives
Cleaning dish and kitchen cabinets		
Frequency	Twice a year	Monthly
Time spent	2 hr. 24 min.	3 hours
Shining silver		
Frequency	Every 2–5 months	Every 1–5 months
Time spent	1 hr. 24 min.	1 hr. 36 min.

It is interesting to note that, except for the few jobs they did every day, the majority of working wives did their housecleaning chores on weekends; and they spent considerably more time at the work than those working wives who cleaned on weekdays. By contrast, the majority of full-time housewives did their cleaning chores on weekdays; and they spent considerably more time at the work than full-time housewives who cleaned on weekends.

Step 3. Before you get too set in your housecleaning ways, experiment a bit. The objective in housecleaning is not to become a slave to the house but to do the work reasonably well in the fastest time with the least effort. As a rule, the fewer steps you have to take and the fewer motions you have to make, the better. It is equally true, on the other hand, that if you do the same job over and over again you develop a kind of rhythm that makes the work go more easily.

For example, some women like to clean one room or one area of the house per day. They figure that they run around less this way and thus save time and energy.

On the other hand, women who make a practice of doing all the bathrooms one day and remaking all the beds on another day and doing all furniture polishing on another day believe that they are saving time and energy, too.

Who's right? Everybody. There is no one way to clean house. So experiment and discover what works out best for you.

Step 4. Get in the habit of bringing with you all the equipment and supplies you will need to carry out the day's work. Then you won't spend so much time running back and forth to the cleaning closet to get something you find you need. Ideally you should have more or less duplicate sets of cleaning equipment in two parts of the house. Two vacuum cleaners are especially desirable—particularly if you live in a two-story house.

But if you can't bring yourself to make such a large outlay for cleaning equipment, you should at least acquire a basket to carry all equipment with you as you move around. Maybe, if you live in a one-story house, you should ask your husband to make a cleaning cart like those used in motels and hotels.

Step 5. Learn not to get sidetracked as you go about your work. Or putting it another way: Do what you set out to do on a given day and don't do any more even if you see something you think should be done.

The reason for this rule should be obvious: Once you stray from routine, one job will lead to another and you will never get done.

Your housecleaning schedule should be set up so that one or two days each week are set aside pretty much for special cleaning chores. Save your spur-of-the-moment ideas for these.

Cleaning living rooms, dining rooms, bedrooms. Although there are different cleaning jobs to be done in all these rooms, the basic approach to each room is the same.

Tidy up daily as necessary. This includes making beds, picking up and putting things away where they belong, plumping cushions, cleaning ash trays, airing out smoke, collecting fallen flower petals, and other necessary tasks to keep the house presentable.

Run your vacuum cleaner or carpet sweeper over rugs two or three times a week—whichever is necessary to get rid of dirt and dust before it is ground into them.

Dust the tops of furniture, windowsills, the mantel, shelves, baseboards, and other exposed horizontal surfaces twice a week.

How often you must do a good cleaning job varies with the room and how hard it is used. Family rooms might need more attention than living rooms. Bedrooms might need more attention than dining rooms because bedmaking stirs up dust. On the other hand, if the dining room is used regularly, the floor certainly needs heavy vacuuming at least twice a week and probably more often to pick up food particles.

In any event, when you do undertake to clean these rooms, you should proceed as follows:

1. Do the things that stir up dust— cleaning venetian blinds or shoveling ashes out of the fireplace, for example.

2. Starting at the high points in the room (ceiling, tops of floor lamps, etc.), dust down to the floor. Use a vacuum cleaner brush as much as possible.

3. Vacuum the entire floor (bare wood and rugs).

4. Sponge fingerprints and smudges from woodwork, around light switches, etc.

5. Polish tops of tables, bureaus, and other pieces, as necessary.

Cleaning bathrooms and kitchens. These rooms require more attention than any others. See *Bathroom Cleaning* and *Kitchen Cleaning.*

Housecleaning Services. Of the many services available to homemakers in most parts of the country, but especially in metropolitan areas, none has been in greater demand in recent years than those that do cleaning. The specific services offered are as follows:

Complete housecleaning. These services bring to your home a crew of men and women who go right through room after room vacuuming, dusting, washing, polishing, etc. The principal advantage of hiring such a service rather than a cleaning woman is that you don't have to provide transportation or lunch, or pay Social Security taxes. And you don't need a big stock of cleaning supplies and equipment because the services provide their own.

Cleaning services are generally available on two bases: You can schedule them to come in every week, two weeks, or month to do a routine cleaning job in the rooms you specify. Or you can employ them to come in on a one-time basis to do a special cleaning job, such as giving the house a really thorough going over or getting rid of the sooty film that covers everything after an oil burner backfires.

The cost of a complete cleaning service obviously varies with the extent of the work done. You may also expect to pay more for special cleaning than scheduled cleaning.

Window cleaning. Window washing is a boring job and a dangerous one if you must climb a ladder. That's why window-cleaning services are so busy all the time, but especially in spring and fall. One other thing to be said for such services is that they wash windows better than most housewives and handymen.

The cost of a window-cleaning service is based on the number of windows and their size. Storm windows cost extra. You can usually arrange to have windows washed on only one side, which of course reduces the cost.

Carpet cleaning. Most of these services will clean carpets in your home or in their shops. They prefer the latter because they feel they can do a better job; but if you don't want to roll up and relay the carpet yourself, you will pay a little extra for having it done. And you are without the carpet for a longer period (if it is cleaned on the floor, you can walk on it within 24 hours).

There is little question that professional carpet cleaning is far superior to home cleaning; but it is not cheap under any circumstances.

Upholstered-furniture cleaning. This service is offered by firms that do nothing else and also by carpet cleaners. The work is generally done in the home.

Drapery cleaning. You can get draperies and curtains cleaned by regular dry cleaners and also by drapery-cleaning specialists. The work is done out of your home; and as a rule, you're expected to take down, deliver, pick up, and rehang the draperies yourself.

Venetian-blind cleaning. Since venetian blinds are difficult to clean well, this is an exceptionally useful service. The cleaning may also include complete replacement of tapes and cords. The work is done in the service firm's shop.

Floor waxing. This service may also

include cleaning, stripping, or simple buffing. The workmen use special cleaners and waxes, which are much better than those available to home owners; and they have heavy, powerful equipment that gets rid of all dirt and polishes floors to a beautiful, durable sheen. A housewife cannot come close to doing such a good job.

Marble cleaning. This is done by marble dealers or marble finishers in their own shops.

Steam cleaning. You might need this service if you live in a masonry house in a filthy city. It may be the only way you can get the grime off the house.

Steam-cleaning firms may also do sandblasting. The latter work is sometimes necessary if you want to remove a paint finish from masonry.

Before you employ a cleaning service. Check its performance and reliability with others who have used it. Remember, however, that the large complete housecleaning services employ a number of workers. Remember also that the turnover of workers in the cleaning services is extremely high. So the fact that Mrs. Jones liked a certain service a month ago doesn't mean you're going to like it equally well, because you may not get the same workers.

Find out whether the service has bonded its workers. If it hasn't, that doesn't mean the people are not to be trusted. But bonding is a plus for a service.

Make sure the service carries insurance on its people. This is particularly important in the case of window cleaners.

Housekeeping Schedules. "Housekeeping" is sometimes confused with "housecleaning." Actually, housekeeping encompasses housecleaning as well as cooking, marketing, shopping, clothes washing and ironing, mending, and bed-making. We might even stretch a point and say it also includes all phases of decorating and flower-arranging because making a house attractive is certainly important to keeping a house in shape.

Because housekeeping is an extremely varied occupation, it defies rigid scheduling. But a schedule of some sort is essential if you want your home to run smoothly. This is especially important, of course, when big family events such as a wedding or a gathering of the clan at a holiday are impending. On these occasions, it pays to sit down and write out a precise list of things to be done around the house and when they should be done.

In the past, housekeeping schedules usually entailed washing on Monday, ironing on Tuesday, cleaning on Wednesday, maid's-day-out on Thursday (which meant a heavy stint of cooking for the housewife), and shopping on Friday. Today, largely because of new laundry appliances, home freezers, better refrigerators, prepared foods, no-iron fabrics, and automobiles—and, of course, the virtual disappearance of maids—this schedule seems rather ridiculous. Much greater freedom of action is possible. For instance, you can easily get your laundering done in one day. You may go marketing two or three times a week. Meal preparation can be shortened drastically. And so on.

Nevertheless, the old basic housekeeping jobs still remain to be done. When you schedule them depends on whether you have a job or not, how old your children are, your husband's work schedule, etc. As we said earlier, a rigid schedule is impossible and indeed is undesirable because it makes you its slave. There is no real reason why you shouldn't do things differently from one week to the next. But whatever you do, you must make time each week for the major jobs. These are:

Cooking and dishwashing (daily)

Washing, drying, and ironing (once, twice, or three times a week)

Marketing and storing away what you bring home (once or twice a week)

Cleaning bathrooms (once a week)

Vacuuming and dusting (once or twice a week)

Changing beds (once or twice a week)

Washing the kitchen floor (about once a week)

In addition, you must allow time in every month for other major cleaning jobs and shopping for articles besides food.

House Painting. House painting is, though easy, a time-consuming job, but the savings you can realize by doing the work yourself are enormous.

Interior painting. This is more exacting, fussy work than exterior painting because mistakes are more visible and interior trim is generally more elaborate. On the other hand, the work in many ways seems to be simpler—in large part because you are under cover and don't have to do so much climbing on ladders.

Paint to use. The choice is wide. Most people, however, prefer latex paint for walls and ceilings in living and sleeping areas and alkyd paint—because it is more washable—for walls and ceilings in the kitchen and bathrooms. Alkyd is also used for woodwork, doors, and windows. Paneled walls are most easily finished with stain-wax or alkyd paint. For a natural finish on doors and wood windows, apply stain followed by varnish.

Flat paint is used on ceilings and walls in all rooms except bathrooms and kitchens, where there is a great deal of moisture and fairly frequent cleaning is necessary. In bathrooms and kitchens, use semi-gloss or, if you don't mind the very high shine, gloss. Because woodwork, doors, and windows also need to be washed frequently, they should be finished in semi-gloss or gloss paint, too.

Procedure. Prepare the painting surfaces and cover those not to be painted. See *Painting.*

Paint the ceiling first, then the woodwork if it is to be the same color as the walls; then the walls. (Usually the walls are painted before the woodwork if they are of a different color.)

When painting the ceiling, use a brush to paint a stripe around the edges where a large roller cannot reach. Then, starting in a corner, with a roller paint a 3- to 4-foot-wide strip straight across the width of the room. Then return to the wall where you started and paint a parallel strip across the room. Working in this way, you give the paint the least possible time to dry; consequently, the new strip blends in better with the old, and the overlapped area is not so noticeable.

Paint walls in the same way. Paint a stripe around the top, around doors and windows, in corners, and at the top of baseboards with a brush. (This is called "cutting in.") Then, starting in a corner, paint a 4- to 5-foot-wide strip down the wall with your roller. Then another and another. Never leave the work for a long time unless you have reached a point where the joining of the strips will not show.

When painting windows, paint the mullions first, then the frame, and finally the trim. On paneled doors, paint the panels first, then the horizontal rails, then the vertical stiles. All door painting can be speeded up if you roll paint on the large flat areas, then go over it lightly with a brush.

When painting baseboards, keep paint off the floor by holding a piece of shirt cardboard against the shoe molding. Wipe the edge of the cardboard frequently; otherwise the paint on it will mark the floor.

Paint radiators with the same semi-gloss or gloss paint that is used on the woodwork. If it is easy to loosen the radiators from the pipes and pull them out from the wall, do so.

For how to apply varnish, see *Varnish.*

Exterior painting. *Paint to use.* Exterior latex paint is now preferred for all exterior walls, including those of wood if they are first primed with an oil-based primer. The paint dries very rapidly, goes on easily, covers well, and allows moisture in the walls to escape.

Oil-based paint, however, should be used on walls that are chalking or very dirty. It sticks better. Oil-based trim enamel should be used on exterior trim, doors, and windows because it is more washable than latex.

Whether you use a so-called one-coat paint or a conventional paint depends on the condition of the walls. One-coat paints give one-coat coverage only if they are applied over a sound paint surface. If the surface hasn't been painted or isn't sound, you will save money and get just as good results by using a conventional paint and applying two coats.

In an industrial atmosphere, be sure that paints are resistant to fumes. In damp areas, use paints containing a mildewcide.

Stains. Exterior stains used on wood are mixtures of penetrating oil and pigment. Opaque stains containing a great deal of insoluble pigment give a paint-like appearance but do not completely conceal the wood grain. Transparent stains change the color of the wood but are not otherwise visible.

Both types of stain are very popular today because they allow much of the natural beauty of wood to show through; they are easy to apply; and they are very durable. Actually opaque stains are no better than paint in the last respect, but transparent stains may last twice as long—especially if two coats are applied to rough wood within 30 minutes of each other.

Natural finishes. In the past the natural finishes most often used on exterior wood were linseed oil and varnish. They are still used but only to a limited extent because they create problems: Linseed oil turns wood very dark and mildews badly. Varnish breaks down rapidly under the sun's rays and must be renewed almost every year.

The most widely used natural finish today is a so-called water repellent—a colorless liquid that retards natural weathering and thus helps wood to retain something very close to its original color. The repellent also keeps wood from splintering and cracking, and if it contains a mildewcide, it stops mildew formation. Usually two coats are required. See *Water Repellents.*

Another excellent natural finish is called a bleaching oil. Made of a penetrating oil, a bleaching agent, and a little gray pigment, it is designed to give new wood an instant gray, weathered look and also to facilitate natural weathering as the pigment slowly wears off. Apply one or two coats according to the manufacturer's directions.

When to paint a house. As a rule-of-thumb, houses need to be repainted every four or five years. In actual fact, however, houses that are a medium or dark color usually need to be repainted only about every six years.

Painting should be done when the temperature is between 50 and 80 degrees, and at a time when insects are not plentiful. The day should be dry and not too windy.

Procedure. For how to prepare the surfaces to be painted, see *Painting.* In exterior work, it is extremely important to look for blisters in old paint. If you find any around windows, it probably means that rain is seeping in around the frames and that you should check the caulking and flashing. If blisters are concentrated under the eaves, you probably need to check the condition of the gutters and install drip edges (see *Gutters*). On the other hand, if blisters are found in many areas, the chances are that they are caused by condensation inside the walls. For how to stop this problem, see *Condensation Control.*

Wash brown rust and green copper streaks on walls with ½ pound trisodium phosphate in 1 gallon water. Countersink protruding and rusty nailheads; paint them with a rust-inhibiting primer; and then cover them with putty.

Take off shutters, screens, and storm windows.

If you are going to apply a primer and a finish coat, the latter can go on as soon as the former is dry, and it must go on within two weeks. If you wait longer than this, you may find that the finish coat starts flaking off within a few months.

Latex paint can be applied to surfaces that are damp but not soaking. Oil paints, however, can be applied only to completely dry surfaces.

Paint the south and west sides of the house in the morning; the north and east in the afternoon. In this way, you avoid the sun, which makes work hot and difficult.

Begin painting at the upper corner of a wall and finish each day's work at a corner, door, or window in order to avoid obvious laps. You will also avoid laps by painting across the house in deep bands rather than working from the top down. Paint the siding before the trim, windows, and doors; however, you will avoid extra ladder work if you paint the eaves and rakes before you start on the siding.

Paint outside surfaces of doors and windows in the same way as inside surfaces.

Apply stains and natural finishes in the same way as paint.

If you hire a painting contractor. A reputable contractor can offer three kinds of paint job: Premium—a job that will give the most excellent finish possible and that will provide the maximum durability. Standard—a job that has the usual life expectancy of a well-painted surface. Minimum—a job that will improve the present surface but will not last overly long.

Keep in mind that proper surface preparation is your best guarantee of a lasting paint job.

When you talk with a prospective contractor, tell him which kind of paint job you want. It will, of course, affect the price. Have him come to your home and go over the areas you want painted. Find out what kind of paint he intends to use. If you wish to specify a particular brand, it is your right to do so.

Before hiring a contractor, be sure to get a signed proposal, estimate, or contract. The document should include the following items:

1. A specific price.

2. A listing of each area to be painted.

3. A listing of the types and brands of paint to be used if you do not specify them.

4. A statement of the number of coats to be applied.

5. A completion date (but allowance must be made for unpredictable weather).

6. A statement that the contractor will use drop cloths and take other measures to protect your property.

Reputable painting contractors are properly insured for their own protection and yours. The contractor should have proof he has workmen's compensation and employer's liability insurance, as well as public liability and property damage insurance. If the contractor is not properly insured, you could be held liable for accidents occurring on your property.

Warning. Never, never, never allow yourself to get trapped into having your house painted with any kind of "miracle" product that is ballyhooed not only to last forever but also to stop dampness, retard fire, absorb noise, and serve as insulation.

Humidifiers. In winter when the air in your house gets too dry, rugs and synthetic fabrics give off sparks, furniture joints crack, tropical house plants wilt, your nose feels dry, and your resistance to colds drops. It is not a pleasant situation, but fortunately it is a situation that is rather easily avoided.

There is an effective kind of humidifier—not merely a pan of water sitting on a radiator—for every home.

If you have a forced warm-air heating system, you can install in it a humidifier that automatically introduces moisture into the air flowing toward the supply registers. Most units are run by electricity (120 volts) and are connected into the plumbing system. Less efficient units, however, must be filled by hand or are driven by the air in the ducts.

The best humidifier pulls hot air from the furnace through a pad which is kept constantly wet. Minerals released from the water collect in the bottom of the unit and must be cleaned out occasionally.

In another system, water is vaporized and blown into the air stream. These units are less costly but also less efficient and require more attention.

A third type of humidifier, called a pan-evaporator unit, contains plates that suck up water from a tray and release it into the moving air. Cost is low; efficiency, even lower. And because the plates become clogged rapidly, they must be cleaned or replaced frequently.

In a house with hot water, steam, or electric heat, you should use a humidifier that vaporizes water and sprays the mist directly into the house air. The available humidifiers range from small, lightweight, portable units big enough to humidify a single room to roll-around console units with an output equal to the best built-in system. Most units must be filled manually, but some can be connected into a cold-water supply line by a small copper tube. A few have humidistats that turn the units on and off automatically as the relative humidity falls and rises.

Whatever the type of humidifier, the one you buy should be made of materials that resist corrosion. They should also resist clogging and be easy to clean.

Humidifiers are rated by the gallons of water they can deliver per day. The smallest models have a capacity of about 1½ gallons; the largest, 15. To humidify an entire house adequately, you need a humidifier that will deliver roughly 1 gallon per room.

Hutch. A tall, shallow piece of furniture used for storage and display of china, books, ornaments, etc. It usually stands on short legs, and has drawers or cabinets in the bottom section and open shelves above. For how to take care of a hutch, see *Furniture, Wood.*

Hydraulic Cement. See *Concrete.*

Hydrochloric Acid. See *Muriatic Acid.*

Ice Buckets. Most ice buckets made today have plastic liners, but some have glass. If the latter are broken, try to have them replaced by the maker. If a plastic liner is cracked, coat the break liberally with plastic-mending adhesive. If this doesn't work, spread on a layer of silicone caulking compound.

Plastic-lined buckets can be washed in hot water and mild detergent; but use only lukewarm water on glass liners. Always empty and dry ice buckets well after use, and leave the top off until they are completely dry. They may mildew otherwise.

Ice-Cream Freezers. The ice-cream freezer of today is virtually identical with that of yesteryear. True, wooden freezers are now lined with plastic to prevent sweating and leaking. And there are also less expensive freezers with a tub made entirely of plastic. But changes in form end there.

Electrically driven freezers that plug into any outlet turn out ice cream in a matter of minutes. Hand-cranked freezers obviously require more effort—but that is part of the fun of making your own ice cream. Both types are available in 4- and 6-quart sizes.

Ice-cream freezers are virtually indestructible. Just remember to wash them out. Use detergent solution on the cream can, lid, and dashers and rinse well. Then dry. Store in a dry closet if you don't want to repeat the process to get rid of musty odors when you make ice cream again.

Ice Crushers. Here are three ways to crush ice cubes effortlessly, thoroughly, and quickly: (1) With a special ice-crushing attachment that fits on a blender in place of the glass mixing jar. (2) With a tabletop appliance that does nothing but crush ice into a small slide-out bin. (3) With a food preparation center—a multi-purpose appliance with such interchangeable attachments as an ice crusher, meat grinder, and knife sharpener. All these units are electrically driven.

There are also ice crushers that are driven by a hand crank.

And if you want chipped rather than crushed ice, you can buy aluminum ice trays with closely spaced dividers that produce neat slivers of ice when you pull the handle.

Although ice crushers are made of corrosion-resistant material, dry them as thoroughly as possible after every use. If a crusher "walks" when in operation (it shouldn't, but any electrically driven device can become unbalanced), have it repaired or at least hold it firmly so it does not do real damage to itself or other utensils on the counter.

Ice-Makers. Most families who want an automatic ice-cube-maker are content to buy a refrigerator incorporating one in the freezer compartment. It is now also possible to buy a refrigerator without an ice-maker and to add the ice-maker at a later date (see *Refrigerators*). But completely separate ice-making appliances are also available for residential as well as commercial use.

Residential ice-makers are designed to produce from about 6 to 50 pounds of ice cubes a day. The smallest appliance is a countertop unit resembling a countertop refrigerator. It contains the same ice-cube-making device that is used in full-size refrigerators. There is additional storage space in the cabinet for ice cubes stored in bags or bins or for frozen foods.

The largest residential ice-maker is about 18 inches wide and is designed for installation under a kitchen counter, though it can also be freestanding. The cubes drop into a permanent bin with access by a let-down door. The appliance requires a drain, which empties into a standpipe or laundry tub on the floor below.

In-between sizes of ice-maker are, like the largest unit, used for making and storing ice only. They may be built-in or freestanding. No drain is required.

All ice-makers can be plugged into a 20-amp small-appliance circuit. They are permanently connected to a cold-water supply line by a ¼-inch copper tube.

Commercial ice-makers are much larger; they make from about 120 to 1200 pounds of ice cubes a day.

If something goes wrong. Make sure the ice-maker is plugged into a live circuit and water is flowing through the main supply pipe. If it still doesn't work, call a serviceman. This is a tricky and sometimes ornery little appliance.

Ice Trays. Although there have been countless designs, the perfect ice tray has yet to be invented. The best presumably is a $3 aluminum tray that ejects eighteen cubes when you press lightly on a lever. The tray is frequently sold with a plastic chest that holds four trays of cubes.

But a simple one-piece tray molded from styrene and costing only about 50 cents is equally good. For one thing, the ice-cube compartments are completely separated. This means that when you carry a tray from the sink to the refrigerator, the water does not slosh back and forth and over the sides as in conventional trays. For another thing, there are no moving parts to wear out as in aluminum trays. You can also eject one or two cubes at a time without dislodging the rest. To eject cubes, you twist the tray.

Whatever kind of ice trays you own, you should not clean them with any abrasive or fill them with very hot water. Both of these things destroy the finish that permits quick release of cubes.

Ice-Water Dispensers. Many families—especially those in areas where the drinking water is not highly potable—have installed old-fashioned bottled-water coolers; and encouraged by this trend, manufacturers of coolers are beginning to dress up the appliances by concealing the water jug inside.

A newer type of water dispenser is a small under-the-sink refrigerating unit that chills the water passing through it when the faucet is opened. The chiller can be connected to the cold-water faucet, a separate faucet, or a fountain bubbler.

Ice-water dispensers are also built into the sides of certain deluxe refrigerators. In one case, the dispenser also produces ice cubes.

Illusion. A net-like fabric of silk, nylon, or cotton with tiny square openings. It is used in veils. Dry-clean when soiled.

Imitation Fur. Imitation furs are made of a variety of fibers—either 100 percent synthetics such as polyester and modacrylic, or blends of synthetics, or synthetics and natural fibers. A few can be hand-washed in warm water, but dry-cleaning is generally safer.

Imitation Leather. The most realistic imitation leathers are made of vinyl and urethane. They can be cleaned with a damp cloth or mild detergent solution. If pieces are torn, glue them together or patch them with plastic-mending adhesive.

Imitation suede is made of cotton. It can be machine-washed in medium-temperature water and tumble-dried at medium heat.

Incinerators. Although the modern domestic incinerator produces virtually no smoke, fly ash, or odors, it is banned from use in many communities. On the other hand, it is permitted in many others and actually encouraged in some. In short, if you are thinking of installing one, you should check first with your local health or air-pollution authority.

Incinerators are designed to dispose of all combustible refuse, such as wet and dry garbage, paper, food wrappings, and fabrics. They cannot dispose of cans, bottles, and metal foil, and aerosols must never be incinerated. The waste is reduced to ashes which collect in an ash drawer that must be emptied every two to four weeks.

All incinerators are alike. Most burn gas, but a few operate on electricity. Combustion is accomplished by a primary burner which burns up the trash and a secondary burner which consumes the by-products of the first burning process. To operate the appliance, you load in the refuse—up to about 1½ bushels at a time—set a timer, and, on gas models, light the burners with a pilot. The gas turns off automatically at the end of the selected time period. Cost of operation runs about $1 to $2 a month.

The efficiency of burning is improved if

packages of wet garbage are well separated by dry refuse. All ashes should be sifted through the grate before each burning, and the ash drawer must not be allowed to overflow. If some debris is not burned, it may mean you did not set the timer dial high enough. However, unburned garbage left in the incinerator should be dry enough by the next day so that it will be consumed rapidly.

Installation of an incinerator (which measures roughly 20 inches square and 36 inches high) is usually made in a basement or utility room. The unit must be vented into a Class A chimney (tile-lined, masonry construction). A Class B vent is not suitable. If your house lacks such a chimney, it is possible to install a prefabricated unit, or you may be able to install the incinerator in a fireproof building away from the house.

Trash burners. These are large steel cans, often home-made from oil drums, that admit air at the bottom and emit smoke through a top screen or grille. They are highly inefficient and slow—and bear no resemblance to an incinerator. Nevertheless, they are often used by rural families in areas not covered by air-pollution ordinances.

Indian Head. A cotton fabric used for many purposes and made by the company of the same name. It is laundered like cotton.

Insecticides. See *Pesticides.*

Insulation. The best time to insulate a house is when it is under construction; and the best kind of insulation to use for most purposes is either urethane foam or fiberglass.

Urethane has twice the insulating value of fiberglass but costs more. Applied by trained applicators, it is sprayed onto the back of roof and wall sheathing. It foams up instantly to form a thick, warm blanket which also acts as a vapor barrier.

Fiberglass insulation comes in batts or blankets that are placed between the studs and joists. The strips may or may not incorporate a vapor barrier of heavy, treated paper that also serves as a nailing flange. Fiberglass insulation is also available as loose fill which can be poured or blown into spaces.

Two other kinds of insulation that are used for special purposes are rigid boards. One of these, made of vegetable fibers, forms the roof deck and finish ceiling in houses in which the rafters are left exposed. It also contains a vapor barrier. The bottom surface can be painted. Roofing is applied directly to the top surface. Thicknesses range from 1½ to 3 inches. The other board insulation is made of polystyrene or urethane and is used to insulate the edges of a concrete slab under a house. It may also be used to insulate basement walls on the inside. It comes in 1- to 3-inch thicknesses. See *Walls, Fiberboard.*

Insulation should be installed in all parts of the house through which heat and cold may pass between outdoors and in. These include the roof or top-story ceilings; the exterior walls; floors over unheated spaces; and concrete floors laid on the ground. The walls in unheated basements should also be insulated, although they usually are not.

The optimum amount of insulation called for depends on where the insulation is to go and on the fuel you burn. This is stated in terms of the insulation's resistance value, or R value. (No matter what insulation is made of, those with similar R values are equal in effectiveness.) The R values recommended are as follows:

	In homes heated by gas or oil	In homes heated by electricity and in Southern homes which are air-conditioned
Roof or top-story ceiling	R-13	R-19
Exterior walls	R-8	R-11
Floors over unheated spaces	R-9	R-13
Concrete floors laid on the ground	R-9	R-13

The higher R values (indicating greater insulating effectiveness) are needed in electrically heated homes and air-conditioned homes in warm climates because electricity costs more than oil or gas, as a rule. Insulation with higher R values may also be installed in gas- and oil-heated homes, but the savings in fuel costs hardly justify the higher initial cost of the insulation except in very cold climates.

How to insulate an existing house. Attic floor. If the attic is not occupied, the cheapest way to insulate it is to cover the floor. The job is extremely simple and inexpensive. Use fill insulation made of loose fiberglass that comes in bags. Pour this between the floor joists on the ceiling of the lower floor, and rake it smooth.

Attic roof. You should insulate the attic roof and end walls if the attic is occupied. Use fiberglass batts or rolls with a vapor barrier on one side. To install a strip, just push the glass fibers between the rafters, unfold the nailing flanges on the vapor barrier, and staple them to the lower edges of the rafters. For the vapor barrier to be effective, the flanges on adjoining strips of insulation must be overlapped as far as possible and tacked down tight at 6-inch intervals.

Inaccessible roof spaces. Innumerable houses have roof spaces that no one can get into; but this doesn't mean you cannot insulate them. Just hire an insulating contractor to blow in loose fill. He does this by making holes in the roof, injecting the fill by a large blower, and then closing the holes. The ceilings underneath must be covered with a vapor barrier of paint. See *Condensation Control—Install vapor barriers.*

Exterior walls. If the walls have no interior surface, install fiberglass batts with a vapor barrier on the inside. If the stud spaces are closed, have loose fill blown into them. In this case, make sure the inner surfaces of the walls are covered with a vapor barrier of paint or vinyl wall covering.

Floors over crawl spaces and other unheated spaces. If you can get at the underside of the floors, install fiberglass batts between the joists. A vapor barrier should be on the upper side of the insulation. To prevent the batts from falling out of the joist spaces, tack chicken wire below them.

Edges of a slab. If a slab feels uncomfortably cold underfoot, you can probably improve it by covering the edges with rigid urethane or polystyrene insulation board. Use 2-inch thickness except in mild climates, where 1-inch is adequate. In very cold climates, use 3-inch. The boards should extend from the bottom of the siding to at least 1 foot below grade level. Secure the boards to the concrete with roofing cement. To protect the insulation against lawn mowers, cover it with asbestos-cement board.

Unheated basement. Glue urethane or polystyrene boards to the inside surfaces of the walls. The cheaper but more troublesome alternative is to nail 2-by-2-inch vertical furring strips to the walls on 16-inch centers and staple fiberglass blankets in between. The blankets should have an R value of 8 in most areas; but use R-11 in extremely cold climates.

Insulation Board. See *Walls, Fiberboard,* and *Insulation.*

Intercoms. With an intercom, you can talk between rooms in the house; converse with someone at the front door while you are still in the kitchen; listen to the baby in his crib; or pipe music throughout the house. Some systems even serve as fire alarms.

Intercoms of two slightly different types are available. One is installed by the telephone company and operates through the telephone receivers and wires in the house. The other is installed by an electrical contractor and operates through its own wires, transmitters, and receivers.

An intercom can be installed in any house. If the house is under construction, the wiring can be concealed completely. In an existing house, it can be mostly concealed.

Ironers. The electric ironer—or mangle, as it is sometimes called—has just about disappeared from use, though it is still made. Several things contributed to its downfall, but especially new fabrics that require little or no ironing.

Most of the ironers in service are fairly heavy, portable units with a large, revolving, muslin-covered roll and a heated steel shoe. Fabrics spread on the roll pass under the shoe and are pressed flat. The heat is thermostatically controlled.

Ironers are particularly useful for pressing large flat pieces such as sheets, towels, and table linens; but with practice you can also use them for shirts, dresses, and just about anything else. They not only speed up pressing but also make it less wearisome because you sit down as you work.

A separate wiring circuit is not needed for an ironer, but you should plug it in only to a 20-amp appliance circuit.

Ironing. See *Laundering.*

Ironing Boards. See *Laundering.*

Irons. Unless you want to save $3, there is no reason today to buy an ordinary dry iron. The steam iron is far more useful because you can use it as a dry iron and as a steam iron. A third type, also a steam iron, is the most versatile since it can be used as well to spray clothes (hence the name that is sometimes used: steam-spray-dry iron).

Aside from the steam iron's versatility, its main advantage is that when it is steaming, you can safely and easily iron materials that would be damaged by a dry iron—wool, silk, rayon, and other synthetics. You do not need a pressing cloth, although this does provide further assurance against damage to fabrics.

You can also use the steam iron to eliminate dents in carpets and to rejuvenate velvet and other pile fabrics that are matted down.

Finally, although a steam iron does not obviate the need for sprinkling cottons and linens, the spray nozzle in the front of the handle permits you to moisten dry spots while you continue with your ironing. Sponging is no longer necessary.

Steam iron features. All steam irons are basically similar in design and do the same job. All weigh close to 4 pounds empty. The major differences are in the size of the water reservoir; in the composition of the soleplate; and in the inclusion of a filter in the best irons to keep the spray nozzle from clogging.

Soleplates are made of, from least good to best, polished aluminum, chrome-plated steel, Teflon on steel, and stainless steel.

Use and care of a steam iron. Modern steam irons have been improved to the point where you can use almost any water

in them without danger of clogging the steam ports. But if your water is very hard, don't take chances: use distilled water or mix your tap water with a so-called steam-iron filter which neutralizes the minerals in the water. Should the ports become clogged despite your best efforts, fill the iron with equal parts of water and white vinegar; and let the iron steam until steam no longer escapes.

Do not iron over zippers or metal snaps lest you scratch the soleplate. If in time a metal soleplate does become scratched, you can smooth it with a very fine emery cloth. Then heat the iron slightly and run it over a piece of wax paper.

To remove burned-on starch from a metal soleplate, rub the plate with very fine steel wool. On a Teflon soleplate (which is less likely to pick up a coating of starch), use a heavy-duty detergent.

Do not let the cord become kinked, especially at the handle, because the wires may eventually break. A cord minder, which holds the cord high above the ironing board, helps to prevent tangling and also gets the cord out of the way so you are less likely to iron over it. Should the cord become frayed or broken, open the back of the handle on the iron, detach the cord, and replace it with a new heavy-duty one. Never use an ordinary lamp or extension cord.

If using the iron at a distance from an outlet, connect it to the outlet with a heavy-duty cord. Again, never use an ordinary lamp or extension cord.

Empty the iron after each use and store it standing on its heel.

Ironstone. A type of stoneware. See *Stoneware.*

Ivory. In the past, the most common use of ivory in the home was in piano keys, but now these are made of plastic. The supply of elephant tusks has dwindled, and now ivory is usually seen in only a few ornaments and knives with ivory handles.

To clean ivory, wash it with a mild detergent solution. If it begins to turn yellow—as it inevitably will with age—you can try exposing it to sunlight and cleaning it with alcohol; but don't count on success.

If an ivory piece breaks, reglue it with cellulose cement or epoxy glue. The tops of old piano keys can be glued down with the same materials, but be sure to clean off the old adhesive first.

Jade. A beautiful semi-precious stone—usually green but sometimes pink or white—which is used in jewelry, lamps, and various art objects. To clean it, simply wash with detergent solution. Scratches on highly polished surfaces should be repaired only by a jeweler.

Jalousies. A jalousie is a window with glass louvers that work up and down. It can be installed in any standard-size window opening, and may also be set into a hinged door. See *Windows.*

Jaspé Cloth. A firm, durable rayon or cotton fabric with stripes of various colors. It is used in upholstery and draperies. Launder like rayon or cotton.

Jasper. A variously colored, extremely hard quartz which is sometimes used in art objects, mantels, columns, etc. Wash with detergent solution when dirty.

Jersey. Any close-knitted fabric. Jersey should be dry-cleaned or laundered according to the maker's instructions.

Jet. A hard black coal which, in highly polished form, is occasionally used to make buttons, jewelry, and art objects. To clean, wash with detergent solution. Scratches should be obliterated by a jeweler.

Jewelry. Most jewelry can be very easily kept clean by scrubbing with a small, soft brush in a warm, mild detergent solution. The addition of a few drops of ammonia will help to cut the dirt, but ammonia should never be used for cleaning pearls.

Another excellent way to clean jewelry—especially if it is intricate—is to use an ultrasonic cleaner filled with mild detergent solution. This type of cleaner should not be used, however, for costume and other jewelry that is put together with cement or glue.

Diamond, and only diamond, jewelry that is very dirty may be dipped momentarily in a boiling soap-and-water solution, rinsed when cool, and then dipped in alcohol.

To remove tarnish on metals, rub with ammonia or silver polish, and rinse.

When a stone falls out of costume jewelry, clean off as much of the old cement

as possible and reglue with cellulose cement. Precious jewelry should be repaired only by a jeweler. Actually, you should have a jeweler check the settings of all articles that are worn regularly about once a year. The strings of good necklaces should be checked at the same time.

To protect jewelry from scratching and chipping, don't jumble all pieces together in a box or drawer. Use a cloth-lined box with spaces for individual items, or wrap each piece separately in a bit of tissue paper.

Juicers. An electric juicer quickly and easily squeezes all the juice from citrus fruits as you press the halved fruit down on a revolving reamer. Some juicers start automatically when the fruit is pressed against the reamer and stop when the pressure is removed; others are controlled by a switch. The juice goes through a strainer into your waiting glass. Some juicers have two reamers—a large one for grapefruits and oranges and a small one for lemons and limes.

Juicers most often are available as a separate appliance, but may be combined with other appliances such as can openers and mixers.

The best kind of hand juicer operates like a potato masher: you put half an orange in the juicer head and squeeze down on it with a pusher.

Citrus juice and pulp are often rather difficult to clean out of juicers; but if they're not cleaned out, they soon mildew. So wash all juicers well under a stream of hot running water, and scrub them occasionally with detergent solution. Dry thoroughly.

Kapok. This is a silky fiber from the ceiba tree which is used to fill cushions. When such cushions become soiled, they should be dry-cleaned.

Kerosene. A petroleum derivative which may be used to remove grease, oil, and wax from surfaces. It may also be used instead of mineral spirits or turpentine to partially clean paintbrushes. It is nonexplosive.

Kettlecloth. A fabric resembling a very firm, crisp gingham with a grainy texture. It is made of a blend of cotton and polyester and is used in clothing and bedspreads. Launder like permanent press.

Kitchen Cabinets. The typical homemaker is vaguely dissatisfied with her kitchen cabinets; and when she remodels her kitchen, she spends much time wondering and worrying about "What is the best kind of cabinet?" There is no real answer.

Whether they are made of wood, steel, or plastic, all quality cabinets are equally good; and whether they are made of wood, steel, or plastic, all cheap cabinets are equally unsatisfactory.

Wood cabinets are most popular—natural wood finishes have been in vogue for a good many years. But as on all wood furniture, the finish gradually becomes scratched and eroded by the oils and salts in human skin. Painted wood cabinets are also available but are less desirable because the paint—an enamel—tends to chip. Fears that the doors and drawers in wood cabinets tend to bind and warp are rarely justified.

Steel cabinets have a baked-enamel finish like that used on major appliances. It is very tough and long-lasting but over a period of time may have to be renewed. Because steel cabinets are mass-produced, they are available in somewhat fewer sizes and designs than wood and plastic cabinets, which can be a drawback. Steel cabinets are occasionally made with wood fronts.

Plastic cabinets are actually made of particle board surfaced on all sides with laminated plastic sheets similar to those used on kitchen counters. The plastic usually has a wood grain. It is easy to clean and never needs to be refinished. There is, of course, some possibility that the plastic sheets will delaminate, but such failures are actually very rare. Homemakers owning plastic cabinets seem to be remarkably happy with them.

A slight but important difference between cabinets is in the way the doors and drawers are installed. Cabinets with flush door and drawer fronts are, in effect, completely smooth. The frames are invisible. These cabinets must be installed with filler strips in the corners and between the cabinets and walls; otherwise the doors and drawers at those points will not open.

Lip doors and drawer fronts project slightly from the cabinet frames, which are visible. Depending on the width of the frames, filler strips may or may not be necessary to provide clearance for the doors and drawers.

Cabinet sizes. See *Kitchen Planning.*

Cabinet features. Easy-sliding drawers, sure catches, and well-designed handles are typical of the features you would naturally look for when shopping for cabinets. Several special features are also desirable:

Adjustable shelves, especially in wall cabinets, allow you to make maximum use of storage space. They also permit easier storage of those big economy-size boxes, blenders, mixers, and other tall items.

Sliding shelves in base cabinets save stooping and fumbling.

Wire shelves with stainless-steel or plastic finish collect much less dirt than solid shelves and are easier to clean besides.

Sliding glass doors on wall cabinets. For normal installations, hinged doors are superior because they allow you to reach into the entire cabinet. But in special situations—such as narrow pantries—sliding doors are extremely useful.

Special cabinets. Many are available, although not all from a single manufacturer.

Corner wall cabinets with revolving shelves not only make better use of space but also allow you to get at things more easily. In cabinets with 90-degree inside corners, the doors revolve with the shelves. In those with a door diagonally across the corner, the doors open to reveal a lazy-susan shelf behind. Revolving-shelf cabinets are made for both wall and base installation.

Wall and base cabinets with doors on both sides are used in peninsulas dividing the kitchen from an eating area. You can put in washed dishes from the kitchen side and take them out from the other side, thus saving steps.

Linen cabinets with closely spaced sliding shelves. These are designed for base installation.

Four- and five-drawer base cabinets.

Spacemaker cabinets that fit under wall cabinets. The newest type, made of plastic, has drawers that slide out and tilt slightly downward. They are excellent for storing bread, food wraps, etc.

Mixer cabinet is a base cabinet with a lift-up shelf like that in typewriter desks.

Narrow utensil cabinet is a base cabinet with a vertical slide-out panel on which you hang strainers, spatulas, knives, and other items.

Tray cabinet has dividers for storing trays. It is a base unit.

Pantry cabinet is 7 feet high, 2 feet deep, and 2 feet wide. It has four tiers of shelves for packaged foods. Three of them swing out.

Cabinet accessories. Some accessories are sold by kitchen cabinet manufacturers; many others are to be found in hardware and department stores. The following are recommended:

Cup hooks. A basic necessity. Use the largest size.

Sliding cup racks.

Sliding towel racks.

Sliding wastebasket racks.

Sliding lid racks.

Sliding drawers of various designs and depths. They make it easy to get at things stored on the bottom shelf of base cabinets.

Back-of-door racks for spices and other small items.

Drawer dividers.

Storage turntables. They can be used anywhere but are especially good for converting dead space in corner cabinets into useful storage space. They are an excellent substitute for corner cabinets with revolving shelves, and much, much cheaper.

How to install kitchen cabinets. Base cabinets. Remove the baseboards and seal up any holes to keep out mice.

Set the cabinets in place exactly where they are to go and push them tight together. If there is a wall at one end of the row of cabinets, you will probably have to insert a filler strip between the wall and the last cabinet.

Lay a carpenter's level across the last cabinet and make sure it is level. Then measure the width of the gap between it and the wall and cut the filler strip end to end to this width. If the wall is straight, you can then fasten the strip to the side of the cabinet and flush with the face of the

cabinet. Plastic and wood fillers can be fastened with nails or screws. Use sheet metal bolts for steel.

If the wall is crooked, hold the filler strip against the front of the cabinet parallel with the edge. Open a pair of dividers to the widest point of the gap between the wall and the cabinet. Then, holding one leg of the dividers against the wall and the other on the filler, draw the dividers down the wall. Cut the filler along the line scribed on it by the dividers. Then fasten it to the cabinet.

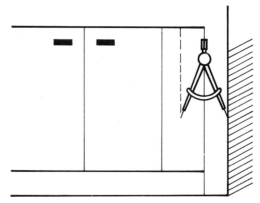

INSTALLING FILLER STRIPS FOR KITCHEN CABINETS

Instead of providing separate filler strips, manufacturers of wood and plastic cabinets often make cabinets that are to be placed against a wall or in a corner with extended stiles. The stiles are the equivalent of built-in filler strips and should be scribed and cut in the same way.

Find the highest point in the floor line along the line of cabinets. The cabinet at this point is the first to be installed permanently. Level it carefully side to side and front to back with your carpenter's level. Then fasten it to studs in the wall with two long screws.

Set the adjacent cabinets alongside and shim them up as necessary with wood shingles so all are level and horizontal. Screw them to the wall and fasten each pair of cabinets together with two bolts driven through the sides at top and bottom.

Continue in this way until all the cabinets are installed. If there is an appreciable crack between the base of the cabinets and the floor, it can be covered with a quarter-round molding. Or you may have the flooring flashed up on the toeboards.

The kitchen counter is fastened to the top of the cabinets with screws driven up into it.

Wall cabinets. You will need a helper to hold these while you install them.

Filler strips should be fitted and attached in the same way as for base cabinets.

With a carpenter's level, draw a level line across the wall at the bottom of the cabinets (usually 54 inches above the floor). Holding the cabinets to this line, attach them to the wall with four 4-inch screws driven into the studs. If you can't drive all the screws into studs, use split-wing toggle bolts. Bolt each adjoining pair of cabinets together.

(Note that screws rather than nails should always be used to install all kitchen cabinets. For one thing, they hold better. They can also be removed without damaging the cabinets if you remodel the kitchen.)

The soffits (or false fronts) between the tops of wall cabinets and the ceiling are most easily made with 1/8-inch hardboard cut to fit the space. Nail 1-by-2-inch cleats to the tops of the cabinets 1/8 inch back from the face. Nail additional cleats to the ceiling directly above. Then nail the hardboard to the cleats with small brads. If the hardboard fits tight against the cabinets and ceiling, the job is done. If not, the crack at the top of the cabinets should be covered with a small molding (which may be supplied by the cabinet manufacturer). Use a quarter-round or some other small molding at the ceiling line.

How to take care of kitchen cabinets. Wipe the doors and other surfaces frequently with a damp sponge to remove fingerprints, etc. Go over them with a mild detergent solution about every two weeks and then rinse. The alternative—especially recommended for steel and wood cabinets—is to use a white appliance wax.

Clean drawers and the insides of cabinets about once every two months. Dusting may be sufficient, or you may need a damp sponge and occasionally detergent solution.

Wipe up grease and wet food spills at once. They may attract ants. Worse, they may permanently stain or damage an enamel or transparent finish.

For how to tighten loose knobs, see *Knobs and Pulls.*

How to repair cabinets. If magnetic catches make too much noise when the doors are closed, cover the little plates on the doors with cellulose tape. If the doors make noise because they are striking the frames of the cabinets, glue squares of tire tube to the frames with rubber cement.

If paint is chipped, sand the edges surrounding the area carefully. Then apply touch-up enamel (which should be available from the cabinet-maker). Touch up scratches in a natural finish on wood cabinets with stain and lacquer.

When cabinets need to be completely repainted, the ideal solution is to remove them and have them repainted in an automobile body paint shop. The only other thing you can do is to sand all surfaces thoroughly to smooth chipped areas and roughen the rest of the paint slightly. Wash with detergent solution, rinse, and dry thoroughly. Then paint the cabinets with a spray gun or aerosol can. You can paint them with a brush, but the finish is less smooth.

If the cabinet door and drawer fronts are in really dreadful shape, it may now be possible to have them replaced by new drawer and door fronts. This new service is offered by some large cabinet dealers.

Kitchen Cleaning. Your kitchen, alas, is one room that needs some sort of cleaning every day.

Counters. After every meal, wipe off those you have used. If you don't, you may have a surprise invasion of ants, flies, cockroaches, and other pests. Usually a clean sponge wet in water takes up the mess. But you should also wash all counters with detergent solution every two or three days.

Treat a breakfast table in the same way.

Sink. Empty the strainer after every meal and swish water inside the basin. Wash basin and strainer with detergent solution after doing the dinner dishes.

Range. Wipe up spills on the top surface at once. Sponge off the top with detergent solution after dinner. For additional cleaning requirements, see *Ranges.*

Refrigerators. If you are not tall enough to see the top of the refrigerator, remember that a layer of greasy dust forms on it very quickly. Weekly cleaning with detergent solution is necessary. See *Refrigerators.*

Cabinets and dishwasher. See *Kitchen Cabinets.* The dishwasher front should be wiped off in the same way. It is rarely necessary to clean the tub unless you have hard water. In that case, go over it with a sponge and cleanser. If the dishwasher has a strainer, clean it every couple of days. Also see *Dishwashers* (page 67).

Floor. This is the biggest cleaning job in the kitchen and certainly the most tedious. See *Floors, Resilient.*

To prevent excessive soiling of the area immediately in front of the sink, cover it with a decorative rubber mat about 24 by 16 inches.

To keep grease from splattering on the floor in front of the range, cover that area with newspapers when frying hamburgers and other greasy foods.

Windows. Wash the glass when you wash the rest of the windows in the house. Wash the sills and horizontal mullions about once a month with detergent solution to remove the grease film that forms on all horizontal kitchen surfaces.

Walls and ceiling. How often the walls and ceiling need to be washed depends on how often you cook greasy foods, but it is rarely as frequently as once a year except in the immediate vicinity of the range and ventilating fan. For how to wash these surfaces, see *Ceilings* and *Walls, Interior.*

Ventilating fan. This usually needs to be cleaned once a month; sometimes more often. For how to go about it, see *Fans, Ventilating.*

Kitchen Organization. Kitchen organization is dictated by your own working habits, size, and physical disabilities (if any); the layout of the kitchen and its storage facilities; how much kitchen equipment, china, and glassware you own; and by your food-buying habits. For example, home economists usually suggest that some foods are best stored near the sink, some near the refrigerator, and some near the range. But if you don't ordinarily stock up on large quantities of canned and packaged foods, it is generally simpler to concentrate all of them in one cabinet—close to the refrigerator, if possible, where all other foods are stored.

Kitchen organization is a process of trial and error, give and take. It is never perfect, no matter how well-planned and equipped your kitchen is, simply because few things that you use are used in just one place.

General rules for organizing a kitchen.

1. Because wall cabinets are easier to use than base cabinets, store as many things as possible in them. If wall cabinet space is limited, however, use it for the high-priority items: canned and packaged foods, everyday china and glassware.

2. Use drawers in base cabinets for all articles listed under *Kitchen Tools* except the sifter, canister set, salt and pepper shakers, and possibly the food grinder. Use drawers also for towels, sponges, food wraps, and garbage bags. If you eat in the kitchen, drawer space is also needed for tableware, mats, and napkins.

3. Store the following under the sink: garbage can, dish rack, brush, scouring pads, detergents, and vegetables and fruits that are not refrigerated.

4. These items should be near the sink: towels, paper towels, sponges, strainers, garbage bags, refrigerator containers, colander, everyday china and glass, serving dishes, juicer, teakettle, coffeepot, pitcher, saucepans, kettle, double boiler, butter dish, salt and pepper shakers. Bread should also be stored here if it is used mainly for toast in the morning because you can then put it on one of the stored bread-and-butter plates and take it directly to the table.

5. Store the following near the range: one large spoon, one small spoon, large cooking fork, one small fork, ladles, potato masher, pancake turner, one set of measuring spoons, one measuring cup, tongs, timer, wire whisk, carving knife, skillets, roasting pans, griddle, cake cooling

rack, hand mixer, grease can, paper towels, pot holders, salt, pepper, other seasonings applied to cooked food, instant coffee and tea, cornstarch, shortening.

6. Near the refrigerator store carbonated beverages, bottle opener, ice-cream scoop, ice bucket.

7. Every kitchen has a main food-preparation area. Usually it is near the refrigerator, unless that appliance is in an isolated location. You should store the following items wherever you prepare most foods: all canned and packaged foods including those which are ready to be eaten or cooked and those that are to be mixed with other foods, onions, garlic, food wraps, knives, forks, spoons, spatula, scissors, skewers, sharpening stone, one set of measuring spoons, one measuring cup, sifter, grater, beater, cutting board, rolling pin, pastry blender, canister set, lemon squeezer, apple corer, bean slicer, mixing bowls, baking dish, casseroles, pie plates, cake pans, cookie sheets, muffin pans, mixer, can opener, waffle iron, sandwich grill, cookie jar. Bread should be stored here if it is used more for sandwiches than for breakfast.

Kitchen Planning. As the major work center of the home, the kitchen not only should include all the mechanical servants that are available to simplify the housewife's work but must also be planned with more attention to detail than any other room. Careful planning is especially important now that the kitchen has become a major living center, too.

In designing your dream kitchen, your first consideration should be its location in the house—both in respect to the yard and to the other rooms. There are no definite rules to guide you here, but these points must be considered:

1. Where is the main outdoor play area? The kitchen should be nearby so you can keep an eye on the children, and so they can be near the refrigerator and sink.

2. If you like eating outdoors, where do you do it? The closer the kitchen is, the easier it is to cook, serve, and clean up outside.

3. On the other hand, if you don't have small children and don't eat outdoors

often, the kitchen may be better on the side of the house away from the lawn and garden.

4. Do you like to keep an eye on neighborhood activities and be able to see who is coming up the walk? Then the kitchen belongs in front.

5. Where is the best view? Since so much time is spent in the kitchen, you might as well be able to enjoy the outlook from there.

6. Where is the garage? The kitchen should be close by. Grocery delivery is easier.

7. Which is the west side of the house? Although you can screen out the sun and install air conditioning, it's a good idea to locate the kitchen on a cooler side of the house.

8. Because the kitchen is the hub of activities inside the house, it should be centrally located in relation to other rooms. In a small, compact house this is not so important; in a large, sprawling house it is.

9. The kitchen must be close to the dining room.

10. Do you want to separate family activities and assure more privacy for all? In one-story houses the kitchen can often serve as a buffer between the grownups in the living room and the children in the bedroom area.

Obviously, there is a conflict between many of these ideas; so the location of your kitchen is almost certain to be a compromise. But a compromise based on a careful weighing of all needs and desires will result in a kitchen you can be happy with.

Size of kitchen. The size of the kitchen depends on what you want the kitchen to be. If it's strictly a work room, it can be as small as you like so long as there is enough space for the cabinets, appliances, and yourself. Average appliance widths are as follows:

	Size (inches)
Refrigerator	27 to 36
Range	20 to 40
Built-in oven	24 to 30

	Size (inches)
Built-in cooktop	22 to 33
Single-basin sink	24 to 30
Double-basin sink	33 to 36
Dishwasher	24
Upright freezer	32
Chest freezer	46 to 60

Base and wall cabinets range from 12 to 60 inches wide. Each larger size is 3 inches wider than the previous size.

These widths, however, are not the final factor in determining kitchen size. To be usable, all appliances require adjacent counter space. The minimum counter spaces are as follows:

Range—If burners are on one side, provide 24 inches on that side and 12 inches on the other. If burners are centered, 18 inches on both sides.

Built-in oven—18 inches on one side or the other.

Refrigerator—24 inches on latch side.

Sink—30 inches on each side.

Dishwasher—24 inches on one side or the other in addition to counter that forms top of dishwasher.

Upright freezer—24 inches on latch side.

Chest freezer—24 inches on one side (either one), or divided.

Note that these minimums can be reduced slightly if one counter is adjacent to two appliances.

Counters are 25 inches deep. The standard depth of ranges, sinks, dishwashers, and base cabinets is 24 inches. Some refrigerators and freezers are the same depth, but many are deeper. Remember, however, that most base cabinets and appliances have doors that open out. So your floor space must be at least 48 inches wide to give you enough space to move around easily.

If the laundry is incorporated in the kitchen, you must provide additional floor space for the washer and dryer and an area in which to do the ironing.

If you want to eat in the kitchen, allow space as follows:

Bar—Minimum depth, 18 inches. Width per person, 24 inches.

Rectangular table for two—24 by 30 inches.

Rectangular table for three or four—30 by 36 inches.

Square table for six to eight—48 by 48 inches.

Rectangular table for six—42 by 60 inches.

Round table for four—31- to 37-inch diameter.

Round table for five—38- to 45-inch diameter.

Round table for six—46- to 52-inch diameter.

Round table for seven—53- to 60-inch diameter.

Round table for eight—61- to 68-inch diameter.

Chairs—allow 24 inches from edge of table to back of chair.

Stools—allow 20 inches from edge of bar to back of stool.

If you want a planning desk in the kitchen, allow at least 18 inches for depth and 30 inches for width.

Don't forget that all the above dimensions are minimums. If your kitchen is distinct and separate from any other room, you should not try to squeeze it down in size beyond the point permitted by these dimensions. The only way you can save space is by making the kitchen part of the dining room. In this case, the space that the appliances and cabinets take up is the same, but the area you require to walk around in can be reduced because it is doing double duty.

Most people have found, however, that a minimum kitchen does not suit their modern way of living. It may make for greater convenience by saving steps, but it does not make for greater family livability. The kitchen today is not just the housewife's workshop; it is used by the entire family. Hence it is well to allow at least 100 square feet for the kitchen.

Arrangement of appliances. The convenience and efficiency of a kitchen depends on the arrangement of the appliances in it. Unfortunately, most people have heard so much about the merits of U-shaped, L-shaped, and straight-wall kitchens that they decide arbitrarily that they must have one of these for themselves. This does not always produce the desired results. It is quite possible that some other arrangement—probably a variation of the U or L—will serve them better.

To determine the ideal layout of appliances and cabinets, you must take into consideration the size of the room, location of doors, windows, and heating outlets, your own working habits, whether you are right- or left-handed, and so on. You may have to draw your plans over and over again before you hit on the best solution. Use these rules for a guide:

1. Ideally, the counters should be continuous from one appliance to another. But don't worry if you must break the line to allow for a door.

2. The sink is the hub of most kitchen work. Consequently, it should be placed between the range and the refrigerator.

3. The refrigerator should be 4 feet to a maximum of 7 feet from the sink; the sink, 4 to 6 feet from the range; the range, 4 to 9 feet from the refrigerator.

4. The range should be closest to the dining room door; the refrigerator closest to the door through which groceries are delivered.

5. If a built-in range is used, the burners should be installed near the sink (in the same position that you would place a conventional range). The oven can be installed elsewhere in the work area as long as it is not too far from the sink.

6. The refrigerator must be placed so you don't have to walk around its door to get into it. If such placement is impossible, buy a refrigerator with a door that swings away from the counter alongside. Left- and right-hand-door models are available.

7. The dishwasher should be next to a sink, but it does not have to be the sink in the work area between the refrigerator and range. It might be placed next to a second sink located outside the work area.

8. The sink does not need to be under the kitchen window.

9. A counter near the grocery delivery door is desirable.

Once you have laid out the kitchen work area, including range, refrigerator, and sink, you can decide on the location of other appliances, the eating space, etc. These should not be right in the work area.

Doors and windows. Many kitchens are ruined because doors and windows are put into fixed positions before the appliances and cabinets are laid out. You can lose valuable cabinet space or break the continuity of a counter by poor placement of a door or window.

There is rarely an incontrovertible reason why a door or window must be in a certain place. They can usually be moved a few inches to one side or another to allow for a better appliance arrangement. Even in an existing house, the cost of moving a door or window is low.

Storage space. Provision of ample base and wall cabinet space is essential. You need a minimum of 12 running feet of wall cabinets that are at least 30 inches high and 6 running feet of base cabinets. Open shelves and short cabinets over or under appliances are not considered a substitute for full-size cabinets.

For maximum convenience, about one-half of the total cabinet space should be adjacent to the three main appliances. (See *Kitchen Organization.*) Other cabinets for less frequently used things can be installed anywhere else. If your house is not cramped for space, a separate pantry between the kitchen and dining room is an excellent addition. (It is also a good location for the dishwasher and a second sink.) Even more storage space for canned goods, bottles, glassware, etc., can be provided between the studs on inside walls. Nail shelves between the studs and cover with plywood doors.

To make use of "dead" corners, install cabinets with revolving shelves. Or you can install a standard 24-inch cabinet that opens into the adjoining room or area.

Standard wall cabinets are 12 inches deep and 30 to 36 inches high. They should be installed 18 inches above the counters. The space above the cabinets may or may not be closed in by a soffit. Soffits prevent dust and grease from collecting on top of the cabinets. They can also be used for dead storage space if equipped with doors.

A 24-inch-high wall cabinet can be installed 24 inches above an electric range; but no cabinet should be used over a gas range. Cabinets 15 or 18 inches high are used over refrigerators.

In selecting wall cabinets, use the largest possible sizes. They are proportionally cheaper than several smaller cabinets totaling the same width, and provide a greater stretch of unbroken shelf area.

In selecting base cabinets, remember that drawer types are more usable (and more expensive) than door types. Both are needed, however.

Filler strips 1 to 2 inches wide should be used between cabinets and side walls and in the corners of U- and L-shaped kitchens. They provide clearance for doors and drawers to open. Filler strips are also used between cabinets to fill a wall space exactly.

Also see *Kitchen Cabinets.*

Open kitchens. In an effort to make a house feel larger than it is and to permit the housewife to join more completely in her family's activities, many architects and builders provide instead of a door an extra-wide opening between the kitchen and dining room. This creates problems: Odors and water vapor can circulate freely through the house. The noise of kitchen activities may be annoying. The sight of a messy kitchen is objectionable.

Ideal answers to these problems have not been worked out, but matters can be improved by installing an ozone lamp to kill odors and a powerful ventilating fan to handle odors and water vapor (see *Fans, Ventilating*); using acoustical tiles on the ceiling to absorb noise; installing some kind of drapery or screen that can be pulled across the wall opening.

Actually, the desire for openness in the kitchen can often be satisfied very simply by providing a pass-through in the dining room wall. This can be as large as you like. It is closed by a door when occasion demands. Built above a kitchen counter, the pass-through also simplifies serving and table-clearing operations.

Special installation requirements. Space provided for a conventional refrigerator and upright freezer should be 3 inches wider than the width of the box. This provides an escape for heat generated by the unit.

The range must be placed so there is counter space on both sides of the burners. Do not jam the burners next to a wall. Do not place the range so there is a door or passageway next to the burners.

If possible, don't put the range under a window. Curtain materials may be ignited.

If possible, place the dishwasher to the left of the sink if you are right-handed; to the right if you are left-handed.

Garbage disposers fit into any standard sink and can be adapted to most old sinks. See *Garbage Disposers.*

Heating and cooling the kitchen. When building a new house, you should decide how you will heat and/or cool the kitchen after the kitchen is planned. The reason for this is that radiators and warm-air registers often are located on walls where they interfere with the placement of cabinets or appliances. Actually, there are many ways to heat and cool kitchens other than with conventional outlets. For instance, you can install electric heating wires in the ceiling; electric and gas heaters in the walls above counters; electric and hot-water baseboard radiators at the ceiling; electric heaters in the floor; heat pumps and air conditioners in the walls over doors or windows; and so on. And, of course, after you have laid out a kitchen, you may well find that there are some open wall spaces where you can use conventional heating units at floor level.

In an existing kitchen which you are remodeling, it is sometimes possible to relocate radiators and registers. But in many cases, the only solution is to remove them, cap the pipes or ducts leading to them, and install new outlets of one of the types described above. Such measures are fairly expensive, of course; but if you get a better kitchen as a result, the expense is worthwhile.

Wiring and lighting the kitchen. See *Electrical System, Household,* and *Lighting.*

How to draw kitchen plans. Most amateur planners prefer to use graph paper with four squares to the inch; but with a bit of practice, you will probably find it is just as easy to work on unlined paper with a ruler and a triangle.

In any case, draw an accurate plan of the

room in which the kitchen will be built; then, to spare yourself the nuisance of redrawing this repeatedly, cover it with tracing paper and work out the kitchen plan on this.

First, locate the sink, refrigerator, and range and draw in the counters. Try several arrangements. Draw in wall cabinets with dotted lines. Then draw in the eating area, freezer, etc., outside the kitchen work area.

Study the plan. Consider how well you could work in the kitchen. Note problems. Then draw a new plan in the same way and study that. If you hit upon a plan that you like very much, put it aside and don't look at it for a day or two; then study it some more.

No one ever draws a perfect kitchen plan the first time. Even people who are supposed to be expert kitchen planners must draw four or five—sometimes as many as a dozen—before they arrive at the best possible design. When at last you do reach that point, redraw the plan accurately to the last half-inch; indicate switches, outlets, lights, heat outlets, etc.; list the types and sizes of appliances and cabinets you want to install.

If you have the slightest doubt about the plan, you should now talk it over with a professional kitchen planner. The man you hire to install the kitchen should develop the final working drawings.

How to measure a kitchen to be remodeled. This is an essential and critical step if you intend to make over an old kitchen. You will need a 6-foot rule, pencil, and sheet of graph paper. First measure the overall length of all walls—making the measurements just above the baseboards—and draw a scale plan of the room. Then go back to each wall and measure each segment of it: the distance from a corner to a door; the width of each door and trim; the width of each window and trim; the space between windows; etc. Draw the doors, windows, etc., on the plan and mark down their width; also indicate the width of all other wall segments.

On the plan, mark down the exact location of heating outlets, thermostats, lights, switches, electric outlets, drains, the ventilating fan—everything that may be included in or interfere with the new kitchen.

Measure the ceiling height; door height to the top of the trim; height of windows at the sills and at the top trim. Note these measurements in the margins of the plan.

You now have a complete, accurate plan of the kitchen as it is, and you are ready to start developing a new kitchen plan in the way previously outlined.

Kitchen Tools. (Also see *Kitchen Utensils.*) In time, most homemakers acquire an enormous collection of kitchen tools. This is not because foods and cooking methods keep changing, thus necessitating new tools, but because inventive people are forever looking for better tools to replace their old ones. In addition, since World War II, a great many old but essentially unknown tools have been imported into the United States from abroad.

For the beginning homemaker who intends to do a fair amount of original cooking, the following kitchen tools are almost essential:

Paring knife
Utility knife
Roast slicer
Boner (knife)
2 large spoons
Cooking fork
Slotted spoon
2 cheap dinner forks (for scrambling eggs, etc.)
2 cheap dinner knives (for spreading sandwich fillings, etc.)
2 cheap dessert spoons (for testing gravy, etc.)
Large ladle (for soups, stews)
Small ladle (for gravy, sauces)
Pancake turner
Narrow metal spatula
Rubber spatula
Wire whisk
Kitchen scissors
Vegetable peeler (preferably floating-blade)
5-cup flour sifter
Flat grater (doesn't work any better than other graters but is easier to store)
Regular can opener
Juice can opener

Corkscrew

2 sets of measuring spoons with long handles

Kitchen tongs

Minute timer (if not built into the range)

Canister set

Cutting board

Rolling pin

Beater

Food grinder

Pastry blender

Wooden spoons—2 or 3 of different sizes

2 kitchen brushes (for vegetables and cleaning)

Lemon squeezer

Sharpening stone

Skewers

2 sets of salt and pepper shakers

3 or 4 pot holders

Other kitchen tools you will find useful at some time are:

Apple corer

Nutcracker

Nut grater

Ice-cream scoop

Garlic press

Egg slicer

Poultry shears

Meat thermometer

Candy thermometer

Cake-decorating set

Cookie cutters

Pastry brush

Pepper grinder

Potato masher

Meat turner (a large, curved kind of spatula which is very useful for lifting and turning big roasts, etc.)

Adjustable notched-tooth, screw-top opener

Funnel

Bean slicer

Scale

Since kitchen tools receive hard wear and are sometimes tossed out with the garbage, there is no need to buy the best quality except in the case of cutting knives and the beater. On the other hand, there is no sense abusing even the inexpensive items, for considered as a collection, kitchen tools represent an investment of not inconsiderable size.

Dry tools well after washing.

Do not soak those made of wood in water. Take particular care not to put fine wood-handled knives and cutting boards into the dishwasher.

Empty the canister set occasionally and clean the insides well.

Do not rest plastic handles on the rims of hot frying pans or pots: they melt.

Kitchen Towels. These are made of cotton, cotton terry, and linen. Cotton terry is most absorbent, but linen is better for drying glassware because it is lintless.

Normal sizes are roughly 16 by 30 inches and 20 by 30 inches. There are also extra-large towels of about 24 by 36 inches.

Like bath towels, kitchen towels dried in a dryer at high heat are particularly soft and absorbent.

Kitchen Utensils. (Also see *Kitchen Tools.*) A matched set of kitchen utensils is an attractive feature of any kitchen, but before you invest in one, you should make certain that all the utensils are equally useful and easy to handle. Many home-makers deliberately acquire an odd collection of utensils simply because they feel each piece has unique utilitarian merits.

Whatever the design of the utensils you buy, these are the pieces that the average homemaker who does a reasonable amount of cooking needs:

Teakettle—2- to 3-quart size

8-quart covered kettle (also called a sauce pot). It is a little hard to store but preferable to a 5-quart kettle (also called a Dutch oven) because it can be used for the same things and many more.

1-quart covered saucepan

2-quart covered saucepan

3-quart covered saucepan

Double boiler—2-quart base; 1½-quart top

Covered skillet—10-inch

Electric frying pan—12-inch

Roasting pan—about 9 by 12 inches (may be covered)

Roasting pan—about 12 by 17 inches (may be covered)

Meat rack

1½-quart rectangular baking dish

1½-quart round covered casserole

2-quart round covered casserole

Two 9-inch pie plates

Two 8-inch layer cake pans

9-inch square cake pan

Wire cake racks

Two cookie sheets

Muffin pan to make 12 muffins

Set of four mixing bowls

Set of metal cups for dry measure

Two 8-ounce measuring cups or one 8-ounce and one 16-ounce

Colander

Large strainer

Tea strainer

Toaster

Mixer

Can opener

Coffee-makers

Many of the above utensils come in other sizes that you may someday find useful. In addition, you may someday need many other small electrical appliances as well as the following nonelectrical items:

Cookie jar

Cake plate with cover

Refrigerator storage containers

Dry-goods storage containers

Loaf pan

Sponge-cake pan

Spring-form cake pan

Soufflé dish

Griddle

8-inch skillet

Teapot

3- or 4-quart casserole

Omelet pan

Custard cups or ramekins

Molds

Egg poacher

Food mill

20-quart stock pot or canner

Also see entries for specific appliances, such as *Blenders; Can Openers; Mixers, Electric.*

When buying kitchen utensils, make sure they are made of quality material that isn't going to chip, bend, dent, or break in short order. The utensils should be well balanced. They must be easy to handle and stand upright when empty and full (for example, a tea strainer that has such a heavy handle that it won't sit on top of a pot unless held is a pretty annoying thing). Handles should be heat-resistant; covers should fit tight. Bottoms of utensils used on the range surface must be flat and rigid so they can be used efficiently on electric ranges and on all burners with thermostatic controls. The bottoms should also fit the burners.

Utensils are made of a variety of excellent materials.

Aluminum is the choice of many home economists because it distributes heat well, is lightweight, and is reasonably easy to take care of. The best utensils are made of cast aluminum. Sheet aluminum is second-rate because it is so easily damaged. Aluminum's worst drawbacks are its tendency to darken when exposed to alkalies and to pit if salty foods are left standing in the utensil.

Cast iron is very heavy and requires a strong arm; but it also distributes heat well, though slowly, and is very durable. It rusts badly, however, if it is not well seasoned with oil and/or if it is washed in a dishwasher. Most new utensils come preseasoned. If you find one that is not or if you inherit an old utensil, wash it thoroughly, swish some salad oil all over the inner surface, and put the utensil in the oven at low heat for 2 or 3 hours. Then wipe off the oil with paper towels.

Copper utensils are rather rare but excellent if made of thick metal that is tin-plated on the inside. (The copper molds made for decorating a wall are not designed for cooking.) Heat distribution is excellent, but even the best weight of metal can be dented with reasonable ease. If used frequently, the tinplate will eventually wear off, but it can be renewed.

Enamelware is made of porcelain-coated sheet steel, cast iron, or cast aluminum. It is very colorful and good-looking, but even the best grades of enamel can be chipped or crazed. They are also sometimes stained by acid. Cast-iron utensils are the best; aluminum the next; sheet metal a poor third.

Another kind of enamelware actually should not be called enamelware because the finish is made of plastic rather than porcelain; however, it looks like enamelware and can be distinguished from it only by the fact that it is made of rather thin aluminum and is less expensive. The finish is considerably less durable than porcelain.

Heat-resistant glass is an old favorite for baking. Foods cook at temperatures 25 degrees lower than in metal. The utensils are easy to clean and retain their original appearance for a long time, but will eventually become a little cloudy from scratching with abrasives and kitchen tools. On the minus side is their breakability.

Glass-ceramic is a new material with the same qualities as glass, but it is much more durable. Utensils can be used on the range surface as well as in the oven right after you remove them from the refrigerator. The material is also attractive enough for the utensils to be used as serving dishes.

Pottery baking dishes have been in use for centuries. They hold heat well but break easily. Only glazed pottery is easy to clean.

Stainless steel is the strongest, most durable and damage-resistant material used in cooking utensils, but it is not a first-class distributor of heat. For this reason, the bottoms of saucepans and other surface-cooking utensils are commonly made of copper, aluminum, or heavy steel (although these materials are not always visible). Baking utensils and mixing bowls, however, are stainless steel throughout.

Stainless steel is easy to clean and is not harmed by scouring, but it may develop dark heat spots which can be extremely difficult to remove. Copper bottoms also become dark and are likely to flake if you leave an empty pan on a hot burner; but the pans are easy to clean with a cleaner made especially for stainless-steel utensils.

Teflon is a plastic coating applied to the inner surfaces of some utensils. It prevents food from sticking and thus makes cleaning easier. Very little if any fat is needed in cooking. But even the newest type of Teflon is not impervious to scratching by kitchen tools.

Tinware is lightweight steel with a plating of tin. The material is used mainly for cake and pie pans, cookie sheets, and similar utensils. These dent and warp easily and may rust if you cut through the tinplate; but they are indispensable and cheap to replace.

How to take care of kitchen utensils. While most utensils other than glass are tough enough to be thrust under a stream of cold water when they are delivered scalding hot from the range, it is just as well to let them cool a bit first. Then the chances of warping and breaking are reduced, and you don't fill the kitchen air with steam and flying grease.

Wipe grease out of utensils with paper towels. Scrape off baked-on food with a spatula. Many utensils can be washed under a stream of hot water; others need to be scrubbed in detergent solution or with a cleanser and even a scouring pad. Utensils that are not covered with burned-on food can be put in the dishwasher provided they do not have wooden handles.

Use special plastic scouring pads on Teflon—never anything more abrasive. If a Teflon pan loses its finish, you can apply an aerosol nonstick spray. The same spray can be applied to all other kinds of utensils and tools.

For more about the care of kitchen utensils, see the entries for the materials of which they are made. Also see *Dishwashing.*

Knife Sharpeners, Electric. Sharpening knives is a job often put off and neglected. Electric sharpeners are quick and efficient, but unfortunately many people use them badly and thus ruin knives rather than improving them.

To use a sharpener, you merely draw the knife along a slot containing a rotating wheel. Some units sharpen one side of the blade at a time; others sharpen both simultaneously. Although scissors also can be sharpened on most units, your best scissors should be sharpened by a professional.

Knife sharpeners are available as a separate appliance but are often combined with another, particularly a can opener. Some mixers are also equipped to sharpen knives.

For how to sharpen knives well, see *Knives, Kitchen.*

Knitted Fabrics. Knitted fabrics can be produced from any kind of fiber, but in the past have been most commonly made of cotton, wool, silk, and nylon. Recently polyester has come into vogue. All are formed by interlocking loops of yarn.

Cotton knits are washed in warm water and dried at moderate heat. Wool knits are most safely dry-cleaned but can be washed by hand in cold or lukewarm water and rinsed in cold. The water should then be pressed out of them gently and they should be stretched to shape, laid flat, and allowed to dry naturally.

Synthetic knits are laundered like permanent press. Wash in warm water and remove from the tub as soon as they are rinsed. Dry at low heat for about 15 minutes; then continue tumbling without heat for 10 minutes. Remove the articles from the dryer immediately.

Knits rarely need pressing except to smooth out occasional stubborn wrinkles.

Holes and tears in knitted fabrics are mended with either a knit stitch or blanket stitch. The latter is easier, but the former produces a more elastic, less conspicuous mend.

Knives, Electric. Electric knives are useful not only for such major productions as carving a roast but also for many preparatory slicing jobs such as slicing tomatoes and onions.

The basic part of the knife consists of two linked, serrated blades which move rapidly in opposite directions when in use. They fit into a handle that plugs into an electric outlet or is cordless and operates on rechargeable batteries. The cordless models are recharged while in their storage base, which is connected to an electric outlet. The advantages of a cordless knife are that there is no cord to get in the way and you can use the knife where an outlet isn't available—on the patio or at a picnic.

Features you should look for in an electric knife include good balance and a comfortable handle. The knife should have a guard on the end of the blades near the handle to keep fats and juices away from the unit itself. The blades should be easy to insert and remove. (A few models have a sheath to cover the blades while you're doing this.) A safety-lock switch, which prevents the knife from being turned on accidentally, is particularly important for the cordless models. Other models should be unplugged when you remove or insert blades.

Most slicing knives come with a storage unit for handle and blades; in cordless models it provides the contact for recharging. This storage unit may sit on a counter, hang on a wall, or fit in a drawer. It should be designed to shield the cutting side of the blade from an unwary hand.

To clean an electric knife, unplug it, remove the blades, and wash them in warm detergent solution. Do not soak them or put them in the dishwasher. Dry well. The knife handle is wiped off with a damp cloth.

To preserve the edges of the blades, which cannot be resharpened, carve on a wood board rather than on china or metal. This also helps to preserve platters, which may be damaged by the blades. Don't cut bones or frozen foods.

Knives, Kitchen. There is an amazing difference between good knives and poor. To begin with, the good knives cost much, much more. But after you recover from the shock of their expense, you will find that you never use any other knives in the kitchen, even though you have a drawer full of cheap ones. The good knives are a pleasure to use. They save time and they are safer. Why? Because they hold a sharp edge for a long time. (This not only facilitates cutting but also helps to prevent accidents because a sharp knife cuts what it is supposed to cut—it doesn't "bounce" off the food and slice your finger.) They are balanced better and handle better. And they are made of sturdy metal which doesn't break.

A further advantage of good knives is that you don't need very many of them. Exactly what you do need depends on what you cook and the way you cook. Basic types of knife include the following:

Paring knife, generally with a 3-inch blade.

Utility knife with a blade 4 to 7 inches long.

Roast slicer with 8- to 12-inch blade for carving.

Ham slicer with 10-inch blade rounded at the end.

Boner, or trimmer, with a heavy 6-inch blade.

French cook's, or chef's, knife, usually with an 8-inch triangular blade that is wider than the handle where they join.

Butcher knife with a wide 7-inch blade.

Bread knife with scalloped or saw-toothed blade.

Grapefruit knife with a short, curved blade with serrated edges.

Selecting knives. The best material for knife blades is high-carbon steel. It will rust; but it takes a sharp edge easily and holds it for a long time.

Stainless steel is prettier and rust-proof, but doesn't stay sharp so long. High-carbon stainless steel is better but still not up to high-carbon steel. The same is true of vanadium steel. Ordinary sheet steel and iron are not desirable.

Hollow-ground blades, which are slightly concave, are a bit better than other blade shapes. Serrated blades are claimed to be better than straight-edged blades because they stay sharp and never need sharpening; but this is a gross exaggeration.

Wood handles are handsome but you should not put them in the dishwasher because the hot detergent solution bleaches and roughens them. Plastic or hard rubber handles are better. Be sure that the handle fits your hand and that the knife feels nicely balanced. For strength and durability of larger knives, the tang (an extension of the blade) should run up through the center of the handle for its full length. On small knives it need extend up into the handle for about half its length. Rivets should be used to fasten the handle and tang together firmly.

How to take care of good knives. Keep them in a case or rack separate from one another—not jumbled together in a drawer where they will quickly lose their edge. Magnet holders are undesirable because they can dull the edge. Furthermore, it is possible to knock a knife loose from them—perhaps on to your hand or feet.

Use a cutting board to cut on.

Don't soak knives in water. Wash them soon after you're through with them—before food hardens on them and you have to struggle to get it off. Dry thoroughly—the handle, too.

How to sharpen knives. Electric sharpeners and stationary sharpeners made of steel circles through which you draw the blade several times produce sharp edges; but usually wreck the blades in time. This is mainly because people don't maintain an even pressure on the blades at all points, and as a result, they develop a scalloped look.

The best way to sharpen knives is on a sharpening stone—preferably one measuring 2 by 6 inches with a coarse grit on one side and fine grit on the other. Wet the stone with water to prevent filling the pores with particles of steel and stone.

Lay the blade flat across the coarse side of the stone and tilt up the back edge at a 20-degree angle. Then move the blade in circles toward the sharp edge. Start at the tip of the blade and work toward the base in a spiral motion. Pressure on the blade should be somewhat heavier on the forward part of the stroke than on the backward part.

After sharpening both sides of the blade, turn the stone over and repeat the process on the fine side of the stone. Test for sharpness with your thumb.

Carving knives are also sometimes sharpened on a steel—a long, round rod finished like a very fine file. This does not produce as good an edge as a stone, but is useful for touching up knives that are getting a little dull.

The steel should have a guard above the handle. Hold the steel in your left hand, pointing up and away from you at a 45-degree angle. In your right hand, hold the base of the knife blade to the tip of the steel and bring the blade down and to the right in a sweeping motion that ends with the blade tip near the guard on the steel. Sharpen the right edge of the blade on the top of the steel; the left edge on the bottom. Alternate one stroke on each side.

Knobs and Pulls. Don't just get disgusted with the way the knobs and pulls on your furniture, cabinets, doors, etc., are forever coming loose. Do something about them.

Remove the bolt that is usually driven into the back of the knob (or pull). Dab a very little silicone caulking compound on the back of the knob, well away from the exposed edges. Set the knob in its proper position and replace the bolt and tighten it well. Do not turn the knob; only the bolt.

One slight disadvantage of this repair is that if you ever have to remove the knob, you will find it a bit hard to do. The caulking is a strong adhesive.

If the threads of the bolt are worn and do not hold tightly in the knob for that reason, rub silicone caulking compound into them before tightening.

Similarly, if the bolt at the back of a pull has such worn threads that the nut will not hold on the other end, screw the nut as tight as possible and then dab caulking compound on it and on the exposed threads. The alternative is to apply plastic metal.

If a doorknob spins without moving the latch, tighten the screw in the base of the knob. Should the knob continue to spin, unscrew it from the spindle. Then unscrew the other knob and replace the spindle.

Knots. Knot-tying is a lost art. But there are still several knots besides the bow knot which almost everyone should know and has occasion to use.

Square knot is used to tie together the ends of a string or rope or to join two pieces. To tie, cross the ends and bring the bottom piece up over, around, and under the top piece. Bend the two ends toward each other and bring the top piece over, around, and up over the bottom piece. Pull the ends in opposite directions. The knot looks like two neat interlocking loops.

Many people make the mistake of starting the top piece under the bottom piece. This forms a granny knot, which has no strength.

Bowline is tied to form a nonslip loop in a string or rope. Make an overhand loop with the end of the rope held toward you. Then pass the end up through the loop, around behind the standing part, and down through the loop again. Pull tight. If you want to anchor yourself on a steep roof, you should loop a rope around your waist and tie a bowline.

A pair of half hitches is used to draw a rope tight around an object. It is, for instance, a good knot to use to hang a swing from a tree limb. To tie, pass the end around the object and then halfway around the long length of rope and

through the loop thus formed. Draw tight. Then double the end back and under the long length of rope again; up and through the new loop. Draw tight once more.

Clove hitch is used for the same purpose as a pair of half hitches. It can be tied in the middle of a rope or at the end, but has a tendency to slip when tied too close to the end. Wrap the rope around the object and over itself. Then wrap the rope around the object a second time and pull the end under itself and draw tight. No matter whether you now pull on the right or left end of the rope, it tightens down on itself and holds the object securely.

Knot Sealers. See *Painting (Prepare the surface with care*, step 9).

Kraftfiber. A fibrous material made from wood pulp. It is dyed and woven into rugs that are used on porches and in other informal areas indoors and out. Since the rugs fade badly in sunlight and soak up moisture, they should be coated with vinyl.

Vacuum rugs of kraftfiber regularly to keep dirt from penetrating the fibers. Sponge with water or mild detergent solution to remove soil.

Labeling. Labels help to take some of the chaos out of daily life. But unfortunately, although labeling is a very simple task, it is usually very badly done—if done at all.

In the well-equipped household, a small supply of labels of various kinds should be maintained at all times. The most useful, inexpensive labels are: (1) Paper labels with self-adhesive backing. These stay stuck down better for a longer period of time than labels that must be moistened. (2) Lightweight cardboard shipping tags with reinforced punch-outs through which twine or wire is looped. (3) Round, metal-rimmed tags designed especially for use on articles that receive considerable handling—for example, keys.

A very popular type of stick-down label is a plastic tape that is run through a small embossing machine called a tapewriter, or labelmaker. The main advantage of these labels is that they are legible, neat, and permanent. They are also fun to make. But they are a little more expensive than some other methods.

TYING KNOTS

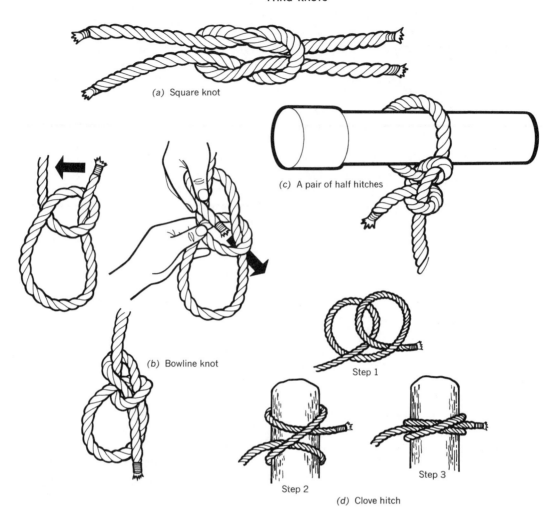

(a) Square knot

(c) A pair of half hitches

(b) Bowline knot

Step 1

Step 2

Step 3

(d) Clove hitch

Labels are generally needed for the following things:

Keys not in key cases. Use metal-rimmed tags. Or hang the keys on a keyboard inside a closet and paste labels on the board above them.

Electrical circuits. Post individual labels or one large printed list inside the cover of the circuit-breaker panel or fuse box.

Plumbing valves in the basement, utility room, and pump house. Use tie-on tags and spray them with clear lacquer to keep them from becoming so grimy you can't read them. An excellent alternative is to use embossed labels.

Boxes, trunks, chests in which things are stored. Attach labels listing the contents.

File boxes, albums, or other containers for photographic slides, prints, negatives, or films.

Boxes, jars—whatever containers you use—of nails, screws, bolts, tacks, etc.

Paint cans. Label with the name of the room in which each paint was used.

Filing-cabinet drawers. Also, of course, each filing-cabinet folder.

Plants inside and outside the house. It is silly not to know their names when somebody asks. Use wood or plastic plant labels.

Lace. Lace is a net-like fabric with an ornamental design worked in. It is made of silk, cotton, nylon, and acetate. Lace articles can be dry-cleaned but may also be hand-washed in lukewarm water and light-duty detergent. Lay them flat on a towel to dry. Press when slightly damp. Lift and lower the iron; do not slide it.

Valuable lace that is stored for long periods should be laid flat or, if the piece is large, rolled loosely in a white terry towel or piece of white felt. Seal from the air—you can wrap it in paper or a plastic bag.

Lacquer. Lacquer is a clear or pigmented finish that is widely used in industry but is rarely used by the home handyman except to finish furniture and to waterproof non-washable wallpaper. Its special virtues are durability, resistance to alcohol, and beauty. There are lacquers that are so clear and colorless that you cannot tell they have been used except by the shine of the surface. All lacquers are sensitive to heat.

Some lacquers are available in aerosol sprays. Others can be applied by spray gun. But the lacquers most used in furniture work are called brushing lacquers. These dry more slowly than other lacquers, but even so, they are tricky and you should practice with them a while before you go to work in earnest.

Lacquer can be applied over shellac but not over most other finishes because it eats right through them. This means you must either cover an old finish with shellac or remove it entirely. If using a stain under clear lacquer, use one with an alcohol or water base.

The room in which lacquer is applied should be warm, dust-free, and well ventilated. Because the finish is very volatile, do not smoke or work near a fire. Thin the lacquer with lacquer thinner according to directions on the can. It will be very runny, which is one reason for practicing before tackling a job.

Use a first-class brush and clean it thoroughly in lacquer thinner. Then load it full and flow the lacquer on the surface in swift, even strokes. Because lacquer dries rapidly, you must work fast. Overlap parallel strokes just enough to eliminate bare spots. Work from the high point of the surface downward. Do not try to brush the lacquer out unless it runs. The finish should level itself.

Allow each coat at least as much drying time as the directions call for. Usually an hour is about right. Then rub it down carefully with fine sandpaper or steel wool and apply a second coat. Because the lacquer is thin, you may need three or four coats to achieve the desired effect. Sand each coat except the last. This may be left with its natural glassy look. For a velvety look, rub it down with pumice stone or rottenstone (see *Abrasives*).

Scratches on a lacquered surface can generally be obliterated by rubbing a cotton swab dipped in lacquer thinner over them. The thinner dissolves the lacquer and makes it flow together. On larger damaged areas apply matching lacquer which is well diluted with thinner.

Ladders. In 1968, the extension ladder on which a New England paint dealer was painting his own house suddenly slipped, buckled, and came crashing to the ground. One year later the paint dealer was still encased in plaster when he wasn't undergoing surgery.

Such accidents are not rare. Ladders are lethal. And the only way you can protect yourself is to buy the best and use it cautiously.

Stepladders. Stepladders are made of wood and aluminum. The latter are lighter, more durable, and more rigid. But they have a tendency to "walk"; and even though the steps are grooved, they are more slippery than wood steps.

Conventional stepladders come in 2-, 5-, 6-, 7-, and 10-foot heights. Taller ladders are available, but for the majority of families a 5-footer is adequate. A 2-foot ladder is useful in the home primarily for cleaning ceilings and blinds and reaching things on the top shelves of tall closets and kitchen wall cabinets.

An unusual type of stepladder converts to an extension ladder. It can also be used as two single ladders, and used on stairs. A 6-foot size extends to 11 feet.

When using a stepladder, always open it all the way and lock the extension arms. Then make sure the ladder is standing firmly on all four legs and is not leaning to one side or forward (a very slight lean backward is not so dangerous but should be avoided). If it is leaning, put a wide board under the downhill legs.

Don't stand on the top step of a ladder unless someone is holding it for you. Even when you are on the next-to-the-top step, assistance is desirable.

Extension ladders. Aluminum ladders have just about pushed wood ladders off the market because they are so much easier to handle. Magnesium ladders are still easier to handle but their cost is high.

Actually, for a heavy man, a wood ladder is still the best buy because while it may not really be stronger than a top-quality aluminum ladder, it feels sturdier when you are on it. But a wood ladder over 24 feet in length is no fun to handle.

Aluminum extension ladders are available in 16-, 20-, 24-, 28-, 32-, 36-, and 40-foot lengths. Their maximum extended length, however, is 3 or 4 feet less than their nominal length. If you are buying a ladder to climb up on a roof, measure the height of the roof at the eaves and add 4 feet to allow for the fact that the ladder will be slanted and should rise well above the eaves so you can climb onto the roof safely. You need a ladder with a maximum extended length equal to this figure.

A useful optional accessory for an extension ladder is a standoff stabilizer. When attached to the top of a ladder, this wide, bow-shaped device holds the ladder away from the wall about a foot. The ends will straddle a window about 45 inches wide or reach over gutters.

To erect a ladder, brace the bottom end against a rock or curb, then lift the top end and walk forward under the ladder, raising it rung by rung until it is vertical. You can then carry the ladder to the house wall by reaching through it with your right arm and grasping a rung level with the top of your head. Don't try to carry a ladder in this fashion, however, if it is extended.

To extend a ladder, hold it upright and then pull up the top section with the rope that runs through the pulley at the top of the bottom section. Make sure the top section is locked securely in place; then let the ladder slant forward. The distance from the bottom of the ladder to the house wall should equal one-fourth the extended height of the ladder. If the ladder is further from the wall, it may break; and if it is closer, it may topple backward.

Make sure the ladder is not slanting to one side or the other and that it is on a firm base. If the ground is soft, place a wide plank under the legs. If the base is smooth, you must do something to keep the legs from skidding. Have someone hold the ladder; or nail a thick cleat of wood behind the rails; or lay a bag of sand behind them; or loop a rope around the bottom rung and tie it to a post, tree, or shrub between the ladder and the house.

If you place a ladder against a tree, make sure that the top ends of both rails rest firmly on the trunk and/or a sturdy branch. If only the uppermost rung rests on the trunk, the ladder can slip from side to side or may twist around the trunk.

Before climbing a ladder, be certain that the soles of your shoes are clean and dry. Wear thick leather-soled shoes if you will spend a long time on the ladder; the rungs won't tire your feet so much. As you climb, use both hands to grasp the rungs. Keep tools in your pockets. Pull up large tools, pails of paint, etc., by a rope.

Never climb above the third rung from the top. Keep both feet firmly on the rungs when working. Don't stretch too far to either side.

When working on a steep roof, use one section of an extension ladder to climb on. To hold the ladder securely, tie a stout manila rope to the top rung, toss the free end over the ridge, and tie it to a tree on the other side of the house. If there isn't a tree, run the end of the rope through a window and tie it to a long 2-by-4 laid horizontally across the interior window trim and adjacent walls.

Always store ladders under cover so they won't rot or corrode. Hang an extension ladder horizontally and flat against a wall on large L-shaped shelf brackets.

If the rails on a wood ladder are cracked or rotten or if those on a metal ladder are even slightly bent, don't take chances and try to brace them. Buy a new ladder.

If a rung on a wood ladder is cracked or broken, the only safe way to replace it is to drill out the ends by drilling all the way through both rails. Then insert a new rung of oak of the same size. If the rung on a metal ladder is broken, have it repaired or replaced by a metal-working shop.

Remember: Ladders are lethal. Don't take chances with them.

Lamé. A beautiful silk or rayon fabric glittering with metal threads, lamé is used in clothing. It must be dry-cleaned.

Laminated Fabrics. A laminated fabric is almost always made of different materials and may be two or more layers thick. It is made by bonding one fabric to another with an adhesive or by bonding fabric to foam with heat.

Although there are occasional problems with delamination, all laminated fabrics can be laundered in automatic washers and dryers in the same way as permanent press. The only difference is that the laminates must be handled very gently and in small loads. Use slow speeds. Fabrics made with foam should be treated like delicate silks and nylons. A cool-down period at the end of the rinse and drying cycles is required for some fabrics but not all.

Laminated Papers. See *Wall Coverings.*

Laminated Plastics. See *Plastic Laminates.*

Laminated Wood Veneers. See *Wall Coverings.*

Lamps. See *Lighting.*

Lampshades. See *Lighting.*

Latex Cement. See *Concrete.*

Lauhala. A glossy yellowish-brown material made from the leaves of a Hawaiian tree. The leaves are folded into 1-inch strips and plaited into thin mats that can be used as rugs and screens.

Vacuum to remove dirt and grit. Wash with water or detergent solution frequently. This not only keeps the material clean but also prevents it from getting brittle. The tendency to brittleness is stronger in hot climates than cold.

If a strip is broken, it can generally be glued to the strip underneath with white wood glue. Or you can cover the break on the back side with a patch of almost anything.

Laundering. Laundering consists of washing, drying, and ironing items made of fabric. The first ingredient in laundering is water. It is essential that you have:

1. Enough water. A 15-pound automatic washer going through a complete wash-rinse cycle with a full tub uses about 60 gallons of water; and if you add a soak cycle, the washer uses another 30 gallons. Of course, if you buy a washer with a suds-saving feature, and if you have a big enough laundry tub into which the suds water can be pumped, you reduce your water needs about 30 gallons on a *second* wash load. If you have a nonautomatic washer (wringer or spinner model), you can also reduce water consumption on a *second* load. Nevertheless, washing clothes requires a good supply of water.

2. Reasonably soft water. Water hardness is measured in grains (see *Water Softeners*). If your water has less than 15 grains of hardness, almost any detergent you use will soften it adequately. Above 15 grains, however, you should either install a water softener on the supply line or use a packaged nonprecipitating water softener in the wash cycle. For water with 15 grains hardness, use ¼ cup; 20 grains, ½ cup; 25 grains, ¾ cup; 30 grains, 1 cup. Above 30 grains, add 1 tablespoon of softener for each additional 5 grains hardness.

If you use soap rather than a detergent, you should add 3 tablespoons water softener to water of 5 grains hardness. Above that, use softener as follows: 10 grains hardness, 1/3 cup; 15 grains, 2/3 cup; 20 grains, ¾ cup; 25 grains, 1 cup; 30 grains, 1¼ cups; each additional 5 grains, 1 tablespoon. The softener should be used in both the wash and the rinse waters, but especially the rinse water.

3. Hot water. Water used for clothes washing should be between 140 and 160 degrees. Since water loses temperature on its way through the pipes from the water heater to the washing machine, your water heater thermostat should be set at 160 degrees minimum.

Of course, cold-water detergents are available; and if for some reason it is impossible to raise your water temperature, you can use these. But don't expect your cottons and linens to come out as well as if you used hot water. Cold-water detergents are fully effective only when used to wash woolens and other fabrics that require cold-water washing.

Soaps and detergents. Soap is best used only if your water is naturally soft or goes through a mechanical water softener before it reaches the washer. If you have to take the time to pour a powdered water softener into the washer at the start of the rinse cycle, you lose some of the convenience an automatic washer is supposed to give.

Soaps are classified as heavy-duty, or all-purpose, and light-duty, or fine-fabric. The former are used for washing cottons and linens; the latter for silks, rayons, and other fine fabrics, delicately colored cottons, linens, and lightly soiled articles.

Detergents can be used in soft water and are especially recommended for water with any degree of hardness. Some are dry powders; some, liquids; and a few are in tablet form.

As noted earlier, there are cold-water detergents and also two other types of detergent that are classified like soaps, as heavy-duty or light-duty, and used in the same way. Of these, the heavy-duty, or all-purpose, detergents break down into three types: high-sudsing, controlled-sudsing, and low-sudsing. The degree of sudsing has no effect on the cleaning ability of a detergent. It's a matter to be considered only if your water is very soft, thus producing an objectionable amount of suds.

To complicate the detergent picture further, many manufacturers are now selling detergents containing enzymes. Known as enzyme-active detergents, these are especially effective in removing blood- and milk-based stains from fabrics; but they cannot be used with chlorine bleach, because the bleach kills the enzymes. (The only way to benefit from the cleaning action of a bleach as well as enzymes is to add the bleach to the wash cycle 5 minutes or more after the cycle starts.)

Which detergent or soap you use is a matter of personal experience: use the one that does the best job for you. And stick with it, because if you switch back and forth—especially between detergents and soaps—your clothes may develop a gray or yellow cast.

For a brief discussion of the water-pollution problems caused by detergents, see *Detergents*.

Enzyme presoakers. These have recently arrived on the laundering scene and have been welcomed by many homemakers. But they have also been labeled pollutants by conservationists.

The presoakers are powders used to supplement the action of detergents when you must launder very dirty or badly stained fabrics or fabrics such as wool and silk that are sensitive to chlorine bleach. The enzymes are particularly effective in the removal of protein stains such as blood, milk, gravy, and urine. But they have no germicidal powers.

To use enzyme presoakers, you simply fill a basin or washer tub with warm water, add the presoaker according to the maker's directions, and allow the clothing to soak for *at least* 30 minutes, but preferably overnight. Chlorine bleach should not be added to the solution.

Bleaches. A bleach does not remove soil but does remove stains and helps to restore or maintain whiteness in fabrics, and a chlorine bleach has germicidal properties. It must be used with care, however, since it can damage fabrics.

The most common type of bleach is chlorine, which is available in powdered or liquid form. This is an extremely potent chemical and must not be used on silk, wool, acetate, rayon, and various resin-treated fabrics; or with household ammonia or enzyme-active detergents or enzyme presoakers. Follow these rules when using it:

1. Find out what the full-load water capacity of your washer is and use the bleach only in the amounts specified by the maker. (For instance, if your washer holds 25 gallons of water and you are supposed to use only 1 tablespoon of bleach per gallon, you should use no more than 25 tablespoons.) Do not use bleach if the tub contains less than a full load of water unless you are sure about the gallonage of the partial load.

2. If your washer has a bleach dispenser, use it. It is designed to introduce the bleach into the wash water at the correct time. Only liquid bleach is used in dispensers.

3. If you add bleach by hand, dilute it with at least a quart of water and add it only to the wash cycle after activation has started and the detergent has dissolved. (It is possible to add bleach to the wash water before the clothes are loaded in, but this reduces the whitening action of the detergent.)

4. Never pour undiluted bleach directly into the washer or on dry clothes.

Oxygen bleaches are milder than chlorine bleaches and can be used on *all* fabrics. They can also be used with enzyme-active detergents and enzyme pre-soakers.

One of the oxygen bleaches is hydrogen peroxide, a liquid that is most useful for treatment of special stains. The other is sodium perborate, a powder that is added to the wash water with the detergent. Its effectiveness increases with the temperature of the water.

To disinfect clothing, bedding, etc., use chlorine bleach or any of the disinfectants described under *Disinfectants.*

Bluing. Bluing has no cleaning ability. It simply makes laundry look whiter by restoring the blue tones that tend to disappear when white fabrics age and turn yellow. Some detergents contain brighteners that accomplish the same thing.

Dry-bead or flake bluing is added to the wash water with the detergent. Liquid or tablet bluing is diluted in a quart of warm water and added to the rinse.

Fabric softeners. More and more homemakers are using fabric softeners to make fabrics fluffier, reduce wrinkling, and prevent static electricity in synthetics. The softeners are especially effective with pile fabrics and knits; but if used continuously with any fabric, they may cause discoloration and reduce absorbency.

Fabric softeners are used only in the final rinse water. They should never be mixed with detergent, soap, bleach, starch, or bluing; and some should not be used with water softeners. If your automatic washer has an automatic fabric-softener dispenser, use it; otherwise wait until the final rinse and then pour the softener directly into the washer. You can also use a softener when washing clothes by hand.

Starch. Dry and liquid starches have virtually disappeared from supermarket shelves since the advent of spray starch. Although the latter costs more, it is much easier to use and *allegedly* does not scorch. All you have to do is spread a garment out on your ironing board, spray it lightly with the starch, and iron at once. The garment may be dry or damp. The iron should be heated to one setting below that normally used for the fabric.

In addition to its extra cost, a drawback of spray starch is that it does not treat garments as evenly as old-fashioned starches. If you use the latter for small jobs, mix it with water in a bowl or basin. Dip and squeeze damp articles in the solution until they are evenly wet; then wring them well or spin-dry in your washer; and place them in your dryer until they are damp-dry. They are then ready for ironing. If the starched articles are hung on a line, allow them to dry completely; then sprinkle with water; wrap in a damp towel or sheet of plastic for an hour or two until they are evenly damp, and iron.

If starching a large load, wash and rinse the clothes in the usual way. Then reset your washing machine to wash and add the starch after agitation starts. Continue agitating for several minutes; then advance the machine to spin. Dry as above.

After a washing machine is used for starching, it should be cleaned thoroughly by putting it through a complete rinse cycle.

How to wash clothes. Step 1. Sort articles according to fabric, colorfastness, construction, bulk, and degree of soil. The typical family wash is separated into the following groups: (a) white cottons and linens; (b) colorfast cottons and linens; (c) noncolorfast cottons and linens; (d) permanent press; (e) delicately constructed whites; (f) delicately constructed colored items; (g) woolens; (h) baby clothes; (i) heavily soiled work or play clothing.

Test colored articles for colorfastness if you are uncertain by soaking a snip from a seam in a jar of detergent and water of the correct washing temperature for a few minutes. If color appears in the water, wash the article by itself.

No load should consist entirely of large pieces. Very large pieces such as rugs, blankets, quilts, draperies, and slipcovers should be washed by themselves.

Step 2. Make sure that no load is too large. It is far better to underload a washer tub than to overload it: even though you waste water, you get your clothes cleaner and they will set fewer wrinkles.

The maximum load size for your washer is indicated in the instruction manual. Usually this is figured in pounds of dry clothes. If you want to be precise, you can weigh each load before dropping it into the washer; but it is not really necessary to do this if you have a general idea of what washable articles weigh. The table indicates this:

Article	Approximate weight (pounds)	Pieces per pound
Sheet, single	1	1
Sheet, double	2	1/2
Bath towel	1	1
Hand towel (terrycloth)	1/5	5
Pillowcase	1/4	4
Dish towel	1/4	4
Luncheon cloth	1/2	2
Man's shirt	1/2	2
Undershirt	1/4	4
Pajamas	1	1
Woman's dress	1/3	3
Blouse	1/4	4
Nightgown	1/3	3
Slip	1/5	5
Small child's dress	1/4	4
Diapers	1/6	6
Blue jeans	2	1/2

Step 3. Remove unwashable trimmings, delicate buttons, drapery hooks, etc. Zip up zippers; hook hooks. Turn pockets inside out. Turn down cuffs and brush out dirt.

Step 4. Remove stains that will not come out in the wash or that may be set by hot water. See *Stain Removal.*

Step 5. Rub badly soiled areas with a paste of the detergent you use in the washer. The alternative is to soak the articles in an enzyme presoaker or to soak them in detergent with or without agitation.

Step 6. Load washer with the larger articles at the bottom of the tub. Add detergent and perhaps bleach and fabric softener if your machine has automatic dispensers for these. Set controls and start washer.

Step 7. If you are washing permanent press, polyester knits, or laminated fabrics, remove them from the washer as soon as it has run through its complete cycle. They are likely to set wrinkles if left in the tub.

How to dry clothes in a dryer. You will dry clothes much more easily, faster, and better in a dryer than on a line. And there are very few things you cannot dry this way.

Generally, articles that are washed together may be dried together. Clothing that has been starched, however, should be dried separately; and after the load is completed and the dryer drum has cooled down, you should wipe it out with a damp cloth so that any lingering starch will not be transferred to subsequent loads.

Don't overload the dryer, since this slows the drying process and promotes wrinkling of permanent-press fabrics.

If your dryer has an automatic drying cycle, use it as much as possible. It takes the guesswork out of the drying process: clothes come out exactly right every time, and there is no danger of overdrying and thus causing wrinkling, fabric harshness, and possible shrinking.

On the other hand, if you do set your dryer for timed drying, remember that it is better to underdry than to overdry. If a load is still damp when the dryer completes its cycle, it's easy enough to turn it on again for a few more minutes.

When loading the dryer, make sure that no small, loose objects—especially metal objects which might cause a short circuit—get into the drum. Turn pockets or heavy garments inside out.

Clean out the lint trap. Set controls and start the dryer.

At the end of the drying cycle, remove permanent press, polyester knits, and laminated fabrics immediately so they will not set wrinkles.

Many articles, such as permanent press, terry towels, corduroys, knits, seersuckers, and cotton flannels, can be folded and put away without ironing.

How to dry clothes on a line. There certainly are no tricks or secrets about line-drying clothes outdoors or in. But a few points should be borne in mind:

1. A plastic-covered line lasts longer and stays whiter than a cotton line. But if outside, it should be wiped off before each use to remove the dirt that settles on it from our polluted skies.

2. Clothes on the closely spaced lines of a reel or a large "disappearing" clothesline dry more slowly than those on a single line or widely spaced lines simply because they are exposed to less sun and breeze.

3. If you use a portable clothes reel outdoors, tie it securely to a post driven into the ground. The wind may topple it otherwise. A reel with a pole that drops into a pipe recessed in the ground is sturdier and less troublesome.

4. Don't hang colored fabrics in the sun: they tend to fade rapidly.

5. If wet clothes freeze, bring them indoors as soon as possible or they may be damaged.

6. Shake each article vigorously before hanging it. This helps to ease creases and makes for softer fabrics. Then pull articles gently into shape.

7. To keep sheets from getting distorted, hang them halfway over the line and pull the corners together. The alternative is to fold them in half and pin to the line at four places. Then straighten out the edges.

8. Hang shirts by the tail.

9. Hang handkerchiefs at two corners, not just one. They retain their shape better.

10. Hang drip-dry shirts and other garments on hangers; button the collars; and straighten the sleeves and body of the garments with your fingers.

11. Discard clothespins that are rough or broken.

12. To help clothes hung indoors dry faster, set an electric fan about 4 feet off the floor at one end of the line and let it blow toward the other end.

How to iron clothes. Ironing is a tedious job at best, so there is no point in making it worse by starting out badly equipped. You need the following:

A steam iron.

A sturdy, wide-footed portable ironing board that adjusts to various heights so you can iron sitting down or standing up.

The cover should be thick, durable, relatively scorch-resistant, and above all it should fit tight and stay tight. (Avoid built-in ironing boards. They sound like a good idea but are actually extremely unpleasant to work at.)

A sleeve board.

A high chair with a back, and a front rung to rest your feet on.

A laundry cart or basket—preferably a cotton basket hanging in a folding metal rack on casters.

Some sort of temporary storage space for articles that have been ironed.

A sprinkling bottle.

A pressing cloth.

The first step in ironing is to sort the laundry by types of article—shirts, sheets, dish towels, etc., because in ironing similar articles one after the other, you develop a rhythm that saves time and energy.

The next step, which you will probably take simultaneously with the first, is to sprinkle all articles that require it. If you take a little time to do this well, you will save a lot of time when actually ironing.

The best way to dampen laundry is to remove it from the dryer or line while it is still slightly moist. (However, line-dried starched articles should be completely dry.) If you have a dryer with an automatic sprinkler, use that (but not during a regular drying cycle).

If sprinkling by hand, spread the clothes out on a table or counter and go over them evenly with a sprinkling bottle. Dampen both sides of double-thick articles. Starched pieces need to be wet more thoroughly than unstarched. Similarly, pieces that should be pressed perfectly (shirts, for example) need more moisture than those that will be smoothed out fairly crudely (underwear, for example). After sprinkling, roll or fold each article loosely and set it aside for a couple of hours or overnight, so that it will be evenly damp.

When you actually start to iron, it's usually a good idea to begin with those articles that require least heat and proceed to those requiring more. If you work in the reverse order, there is a risk that even though you adjust the thermostat downward, the iron will not cool fast enough and you will scorch the articles requiring lower heat.

If you don't know at what temperature a new fabric should be ironed, start at a low setting and move upwards only if you do not get satisfactory results in short order. Whenever your iron seems to be sticking to the fabric, lower the heat at once.

Here's how to iron various articles laundered in the home. Note that one of the main ideas is to get things smooth without reironing surfaces. This is possible if you sprinkle articles properly, smooth them flat on the ironing board, and iron the top side long enough for heat to get through to the bottom side.

Sheets. Fold in quarters across the width, and sprinkle. When damp, lay the sheet, still folded in quarters, across the ironing board with the top hem up. Iron well, turn entire sheet still folded and iron totally dry. Pick up from board, fold in half so that side edges are together and fold once more across the middle. Fold again as necessary to fit linen closet shelf. Iron as folded.

Pillowcases. Open out on board and iron the top side. Fold in half and iron the side thus exposed. Fold for storage and iron on one side.

Handkerchiefs. Spread open and iron, making sure that corners are straight and hems flat. If edged with lace or embroidery, take care to avoid unwanted pleats or puckers. Fold women's handkerchiefs in quarters. Men's handkerchiefs are folded in quarters or a long rectangle. Iron after folding.

Tablecloths. Fold in half lengthwise, then again in half lengthwise, and sprinkle well. When damp, place the cloth across the board and open it halfway. Iron the entire top side with smooth, crosswise strokes. Lift off board and fold across the cloth so that the ironed side is now inside. Iron both sides of folded cloth. Then fold as desired and iron on one side when folded. Be sure to iron totally dry at all times. To eliminate creases in tablecloths, iron like the following without the towel.

Tablecloths—lace. Open out completely to avoid a middle crease which might, in time, crack. Place on ironing board right-side down over a terry towel. Iron over all.

Be very careful not to rip lace with the point of the iron. When the cloth is totally dry, fold without ironing.

Napkins. Spread open and iron carefully to keep them neat and square. Usually napkins are folded in fourths, but large monogrammed dinner napkins should be folded in such a way that the monogram will be on top. Small tea and luncheon napkins may be folded in fourths and then diagonally to make a triangle. Iron as folded. Lace and embroidered napkins should be ironed over a terry towel face down.

Shirts and blouses. Place collar over the end of the ironing board with body hanging free. Iron both sides of collar, shaping it carefully. Iron from the edge toward the neckline to avoid puckering or rippling.

Place sleeve cuffs over the end of the board (use a sleeve board if you have one) and iron in the same way. Then place the sleeve down the length of the board and iron both sides. If gathered into the cuff, nose the front of the iron into the gathers. Lift garment off board and ease shoulder sections on to the end of the board. Iron. Then pull the entire body onto the board and iron. Hang on a hanger and button neck or waist button.

If garment is to be folded, place it on the board with front facing you and button buttons. Turn over, arrange sleeves lengthwise with angled folds at the shoulders. Turn in even sections of each side, enclosing sleeves as you do so. Then turn up tail about a third of the length of the shirt. Make a second turn the same length.

Sleeves—short plain. Spread on board, press. Turn and press second side.

Sleeves—plain folded. Iron both sides. Then turn the edge back as desired and iron again.

Sleeves—short, puffed. Make fold across sleeve, forming a circle. Working from outer edge, nose iron into the gathers, then press the edge.

Sleeves—long, gathered. Iron like a flat sleeve, but at the shoulder and cuff, nose iron into gathers. Repeat on reverse side.

Sleeves—pleated. Smooth pleats and iron a small section at a time.

Dresses. Iron bodice and sleeves as per

Shirts and blouses and *Sleeves.* To prevent wrinkling, the skirt is the last part of a dress to be ironed. Slide dress over ironing board. Let bodice hang out of the way. Press shirt with long, lengthwise strokes to avoid stretching out of shape. Turn as necessary.

When ironing gathered skirts, nose the point of the iron into gathers. On pleated skirts, smooth the pleats with one hand, hold them if necessary, and iron them in small sections with the other hand.

Skirts. Iron as above. Take care to iron waistband smooth.

Pockets—hanging. Pull out from garment, smooth, and iron on both sides.

Pockets—applied. Smooth and press carefully to keep edges straight. If pocket has a flap, open it before pressing pocket; then close and press flap.

Slacks, trousers, shorts. Turn inside out and iron pockets as they hang free. Then slide garment, right side out, over end of ironing board and iron the waistband, seat as far as possible, and fly. Do not touch iron directly to zipper. Remove garment from board and fold legs carefully along old creases. Spread lengthwise on board and toss top leg back over the waistband. Then iron leg on board up and down and crosswise. Turn garment over and iron other side of leg. Then iron the second leg in the same way.

Gowns and slips. Just slip over end of board and iron. When entire garment is smooth, fold in any way you like and iron lightly.

Brassieres. Hold over end of board and iron cup smooth. Don't press in stiff wrinkles, and don't iron elastic parts. Iron straps. Fold as you like.

Curtains—straight. Always iron with the lengthwise thread. This will help to retain the curtain's shape and prevent puckering and rippling. Don't stretch or pull the fabric. Hang as soon as possible.

Curtains—ruffled. Place ruffle on board and iron it from the edge into the gathers. Then iron top of curtain. Drop ruffle off board and iron the body of the curtain with straight, long strokes.

Draperies—pinch-pleated (not lined). Start with the pleated hem. Iron the flat areas between pleats. Then lay the entire cluster of pleats flat on the board and iron them. Iron the side hems from top to bottom; then the bottom hem. Spread the entire drapery on the board and iron the body.

Draperies—lined. Iron as above; however, the side hems must be carefully checked for evenness. After pressing all hems, turn lining side up, slide it over the board, and iron the lining. Then turn the drapery over and iron the face. Insert hooks and hang drapery as soon as possible. If it does not hang perfectly, give each pleated section a sharp downward pull at the bottom hemline.

How to launder specific fabrics. Cotton and linen—whites and light colors: Hot wash. Warm rinse. Normal agitation for 8 to 10 minutes. Normal spin. Heavy-duty detergent. High drying heat for 40 minutes. High ironing temperature.

Cotton and linen—bright and dark colors. Warm wash. Warm rinse. Normal agitation for 5 to 8 minutes. Normal spin. Heavy-duty detergent. High drying heat for 40 minutes. High ironing temperature.

Cotton and linen—noncolorfast. Cold wash. Cold rinse. Normal agitation for 5 to 8 minutes. Normal spin. Cold-water detergent. High drying heat for 40 minutes. Low ironing temperature. Wash and dry these articles by themselves.

Cotton with easy-care finish. Warm wash. Warm rinse. Normal agitation for 5 to 8 minutes. Normal spin. Heavy-duty detergent. High drying heat for 40 minutes. Low ironing temperature.

Wool. Tepid wash. Cold rinse. Gentle agitation for 2 minutes. Normal spin. Light-duty or cold-water detergent. Air-dry. Low ironing temperature.

Silk. Tepid wash. Cold rinse. Gentle agitation for 2 minutes. Slow spin. Light-duty or cold-water detergent. Low drying heat for 15 minutes. Low ironing temperature.

Acetate. Warm or cold wash. Cold rinse. Gentle agitation for 3 to 5 minutes. Slow spin. Light-duty or cold-water detergent. Low drying heat for 15 minutes followed by a 10-minute cool-down. Low ironing temperature.

Anidex. Hot wash. Warm rinse. Normal agitation for 5 to 8 minutes. Normal spin.

Heavy-duty detergent. High drying heat for 30 minutes. Medium ironing temperature.

Triacetate. Warm wash. Cold rinse. Gentle agitation for 3 to 5 minutes. Slow spin. Light-duty detergent. Low drying heat for 15 minutes. Low ironing temperature.

Acrylic. Warm or cold wash. Cold rinse. Gentle agitation for 3 to 5 minutes. Slow spin. Light-duty or cold-water detergent. Low drying heat for 15 minutes followed by 10-minute cool-down. Low ironing temperature.

Modacrylic. Warm wash. Cold rinse. Gentle agitation for 3 to 5 minutes. Slow spin. Light-duty detergent. Low drying heat for 15 minutes followed by a 10-minute cool-down. Low ironing temperature.

Nylon. Warm wash. Cold rinse. Gentle agitation for 3 to 5 minutes. Slow spin. Light-duty detergent. Low drying heat for 15 minutes followed by a 10-minute cool-down. Low ironing temperature. Wash whites and colors separately.

Polyester. Warm wash. Cold rinse. Gentle agitation for 3 to 5 minutes. Slow spin. Light-duty detergent. Low drying heat for 15 minutes followed by a 10-minute cool-down. Low ironing temperature.

Rayon. Warm or cold wash. Cold rinse. Gentle agitation for 3 to 5 minutes. Slow spin. Light-duty detergent. Low drying heat for 15 minutes followed by a 10-minute cool-down. Low ironing temperature.

Spandex. Hot wash. Warm rinse. Gentle agitation for 4 to 6 minutes. Normal spin. Light-duty detergent. Low drying heat for 15 minutes followed by a 10-minute cool-down. Do not iron.

Blends. Launder a blend as you would the most sensitive fiber in the blend. In other words, if it is a blend of cotton and acrylic, launder like an acrylic.

Permanent press and laminated fabrics. Warm wash. Cold rinse. Gentle agitation for 3 to 5 minutes. Slow spin. Light-duty detergent. Low drying heat for 15 minutes followed by a 10-minute cool-down. Low ironing temperature if ironing is needed.

Fiberglass. Unless manufacturer says article can be machine-washed and gives directions, wash by hand in a tub of warm water with light-duty detergent. Dunk up and down; squeeze suds through material. Rinse in warm or cold water. Hang to dry. Do not iron.

Corduroy. Hot or warm wash depending on colorfastness. Warm rinse. Normal agitation for 8 minutes. Normal spin. Heavy-duty detergent. High drying heat for 30 minutes. If removed when slightly damp, little ironing will be needed. Wash one color at a time and turn garments inside out.

Vellux. Warm wash for normal soil; hot for heavy soil. Warm rinse. Normal agitation for 6 to 8 minutes. Normal spin. Heavy-duty detergent. Medium to high drying heat for 30 minutes.

Knits—fine wool and all loose types. Wash by hand in cold or tepid water with cold-water or light-duty detergent. Press damp-dry in towels. Block to shape, lay flat, and air-dry.

Knits—polyester. Warm wash. Cold rinse. Gentle agitation for 3 to 5 minutes. Slow spin. Light-duty detergent. Low drying heat for 15 minutes followed by a 10-minute cool-down.

How to launder specific articles. Pleated garments. Hand-wash in warm water. Warm rinse. Light-duty detergent. Drip-dry on hangers. Support skirts at waistband at three places at least. Low ironing temperature. Press on reverse side with a damp pressing cloth. Handle as little as possible while garment is warm.

Fleece garments. Check whether garments are washable. Machine-wash in warm water. Cold rinse. Gentle agitation for 5 minutes. Normal spin. Heavy-duty detergent. Low drying heat for 10 minutes. Remove while damp-dry; shape; and continue drying on a hanger.

Neckties. It's better to dry-clean neckties but they can be laundered if made of cotton, acrylic; or other washable fabric. If you're not certain whether they are colorfast, soak a part of the narrow neckband in detergent solution to test. Hand-wash and rinse in warm water. Light-duty detergent. Do not twist, rub, or wring. Use a soft brush on badly stained areas. Squeeze dry, then shape and hang on a coat hanger to dry completely. Press under a pressing cloth with a steam iron. To prevent seams on back side from showing on the front, insert in the tie a piece of stiff shirt cardboard cut to the proper shape.

Diapers. Rinse immediately. Soak in 1 gallon water, 2 tablespoons borax, and ¼ cup detergent until ready to wash. Wash in hot water. Warm rinse. Normal agitation for 12 to 14 minutes. Normal spin. Heavy-duty detergent. High drying heat for 40 minutes.

Blankets—woolen. Warm wash. Cold rinse. Gentle agitation for 2 minutes. Normal spin. Light-duty detergent. Dry on line. If using a dryer, place half a dozen large terry towels in drum. Heat them for 5 minutes at high heat. Then put blanket in drum and continue heating for 15 minutes. Remove blanket at once and block it to shape. Press binding with cool iron. Wash and dry only one blanket at a time.

Blankets—synthetic. Warm wash. Cold rinse. Gentle agitation for 5 minutes. Normal spin for 3 minutes. Light-duty detergent. Line-dry or dry in dryer at low heat for 10 minutes. Remove at once. Press binding with cool iron. Wash and dry only one blanket at a time.

Blankets—electric. If washable, wash and dry like woolen blankets.

Quilts. Hot or warm wash depending on colorfastness. Warm or cold rinse. Gentle agitation for 6 to 8 minutes. Normal spin. Light-duty detergent. Low drying heat for 15 to 20 minutes if synthetic. High drying heat for 40 minutes if cotton.

Pillows—feather. Warm wash. Warm rinse. Normal agitation for 6 to 8 minutes. Normal spin. Light-duty detergent. High drying heat for 60 minutes or more. Wash and dry two pillows at a time. Before washing, hold them down in bottom of tub for a few minutes until saturated. Turn them over halfway through wash.

Pillows—polyester. Hand-wash in warm water. Heavy-duty detergent. Do not twist; force suds through pillow by pushing. Thorough warm rinse. Spin-dry in washer. Low drying heat for 20 minutes or longer.

Rugs—cotton. Hot or warm wash depending on colorfastness. Warm rinse. Normal agitation for 10 minutes. Heavy-duty detergent. Normal spin. High drying heat for 40 minutes.

Rugs—acrylic. Warm wash. Cold rinse. Gentle agitation for 5 minutes. Normal spin. Light-duty detergent. Low drying heat for 15 to 20 minutes. Remove while damp, shake, and lay flat to prevent matting of fibers.

Washable rainwear. Warm wash. Cold rinse. Gentle agitation for 3 to 5 minutes. Double rinse. Slow spin. Light-duty detergent in sparing amount. Low drying heat for 15 minutes followed by a 10-minute cool-down. Low ironing temperature.

Plastic articles (shower curtains, baby pants, lined bibs, etc.). Warm wash. Warm rinse. Normal agitation for 4 minutes. Normal spin. Light-duty detergent. Line-dry.

Slipcovers. Be sure of colorfastness. Warm wash. Cold rinse. Normal agitation for 6 to 8 minutes. Normal spin. Low drying heat for 15 minutes if synthetic. High drying heat for 30 minutes if cotton. Remove while slightly damp. Press ruffles and pleats with cool or hot iron. Replace on furniture while still slightly damp to reduce chance of shrinking. Smooth carefully, and allow to finish drying. Launder sofa slipcovers one at a time.

Curtains and draperies—fiberglass. Hand-wash in warm water; rinse in cold. Light-duty detergent. Hang to dry. Do not iron.

Curtains and draperies—permanent press. See directions for permanent-press fabrics.

Curtains and draperies—sheer synthetics. Follow directions for appropriate synthetic fabric.

Curtains—cotton. If reasonably new, launder like cotton fabrics. If curtains are old or weakened by sun, launder like permanent press.

Reconditioning fabrics. Fabrics may turn yellow or gray if washed in water that is too cold; or if washed with too little detergent; or if washed in hard water; or if not rinsed sufficiently. Switching from one detergent or soap to another may also cause discoloration.

To correct yellowing or graying, put articles through a full wash cycle using hot water and extra detergent. Then wash in hot water and 2 cups of nonprecipitating water softener. Add ½ cup ammonia if items are very badly discolored. Wash once more in hot water and detergent with bleach.

Fluffing and airing articles. This can be done in most dryers simply by tumbling the articles without heat for 5 to 10 minutes. It does an excellent job on pillows.

Laundry Planning. The average housewife spends in the neighborhood of 10 hours a week doing the laundry. This means the laundry area should be well equipped, conveniently located, and comfortable to work in.

The least desirable location for a laundry is the basement. Heavy loads of clothes must be carried up and down stairs (even if you have a laundry chute, you must carry the clothes upstairs). You are away from the phone, the front door, and the children. But there is usually ample space and, if you are not a particularly tidy person, you are under no compulsion to keep the area neat.

A much better location is on the first floor. Unless space is confined, the utility room is excellent. The kitchen is equally good, though you may object to doing the washing and drying in the same room where you do your cooking. (This feeling can be ameliorated somewhat, however, if the laundry equipment is placed outside the kitchen work area.) If a pantry is available, it can do double-duty as the laundry.

Theoretically, a bathroom in the bedroom area is an ideal laundry location because it is near the main source of soiled clothes. But unfortunately, few bathrooms have the space to accommodate even the minimum laundry equipment needed—not to mention space to set up an ironing board.

Another possible location in the bedroom area is in a wide closet opening off the hall. But here again, you must do your ironing elsewhere and you are almost certain to make a mess every once in a while.

The only other remaining possible laundry locations are on a back porch or in a garage. Both are adequate if you live in a warm climate; but not at all pleasant in a cold climate. (Furthermore, you must drain the washer and plumbing after use.)

The list below covers the equipment required for a perfect laundry and its usual dimensions.

	Size (inches)
Automatic washer	30 x 24
Automatic dryer	30 x 24
Combination washer-dryer	30 x 24
Laundry tub (preferably recessed in a cabinet)	24 x 24
Sorting counter with cabinet beneath for supplies, hand iron	24 x 24
Ironing board	15 x 54
Laundry cart	24 x 20
Ironing stool	15 x 15

For a smooth work flow, the laundry equipment should be arranged in the following order: sorting counter, tub, washer, dryer, ironing board. There is no reason, of course, why these have to be in a straight line; but you should provide enough floor space to work comfortably. At the sink, washer, and dryer, you need a space at least 4 feet deep. When doing your ironing, you need a floor space 6 by 6 feet.

If possible, use the wall space above the tub, washer, and dryer for shelves or cabinets where you can store ironed and folded articles as well as myriad cleaning agents. Do not fail to install on an open wall or the back of the laundry door, 5 feet above the floor, one or more large hooks for garments on hangers.

For how to install the laundry appliances, see *Clothes Dryers* and *Washing Machines.*

Lavatories. (These are also called sinks or washbasins.) The best lavatories are made of vitreous china. Porcelain enamel on cast iron and porcelain enamel on steel are second and third choices.

Most families today prefer lavatories that are built into a so-called vanity cabinet. But it's a mistake to think that all such installations are highly desirable. It is true that the piping under the lavatory is concealed and that the floor around it is easier to clean because you don't have to mop around any legs. But unless the vanity is of ample size, counter and storage space provided are of little value.

Freestanding lavatories are less expensive, and if they have wide rims, they offer as much "counter space" as many vanities. Most freestanding lavatories have legs; but some are hung from the wall.

How to clean a clogged lavatory drain. In lavatories, clogging is most often caused by hair snarled around the base of the stopper. Simply remove the stopper and clean it with toilet paper.

Depending on their design, pop-up lavatory stoppers are removed by lifting straight out; by turning one-quarter turn and lifting out; or by loosening a nut on the waste pipe under the lavatory, pulling out the horizontal rod running through it, and lifting out the stopper.

If the stoppage is below the stopper, proceed as follows:

1. Form a hook at the end of a long, stiff wire; poke it down the drain and fish the stoppage out.

2. If the stoppage is deep down and the U trap below the lavatory has a clean-out plug, place a pail under the trap, unscrew the plug, and reach up the trap with your bent wire.

3. If the trap does not have a clean-out, partly fill the lavatory with water, place the suction cup of a plunger over the drain opening, and pump the handle up and down. The suction may loosen the stoppage enough so that it can be washed away.

4. If all else fails, the straight waste pipe directly below the lavatory bowl and the trap underneath can be removed by unscrewing the large nuts that hold them. This is not a difficult job, but take care not to bend or mar the pipes or nuts, which are made of lightweight metal and are chrome-plated. When the pipe is open, insert a coiled plumber's auger and crank it down the drain until it breaks through the stoppage or pulls it back out.

How to stop faucet drips. Compression faucet. This is the common, familiar type of faucet used on almost all old fixtures and a substantial percentage of new ones.

Turn off the water to the faucet. Remove the faucet handle and escutcheon cap, if any. Unscrew the large packing nut on top of the faucet assembly. (If the nut is not concealed under an escutcheon, wrap adhesive tape around it before applying your wrench. This will prevent marring of the finish.) Screw out the stem assembly.

Unscrew the washer on the end of the stem. If the screw head has corroded, the threads can usually be unscrewed with pliers. If there is nothing for the pliers to grab, however, put the stem assembly in a vise and, with a small metal drill, carefully drill out the threaded portion of the screw. (This is difficult and not always successful, but it is worth trying before you buy a new faucet.) Replace the old washer with a new one of the same size. Hold it in place with a new brass or bronze screw. Then reassemble the faucet.

If the new washer fails to stop the drip, the valve seat against which it presses is probably worn and uneven. If the faucet was made before World War II, the valve seat can be smoothed with a special tool called a valve-seat grinder. Postwar faucets, for the most part, have renewable seats—that is, the old seat can be removed and replaced. In either case, the work is best done by a plumber.

American-Standard Aquaseal faucet. In this faucet, a rubber diaphragm takes the place of the washer and valve seat in a compression faucet. Turn off water supply. Lift off the faucet handle and tighten the large cap nut slightly. If this does not stop the drip, unscrew the cap nut and lift out the valve stem. Pry out the rubber diaphragm in the valve body below the stem (it may, however, come out with the stem). Replace it with a new one.

American-Standard single lever faucet. In this mixing unit, both hot and cold water are controlled by a single handle which tips back to turn on the water and swings to right or left to control the temperature. Shut off both hot- and cold-water lines before making any repair. Then remove the escutcheon and unscrew the two large cap nuts on either side of the faucet assembly. Lift out the wire mesh screens and wash them. Take out the stainless-steel valves and polish the faces with an eraser. Clean the valve seats with an eraser. Then replace the parts.

American-Standard push-pull faucet. Water flow is controlled by pulling the handle out or pushing it in; water temperature is regulated by turning the handle to right or left.

Instructions for stopping a faucet drip are printed on a small slip concealed behind a removable plate in the back of the faucet. These read as follows: Turn off water supply. (1) Disconnect pop-up rod underneath the lavatory and remove pop-up rod by lifting out and through the top of the spout. (2) With a 3/16-inch Allen wrench remove the pop-up bushing. (3) Grasp the front of the spout with a slight rocking action, lift spout directly up, thus separating it from the escutcheon and body. This reveals two screen-covered projections on the bottom of the spout. (4) Remove the screens and valve stem and spring assemblies. Clean rubber surface of the valve seat. The eraser end of a pencil makes a good tool. (If the seat is damaged, remove with a 5/16-inch Allen wrench and replace.) (5) Replace stem assemblies and screens. Slightly deform screen to an oval shape so it will fit tightly.

Crane Dial-ese faucets. Turn off water supply before beginning. (1) Remove handle screw and lift off handle. With a wrench, remove lock-nut by turning it counterclockwise but leave gasket in position. (2) Remove Dial-ese control unit with a wrench. (3) Unscrew the large piece at the top of the control unit and then pull the rest of the unit apart. (4) Replace the small seat ring near the bottom of the control unit with a new ring of the same type. (5) Apply a little heavy grease to the threads of the long, narrow stem piece; then reassemble the entire control unit. The large top piece should be screwed hand-tight, no more. (6) Replace the control unit in the faucet and screw on the lock-nut.

Moen single-handle faucets. Turn off hot and cold water. Remove handle cover, handle, and stop tube. Lift out retainer clip and pull the valve cartridge out of the body. Push new cartridge all the way into the body until the front of the ears on the valve cartridge are flush with the body. Replace the retainer clip so that the legs straddle the cartridge ears and slide it down in the bottom slot in the valve body. Replace stop tube, handle, and handle cover. When mounting the handle, the red flat surface on the stem of the valve cartridge must point up.

Delta faucets with single lever handle. Turn off hot and cold water. Loosen small set screw in handle and pull off handle. Unscrew the round cap under the handle. Pull up on the stem. This removes a cam and the ball to which the stem is attached. From the body of the faucet lift and replace the two rubber seat-and-spring assemblies. If the ball on the stem is rough around either of the two small holes, it should also be replaced. Then reassemble, making sure that the slide in the side of the ball is inserted over the pin in the body above the seat assemblies, and that the lug on the side of the cam is inserted in the slot on the side of the body. Make sure the round cap is tight before replacing the handle. Also tighten the adjusting ring in the top of the cap.

Delta faucets with single knurled handle. Turn off water. Pull out plastic cap in top of handle, remove the screw that is exposed, and lift off the handle. Then follow directions above for lever-style handle.

Delta two-handle faucets. Turn off water. Take out cap in top of handle, remove screw, and lift off the handle. Unscrew the topmost nut that is exposed. Note carefully how the stem assembly is installed; then pull it out. Remove the seat and spring assembly in the body of the faucet and replace it. Then replace the stem in the same position as you found it, and tighten the nut around it securely.

Bradley faucets with single knurled handle. Turn off water. Pull out cap in top of handle, remove the screw underneath, and lift off handle. Remove the three screws at the base of the cam bearing and lift off the bearing. Then remove the cam, sleeve, and cartridge from the faucet body. Install a replacement sleeve. Be sure to line up the flat on the serrated end of the cam with the flat in the serrated hole in the knob. Reassemble handle.

Bradley faucets with single lever handle. Turn off water. Pull out cap in top of handle, remove the screw underneath, and lift knob and lever handle from the serrated end of the cam. Press the cam down. Swing knob and lever back roughly 90 degrees, slide them to the right, and remove the lever. Then remove the three screws at the base of the cam bearing and proceed as with a Bradley knurled handle.

Leak around compression faucet stem. Remove the faucet handle and escutcheon (if any) and tighten the packing nut slightly until the drip stops. If this does not work, unscrew the nut and pull out the packing inside. Wrap graphite wicking around the faucet stem several times, push it up under the packing nut, and screw the nut back on the faucet body.

Temporary repairs can be made with soft cotton string instead of graphite wicking.

How to clean lavatories. See *Bathroom Cleaning.*

Lawn. A very fine, sheer fabric with a somewhat crisp feel. Made of cotton, linen, or synthetics, it is used in clothing and sometimes in curtains. Laundering varies with the fiber in the material.

Lead Anchors. See *Wall Anchors.*

Leather. *How to clean.* Smooth leather that is soiled can usually be cleaned with saddle soap, a spray-on leather conditioner, or a mild detergent solution. Then, to keep the leather pliable, rub neat's-foot oil or lanolin into it and let it stand overnight. Then buff with a cloth.

Stains on leather are very difficult to remove. Try brushing rubber cement on them and peeling it off. If this doesn't work, try a little cleaning fluid or the cleaner that is sold with kits for coloring leather.

Leather garments—especially suede garments—should be cleaned professionally.

Clean and polish leather table tops with paste wax.

How to press leather. Cover it with brown wrapping paper and press with a dry iron at the lowest setting.

How to recondition leather. When leather dries out, it cracks and turns to powder. To keep it pliable and beautiful, rub neat's-foot oil or lanolin into it and let it stand overnight. Repeated applications may be necessary on very tired material.

Note that leather treated with lanolin is easier to polish than that treated with neat's-foot oil.

How to repair leather. If torn, leather that is soft and thin can be mended with needle and thread. Otherwise, paste a scrap of chamois or cotton fabric to the back with rubber cement or fabric-mending adhesive.

If leather is torn from wood or other material to which it is bonded, reglue it with rubber cement.

If a leather bookbinding starts to turn powdery, smooth it carefully with very fine emery cloth. Then make several applications of neat's-foot oil. When this is dry, spray the bindings with a thin colorless lacquer.

How to paint leather. Buy a leather-coloring kit sold in shoe, drug, and variety stores, and follow directions.

A clear finish on leather table tops and other rigid surfaces may be applied by spraying with several thin coats of the clear varnish or lacquer used for fixing (protecting) pictures. Clean the leather with a spray-on leather conditioner first.

How to store leather articles. Keep them out of a hot, dry attic or damp, cool basement. Store them anywhere else and don't pack the articles in so tightly that air cannot circulate around them.

Take care not to scuff leather luggage when taking it out of storage or returning it to storage.

Also see *Imitation Leather* and *Leatherette.*

Leatherette. An imitation leather. Clean it with a sponge dampened with detergent solution. If torn, paste a scrap of fabric to the underside with fabric-mending adhesive.

Lenox. China made in New Jersey by the Lenox Company. The same firm also produces other kinds of ceramic ware. See *China.*

Levels, Carpenter's. See *Tools, Workshop.*

Lighting. Good lighting can do wonders for you and your home. It makes your rooms seem larger. It brings out colors and textures that add beauty to the home. It can be used for decorative effects just like paint or fabrics. But most important, it helps you to see what you are doing—with a comfort that you ordinarily experience only in the best-lighted factory or out of doors. This does much to make the complex, multi-faceted job of homemaking easier.

There are, of course, many ways to light a home properly. But these suggestions, developed by the Illuminating Engineering Society, are the most practical, moderate-cost answers to most lighting problems. They can be adapted to any house.

First consider a few precepts: (1) Good lighting means a high level of illumination: plenty of light so you can see what you are doing. But it must be glareless light. And it must fill the entire room to prevent the eyestrain caused by strong contrasts between light and dark areas. (2) Good lighting is flexible. You can choose between many light sources and vary the light level up and down to suit your needs and moods. (3) Good lighting is a combination of general room lighting and local lighting for specific visual tasks. The former is best done with built-in fixtures; the latter, with portable lamps. You can, of course, build in all your lighting, but unless skillfully done, the effect may be monotonous. (4) Good lighting depends not only on using the right size bulb in a well-designed fixture but also on using light-colored reflecting surfaces. Dark walls, ceilings, and floors soak up light; light to medium shades reflect and spread it. In actual practice, your ceilings should be white or very light colored; walls can be slightly darker; floors can be darker still. The popular cocoa color is about as dark as a floor should be. (5) Good lighting requires that the bulbs be shielded from the eyes except in certain cases.

Bear these requirements in mind as you study the following good-lighting practices:

General lighting. General lighting is soft, rather low-level lighting—not sufficient for specific close work but bright enough so you can see and move around easily. It serves as background lighting when you are sitting or working in a room and as see-your-way lighting when you are moving through the house. It is best provided by the following:

Fixtures attached to the ceiling. These should hang 3 to 12 inches below an 8-foot ceiling and should have diffusing bowls of flashed opal glass, ceramic-enameled glass, or medium-dense plastic. In rooms of over 100 square feet, use fixtures accommodating a total of 150 to 300 watts in incandescent bulbs, or 50 to 100 watts of fluorescent. In smaller rooms, use smaller fixtures. One centrally located fixture will serve a room of up to 250 square feet. For larger rooms, or if a room is 60 percent longer than it is wide, use two fixtures. In narrow halls over 12 feet long, install two small fixtures. On stairways, use fixtures at top and bottom.

Ceiling fixtures are the least expensive type for general lighting purposes. They can be used in any room, but are best suited to bedrooms, dining rooms, bathrooms, and kitchens.

Ceiling-attached fixtures in garages, utility rooms, and unfinished basements do not require shielding, but for best results should have reflectors to direct the light downward. In one-car garages, place the fixtures on both sides of the car about 6 feet back from the front bumper. In two-car garages, place a third fixture between the cars near the rear bumpers. All fixtures should use 100-watt incandescent bulbs.

In basements, use four or more fixtures evenly spaced. Only one needs to be switch-controlled. Others can be operated by pull cords.

In utility rooms, center a single fixture on the ceiling.

Recessed lighting fixtures do not spread the light; consequently, it takes two to four fixtures (the exact number depends on their size) to give as much light as one surface-mounted fixture. A single recessed fixture may, however, be used to light a tiny room.

Luminous ceilings are oversize recessed fixtures. Fluorescent tubes are mounted above large panels of translucent plastic or perforated material. The fixtures are put together in the house. They can be any size from about 2 by 4 feet up, but are most effective when they form an entire ceiling.

They are expensive but give a very high level of illumination; consequently they are especially adapted to family rooms, playrooms, bathrooms, and kitchens. Small panels are excellent over dining tables, plant pockets, etc., where both general and specific lighting are needed.

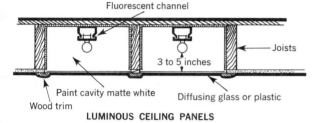

LUMINOUS CEILING PANELS

Lighted wall valances are used over windows. They are usually designed to throw light up on the ceiling and down on the draperies. They should be mounted no less than 10 inches from the ceiling. If the space is less than this, a top should be put on the valance. Use fluorescent tubes placed end to end.

Lighted valances can be installed anywhere but are particularly effective in living rooms. Because they cast most light on the wall, the wall seems to recede and the room looks larger.

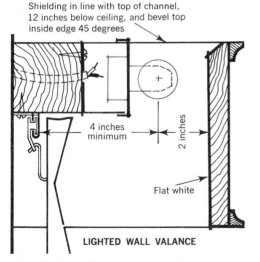

LIGHTED WALL VALANCE

Lighted wall brackets are the same as lighted valances except that they are mounted on blank walls. They are also used for specific local lighting. Ready-made wall brackets and short valances are

on the market; or you can make your own with wood and fluorescent channels. In the latter case, paint the inside surfaces white.

Lighted cornices are similar to lighted valances and brackets except that they are mounted against the ceiling. All light is directed downward. Visually and from a lighting standpoint, their effect is best when they run the full length of a wall. Cornices should be painted white inside.

Note that in living rooms and other large rooms, you should provide a minimum of 16 feet of valance, bracket, or cornice lighting. Use the three types of fixture together or separately. No single fixture, however, should be less than 4 feet long. In rooms of less than 125 square feet, use a total of 6 to 12 feet of wall lighting.

Lighted coves are inverted cornices and throw all light upward. They are not recommended for general lighting since they are about half as efficient as other wall lighting. They are also dreadful dust collectors.

Local lighting. Local lighting is high-level illumination needed for specific visual tasks. Fixtures should be built in the following rooms:

Kitchen. To light counters, install fixtures directly under the wall cabinets. One fixture is needed for each counter, but for long counters, use one fixture every 4 feet. Use one 20-watt fluorescent tube or two 40-watt incandescent bulbs per fixture. Fluorescent tubes don't have to be shielded if mounted close up under the cabinets, but it is better if they are. Incandescent fixtures must be shielded always.

If there are no cabinets above a counter, follow directions for lighting a sink.

To light a counter-height range (lamps built into such ranges are inadequate), mount a 25-watt fluorescent bracket on the wall over the range. The tube must be shielded. The bottom edge of the shield should be 58 inches above the floor. The bracket may be left open at the top or covered with frosted glass.

To light a sink in front of a window, mount two 25-watt fluorescent tubes or two 75-watt R-30 incandescent floodlamps on the ceiling or bottom of the soffit, and shield them with an 8-inch board. You may also recess fixtures equipped with glass or louvered shielding in the ceiling or soffit. If the sink is not in front of a window, follow directions for lighting the range.

Laundry. In an unfinished utility room, install a ceiling-attached fixture directly over the tub, washer, and dryer and 4 feet above them. Use a 150-watt silver-bowl incandescent bulb or two 25-watt fluorescent tubes. The fixture must be shielded only on the sides. In a laundry that has been finished off, use a recessed ceiling fixture or close-to-the-ceiling semi-direct fixture. More wattage is required.

An additional fixture of the same type is needed at the ironing area. Center it 4 feet above the ironing board.

Workshop. Over the workbench and large power tools, install side-shielded ceiling-attached fixtures using two 25-watt fluorescent tubes. Center over the bench or tool with the bottom of the shield 4 feet above the work surface. The fixture may be hung on pipes so it can be moved sideways.

Bathrooms. To light an average-size mirror, install fixtures on the wall on both sides. The fixtures should be 30 inches apart and centered 5 feet above the floor. A third fixture should be mounted on the ceiling, directly over the sink and 12 to 18 inches out from the wall. Each fixture should use one 20-watt fluorescent tube, or one 60-watt incandescent bulb, or two 40-watt incandescent bulbs. Incandescents must be shielded with translucent glass or plastic. Shielding is desirable but not mandatory for fluorescents.

If a mirror is extra-wide, install a luminous ceiling. Or use a single ceiling-attached or recessed fluorescent fixture with two rows of tubes extending the length of the mirror. Install the fixture 1 foot out from the wall.

Dining room. Over the dining table, use any type of ceiling-attached fixture or a luminous fluorescent panel at least the size of the table. If the table is off center in the room, use a recessed incandescent downlight with a 1- to 6-inch opening. Center the fixture over the table.

To raise the overall level of light in the room, install a lighted valance over the windows or a lighted wall bracket over the buffet.

Other local lighting. Other local lighting may be done with portable lamps or built-in fixtures. If the former are used, provide outlets near the point of use. For reading, sewing, writing, piano playing, use lamps with properly designed diffusing bowls, or an R-40 indirect white incandescent lamp, or a PS-25 incandescent lamp, or a 32-watt circline fluorescent tube. Incandescent bulbs should be of 50-100-150 watts or 100-200-300 watts.

Lamps should be placed beside all reading chairs and the piano. For desk lighting, use a table lamp or a pair of pin-up lamps. For work at a sewing machine, use a floor lamp or pin-up lamp. For reading in bed, use a lamp on a bedside table or a pin-up lamp. For dresser or dressing-table lighting, use a pair of incandescent lamps.

In closets, center an inexpensive incandescent lampholder with a pull cord above the door, either on the ceiling or wall. A 25-watt bulb is usually large enough.

Install wall fixtures using 40- or 60-watt incandescent bulbs on both sides of exterior doors. The fixtures should be shielded with etched or diffusing glass or plastic, but should be open at the bottom for downlighting. Mount the lights 66 inches above the doorstep. If only one light can be used, place it on the latch side of the door.

Recessed fixtures may also be used over covered entrances.

Basic facts about incandescent light. 1. Most incandescent bulbs for household use have an operating life of 750 to 1000 hours. So-called long-life bulbs will, of course, last longer than this; but most of them have a lower light output (the major exceptions are those containing Krypton). They should be used, therefore, only in places which are hard to get at or where you do not need a great deal of light.

The average light output and life of every bulb now manufactured is printed on the container in which the bulb comes.

2. For the best balance of bulb life and light output, be sure to use bulbs of the

same voltage as that supplied by the electric utility serving your area. In the majority of communities, 120 volts is standard, so most light bulbs sold are designed for 120 volts. But in a few communities, where the voltage supplied is 125 volts, you should buy 125-volt bulbs.

3. If you use anything larger than a 25-watt household bulb outdoors, it must be protected from rain and snow; otherwise it will break when turned on. The only bulbs that are safe to use in an exposed location are PAR bulbs, which are made with tempered glass.

Basic facts about fluorescent light.
1. Fluorescent tubes will operate about seven to ten times longer than incandescent bulbs. And they will last even longer if you let them burn rather than turning them on and off.

2. One of the advantages of fluorescent tubes is that they give off much more light per watt than incandescent bulbs yet do not produce as much heat. This makes them particularly desirable for use in kitchens, where temperatures often rise uncomfortably high.

3. For most homes, the best type of fluorescent tube is called the Deluxe Warm White. This has a slightly pinkish tone which blends well with incandescent light and enhances complexions, food colors, and other warm tones. In rooms with a great deal of green or blue, however, use Deluxe Cool White tubes.

4. Most small fluorescent tubes are of the preheat type which require starters (little metal cans inserted in the fixture) and take several seconds to light. Rapid-start tubes do not require starters and light almost instantly, but are available only in larger sizes above 30 watts.

Circular fluorescents, called circline tubes, are rapid-start lamps that will operate in all circular fixtures, although there is a delay when they are used in fixtures with starters.

5. To install a fluorescent tube in a fixture, hold it as close as possible to the ends, slide the two pins in the ends up into the sockets, and twist the tube in either direction until it snaps into place.

To install a circline tube, face the fixture so you can see the four holes in the socket. Hold the tube with the base facing you and the tube marking downward. Then turn the tube upward, insert the prongs in the fixture, and push the tube into the support clips.

6. Fluorescent tubes must be handled with care, because if they should break in your hands and cut you, the phosphors coating the inside of the tubes might poison you.

How to replace a lighting fixture. Turn off the current at the circuit-breaker or fuse box. Remove the fixture from the ceiling or wall by loosening the nuts or screws holding it. Separate the two fixture wires from the wires in the outlet box. Attach the black wire in the new fixture to the black circuit wire; the white wire to the white circuit wire.

Use solderless connectors, which are also called wire nuts, to connect the wires. The best connector has a steel coil inside a plastic cap. Hold the bare ends of the wires together and twist them around each other once or twice; then insert them in the connector, and screw it on tight. When the connection is completed, the bare wires should not be visible. If they are visible, unscrew the connector, nip a bit off the ends of the wires, and attach the connector again.

Never try to connect a lighting fixture simply by twisting the wires together and wrapping them with electrical tape. Such a joint has no strength. The only way to make a joint in this way is to solder the wires before taping them.

When installing a fluorescent fixture, the long metal box, or channel, containing the wiring and ballast must be opened. The channel is then attached to the outlet box with a lock nut; and for safety's sake, because the fixture is heavy, it should also be attached to the ceiling or wall with a couple of long screws. Note, however, that if the ceiling or wall is made of combustible material, the channel must be furred out from it ½ inch so that air can circulate behind it.

The wires inside the channel are connected to the circuit wires—black to black and white to white—with solderless connectors. Then screw the cover back on the channel.

How to repair lighting fixtures. If a pull chain breaks off inside a fixture, turn off the current, take the fixture down, and open it. You will probably find the end of the chain clamped into a kind of trigger. Pry the slot in the trigger open just enough to release the chain. Thread a new chain into the fixture from the outside and clamp it into the trigger.

If the diffuser on a fixture is broken, it is wise to replace it. But it can be repaired, if made of glass, by gluing with cellulose cement. On a plastic diffuser use plastic-mending adhesive.

If a fluorescent tube blinks on and off, the chances are that the starter is worn out. First remove the tube; then press down and twist the starter until it comes out. Replace it with a new starter of the same number. If the light continues to blink, replace the tube.

The starter should also be replaced if a fluorescent tube lights at the ends but not in the middle.

How to repair portable lamps. Disconnect a lamp before making any repairs.

If a bulb breaks, leaving the metal base in the socket, you can usually remove the base by pressing a finger firmly against the inside surface and twisting. If this doesn't work, grasp the top edge of the base with pliers and twist it out.

To replace a defective socket, remove the bulb and pull off the outer metal shell of the socket and the inner cardboard shell. Unscrew the wires and lift the socket body out of the bottom half of the socket shell. It is not necessary to replace the entire socket—just the body. Bodies are interchangeable provided they have the same kind of switch. Wrap either wire clockwise around either screw and tighten in place. Then replace the cardboard and metal shells.

In replacing a defective lamp cord, the trick is to thread the new cord through the lamp. This is easy enough if the lamp base is straight: after removing the old cord, you just push a cord into the lamp from the bottom up. However, if the socket is mounted on an arm, as in a student lamp, you must first disassemble almost the entire lamp by screwing apart the various sections. In either case, the new cord is attached to the socket by removing about ½ inch of insulation from the ends of the two wires. Twist the strands together; then wrap one wire clockwise around either of the two screws, the other around the other screw.

To steady a lamp with a large cylindrical base that has a tendency to topple over in a breeze, fill the base partly with sand.

For mending diffusing bowls, see above—"How to repair lighting fixtures."

To clean lighting fixtures and lamps. Clean incandescent and fluorescent bulbs with a cloth dampened with detergent solution. Diffusers, fixtures, and lamps are cleaned in the same way.

If pendants on crystal chandeliers are not difficult to remove, take down a few at a time, dip in warm water to which a little ammonia or vinegar has been added, and dry. Do not touch with your hands when rehanging them. The alternative, which is more laborious, is to wipe the pendants off with a damp cloth while they are on the chandelier. (In either case, the task is so tedious that you should think twice before installing a crystal chandelier.)

If plastic, metal, or parchment lampshades become soiled, go over them with a damp cloth and a little detergent.

Dust all lamps and fixtures about once a week. Because of their rather intricate shapes and the heat they give off, they attract more than their share of dust.

Lightning Protection. Houses in built-up areas generally do not have lightning rods. Out in the country, however, rods can be extremely valuable.

If you feel you need them, call in a firm that specializes in making installations. Effective systems are quite complicated and must be designed especially for each house.

Limoges (lim-*mohzh*). A beautiful French china. See *China.*

Lined Fabrics. These are the same as laminated fabrics (which see).

Linen. Linen is a very strong, durable fabric woven from flax fibers. The characteristics of the fabric depend on the way it is woven.

Like cottons, linens are washed in hot water; dried in a dryer at high temperature for about 40 minutes; and pressed with a hot iron. White linens should be bleached occasionally to keep them from reverting to linen's natural grayish-tan color. You may add bluing if you want to enhance the whiteness.

Because linens are naturally rather crisp, they are rarely starched.

Anything made of an Irish linen known as Moygashel should be dry-cleaned to keep its fine finish.

Linen Closets. Because a linen closet is used mainly—if not exclusively—for storing bed and bath linens, it should be located in a hall in the sleeping area where anyone can get at it. In a new house, the closet should not be more than 12 to 20 inches deep. Anything deeper is hard to see into and makes storage and removal of linens at the backs of shelves difficult. To make maximum use of the closet, the door should extend to the ceiling and should be almost as wide as the closet.

Shelves of ½-inch plywood are adequately strong. If you hang them on adjustable hangers, storage flexibility is greatly improved (see *Closets* and *Shelves*). Paint them with gloss paint or cover with vinyl.

If you want to store linens in a bathroom, a 30-inch-high, 24-inch-wide kitchen wall cabinet installed over the toilet tank (5 feet above the floor) provides a surprising amount of space.

Linens. For the many types of linens used in the home, see *Bedding; Kitchen Towels;* and *Table Linens.*

Linoleum. See *Floors, Linoleum.*

Lowestoft. A celebrated china presumably produced only in the little town of Lowestoft, England, but actually originated by the Chinese. It is no longer made.

LP Gas. LP, or liquified petroleum, gas is also called bottle gas, tank gas, butane gas, propane gas, or LPG. It is a liquid gas, derived from petroleum or natural gas, which is stored in a steel tank outside the home. When a gas burner inside the house is opened, the liquid turns into and emerges as a gas which burns like natural gas.

LP gas is used for heating, water heating, cooking, clothes drying, and inciner-ation—mainly by people who live out in the country where there are no gas mains. Although it generally costs a bit more than oil and electricity, it enjoys one advantage over those fuels: as with natural gas, the supply into the house is not interrupted by power failures.

LP gas is delivered to large users by tank truck and is pumped into a big tank installed above or below ground. Small users can buy the gas in small prefilled cylinders, which are generally placed outside the back door in a rack. When one cylinder is emptied, the user turns on a second and then calls the dealer to bring a replacement for the empty.

Equipment used with LP gas may or may not be usable with natural gas. For example, modern gas ranges will burn either fuel. On the other hand, LP gas dryers are slightly different from those burning natural gas.

The rules for using LP gas are the same as those for using natural gas. (See *Gas.*) The only real difference is that if there is a gas leak, you call the LP gas dealer rather than a gas utility. At the same time, you should cut off the supply of gas from the tank.

Lubricants. Many things around the house need to be lubricated from time to time. They include hinges, door latches and locks, garage-door hardware and tracks, window hardware, some electric motors and appliances, workshop and garden tools, window stiles, drawers, and even squeaky floor boards. Directions for lubricating all articles that require it are given in the listing pertaining to that article. A number of lubricants may be used:

Lightweight household oil comes closest to being an all-purpose lubricant. Use it on small motors, hinges, latches, etc. It is also wiped or sprayed on tools to keep them from rusting. A very thin film is enough.

SAE No. 10 and No. 30 are heavier oils for large motors and gasoline-driven garden tools.

Silicone spray lubricates hinges, latches, and locks; makes drawers and windows slide; protects metal against rusting. If squirted into cracks between floor boards, it helps to silence squeaks.

Powdered graphite comes in a pencil-like

squeeze dispenser. Use it to lubricate the insides of latches and locks and swinging door springs. It also stops floor board squeaks. But it is very messy.

Automobile grease applied to garage-door tracks facilitates movement of the doors. **Petroleum jelly** can be used in the same way on tracks for all types of interior sliding doors.

Paraffin, or candle wax, is rubbed into the pulley stiles of double-hung windows to make the sash work more easily. It is also coated on runners and sides of drawers that stick.

Penetrating oil serves as a lubricant but is used primarily to help open metal joints that are stuck together by corrosion. For instance, if you can't unscrew a rusted nut and bolt, pour oil on the joint and let it stand for a minute or two; then tap the nut several times to set up vibrations and allow the oil to penetrate further into the joint. You can then unscrew the nut with pliers or a wrench.

Penetrating oil is also useful for cleaning gummed-up metal, as in typewriters, rifle barrels, fishing reels, etc.

Lucite. DuPont's trade name for a transparent colorless acrylic which goes into clock faces, picture frames, and many other home-furnishing items; it is also used in a latex paint.

Lumber. See *Wood.*

Lycra. Name for a brand of spandex stretchable fabric (which see).

Madras. Originally made of cotton, madras is now also made of rayon. It is a thin, tight material with spaced cords or woven stripes. Wash like cotton or rayon.

Be careful of "bleeding madras," which is used widely in sports clothes. Wash it separately in lukewarm water. The colors are meant to run.

Majolica. Also spelled maiolica, this is a beautiful type of earthenware with an opaque glaze. It is, as a rule, highly decorated. Wash it in detergent solution but not in a dishwasher. Glue broken objects with cellulose cement.

Marble. This classic, handsome stone is used to cover floors, walls, fireplace breasts, counters, tables, and windowsills. And because of the recent interest in luxurious bathrooms, it is often used to build tubs and shower stalls. Outside the house it is most often used in steps.

How to repair marble. If a piece is broken, clean and dry the edges; apply epoxy cement; and press edges firmly together. Do not disturb for 24 hours.

If a piece separates from a base, such as a floor, ·clean the back and sides thoroughly and clean the base. Apply silicone rubber adhesive to the back of the marble, set in place, and weight or clamp for 24 hours. Fill the joints around the edges with cement grout as used for ceramic tile.

To obliterate small scratches, sand with extra-fine sandpaper. Then dampen a rag in water, dip in tin oxide powder, and rub vigorously until the surface is smooth and shiny.

When marble becomes badly pitted and scratched, it should be repolished by a marble dealer or finisher, for the work is difficult. Instead of hand-polishing part of a piece, for example, professionals generally prefer to do over the entire piece with a machine. However, because so many do-it-yourselfers have tried to polish marble, the Marble Institute of America has prepared the following instructions:

"The task for the inexperienced person at home is difficult, requiring patience, hard work, proper materials, and observance of simple rules of procedure. Since water is required as a lubricant for the polishing abrasives, a certain amount of sloppy waste material should be anticipated and provided for. Work should be done in a workshop or basement room where the marble surface can be held securely in place and where clean-up is no problem.

"The secret of polishing marble is to buff or rub the surface persistently and evenly with abrasive materials of successively finer grit sizes. The coarse abrasive materials are usually purchased in the form of small hand-size bricks, each brick being composed of abrasive grit of a specific size. Those used in marble finishing range from the coarsest, No. 45, through 120, 220, and 280 to the finest grit size brick, which is called hone. Finally, polishing powder composed of tin oxide to which has been added a few grains of oxalic acid is used during the final polishing stage to give the marble its glossy, high-polished finish. No oxalic acid should ever be used with the tin oxide for polishing green marble or any marble which is to be outdoors.

"The following procedure should be followed in order to achieve the best possible results.

"1. Examine the surface carefully to determine how much buffing or polishing will be required. Rough surfaces, containing swirl marks, deep scratches, and pits will require extensive effort and a great deal of time to bring them to a final smooth, high polish. Polished surfaces with only faint ring marks, or with small spots only slightly rough to the touch, can often be buffed to a shine with polishing powder alone.

"2. The condition of the surface will determine which abrasive material to start with. On a very rough surface the No. 45 or 120 grit size brick should be used first to rub the surface evenly and persistently so that all scratches, marks, and blemishes, except of course those left by the brick itself, are rubbed away. The remaining abrasive bricks in the series should then be employed successively. These remove the marks left by the previous abrasive until a smooth but nonglossy surface, known as a hone finish, is achieved. Remember that the lower-numbered, coarser abrasive bricks should be used first; the higher-numbered finer abrasive bricks last. A back-and-forth rubbing motion rather than a circular motion is recommended. Water should be applied frequently to the face of the stone during the rubbing process. Abrasive residue should be sponged away to prevent clogging of the surface of the brick in contact with the marble. Work on only about 4 square inches of surface area at any one time; then move on to the adjacent area.

"3. Once a honed surface has been produced, the surface of the marble should again be sponged thoroughly to remove all grit. The surface should be carefully reexamined to make sure that all spots, pits, and scratches have been removed, otherwise they will show through the final polish. Expert hand polishers agree that the smoother the hone finish, the better the final high polish. The final hone should have a satin finish which, though not glossy, does have a slight luster.

"4. The final polish is achieved by steady and persistent buffing or rubbing with polishing powder. After sprinkling the powder lightly on the surface, use a pad of medium-hard felt, hard wool carpeting, or chamois which has been dampened with water to do the actual buffing. The best buffing pad is one which has been saturated and compacted with polishing powder and water. Add a few drops of water whenever additional lubricant seems necessary. More powder may also be added so that a thin, dry slurry appears over the surface of the marble. After a lengthy period of vigorous rubbing, the surface will start to take on the characteristic shine of polished marble. Continue rubbing until the shine is uniform, then rinse the surface and dry it with a soft cloth.

"Abrasive bricks and polishing powder can be obtained from any member of the Marble Institute of America as well as from many hardware stores, masonry supply dealers, and building materials dealers. Several marble-polishing kits are on the market."

How to clean marble. To help prevent staining and accumulation of dirt, new marble should be sealed with a special marble sealer. This should be renewed every six months or whenever the marble is washed thoroughly. On floors, it should be applied about every four months. No other type of finish or polish should ever be used on marble.

Wipe up spills as soon as possible after they occur. Lemon juice, vinegar, other acids, carbonated drinks, fruit juices, and the like etch marble, producing dull spots.

To remove soil, try water first, then, if the water doesn't work, a mild detergent solution. Do not use ordinary detergents repeatedly, however, because some of them yellow certain kinds of marble. It is better to use a special marble detergent.

If marble is covered with grit or dust, vacuum it off before washing. The stone is relatively easy to scratch.

How to remove stains. Special agents for removing stains are available from marble dealers and finishers and also by mail from Vermarco Supply Company, a division of the Vermont Marble Company, Proctor, Vermont.

Grease. Scrub with a liquid marble cleaner; let stand for a few minutes; then rinse. If repeated treatments fail, mix the cleaner with whiting or marble detergent to make a paste and apply in a ½-inch layer over the stain. Cover with a damp rag for 24 hours. Then scrape off and rinse.

Rust and ink. These require a special Vermarco cleaner.

Coffee, tea, wine, fruit, and other organic stains. Pour hydrogen peroxide on the stain and add a few drops of household ammonia. When solution stops bubbling, rinse it off. For stubborn stains, mix peroxide with whiting and apply a thick poultice to the stain. Add a few drops of ammonia. When bubbling action stops, scrape off and rinse. Throw the old poultice outdoors at once to allow it to cool down. Note that the peroxide may etch the marble slightly, in which case you will have to repolish it with tin oxide powder.

Paint. Scrape off with a razor blade. Clean with liquid marble cleaner.

Smoke. Clean with liquid marble cleaner and, if necessary, apply a poultice of the cleaner.

Marquisette. A fine, open, diaphanous fabric used in curtains and clothing. It is made of many materials but most commonly of polyester. Some marquisettes can be machine-washed in warm water at slow speed and tumble-dried at low temperature. Others should be hand-washed and drip-dried. Press with a warm iron.

Matelassé. (*maht*-uh-lah-*say*). A double fabric with a surface that is raised to give a puckered or quilted effect. Fabrics of this type are made of several fibers and are used in clothing, upholstery, and draperies. They should be dry-cleaned.

Mattresses. Mattresses and springs are fairly expensive items and they will last longer and remain comfortable if you take care of them.

Make it a habit not to sit on the edges of beds; and see to it that the other members of your family do likewise.

Turn mattresses side to side about once every two months; and also turn them end to end every four months.

Strip beds occasionally and leave mattresses exposed for a day so they can air. If you can move them outdoors into a sunny, airy spot, so much the better.

Protect mattresses on children's beds with rubber or vinyl pads. If the mattresses are wet, sponge the spots with detergent solution and allow to dry thoroughly.

If buttons come off mattresses, no immediate harm is done; but don't wait too long before making repairs because the padding and springs may start to shift. Buttons are attached in pairs. With a long needle or wire, pull a piece of strong twine or thread through the mattress and tie it to the top button. Then draw up tight on the twine and tie it to the bottom button.

An old mattress that becomes lumpy can be improved greatly if you cover it with a 1-, 2-, or 3-inch topper of urethane foam.

Mattresses and springs should be stored flat if space is available. Wrap them well with kraft paper or polyethylene film to keep out dirt and discourage mice; or put them in the boxes in which they came (unfortunately, these are rarely saved). Place the springs on the bottom and raise them off the floor a couple of inches so air can circulate underneath. Store the mattresses directly on top.

If space is not available, place the wrapped mattress against a vertical wall; place the spring against it; and tie them to screw eyes driven into the wall so they will not sag.

Meat Slicers. Here is the quick-and-easy way to slice not only meats but also breads, cheeses, fruits, and other solid foods. Slicers made for home use are either hand-cranked or driven by a small electric motor that plugs into any outlet. They have 6¼- or 7½-inch revolving blades. The feed mechanism can be set so you can slice meat that is almost thin enough to see through up to meat ¾ inch thick.

Meat slicers have legs that grip tight to the counter top. A safety guard prevents slicing unless your hand is safely out of the way. After use, the blade is easily released for washing in detergent solution.

Melamine. Melamine is a hard, fairly scratch-resistant, strong plastic that can withstand continuous temperatures just below the boiling point. It is not affected by detergents, cleaning fluids, oils, alcohol, or nail polish. The material can be made in all colors and has a glossy surface.

Melamine is used to make laminated plastic panels that are installed on counters and the tops of furniture, but it is best known as a lightweight, colorful dinnerware.

Laminated plastic surfaces are washed with any detergent solution. Tableware may be washed in the dishwasher. You should not, however, use abrasive cleansers or scouring pads on any melamine. Neither should you cut on it with a sharp knife. Tableware should not be put in an oven or on a range burner.

Melamine articles that are broken can be glued together with plastic-mending adhesive; but since the plastic is usually very thin, the glued joint will soon break again.

Melton. A heavy wool fabric with a smooth, dense, felt-like surface that is used in coats. It should be dry-cleaned.

Mending Plates. The articles most commonly known as mending plates are flat steel plates, such as angle irons and T's, that are used to hold together or reinforce pieces of wood. (See *Wood—Miter joints.*) They can also be used for the same purposes with plastics and metals.

A less familiar kind of mending plate is made in two half-circles. These are bolted around a pipe, over a rubber gasket, to stop a leak. Different sizes are available to fit iron and brass pipes of various sizes. They can also be used around copper tubes.

Metal Fasteners. Metal is fastened to metal by welding, brazing, soldering, and also by a variety of special fasteners. Some of these are also used to join metal to wood or plastic.

Nuts and bolts are used to make a very strong joint that can be opened at any time. There are three kinds: (1) Stove bolts are the smallest, with slotted heads like screws. The bolts you are most likely to use have round heads, but those with flat heads may be used in wood or in metal if the holes in the latter have been beveled. (2) Carriage bolts have smooth oval heads with a square collar directly beneath. This bites into wood and keeps the bolt from turning; but a square opening must be cut in metal for the collar. (3) Machine bolts are very large bolts with square heads.

To install a bolt, drill a hole the size of the bolt shank or a little larger; insert the bolt; and screw on the nut. If two pieces of metal are being joined, it generally is not necessary to separate them from the head of the bolt and the nut by flat washers; but you usually do need a lock washer under the nut to keep it from coming loose. Flat washers may be used, however, to separate the head of a bolt or nut from wood. In this case, you need a lock washer between the nut and the flat washer.

(Lock washers of two kinds are used. One is an incomplete circle of steel with the ends sprung to the sides. The other is a thinner, slightly convex circle with teeth. You can buy assortments of both kinds.) **Sheet-metal screws** are threaded for their entire length and are self-tapping. You just make a hole in the metal and then drive the screws in with a screwdriver. The screws are very commonly used in major appliance cabinets.

(Unlike sheet-metal screws, machine screws are not self-tapping; so you will probably never use them except to replace an old screw.)

Rivets used in the home workshop are fairly small fasteners of steel, aluminum, or copper. Drill a hole to receive the rivet shank; insert the rivet and place it head down on a piece of steel; clip off the excess shank so it sticks out only about 1/8 inch; then tap it down with a hammer. Since the rivet metal is soft, you don't need to hammer hard. The end should be rounded, not flattened.

Once a rivet is installed, it can be removed only by filing off one of the heads.

Rivets are also used to join leather, fabrics, and plastics. These rivets, however, are made in two pieces, each with flat heads. Slip the shank of one into the shank of the other. Then give one of the heads a swat.

Cotter pins have a split shank. After this is inserted through a hole in metal, the two arms are spread outward. Cotter pins are used to join metal pieces that will have to be separated at some future date. The joint is loose.

Metallic Cloth. A fabric containing metal threads. It may be used in clothing, clothing accessories, and draperies. It should be dry-cleaned.

Metallized Fabric. This is a new kind of fabric stemming from the development of a superinsulation material for the space program. It is made of nylon coated on one side with a thin, porous film of aluminum. The other side is dyed any color. The material has excellent insulating characteristics, is waterproof, yet air will pass through it. Used in clothing, the metallized side is against the body; in draperies, it faces outdoors, consequently the fabric turns back many of the sun rays that fade carpets and furniture. In summer, it also helps to keep out heat. Light comes through, however.

The new material is best dry-cleaned when soiled; but it can be machine-washed in cold water and cold-water detergent. Dry on a line.

Milium-treated fabric is an older metallized material differing from the new one in that the aluminum is applied in the form of paint. The fabric does not breathe and should not be laundered.

Metal Polishes. There are a lot of ancient recipes for cleaning metal and a lot of new polishes, liquids, and even an electrical appliance (see *Ultrasonic Cleaner*) for doing the same thing. The simple creams or pastes that have been on the market for a number of years are as good as anything. Don't fall for loud claims and sky-high price tags.

Most metal polishes will clean most metals, solid and plated, although you can't be sure until you read the label. They should not be used on metals that have been lacquered. If you have many pieces of one particular kind of metal, however, you may want to use polishes recommended particularly for that metal. Chrome and aluminum polishes, for example, are especially effective for restoring a shine to window and door frames and outdoor furniture that has become pitted and dull.

Some polishes contain tarnish-preventive ingredients. If you use one that does not, you can protect the metal with a tarnish-preventive aerosol spray. But it is easier to prevent tarnish simply by keeping metal pieces that are not on display in cloth or plastic bags or tarnish-proof paper.

Micarta. A laminated plastic made by Westinghouse.

Mice. See *Pest Control.*

Mildew. Unless you take proper precautions, mildew is likely to raise havoc with your clothes, bedding, and woodwork in the summer.

As most homemakers have discovered to their sorrow, the molds that cause mildew will grow on almost anything—cotton, linen, silk, leather, paper, wood—if they have dampness and warmth to thrive on. That's why you will find them flourishing in warm weather, especially in a house that has been closed up. They're also likely to grow in new houses because of the moisture in the building materials.

It is not difficult, however, to prevent or get rid of the discolorations, musty odors, wood decay, and rotting cloth caused by mildew. Here is the way to go about it:

Preventive measures. Remove causes of dampness in the home wherever possible. Ventilate the house only when the air outside is cooler and drier than that inside—on cool evenings, for example. If airing does not get rid of dampness, heat the house for a short time; then open doors and windows to let out the warm air that has taken up the extra moisture. Use an electric fan to force the air out more quickly.

Leave closet doors and bureau drawers open occasionally to keep moisture from gathering and to stir up the enclosed air. Run an electric fan in places that cannot be exposed to outdoor breezes. To dry out musty closets, burn a 60-, 75-, or 100-watt incandescent bulb continuously in them, or place an open container of calcium chloride in the closet with the door closed.

Musty odors in basements usually disappear if the house is well heated and dried and the basement itself is ventilated. If the odor persists, sprinkle calcium chloride over the basement floor and let it stand until the mustiness is dispelled. In closets and other fairly confined areas, you can also burn an ozone lamp to kill the musty odor. If a ready-made fixture is not available, you can make your own by wiring a standard lamp socket and intermediate lamp socket in series. Screw a 40-watt incandescent bulb into the former; an ozone lamp into the latter. The ozone lamp should be shielded from the eyes.

Never let damp or wet clothing or other articles lie around. Dry soiled clothes before throwing them into the hamper; wash dishcloths and hang them to dry; spread out washcloths; stretch out wet shower curtains; sprinkle for ironing only as many articles as can be ironed in a day (if ironing is delayed, put the damp clothes in your refrigerator).

Wash or dry-clean clothing and other household fabrics before storing them, since soiled articles are more likely to mildew than clean ones. Do not leave sizing or laundry starch in fabrics to be stored since molds feed on these finishes. Sun and air stored articles from time to time.

When you purchase cotton shower curtains, awnings, tents, sails, etc., be sure they have been treated with chemicals to make them mildew-resistant.

To keep books in a closed bookcase from mildewing, dust them occasionally with a small amount of paraformaldehyde or burn an electric light in the bookcase.

To remove mildew. Remove mildew spots as soon as you find them before they have a chance to weaken the material. Take off surface growth by brushing the affected article out of doors (this prevents scattering of spores in the house). Sun and air fabrics thoroughly. Dry-clean fabrics that cannot be washed.

Fresh mildew stains on washable fabrics should be washed at once with detergent. Rinse well and dry in the sun. If any stain remains, sponge with a solution of 1 tablespoon sodium perborate to 1 pint lukewarm water; let stand for a minute or two, then rinse well. On colored material, test the bleach first on an inconspicuous area.

If soiled dishcloths and washcloths get musty-smelling, boil them a few minutes in water to which baking soda (2 teaspoons to a quart of water) has been added. Use a bleach if necessary; then launder as usual.

Soak old mildew stains on undyed cotton, linen, or rayon in a chlorine bleach for a short time; then dip in a weak solution of white vinegar to stop the action of the chlorine; and rinse well in water. Never use chlorine bleach on silk or wool.

Remove loose and embedded mold from outer coverings of upholstered furniture and mattresses with a vacuum cleaner tool. Give them sun and air. If there are stains, sponge lightly with thick suds and wipe with a clean, damp cloth. Wipe upholstered furniture with a cloth wrung out in diluted alcohol. Sop up as much of the moisture as possible with a towel.

Sponge mildewed rugs and carpets with a rug shampoo; wipe with a damp cloth, and dry in the sun. If mildew has grown deep down in the pile, send the rugs to a professional cleaner.

To remove mildew from leather goods, wipe with a cloth wrung out in diluted alcohol or wash with saddle soap. Wipe with a damp cloth and dry in an airy place.

Spread pages of mildewed books out fanwise to air them. If very damp, sprinkle cornstarch or pure talc between the leaves and let stand several hours; then brush off. On white paper, ink eradicator may be used to remove stains.

Wipe mildewed floors and woodwork with a cloth dipped in water to which a little kerosene has been added, or wash with warm detergent solution. Dry well.

Remove mildew stains from painted surfaces inside and outside the house with a mixture of 1/3 cup household detergent, ½ cup oxygen bleach, and 4 cups warm water. Allow the solution to stand for 10 minutes before rinsing. Then to prevent a new attack of mildew, repair the area with a paint containing a mildewcide. The alternative is to add mildewcide to any standard paint you wish to use.

When wallpaper has mildewed, brush off any dry, loose mold with a cloth or brush. Dry the paper and the plaster beneath by heating the room for several hours or even days. If the paper is washable, wipe mildew stains with a cloth wrung out in detergent solution, then with a clean damp cloth. Pat dry with a soft cloth.

Miracle Adhesive. See *Gluing—Silicone rubber adhesive.*

Mirrors. The best mirrors are made of plate glass; less expensive types are of sheet glass. If you have an old plate-glass mirror with a sound finish, it pays to hold on to it because you can always have it cut by a glass dealer to almost any shape. This costs less than a new mirror. On the other hand, it rarely pays to have a plate-glass mirror in poor shape resilvered.

When a mirror is used as the top of a table of any type, make certain the base is smooth and free of gritty dirt before setting the mirror down. If the base is rough, cushion it with newspapers.

There is no trick to hanging a framed mirror on the wall provided the picture hook is large enough to support the weight. Such a mirror should be treated like a picture and dusted, damp-washed, and cleaned behind in the same way.

Installing an unframed mirror on a wall is done in several ways. The simplest is to use L-shaped plastic or metal mirror hangers which are screwed to the wall at the bottom, sides, and top of the mirror. One arm of each L overhangs the front edge of the mirror, locking it in place. The number of hangers needed depends on the size of the mirror. You should probably use three under a large mirror; only one under a small mirror. One on each side and at the top is generally sufficient for horizontal mirrors; but more are needed for tall mirrors.

The number of hangers also depends on the wall. The more hangers that can be screwed into the studs, the fewer you will need. If you cannot screw into the studs, except perhaps in one or two places, and if the screws cannot get a firm grip in the wall surface, coat the back of the mirror with silicone rubber adhesive and glue it to the wall. It is still advisable to use a few hangers, even though the adhesive is strong enough to bear considerable weight.

If you dislike the appearance of small mirror hangers, you may be able to find an unobtrusive stainless-steel channel that is screwed to the wall. The mirror rests in this, almost concealing it. Silicone rubber adhesive must be applied to the back of the mirror to keep it from falling forward.

Yet another way to install mirrors—no longer much used—is to have holes drilled through the corners. Screws encircled by large ornamental washers are driven through these.

Mirrors which are mounted flat on a wall need only to be dusted, washed, and polished.

Superstition to the contrary, a broken mirror may not mean bad luck; but it does mean you should get a new mirror because even though you can glue the pieces together with cellulose cement, the mend will be obvious and unsightly.

Mirror Tiles. These are 12-inch-square mirrors made of sheet glass. They have either a normal mirror finish or decorative figuring and coloring. Application can be made to any smooth, sound wall by sticking double-faced, pressure-sensitive tape to the back of each square and then pressing the square to the wall. Generally, the tiles are installed edge to edge like ceramic tiles, and cover an entire wall. The joints are not grouted.

Miter Box. See *Tools, Workshop.*

Mixers, Electric. A mixer makes many jobs from whipping cream to beating egg whites and mixing batters easier and quicker.

Mixers fall into two basic categories: portable and fixed to a stand.

Portable mixers do an excellent job on most mixing tasks. Their compact size and weight make them easier to use and to store than stand models.

Portable mixers usually have three speeds (although some have as many as twelve and some have solid-state controls). The speed control should be located where it is easy to reach and change with either hand. The beater-ejection button or control also should be easy to reach but not so easy that you might eject the beaters accidentally during operation.

Since you hold the mixer as you use it, its weight and balance are important. A light-weight mixer can be more cumbersome than a heavy one if the weight is poorly distributed. Proper balance also means that the mixer should be able to rest securely on its heel when not in use, both when the beaters are clean and when they are weighted with food.

Portable mixers are available with such attachments as knife sharpeners and drink mixers.

Stand mixers are more powerful. They do everything that portable mixers do and in addition they have the power needed for mixing heavy batter and dough. Most of them are pretty hefty to move around, so it's advisable to give them a permanent place in the kitchen.

Stand mixers usually have two sizes of rotating bowls with provision for changing the position of the turntable so that the beaters circle the side of the bowl rather than the center. Two models have a single wire whisk rather than a pair of beaters. The number of speeds varies, but most models have ten or more. Solid-state controls which maintain the set speed of the mixer and keep it from slowing down as the mixture thickens or speeding up as it thins are becoming more popular.

Stand mixers are available with a wide variety of attachments: a dough hook for kneading dough, blender, food grinder, and juicer, for example.

How to care for mixers. Clean them thoroughly with a wet sponge after each use; otherwise they will become encrusted with food which gets increasingly hard to remove. Clean under the turntable of stand mixers frequently, and lubricate the pivot with a little salad oil from time to time.

Stand mixers that are not stored in a cabinet should be kept covered with a plastic hood when not in use.

When a mixer is operating, never put a metal fork or spoon into the bowl because it may tangle with the beaters. Always use a rubber spatula.

If beaters become bent, you can usually get them back into operating condition by bending them carefully with smooth-jawed pliers. A bent shaft can sometimes be straightened with a hammer or in a vise.

A broken glass mixing bowl can be glued with cellulose cement, but this is a questionable practice, for if the revolving blades happen to strike the sides, it is likely to break again.

Modacrylic. A modified acrylic fiber that is used in draperies, carpets, and imitation fur fabrics. Articles made of it hold their shape well, resist abrasion, and are very resistant to fire. Wash in warm water; dry at low heat. If ironing is necessary, iron at low heat. For how to clean modacrylic carpets, see *Rugs.*

Mohair. The lustrous hair of the Angora goat used to make a smooth, resilient, durable fabric or yarn that goes into clothing, sweaters, and upholstery. It should be dry-cleaned.

Moiré (mwa-*ray*). A silk, rayon, or cotton fabric with a wave-like or watery appearance, moiré is used in draperies, bedspreads, and clothing. Dry-clean it.

Monk's Cloth. A cotton fabric in a coarse, soft, loose basket weave. It is used in draperies. Wash like cotton.

Mopping. No woman has ever been crowned mopping queen of the universe; but there are some who deserve the title far more than others, because when they mop, they get floors really clean. Here are the simple rules they follow when wet-mopping:

1. Change mop water frequently.

2. Rinse the mop frequently.

3. Wring the mop as dry as possible so that you don't damage the flooring or introduce too much moisture into the house air.

4. Try not to slosh water or the mop head on baseboards, appliances, bathroom fixtures, etc. Removing the resulting spots is a needless chore.

The rules for dry- or dust-mopping are:

1. Try using a vacuum cleaner rather than a mop: it does a more thorough job.

2. Shake out the dust mop frequently and thoroughly; and when you do, go outside and close the door behind you so that dust doesn't float back in.

3. Wash the mop when it gets dirty. Use lukewarm water and minimum agitation. When dry, spray it with silicone to pick up and hold dust.

Mops. Wet mops are made of fluffy string or synthetic sponge. Unless you want to pamper yourself a little bit (and not unwisely), you need a string mop only. This is not pleasant to wring out, even if you have a mop-wringer pail, but because it is flexible, it is much more maneuverable than a sponge held in a rigid head. The latter is fine to use in a kitchen; but impossible to work into tight corners behind toilets and sinks.

Unfortunately, many string mops today are made with removable heads that are held in a wide metal clamp. If you're not careful, the clamp will scratch a floor badly. Mop heads that are held in plastic are somewhat better because they don't scratch, but the plastic is prone to break. So if you can find an old-fashioned string mop with the head tied directly to the handle like a fluffy pony tail, grab it.

Sponge mops have hand wringers. In one type of mop, the wringer swings down and over the sponge in a clamshell-like bite. In the other mop, when you push down on the wringer handle, the sponge folds in on itself. This mop has a tendency to get out of whack.

The best dry mops are made with shaggy heads that slip on and off over a wire frame that spreads the heads flat. The heads are removable for washing.

Mosquitoes. See *Pest Control.*

Mother-of-Pearl. The lustrous, white or pastel inside layer of certain shells, usually oyster shells. It is used to make buttons and teething rings and to ornament the backs of hairbrushes and other articles. Clean with a mild detergent solution. Apply cellulose cement to broken edges and press them together for an hour or two.

Moths. See *Pest Control.*

Moving. On the average, Americans move about once every five years. But no matter how many times a family moves, it always finds it a lot of work. Here are the steps involved:

1. Decide what you are going to take with you and what you are going to dispose of or perhaps leave in the house (usually such things as the TV antenna, range, dishwasher, and some light bulbs). If you make a complete list of what you are taking and something turns up missing later, it may help you to remember what you did with the missing item. It might also help you get redress from the mover if he lost the item.

2. If you don't know a reliable moving company, get recommendations from neighbors and friends. Check with the Better Business Bureau. Then ask for estimates from three or four companies. And when the estimators come, be sure to show them everything you are going to move and everything that they will have to pack. In an interstate move, rates are usually based on the weight of the load and the distance you are moving. In a local move, rates are usually based on the time the move will take. An additional charge is made for packing articles. You can save money by packing more things yourself in cartons supplied by the moving company, or by moving things in your car, thus reducing the weight of the load or the time the move takes.

The alternative to hiring a moving company is to rent a truck and move things yourself, perhaps with the help of friends. Many young couples with a limited amount of furniture do this and save a great deal of money. The work, however, is arduous and difficult if you own a king-size bed, piano, or huge sofa.

3. Make arrangements to insure the load. By law, the mover is liable for loss or damage to a maximum of 60 cents per pound. This means that if you don't take out insurance and if a sofa weighing 130 pounds is lost, you would be paid $78 even though the sofa might actually be worth $400. Obviously, therefore, it is wise to insure the load to its full value. The insurance can be purchased through the moving company or your regular insurance broker. Get prices from both.

4. Give your new address to everybody who ought to know it: post office, draft board, motor vehicle department, bank, magazines and newspapers you subscribe to, mortgage company, loan agencies, insurance companies, credit card companies. The post office provides free change-of-address cards.

5. Notify telephone, gas, electric, and water companies to discontinue service at your old address on the day of your move and to start service at your new address. If you are making a very short move and take

possession of your new house before you move, you can arrange with the telephone company to install a phone with your old number in the new house while you still have the phone in your old house. Thus the phone will ring in both places until you move out of the old house.

6. Notify regular delivery services, such as the milk company and fuel oil dealer, to discontinue service.

7. If you are moving out of town, collect medical and dental records, school records, drug prescriptions, and similar things you must take along.

8. If moving out of town, don't discontinue your checking account until after you are well settled in your new home. Opening a new account is a time-consuming little chore. There is no sense or need to bother with it the instant you arrive in a new community.

9. If you hold a garage sale, do so at an early date. Give whatever else you don't need to charitable organizations, but don't expect them to take junk. For income tax purposes, make a list of what you give to each organization, and ask the organization to tell you what the value of each article is.

10. Return whatever you have borrowed.

11. If you are moving out of a region, there are possibly quarantines prohibiting you from taking your house plants and garden plants with you. In that case give them to friends.

12. If you are making a local move and if your rugs, furniture, or venetian blinds need cleaning, have the cleaning services pick the articles up before you move and deliver them to your new home. It will cut your moving expenses.

13. If the cost of your move is based on the time it will take, you can cut the cost by taking down draperies, curtain rods, and pictures, and taking up carpet that is tacked down.

14. Arrange with an appliance dealer to prepare your automatic washing machine for the move. The moving men won't do this.

15. Check whether the mover will move your filled freezer. On a short move he probably will; on a long move, he probably won't.

16. Ask the mover for tags to put on all articles that require special handling, such as storing.

17. Be prepared to take your pets with you; the mover is not allowed to.

18. Start packing. Inasmuch as the mover is not responsible for breaking articles you pack, it's a good idea to let him pack all valuable breakables—china, good glass, good lampshades, paintings, clocks, small appliances, etc.

Cartons that you use for packing should be made of sturdy kraft board and have tops with four flaps. (If a top has been sliced off in one piece with a knife, it is hard to seal and lacks strength.) Don't pack cartons so high that the top bulges. After packing, seal the tops with gummed tape and print on them what is inside.

Pack no more than two dozen books per carton; no more than a 12-inch-high pile of phonograph records. The boxes are too heavy to handle otherwise.

Wrap each individual piece of china, glass, pottery, etc., in one or more full sheets of newspaper or, better, the unprinted packing paper used by movers. Nest plates and place them on edge. Glasses, cups, and vases should not be nested. They are placed top down. Wad more newspaper between all sides of the carton and the packed articles. Glass kitchen utensils and your best metal utensils should also be wrapped individually. They can then be nested.

Wrap hollow ware in the mover's packing paper or in tissue and newspaper. Pack it, with plenty of padding, in a locked trunk or wooden box.

Wrap and pack small pictures like china. Place on edge in the carton. You can move large pictures and mirrors across town in your car if you wrap each one in a blanket or mattress pad.

Close the tops of all medicines, perfumes, and other bottles securely. Seal tops on bottles with cellulose or adhesive tape, and wrap each bottle separately.

Load bureau drawers with as many things as possible, but don't cram them. If you weigh bureaus and other chests and cabinets down too much with heavy articles, you will wind up with a lot of cranky moving men—and an unhappy moving day.

Tie mops, brooms, garden tools, etc., in small bundles.

Take jewelry and valuables from the safe-deposit box with you in your car or send them to your new home by registered mail.

19. If you have filing cabinets or trunks with locks, make sure you have the keys. If you don't, cover the locks with adhesive tape so they cannot be shut and warn the moving men about them.

20. If you expect to arrive in your new town before the mover, remember to give him the address and telephone number where you will be staying so he can notify you if any hitch develops.

21. If you are known to the moving company, it may be willing to bill you after the move. Otherwise you should be prepared to pay off the moving men by certified check, cash, or money order. The maximum amount you are required to pay on a COD shipment equals the amount of the estimate plus 10 percent. If the actual charge is higher than this, you have fifteen days to pay the balance.

22. All articles damaged in transit should be pointed out to the moving men and you should see that they list them in writing. You should then file a written claim with the company within a week. Actually, under ICC rules, you have nine months from the date of delivery in which to file a claim, but the longer you wait the harder it will be to prove your loss. ICC rules also require the moving company to acknowledge a written claim within thirty days and to take some action on it within 120 days.

23. If you have an argument with the mover, you can file a complaint with a local office of the ICC; with the Bureau of Operations, Interstate Commerce Commission, 12th Street and Constitution Avenue, NW, Washington, D.C. 20423; or with the Consumers Service Department, American Movers Conference, 1625 O Street, NW, Washington, D.C. 20036.

Muriatic Acid. Muriatic, or hydrochloric, acid is a dangerous chemical used to clean and etch masonry and metal surfaces before they are painted. It also is used to remove efflorescence from masonry.

You should always buy muriatic acid in a container that gives detailed directions for its use or that is clearly marked as a 20 percent solution. (If the container is not marked in either of these ways, you have no way of knowing how strong the acid is or how it should be diluted.)

Twenty percent muriatic acid should be used full-strength for etching masonry and taking scale off metal. Dilute it half-and-half with water to remove stains. And dilute it with 3 parts water or more to remove efflorescence.

Wear rubber gloves and goggles when working with muriatic acid. Mix it in a plastic pail or glass container. Apply with a bristle brush. Rinse well.

Muslin. An inexpensive, rather coarse, strong cotton fabric used for bed linens and to a limited extent in clothing. Launder like cotton. There is also a sheer muslin resembling stiff voile.

Nails. The size of most but not all nails is described by a number followed by the word "penny" or the letter d. A 2-inch nail, for example, is a 6-penny or 6d nail; a 3-inch nail is a 10-penny or 10d nail.

You can, of course, order nails from a hardware store or lumber yard by length; but if you want to sound like an old pro, you should speak in terms of pennies as follows:

Length of nail (inches)	Penny size (d)
1	2
1¼	3
1½	4
1¾	5
2	6
2¼	7
2½	8
3	10
3¼	12
3½	16
4	20
4½	30
5	40
5½	50
6	60

Over 6 inches, nails are known as spikes and are identified by their exact length.

Brads and wire nails are small nails that are also graded by length.

Most nails are made of ordinary steel. If you need rust-proof nails, specify galvanized steel; it may rust in time outdoors, but if it is kept covered with paint, it probably won't. Aluminum nails should be used when installing aluminum siding, roofing, flashing, etc. Copper nails are used with copper flashing. Stainless steel nails can be purchased but are very expensive.

Which size nails to buy. In various entries in this book you will find that nails of specific size are called for. But unless you have definite directions like these or unless you have someone else's experience to go by, you will have to figure out for yourself what you need.

One point to remember is that the longer a nail of any particular type, the greater its diameter. This makes it stronger. So when you need strength in a joint, use a large nail; but don't make the mistake of using such a large nail that it splits the wood.

If you are fastening a board to a thick, solid base such as a stud or joist, the nails you use should be about three times longer than the thickness of the board.

However, if you are joining two ordinary boards together, you have no need for such a long nail. If you want to clinch the nail so it cannot come out, you need a nail only about ¼ inch longer than the thickness of the two boards. On the other hand, if you don't want the point of the nail to come through, you must use nails that are slightly shorter than the thickness of the two boards. In this case, you need more nails than would be necessary in the former case. The alternative—which is better—would be to fasten the boards together with screws.

Types of nail. Common nails are workhorse nails used for fairly heavy work. The nails are larger in diameter than other types; have round, flat heads. Since the heads are rarely countersunk, except in siding, the nails are usually used only when the heads will not be seen.

Box nails resemble common nails but are a little slenderer. They are used in making boxes and for nailing wood that might be split by common nails.

Wire nails are small, thin, common nails

from 5/8 to 1¼ inches. They are used instead of brads when it is not necessary to conceal the heads.

Spikes are like common nails, but they range from 6 to 12 inches in length.

Finishing nails are the thinnest large nails and have small heads that are easily driven into wood and are then, as a rule, countersunk with a nailset. These nails are used mainly in fine work.

Casing nails are like finishing nails but have slightly thicker shanks. They are used in paneling, cabinet work, and the like. Actually, most people use finishing and casing nails interchangeably. They don't know which is which and it is probable that the hardware dealer doesn't know either.

Brads are very small finishing nails ranging from ½ to 1½ inches in length. They are used for such things as framing pictures, attaching small moldings, and putting latticework together.

Special-purpose nails. Cut nails are thin rectangles tapering from the head to the point. They are used to lay hardwood floors. Sizes range from 6d to 20d.

Ring-grooved nails. These look like lightweight common nails except that the shank is notched in small concentric rings. The nails are recommended for installing gypsum board, hardboard, and other wallboards because they hold securely in the studs and prevent what is known as nail-popping. Ring-grooved nails are also called ringed-shank or annular-grooved nails.

Screw nails have a steep screw thread from the point to the small head. They have great holding power and are used in wood, especially in strip floors. They can be countersunk.

Shingle nails are fairly small galvanized nails used primarily in wood shingles. Asphalt-roofing nails are also galvanized, but have very large heads so they will hold asphalt roofing of all types securely.

Coated nails. These are mainly box or common nails with various kinds of coating to prevent rusting. Cement-coated nails are often used to install gypsum board, but lack the holding power of ring-grooved nails.

Masonry nails are made of zinc-coated hardened steel, have rather short, heavy shanks and large heads. You can drive them into brick, concrete block, etc.

Other special-purpose nails are so highly specialized that the home owner rarely has reason to use them.

Nailsets. See *Tools, Workshop.*

Nainsook. A soft, wispy cotton fabric similar to batiste and used for the same purposes. Hand-wash and press with a warm iron.

Nambé (*nahm*-bay). Nambé is an alloy of eight different metals that is hand-cast in sand molds to make tableware and decorative accessories. It has a silver-like finish with slight pits.

When used for baking or surface cooking, Nambé should be rubbed with a little butter or cooking oil to help preserve the original luster. Wash with hand-dishwashing detergent and dry at once. Because the material shows water spots, washing in a dishwasher is not recommended. Neither is use of abrasives.

If the metal is stained by acid foods, polish with brass polish.

Naphtha. Naphtha and benzine are two very similar petroleum derivatives used primarily for cleaning wood (because they do not raise the grain as water does) and removing wax and furniture polish from various materials. Use it with care because it is flammable.

Napkins. See *Table Linens.*

Needlepoint. A hand-embroidery made usually with wool yarn on open-work canvas. The surface is covered with small, closely spaced stitches. Petit point is needlepoint made with very small stitches. Gros point is made with larger stitches.

Needlepoint is used for many decorative purposes, such as upholstering furniture and making pillow covers, purses, belts, rugs, and wall hangings. If soiled, it must be dry-cleaned. Areas that are burned or damaged in any other way may be reworked.

Ninon (*knee*-non). Ninon is a fabric resembling chiffon but sturdier and crisper. Made of polyester, nylon, silk, or rayon, it is used in curtains and clothing. Launder as you would any delicate fabric. Do not iron.

Nuts and Bolts. See *Metal Fasteners.*

Nylon. Nylon is usually thought of as a plastic filament that is used widely in textiles and carpets; but it is also used in solid articles. The material is tough and resilient; withstands moderate heat; and resists damage by common chemicals, greases, and solvents. It is stained by coffee, tea, mustard, and highly colored foods such as beets. When used in carpets, it often causes annoying static problems which can be corrected only by raising the house humidity or by applying an antistatic spray.

Solid nylon articles are cleaned with a detergent solution or dry-cleaning fluid. Do not use abrasives. Broken articles cannot be glued.

Nylon garments are readily machine-washed in warm water to which a light-duty detergent has been added. A water softener should also be added if the water is hard. Dry in a dryer at low temperature for 15 to 20 minutes and continue tumbling without heat for another 10 minutes. Then remove the garments at once and hang.

If you don't have a dryer, remove nylon garments from the washer after they are rinsed and before they are spun-dry. Then allow them to drip-dry on hangers.

Badly soiled or stained white garments that are not cleaned by this treatment should be soaked overnight, before they are laundered, in a solution of 1 cup dishwashing detergent and 1 gallon warm water. Wash separately from colored garments because nylon quickly picks up and retains colors and soil.

Water-based stains on nylon fabrics are removed by sponging with water. Use a cleaning fluid on oil-based stains. If any stains persist, the article should be dry-cleaned.

Press nylon with an iron at a low setting. To clean nylon carpets, see *Rugs.*

Odor Control. The first line of defense in fighting odors is opening windows and doors. This, in fact, is probably your chief line of defense in living and sleeping areas. But in the kitchen and in all inside bathrooms (without windows) you need ventilating fans. Such fans are also highly desirable in outside (windowed) bathrooms. (See *Fans, Ventilating.*)

Aerosol sprays do not remove odors but conceal them. Called air fresheners, most come in cans of about 7 ounces or more. To use these aerosols, aim at the ceiling and press the spray cap briefly. A more highly concentrated type of freshener is sold in a small aerosol can with a metered valve which prevents overuse of the spray.

Bottles filled with deodorant are not as instantly effective but are helpful. Just remove the cap, pull up the wick, and set the bottle near the source of the odor.

Small ozone lamps are sometimes installed in closets to prevent the musty odor of mildew. They might also be used in musty rooms. (See *Mildew*.)

If you want year-round odor control throughout your house, there is a new electrical appliance that can be installed in a ducted heating or air-conditioning system or mounted on a wall in a central location in the house. The chemical dispersed by the unit neutralizes the odors it encounters; at the same time it adds a slight scent to the air.

Two odors that are particularly difficult to get rid of are stale tobacco smoke and a wood fire. Despite airing and aerosols, these may persist for several days. It is, however, possible to hasten them on their way by setting a bowl of water containing several tablespoons of household ammonia in each affected room.

Oil. See *Lubricants*.

Oilcloth. This is a cotton fabric with a water-tight, shiny, paint-like surface. It is occasionally used to cover shelves and tables. To clean, simply go over it with a sponge dipped in water or mild detergent solution.

If oilcloth is torn, you can mend it by pasting a scrap of fabric of any kind to the back with fabric-mending adhesive.

To keep the shiny surface from cracking, avoid folding oilcloth and don't expose it to too much sun.

Olefin. A class of plastics, including such types as polypropylene and polyethylene. When retailers refer to olefin fibers in carpets or upholstery, they are talking about polypropylene.

Onyx. A beautiful type of stone that is made into ornaments. Wash with detergent solu-

tion. Mend broken pieces with epoxy glue or cellulose cement.

Organdy. A stiff, translucent cotton or nylon fabric used in clothing and curtains. It should be hand-washed in warm water and dried over a line. Press with a hot iron if cotton and a warm iron if nylon.

If organdy loses its stiffness, it should be starched. But this is rarely necessary.

Oriental Rugs. The most beautiful type of rug. (See *Rugs*.)

Orlon. Trade name given by DuPont to its acrylic fiber.

Outdoor Furniture. Whatever it is made of, outdoor furniture must be protected against damage by the sun, rain, wind, dirt, birds, and trees.

The best general rules to follow are:

1. Keep pieces under cover when not in use. If you cannot move them under a roof, cover them with old plastic shower curtains.

2. Keep all lightweight pieces in a wind-proof pocket to prevent them from being blown about like tenpins by driving winds.

3. Dry furniture pieces if rained on.

4. Clean regularly with a damp sponge.

5. Refinish furniture in the spring before taking it outdoors. Some pieces need refinishing annually; others every other year.

Wood. Paint regularly with gloss trim enamel or—not as good because it deteriorates in sunlight—with spar varnish. Make sure nail heads and screw heads are countersunk and covered with putty. If wood cracks, fill the break immediately with plastic wood or water putty.

Although redwood weathers better than most woods used in outdoor furniture, it is easily stained. So cover it with varnish. If stains do appear, sanding with the grain should obliterate them. If not, bleach the stained areas with 3/8 ounce oxalic acid mixed with 1 pint rubbing alcohol.

Painted metal. Paint with trim enamel. If rust spots appear, chip, scrape, and sand the areas thoroughly; apply a liquid or jellied rust remover; wash with naphtha or turpentine; and brush on a rust-inhibiting primer followed by enamel.

Chromium-plated steel needs less attention than most materials but may require occasional treatment with a chromium cleaner and protector.

Aluminum may rub off black on your hands and clothes for some time when new; and if it does, you should wash it well with detergent solution. Rub hard. Thereafter it requires only occasional washing to keep it clean. Polishing with an automobile wax will make it shine.

Vinyl. Clean every couple of weeks with detergent solution or prepared vinyl cleaner.

Polypropylene is used to make colorful webbing for chairs and chaises. It resists soiling to a remarkable degree; can usually be wiped clean with a damp cloth. It disintegrates rapidly, however.

Rattan, wicker, and other woven furniture. The brads used in construction of these pieces are difficult to countersink; so the only way to stop them from corroding and staining the surrounding wood is to apply paint or varnish every spring.

Canvas will retain its appearance for just about one summer, no more—and probably less. Then it needs to be replaced or painted with canvas paint. It can be cleaned, but not easily, by hard scrubbing in a very hot detergent solution.

Glass. Table tops of glass show less soil if they are figured or translucent. Don't place them under brittle trees.

How to repair outdoor furniture. See the entry for the appropriate material.

Outing Flannel. See *Flannelette.*

Ozone Lamps. These are small bulbs used to counteract unpleasant odors. They are also installed in some automatic dryers. See *Mildew.*

Package Wrapping. The next time you receive a package torn and smashed to bits, let it serve as a reminder that if you want to send anything through the mails today, you must wrap it well.

Even if you are mailing a fabric, it should be enclosed in a corrugated board carton (but see below), not just wrapping paper. For nonbreakable material, the carton need be only just large enough to contain the material. But for anything breakable the carton should be at least a third larger than the contents and similar in weight to one of the cartons used for packing liquor bottles. The top of a carton should have four undamaged flaps that fold in toward the center. Cartons that you pick up from grocery and liquor stores usually have been cut open on three sides of the top and are impossible to seal tight.

It is easy enough to reduce the depth of a box that is too big for your needs by cutting down through the four corners for several inches. Be sure the cuts are the same length. Then turn the box on one side, and with a yardstick as a guide cut from one corner to the next with a razor blade. Slice through the top layer of paper only, and fold the upper part of the side inward. Do the same thing on the other three sides. Then cut off the top flaps where they overlap.

The most generally available stuffing in the home is newspaper. Excelsior and shredded paper are better but messy to store and a fire hazard. Crumple up individual sheets of newspaper and place a layer in the bottom of the carton. Then set in the article being mailed and pack more crumpled paper around and over it. When the job is done properly, the article should be well padded on all sides; and when you shake the carton vigorously, nothing inside should move.

For fragile articles, a new stuffing material made of two sheets of plastic film with air bubbles in between is excellent—if available. When this is wrapped around an article once or twice, little additional cushioning is needed.

Flat glass articles, such as mirrors and pictures, should not be sent through the mails unless they are sandwiched between large pieces of 1/8-inch hardboard or ¼-inch plywood. Even with this protection, they must be surrounded with a great deal of cushioning material and packed in a deep box.

When sealing packages, you can use stout string, tape, or both. String alone is better than tape alone; and using both is best of all. Tape alone should be used only on reasonably small, lightweight packages. You definitely should use string—with or without tape—on heavy packages and also on soft packages (which are not recommended in the first place).

If taping cartons, use heavy, kraft gummed tape at least 2 inches wide. Ready-to-stick tape is more convenient than the type you have to moisten, but more expensive. When wetting tape with a sponge, try not to apply any more water than you would with your tongue. A tape that is too wet curls, is hard to handle, and doesn't stick instantly.

The first strip of tape should be centered over the juncture of the top flaps. The flaps should butt. Extend the tape down the sides of the carton for several inches. Then fold a strip of tape lengthwise over each open end joint.

If the flaps on the carton have been torn, it is advisable before taping them down to smear white wood glue on the underneath flaps so they will stick to the top flaps.

If tying a package with string, loop the string once around the ends and once around the sides of the carton if reasonably compact. But if the carton is very long, loop the string once around the ends and twice around the sides near the ends.

The easiest and most secure way to tie a package is to loop string around the sides of the carton and tie the short end around the long end with a single half hitch (see *Knots*). Then tie a knot in the short end so that it cannot slip through the half hitch. Pull the string taut. Then carry it around one end of the box and loop it around the string at the bottom. For extra security, tie a knot at this point. Then bring the string on around to the top of the box; wrap it around the knot; pull tight; and tie two or three half hitches.

It is necessary to wrap a carton in paper only if the cardboard is in less than perfect condition. The best paper to use is a heavy 50-pound weight. It needs to be wrapped only once around a package. Lap the ends 2 or 3 inches. The width of the paper should equal the length of the carton plus its height plus 1 or 2 inches. (In other words, if a carton is 10 inches long and 7 inches high, you should cut the paper to a width of 18 or 19 inches.) Thus, when the paper is folded around the carton, it will completely cover the carton ends yet lie flat. Always seal the end flaps and the top flap of paper with gummed tape.

Address a package on the top only. Because labels may come off, the post office department prefers that you do your lettering—in clear, bold print—directly on the carton or paper wrapping.

If, however, you use a carton that has been through the mails before or that is covered with advertising, and if you do not elect to overwrap it in paper, then you must paste an address label on the top. To guard against loss of the package in the event the label disappears, place inside the carton, right under the top, a printed slip saying, "This package shipped by [your name and address] ."

If you don't use a carton. In addition to giving good protection to packaged articles, cartons are desirable because they are easy to handle, usually can be obtained for nothing, and are simple to pack. But there are two other ways to package nonbreakable items: in rolls of corrugated board and in padded shipping bags, or envelopes.

Unfortunately, the rolled board is hard to work with. The padded bags, on the other hand, are simplicity itself—though a bit costly. All you do is slip the article inside, fold over the open end, and seal it with staples (preferable) or gummed tape.

The bags come in numerous sizes from about 4 by 7 inches up to 14 by 20 inches. They take up almost no space when stored.

Pails. Despite aggressive plastics manufacturers, there is still no substitute for the old-fashioned galvanized pail. It is strong, easy to clean, and lasts forever.

Plastic pails are cheaper and lighter; but they crack readily; melt if you make the mistake of exposing them to direct heat; and when they are full, they balance uncertainly and threaten to collapse.

If you insist on buying plastic, you should at least make sure that the top rim is bent down over a band of steel and that the handle is hooked into the band. When the handle is simply hooked into slots in the plastic, is is likely to come loose at crucial moments.

Very flexible plastic pails are generally made of polyethylene and can be repaired only with heat. More rigid plastic pails can generally be patched with a scrap of vinyl pasted down with plastic-mending adhesive.

Holes in galvanized pails are filled with plastic metal. Clean the surface thoroughly before applying this.

Paintbrushes. A paintbrush is the only all-around painting tool. You can use it to apply any kind of finish to any kind of surface and to achieve any kind of result. With it you can put paint exactly where it is supposed to be—even in hard-to-get-at places. And it is more economical of paint than other tools.

Its principal drawback is that you cannot cover large areas rapidly.

Selecting paintbrushes. If you take care of your brushes, you will never regret spending money for good ones. They do an infinitely better painting job than cheap brushes and last years longer.

Four simple tests should be made to determine whether a brush meets quality standards. First, separate the bristles at the center and look for a solid strip in the heel of the brush. The strip keeps the bristles in shape, helps to carry the paint load, and makes for easier cleaning.

Second, examine the bristles. If they are of animal hair, they should have split ends. Nylon bristles may or may not be split but should definitely be finely tapered.

Third, check the bounce of the brush by brushing the bristles against your hand. They should not fan out excessively but should feel springy and elastic.

Finally, shake the brush vigorously and fan the bristles to see how many fall out. All brushes lose bristles, but cheap ones lose a great many.

The shape and size of the brushes you buy depend on the painting jobs you intend to do. Ask the dealer to help you. The great majority of brushes are rectangular, and come in widths from ½ to 6 inches. Angular brushes are used for painting windows and trim. Oval brushes, called sash tools, are also used for painting window mullions.

How to use a paintbrush. Dip only half of the brush into the paint and slap it gently against the inside of the can to remove the excess. Do not wipe it off on the rim of the can. Apply paint with light,

short strokes. Use only the ends of the bristles. By brushing back and forth, you use all the paint and also make the bristles on each side wear more evenly. After applying paint to a fairly small area, smooth it out with crosswise strokes. Then, to eliminate brush marks almost completely, smooth it out again with strokes in the first direction.

Paint should be brushed on. Enamel, varnish, lacquer, and shellac are applied with a somewhat fuller brush and are flowed on.

How to care for paintbrushes. If you're starting with a new brush, give it a shake to dislodge loose bristles. A nylon brush is then ready to use. A brush with animal hair should be suspended for 12 hours in linseed oil if you intend to use it at first with oil or alkyd paint. If you intend to use it with any other type of finish, dip it briefly in the thinner used for that finish.

The proper thinners for oil and alkyd paints, oil-base stains, enamels, and varnish are turpentine or mineral spirits. Use denatured alcohol for shellac; lacquer thinner for lacquer; water for latex paint.

After you are through painting, soak the brush in the proper thinner. Work it against the side of the can and up and down to get out the paint. Use a putty knife to remove paint caked on the bristles and ferrule. Fan and squeeze the brush with your fingers to work the paint from the heel.

If the thinner is very dirty, rinse the brush in clean thinner.

If you intend to use the brush again the next day, rub it back and forth across several thicknesses of newspaper to dry it out somewhat. If you are going to store the brush, however, wash the bristles in mild detergent solution after they are clean. Rinse them well; dry them on newspaper; and then let them air-dry. When you can no longer feel any moisture, wrap the bristles in heavy brown paper or a plastic bag and store the brush flat in a drawer or hanging by the handle.

How to reclaim an old brush. Suspend it in liquid brush cleaner by drilling a hole through the handle, inserting a wire, and resting the ends on the rim of the can.

Never let a paintbrush stand for long on its bristles, because they will become warped.

When the bristles begin to soften, work the paint from the sides with a blunt-edged scraper run from the ferrule down to the bristle tips. To get out hidden paint, use a steel comb. The whole job takes time; don't expect to accomplish wonders in minutes. Scrape; then soak the brush again in the cleaner.

When the brush is finally clean, wash it in detergent solution and rinse well.

Painting. Also see *Paintbrushes; Paint Rollers; Paint Sprayers; Paint Thinner; Paints; Paint Removal; House Painting.* And for specific recommendations for painting and finishing different materials and objects, see *Wood; Concrete; Aluminum; Furniture, Wood;* and similar entries.

Most home owners today do some or all of their own painting. The explanation is obvious: the work is simple and not arduous; it saves money (the paint used comes to only about 20 percent of the price charged by a painting contractor); and there is a certain satisfaction in being able to say, "I painted it myself."

Strictly speaking, the verb "paint" means to apply the opaque liquid known as paint. But in common usage, the verb is extended to cover the application of all other hard liquid finishes including varnish, shellac, lacquer, stains, and sealers. Although this may be offensive to wordsmiths, it nevertheless makes sense because all these finishes are applied in much the same way as paint.

Choose the right finish. This is the first step in any painting project and it is not always an easy one. If you cannot find the answer under *Paints,* tell a paint dealer what you intend to paint, its condition, where it is located or used, and what you want to accomplish. He can undoubtedly tell you what finish you should use.

The dealer can also tell you how much paint you should buy if you give him a fairly accurate estimate of the square footage of the thing to be painted.

Pick the right conditions and/or location. The way a finish turns out depends on such things as the temperature, air movement, surface condition of the painted object, traffic, etc. Obviously, you have more to worry about when you are painting outdoors than when you are painting indoors. But even inside the house you may run into temperature problems and dust in the air. And there is always a possibility that someone will put his hand on what you have painted or knock it over.

Prepare the surface with care. Your success as a painter actually depends less on your skill in wielding a paintbrush than on the attention you give to preparation of the surface. While there are many differences in finishes and the way they are applied, you can put these down as general rules for starting all paint jobs:

1. Clean the surface completely. Remove dust, dirt, grease, mildew, crayon marks, ballpoint pen marks, etc.

2. Remove wax and polishes with naphtha, turpentine, or a prepared wax remover.

3. Remove old finishes that are in any way defective—loose, powdery, alligatored, etc.

4. Remove all rust from iron and steel; loose, powdery, rough corrosion products on other metals.

5. If an old finish is very hard or glossy, it must be roughened slightly to assure adherence of the new finish. Go over it with sandpaper or steel wool or rub it with a liquid paint sander.

6. Although unfinished wood surfaces may feel smooth, go over them with fine sandpaper to remove tiny fibers that would be raised by the finish. Even after doing this, you will have to sand the first coat to eliminate the fibers entirely.

7. Be sure the surface is dry except when using water-based paints. The latter can be applied to damp surfaces—and in the case of brick should be.

8. Fill holes, cracks, etc., with spackle, patching plaster, putty—whatever is appropriate. If you are painting bare wood, the patching material should be applied after the wood has been primed. In all cases, you should spot-prime the filled areas before applying the final coat of paint.

9. Seal knots in softwoods. Use WP-578

sealer if the wood is unfinished; shellac, a so-called stain-kill, or aluminum paint on finished wood.

10. On porous wood, such as oak, apply a paste filler to fill the pores; otherwise the surface will soak up an unnecessary amount of paint and will look uneven. Brush the filler on with the grain and then across the grain. Wipe it off with rags when it begins to dry; then sand the surface smooth the next day.

11. If you are applying a clear finish, sand the wood to a uniform appearance.

Protect surfaces that are not to be painted. Remove hardware such as doorknobs and escutcheons and switch plates, venetian blinds, shades, curtain rods, etc.

If your hand is not steady, apply masking tape around the edges of floors, lighting fixtures, and other areas and objects.

Cover furniture and large objects with newspapers and old sheets.

Protect floors with a canvas drop cloth or old mattress pads. Newspapers may be used but are too easily scuffed around. Plastic drop cloths are undesirable because they do not absorb paint; consequently, you may get it on your shoes and track it through the house. Whichever type of drop cloth you use, always lay it the same side up throughout the day. If you move it and turn it upside down, the wet paint that has dropped on it will mark the floor.

Apply a primer. Primers and undercoaters are used only with paint and enamel. You may not need them on a surface that already has a sound finish. But if a surface is bare or if the old finish is considerably darker than the new, you do.

The primer used must be compatible with the final finish, so be sure to look for this information on the can containing the final finish. The primer should also be tinted the same color as the final finish but should be a slightly lighter shade. Then when you apply the finish coat, you can see which areas you have and have not covered.

Ready the paint. Read the directions on the can.

If paint or stain has not been stirred or shaken by the paint store, you must mix it thoroughly to blend the pigment with the carrier. Some clear finishes also need stirring. Use a wide stick of wood and move it around and around and up and down. If the can is very full and the pigment in the bottom thick and unyielding, pour half of the paint into another can and stir each of them. Then gradually add the thinner paint to the thicker until you achieve the proper consistency.

Do not thin the paint unless it is very thick or the manufacturer recommends thinning. In that case, always use the thinner specified. (Note that so-called no-drip paints are supposed to be thick and should almost never be thinned.)

If the paint is old and contains lumps and skin, strain it into a clean container. The best strainer is a nylon stocking fitted over the top of the old can. The alternative is to tie several layers of cheesecloth securely to the top of the clean container or to rest several layers of screen wire on it. Once the paint has been strained, do not return it to the original can until that has been rinsed with thinner to remove lumps, etc.

Now paint. For how to go about this, see *Paintbrushes; Paint Rollers; Paint Sprayers; House Painting;* and the entries for specific materials and objects such as *Wood* and *Concrete.*

Clean up afterwards. As soon as you finish painting look around for splatters and wipe them up at once.

Clean your painting tools.

To store paints in the can so that a skin will not form on the surface is difficult. The first step is to wipe all the paint you possibly can from the rim of the can. Then set the lid in place and push it down firmly with your hands or step on it. Do not hit it with a hammer because that frequently bends it. The final step favored by most amateur painters is to cover the top half of the can with aluminum foil and secure it with a rubber band.

Paint Removal. Old paint must be removed from a surface if it is scarred, peeling, checked, alligatored, etc., pretty much all over or if you are going to apply a transparent finish. The first step in removing paint is to take off whatever hardware will get in the way of the work or may be damaged by it.

The second step is to try to remove the

paint by scraping it off with a scraper, putty knife, or knife (but not a piece of broken glass because that may cut too deeply). Sometimes this is surprisingly easy. If not, a third step is in order: you must either dissolve the paint with a solvent or burn it off.

Dissolving paint. Various solvents will soften paint and other hard finishes but prepared paint remover is best. It is not only powerful and fast but is also effective on all finishes and is safe to use on most materials, including wood, metal, and masonry. Use a thick, paste-like remover on vertical surfaces; a liquid remover on horizontal surfaces.

Flow on the remover in one direction with an old paintbrush. Do not go back over it. Let it stand for about 15 minutes until the finish is soft. At this point, you are supposed to be able to remove the finish with coarse steel wool dipped in water or detergent solution. This may not prove to be as easy as the manufacturer implies, however; and if that is the case, use a metal scraper, putty knife, or pocket-knife. Work with the grain as much as possible.

To get an old finish off curved and carved surfaces, use steel wool or a hard toothbrush.

Make repeat applications of remover if the finish does not come off completely.

When the last speck of finish is gone, go over the surface once more with a scrap of terry cloth wrung out in water or detergent solution. Then allow it to dry for 24 hours.

Burning off paint. Removing paint with a solvent is a great deal safer than burning it off; but burning is often preferable if the old paint is extremely thick or the area to be stripped is large. Burning is the standard method for removing paint from the exterior of a house.

You can do the work with a propane torch with a fan-shaped nozzle or with an electric burner that is pushed across the painted surface. The former is faster and more maneuverable because you are not tied to an extension cord; the latter is somewhat less hazardous because there is not an open flame. But the two tools are used in the same way. You simply hold them over the paint until it blisters; then you immediately peel it off with a putty knife.

An infrared heat lamp can also be used to burn off paint. The work, however, goes slowly because the lamp's temperature is low. On the other hand, there is no danger of fire.

Paint Rollers. Do-it-yourself house painting became an accepted fact of life when the paint roller was invented. It turned the once tedious job of wall and ceiling painting into a veritable lark. No longer must you be an expert to cover a lot of ground in a short time. No longer must you be an expert to paint a wall smoothly and evenly.

Selecting a roller. Rollers differ in length, thickness of nap, and price. The biggest is an 18-inch monster for painting sky-high ceilings. The smallest, made for painting in corners, can be used to make a line only a fraction of an inch wide. For general purposes, a 7- or 9-inch roller is about right.

Rollers with short nap are used to apply most paints to smooth surfaces. Those with long nap are used on rough surfaces. In a good paint store, you will find that the rollers on display are marked for specific surfaces and specific kinds of paint.

Quality roller covers cost about $2. They should always be used for applying latex paint because they can be easily washed and reused time after time. Because other paints are much harder to clean out of a roller, however, many painters use cheap throwaway covers for them. But be warned that cheap covers may fall apart when you're only part way through a project, and they do not always give as smooth a finish as you might like.

How to paint with a roller. You need a sloping pan to hold the paint. Fill it only part way so that some of the corrugations at the upper end are exposed. Good pans are designed so that you can hook them safely to the top step of a stepladder.

Roll the roller into the paint to cover the entire nap. Then roll it lightly over the corrugations to remove excess paint.

Apply paint to the wall or ceiling with light pressure. Do not work too rapidly.

Rollers ordinarily do not spatter paint, but if you use too much pressure or roll too fast, they throw a fine, mist-like spray all over the place. They will also drip big globs if loaded with too much paint.

Start each new load a slight distance from the previously painted area and work toward the completed work. Roll in any direction that is easy or necessary to cover the surface. Cross-rolling is permissible. But always finish by rolling all strokes in one direction. If the ends of the roller leave thick lines, these must be rolled out.

To paint ceilings with a roller, screw an extension handle into the end of the roller-holder handle. Although a long extension handle is a little awkward to work with, don't shorten it. The main virtue of a long handle is that you can operate the roller with both hands at the same time. This is less tiring than trying to work with a short handle in one hand.

One excellent use for a roller which is overlooked by many amateur painters is in painting doors and woodwork. Just roll the paint on the flat surfaces; then go over them with a brush to remove the stipled effect and blend the paint in with the areas that can be covered only with a brush. Using this team of tools speeds woodwork painting appreciably.

A drawback of rollers is that they will not paint all the way into a corner or up against the trim. This means you must use some other tool to paint the edges of the room. If you use a paintbrush, there is a noticeable difference between the painted areas and the rolled areas, even though the former may be very narrow. For that reason, many home owners use a narrow cutting-in roller in corners and alongside trim. The alternative—which is not as good—is to use a small flat pad which is dipped in paint and then stroked on the wall.

How to take care of rollers. After finishing a job, if you have been using latex paint, put the pan in a tub and let water run into it slowly while you roll the roller back and forth. This cleans the pan as well as the roller. When the water in the pan begins to clear, pull the roller cover from the handle and run more water through the center hole and over the sides. Then roll the cover on the sides of the tub and then on newspaper to squeeze out the moisture. Stand on one end to drain and dry completely. Don't replace the cover on the handle—unless you are going to paint with it again soon—until it is bone dry.

Rollers that have been used in other paints and finishes must be saturated in the proper thinner in a large glass jar or other container. Work the cover up and down to dislodge the pigment. Don't let it stand in the container very long because the bottom end will become covered with a heavy coating of pigment. When it is finally as clean as you can get it, roll it on newspapers to squeeze out the solvent. Then wash in detergent solution, rinse, and allow to dry.

If you're using a roller to apply oil, alkyd, or similar finish on several successive days, it is not necessary to clean the roller cover every night. Just pour solvent into the roller pan to a depth of about 1 inch; saturate the roller in this and let it stand. Because the solvent is slow to evaporate, the roller should be soft and ready for use the next day.

Paints. Following are brief descriptions of the paints that home owners are most likely to use. Recommendations for painting different materials and articles are also given in the entries for those materials and articles.

Interior wall primers. *Latex primers and primer-sealers.* Especially recommended for use on gypsum board because they do not raise the paper fibers. Also excellent on damp plaster and masonry because of resistance to alkalies.

Alkyd primers and primer-sealers. Suitable for all surfaces except gypsum board and those containing active alkali. Must dry overnight.

Oil primers and primer-sealers. Similar to alkyds but somewhat slower-drying and have more odor. They are losing popularity.

Interior wood primers. *Enamel undercoaters.* May be used under any pigmented interior finish, but especially under gloss and semi-gloss enamels. They have good hiding power and form hard, tight films that prevent penetration of the finish coats.

Clear wood sealers. Usually used under clear finishes but can be used under pigmented materials as well. They are designed to seal the porosity of wood without impairing the natural appearance.

Interior masonry primers. *Block fillers.* In the home, use a latex primer that can be applied either to dry or damp surfaces.

Interior finish coats—gloss. *Gloss enamels.* Usually alkyds, made for application to walls and woodwork. They retain their gloss very well, are easy to wash, and resist yellowing.

Alkyd floor enamels. Fairly fast-drying and have reasonably good resistance to abrasion and impact. Should not be used on fresh concrete or any floors that may become damp.

Epoxy or urethane floor enamels. These may be available in one- or two-part form. The one-part paints are slightly better than ordinary alkyd floor enamels. The two-part paints have extremely high adhesion, abrasion resistance, and resistance to water and solvents. But you must prepare the surface very carefully.

Interior finish coats—semi-gloss. *Semi-gloss enamels.* Use on woodwork and walls that require fairly frequent washing (in the kitchen, for example). The alkyds are considerably better than the old oil-based paints.

Semi-gloss latex paints. Not as good as semi-gloss enamels but may be used for the same purposes if fast coverage is all-important to you.

Interior finish coats—flat. *Alkyd flat wall paints.* These are usually superior to latex paints in hiding power and washability.

Latex flat wall paints. These are the most popular interior flat wall paints because they are so easy to apply and give good results if you are careful. Two points you should note especially when using them are: (1) Don't try to roll or brush them out too much. (2) Don't apply them to very porous surfaces or when the temperature is very high or very low or the humidity is very low.

Latex floor paints. Have only fair abrasion resistance but are useful on damp and fresh concrete floors.

Exterior wood primers. *Fortified primers.* These are better than ordinary oil primers because they dry faster and are more resistant to bleeding, mildew, and moisture.

Exterior masonry primers. The finish paints used on masonry are also commonly used as primers. In addition, you may sometimes need a clear sealer made of phenolic, alkyd, or epoxy. These are particularly recommended for smooth, weathered surfaces.

Exterior metal primers. *Red lead primer.* The oldest metal primer and still considered nearly perfect. The finish paint should be applied over it within six months.

Zinc chromate primers. Also called zinc yellow. They dry harder and faster than red lead.

Exterior finish coats. *Oil-based house paints.* These are made with linseed oil and various pigments. Although they can be applied to any material, they are best adapted to wood. Use on walls only, because they are rather soft, cling to dirt, and are not easy to wash. They look fairly glossy when first applied, then turn fairly flat.

Barn paints. These are much like house paints but are usually barn red. They are formulated to give a uniform appearance over poorly prepared and nonuniform surfaces, but lack the long-term protective qualities of house paints. They are also used on sheet-metal roofs.

Flat house paints. Like oil-based house paints but flat from the start. Particularly recommended for shingles and shakes.

Alkyd trim enamels. The best paints for exterior trim because they are durable, glossy, and easy to keep clean.

Alkyd masonry paints. Similar to alkyd trim enamels but with more pigment. Use only on dry walls.

Latex masonry paints. The outstanding paints for masonry walls provided they are not chalking heavily. They go on easily, dry quickly, and cover well. Have a low sheen.

Latex house paints. Similar in all respects to masonry paints and just as good. Unlike oil paints, they permit the escape of moisture in the walls; consequently, do not blister because of condensation. Colored paints fade less than oil or alkyd flats.

Furniture finishes. *Gloss enamels.* Same as the paint used on interior woodwork. Should usually be applied over an enamel undercoater.

Lead-free enamels. Use on children's furniture, playpens, toys, and woodwork in children's rooms.

Special paints. *Dripless paints.* Various kinds of paint for interior and exterior use are made this way. They are very thick; should not be thinned. They may not drip but they do spatter.

Textured paints. Thick latex paints for application to interior walls. They are used to give walls a textured look and/or to conceal defects in the wall surface. Texturing is done with special rollers, brooms, combs, etc. One type of textured paint contains sand.

One-coat house paints. Heavily pigmented latex or oil paints that cover in one coat provided they are applied over a sound paint surface.

Fire-retardant paints. Paints formulated to keep the materials to which they are applied from catching fire rapidly (but the paints do not prevent fire). One type swells up to insulate the base material; the other releases fumes which smother flames. The paints are used indoors primarily. Color choice is limited; washability is often poor; cost is high.

Paint Sprayers. With a spray gun you can get perfect paint coverage on any surface whether it be a large wall or an intricately carved and creviced piece of furniture. The work goes rapidly, and the resulting finish is almost as smooth as glass.

On the other hand, spray equipment takes time to set up. Because the fine mist of paint is easily wafted through the air, you must cover every surface that is not to be painted. And it is a good idea to wear a mask to protect your nose and lungs from the spray mist.

Spray guns. *Renting a sprayer.* Unless you intend to do a great deal of painting, it is questionable whether you should buy spray equipment. The cost is considerable. You can rent a perfectly good outfit from your paint dealer or rental agency.

How to use a paint sprayer. The paint must be mixed thoroughly and strained through a nylon stocking or cheesecloth to remove lumps. Don't thin it unless the paint dealer so advises. Before starting work, test the spray pattern on a piece of newspaper. You can adjust the nozzle to give anything from a small, more or less round pattern up to a very wide pattern. You can also adjust the quantity of the spray to increase or . decrease coverage.

Spraying is done with a full-arm motion. Hold the gun 6 to 8 inches from the surface and keep it pointed squarely at it. Don't swing the gun in an arc. Pull the trigger before the gun reaches the surface and release it after reaching the end of your stroke. This keeps the paint from building up in one spot. Keep the gun moving whenever you are spraying.

The usual practice is to work first from side to side. Then, if necessary, go over the area from top to bottom. The spray pattern should overlap about one-third.

When you are finished spraying, clean the gun at once so that it will be in good working order for the next user. Empty the equipment and clean it as well as possible with paper towels. Then spray the proper solvent through it until it comes out clear. Wash the exterior of the equipment with solvent, too.

Aerosol sprayers. These are costly but convenient. Read the directions on the cans before using them. Shake well to mix the paint and build up pressure.

The technique of spraying with an aerosol is similar to that used with a big spray gun.

One minor problem with aerosol paints is that they are formulated differently from conventional paints; therefore, you may not be able to get an exact match. The answer is to use a special type of aerosol called a Preval. This consists of a jar with a small container of propellant on top. You can fill the jar with any conventional paint 'that· has been thinned according to the directions that come with the aerosol. Then all you do is screw on the container of propellant, press the trigger that controls the nozzle, and go to work.

Paint Thinner. Strictly speaking, a paint thinner is anything used to thin paint.

Water is a thinner for water-based paints; alcohol, a thinner for shellac; lacquer thinner, a thinner for lacquer; turpentine and mineral spirits, thinners for all other paints.

Usually, however, paint thinner is the name given to inexpensive petroleum derivatives used for thinning oil and alkyd paints, varnish, and oil-based sealers. The same liquids are also used for cleaning paintbrushes and other equipment used to apply these finishes, and for cleaning grease, oil, and wax off wood, metal, stone, etc.

Other names given to paint thinners include mineral spirits, petroleum distillates, and odorless thinners. All are flammable.

Paisley. A light woolen fabric woven with intricate figures or a silk fabric colorfully printed to imitate the woolen. Both materials are used in clothing and as coverings and hangings. They should be dry-cleaned.

Paraffin. (See *Lubricants.*) Windows, drawers, etc., may be made to work more easily by rubbing a cake of paraffin on the sticking surfaces or by melting the paraffin and applying it with a brush.

To melt paraffin for any purpose, place the cake in a pan and heat it over boiling water. Since the wax is very flammable, it should never be heated directly on a burner.

Particle Board. Known also as chipboard and flakeboard, this is a lumber product made by bonding together small waste scraps of wood to form large panels (usually 4 by 8 feet) of various thicknesses.

Particle board has a surprisingly attractive, smooth, yet slightly textured surface. It has considerable strength and durability. But its principal virtue is its excellent dimensional stability (meaning that it expands, contracts, and warps very little). It is good for cabinet doors and large counter, table, and desk tops; is widely used as the base for plastic laminates; and may be used as an underlayment for resilient floors. You might also panel interior walls with it.

The board is easily sawed and planed. If the edges are to be exposed, they should be covered with the thin ribbons of veneer which also cover plywood edges. If used for doors, screw the hinges to the edges as well as to the face of the panels. Exposed panels can be finished with any clear finish or oil-based paint.

Patching Plaster. A rather quick-drying plaster used for patching plaster and gypsum-board walls. It is mixed with water in small batches. Wet the surfaces to which it is to be applied. When it is dry, it can be sanded.

Patching plaster is best used on large or deep holes. Use spackle for small holes. If holes are so deep that the plaster sags, build it up in layers. The second layer can be applied to the first as soon as the latter has set.

Paths. Set flagstones or rough field stones directly in the ground as stepping stones. If you use sawed sections of redwood or cypress logs, set these in the ground in the same way. Remember, however, that wood tends to be slippery when wet; so to make it skidproof, nail a piece of ¼-inch galvanized wire mesh on top of each log and sprinkle it with sharp sand. Somewhat surprisingly, this does not spoil the appearance of the logs.

Paths surfaced with pebbles, crushed stone, or chipped bark should have metal or board edges to keep the fragments in place; and the surface of the paths should be an inch or two below the surrounding ground level. This is less important with bark than with the other materials, however, since it is unobtrusive in appearance and cannot damage a lawn mower.

Patios. See *Terraces.*

Peau-de-Soie (poh-duh-*swab*). A light, soft, satiny fabric of silk or acetate which is used in clothing. It should be dry-cleaned. Press with a cool iron on the reverse side.

Pellon. Proprietary name for a fabric used to line garments. It is made of polyester or a blend of rayon and nylon. Wash this fabric or a garment lined with it in water no hotter than warm and dry at low heat.

Penetrating Oil. See *Lubricants.*

Percale. A strong, durable, lightweight, closely woven cotton fabric used in bed linens, curtains, and clothing. Launder like cotton.

Permanent Press. Permanent press is the

name given to garments and other articles that require little or no ironing after laundering. It is also the name given to a type of fabric. (Durable press is an alternate name for the same things.)

The fabric is usually made by blending cotton or rayon with a thermoplastic fiber such as polyester, nylon, or acrylic. The cotton or rayon makes the fabric comfortable to wear and to sleep on, and when properly finished contributes to wrinkle and crease resistance. The thermoplastic fiber strengthens the fabric, permits it to be shaped, and makes it hold its shape. According to a textile engineer: "A thermoplastic textile has two characteristics—a flow and a memory. By flow, we mean the textile can put itself in new positions when exposed to certain conditions. Thereafter, it remembers to return to the positions in which it was last established."

Leaving the factory, a permanent-press article is, of course, set in a desirable shape; and as long as it is washed and dried according to procedures specified on the maker's tag, it will retain that shape. But if you mishandle it, it may assume an undesirable new shape to which it will cling with annoying stubbornness. For example, if you leave a pair of permanent-press slacks in the washer too long after they are laundered or if you overheat them in a dryer, they are likely to set wrinkles as pronounced and obstinate as any you ever encountered.

A second problem with permanent-press fabrics is that, like wash-and-wear materials, they are hard to get clean. Early permanent-press articles required a good deal of pretreatment or bleaching to make them sparkle. Most articles on the market now, however, are treated with an anti-soiling and/or soil-release chemical which permits removal of soil with little or no pretreatment.

Permanent press is best washed in a washer and dried in a dryer. The following treatment is required:

Don't overload either washer or dryer. The more freely permanent-press articles can tumble about, the fewer wrinkles they will set.

Wash in warm water with a light-duty detergent.

In a washer, spin the articles at slowest possible speed. If hand-washing, squeeze water out of the fabric; do not wring or twist.

Don't allow the articles to sit in the bottom of the washer or laundry tub after they have been washed.

In a dryer, use low heat and dry the articles for about 15 minutes. Then allow them to tumble-dry without heat for another 10 minutes. (Most new dryers have an automatic cool-down period.) Remove the articles as soon as the tumbling action stops.

If drying on a line, hang the articles on hangers or over the line. Don't use clothespins. Shape and smooth the fabric with your hands.

Touch up permanent press if necessary with a warm iron.

Pest Control. If there is one general rule for keeping pests under control, it is: Try to stop them before they multiply. This involves four steps:

1. Keep your house clean. Many pests thrive on dirt.

2. Keep a reasonably close check on the points where pests are most likely to enter the house (for instance, inspect foundation walls for termites).

3. Know the favorite carriers of pests, and inspect them regularly when the pests are usually active. In other words, look out for ticks on your favorite friend Fido in the summertime.

4. Don't hesitate to call an exterminator if pests get out of hand, because once they are firmly entrenched in a house, the pesticides and traps available to home owners are of limited value.

Ants. Outside the house, sprinkle chlordane dust around ant hills; kill swarms with pyrethrin spray. Inside the house, use pyrethrin spray on ants directly, and apply it behind the sink and refrigerator and along baseboards where ants may be entering. Ant traps are also effective when placed where the bugs congregate; but note that they contain poison that is harmful to humans and animals, so keep them out of reach of children and pets.

Carpenter ants bore holes in wood, leaving a pile of sawdust behind. But unlike termites, they do not eat the wood and therefore do less damage. They can be controlled like other ants.

Bats. These foul-looking, smelly, flying animals live in attics and roof spaces. Your best protection against them is to inspect the upper regions of the house regularly for holes and cracks and to seal all you find. To drive bats out of an attic, sprinkle naphthalene flakes liberally around the space.

Bedbugs. Bedbugs are brown, flat, smelly pests which you may carry in on your clothing from trains, buses, theaters, etc. They infest mattresses, bed frames, upholstered furniture. Control them by spraying mattresses on all sides and cracks and crevices in bed frames with pyrethrin. Also spray cracks along baseboards and in walls.

Bees, hornets, wasps. These pests generally build their nests in roof ventilators and under eaves; but if they find a hole in the siding, they may take up residence in the attic. Make sure all ventilators are screened with fine mesh. Look for holes and cracks in siding, under eaves, etc., and plug them with caulking compound. Pyrethrin kills the insects quickly when it is sprayed directly on them. For nests high above the ground, use an aerosol that will shoot a stream for 15 feet or so.

Birds. Although birds can be surprisingly destructive once they get into a house, the number of home owners who are bothered by them is very small. Some of the minority, however, have rather persistent problems with birds nesting in chimneys. These can be driven out by building a roaring fire. Then cover the top of the chimney with chicken wire.

Carpet beetles. Carpet beetles are small, more or less oval beetles which produce larvae that feast on wool, mohair, fur upholstery, carpets, and clothing. To discourage them, vacuum backs and bottoms of upholstered furniture, under rugs, and in closets to remove dust and lint in which the bugs may settle. Clean articles to be stored and enclose them in wrappings with paradichlorobenzene crystals. Mothproofing sprays also control carpet beetles. Pyrethrin sprays kill them on contact.

Centipedes. These are actually beneficial insects since they kill many insect pests. But if they get too numerous in bathrooms, basements, and other damp areas for your peace of mind, you can massacre them with pyrethrin spray.

Cockroaches. The roach is a nasty, foul-smelling insect that contaminates food and ruins books. It finds its way into the house in many ways—frequently on food packages from the grocery. Once established, a colony sometimes seems to be almost indestructible. Pyrethrin spray kills the bugs on contact. You can also control them by applying poison under sinks, kitchen appliances, and radiators; around pipes; inside cabinets and on shelves. First apply boric acid powder through a flour sifter. Then spray with pyrethrin. A combination boric-acid-pyrethrin aerosol spray is available.

Fleas. Your best defense against fleas is to put flea collars on dogs and cats. The collars are effective for two or three months or until they are immersed for some time in water. But use with caution, since some pets, unfortunately, are allergic to them. If yours is one of these, control fleas by spraying pyrethrin on floors and baseboards in the room where the pet sleeps. Wash a dog frequently with flea soap. For cats or dogs, apply a pyrethrin spray.

Flies. The best way to reduce the fly population in and around your house is to install a garbage disposer or to collect and store garbage and other household refuse in large paper garbage bags (see *Garbage Bags*). To control the flies that remain, spray pyrethrin around a room for about 6 seconds; then close the room for 15 minutes or more. An equally good method is to hang one or two sticky flypapers in the room and on porches, and learn to use a fly swatter.

Mice. You can keep mice from getting into the living area of your house if you will take time to search throughout the house for the holes through which they enter. Cover these with pieces of aluminum flashing or a flattened tin can and tack the edges down securely. Holes around pipes can be plugged with wads of coarse steel wool.

Mouse traps baited with smelly cheese or bacon are still the best way to kill mice.

Set the traps every night until they fail to attract occupants for several days. Be careful not to place a trap where it may fall inside a wall or some other crevice from which you cannot retrieve it: a dead mouse is even less attractive than a live one.

An active cat may also catch or discourage mice.

Mosquitoes. Outside area controls for mosquitoes have lost considerable effectiveness since DDT was taken off the market. Do the best you can with what is left. Sprays and foggers appear to be somewhat better than powders which are scattered on plants and ground.

To keep mosquitoes out of the house, make sure your window screens are in good repair and tightly installed, and that screen doors close rapidly and tightly. If a house is swarming with the pests, spray pyrethrin around each room for about 6 seconds; then close the room for 15 minutes or more.

Moths. If you have a wool carpet, treat it with moth spray or have it mothproofed. When storing woolens, furs, and other materials of animal origin, clean them thoroughly by washing or dry-cleaning, and store them in tight containers or wrappings with paradichlorobenzene crystals.

Vacuum closets, trunks, and other storage facilities used for fabrics regularly.

Powder post beetles. These pests look something like a knight in armor. They bore holes into the surface of wood—flooring, woodwork, and furniture, as well as structural timbers—and reduce the wood inside to a powder. To avoid them, always remove bark from any wood you use. Treating wood with preservative is also advisable, especially if you must replace timbers that the beetles have ravaged.

Rats. If you live in an area where rats are a major problem, you will need an exterminator. If you are bothered by only a few rats, place trays of warfarin near their hideouts or wherever they are feeding. Keep the trays filled until there is no more indication that the rats are feeding.

Scorpions. These sometimes large, lobster-like animals carry a poison in their long tail and can cause a painful sting if they hit you. They live mainly in the Southwest and have a nasty way of hiding in shoes, clothing, and other dark places. The best way to get rid of them is to hunt for them throughout the house and mash those you find. Close all holes through which they can enter.

Silverfish. These quick, little, fish-shaped insects dote on paper, starched fabrics, and rayon. They congregate where it is warm and damp—notably in basements—and then spread through the house. To keep them under control, spray breeding areas, bookcases, shelves with pyrethrin. If cottons and rayons are to be stored, clean them well but don't starch them.

Spiders. You can kill spiders easily enough by squashing them. Squash their eggs, too, and destroy cobwebs. Pyrethrin spray will also control the bugs.

Black widow spiders are most likely to be found in rubbish heaps, under stones, and in dark sections of garages and around basement windows. Spray them with pyrethrin. They normally die when the weather turns cold.

Squirrels. Squirrels can be extremely destructive if they take up residence in the house. Keep them locked out by making sure all openings in cornices, walls, etc., are sealed. If a pair does get into the attic, find out where they entered; wait till they come out to go foraging; and close the hole fast. A cat will also drive them out.

Termites. There is no doubt that termites can do serious damage to a house by undermining the structural timbers. But a point you must remember if you discover you have termites is that your house is not going to come tumbling down around your ears tomorrow. This is true regardless of what termite-control firms tell you.

Another point to remember is that some termite-control firms have the ability to see termites where none actually exist. So if you have occasion to engage a firm, ask your neighbors for recommendations; check the firms out with the Better Business Bureau; and ask several firms to look over the house and quote a price for treating it.

Termites are 3/8-inch subterranean insects which resemble ants but do not have an ant's pinched-in waistline. One other difference: whereas flying ants have four transparent wings of unequal size, termites have four translucent wings of equal size.

One way to tell whether you have termites is to inspect the foundation walls, inside and out, for small earthen tubes extending from the ground up to the sills. You can also be pretty sure you have termites if you discover their discarded wings on the ground in the spring. But termites give no visible signs of their presence when they are busily chewing their way through the wood in a house. The only way you can find them then is to jab an icepick into sills, joists, and other vulnerable wood. If the point goes in easily, remove the outer layer of wood. If the inner wood is riddled with tunnels and covered with tiny gray specks, termites have been around.

Termites today are found in all states except Alaska, but they are most numerous and destructive in the south and California. Somewhat surprisingly, they are more likely to attack new houses than old; and they are especially captivated by houses built on slabs.

There are several things you can do to help keep termites at bay:

1. Because the pests love dampness, you must take all possible steps to keep your basement and crawl spaces dry. (See *Basements.*)

2. If you have occasion to do any planting, digging, or tilling around the house, remove all wood scraps you encounter. If you have a brand new house, it is a very good idea to rent a tiller and turn over the soil all around the house for a distance outward of about 25 feet in order to uncover the wood scraps left and covered over by the builder.

3. Plug all cracks and holes in foundation walls with concrete or roofing cement.

4. Look for and remove termite tubes on foundation walls a couple of times a year.

5. If any wood parts of the house are in contact with the soil, dig out under them and pour a concrete block or pier for the wood to rest on. Wood fences, trellises,

dividers, planters, etc., that are in direct contact with the ground and the house should also be raised off the ground or separated from the house by an air gap.

If you have, or strongly suspect you have termites, the soil all around the house must be treated with chlordane or some other chemical proved to be effective against the insects. You can apply the treatment if you have a basement and/or crawl space with a concrete floor under the entire house. Dig a trench 8 inches wide and 12 inches deep next to the foundation walls on the outside. In the bottom, make a series of holes with a crowbar. These should be 1 foot apart and should extend down to the footings. Pour in the chemical at the rate of 1 gallon per 2½ lineal feet for each foot of depth from the bottom of the trench to the footing. Then fill in the trench halfway; pour in ½ gallon of chemical for each 2½ lineal feet; and add another ½ gallon when the trench is filled completely.

Soil treatment should be done by professionals if you have a crawl space that is not paved or if your house is built on a slab.

Soil that is properly treated should keep your house free of termites for about ten years. It should then be retreated.

There are other methods for controlling termites which are just as effective as soil treatment but they are easily applied only in houses under construction.

Ticks. Ticks are nasty insects that infest the city as well as the country. Some carry Rocky Mountain spotted fever. They are usually brought into the house in summer by pets; and if they once become established, they can be eradicated only by an exterminator.

The best way to prevent a tick infestation is to put flea collars on your pets (see *Fleas,* above). The collars are almost equally effective against ticks except during severe infestations. At those times you should also spray animals with a pyrethrin compound available from veterinarians or pet stores (but the sprays alone have little value). The only alternative—a rather hopeless one—is to inspect your pets every night and destroy any ticks you find.

In picking off ticks, if you just pull the

body, the head may be left embedded in the skin. But if you hold a lighted cigarette just behind the body, the heat should force the bug to withdraw its head. Then you can pick it off safely.

Pesticides. Although some pesticides are nontoxic to humans and animals, all should be treated with respect and used with care. Read directions on the containers carefully. Wash hands after use. Store in a safe place out of the reach of children.

The following pesticides are useful around the house:

Pyrethrin. This is an insecticide extracted from the pyrethrum flower. It is applied as a spray against a variety of insects. It is nontoxic to humans and pets, but don't let children get hold of it anyway. Do not use it near fish bowls or ponds without covering them well. Remove birds from the room in which you use the spray, and do not spray around uncovered foods.

Chlordane. This is a useful but dangerous chemical and should generally be used outside the house only. It is very effective against termites and ants.

Warfarin. This is the most effective rat poison yet developed. It comes in powder form. Rats never seem to tire of it, and after they have gorged themselves sufficiently, they die. The material will not kill other animals and humans because they get rid of it by vomiting; but it should be kept well away from them anyway.

Petit Point. An embroidery stitch. (See *Needlepoint.*)

Petroleum Jelly. See *Lubricants.*

Pewter. Pewter is a semi-dull gray alloy used mainly in plates and other tableware, candlesticks, and lamps. The composition of the metal, which is rather soft and has a low melting point, varies. The main ingredient is tin. Two or three hundred years ago, when pewter was most popular, the tin was mixed with copper, lead, or antimony, or a combination of them. The best pewter had little if any lead and was therefore considerably harder and brighter than the later alloys, which often contained a high percentage of lead. Pewter now being produced generally contains little lead.

If solid pewter articles are damaged in any way, let a silversmith or skilled metal

worker repair them. Clean pewter with brass polish. Since it is fairly slow to tarnish, it usually needs attention only two or three times a year. If you have the good fortune to lay hands on an old piece of pewter which is badly darkened, soak it in a strong solution of lye. Then clean it with brass polish, alternated, if necessary, with a household cleanser. Hard rubbing is required.

Pebbled black spots caused by oxidation can rarely be removed by cleaning. But do the best you can. Then leave well enough alone. Don't let anyone work on the spots with acid or a buffing wheel.

Pewter is also plated on other metals. Clean it with detergent solution and, if necessary, brass polish; but don't use cleansers. If the metal is dented, hold a block of wood on the concave side and tap the other side with a rubber mallet or stick of wood. Work from the edges of the dent toward the center.

Phenolics. Of all the plastics in use, the phenolics are among the most common. They are encountered frequently in the home in the form of utensil knobs and handles, molded drawers, washing machine agitators, radio cabinets, and telephones.

Phenolics are poor conductors of heat; excellent electrical insulators; strong; and resistant to water, alcohol, oil, grease, mild acids, and common solvents. While they are not very pretty, they retain their luster and rigidity well.

Clean phenolic parts with a detergent solution. If absolutely necessary, you can scrub them with a mild abrasive or scrape them with a dull knife without doing much damage. Broken articles are mended with plastic-mending adhesive.

Pianos. Pianos, like human beings, are sensitive to changes in the atmosphere. They should be placed near a blank wall as far as possible from heating outlets and windows. The humidity of the room should be moderate. Too much dryness opens joints and may even crack the soundboard. Too much dampness causes rusting and damage to interior parts and sluggish action.

Care for the piano case as you would any other fine piece of furniture. Dust regularly. Remove soil and smudges with a cloth dampened in water or very mild detergent solution. Polish or buff as necessary to maintain a fine luster.

Clean dust out of the soundboard every few months with a vacuum cleaner. Use a soft upholstery brush and touch it only lightly to the soundboard.

Use a mild detergent solution to clean keys. Wring the cloth out well and rub the keys front to back. Since a bit of the black may come off on the cloth, use one cloth for the black keys and another for the white. Avoid getting water between the keys. Dry them well.

If the keys turn very yellow—a problem on old instruments with ivory keys—keep the top open and expose them to as much light as possible. But don't expect miracles.

The National Piano Manufacturers Association recommends that a piano be tuned by a professional four times in the first year after you buy it. Thereafter it should be tuned at least twice a year.

Picture Framing. Buy frames or have them made for you by an art supply store. They have a much wider choice of framing materials than you can track down on your own. And the frames are made better.

The glass is usually cut from lightweight picture glass but in certain situations, where light reflections on the glass obscure the picture, you may find that a nonreflecting glass is desirable. (Note, however, that this raises problems, too: viewed from the side, the picture may also be obscured. This glass is best used only for black and white pictures, since it can distort colors. And it should always be used with a thick mat.) In any case, the glass should be a fraction of an inch smaller than the rabbeted opening on the back of the frame.

Use the glass as a pattern for trimming the picture. As a rule, if there is a border around the picture, it should be the same width on all sides. However, if the picture is not of the same proportions as the frame, you should have equal borders on the sides and hopefully at the top. The widest border should then be at the bottom.

After making sure the glass is spotless, place the picture behind it; and over the back lay a piece of smooth gray or white cardboard of the same size. Lay a second piece of cardboard of the same type on top, or use corrugated board. (You should not place corrugated board directly in back of a picture, however, because it may not be completely flat.)

Hold the picture and cardboard in the frame with brads about ¾ inch long. Lay the brads flat on the cardboard and drive them into the frame with the thin edge of a screwdriver or chisel. Space the brads about 3 inches apart all the way around.

To keep out dust and sometimes insects, paste a sheet of kraft paper to the back edges of the frame with white wood glue. Then drive tiny screw eyes or tacks into the back of the frame and attach woven picture wire to them. The screw eyes should be located about one-fourth of the height of the frame from the top. The midpoint of the wire should be at least 1 inch below the top of the frame so the picture hook will be hidden. It can, of course, be lower than this.

How to mat a picture. Buy matboard at an art supply store. You might use heavy paper, but since it is not as thick as matboard, it does not give a picture the same sense of depth. Furthermore, it may not lie flat.

Cut the matboard the same size as the picture glass. Then place the board front side up on a piece of smooth plywood and draw an outline of the opening to be cut. Use a metal-edged ruler and make light pencil marks where you need them to guide you and no place else.

Place the ruler along one of the lines and secure it at both ends to the plywood with C clamps. These will keep both the ruler and the matboard from slipping. Then cut from one end of the line to the other with a sharp razor blade. Hold the blade at a slight angle so that the cut edge is beveled—slightly wider at the front of the board than at the back.

Cut the other sides of the opening in the same way. Then clean the surface of the mat with art gum. Position the picture behind the opening and fasten it at the top edge to the back of mat with a strip of masking tape. This will keep it from slipping. The other sides should not need to be fastened down if the backing cardboard is flat and stiff.

How to repair picture frames. Corner joints open. Open them a bit further so you can smear a little white wood glue on one of the mitered edges. Then press the moldings together and tap in the little brad which originally fastened the moldings.

Finish marred. Remove the picture and glass. Sand or steel-wool the old finish until it is smooth. Then apply enamel or any other finish.

Molded area of gilt frame damaged. Remove any weak or loose surrounding material. Then mix water putty with water to form a moderately stiff putty and apply it to the break with a tiny spatula, a small screwdriver with rounded edges—anything you choose. Mold it to match the old ornamentation, and when it is nearly set, smooth it off as necessary. Then allow it to dry at least 24 hours and apply gold paint.

Pictures.

How to hang pictures. Use picture hooks that are secured with small nails. The type that is pasted to the wall is not reliable. To keep from cracking a plaster wall unnecessarily, paste a little patch of masking tape to the wall and drive the picture hook nail through it.

Picture hooks are available in various sizes and are graded by the weight they will support. Although it is unnecessary to weigh each picture before hanging, don't hang too heavy a picture on too small a hook. If you just can't wait to buy a larger hook, use two small hooks and space them about 6 inches apart.

On thin wall surfaces such as hardboard, ¼-inch plywood, or 3/8-inch gypsum board, picture hooks should not be used at all if the picture is heavy and the nail cannot be driven into a stud. In this situation, you should substitute a split-wing toggle bolt or hollow-wall screw anchor. See *Wall Anchors.*

How to care for pictures. Pictures collect dust like everything else. They may become smudged with grease or fingerprints, too. Dust or vacuum them every couple of months; and go over the glass and frame with mild detergent solution when they are soiled. Use a cloth or sponge that is well wrung out. Rinse with clear water. Then dry with a chamois or paper towels.

Take pictures down from the wall every six months or so and vacuum the backs as well as the wall.

Oil paintings should be cleaned professionally every few years. Between times, about once a year, you can sponge them lightly with lukewarm water. Wring the cloth—a very soft cloth—almost dry. Don't scrub. Dry with a kind of patting motion.

If an oil painting on canvas begins to wrinkle or belly, take it down from the wall and tap in the wedges in the back corners of the stretcher. Don't stretch the canvas drumhead tight.

Pillows.

A good pillow is reasonably firm and resilient; not floppy or saggy. It is covered with tightly woven, nonslippery fabric with tight, strong seams. A removable cover of permanent-press fabric is desirable because it further protects the pillow and is itself easy to wash; but the extra layer of fabric adds a little stiffness to the pillow.

Pillows stuffed with goose or duck down are the most luxuriant and expensive you can buy. Some are machine-washable and -dryable.

Down mixed with goose or duck feathers is slightly less expensive. The pillows are firmer than those made with down alone and also more resilient.

Pillows stuffed with duck or goose feathers alone are about half the price of down pillows but a very good buy. Those made with chicken or turkey feathers, however, are a poor choice because they pack down and get lumpy. Feather pillows can be laundered.

Foam pillows are made of molded foam or shreds. You can purchase pillows of almost any degree of firmness. But the main advantage of foam is that it is nonallergenic. In price, the pillows are about on a par with feather pillows.

Polyester pillows are also nonallergenic and considerably lower in price. The pillows are lightweight, have satisfactory resilience, and can be washed and dried easily.

Pillow sizes. Bed pillows are sold in five sizes:

	Most common dimensions (inches)
Standard size for single and double beds	20 x 26
Queen size	20 x 30
King size	20 x 36
Junior size	16 x 20
Tiny size	12 x 16

How to take care of pillows. See *Laundering.* But dry-cleaning is easier than washing them yourself.

If you are thinking of re-covering pillows, think again: it's a miserable chore, unless your pillows are of molded foam. The new cover should be made with welted seams. You then make a small opening in the end of the old cover and stitch it to the new cover. Then slowly work the stuffing from the old cover into the new. Since you are, in effect, working in the dark, you can imagine the problems involved in getting the stuffing distributed properly inside the new cover.

Piqué. A fabric with a neat, small embossed design in lines or patterns. Made of cotton, silk, rayon, or a blend of cotton and polyester, it is used in clothing, bedspreads, and draperies. The method of laundering depends on the fibers used. Do not use a chlorine bleach.

Planes. See *Tools, Workshop.*

Plaster Objects. Plaster is sometimes used to make ornamental objects, figurines, and picture frames. If these are painted, as they almost always are, they can be cleaned by washing with a minimum amount of mild detergent solution. Rinse and dry thoroughly.

If an object is broken, coat the edges with cellulose cement and let it dry. Then apply a second coat of cement to one surface, and press the pieces together.

Chipped areas can be repaired with plaster of paris.

Plaster of Paris. A white powder that is mixed with water and used to patch holes in plaster or gypsum board. It sets in 10 minutes, so mix in small quantities. Wet surfaces to which it is to be applied. Patching plaster is easier to use.

Plastic Anchors. See *Wall Anchors.*

Plastic Films. The plastic films we use and sometimes must contend with in the home are polyethylene, cellophane, saran, and vinyl. The last is such a heavy material that it probably should not be called a film. (For more about these materials, see the named entries. Also see *Food Wraps.*)

One important point about plastic films must be stressed: children often find them attractive to play with, and several years ago a number of children were suffocated when they put their heads inside cleaner's bags. Since then, cleaner's bags have usually been perforated. But all plastic bags are not; and in any case, it is still possible for a child to get himself so swathed in plastic film that he cannot breathe or extricate himself. In short, don't keep plastic films within reach of children.

Plastic Laminates. Plastic laminates are thin, rigid sheets formed of several thinner layers bonded together. The laminates are then usually glued to a firm base of plywood or particle board or, in some instances, to a thin layer of foam plastic, which is in turn glued to a wall.

Plastic laminates are strong, durable, easy-to-clean materials used for kitchen and bathroom counters and to cover kitchen cabinets, doors, walls, tables, and desk and chest tops.

To clean a plastic laminate, simply wipe it off with a damp sponge or a sponge dipped in detergent solution. If dirt or stains persist, use a mild powdered cleanser.

Holes, burns, and dents in laminates are impossible to repair perfectly. Some handymen have cut out the broken material and set in a patch; but the work is very, very difficult and the patch cannot be concealed. An easier solution—though still not a perfect one because the repair is visible—is to fill holes with a material that comes in tubes called Kampel Seamfil (Kampel Enterprises, Dillsburg, Pennsylvania). This must first be mixed to the desired color. It is then spread into the holes and smoothed with a small spatula.

If a laminated plastic sheet comes loose from the base to which it is bonded, scrape out the old adhesive and let the surfaces dry thoroughly if they are wet. Then spread a thin layer of waterproof countertop adhesive on the exposed base, press down the plastic, and weight or clamp it in place for 24 hours.

Plastic Metal. See *Gluing*.

Plastics, Solid. These are the materials most of us first think of when the word "plastics" is mentioned. They are the plastics used to make radio cabinets, utensil handles, eyeglass frames, lampshades, light diffusers, squeeze bottles, toys, etc.

Most of the plastics that are common in the home—vinyl and polyethylene, for example—are described elsewhere in this book. But unfortunately, no mere word description can help the layman differentiate among plastics. In fact, even experts must on occasion put plastics through tests before they can be sure what they are dealing with.

At first glance, this problem of identification might appear to make the job of cleaning and repairing plastics almost impossible. Actually, it does not. Dirt and most stains can be removed from all solid plastics simply by washing them with a mild detergent and warm water. Do not use abrasives.

Most broken plastics can be glued together with plastic-mending adhesive.

Plastic Wood. Sometimes called wood dough, this is a prepared damp dough made of tiny wood fibers and chemicals. It is used mainly to fill holes and cracks in wood; but it sticks to almost any surface, including glass. It dries rapidly to a hard, waterproof surface which can be sanded, sawed, or drilled.

Ordinary plastic wood is a dirty yellow. It can be painted but not stained. However, the material is also made in colors to match many woods. You should use these in making repairs in wood with a natural finish.

Plexiglas. Trade name of an acrylic produced by Rohm & Haas.

Pliers. See *Tools, Workshop*.

Plissé (pliss-*say*). A lightweight cotton or rayon fabric with a puckered or crinkled effect. It is used in bedspreads, curtains, and clothing. Wash like ordinary cotton or rayon. No ironing is necessary, especially if the material is dried in a dryer.

Plumber's Friend. A tool for opening clogged drains. It consists of a straight wooden handle on the end of which is a large, rounded rubber cup. In using it, you fill the plumbing fixture with a little water, place the cup over the open drain, and pump the handle up and down. The suction created in the drain loosens—or at least is supposed to loosen—the clog.

Plumbing System, Household. A good plumbing system is essential to the health not only of the family in whose house it is installed but also to the community at large. This is the most important reason for having an experienced licensed plumber put in a new system or remodel an old one.

The second reason for employing a licensed plumber is that a plumbing system is complicated. It is often difficult to fit into the structure of a house. It requires manual skill and strength and special tools to put it together. Its life and efficiency depend on the installer's knowledge of certain physical laws and familiarity with bacteriology and chemical science.

The fact that plumbers are widely ridiculed is no excuse for even considering doing your own plumbing (except simple repairs). True enough, not all plumbers are good. But in most parts of the country they are at least required to have gained practical experience and to have passed a test before being allowed to go into business. This in itself is reasonable assurance that your plumbing system will be safe and efficient.

Unfortunately, however, even though all plumbers in your community may be licensed, it is difficult to tell the good workmen from the poor. The prices bid on a job are no criterion. Neither are appearances, speech, or general attitudes. The only way to find out is to ask the opinion of people for whom the plumbers previously worked. Have they had any trouble with the systems the plumbers installed? Did the plumbers get their work done on schedule? Were they careful about protecting other parts of the house and neat in cleaning up after their work? Were their final charges close to estimates?

Local plumbing codes. Throughout most of the country, plumbing systems must be installed strictly in compliance with codes. To make sure that they are, building and/ or health inspectors look over each system and okay it before it may be put into service.

In rural areas, where there may be no codes or inspections, it is a wise precaution to insist that your installation be made in accordance with the National Plumbing Code, which sets up nationally recognized minimum requirements for plumbing.

Code requirements vary between localities, but in all cases they are extensive and often rather arbitrary. This may be annoying, especially when they prohibit the use of new materials and equipment; but if they serve their purpose of safeguarding health, there can be no real complaint.

Cost of plumbing. The plumbing system is one of the most expensive parts of any house. It accounts for just about 10 percent of the total cost of a small house built in an area served by a municipal water system and sewer; and the figure can go higher if you have to develop your own water supply and septic system, if you treat the water in any way, or if you install three or four bathrooms.

You can, of course, reduce the initial cost to some extent by selecting less expensive fixtures and fittings; but your subsequent repair bills will make you regret this action. A far better way to save money is to plan your home so that the entire plumbing system is concentrated in a small area. Place the bathrooms, kitchen, and laundry back to back or, in a multistory house, one over the other. In each bathroom, place the fixtures side by side so that all are connected directly through the same wall into the main supply lines. Install the water heater as close as possible to the fixtures that use hot water.

Piping. The piping in a plumbing system consists of:

Hot- and cold-water supply lines.

The house sewer, which begins at the foundation wall and ends at the municipal sewer or septic tank.

The house drain, through which all soil and waste water is carried to the house sewer. It is also known as the collection line. Installation is made under the floor or along the basement ceiling.

The soil pipe, which carries the discharge of toilets to the house drain.

The waste pipes, which carry the discharge of all other plumbing fixtures either into the soil pipe or the house drain.

The vent pipes, which ventilate the drainage system.

The supply lines are made up of small diameter pipes or tubes through which water rushes under pressure. The pipes are laid out in horizontal runs (although they are not completely horizontal, because all must slope slightly to one point at which they can be drained) and in vertical branches known as risers.

The drainage lines are made up of large diameter pipes which are sloped to carry waste liquids and solids by gravity to the sewer or septic system. The part of the soil pipe that runs vertically up through the house is called a stack.

The layout and construction of the drainage system is of critical importance. U-shaped traps are installed below all fixtures (toilets have built-in traps) and a large trap is also installed in the house drain just inside the foundation wall. The purpose of the traps, which should always be full of water, is to keep noxious sewer gases out of the plumbing system and the house.

The drainage system must be ventilated to maintain atmospheric pressure within it and thus to prevent loss of water in the traps, slow movement of wastes through the pipes, and deterioration of the pipes by the chemical elements in the wastes. The vent pipes, which also carry off gases, are installed on the sewer side of each trap and are connected into a large central stack (a continuation of the soil pipe stack) which extends through the roof.

Piping materials. Pipes in the home plumbing system are commonly made of copper, galvanized steel, cast iron, brass, vitrified clay, plastics of various composition, bituminized fiber, and asbestos cement.

Copper currently is the most popular material for all supply lines and also for interior drains; but recent developments in the plastics industry are likely to push plastic supply lines and drains into the No. 1 position sometime in the future.

Outside the house, flexible plastic tube is used widely to bring water underground to the house. Drains are made of cast iron or composition material.

If you live in an old house, you may find that you have a mixture of piping materials. Or if you must make changes in the plumbing system, you may find it expedient to install a new material yourself. This can be done provided you do not attach one kind of metal directly to another kind of metal. This would set up an electrolytic reaction that would bring on a serious case of corrosion. To prevent this problem, insulating fittings should always be inserted between different metals.

Pipe sizes. Copper drains are generally 3 inches in diameter and can be installed in any standard stud wall. But cast-iron drains are 4 inches in diameter inside and 6 inches outside—which means that the walls through which they run must be extra thick.

The average home is served by a 1-inch main supply line and a system of ¾-, ½-, and 3/8-inch branch lines. But a system that is adequate for the average home is not necessarily adequate for you.

The sizes of pipes that should be used in your house depend on the types of outlets to be served, the total number of outlets, the water pressure, and the distance the water must be piped. If your family living habits are unusual, they, too, must be taken into account.

Your plumber should work out the answer for you. But under no circumstances let him come up with a skimpy one. It is always safer to oversize pipes than to figure them too tight.

Valves. Plumbing valves are expensive and for this reason the plumber and home owner are sometimes inclined to eliminate as many as possible. This is wrong. Valves are useful not only when repairs are to be made but also for controlling the flow of water at the outlets.

A gate valve is needed on the main supply line where it enters the house. (If the water is metered, the valve goes on the house side of the meter.) This permits shutting off the entire water supply.

Globe and stop valves should be installed on all main branch lines and on important sub-branches. They are needed to shut off water entering the water heater, house heating boiler, bathroom, kitchen, and laundry fixtures, and outdoor faucets. Valves on the main branches are best equipped with small bleeder valves to permit draining of individual sections of the plumbing system.

A drain valve should be installed on the house side of the meter so that the entire system can be drained.

If your pressure varies over too wide a range and thus causes an uneven rate of flow from the outlets, you should also install water flow control valves in the supply lines. If you have a private water supply, the valve may be installed at the pump. Otherwise the valves are usually installed just below the outlets.

Piping identification. To facilitate repair work and in case of emergencies, all valves should be tagged with the names of the outlets they control. Painting the pipes is also recommended. Use red for hot-water supply lines; blue for cold-water supply lines; yellow for waste lines; and black for vent pipes.

Water pressure. In a public water supply, provisions are made to deliver water at adequate pressure to all users. Nevertheless, the pressure is not the same for all buildings served, nor is it the same every minute of every day.

In houses with their own wells, there is also variation in the water pressure. It may drop 20 to 30 pounds from the time the pump shuts off after filling the pressure tank until it turns on again after the water has been drawn off.

The minimum desirable water pressure in a home is 20 pounds; the maximum, 75 pounds.

If you have your own well and pressure tank, water pressure can be raised or lowered at both the pump's starting and stopping points simply by adjusting the air-pressure switch.

If the pressure in the city water main outside your house is low, it can be compensated for by installing a supply line of larger diameter than would normally be used. Another solution is to install an electric pump that carries water from a tank connected into the supply line to a small pressure tank from which it is distributed through the house.

If over a period of years your water pressure gradually drops, clogging of the pipes is probably to blame. Examination will show that the scale deposits are thickest at the elbows, but they may be fairly uniform throughout much of the system. Replacement of the pipes is the only solution.

If your water pressure is too high, causing the water to spurt out of faucets at objectionable velocity, it should be cut down by the installation of a pressure regulator on the main supply line.

Water hammer. The pounding noise that sounds when a faucet is shut off should be prevented at the time the plumbing system is put in by installing air chambers on top of each hot- and cold-water supply branch to each fixture. These chambers are nothing more than short sections of capped pipe in which air is trapped when the piping system is filled with water.

In an existing house, if pipes bang noisily when a faucet is turned off or turned partly on, the washer may be worn or the packing nut may be loose. Should the noise continue after you check these points, turn off the water at the main valve, open all faucets to let air into the pipes, and then drain the entire system. This should replace the air in the air chambers and stop the thumping. If not, call in a plumber.

Back siphonage. This dangerous problem arises when there is a drop in the water pressure and when the spout of a faucet running into a sink or other fixture is below the water in the sink. The pressure drop precipitates a siphon action which draws the water in the sink back into the piping system, thus contaminating the fresh water supply.

To prevent back siphonage, modern plumbing fixtures are designed so that there is an air gap between the faucet and the rim of the fixture. But old fixtures often were not designed in this way; and if you happen to have any in your house, you ought to call in a plumber to correct the situation.

How to correct plumbing problems. Shutting off the water. If a plumbing system is properly equipped with valves, the water can be shut off at the main supply line (near the meter), on any branch line, or just below the outlets.

The main valve is closed only if the entire plumbing system is to be drained or if major overhauls are to be made.

The valve on a main branch is closed for repairs to any part of that branch or to bathtubs served by the branch (unlike bathroom and kitchen sinks and toilets, tubs do not normally have shut-off valves below the faucets).

For repairs to washbasin or sink faucets or toilets, the valves immediately below the fixtures are closed. If a conventional faucet needs to be fixed, only the valve that controls that faucet is closed. But if the faucet is of the single-control type, both the hot- and cold-water valves must be closed even though the difficulty is only on the cold-water side or the hot-water side.

Leaks in lengths of pipes or tubes. For an emergency repair, shut off the water to relieve the pressure. Drain the pipe if possible. Dry the pipe and wrap friction or adhesive tape around the pipe. Coat with shellac if available.

For a more permanent repair, buy a mending plate to fit the pipe. Place the rubber gasket that comes with the plate over the hole in the pipe. Fold the plate around the pipe, over the gasket, and lock it in place with bolts.

If you can't buy a mending plate, use a clamp of the type used to join flexible plastic water pipes to plastic fittings. Put a rubber gasket over the hole, wrap the clamp around it, and screw it tight. You can use a series of clamps side by side if the break in the pipe is large.

To buy mending plates, faucets, or fittings, you must be able to tell the plumbing supply house which size of pipe you are working on. The easiest way to find out is to tie a knot in a piece of string and wrap the string once around the pipe until it touches the knot. Remove the string from the pipe and measure from the touching point to the knot.

If string measures:

Pipe size (inches)	on iron or brass pipe (inches)	on copper tube (inches)
3/8	2 3/16	1 9/16
1/2	2 5/8	2
5/8	—	2 3/8
3/4	3 1/4	2 3/4
1	4 1/8	3 7/16
1 1/4	5 1/4	4 5/16
1 1/2	6	5 1/8

Leaks at unions. (A union is a fitting with one large central nut and two small side nuts.) Shut off the water and drain the pipe. Loosen the large central nut. Pull the opposing pipes slightly apart and clean the faces of the union. Bring the pipes together again, make sure they are in line, then tighten the nut. If the opposing faces of the union are badly corroded, cut a rubber gasket to fit on the male face.

Leaks at other joints. If there is not a union in the pipe run in which the leak occurs, even an emergency repair is difficult. However, you can make a stab at it. Do not clean the exposed threads or joint: you may only make the leak worse. Wrap cotton wicking or string soaked in pipe dope (pipe compound) into the threads and build up the cotton coil to make it reasonably smooth. Then overwrap with friction or adhesive tape. Call a plumber to make permanent repairs.

If there is a union in the pipe run in which the leak occurs, you may be able to stop the leak, but be prepared for major trouble because the pipe threads may be so badly corroded that the pipe will break. Shut off the water and drain the line. Open the union. The pipe can now be unscrewed at the leaking joint with a pipe wrench. Clean the threads lightly with a knife or wire brush. Wrap a white fabric tape known as tape dope once around the male threads. Screw the pipe into the fitting by hand, then tighten with your wrench. Do not tighten too much: at least two threads should show outside the fitting. Then rejoin the union.

Leaks in bleeder valves. As noted earlier, bleeder valves are small, cap-like devices sometimes used on large valves to permit draining of pipelines. If a bleeder valve is dripping, simply turn it to the right. If the dripping doesn't stop, close the main valve and turn the bleeder valve to the left until it comes off. Cut a small round patch from a tire tube or rubber gasket material to fit inside the valve. Then screw the valve back in place and open the main valve.

Sweating pipes. If cold-water pipes sweat in summer, wrap them with strips of fiberglass insulation. (The same material is used to insulate hot-water lines against heat loss.)

Frozen pipes. To prevent freezing, wrap pipes with electric heating cable made for the purpose.

For installation on the outside walls of a house use a nonfreeze faucet with a built-in shut-off valve to protect against freezing inside the faucet and the connecting pipe. It is installed at a slight downward angle that allows the water to drain away naturally when the valve has been closed.

To thaw frozen pipes, open all faucets on the line. Apply heat from the faucet end toward the supply end (but in the case of drains, apply heat from the house end and work toward the sewer end).

Do not use a blowtorch of any kind on a frozen pipe. Use electric heat lamps or heating cable. Supplementary heat can be supplied by wrapping the pipe in cloths and pouring on hot water.

How to drain the plumbing system. If a house is empty and unheated in the winter, all pipes and fixtures must be drained. But it is not enough just to shut off the main supply line valve, open the faucets (to provide air pressure), and drain off the water. The traps and toilets must also be drained, and this calls for a plumber with a siphon and force pump.

Some kind of anti-freeze, preferably glycerin, is then poured into the traps and toilets to assure that any remaining water will not freeze.

Plywood. Plywood is made of three or five thin plies (layers) of wood glued together under pressure in large panels. The standard panel measures 4 by 8 feet, but other sizes are sold.

What might be called general-purpose plywood is made of softwood. For years it was made almost entirely of Douglas fir and consequently was called fir plywood; but today other softwoods are also used. Plain softwood plywood is used for such things as sheathing, subfloors, roof decks, built-ins, and cabinet doors. Softwood plywoods with special textured surfaces on one side are used for exterior siding and interior wall paneling.

Hardwood plywood is used primarily for interior wall paneling and built-ins. The surface ply is made of hardwood or occasionally of a select softwood; the inner plies are softwood. The panels are generally ¼ inch thick, although other thicknesses are available. Some are factory-finished. For how to install and finish hardwood plywood, see *Walls, Plywood.* The same directions apply to the use of textured softwood plywoods on interior walls.

Almost every home owner who works around his home has occasion to use plain softwood plywood. In deciding what kind of plywood to buy, remember first of all that it is made either for exterior or interior use. Exterior plywood is put together with glues that will not loosen when exposed to moisture; interior plywood is not. It follows that you must use interior plywood indoors only—and only in situations where it will not get damp. Use exterior plywood in all exterior construction and also indoors in potentially damp situations. (For example, if you lay wall-to-wall carpet directly on a subfloor of plywood, you should use exterior plywood because it will shrug off the water used when shampooing the carpet.)

The second point to decide is what sort of surface the plywood should have. The way in which softwood plywood is graded is quite complicated and you gain little by trying to understand the system. Just remember that some plywood panels have smooth surface veneers that are completely free of defects. Others have surface veneers with defects that have been repaired with fillers or plugs. Others have surface veneers pock-marked with open splits and knot holes.

Remember also that plywood panels may be sound on one side but not on the other, or that they may be sound or unsound on both sides.

Obviously, when buying plywood, you should inspect the panels to make sure you get the surface or surfaces you need—and no better. For example, if you are constructing a built-in desk which is to be stained, you need plywood that has a perfect natural finish on one side only. If you are painting the desk, you need a smooth surface but it can have defects that have been neatly repaired.

The final point to think about when buying plywood is what thickness you need. The most common thicknesses are ¼, 3/8, ½, 5/8, ¾, and 1 inch. In construction, there are some pretty definite rules about the thickness of plywood to use in subfloors, roof decks, and sheathing. The key to the decision is the spacing of the joists and studs. If you know what the spacing is, your lumber dealer can tell you what plywood you need.

For paneling interior walls, ¼-inch plywood is thick enough. For built-ins and other purposes, use ½-, 5/8-, or ¾-inch plywood as your judgment indicates. The more the piece you are building is to be braced, the thinner the plywood can be.

How to work with plywood. Sawing. Support the plywood panel well to prevent sagging and twisting. If cutting off a large piece, have someone support it—especially as you get near the end of the cut.

Use a circular saw with a combination blade if possible; otherwise, a fine-toothed (preferably 10-point) crosscut hand saw. Saw with the good surface up.

Fastening panels together. Use finishing nails or screws, and countersink the heads. Both hold well when driven into the face of a panel (at right angles to the plies); but they are not so reliable when driven into the edges (parallel with the plies). When making a hinged door of plywood, therefore, you should use hinges that are fastened to the front or back surface.

Glue provides strong reinforcement for all joints. Use white wood glue indoors; waterproof glue outdoors. Glue joints first and then drive in nails or screws.

Corner joints. The simplest joint is an ordinary butt joint. It is not as strong as some other joints, but can be reinforced by nailing a strip of wood into the inside corner. Make the joint with glue and nails or screws. The end grain will be difficult to conceal, but see below.

A mitered joint is only a bit stronger than a butt joint, but the end grain is completely concealed. Unfortunately, you need power tools to make a mitered joint.

Center joints. When one piece of plywood meets another to form a T (as when you install a middle shelf in a bookcase), you can simply butt the center piece to the end and secure it with glue and nails. Installation of a cleat under the joint adds great strength.

But the dado joint is preferable—provided you have power tools.

(For illustrations of joints, see *Wood.*)

Covering plywood edges. Fill voids with water putty. When dry, sand the edges smooth. If you are not fussy about appearances, you can now apply three coats of oil paint. But for a really smooth edge, sand the edges and then apply a paste filler to fill all pores. Allow this to dry, sand again, and then paint.

A better way to edge a shelf, table top, and the like is to glue on wood-veneer edging tape—a ribbon-like strip of wood of various species. First sand the plywood edge thoroughly; then cover with an even layer of white wood glue or contact cement; center the strip over the edge and smooth it down. When the glue dries, carefully trim the edges of the strip with a razor blade or sharp knife. Then sand them down level with the plywood surfaces.

A more durable joint of the same type is made by gluing and nailing a strip of solid wood to the plywood edge.

How to finish plywood. Sand with fine sandpaper to remove defects and fuzz. To control the grain so it doesn't show through the final finish, apply one of the resin sealers made for the purpose. Then apply two or three coats of oil or alkyd paint.

For a clear finish, use oil stain or a stained resin sealer. Then apply varnish or shellac.

Pocketknives. See *Tools, Workshop.*

Polycarbonate. This is an unusually strong, rigid, stable plastic which is used in such things as tool handles, home appliances, light diffusers, and air-conditioner cabinets. Flat sheets are frequently used in place of glass to glaze windows that are frequently broken.

Polycarbonates can be struck with a hammer and will not break. They also have good resistance to heat, oil, and stains. Clean with detergent solution.

Polyester. Polyester plastic, reinforced with glass fibers, goes into a variety of solid articles. It is also formed into a yarn that is woven and/or knitted into fabrics.

The solid articles are tough, strong, and resistant to most acids and solvents. For how to clean and repair them, see *Fiberglass-Reinforced Plastics.*

Polyester fabrics are laundered like permanent press.

Polyethylene. Polyethylene is a widely used plastic which is made into moisture barriers used under houses and in house walls; food wraps; freezer containers; flexible ice trays and tumblers; squeeze bottles; pipes and tubing. It is strong and tough, is not affected by very low temperatures, and resists damage by food acids and chemicals, but generally is damaged by heat over 212 degrees.

Polyethylene can be cleaned with warm water and mild detergent. Don't use abrasives on it.

Films of polyethylene can be sealed or repaired by placing two layers together, covering with a sheet of paper, and pressing for a few seconds with a medium-hot iron. To repair heavier grades, oxidize the surface by playing a flame (as from a propane torch) very lightly over it. Take care not to melt the plastic. Then apply a drop of water to the surface. If this spreads, the polyethylene can be glued; if not, heat the surface again slightly. Use plastic-mending adhesive.

Polypropylene. This is a plastic which goes into solid articles, such as thermos bottles, and which is also made into fibers.

Solid polypropylene is cleaned with a mild detergent solution and it can be sterilized in boiling water. Broken articles cannot be mended.

The fibers, which go into indoor-outdoor carpets and upholstery fabrics, are extremely resistant to dirt and stains. They can usually be wiped clean with a cloth dipped in water.

Polyurethane. Correct name for the plastic commonly known as urethane (which see).

Pongee. A silk fabric similar to shantung (which see).

Poplin. A tightly woven, crisp fabric with small crosswise ribs. Poplin today is usually made of cotton and sometimes of rayon. It is used in clothing. Launder cotton poplin like cotton; rayon poplin like rayon.

Porcelain. Another name for china. For how to wash and repair porcelain, see *China.*

Porcelain Enamel. This is a form of glass that is fused to metal at high temperatures. It is dense, hard, durable, heat-resistant, stain-resistant, and color-retentive; and for these reasons, it is applied to such things as lavatories, sinks, bathtubs, and ranges.

Porcelain enamel is quickly cleaned with water or detergent solution. Use a non-abrasive cleanser to get rid of stubborn soil and stains. Many stains can also be removed with household ammonia or with 3 tablespoons Javel water in 1 quart water.

If porcelain enamel is chipped, touch up the bare metal with epoxy or porcelain glaze. Do not try to repair scratches or craze marks.

Portland Cement. See *Concrete.*

Pottery. Anything made out of baked clay, including the finest china, is pottery. But today the word is often restricted to a form of thick or heavy earthenware. Some pottery made is for dinnerware; and there

are also pottery vases, bowls, pitchers, ornaments, and baking dishes.

Pottery that is not glazed stains readily and must be given a hard scrubbing to get off ordinary dirt. Glazed pottery is easily washed in detergent solution and resists staining.

If a piece of pottery is broken, repair it with epoxy glue or cellulose cement. Very coarse, heavy pieces can also be mended with silicone rubber adhesive.

For a discussion of what pottery dinnerware a family should buy, see *Dinnerware.*

Powdered Graphite. See *Lubricants.*

Powder Post Beetles. See *Pest Control.*

Pressure Cookers. If you prefer fresh foods to frozen or canned, a pressure cooker is a real time-saver. It also makes cheap cuts of meat more edible, and because you cook with less water, there is less vitamin loss than with other methods of cooking.

Electric pressure cookers plug into a 120-volt outlet; nonelectric cookers are used on the range. Most cookers have a capacity of 4 or 6 quarts. Smaller sizes are available; also very large sizes for canning.

A few pressure cookers have a gauge to tell you what the pressure is; you adjust the heat to raise or lower the pressure. Other cookers have a pressure regulator. These operate at one pressure. All cookers have a safety valve in case the pressure gets too high.

In using a pressure cooker, be sure to follow the maker's directions carefully and keep an eye on the clock. A timer is almost a necessity.

Clean pressure cookers in the dishwasher or in the sink. Since they are made of aluminum or stainless steel, they can be scrubbed with an abrasive. (Electric controls must first be removed, of course.)

Pressure-cooker lids should be washed in the sink. Don't immerse the pressure gauge. Clean the gasket with a soft brush. Clean the vent tube also.

Don't. store a cooker with the lid screwed on tight.

When the lid gasket becomes worn and begins to leak steam, you can probably pull it off and replace it; but it is sometimes surprisingly difficult to achieve a tight seal. If you run into this problem, let the dealer replace the gasket.

Pumice Stone. See *Abrasives*.

Putty.

Oil putty. The original putty was a mixture of whiting or white lead and linseed oil which was used to fill holes in painted wood and to set windowpanes. It can still be used for the same purposes but is generally confined to hole filling.

When oil putty is used on bare wood, the wood should first be brushed lightly with linseed oil or oil paint. This keeps the wood from drawing oil out of the putty.

Putty that becomes stiff with age can be softened by mixing with linseed oil; but use very little oil because it goes a long way. Remove the putty from the can and knead it on a pane of glass. (It actually is much simpler to buy a new can of putty.) **Latex putty** is commonly called elastic putty. It is used for glazing windows. The mullions should be painted with oil paint if the wood is bare or dried out.

Don't mix latex putty with oil or try to rework it if it becomes too stiff. However, an advantage of latex putty is that it does not become very stiff with age and therefore helps to cushion window and door glass against slamming.

Both latex and oil putty should be allowed to dry fairly hard before they are painted. When the putty doesn't dent easily under your finger, it is ready.

Do not try to use these materials in freezing weather.

Water putty is sometimes called wood putty (as if oil and latex putties were not wood putties, too). It is a dry white powder that is mixed with water to form a thick paste. It must be used soon after mixing; it cannot be saved.

Water putty is good for filling holes in wood. But its unique advantage is that it can be shaped like modeling clay; and once it hardens, it holds its shape and is very durable. This makes it ideal for filling gaps in broken moldings, replacing capitals on columns, etc.

Wood to which the putty is applied should first be wet with water. If the mixture is too thin and sags, build up the necessary thickness by layers. As soon as

the putty begins to stiffen, it can be shaped and tooled with fingers, a knife, small spatula, or a pencil point. When it is hard, sand it smooth. Sanding may be a little easier if you dampen the putty slightly.

You can paint the putty as soon as it is hard and dry.

Putty Knives. See *Tools, Workshop*.

Pyrex. Corning Glass Works' name for glass used in cooking utensils and outdoor floodlights. See *Glass*.

Pyroceram (pye-roh-sur-*ram*). Trade name for a type of glass-ceramic invented by Corning Glass Works. See *Glass-Ceramics*.

Qiana. A superb nylon fabric with the lustrous appearance and feel of silk. It can be machine-washed like nylon. But since Qiana garments are often made with unwashable trimmings and fastenings, drycleaning is wiser.

Queensware. An English earthenware. See *Earthenware*.

Quilted Fabrics. These thick, soft, warm, three-ply fabrics are made of various materials. Most can be machine-washed and dried (but be careful that they do not shrink); some should be dry-cleaned. They are not ironed.

Quilts. See *Bedding*.

Radiators.

How to paint radiators. Never use metallic paint: it reduces heating efficiency (but once you paint over it with another paint, efficiency is restored). And don't use latex paint, because the water in it is likely to cause rusting. Use a good oil- or alkyd-based paint of any desired color. So-called radiator paints offer no advantages.

Turn off the heat before working on a radiator. Remove radiator from wall (see following).

Scrape and sand the radiators thoroughly to remove all loose and scarred paint. Eradicate rust spots with steel wool and rust remover. Then clean the radiators thoroughly with a vacuum cleaner and brush. If an old paint film is intact, wash radiators with detergent solution, rinse, and allow to dry half a day or more. If the bare metal shows, however, wash with turpentine or paint thinner.

Apply paint with an old, small brush.

Use a spray gun or aerosol to paint the hard-to-get-at inner surfaces.

How to correct problems. If a hot-water radiator does not heat properly, open the small valve in one end until all the air trapped inside is exhausted. If a steam radiator doesn't heat properly, remove the vent valve, shake out accumulated water, and pick dirt out of the vent hole with a pin. If the radiator is still sluggish, soak the valve in gasoline for a few minutes. If trouble continues, buy a new valve—preferably an adjustable valve.

If a steam valve drips water, adjust it to a slower venting opening or close the radiator inlet valve slightly. If this doesn't work, replace the valve.

If a steam radiator or pipe bangs, the radiator must be raised and slanted slightly toward the boiler so that water will not stand in it. Insert ½-inch wood blocks under the radiator legs at the pipe end; slightly thicker blocks under the legs at the valve end. Then check the radiator with a carpenter's level to make sure it is pitched properly.

If water leaks from around the large packing nut on the inlet valve of a hot-water or steam radiator, unscrew it with a large wrench and remove the old packing. Then wrap graphite wicking several times around the valve stem and replace the packing nut. Do not screw it so tight that you cannot turn the valve handle. This repair should be made when the heat is off.

How to remove a radiator. There is nothing to this: just unscrew the large nut securing the radiator to the pipe (or pipes), pull the pipe away, and pull the radiator out from the wall.

It is always advisable to remove radiators when you are painting them or papering or painting a room.

Radios. Radios should not be exposed to direct heat, and the vents in back should not be obstructed. If you build in a set, allow ample space within the built-in and provide good ventilation.

Clean plastic cabinets with detergent solution; wood cabinets with white appliance wax or furniture polish. If a plastic cabinet is broken, it can be repaired with plastic-mending adhesive.

Ranges. Despite the enormous improvements that have been made in kitchen ranges, it is worth noting in passing that wood and coal stoves very much like those our great-grandparents used are still sold. They have no conveniences and they are not easy to clean; but they cook very well once you master them. Cooking with electricity or natural or LP gas is, however, a great deal simpler and more accurate.

Types of range.

Freestanding ranges are by far the oldest type. They can be installed anywhere in the kitchen—between counters, at the end of a counter, or by themselves. They are easy to pull out for servicing; but since there is no practical way to close the cracks between the range and adjacent counters, food spills down into them.

The smallest ranges are about 20 inches wide and have three or four burners. Other standard sizes are 24, 30, 36, and 40 inches wide. Most of these ranges have four burners but a few have as many as six. The larger ranges may have two ovens.

Slide-in ranges are freestanding units but designed so that they fit tight against the adjacent counters and cabinets. They look built-in but are not.

Two-oven, eye-level ranges are also freestanding with a built-in look. Up to the surface units, they are a conventional four-burner range; but above the surface units, projecting out from a high backsplash, is a second oven with or without broiler. The control panel is alongside.

Eye-level ranges have proved very popular because you can have two ovens and one or two broilers in a 30- or 36-inch space. Some models even include a built-in ventilating hood.

Stack-on ranges are similar to two-oven, eye-level ranges without the bottom oven. In other words, the range consists of four surface units which are placed atop a 30-inch-high base cabinet and an eye-level oven and broiler. It looks built-in, and although it isn't, it might as well be because you can't take it out without leaving a glaring hole in a kitchen.

There are also stack-on ovens—boxy units that are placed directly on a counter top and are used for nothing but baking and broiling. Sometimes they are called portable ovens but they fit the term only if you happen to be a giant.

Drop-in ranges are built-ins that incorporate in one 20- to 30-inch-wide unit four burners and an oven. The ranges slip into a niche between counters and are supported above the floor on a platform beneath which there may be a shallow cabinet drawer. Drop-ins generally do not have backsplashes, which makes them ideal for installation in islands and peninsulas. As opposed to a conventional built-in range, they are very inexpensive to install because they require only one electrical connection and no elaborate cabinets.

Built-in ranges are not one thing but two: an oven that is recessed in a special cabinet or a wall, and a cooktop that is dropped into the top of a counter. Usually the two units are rather well separated—and for some people that is probably their main advantage, for it permits unusual flexibility in using the kitchen. Another advantage is that the oven can be mounted at any height that is most convenient for you to see and reach into. The cooktop can also be mounted at any height simply by raising or lowering the counter into which it is set.

Built-in cooktops have from two to seven burners. A few also have a barbecue grill. They range up to 42 inches in width. Oven units have one or two ovens and broilers. In the double-oven units, the ovens are usually placed one over the other, but in a few cases, they are side by side. Except for the side-by-sides, the ovens generally fit into cabinets 24 or 27 inches wide and 24 inches deep.

Because of the depth of the oven cabinet and because it is usually 8 feet high, it dominates the kitchen from the appearance standpoint; and if it isn't carefully placed, it often interferes with the flow of work. Like a refrigerator, it should never be placed in the middle of a counter— always at an end. The deep storage space above the oven is only moderately valuable because it is hard to reach into; and the space below is not much more accessible.

Electronic ovens. These are relatively small, stack-on ovens that plug into any 120-volt circuit. They cook by sending high-frequency microwaves through the food. Heat is created only in the food; not in the oven or the utensils holding the food.

The principal advantage of electronic ovens is that they are incredibly fast; they will, for example, cook a 5-pound roast in a little more than 35 minutes. Since the oven is cool, food can be cooked on the platters on which you intend to serve it. This cuts down after-cooking clean-up. The oven itself can be wiped clean with a damp sponge.

Despite these advantages, the ovens have not proved very popular because they are expensive; and while they cook meat well, it does not come out an appetizing brown. Furthermore, they are too small to cook, say, a large turkey.

Recently some persons have expressed fears that the microwaves present a potential health hazard. But ranges now on the market have been cleared by the U.S. Department of Health, Education, and Welfare.

Cooking features. It is probably harder to select a range than any other appliance. First you must decide which basic type of range you want. Then you must decide which of many, many features promise to be most useful. Here are some of the most important:

Number and arrangement of cooking units. The average range has four surface burners, one oven, and one broiler. You can have more or less depending on the type of range.

Surface burners (the electrical industry dislikes the word "burner" and prefers "unit" instead) are placed in many ways, for each of which the manufacturers can usually present sound arguments. In point of fact, one arrangement is not much better than the next.

As a rule, surface burners are at standard counter-top height—36 inches; but they are sometimes dropped a few inches.

Oven and broiler sizes vary. In ranges with two ovens, the ovens are almost never the same size. Check this point carefully.

Controls. On gas ranges you can generally adjust the flame to any height; on electric ranges there is usually only one (at the most) surface unit giving equal flexibility. It is doubtful, however, whether many homemakers take full advantage of this feature. The set temperature settings provided on most electric ranges and on many gas ranges give a more than adequate choice of cooking heat.

Deluxe gas and electric ranges usually offer one thermostatically controlled surface burner. This brings food to correct cooking heat and then automatically holds it at that point. Boiling over, burning, and sticking are thus prevented.

On eye-level ranges, controls are usually mounted at eye level where they are easy to see and adjust, and where they escape soiling by spills and flying grease. On other ranges, the controls are mounted on the backsplash, range surface, or a front panel just above the oven. None of these arrangements is ideal.

Backsplash controls are easier to see, safely out of the reach of small children, and collect a little less grease because most people use back burners less than front. On the other hand, you must reach across steaming hot pots to turn them.

Surface controls are easy to see, a little less safe as far as children are concerned, but a little safer to use for you. But they become badly splattered by grease.

Front-panel controls are hardest to read, not at all safe from children, but very safe to operate. They are splattered by grease from pans on the front burners.

Automatic oven. An automatic timer which turns the oven on and off at predetermined times is a feature of most medium- and high-price ranges. Expensive models also have a so-called automatic cook-and-hold oven which starts cooking at the time you select, cooks for the desired length of time, then turns down and holds at a gentle warming temperature until you are ready to serve.

Some ranges also have an automatic probe which is stuck into a roast to assure proper cooking. (See *Thermometers.*)

Broiling. Broiling in gas ranges is smokeless because the flame consumes the smoke. In an electric range, however, you may get considerable smoke unless special provision is made to prevent it.

Broiling speed depends on the size or wattage of the burner. In some ranges, broiling time can be cut in half because there are two burners—one above and the other below the food.

Cleaning features. For many years the only cleaning features that ranges boasted included such things as pull-off control knobs, throwaway reflector pans, removable oven doors, and no-stick oven walls. These were not without value; but neither did they contribute greatly to the housewife's natural desire to simplify her clean-up chores.

Two more recent developments, however, are making a great change.

Seamless range surface. The range top consists of a large, smooth, flat sheet of glass-ceramic sealed into a flat, chromium-plated frame. Spills and spatters can be wiped off with one swish of a damp cloth. There is no place for grease, water, or food particles to hide.

The four electric heating elements—each with its own thermostat—are mounted beneath the surface. Their location is indicated by four sunburst designs. When the elements are on, the sunbursts glow yellow; areas in between remain cool.

Automatic oven cleaning. Although this adds substantially to the cost of a range, it has proved so popular that a large percentage of all ranges sold incorporate it.

Two types of automatic-cleaning oven are manufactured. The self-cleaning, or pyrolitic, oven was the original. After the heavily insulated oven has been used for cooking, it is switched to a special locked-door cleaning system which provides temperatures from 850 to 1000 degrees for a period of about 2 hours. At the end of the cycle, all that remains of the grease, sugar, and food particles that had been on the oven door, liner, and racks is a powdery ash which is easily removed with a damp cloth.

In a continuous-cleaning oven, the oven cleans itself at normal cooking temperatures during regular cooking operations. This is also known as a catalytic oven, because theoretically a catalytic material is mixed into the porcelain enamel on the oven panels. This causes a chemical reaction which oxidizes food soils. In actual fact, many catalytic oven finishes do not contain a catalyst although they have been formulated to clean themselves as if they did.

Although continuous-cleaning ovens keep themselves clean during normal usage, the cleaning action is not as effective as that of self-cleaning ovens. For one thing, they do not clean away heavy spillovers or carbohydrates, but only moderate accumulations of grease. Chromium-plated racks and door glass must be cleaned by hand. Oven bottoms lift out for cleaning or are lined with throwaway aluminum foil.

Self-cleaning ovens, on the other hand, can get rid of heavy accumulations of all kinds of soil. All oven surfaces are cleaned. In fact, manufacturers also recommend that drip pans under surface burners be cleaned in the oven, too.

Using a range. A gas range must be connected to a gas line; and all except the simplest models must also be connected to a 120-volt, 15-amp lighting circuit.

An electric range requires a 240-volt circuit fused to handle the maximum load of the range. If you install a built-in range, the cooktop and oven are served by separate 240-volt circuits.

Before installing a range between counters, inspect the walls and floors of the niche and close up all holes you find with pieces of aluminum flashing tacked down tight. Be sure to place a patch around the opening through which the gas pipe or electric cable enters. Reason: Ranges do not have back panels or bottoms; consequently, mice can easily get into the storage drawers.

Make sure the range is leveled carefully with wood shims.

Avoid using just one or two burners most of the time. If you use all the burners about equally, the controls will last longer. So will electric elements.

Utensils should not overhang the burners more than 1 inch, especially if you are cooking at high heat for extended periods.

The heat will build up and may cause the porcelain-enamel surface to craze or discolor.

Aluminum foil may be used to line the bottom of an electric oven provided the foil is placed under the element and does not touch it. Never place a large sheet of foil over the element. Never line any oven shelves with foil.

If aluminum foil is used to line drip pans under surface burners, it should conform exactly to the pans and have a hole in the middle. Use of preformed throwaway aluminum reflector pans is preferable.

Electric elements are self-cleaning, though they may be quite odorous in the process. It won't hurt to wipe them off with a damp cloth when they are cool; but don't use cleaning agents on them. Wipe gas burners off every week with a damp cloth. If the ports become clogged, remove the burners and wash them in detergent solution at the sink. Rinse well and dry.

Clean the porcelain-enamel finish with a damp cloth or cloth dipped in detergent solution. It is not damaged by most spills; however, acids should be wiped up immediately. If the surface is hot, use dry paper towels—water or detergent might craze the finish.

Clean the control panel frequently with detergent solution: it gets fouled up with grease very quickly. Removing the knobs simplifies cleaning.

Reflector pans and oven racks should be cleaned with detergent solution after spillovers occur. If food bakes on, use scouring pads or cleansers. Clean the surface under the burners frequently to remove grease which might ignite.

If you don't have an automatic cleaning oven, clean the oven surfaces after every use when they are cool. Use detergent solution and rinse well because detergent left on the surfaces may cause additional stains. If you do this little job as a matter of routine, you won't have to do a major cleaning job so often.

If soil in the oven or broiler is stubborn, try scrubbing it with ammonia; then try leaving a saucer full of ammonia in a closed oven overnight. If you still haven't made progress, go to work with any of the special oven cleaners you think well of.

These cleaners come as aerosol sprays or brush-on liquids. Though the latter take longer to apply, they are more effective and less hazardous to use. You can control the application better and achieve a more uniform coating. (It is advisable to keep oven-cleaning solutions away from electrical connections, aluminum parts, interior lights, surrounding trim, and the floor.) If the oven is heavily soiled, don't expect one application of either spray or brush-on cleaners to remove all the residue without scrubbing.

Oven cleaners contain very strong chemicals. Follow label instructions exactly. Store them out of reach of children.

If something goes wrong. Before calling a serviceman, check whether the gas pilot light is on or that the fuse in the range circuit has not blown.

Make sure electric elements, if removable, are plugged in. On other electric ranges you may find that the leads to the surface units have broken.

If foods do not seem to cook properly in the oven, read the instruction book to determine if the trouble is with the utensil you are using rather than with the oven itself.

When the oven light burns out, replace it with a new oven light, not an ordinary household bulb. If the glass has broken out of its base, which is left in the socket, disconnect the fuse before replacing the bulb.

Patch chipped areas in porcelain enamel with epoxy touch-up enamel.

Rats. See *Pest Control.*

Rattan. Rattan is a tough, fibrous, woody material split from the long, climbing stems of certain kinds of palms. It is made into furniture and baskets, among other things.

When rattan is soaked in water for a long time, it becomes quite pliable; but when dry, it is stiff yet springy, and when it breaks, it breaks sharply across the grain. This makes repairs difficult.

For instance, if a strip of rattan breaks, say, in the middle of a chair seat, the only way to mend it is to bring the ends together, lay an overlapping strip of thin but stiff wood underneath, and glue the two layers together with epoxy glue.

If a strip that is wrapped around wood breaks loose at one end, it should be anchored again as soon as possible—before it unravels further. Dab epoxy glue on the underside; and tack down the end with a small brad.

To clean rattan, sponge off with a detergent solution. If the article is covered with a clear finish, as it usually is, sand areas that have chipped and apply varnish. This is especially important on outdoor furniture, because the finish is needed to keep the brads and nails in the furniture from rusting and making permanent black stains.

Rayon. Rayon is an old and variable synthetic fabric with a resemblance to silk. It has many uses.

The material is usually safe to wash, although rayon fibers lose strength when wet and articles must therefore be handled carefully. Use warm water, a light-duty detergent, and gentle wash action. Hang to dry or place in a dryer at low temperature for about 15 minutes. Iron on medium heat.

Record-Keeping. You will save time, inconvenience, exasperation, and money if you keep in some easy-to-remember place the following essential information about your home:

Name of builder if the house is new.

Blueprints and specifications if you had the house designed and built for you.

Names and telephone numbers of all subcontractors, workmen, and servicemen who have done good work for you.

Bills for all guaranteed items (so you can prove when you bought them).

Manufacturer's use-and-care literature.

Parts lists supplied with equipment bought by mail order.

Samples of wallpaper you have hung. Note on the back the name and number of the pattern, manufacturer, and run number.

Names of paints you have used. If paints have been specially mixed, try to keep a wet sample in a can so that it can be easily matched.

Record Players.

How to take care of equipment. Handle the tone arm with care. Don't drop it on a record or turntable: this may damage the cartridge or scratch the record. Don't interfere with the action of the tone arm while the record is playing or the automatic record changer is operating. Follow the manufacturer's specific instructions for lubrication of phonograph equipment to keep it running smoothly.

To protect your records and to ensure sound quality, the stylus should be checked for wear and replaced when necessary. How long it will last depends on several things: the hours of use you give it, the quality of your equipment, the condition of your records, and the material and design of the stylus tip.

A good rule-of-thumb: Have a diamond-tipped stylus checked at least once a year if you give your record player average use; have it checked twice a year if you play records very often. To have it checked, remove the cartridge assembly from the tone arm and take it to a dealer. He will examine it under a microscope for signs of wear and replace the stylus if necessary. A sapphire-tipped stylus should be replaced after about 50 hours of playing.

For the best sound production, the record player should be on a heavy, solid surface that will resist vibration. If you have an automatic record changer, follow the manufacturer's recommendations for the maximum record load; don't overload it.

Dust and polish a wooden record player cabinet as you would any other piece of furniture. Plastic cabinets are washed with detergent solution.

Records, Phonograph.

Cleaning. Dust, dirt, or an accumulation of oil from your hands in the record grooves or on the stylus or needle of your record player can be damaging to records and to the stylus, and can distort sound reproduction. Keeping records clean is even more important if you have an automatic record changer. Surface dirt can be ground into the grooves when the records are dropped during changing.

Records collect static electricity, which draws particles of dirt and dust to the surface and keeps them there. A variety of special record-cleaner products are designed to help control this static charge as well as keep the records clean. For normal upkeep of records, there are liquid cleaners, sprays, treated cloths, nylon rollers, and brushes. There are also brushing devices that keep records clean by brushing a path ahead of the stylus as the record plays.

Records that have been neglected need actual washing in a special record-cleaning detergent or light-duty laundry detergent. To wash, stand the record on its edge in the solution and clean gently in the direction of the grooves with a clean sponge or special brush. Rinse in cool, clear water, shake off the excess, then blot until nearly dry with a lint-free cloth. Stand the record upright in a rack to finish drying.

Keep the stylus tip free of dust and oil by cleaning it with a small, soft brush. Don't use your fingertip: you will leave an oily deposit.

How to store and handle records. Records should stand upright in their jackets in a record rack or cabinet away from direct sunlight and extreme heat. Handle records only on their edges or on the label. Oil from the skin adheres to the grooves and collects dirt. Friction between the jacket and record creates static electricity, but you can prevent some of this by bulging the jacket slightly as you remove or replace a record.

Stereo and monaural records. Stereophonic records should be played only on stereo record players. Monaural records can be played on any record player, but the records are no longer produced.

Refrigerators. With the rising cost of food dealing family budgets a serious blow, wasting food—either in storage or in cooking—is an extravagance few can afford. For many, bulk shopping to save money has become a way of life. But your refrigerator has to have enough space to hold and keep those extra amounts of food you purchase at a savings, and freezer space must accommodate extras, such as a quantity of meat bought at a special price.

Before you actually shop for a refrigerator, measure the space where it will be used. Also measure the doorways it will have to go through when delivered.

Today's refrigerators (and freezers) come in a wider range of sizes than they used to and are designed to fit a variety of spaces. Insulating materials are more compact; walls are thinner; door hinges are designed so that the door is flush with the side of the appliance when it is open and doesn't take up extra space.

An aid in comparing refrigerators of different brands is to look for a certification seal from the Association of Home Appliance Manufacturers (AHAM). This assures you that the cubic-foot capacities listed have been determined by standards set by the association. Cubic-foot ratings include the space that is occupied by shelves, crispers, and ice trays or ice-makers.

Refrigerator-freezer combinations. If you need both a refrigerator and a freezer, the refrigerator-freezer combination is probably your best choice. In the freezer compartment there is adequate room for the food an average-size family would freeze. The freezer, separated from the refrigerator part of the appliance by its own door and by insulation, can maintain the zero-range temperature necessary for long-term, efficient frozen-food storage.

Refrigerator-freezer combinations are of three basic designs, depending on where the freezer compartment is located—at the top, at the bottom, or side by side with the refrigerator section. You can choose nearly any capacity, from about 11 to 30 cubic feet (the figures include both refrigerator and freezer space).

Top-placed freezers are easy to see into and use. Most standard models have a storage rack in the door plus a shelf that bridges the ice-cube trays in the compartment. Deluxe models often feature additional door racks and shelves inside the freezer compartment.

Freezers underneath the refrigerator are not as easy to see into and get things out of, but the fresh-food section, which you use more frequently, is more accessible than is the case in other designs. Some bottom freezers have a drawer opening.

Side-by-side models are divided into two vertical sections, one a refrigerator and one

a freezer, usually with each door hinged at the outside wall. The largest of this type of appliance has more space, particularly in the frozen-food section, than other combination designs. There are more shelves in the freezer section, but the shelves inside both the freezer and refrigerator are narrower. When you consider this type, you must decide whether the shelves can hold your largest mold or casserole or a holiday turkey. Another feature to watch for: in all but a few models one of the doors is hinged to open the "wrong" way in your kitchen, making it cumbersome to use.

In any of the three basic combinations, here are some of the features to look for.

Inside the freezer compartment. No-frost operation. Manufacturers usually include a no-frost feature on most of their models. A refrigerator with this feature costs more, and because of its automatic action it is more expensive to operate. If defrosting is a household task that irks you, this feature will have special appeal. (When the freezer section is no-frost, the companion refrigerator is too.)

Packages in the freezer never become frost-coated or freeze together; labels stay easy to read; no freezer space is lost to layers of frost. Because of the forced air circulation, temperatures are more uniform throughout the freezer and fresh-food sections, including the door racks. And temperatures return to normal more quickly after a door has been opened. But because of this same forced-air circulation, foods will dry out more quickly and need to be especially well wrapped or covered. Foods left in the freezer for several months will deteriorate somewhat in quality because of the slight rise in temperature during each defrost cycle.

Manual defrost operation. Even without the no-frost feature, freezers need not be defrosted nearly as frequently as the freezer section of a conventional one-door refrigerator. Because the freezer section is exposed to room-temperature air only when its own door is opened and doesn't pick up moisture from food in the fresh-food section, defrosting is necessary only a few times a year.

Automatic ice-makers are available on many models of combinations. In several brands the ice-maker accessory can be installed later on, if you decide you want it. Some ice-makers are more elaborate than others, but their main appeal is the same: they eliminate the annoyance of refilling trays and of trailing water from sink to refrigerator; they make ice cubes as you use them—you're never out of ice.

For the ultimate luxury in automatic ice cubes, a few new side-by-side deluxe models have a dispenser recessed on the outside of the freezer. This feature allows you to get ice cubes (on some models, crushed ice or ice water as well) without opening the freezer door.

An ice-maker can add about $50 to the initial price of the appliance, and there's additional expense in connecting it to a water line. Along with its storage bin, it also takes up more space than standard ice-cube trays.

Ice trays. Even without the luxury of automatic ice-making, handling ice cubes and trays is much easier than it used to be, with practically no wrestling and coaxing necessary. The new trays have coatings that keep cubes from sticking, and many trays are made of flexible plastic so you can pop the cubes out easily. Some trays are emptied by inverting them over a storage container and pulling a lever.

Inside the refrigerator compartment. Shelves. For the most flexibility in what you can put in your refrigerator, look for shelves that are adjustable and removable. This feature will be important when you need to store something big, such as the Thanksgiving turkey, or extra supplies for company. In some refrigerators, only minor changes can be made in shelf positions. Many new models feature cantilevered, adjustable shelves attached at their back corners to a support track on the back of the refrigerator. Some models have one or more half-width shelves that can be staggered in height or placed at the same level to make one wide, flat shelf. Others have one or more slide-out shelves, making their contents easy to see and easily accessible. (These slide-out shelves are more convenient if they have some type of

guard rail at the back to keep food from falling off when you pull shelves forward.)

The shelving arrangement on refrigerator doors varies from model to model. It usually includes compartments for butter, cheese, and eggs. Deluxe models frequently have one or more shelves of the adjustable cantilevered type; on less expensive models, shelf positions are permanent. Most models have at least one shelf that will hold tall bottles or half-gallon milk containers. In a few, the shelves are deep enough to hold a gallon container. When you are examining door storage, check whether the support strips are sufficiently high and attached securely at the sides to prevent foods from spilling out when the door is opened or closed.

Special butter and egg storage. Compartments for storing these foods are basic to most refrigerators. But deluxe models may include a compartment in the door that holds butter at a warmer, spreadable temperature. (Only small amounts for current use should be kept there, since butter won't keep as long at that temperature.) When egg bins are removable, they are easier to fill, use, and clean.

Meat keepers. Most refrigerators have a meat-storage compartment intended primarily for convenience. But some meat compartments are designed to maintain a colder temperature than the rest of the fresh-food section (30 to 35 degrees). This keeps fresh meat cold enough to store safely for up to a week. Some of these special compartments can be converted to vegetable-storage space by moving a control that cuts off the cold-air flow into the compartment.

Vegetable crispers. Although these are standard equipment with most refrigerators, they don't always do their job well, which is to maintain a slightly higher temperature (40 degrees) than the rest of the refrigerator in order to keep vegetables moist, fresh, and crisp. Although you can't gauge the temperature accuracy of the crisper merely by looking, you can check to see if the vegetable drawer fits tightly—a good test of its efficiency.

Temperature controls and lights. Larger models often have separate temperature controls for the refrigerator and freezer so that you can change the temperature in one without affecting the other. The controls should be well marked and easy to read. The controls and interior lights also should be located so that normal loading of food or packages will not make the controls impossible to reach or obscure the light.

On the outside. A very few combination refrigerator-freezers can be completely built in; many have a built-in look. Their condenser coils are at the bottom rather than on the back, thus allowing the appliance to be placed flat against a wall.

Although a right-hand door opening is standard, you can order a left-hand door if you need it to fit your space. Most of the side-by-side models have double "French" doors that open from the center. Those with freezers placed at the top or on the bottom usually open from just one side (bottom freezers may have a drawer opening), although a few of the larger models have French doors on the refrigerator section above and a roll-out freezer drawer below.

The door opening usually cannot be changed once you have the appliance home, but some manufacturers have designed door hinges that can be reversed at any time, and some are so simple to reverse that you can do it yourself without calling a serviceman. This feature can be very helpful if you move or remodel your kitchen.

Many manufacturers include rollers as standard or optional equipment so you can roll out the appliance when you want to clean around and under it.

Conventional refrigerators. These appliances have only one outer door, with a frozen-food compartment inside (usually at the top of the refrigerator). The largest have a capacity of about 13 cubic feet. If you have a separate freezer, or if you don't intend to keep a large stock of frozen food on hand, a conventional refrigerator will serve your needs well, and at a lower price

than a combination refrigerator-freezer. The temperature in the freezer compartment is too high for long-term frozen-food storage. At this higher temperature (15 to 20 degrees), foods deteriorate in color, texture, flavor, and nutritive value after a few weeks. While they would be safe to eat, they would not be so attractive or palatable.

In the fresh-food section of the refrigerator, there are standard features such as a vegetable crisper, meat keeper (which often is a tray directly under the freezing compartment), three or four shelves that may slide out or be adjustable in height, door shelves divided into compartments to hold items such as large bottles, butter, eggs, and cheese.

If you want more fresh-food storage and your freezing needs are minimal, there are "all-refrigerator" models, with an extra-small frozen-food compartment that holds ice-cube trays and only a few packages of frozen food.

Compact refrigerators. These scaled-down appliances are an ideal solution if your space or needs are limited. The largest of them can slip under a standard kitchen counter or stand by itself. Smaller units are designed to sit on a counter or rolling cart or on their own stand or legs. Capacities range from about 1½ to 7 cubic feet. With variations, they duplicate in small scale the features of conventional refrigerators. A few deluxe models are equipped with no-frost operation and automatic ice-makers.

Operating a refrigerator. Modern refrigerators are designed to operate in rooms where the temperature does not dip below 55 degrees.

Conventional refrigerators can be plugged into a 20-amp appliance circuit that is also used for small appliances. But large no-frost refrigerators should be connected to their own individual 20-amp circuits. Do not connect refrigerators with extension cords.

The dealer should level your refrigerator upon delivery. If he fails to do the job properly or if the floor should settle slightly, you can make your own adjustment by removing the grille below the door and turning the leveling screws.

When starting a new refrigerator, set the temperature controls at midpoint and allow the refrigerator to run for 24 hours. Then raise or lower the temperature as desired. A freezer compartment should run no higher than 5 degrees. Ideally it should be at zero. The fresh-food section normally runs at about 38 degrees.

Wipe up food spills as they occur. Use a sponge dipped in plain water. Wash walls, shelves, compartments, drawers, and door gaskets about once a month with a solution of baking soda and water. Odors can be removed by placing a saucer of crumbled charcoal or an opened package of baking soda in the box.

Keep the outside of the refrigerator clean by washing with mild detergent solution. Greasy dust accumulates on the top quite rapidly. To protect the finish, apply a white appliance wax, especially around the door handles. Pull the refrigerator out from the wall about every six months to get at the dirt and cobwebs behind and underneath it. At the same time, wash that part of the side panels that has been hidden by the adjacent cabinets.

If your frozen-food compartment is defrosted manually, the job should be done whenever frost has built up to about ¼ inch thickness. With a greater frost build-up, the appliance has to work harder, causing extra wear and tear on the refrigerating mechanism.

Plan the defrosting in advance and try not to have too much food in the freezer at that time. Turn the freezer off and remove all food packages. Either wrap these in newspapers or put them in insulated bags. Leave the door open to hasten thawing. Pans of hot water will speed the process, but don't fill your ice-cube trays with hot water, because that may remove the nonstick coating. Never use an electric defroster: more refrigerators have been wrecked by that little "convenience" than dealers and manufacturers care to count.

After all the ice has disappeared, wipe out the inside surfaces, compartments, and shelves with baking soda and water.

The condenser coil and grille should be vacuumed from time to time to remove lint and dust, which affect the efficiency and operating cost of the refrigerator. On no-frost models, the evaporator pan at the bottom should be washed when you clean the grille. Check the use and care booklet.

Examine the tightness of the door gaskets occasionally. If they don't seal the door tightly, warm air will get in and cold air will escape. On most models, you can test this by slipping a new dollar bill between the gasket and the door jamb. If you can pull it out easily, the gasket needs replacing.

Repair broken plastic parts with plastic-mending adhesive; but don't count on their lasting much longer.

If the finish is scratched, apply touch-up enamel promptly, before rust sets in.

If you leave home. If you are planning to be away from home for one to four weeks, it's safe to leave a refrigerator (and freezer) in normal operation; but all perishable foods should be removed from the fresh-food compartment. If you have an automatic ice-maker, turn it off.

If you will be away from home longer than a month, you should remove all food, disconnect the appliance, and wash the interior with baking soda. Be sure all ice trays and bins are empty. Shut off the water to the ice-maker. For safety and to keep the interior fresh-smelling, prop the door open.

What to do with an old refrigerator. Getting rid of an old refrigerator or freezer can present a problem. If you are purchasing a new model, the dealer may take the old one as a trade-in or dispose of it for you. If not, contact your local sanitation department for information on how you should dispose of it.

Never discard an old refrigerator or freezer or store it temporarily—even for a few hours—with its door intact. To a child, that cubicle is an enticing retreat. Neither the child who may crawl in nor his friends will realize that once the door is closed, the compartment is airtight. Older appliances with a latch closing cannot be opened from within, and suffocation can occur in as little as 10 minutes. Today's models have a magnetic closure that can be pushed open from the inside, but a child may not have the presence of mind or strength to do this. So, if you discard the refrigerator, remove the door completely (this is a law in some states). If you are storing it, remove the door or latch.

If anything goes wrong. Before calling a serviceman be sure about the following:

The refrigerator is plugged in.

The fuse has not blown.

The control or controls are properly set.

The door has not been left open or has not been opened and closed very often.

Lint and dust have not accumulated in great amounts around the compressor.

Registers. If the wall or ceiling around a warm-air register gets dirty, it's a sure sign that you are not cleaning the furnace filters regularly. Do so at once and from now on.

You should also remove the grilles on the registers, clean them well, and put your vacuum cleaner hose down the ducts to get out dirt that has lodged inside. If the wall is washable, sponge it with water or detergent solution. Use a dough cleaner on non-washable wallpaper.

Revere Ware. Trade name of well-known stainless-steel cooking utensils with copper bottoms. They are easily cleaned with detergent solution; can be scoured with fine steel wool or cleansing powder. To remove stains, use a stainless-steel cleaner made specifically for use on the ware.

If an empty utensil is left on a hot burner, the copper will crumble and flake, but this does not damage the utensil seriously.

Revere Ware is also made with a Teflon coating.

Rivets. See *Metal Fasteners.*

Roasters. Roasters are thermostatically controlled electrical appliances used for baking. They are big enough to hold a turkey—even a complete meal for a family of six. The cooking well is removed for washing. Polishing the enamel exterior with white appliance wax helps to preserve the finish.

Roofs, All Types.

How to keep water from backing up under roofing. When ice dams form in gutters or on the lower edges of a roof, water running down the roof is unable to fall to the ground and may back up under the roofing and then drip down through the ceilings and walls below. You can prevent this when you are roofing a house by laying a flashing strip of asphalt-roll roofing along the eaves. This should extend from the edges of the roof up to a point 1 foot inside the inside wall line.

On an existing roof, lay electric heating cable in a zigzag pattern along the edges of the roof. See *Gutters.*

How to protect eaves and rakes. To force water dripping from the roof to drop straight to the ground rather than curling back and running down the fascia or the walls, install aluminum drip edges shaped roughly like an L. The wide upper flange is inserted between the roofing and the sheathing; the narrow bottom flange hangs over the roof edge, pointing down. Drive nails through the wide flanges at the ends of all strips to keep wind from ripping them out.

How to find leaks in a roof. These may be obvious. If not, try to get up under the roof and look for water stains on the underside of the sheathing or pinpoints of light coming through. Push a wire up through the holes so you can locate them quickly when you are on the roof.

If you cannot get under a roof, your only hope is to hunt around on top and plug every possible hole in sight. Although leaks may occur anywhere, the chances are that they are in roofing that has buckled, split, or worn away. They may also be in the flashing. See *Flashing.*

How to keep moss from growing on a roof. If the roof is covered with wood shingles, remove the moss with a stiff bristle brush. Then apply a wood preservative containing pentachlorophenol. On other roofs, brush off the moss and apply a solution of ½ ounce sodium arsenite in 10 gallons water. Take care not to drip either chemical on plants.

How to work on a roof. Don't take chances. Wear rubber-soled shoes or go barefoot. Tie a rope around your waist, toss it over the ridge, and tie it to a tree on the other side of the house. If there isn't a tree, tie it to a long 2-by-4 stretched across the inside of a window on the other side of the house. See *Knots.* When making extensive repairs or laying a new roof, work from a ladder that is roped to a tree on the other side of the ridge. See *Ladders.*

Roofs, Asbestos-Cement. Asbestos-cement shingles are available in various widths, but are laid to look like wood shingles. They are heavy, fireproof, and last forever if not broken. Asbestos-cement roofs should be laid by a professional.

To replace a broken shingle, remove all pieces and cut the nails that held it with a hacksaw blade slipped under the shingles in the next course above. Put a large dab of roofing cement on the roof deck to help hold the new shingle when it is inserted in the gap. Then drill a hole through the joint between the overlapping shingles and through the upper edge of the new shingle. Drive a galvanized nail through this. To keep water from leaking through the nail hole, insert a piece of aluminum flashing under the overlapping shingle over the nail head.

Roofs, Asphalt-Roll. Asphalt-roll roofing is similar in composition to asphalt shingles but is laid in long rolls 1½ or 3 feet wide. Since the material is quite unattractive, it is generally used only on roofs of simple vacation homes. Life expectancy is about twenty years.

How to install roll roofing. The roof should have a minimum pitch of 2 inches in 1 foot. Although the roofing can be laid over asphalt and wood shingles, it is better practice to remove all old roofing, including roll roofing.

The temperature should be no lower than 40 degrees when you lay the roofing. If it is under 60, store the roofing rolls in a warm place before unrolling them. If the day is very hot, wear soft-soled shoes so you will not dent the roofing.

All valleys should be flashed with roll roofing before the rest of the roof is covered. First lay an 18-inch strip granule side down. Cover this with a 36-inch strip granule side up. Nail each sheet along the edges at 18-inch intervals. Strike chalk lines 12 inches from the center of the valley from the ridge to the eaves to guide you in cutting the roofing to be laid.

Lay the first roofing strip along the eaves. It should overhang the drip edge about ¼ inch. Make sure the strip is straight and flat. Then nail along the top edge every 24 inches. The nails should be 1 inch in from the edge. Apply all subsequent strips in the same way. In a normal installation, the upper strip laps the one just below it by 2 inches.

When the strips have been laid all the way up the roof, apply a heavy, continuous ribbon of roofing cement 2 inches wide along the top edge of each sheet and press the upper strips into this. Then nail down the edges with galvanized roofing nails. Use 1-inch nails unless you are laying the roofing over old roofing, in which case use 1½-inch nails. Space the nails 2 inches apart. Work from the center of the strips toward the ends. The strip along the eaves is nailed in the same way.

If it is necessary to lap strips at the ends, make the laps 6 inches wide. Cement and nail the strips in the way horizontal joints are made.

End laps at valleys should also be 6 inches wide. Nails should be 3 inches back from the chalk lines. Over metal flashing, make laps 6 inches wide and use plenty of cement. No nails should be driven through metal flashing.

Hips are covered from top to bottom with 18-inch roofing strips. Cement down the edges and secure them with nails spaced 2 inches apart.

Ridges are covered with two 18-inch strips. The first needs to be nailed only enough to hold it in place, but the edges should be cemented. The second strip

APPLICATION OF ROLL ROOFING BY THE EXPOSED-NAIL METHOD (PARALLEL TO THE EAVES)

Wood deck

Preliminary nailing: nails 18 inches apart

Lap cement →

Nails staggered: rows 2 inches apart

2-inch head lap

4 inches

2 inches

6-inch end lap

Nails 2 inches apart in row 1 inch from edge of roofing

Sheets overhang eaves and rake edges ¼ to ⅜ inch

should be cemented and nailed at 2-inch intervals.

Roll roofing may be applied on roofs with a minimum pitch of 1 inch if you use 19-inch-selvage double-coverage roofing. These sheets are 3 feet wide and are divided lengthwise into a 17-inch mineral-surfaced strip and a 19-inch smooth-surfaced selvage.

The first strip laid is a starter strip made by cutting the 19-inch selvage from a full strip of roofing. Lay this along the eaves and fasten it down with three rows of nails.

Apply the first full strip of roofing over this. It should project slightly beyond the eaves edge. Nail it in the selvage with two rows of nails. The first row should be 4¾ inches below the top edge of the strip; the second row, 8½ inches below this. Space the nails 12 inches apart.

Lay subsequent strips in the same way. Each strip should overlap the selvage of the previous strip. When all the strips are down, lift the bottom edges of the strips and apply roofing cement to the selvages. Cover them completely. Then press the strips into the cement. No nails are exposed.

How to repair roll roofing. If nails pop out, replace with longer roofing nails and coat the shanks with roofing cement.

Fill small holes with roofing cement. If the roofing is torn, cut a patch of roll roofing several inches longer and wider than the tear. Smear asphalt-roofing cement under the torn edges, and on the top of the patch. Then insert the patch

DOUBLE-COVERAGE ROLL ROOFING

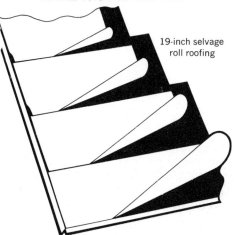

19-inch selvage roll roofing

under the roofing and press the roofing down. It should not be necessary to nail down the edges.

Roofs, Asphalt-Shingle. Asphalt shingles are the most widely used roofing material today. They are inexpensive, easy to install and repair, and last for about twenty-five years. Many colors are available. The light shades are commonly used on air-conditioned houses because they reflect the sun's rays and help to reduce attic temperatures in summer.

How to reroof with asphalt shingles. Purchase shingles weighing at least 230 pounds per square (a square is 100 square feet). If you live in a wind-swept location, use shingles with seal-down tabs which will not lift in the wind.

To determine how many bundles of shingles you need, measure the height of the roof and double the figure to include both sides. Measure the width and multiply it by the doubled height to find the total area in square feet. Add 10 percent for waste if the roof is unbroken except by a chimney; 15 percent if it is cut up. This gives you the total square footage required. Then divide by the square-foot coverage of the bundle, which varies from about 25 to 33 square feet.

Asphalt shingles should be used only on roofs with a pitch of at least 4 inches per foot. The roof deck must be sound (replace rotten and weak boards) and as smooth as you can make it. Old asphalt shingles or roll roofing need not be removed unless the deck and rafters are not strong enough to bear the weight of the additional shingles or unless the deck is in serious need of repair. But you should cut out all loose, curled, and lifted roofing; pull protruding nails; take off badly worn edging strips; and remove the cap strips on ridges and hips.

It is also possible to lay asphalt shingles over old wood shingles; but you must nail wedge-shaped feathering strips under the butts. It is easier to rip off the old shingles.

On roofs from which shingles have been removed entirely, lay 15-pound asphalt-saturated roofing felt over the wood deck.

To protect eaves and rakes and improve the roof's water-shedding ability, install aluminum drip edges over the edges of all eaves and rakes. Nail the wide upper flange to the roof at several points; the narrow bottom flange hangs over the roof edge, pointing down.

If it is necessary to remove old shingles along the eaves, a flashing strip of asphalt-roll roofing should be laid over the drip edges. This overhangs the drip edges ¼ inch and should extend up the roof to a point 1 foot inside the inside wall line. The purpose of the flashing strip is to prevent water from backing up under the shingles when the gutters are clogged with ice and dripping down through the ceilings and walls below.

Sweep the roof well before starting to lay shingles.

The first row of shingles is a starter course laid along the eaves with butt ends

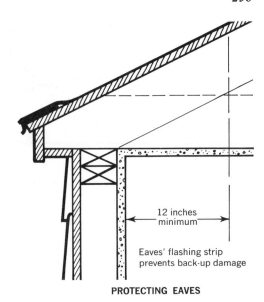

12 inches minimum

Eaves' flashing strip prevents back-up damage

PROTECTING EAVES

up. Cut 3 inches off the end of the first shingle strip. Lay the shingles flush with the eaves flashing strip. If there isn't a flashing strip, the shingles should overhang the drip edge ¼ inch.

The first exposed course of shingles and all subsequent courses are laid butt ends down. Start at the most visible rake and work toward the valley or the other end of the roof. If both rakes are equally visible, start midway between them and work both ways.

Before starting on the second course of shingles, snap a chalk line across the first course to mark the position of the butts. Thereafter, in order to keep the shingles in straight lines, snap chalk lines for every third or fourth course.

Shingles must, of course, be staggered so that cut-outs do not line up. Cut the first tab of the starting shingle in the second course in half, and align the cut edge with the rake. From there on, start all odd-numbered courses with a full shingle; all even-numbered courses with a full shingle minus half of a tab.

Follow the manufacturer's directions in determining how much of the shingle to expose. In average installations, 5-inch exposure is used; in windy locations, 4-inch.

Proper nailing is essential to a tight roof.

Use 1-inch galvanized roofing nails on new roofs; 1¾-inch galvanized nails for re-roofing. Square-butt shingles (the most common type) require six nails per strip. Drive the nails 5 5/8 inches up from the butt ends and 1½ inches from the cut-outs and ends of the shingle strip. After placing a shingle and aligning, start nailing from the end nearest the shingle previously laid and proceed across. If you nail from the two ends toward the middle, buckling may result. Drive nail heads flush with the surface of the shingle, not into the shingle.

NAILING SHINGLES

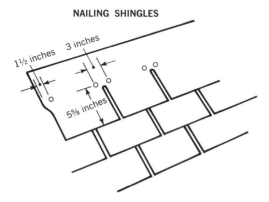

Do not nail shingles where they overlap flashing. Bed them in roofing cement instead. When shingling over valley flashing, snap chalk lines down the full length of the valley on each side. Space the lines 6 inches apart at the ridge and spread them an additional 1/8 inch per foot as they descend the roof. (Thus if a valley is 12 feet long, the shingles are spaced 6 inches apart at the ridge and 7½ inches apart at the bottom.) Trim shingles in each course to align with the chalk lines. Clip 1 inch diagonally off the upper corner of each shingle.

When laying shingles around chimneys, plumbing vents, and along side walls, fit them over or under the original flashing in the same way the old shingles were applied.

Special shingles are made for application on ridges and hips, but it is just as easy to cut square-butt strip shingles into three equal lengths. Bend each cut length down the center so that it laps over the ridge or hip an equal distance on each side. Begin-

ning at the rake end of the ridge or at the bottom of a hip, apply shingles with 5-inch exposure to the weather. Nail each shingle with one nail on each side. Place nails 5½ inches back from the exposed end and 1 inch up from the side edges.

How to repair an asphalt-shingle roof. Finding leaks. See *Roofs, All Types.*

Stopping leaks. If the hole is small, raise the shingle butt carefully and smear asphalt-roofing cement underneath. Use thick cement that is reinforced with fibers.

In the case of larger holes, spread roofing cement under the shingle butt and embed in it a piece of aluminum flashing cut just a bit smaller than the butt. The top edge of the metal should extend up beyond the butt end of the shingle in the next course above. Dab more cement on the top of the metal to hold the shingle down.

Shingles torn. Put asphalt cement and metal flashing underneath in the manner described in the preceding paragraph.

Shingles buckled. Cut through the center of the bulge; then put asphalt cement and metal flashing under it.

Butts curl in the breeze. Dab asphalt cement under them and stick them down tight.

Shingle missing. It must be replaced, obviously. To do this, pull out whatever nails you can get at without damaging the surrounding shingles. You will then probably have to trim back the top edge of the new shingle somewhat in order to get the butts positioned properly. You may also have to drive nails through the exposed butts of the shingle in the next course above. If so, dab roofing cement under the tabs to keep water from dripping down through the nail holes.

How to extend the life of an old roof. If the roof is worn but still sound, you can lengthen its life five or ten years by applying an asphalt-based aluminum roofing paint. Use a paint containing asbestos fibers if the roof is slightly cracked and pocked; nonfibered paint otherwise.

Repairs that are needed should be made before painting. The paint is applied with any kind of paintbrush. Do not try to

REPAIRING HOLES IN ASPHALT-SHINGLE ROOFS

To stop a large leak in a shingle roof, spread roofing cement over it and slide a piece of metal flashing up under the shingles.

brush it out too much. Coverage ranges from 50 to 150 square feet per gallon.

Roofs, Built-up. A built-up roof is made of alternate layers of building felt or fiberglass fabric and asphalt, and then covered with gravel, slag, or stone chips. The roofing is most often used on flat or almost-flat roofs. It should last about twenty years. It should be installed by a professional.

Do not use a roof deck covered with built-up roofing as a porch unless you cover it with wood grating. See *Decks.*

If holes develop in built-up roofing, scrape the gravel aside and apply fibered asphalt-roofing cement. Then replace the gravel.

If the roofing blisters, scrape off the gravel and cut through the blister with a knife. Spread roofing cement underneath and in the slit. Weight down until the blister disappears. Then replace the gravel.

Roofs, Cedar-Shingle.

How to reroof with cedar shingles. Cedar shingles are available in 16-, 18-, and 24-inch lengths. Each bundle covers 25 square feet and contains shingles of different widths.

Cedar shingles should not be used on roofs with a pitch of less than 3 inches in 12 inches. If the pitch is from 3 to 5 inches, 16-inch shingles should be laid with an exposure of 3¾ inches; 18-inch shingles should have a 4½-inch exposure; 24-inch shingles should have a 5¾-inch exposure. If the roof pitch is 5 inches or more, allow a 5-inch exposure for 16-inch shingles; 5½-inch for 18-inch shingles; 7½-inch for 24-inch shingles. All these roofs are equally tight and waterproof. Your choice of shingle length depends on the effect you wish to achieve.

To determine how many shingles to order, calculate the square footage of the first floor of the house and add the square footage of the roof overhangs. To the total, add 3 percent if the roof has a 3-inch pitch; 5½ percent for a 4-inch pitch; 8½ percent for a 5-inch pitch; 12 percent for a 6-inch pitch; 20 percent for an 8-inch pitch; 42 percent for a 12-inch pitch; 60 percent for a 15-inch pitch. Divide this grand total by 25. The answer is the number of bundles you should order if the roof pitch is 5 inches or more. If the pitch is less than 5 inches, add one-third more bundles to make up for the reduced exposure. You will also need one extra bundle for every 25 running feet of hips and valleys.

If the old roof is in very bad shape or if it has already been covered by two applications of shingles, strip off the old shingles. But if the old roof is reasonably sound and only one-application thick, you can apply the new shingles directly on top. You should, however, take the following steps: (1) Cut out the first course of shingles at the eaves and cut those at the rakes back 6 inches. (2) Replace the cut-out shingles with boards. (3) Remove the ridge strip of shingles and replace them with lengths of beveled siding installed thin edge downward. (4) If the valley flashing is badly worn, cover it with boards and lay new metal flashing.

RESHINGLING OVER OLD SHINGLES

Install the new shingles with 5d (1¾-inch) galvanized shingle nails. Use two nails per shingle regardless of the shingle's width. The nails should be driven no more than ¾ inch from the edges and should be at least ¾ inch above the butts of the overlapping shingles. However, when applying shingles over flashing, the nails must be placed more or less one above the other in order to avoid driving them through the flashing.

The starter course at the eaves should be two shingles thick. To speed installation of subsequent courses and make sure they are straight, nail a board across the roof and butt the shingles to this. Space adjacent shingles ¼ inch apart to allow for expansion. The joints in successive courses should be at least 1½ inches apart; and you should never have two joints in a line if only one course of shingles separates them.

Hips and ridges are capped by shingles laid lengthwise. The shingles on each side of the peak are carefully fitted and butted to make a tight joint.

There is no need to apply a finish on a

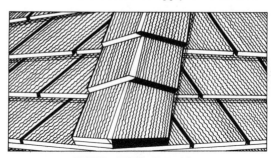

BUTTED JOINTS IN SHINGLES

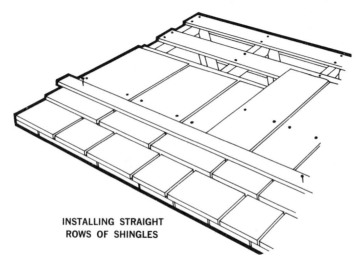

INSTALLING STRAIGHT
ROWS OF SHINGLES

wood-shingle roof; however, you may extend the life slightly if you do. For a more or less natural finish, just brush on a wood preservative containing pentachlorophenol. For a colored finish, apply an oil stain mixed with wood preservative.

How to repair a cedar-shingle roof. Shingle split. Drive in nails on either side of the split. Place the nails as close as possible to the butt of the overlapping shingle. However, if the split is in line with a joint in the next two courses above or below, you should first insert under the shingle a piece of aluminum flashing.

Roof leaks. Push a piece of aluminum flashing up under the shingle over the hole. The top of the flashing should be above the shingle butt in the next course above.

Shingle missing. With a hacksaw blade, reach up under the overlapping shingle and cut off the heads of the nails that held the shingle. Then insert a new shingle. It may have to be cut back at the thin edge if it strikes nails in courses further up. Hold it in place with nails driven just below the butt of the overlapping shingle.

Moss on shingles. This is more of a problem on wood shingles than on other roofing materials, especially in damp, shady locations. For how to correct the problem, see *Roofs, All Types.*

Roofs, Clay-Tile. Tiles used on roofs may be flat rectangles or specially shaped (usually barrel-shaped). They are heavy, durable, and fireproof, and a roof made of them should last indefinitely. It should be installed by a professional.

To stop a leak in a tile roof, slip a sheet of aluminum flashing under the tile. It should extend up beyond the butt of the tile in the next course above. Hold the metal in place with a dab of roofing cement.

If a tile is broken, you may be able to glue the pieces together with epoxy glue or silicone rubber adhesive. If this doesn't work, call in a professional roofer.

Roofs, Fiberglass-Reinforced Plastic. Plastic roofing comes in corrugated, translucent sheets which are used only on terrace roofs. For how to install and care for them, see *Fiberglass-Reinforced Plastics.*

Roofs, Metal. Metal roofs are made of galvanized steel, terne (steel coated with a lead-tin alloy), aluminum, and copper. Installation should always be by a professional.

Small holes are repaired by cleaning the surface thoroughly and applying plastic metal. Large holes and tears can be repaired temporarily by embedding a patch of the same metal in plastic metal or silicone caulking compound.

Paint steel roofs every three or four years with a red-lead primer and a good grade of exterior oil paint. Paint terne roofing every ten years with exterior acrylic-latex paint. If aluminum with a natural finish corrodes badly, paint it as you would steel. Aluminum with a factory-applied baked-on finish may need to be painted ten to fifteen years after installation; thereafter, it needs painting every three to four years to look well. Copper is not finished in any way.

Roofs, Shake. Shakes are thick, hand-split, wood shingles with a very rough texture. They are used on roofs with a minimum pitch of 4 inches per foot, and also on walls. The maximum exposure recommended for 32-inch shakes is 13 inches; for 24-inch shakes, 10 inches; and for 18-inch shakes, 8½ inches.

If you reroof with shakes, the old roofing should be removed down to the deck. Lay a 36-inch strip of 30-pound roofing felt along the eaves where you start work. Then nail 18-inch cedar shingles along the eaves. On top of these nail the first course of shakes.

Use 6d (2-inch) galvanized nails and drive two through each shake. The nails should be 1 inch from each edge and 1 to 2 inches above the butt of the shakes in the course next above.

Space the shakes ¼ inch apart. Joints in adjacent courses should be offset 1½ inches, and should not be in direct alignment in alternate courses.

The top of each course of shakes is covered with an 18-inch strip of roofing felt. The distance from the bottom edge of the felt to the shake butts should equal twice the exposure. (For example, if the shakes have a 10-inch exposure to the weather, the felt should be placed 20 inches above the butts.) The top edge of the felt is extended up on the sheathing and held in place with a few scattered roofing nails.

At ridges and hips you will save work if you install prefabricated ridge and hip units. Or you can cover the ridges with shakes handled like cedar shingles. Before installing any shakes, install a strip of roofing felt at least 1 foot wide over the roof peaks.

How to repair a shake roof. See *Roofs, Cedar-Shingle.*

Roofs, Slate. Slate shingles vary in size, color, and texture; but all are handsome, fireproof, and durable. They must be installed only on a solid deck with a pitch of at least 4 inches. If the slates are unusually thick, additional framing is needed to support them. Installation should be by a professional roofer.

To stop a leak in a slate roof, insert a piece of aluminum flashing metal under the slate, over the hole, and secure it with a dab of roofing cement. The metal should extend up beyond the butt of the shingle in the course above.

If slates are broken, have a professional roofer replace them.

Roofs, Urethane. Urethane foam can be sprayed on any roof to keep out moisture and the sun's heat; but at present it is most commonly used on flat or nearly flat roofs in place of built-up asphalt and gravel. The foam is applied with special equipment by trained applicators in thicknesses of 1 inch

or more. It must be covered with a thin film of silicone or epoxy to protect it from destructive ultraviolet rays.

On new roofs, the foam is sprayed directly on the roof deck. On old roofs, it can be applied over the old roofing material provided that is clean, dry, and sound.

Cost of a foam roof is generally less than the cost of a built-up roof plus fiberglass insulation. Installation can be made in a few hours. One of the advantages in applying foam to an old roof is that it not only seals out moisture and heat but also fills holes in the old roofing, adds to its strength and rigidity, and prevents it from expanding and contracting and opening up new holes.

The life expectancy of a urethane roof has not yet been determined; but it has already proved more durable under blistering sun than asphalt and gravel.

Roofs, Wood-Shingle. See *Roofs, Cedar-Shingle* and *Roofs, Shake.*

Rope. Manila rope is the standard by which all other ropes—and there are a great many—are judged.

Manila is an all-purpose rope which handles and flexes superbly. It is factory-lubricated to give it long life; has good resistance to water and abrasion. A ¼-inch rope can safely support about 120 pounds; ¾-inch, 270 pounds; 1-inch, 530 pounds.

Manila is considerably stronger than sisal rope, but weaker than all synthetics. Among the latter, nylon is outstanding. It is one and a half to two times stronger than manila, extremely resistant to abra-

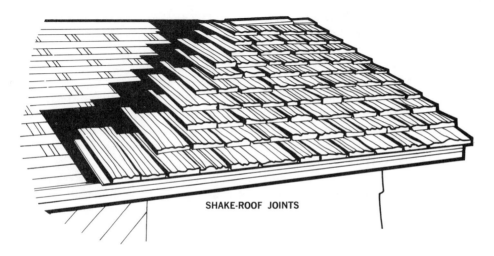

SHAKE-ROOF JOINTS

sion, won't rot, and is not affected by common solvents and alkalies. It also is much more elastic than manila, which means that you can jerk it much harder without breaking it. On the other hand, elasticity is a drawback in some situations.

Polypropylene is also stronger than manila. It has many of nylon's characteristics, but stretches less. You can easily wash it clean. It is lighter than any other rope.

Manila, sisal, and synthetic ropes (which are also made of polyester and polyethylene) are generally made with three strands twisted around one another. The easiest way to keep the ends from raveling is to wrap them two or three times with friction tape or plastic electrical tape. The synthetics can also be kept from raveling by touching a hot iron to the cut ends.

Cotton is used to make braided rope up to ¼-inch diameter. It is good for clothes lines, sash cords, and other uses where great strength is not required.

Small braided nylon rope is also available. It is much stronger than cotton and more resistant to the weather. It is also a lot more expensive.

Either of these ropes is superior to a small rope made of lightweight wire covered with smooth plastic. This rope, however, is very good for clotheslines because it sheds dirt and can be wiped clean with a damp cloth.

Rottenstone. See *Abrasives.*

Royal Copenhagen. A Danish china. See *China.*

Royal Doulton. A well-known English china. See *China.*

Rubber. Articles made of rubber last longer when kept cool and damp than when they are hot and dry. If they do deteriorate, they cannot be salvaged.

To glue two pieces of rubber together or to glue rubber to another material, coat both pieces with rubber cement and stick them together while the cement is tacky (slightly sticky). Ordinary rubber cement is generally satisfactory; but for the strongest joints, use special rubber cements such as those used for patching tire tubes.

Small holes in rubber articles, such as hoses and boots, can be sealed by coating with liquid neoprene or plastic rubber. (The same material is excellent for sealing holes in metal flashing, weatherproofing outdoor electrical boxes, etc.) For large holes, clean both surfaces and roughen them with sandpaper. Then apply a patch from a tire-tube patching kit.

Rubber Cement. See *Gluing.*

Rubber Tile. See *Floors, Rubber.*

Rug Cushions. Rug cushions made of sponge rubber are preferable to those made of jute and hair (even if the latter are rubber-coated) because they are more resilient, will not fray, resist matting, and are non-allergenic. And moisture cannot sink through them to damage the floor underneath.

To allow for stretching, rug cushions should be cut about 2 inches smaller than the rugs. Two or three small pieces can be used under a rug just as well as one large one if you butt the edges.

Rugs. The rugs and carpets in your home are a major investment. You should buy them with care and treat them well.

Whichever type of rug you buy, don't just look at it and perhaps run your fingers over it. Pick it up, bend it sharply, and inspect the density of the pile. The thicker it is, the better. Remember, however, that the thickness and depth of a pile are not the same thing. A deep pile may or may not be thick. And even if it is thick, it may not be as desirable as a rug with a shallow pile, because while it is more luxurious, it crushes more easily, wears more, and is harder to clean.

After inspecting the pile, turn the rug over and inspect the back. It should be tight and firm—with a secure grip on the pile. On many carpets, the backing is covered with latex.

Finally, consider the price. This is figured on a per-square-yard basis, although it may not be quoted in that way. Generally, the higher it is, the better the carpet.

Wall-to-wall carpet versus rugs. If you are having a house custom-built, you will save money—not as much as you may think, but some—by laying wall-to-wall carpet on a plywood floor. If you move and take the carpet with you, however, you may meet resistance from would-be buyers who would prefer oak floors.

In an existing house, if a floor is in bad condition, you may save money by putting in wall-to-wall carpet rather than having the floor refinished and laying down a rug. But the only way you can be sure of this is to get prices for both.

In an existing house with good floors, you will obviously save money initially by using rugs. And if you move, you can take the rugs with you and probably use them again without cutting them. On the other hand, if wall-to-wall carpet is not left behind when a family moves, it almost always has to be cut; that's why families in which the man is frequently transferred by his employer rarely buy wall-to-wall carpet.

But wall-to-wall carpet does have advantages: (1) You can clean it faster than you can clean a rug plus a fringe of bare wood floor simply because you need only one tool. (2) You don't have to go to the bother of moving the furniture, turning back the rug, and polishing the wood floor.

Rug fibers. Wool is still outstanding despite the development of many fine synthetics. It is extremely resilient and resistant to crushing and soil. It is also easy to clean and durable, although it is not as resistant to abrasion as some other fibers. But it must be mothproofed.

Acrylic has considerable resemblance to wool: it is resilient, resistant to crushing and soiling, durable, and easy to clean. In addition, it is not attacked by moths or mildew. Thick new rugs, however, are likely to shed excessively for a while.

Modacrylic is quite similar to acrylic but lacks resilience and pills readily.

Nylon has outstanding resistance to abrasion plus the other advantages of acrylic. Its worst drawback is the sparks it gives off when you walk across it.

Polyester combines many of the good features of wool and nylon at a low price.

It is very crush-resistant but has rather poor stain resistance.

Polypropylene is used for outdoor as well as indoor carpets. It is easy to clean and resistant to staining. Its good wearability is not matched by its resistance to crushing, however.

Saran has good soil and stain resistance but only fair abrasion resistance. It tends to darken in color.

Rayon is inexpensive, and is best used only in low-traffic areas. It crushes badly except when the pile is made of dense, short loops.

Cotton is also extremely crushable and soils badly. But it is durable and easy to wash.

Rug construction. Genuine oriental rugs are unmatched in beauty and durability. They are hand-made. Each tuft of wool, silk, or silky animal hair is knotted to the backing.

Most modern rugs are also tufted, but the tufts are inserted into the backing by machine. The backing is usually coated with latex for extra strength. Modern tufted rugs are much less expensive than Oriental rugs and also generally less expensive than woven rugs. They are classified, according to their surface texture, as plush, loop, twist, and shag.

Axminster, velvet, Wilton, and chenille are woven rugs. The first two are the least costly of the four. They have the best carpet yarn only on the surface. Wilton and chenille are top-quality rugs. The latter is commonly made to order.

Braided rugs are made by twisting fibers together into thick braids and then looping the braids around and around in concentric circles. The rugs lack the resilience of woven and tufted rugs, and the braids, which are sewn together, sometimes come apart. But the rugs are otherwise durable. They may be reversible.

Hooked rugs and vegetable fiber rugs such as sisal are also available.

Broadloom is not a special type of rug. It is simply a rug that was made on a wide loom.

Kitchen carpet. This may be comfortable

underfoot and it may not show dirt and spills, but it is a poor investment because it doesn't wear as well as resilient and seamless flooring and, despite claims, it requires considerable attention to keep it clean.

Acrylic is the best fiber for kitchen carpets. Polypropylene should not be used.

How to take care of rugs and carpets. *Vacuuming.* Regular, thorough vacuuming to remove dirt is vital to the life and good looks of your carpeting. The most damaging kind of dirt is grit, such as sand, because it can cut carpet fibers. If there are traffic paths and spots that get regular heavy use, give them a once-over-lightly cleaning each day to pick up surface litter and dust. For this kind of quick cleaning you can use a regular vacuum cleaner, a less cumbersome lightweight vacuum, or a carpet sweeper. Don't waste your time sweeping a rug or carpet with a broom; it simply pushes dirt around and often drives it farther down into the fibers.

At least once a week you should give the entire carpeted surface a thorough vacuum cleaning—up to seven strokes over each section. To give the pile a neat, uniform surface, make the last stroke in each section you work on follow the same direction. For this kind of cleaning you need a regular, full-sized vacuum cleaner. An upright is the best choice because it does a better job of lifting up and removing deeply imbedded dirt and grit.

Shampooing. Even with the most diligent regular vacuuming, rugs and carpets need occasional shampoos. Grease, soot, and other pollutants in the air settle on and into rugs and carpets, dulling colors and damaging their fibers. How often shampooing is necessary depends on where you live and how clean the air is.

You can shampoo carpets yourself or have it done professionally. The latter is usually the better choice. A professional cleaner can do a more thorough job, with less chance of shrinking, fading, or staining the carpet. Because of the cost, however, you may find it practical to alternate professional cleaning with a do-it-yourself method. Professional rug cleaners can do the work either in their own plants, which

is preferable, or in your home, if it's too difficult to take up the carpet.

Rug-cleaning products for home use come in powder, liquid, and aerosol-spray forms, and all of them vary in their ability to clean and to prevent a build-up of future dirt. Some shampoos contain an effective soil-retarding ingredient; others may leave a sticky residue behind that actually helps dirt adhere to it. Before you use a shampoo for the first time, be sure to test it in an inconspicuous spot, preferably on a carpet swatch. Check the results for color, texture, and general feel. Whatever type you use, vacuuming is the final step that removes both the cleaner and the dirt.

Dry or powdered shampoos often are recommended for wool carpets since they are least likely to cause matting of the fibers. (When you use liquids and aerosol sprays you have to guard against overwetting the fibers.) The time between applying dry shampoos and final vacuuming is only about an hour.

To use the powder, vacuum first, then sprinkle the powder generously onto a section of the rug and work it in with a soft-bristled brush or special applicator. (A few types come packaged with an applicator that dispenses the powder and works it into the carpet at the same time.) Allow the powder to set about an hour; then vacuum thoroughly. (Be sure you have extra vacuum-cleaner bags on hand. The powder fills up the bags quickly.)

Liquid shampoos, which seem to be the most popular, are concentrated detergents that you dilute with water according to package directions and apply as a "dry" foam. You can whip the solution into foam yourself, using an egg beater or wire whisk, or use an appliance that turns it into foam as it dispenses it.

If you shampoo often or have a large expanse of carpet, a rug shampooer applies the cleaner more evenly. There are both electric and non-electric types. Some are combination floor polishers and rug shampooers. For infrequent jobs, you can rent a shampooer from many hardware stores or rental services.

Aerosol sprays, like other aerosol

products, are ready for instant use—the product emerges from the container as a foam. Follow package directions when you spray. If you are careless, it is possible to overwet the carpet when you use either the liquid-foam or aerosol spray.

Using liquids and aerosols. Either liquid foams or aerosols can be worked into the carpet fibers with a sponge, soft-bristled brush, or rug shampooer. Some products come packaged with special applicators.

Before applying either type, vacuum the carpet thoroughly. Move the furniture off the carpet, or put pieces of aluminum foil or plastic wrap under and around furniture legs. Apply the shampoo in even, overlapping strokes. As you work in the shampoo, finish each section by stroking the pile in the same direction. Let the carpet dry thoroughly—and don't let anyone walk on it while it's wet. Drying time can vary from a few hours to overnight, but you can speed drying by using a fan or by opening windows. When the carpet feels dry, vacuum thoroughly.

Laundering small rugs. See *Laundering.*

How to treat spots and stains. Removing spots from any fiber product, including rugs, always is a gamble because the elements are unpredictable: what was spilled, what it was spilled on, and the timing of the remedial treatment. What works well on one spot and one rug may be only half successful in another situation, or it may not work at all. Before trying to remove a large, disfiguring spot you may want to consult a professional rug cleaner after the preliminary sopping up. But for small accidents there are several at-home treatments that have a good chance of succeeding.

When anything is spilled or whenever you notice a stain, treat the spot immediately. Even some substances that you might think will be invisible when dry can eventually discolor the carpet. Liquids containing sugar, for example, will turn brown in time, as the sugar caramelizes. If a guest spills something, you can take quick, calm action and still put him at ease. At least blot up the moisture or rinse the spot with cool water. (A good emergency technique is to cover the area with about a ½-inch thickness of white paper toweling and weight it down with books.)

Some basic procedures apply no matter what the stain or the cleaning solution you're using:

First blot up any excess liquid with paper toweling. If the material is solid, scoop it up with a spatula or knife. Use any cleaning solution sparingly; don't let the carpet get too wet. Apply the cleaner with a clean, soft white cloth or paper towel. Turn the cloth to a clean spot as it picks up dirt. Blot the stain; don't rub or brush. Excess rubbing can distort the pile and cause it to mat. Work on the stain from the outside toward the center. Starting at the center and working outward will enlarge the area of the stain. To dry the carpet afterward, cover the spot with about a ½-inch thickness of white paper toweling and weight it down with heavy books.

There are two basic cleaning solutions that you should keep on hand for spot removal: dry-cleaning solvent and a detergent-vinegar solution. The dry-cleaning fluid or solvent should be the same type used to remove spots from clothing (*never* use carbon tetrachloride). To make the detergent-vinegar solution, add one teaspoon of a powdered neutral detergent (the kind recommended for fine fabrics) and one teaspoon of white vinegar to a quart of warm water. These two solutions work well on a wide range of stains, they are safe to use, and are not likely to damage the carpet.

Besides these two standard spot removers, there are a number of special products available for treating rugs. If you've already found one that works well, don't try an unfamiliar product before testing it first in an inconspicuous spot.

As a general rule, use the detergent-vinegar solution for water-based stains and the cleaning fluid for greasy ones. Some specific procedures for some common causes of spots and stains follow.

Oily foods and materials. Examples: butter, oily liquids, hand or face cream, ball-point-pen ink. Remove the excess and apply the dry-cleaning fluid. Dry the carpet with paper toweling and weights. Apply the fluid again if there's still a trace of the spot. After it's dry, brush the pile gently to restore fluffiness.

Starchy or sugary substances. Examples: soft drinks, alcoholic beverages, candy, fruit stains, washable ink. Blot up or scrape off excess. Apply the detergent-vinegar solution and dry the carpet. Apply more solution if necessary. After drying the carpet, brush the pile gently.

Protein-based substances and some oily foods. Examples: coffee, milk, tea, chocolate, blood, eggs. Blot up or scrape off excess. Apply detergent-vinegar solution. Dry the carpet. Apply dry-cleaning solvent. Dry the carpet again; then brush gently.

Lipstick, crayon, paint, tar, heavy grease, chewing gum. Blot up or scrape off excess. Apply dry-cleaning fluid. Dry the carpet. Apply detergent-vinegar solution. Reapply dry-cleaning fluid. Dry the carpet; then brush the pile gently.

Urine. Blot up as soon as possible. Apply detergent-vinegar solution. After drying, brush the pile gently. Prepared puppy-stain removers are excellent and convenient.

Vomit, excrement. Get after these immediately: they will leave permanent stains on almost any carpet otherwise. Scrape up completely. Apply detergent-vinegar solution. Blot up. Then apply solution of 1 tablespoon ammonia in ¾ cup water. Blot up. Then rinse with 1 part white vinegar and 2 parts water. Blot up once more and allow to dry. Then fluff up the pile.

Signs of age and wear. From the moment your carpet is in use it starts to undergo natural changes in appearance. Here are some of the signs of change you can expect and what you can do about them:

Shedding. Any new carpet contains many fiber ends that weren't removed during manufacturing or it may have excess loose fibers in the weave. Shedding is to be expected, particularly during vacuuming, and it's nothing to worry about. As the carpet is used and cleaned, the amount of shedding gradually will diminish and eventually stop.

Sprouting. Tufts that extend above the rest of the pile are called sprouts. Simply snip them off, even with the rest of the pile. Do not pull them out. Smooth the snipped area gently with your fingers to blend the fibers with the rest of the pile.

Pilling. Little balls of fiber, or "pills," occur when one end of a long fiber works loose and becomes entangled with other fibers or with lint on the carpet. Vacuuming frequently will break off and remove these pills. If some should persist even after vacuuming, you can either pull them off or lift them up and cut loose the tangled fibers.

Shading. As a carpet is used, particularly if it is a solid color and has a uniform pile, it may appear to change color in certain areas. This shading is caused by the pressure of footsteps pushing the tufts in different directions. The way light is reflected from the sides and tops of the slanted tufts causes the apparent difference in color. Once shading starts or becomes pronounced, it cannot always be corrected. To prevent it, vacuum frequently and always finish your vacuuming stroke in the direction the pile should lie.

Pile crushing or indentations. Pile in heavy-traffic areas or where furniture stands in one place for some time becomes crushed and distorted. If you want all parts of your carpeting to get uniform wear, rearrange the furniture occasionally or rotate the rug to prevent permanent indentations from furniture legs and to equalize wear in regular-traffic paths. To restore the pile's surface, moisten the area with steam by holding a dry iron over a damp cloth—or a steam iron over a dry cloth—about ½ inch above the carpet. (Do not press the hot iron down on the carpet.) After steaming, brush the fibers gently to restore the nap. (In spots that are very worn or heavily indented, this technique will not completely restore the nap.) The same procedure helps to flatten curling rug corners.

A special rug rake may be used to bring up the pile on shag rugs.

A cushion under rugs or carpets helps to preserve their appearance, makes the surface more comfortable to walk on, and helps to protect the floor underneath. A cushioned pad under an area rug also keeps it from slipping. (Other ways to skidproof rugs are to paint liquid rubber on the back or to apply anti-skid tapes to the edges.)

Fading. As much as possible, protect carpet from constant exposure to direct sunlight, which will cause the colors to fade.

How to repair rugs. Burns. You can camouflage these to some extent by snipping off the charred edges of the fibers. Be careful not to cut too deeply. Then apply the detergent-vinegar mixture as for removing stains.

A better solution, though more difficult, is to try to reweave the spot with fibers pulled from a scrap of the carpet. First, clip off the charred ends. Then lift the carpet from the floor and, with a needle, thread the fibers through the hole. When the hole is filled, trim the fibers even with the surrounding pile. Glue the bottom ends to the rug backing with rubber cement. This repair is best made by two people, one on either side of the rug.

Frayed edges. Whipstitch them with heavy thread or press on gummed carpet binding.

Worn spots. The only thing you can do about these is to camouflage them temporarily. Make a dye solution to match the rest of the carpet and paint it on with a paintbrush.

Scalloped edges. Rug edges often become scalloped after cleaning. There is very little you can do about this. Try steaming with a steam iron. Or try cutting the rug cushion back slightly under the low edges of the rug. If the problem persists, you had better give up and tack down the edges.

How to store rugs. Clean them first. Then roll them into a compact bundle and tie in several places. Never fold rugs with a backing and don't bend a rolled rug sharply, especially if it has a latex-reinforced backing.

Wool rugs, unless mothproofed, should be well sprinkled with paradichlorobenzene crystals before they are rolled. Wrap them securely in heavy kraft paper

and seal the edges. Other rugs do not need to be mothproofed but a paper covering will keep them clean in storage. It will also help to discourage mice from taking up residence between the folds.

How to take care of vegetable fiber rugs. See entry for the appropriate fiber.

Rug Shampooers. The best rug shampooers are electrical appliances that are also used for polishing floors. They have flat, round brushes that revolve horizontally. (See *Floor Polishers.*)

Nonelectric shampooers resemble a carpet sweeper with a flat plastic tank on the handle. These have rigid brushes that lift the rug pile, and revolving rollers that spread the shampoo. The shampoo is released from the tank by finger-control at the handle.

Rules. See *Tools, Workshop—6-foot rule.*

Rush. Rush is a tough marsh plant which is woven into mats, rugs, baskets, and chair seats. It has surprising strength when new; but with age it tends to ravel and break.

Vacuum articles made of it frequently because they are dust collectors. When the rush becomes soiled, sponge it with a heavy-duty detergent solution.

When strands break, you can usually cut them out without spoiling the appearance of the article. Or you can glue the ends together with white wood glue. If you can find a craft or furniture shop that sells rushes, new strips can be woven in with the old.

Rust. See *Corrosion.*

Safety in the Home. For how to protect your home against fire, see *Fire Prevention.* Other recommendations for improving home safety are made in other entries such as *Gas; Refrigerators; Electrical System, Household.*

Here are twenty-one repairs or improvements you can make in an existing home to prevent accidents:

1. Build railings on all unprotected stairs and porches. They should be 32 inches high. Close in the space below the handrail with balusters or additional rails to keep children from falling through. Make sure existing railings are strong.

2. Install lights in all stairways so that

the treads are clearly visible. The lights should be controlled from both the top and the bottom of the stairs.

3. If the floor level changes abruptly, do something to make the change obvious. You might, for instance, place a piece of furniture in the obvious travel path. Or you might paint a bright stripe on the edge of the step and also on the riser.

4. Nail down loose and protruding floor boards. Replace floor boards and stair treads that are weak, splintered, or rotten.

5. If floor wax is extremely slippery, strip it off and replace it with nonskid wax.

6. Repave broken areas and low spots in walks. If brick paving is used in a shady or damp location, top it with concrete (damp bricks are extremely slippery).

7. Apply anti-skid backing or tapes to small rugs that slide, or tack the rugs down.

8. Repair or replace worn carpets.

9. Paint low-hanging pipes and ducts, low doorways, and low ceilings on stairways a bright color. Yellow and black stripes are a traditional caution signal. Use fluorescent paint for extra visibility.

10. Build a locked cabinet for dangerous medicines. Build another locked cabinet for other poisonous materials.

11. Build a locked cabinet for all firearms.

12. Replace conventional plate glass in sliding glass doors and full-length windows adjacent to the doors with safety glass. Glass shower doors should also be equipped with safety glass or plastic.

13. Install window guards on second-story windows with sills lower than 30 inches. This is especially important in children's rooms.

14. If room doors open into a hall, rehang them to open into the rooms. (Closet doors cannot be changed, however.)

15. Install a straight, vertical grab-bar in all shower stalls and tubs used only for tub-bathing. In tubs that are also used for shower-bathing, install L-shaped bars.

16. Paste skidproof plastic patches in the bottom of tubs and shower stalls. They are more reliable than ordinary shower mats.

17. Move light switches at least 3 feet away from all lavatories, tubs, and shower stalls and the kitchen and laundry sinks.

18. Replace all broken, frayed, or defective electric cords, plugs, outlets, switches, lighting fixtures.

19. If possible, replace conventional electric outlets with grounded outlets.

20. Put safety caps on outlets accessible to children.

21. For maximum protection against shocks, have ground fault circuit interrupters installed on kitchen, laundry, and workshop wiring circuits.

Sailcloth. A smooth, stiff fabric made of cotton or cotton and rayon which is used for draperies, slipcovers, and clothing. Launder like cotton.

Sandpaper. See *Abrasives.*

Saran. Saran is a type of vinyl which is made into a film and sometimes produced as a fiber. The film is a popular kitchen wrap because it sticks to itself and other materials and thus can be used to seal foods from the air.

Sarasa. Sarasa, or E-Sarasa, is a Japanese dying process similar to batik. It can be used to make bedspreads, curtains, hangings—whatever you like. The best fabrics to work with are unbleached cottons, linens, and silks.

The fabric is first coated with skimmed milk and allowed to dry. Appropriate dyes are then applied and covered with flour paste when dry. The fabric is then folded into a small bundle and placed over steam for 45 minutes to set the dye. Finally, it is soaked in cold water to remove the paste.

The dyed fabrics should be dry-cleaned, not washed, when they become dirty.

Sateen. A satin-like fabric generally made of cotton and given a special finish to make it lustrous. It is used to line garments and draperies and is also used by itself. Launder like cotton.

Satin. A soft, lustrous fabric produced in various forms, fibers, and weights and used in clothing, draperies, bedspreads, and upholstery. The material is usually dry-cleaned.

Sawhorses. See *Tools, Workshop.*

Saws. See *Tools, Workshop.*

Scales. The most accurate bathroom scale is a doctor's beam scale. A tall, springless mechanism, it is adjusted by means of weights to within ¼ pound.

Spring-type scales that sit flat on the floor usually are portable; but models that fold out from a built-in wall cabinet are available. These are accurate to within about a pound for a number of years until the spring weakens.

Kitchen scales are also of the spring type. A small table model weighs up to 25 pounds. A hanging model like the old-fashioned peddler's scale weighs up to 60 pounds. There are also kitchen beam scales on the same principle as a doctor's scale.

Scissors. There is a technical difference between scissors and shears: scissors are under 6 inches in length and have handles of the same shape and size; shears are over 6 inches, and have a small handle for the thumb and a larger handle for the fingers.

The best scissors and shears are made of stainless steel. Next best are chrome-plated steel. Then comes nickel-plated steel. Anything else is pretty much a waste of time.

If there is an all-purpose scissors, it is a pair of so-called straight shears. You can buy 6-, 7-, and 8-inch sizes. Still larger sizes are made for special purposes. This is an essential tool for cutting fabric, paper, foods, food wraps, string, etc.

Poultry shears are a help in the kitchen.

Pinking shears with saw-toothed edges are used to cut fabric so it won't ravel.

Embroidery scissors up to about 5 inches in length are needed in the sewing kit.

Electric scissors are a convenience for the enthusiastic seamstress because they slice right through many layers of fabric in short order. The best units have self-sharpening stainless-steel blades. Some models work on rechargeable batteries.

If hand-operated scissors don't cut well, try tightening the screw holding the blades together. You can sharpen the blades a little by cutting through medium-weight sandpaper several times; but for a real sharpening job, look for a scissors grinder.

Scorpions. See *Pest Control.*

Scouring Pads. For really difficult scouring jobs, use a coarse stainless-steel pad. It is about the toughest thing made, outlasting steel wool and other metal pads.

For normal scouring, steel wool is as good as anything. Another good material is a terry cloth with a specially treated, stiff, almost wire-like nub.

Scouring pads for Teflon and other materials that are easily scratched are made of mylar or nylon web.

Scrapers. See *Tools, Workshop.*

Screen Doors. Some screen doors serve also as storm doors. They consist of a door-size frame with removable screen and glass panels. Most such doors are made of aluminum but some are wood.

Conventional screen doors also have aluminum or wood frames. The screen cloth is permanently installed. You hang the doors in the door frame in the spring; take them down in the fall.

Screen doors are repaired and finished in the same way as window screens (see *Screens, Window*). If a door sags, it can be pulled back into square with a metal door brace and turnbuckle. The brace is a long two-piece rod with screw eyes in the ends. Attach one piece to the sagging corner; the other to the upper corner diagonally opposite. The turnbuckle joins the two rods. As you screw up on the turnbuckle, it pulls the rods together, straightening the door.

If a door slams shut, loosen the coil spring; let it return to its normal length; and screw it to a new position on the door framing. (In other words, when the door is closed, the spring should not be under tension.) You can, of course, substitute a pneumatic closer for the spring.

Screen doors should be stored flat in U-shaped hangers or on top of sawhorses. Space the hangers about 42 inches apart. The doors should be separated by boards; otherwise the hardware will not allow them to lie flat.

Screens, Window. Although all screens keep bugs out of a house in the same way, they are built and hung in several ways.

Combination screens and storm windows with aluminum frames are used in colder climates, where they are permanently installed outside double-hung and sliding windows. Most combinations have three tracks—two containing glass panels that cover the window in winter; the third containing a screened panel that covers one-half of the window in summer. In winter, the screened panel is stored in its track at the top of the window.

Wood-framed screens have been in use ever since screen cloth was invented; but they are less widely used today because they are a bit heavy and awkward and need to be painted frequently.

Aluminum-framed screens have very narrow frames in natural aluminum or, much better, aluminum with a baked-enamel finish. Like wood-framed screens, they are usually taken down every fall and put up every spring. They are lightweight, inconspicuous, and strong. If you don't want combinations, this is the best type to use.

Tension screens have no frames. They are fastened only at the top and bottom of the window frame. The sides simply press against the frame. Despite this, they keep out most insects well enough. But they are

flimsy and not so easy to store as one might expect.

Roll screens are like window shades. They roll up to the top of the window when not in use, and are pulled down in summer. The side edges are held in channels. These are efficient units but expensive and uncommon.

Screen cloth can be made of aluminum, copper, galvanized steel, or fiberglass.

How to make aluminum-framed screens. Use do-it-yourself aluminum screen sections and fiberglass screen cloth. Measure the opening just inside the window casing and deduct 1/8 inch from both the width and the height. Pry the splines (slender metal strips) from several framing sections, and then cut the sections to the right length with a hacksaw or fine-toothed backsaw. The cuts should be made at 45-degree angles. Smooth the rough edges with a file.

Assemble the four pieces comprising the frame by inserting L-shaped corner locks in the corners. If the screen is over 6 square feet, it is advisable to add a U-shaped brace across the middle. Notch the ends to fit over the side framing members; and screw them in place with sheet-metal screws.

Cut the splines to the proper length. The ends are butted, so the cuts are made at 90-degree angles.

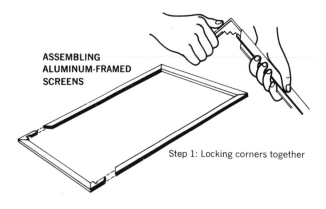

ASSEMBLING
ALUMINUM-FRAMED
SCREENS

Step 1: Locking corners together

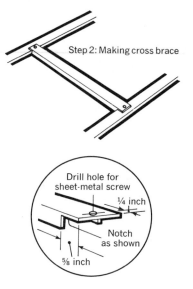

Step 2: Making cross brace

Drill hole for
sheet-metal screw

¼ inch

Notch
as shown

⅝ inch

Cut the screen cloth to the outside dimensions of the frame. Place the frame on a table or floor, groove side up, and check the corners with a try square. Then position the screen cloth on top.

Place one of the long splines over one side of the frame and press it into the groove with the screen cloth underneath. You can start this operation with your fingers; then, after the spline is part way in, place a block of wood on top and tap it with a hammer until the spline is level with the frame. Work from one end of the spline to the other.

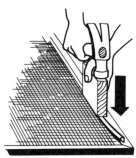

Step 3: Tapping in spline

Repeat this operation at the other side and then at the two ends. It is important to keep the screen cloth straight and taut; but don't pull it so tight that the frame is bent.

When the screen cloth has been "tacked" down along all edges, check once more to be sure the frame lies flat. Then with a razor blade, trim off the screen cloth along the outside edges of the splines.

The screen can be hung with the hanger kit made by the manufacturer of the screen framing. The alternative is to hold it in the window with four screws driven into the casing snug against the aluminum frame.

How to repair window screens. Holes in screen cloth. If the mesh is not broken, simply push it back into position with the point of a nail. If the mesh is broken in a metal screen, buy small, square screen patches and hook the ends into the screen cloth.

If the mesh in fiberglass screen cloth is broken, it is possible to fuse a fiberglass patch to the screen with a warm iron. But practice making this repair on waste material first. Hold a flat piece of metal under the hole; lay the patch on top; and touch it lightly with the tip of the iron.

To replace screen cloth. In metal frames, the cloth is generally held in place by splines. Pry these out carefully; remove old screen cloth; and then apply new cloth in the way described for making screens. Note that there is no reason why you should not use aluminum screen cloth rather than fiberglass (although the latter is a little easier to handle and never needs finishing). If you do, cut the cloth with a sturdy, sharp knife rather than a razor blade.

In most wood frames, the screen cloth is tacked either to the face of the frames or into rabbets along the inside edges. The edges of the cloth are covered with wood molding strips which are held down with brads. Pry the strips up gradually: they break easily. Then remove the screen cloth and all tacks or staples.

Place the new screen cloth over the frame and fasten it down at one end and then at the other. Pull it as tight as possible but don't warp the mesh. Then fasten the sides. You can use tacks; but if you have a stapler, the job goes much faster. Renail the moldings over the edges of the cloth; and then cut the cloth along the outer edges of the moldings with a razor blade or knife.

If frames are wobbly. Aluminum frames are so slender that they are normally somewhat wobbly. You can brace them, if you wish, in the way described for making new screens. But usually there is no need to worry about them.

Wood frames should be rigid. If they loosen at the corners, you may be able to correct matters by forcing white glue into the joints and then driving very long finishing nails through one rail into the other. If this doesn't work, screw angle irons into the corners.

How to refinish screens. Paint wood frames every two years with exterior trim enamel. Unfinished aluminum frames need not be painted or finished, but look better if they are. In salt air and corrosive atmospheres, some sort of finish is essential. See *Aluminum.*

Fiberglass screen cloth is never finished. Metal cloth should be to prevent corrosion. Unfinished copper screen cloth may stain the screen frame and windowsill green; unfinished galvanized-steel screening makes brown stains.

Metal screen cloth needs to be refinished every two or three years, as a rule. First brush it vigorously to remove dirt and the products of corrosion. If you want a clear finish, apply spar varnish. For a paint finish, use a screen enamel or zinc dust paint. All finishes are most easily applied with a scrap of carpet.

How to store screens. To get screens out of the way and also to keep them safe, it is a very good idea to suspend parallel pairs of U-shaped wood racks from a basement, attic, or garage ceiling. The screens are placed flat in these.

If the screens do not have any projecting hardware, such as screw eyes, hooks, or hangers, they can be stored one directly on top of the other. But if they have hardware, separate each screen from the next with a couple of boards.

When hanging screens, dust them well with a brush. Then wash with detergent solution and rinse under the stream of a hose.

Screwdrivers. See *Tools, Workshop.*

Screws. For information about self-tapping sheet-metal screws, see *Metal Fasteners.*

Wood screws are used when you want to hold two or more pieces of wood together very securely. They are also used in work that you may some day want to disassemble. For example, kitchen cabinets should always be installed with wood screws so you can take them out without damage either to the cabinets or to the wall behind them.

Wood screws are made of steel, brass, bronze, and aluminum. The steel screws come in several rust-resistant finishes as well as ordinary steel.

Screw heads are flat—designed to be sunk flush or below the surface of the wood; oval—designed to be partially sunk into wood; and round—protruding completely from the wood surface. Most screws have a single slot; but the Phillips screw, which is more commonly used in metal than wood, has two slots which cross.

Lag screws are very large, heavy screws with an unslotted square head which is grasped in a wrench. They are used for joining large timbers.

The length of wood screws is measured from the point to the widest part of the head. Lengths range from 3/16 to 5½ inches. The diameter, or gauge, of a screw is identified by a number from 0 (very small) to 24 (quite thick). No single design of screw is available in all sizes.

There are no exact rules for what gauge and length of screw you should use where. The main thing is to get one that is long enough to penetrate deep into the wood piece at the pointed end. This doesn't mean that if you are screwing a 1-inch board to a 2-inch timber, you should use a screw that goes almost through the timber. As a rule, a screw that went halfway through the timber would be adequate. On the other hand, if you are attaching the board to the end of the timber, you should use a longer screw because screws don't hold as well in end grain as in cross grain.

Large-diameter screws are used when you need extra holding strength and extra resistance to lateral stress. The threads are deeper than on smaller screws. And, of course, the greater thickness of the metal makes for greater strength.

If wood is very soft, you can drive in a short screw simply by making a small starting hole with an awl. Generally, however, you can save time and energy by drilling holes. The first hole, sometimes called the pilot hole, is slightly smaller and shallower than the screw threads. You can usually drive a screw into this without any trouble; but if you are feeling weak, you can then drill a slightly larger hole the same diameter as the smooth screw shank and no deeper. To countersink a flat or oval screw head, your final job is to drill a shallow, wide hole with a countersink bit.

When driving screws and when removing them, use a screwdriver with a square blade with square corners. A worn, rounded blade may ruin the screw head before you finish your work.

Sealers. A sealer is a varnish-like finish formulated to penetrate and seal the pores of the material to which it is applied. Thus it helps to prevent staining of the material and makes for somewhat easier cleaning.

Most sealers are colorless but some contain pigments. They are made for use on wood (especially floors) and masonry. Application is best made with a brush. Materials that are given two coats need no other finish. Occasionally, however, sealers are used as a prime coat under another type of finish.

Secretary. A tall, decorative desk with a fold-down writing surface above which is a tier of shallow shelves behind doors and below which are two or three drawers. For how to take care of a secretary, see *Desks* and *Furniture, Wood.*

Seersucker. A lightweight fabric with crinkled, lengthwise stripes which is used in clothing and bedspreads. Commonly made of cotton, it is laundered like that material; blends of cotton and polyester may be laundered like permanent press.

Serge. A heavy clothing fabric with diagonal lines. It is usually, but not always, made of wool. In any case, it should be dry-cleaned.

Settle. A long wooden bench with a high solid back, arms, and often with an enclosed foundation that can be a chest. For how to take care of one, see *Furniture, Wood.*

Sewage System. If your house is connected to a municipal sewer, the only problem you may run into (short of paying the sewer tax) is clogging of the large drain running from the house to the sewer. If this happens, you need a long, heavy steel snake to break through the clog—and even with that you may not succeed. So it is much smarter to call a sewer-cleaning service.

If you live beyond the town sewer zone, you must build and maintain your own sewage-disposal system. This can be a cesspool or a septic system.

Cesspools. A cesspool is a covered pit lined on the sides with masonry blocks, bricks, or stones laid up without mortar. Solid particles of waste settle in the bottom of the pit, where they gradually disintegrate; the liquid portion of the waste seeps out through the sides into the surrounding soil.

Cesspools today are frowned upon as unsafe and objectionable, and in many parts of the country they are outlawed. Where they are permitted, they must be located at least 15 to 20 feet from the house and 150 feet away from all water sources. They can be installed only in sandy, gravelly, or other very porous soil.

In time, all cesspools clog up and need to be pumped out (treatment with chemicals that are flushed into the pit does little good). But clogging soon occurs again because the cracks in the sides and the surrounding soil have become saturated with matter. When this happens, a new cesspool must be dug.

Septic systems. A septic system is the only really safe, sanitary, and permanent way to dispose of sewage if you cannot connect into a town sewer. The system consists of a big watertight tank into which the house drain empties. A bacterial action in the tank breaks the waste matter down into sludge, liquid, scum, and gases. The sludge settles to the bottom of the tank beneath the liquid and the scum that forms on top. Excess liquid, known as the effluent, flows out through the other side of the tank into a network of large underground drains comprising the disposal field. The gases escape back through the house drain and up through the vent stack into the open air.

Septic systems must be built by qualified sewage-disposal firms in accordance with local building and health laws. If properly constructed, they present no problems, although tree roots sometimes invade the disposal lines and must be cut out by a sewer-cleaning service.

The tank, however, must be pumped out to assure its proper performance. Most authorities recommend that this should be done every twelve to eighteen months by a professional septic-tank cleaner during warm weather. If cleaned in the winter, the cold may slow the bacterial action in the tank.

Chemicals and bacterial substances advertised as miraculous septic-tank cleaners are of dubious value. They may help a bit but they are not a substitute for pumping. The same is true of yeast, which some people add to septic tanks.

Shantung. Originally a silk fabric, shantung is now also made of acetate and rayon. It has a crisp texture and small, irregular ribbing, and is used in clothing. Wash like silk.

Sharkskin. A firm, tight fabric resembling the skin of a shark and made of de-lustered wool, cotton, and acetate. It is used in clothing. Dry-clean.

Sharpening Stones. See *Tools, Workshop* and *Knives, Kitchen.*

Sheets. See *Bedding.*

Sheffield. A famous type of silverplate originated in Sheffield, England. The silver is plated on copper. See *Silver.*

Shellac. Shellac is an alcohol-based finish used for finishing furniture and paneling, sealing knots and stains, and as a base for varnish and paint. It is also used for finishing wood floors but is not recommended because it is damaged by water and scratches rather badly.

Natural shellac is transparent and orange colored; but white shellac, which is colorless, is more generally used. Neither type should be applied if it is more than six months old.

Another shellac-based finish which contains a white pigment is called a "stain killer" and is used mainly for priming wood.

Transparent shellac is generally sold in 4- or 5-pound cuts. (This means it is made of 4 or 5 pounds of shellac gum dissolved in 1 gallon of alcohol.) When used as a finish on furniture and paneling, you should first mix 1 quart 5-pound shellac with 1 quart denatured alcohol; or you should mix 1 quart 4-pound shellac with 3 cups alcohol.

The diluted shellac should be applied in from three to six very thin coats. As soon as each coat has dried for 3 hours, go over the surface with fine sandpaper or steel wool. After the final coat has been rubbed down, apply wax.

If you want to change the color of wood before applying shellac, use a water stain. Oil and alcohol stains are less reliable under shellac.

Shellac is best applied in a dry room at a temperature of 70 degrees. If applied in damp weather, a "bloom," or white clouding, may develop on the surface. Should this happen, try wiping it off with alcohol.

Shellac finish that is scratched or damaged can be easily touched up by brushing on diluted fresh shellac. Since the new shellac dissolves the old, the two blend together without obvious laps.

Shellac can be removed by rubbing with alcohol or applying paint remover.

Shells. Shells are used as small baking dishes, ash trays, and ornaments. You can wash them to your heart's content in the dishwasher or detergent solution; and you can use cleansers on those with a rough surface. But avoid getting vinegar or citrus juice on polished shells, because they will etch the surface. If an ornamental shell is broken, it can be glued with cellulose cement.

Shelves. If a shelf is to be of any value, it must be constructed of material that is strong enough not to break or bend, and it must be anchored firmly so it won't come down.

Shelving material. As a rule, the heaviest articles that are stored on shelves in the home are books, phonograph records, and paint. Books of average size covering a square foot of shelf space weigh approximately 20 pounds; a foot-high stack of 12-inch records in cardboard covers weighs 45 pounds; 4 gallons of paint (which occupy about 170 square inches of shelf space) weigh 44 pounds.

A 1-inch white pine board is strong enough to carry any of these loads without bending if it is supported at 3-foot intervals. A 1¼-inch board would need to be supported at 5-foot intervals.

One-half-inch plate glass could also carry these loads if supported at 3-foot intervals. If you used ¼-inch plate, however, the distance between supports would have to be reduced to 15 inches.

Steel shelving is usually very thin and pliable but has great strength and stiffness because the front and back edges are folded down.

Shelf supports. Shelf supports of many kinds are used. Wood cleats are the simplest. They can be cut out of any small board, but a 1-inch width is perfect.

Shelf molding is a special wood molding with a rabbet cut in one face. The shelf board rests in this.

L-shaped shelf hangers are little metal gadgets that plug into holes that you drill in the sides of bookcases and cabinets. The holes are in vertical rows and spaced about 2 inches apart so that the shelves can be adjusted up and down.

Shelf-support strips are an elaborate substitute for the L-shaped hangers. They are narrow metal strips with horizontal slots from top to bottom. The strips are screwed to the sides of a bookcase or cabinet, and V-shaped clips are then inserted in the slots to support the shelves. The shelves can be adjusted up and down in small increments.

Slotted metal standards are similar to support strips but used to support cantilevered shelves. The standards are, as a rule, long strips of metal with closely spaced vertical slots from top to bottom. Metal brackets hook into the slots. Depending on the size of the brackets, they can support shelves from about 4 to 20 inches deep. The number of shelves installed in each set of standards depends on the size and weight of the articles on the shelves.

Slotted standards are normally screwed to a wall, but special standards which wedge between the floor and ceiling are available. These are used to make freestanding shelves anywhere in a room.

Shelf brackets are screwed to walls in pairs to support single shelves. The simplest brackets are L-shaped and ugly. More ornamental designs are available.

U-shaped shelf hangers made of heavy steel wire are used to suspend shelves below the basement ceiling joists. You can make the same kind of hangers by nailing three narrow boards together.

How to build bookshelves. This is an easy job, but before you rush into it, make up your mind on the following points:

Location: You can build bookshelves almost anywhere but don't make the mistake of putting them in an inaccessible spot. You should be able to get at them without moving furniture. And the light should be good enough so that you can read the titles.

Materials: Most bookshelves are built of white pine boards that are either painted or stained; but you can use birch, mahogany—anything you like. One-inch lumber is thick enough.

Design: If you are a great book collector, you will probably want shelves that run from floor to ceiling (actually, the bottom shelf is placed just above the top of the baseboards; the top shelf should not be more than 78 inches above the floor). But there is no reason why your shelves should not be long and low if that is what best suits the room; or why you should not place the shelves above a deep cabinet with doors that is used for storing games, photographs, etc. In other words, you can build bookshelves in any way you like; but don't actually start the job until you have figured out on paper exactly what the design will be.

Bookshelves should be 9 5/8 inches deep (made with 10-inch boards) to accommodate most book sizes. If the shelves are fixed, space the lower ones 11 inches apart; the upper ones, 9 inches apart. Adjustable shelves may be preferable because they save space.

Bookcases commonly extend from a corner of a room to a door or window. From the construction standpoint, this is an excellent location because the boards that form the sides of the bookcase can be nailed securely to the wall at one end and to the door or window trim at the other. There is little chance that the weight of the books can bring down the bookcase. But if it is impossible to nail one end of a bookcase into something solid, you must anchor it to the back wall or ceiling. This can usually be done with large angle irons screwed to the sides and through the wall or ceiling into a stud or joist.

Erect the sides of the bookcase first; then the shelves. The bottom shelf rests on cleats nailed to the sides and on a toeboard which encloses the space underneath. If the other shelves are permanent (and are over 3 feet long), support the ends on cleats or shelf molding and place a third cleat under the back edge. It can extend the length of the shelf or be placed just under the midpoint.

If the shelves are adjustable, use L-shaped hangers or shelf-support strips at the ends; and if the shelves are over 3 feet long, support them at the middle of the back edge also. The hangers or support strips should be installed 1½ inches in from the front and back edges of the sides.

The space between the books on the top shelf and the ceiling is usually closed in. A fluorescent cornice light projecting in front of the shelves at the ceiling line may be installed to throw light downward on the books.

How to build cantilevered shelves. Cantilevered shelves have come into vogue in recent years because they are decorative and very easy to build. If properly constructed, they are sturdy enough to support considerable weight.

Slotted standards come in lengths up to 12 feet and are easily trimmed with a hacksaw. Conventional standards are designed to be screwed to the wall. Use the screws that come with the standards and install them in all screw holes. If walls are made of wood or plywood at least ½ inch thick, the standards can be installed anywhere; but if the walls are of gypsum board, plaster, hardboard, or thin plywood, the standards must be placed over studs and the screws driven into the studs. On masonry walls, the screws are driven into lead or plastic screw anchors.

In erecting the standards, make sure you have them right end up. Fasten the first standard to the wall at the top; then with a carpenter's level or a plumb line, position it straight up and down and drive in the bottom screw. After the remaining screws are in, install the next standard. Be sure it lines up exactly with the first. Don't trust your eye; don't try to measure down from the ceiling or up from the floor. Use a carpenter's level and draw a faint line across the wall from the top slot of the first standard to the top slot of the next.

Install the second, third, and all other standards like the first. A 32-inch spacing between standards is satisfactory for almost all cantilevered shelf arrangements; but if you are planning to store a great many books or records from floor to ceiling, a 16-inch spacing is better.

A special kind of slotted standard known as a Porta-Post can be used in apartments where you are enjoined from drilling too many holes in the walls. The post is bent outward at the bottom and rests on the floor. Thus much of the weight on the post is borne by the floor rather than the wall. Only a single screw at the top of the post is needed to hold it in place against the wall.

How to build a closet shelf. The average closet shelf is 12 inches deep and 68 inches above the floor. If made of wood, the cleats or shelf molding under the ends should extend from the back wall of the closet to the front so that they can be nailed securely to at least two studs. If the shelf is over 4 feet long, support the back edge also.

An easier way to build a closet shelf is to buy a prefabricated steel shelf with baked-enamel finish. These come in several adjustable lengths. They are quickly installed with two end brackets and a back-wall bracket.

How to build utility shelves. If you need one or two shelves, screw L-shaped brackets to a wall and screw a board to the top. If you need a bank of shelves, save time, energy, and money and buy knock-down steel shelves. Be sure to anchor the assembled unit to the wall; otherwise it may tip forward.

Another easy way to build utility shelves is to hang U-shaped shelf hangers from the joists.

How to build back-of-door shelves. These are useful for storing small items on the backs of hinged closet doors. Make them of ½-inch white pine boards no more than 4 inches deep or of tempered hardboard.

Cut the boards and nail them together to make a frame about 18 inches wide and 4 feet high (it can be slightly larger or smaller than this). Cut additional boards for shelves and nail them into the frame with finishing nails. Then cut strips of hardboard about 2 inches wide and 18 inches long, and fasten them to the fronts of the shelves with brads to keep things from falling on the floor. If you want to put a back on the shelves, use hardboard.

Attach small, flat, straight steel mending plates to the back edge of the two uprights. They should project above the top about 1 inch. Drive screws through these to hang the shelves on the door.

Shelf finishes. A good shelf must not only be strong but it must also be tough enough to resist scratching, spills, and the frequent washings needed to get rid of the dust and grease that are forever accumulating. This is one reason that glass shelves and steel shelves with a baked-on factory finish are desirable.

If wood shelves are painted, use semi-gloss or gloss enamel. For a clear finish, use urethane varnish. In situations where an extra-durable surface is required, cover the shelves with laminated plastic sheets or Class A vinyl wall covering.

Shelving paper. Shelving paper is unnecessary if you take the time to cover shelves that get hard wear and collect a lot of dirt with permanent plastic, as above.

If you don't do this, use one of the following: (1) Rubber sheeting. It is rather expensive and not as easy to wash as it should be; but it is excellent in china and glass cabinets because it cushions fragile articles. (2) Vinyl sheeting. It lies flat, won't tear like paper, and cleans readily. Some kinds have an adhesive backing. (3) Paper. Cheap, but a short-lived nuisance.

Shower Curtains. Shower curtains have two principal drawbacks: they allow water to escape from the shower and they mildew.

The first problem is readily solved by using two curtains on each tub or stall: one a decorative curtain hanging outside the tub, the other a lightweight vinyl liner on the inside. The liner can be made more effective in containing moisture if the bottom edge is weighted, preferably with magnets that will make it adhere to the side of any metal shower stall or tub made internally of iron or steel.

Mildewing of a shower curtain is almost impossible to prevent, even if you spread the curtain out after using the shower. You can slow the process considerably, however, if you rub a cloth dipped in a solution of chlorine bleach down the inner face of the curtain about once every two weeks. In addition, you should take the curtain down and wash it in detergent and bleach every two or three months.

Tears in curtains, which are now made almost entirely of vinyl, can be patched with a scrap of vinyl and plastic mending adhesive.

Shower Doors. Shower doors are made with chrome-plated steel or anodized aluminum frames and plastic or glass panels. The glass should be tempered to resist breakage, although in cheaper doors it usually is not. Because water spots, soap drips, and hand prints stand out on clear glass and plastic, you will save yourself a lot of cleaning if you use translucent or textured glass or plastic.

On shower stalls, the doors are customarily hinged to swing outward. A less common type of door is a bi-fold unit that opens inward like doors in telephone booths. All have some sort of arrangement to prevent water from leaking under the doors, but this is often ineffective.

Doors for shower enclosures over tubs are of several designs. In the most common type, two panels slide back and forth in a metal frame that fits from one end of the tub to the other. This is a very undesirable arrangement because you can clean only half the tub and walls at a time.

The two other types of door are better because they open wide to permit full view of and access to the tub and enclosure. One door is made of narrow panels which fold back to the ends of the tub accordion-fashion. The other door has two large panels hinged at the middle which fold back to the back of the tub like a bi-fold door.

All shower doors need to be washed down with water to remove spots. The bottom tracks in which tub doors slide must also be cleaned about every month to remove accumulated dirt, soap, etc. Use a detergent solution and an old toothbrush.

Shower Heads. Modern shower heads are resistant to clogging; but if trouble does occur, it is a simple matter to take them apart and clean them out. The way in which this is done varies with the design, but is obvious upon close examination.

In older shower heads, the water issues through small holes in the face of the head. These are likely to clog, particularly if the face is made of metal and your water contains sediment or is hard. To prevent this, unscrew the head every six months or so and flush it out. If the head is "frozen" to the pipe, stick a pin through the holes from below.

If it is difficult to adjust the direction in which a shower head is aimed, screwing the head slightly to the left relieves the pressure against the ball joint and allows you to swivel the head as you wish.

Shower Stalls. Many people prefer shower stalls to tubs with showers; but for most people, the principal advantage of stalls is that they take up relatively little space. Thus they make it possible to install a complete bathroom in tight quarters or to add a second bathing unit in an existing bathroom.

Of the two basic types of shower stall, the prefabs are the more popular because they cost less. Most are made of steel with a baked enamel or porcelain enamel finish. They range in size from about 30 to 40 inches square, and are available with glass or plastic doors or with an opening that you curtain.

One of the drawbacks of metal stalls—at least of the cheapest models—is that they may in time rust out. But this can be prevented by touching up chipped spots as soon as you find them with a metal primer and epoxy or porcelain glaze

New fiberglass stalls are an improvement over metal because they can be molded in one piece (not all are, however). This eliminates the joints between the stall walls and the base, known as a receptor. Because fiberglass is easy to shape, it also permits ingenious designers to make stalls in new shapes (one round model, for example, is shaped something like a conch shell and consequently does not require any door or curtain).

Shower stalls built from scratch in the bathroom are generally more luxurious than prefabs. You can have them built to any size and in any shape if the base is made of ceramic tile embedded in cement over a pan of sheet lead. But if you buy a prefabricated receptor of man-made "stone," the stall cannot be any larger than a metal or fiberglass prefab unit.

Walls of site-built shower stalls are almost always made of ceramic tile, which should be laid up in Portland cement. Sheets of laminated plastic or enameled hardboard might be used; but because it is difficult to make watertight corners with these materials, their use is not recommended.

Doors are of plate glass or plastic in chromium steel or anodized aluminum frames.

Tile shower stalls should remain watertight as long as the mortar joints are sound. So cast an eye on these from time to time, and fill them with tile cement whenever they crack open or begin to erode.

If a prefabricated receptor is installed, you should also watch out for leaks around the rim. (The same problem may occur in metal stalls.) Apply silicone caulking compound if any show up.

Shutters.

Exterior shutters. Louvered shutters for exterior use are made of wood, plastic, or aluminum.

Wood shutters must be painted or given a clear finish; and thereafter they need to be refinished about every three years. This is a tedious chore, even though the shutters are generally installed with hinges so they can be taken down to work on.

Plastic shutters are colored integrally and never need finishing. Aluminum shutters have a tough, baked-on finish which should last for years. However, neither looks "authentic." This is partly because they are too smooth and too perfectly formed and partly because they are mounted tight to the wall. (Because of this tight mounting, it is harder to paint the house walls around plastic and aluminum shutters than around movable wood shutters.)

Solid-paneled shutters of wood are also available. They are much easier to paint than louvered shutters but more expensive originally.

Probably the commonest mistake people make when installing shutters is to buy units that are too narrow in relation to the window. Shutters should be sized so that if they were closed, they would exactly fill the window opening. In other words, each shutter should be half the width of the window. Their height should equal the distance from the sill to the bottom of the top casing.

All exterior shutters soil rapidly and need to be washed once or twice a year. The best way to do this, especially if they are louvered, is to hose them down under a hard stream before you wash the windows.

Interior shutters. These are narrow, folding wood units. They may have adjustable louvers; or they may come with empty center panels in which you stretch a decorative fabric. In either case, the wood may be painted or given a clear finish.

The shutters can be used to cover only the bottom half of the windor or the entire window. If you use full-height shutters inside the frame, measure the width and height of the opening and order the exact size or the next size larger. For shutters that are mounted on the trim around the opening, measure the opening and order a pair of shutters 2 inches larger.

Inside shutters should be vacuumed about every other week to remove dust. Wipe them with a cloth dampened in mild detergent solution every month or so or use a white cleaning wax.

Also see *Sun Control.*

Sideboard. A large piece of dining-room furniture, with a tabletop for serving and usually storage drawers and cupboards. See *Drawers* and *Furniture, Wood,* for how to take care of a sideboard.

Silicone. Silicone is a tough, durable, water-repellent, weather-resistant plastic that can be used in the following ways:

As caulking around bathtubs and in other places where you require a sealant with great adhesiveness, flexibility, and durability. It can also be used to seal holes in such things as pails, ice buckets, and vases. Both white and clear types are available. Most brands are not paintable. See *Caulking.*

As an adhesive. See *Gluing.*

As an invisible, colorless damp-proofer on masonry walls. See *Walls, Brick,* and *Water Repellents.*

As a water-repellent coating for fabrics and leather. Applied by aerosol, it can also be used to protect metal against rust and tarnish.

As a lubricant to prevent squeaks in hardware and floor boards and to make windows and drawers slide more easily. (This is the same material as the water-repellent coating.)

As a flexible, long-life roofing material that is applied directly to a plywood deck. When reinforced with mineral aggregates, the same coating may be used to surface sun decks, porches, terraces, or the garage floor.

Silk. This very beautiful, lustrous, soft yet amazingly strong fabric deteriorates if it is not kept clean. Clothing, bedspreads, and draperies made of it should, therefore, be sent frequently to the dry-cleaner. Or you can launder them yourself if you handle them gently.

Use tepid water and a light-duty detergent. If hand-washing, avoid scrubbing. If machine-washing, use a slow agitator and spin speed. Dry over a line or in a dryer at low heat for about 15 minutes. Press with an iron set at moderate heat.

If white silks need to be bleached to get rid of a yellow cast, use hydrogen peroxide or sodium perborate only.

Silver. You can make a few minor repairs in silver knives, forks, and spoons (see *Flatware*), but let a silversmith take care of everything else. The metal is too valuable to play with.

When silverplate becomes worn, exposing the base metal, have the piece replated. The cost is modest.

To clean silver, use a good paste or liquid silver polish. Rub vigorously until a clean cloth will show no dirt. Use a soft toothbrush to get into crevices.

Electrolytic cleaners in which silver is dipped are effective, but over a long period they damage the metal. An ultrasonic cleaner may be used to remove dirt and tarnish, but you should apply a little polish afterwards to make the metal glow.

Tarnish is not preventable, but you can slow its development if you keep pieces in tarnish-resistant paper or silver bags.

Salt problems. Salt is an enemy of silver if left in contact with it for very long. To prevent trouble, make a practice of emptying silver salt cellars and shakers; that is, do not let salt remain in them overnight. Empty and rinse the pieces thoroughly. Silver salt spoons should also be washed after every use.

Glass liners in salt cellars provide little protection, because a few salt crystals inevitably work their way under them. Silver tops on glass salt shakers also become corroded in time even though the salt is not in constant contact with them. Consequently, you should wash these pieces very frequently.

Silverfish. See *Pest Control.*

Sinks. Kitchen sinks are made of porcelain enamel on cast iron, porcelain enamel on steel, and stainless steel. Despite the popularity of the last, they are more difficult to keep looking clean than enameled sinks, and in time become covered with tiny scratches. On the other hand, if you want a sink of special design, you are more likely to find it made in stainless steel than in porcelain. Of the enameled sinks, those made with cast iron are the better.

Except for special purposes, single-bowl sinks that drop into a 24-inch cabinet are about the smallest practical size. The largest single-bowl sink goes into a 33-inch cabinet.

Double-bowl sinks fit into cabinets ranging from about 33 to 54 inches wide. And triple-bowl sinks fit into cabinets from about 45 to 60 inches wide.

Most modern sinks do not have attached drainboards but a few do. In double- and triple-bowl sinks, there is wide variation in the size, depth, and even shape of the bowls. Several double-bowl sinks are designed for installation in corners.

Multi-bowl sinks are especially desirable if you don't have a dishwasher; but if you have a dishwasher, they lose much of their value. This is not to say that you would not find them useful, but it is quite possible that you would get greater use out of two single-bowl sinks placed in different parts of the kitchen. You could then use one sink almost exclusively for the preparation of food; the other for dishwashing, drink-mixing, flower-arranging, soaking kibbled dog food, children's hand-washing, etc.

Kitchen sinks are normally installed with the rim 36 inches above the floor. If you are very short or very tall, however, you can make a sink more comfortable to work at by lowering or raising it several inches. But a better solution, as a rule, is to install a sink with a bowl a little shallower than the standard 7½- or 8-inch depth.

In addition to kitchen sinks, several other types of sink are used in the home. Laundry sinks, also called laundry trays, have one or two very deep bowls. One of the newest models is a wall-hung unit made of thick, reinforced plastic. Bar sinks are very small, usually deep sinks with high gooseneck faucets. They have single or double bowls. Floor sinks resembling small, low-sided bathtubs are used for filling buckets, cleaning wet mops, washing pets, draining rain-soaked clothing, etc.

For bathroom sinks, see *Lavatories*.

How to correct sink problems. Flow of water from faucet is slow. The faucet aerator in the spout is probably clogged. Unscrew the aerator by hand, or if it is stubborn, wrap it with adhesive tape and use pliers. Remove the strainers from the aerator, noting the positions which each occupied, and wash them under running water to remove sediment. Then replace them in the same order and screw the aerator back on the faucet.

Faucets leak. See *Lavatories*; sink faucets are repaired in the same way.

Drain clogged. Kitchen sinks are most likely to be clogged by grease which congeals in the waste pipe well below the trap; however, if there is reason to believe the stoppage is in the trap, try steps 1, 2, and 3 for removing lavatory stoppages. See *Lavatories*.

If the stoppage is in the waste pipe below the trap: (1) Drop a tablespoonful of chemical cleaner down the drain, add a cup of cold water, and let it stand for 30 minutes. But do not use any chemical cleaner in a sink with a garbage disposer, because it may corrode the metals of the disposer. (2) If the chemical is not effective, pour boiling water with a little household ammonia into the drain to soften the stoppage. Then fill the sink partly with water, place the cup of a plumber's friend over the drain opening, and pump it up and down. (3) If the drain is still clogged, remove the U trap and insert a coiled spring auger in the drain. Crank it down through the pipe until you bore through the stoppage.

How to clean sinks. See *Stainless Steel* or *Porcelain Enamel*.

Sisal. Sisal is a strong, tough plant fiber which is used to make rope and rugs. Because it takes dye well, rugs made of it are available in many more colors than you usually find in similar kinds of rugs. The rugs are also very durable and can be used outside as well as in.

Clean and repair like straw (which see).

Skotch Fasteners. See *Wood Fasteners*.

Skylights. Skylights are not only an excellent means of illuminating dark rooms or dark corners of large rooms but also of venting the hot air under the roof. They permit installation of fewer and smaller windows. They even admit a view of the most glorious part of our world, the sky.

The most popular skylights are plastic domes. These come in a wide range of sizes; and in squares, rectangles, and rounds. They are mounted either directly on the roof or on frames a few inches above it. Some models can be opened.

For a summer cottage, a dome with a single plastic shell is adequate, but for a year-round home, use a double-shelled unit which prevents heat loss and condensation.

Other skylights adaptable to homes are flat, rectangular units that parallel the roof line. These can be mounted on flat roofs; but unlike the domes, are especially suited to steep roofs. They, too, come in many sizes and with either single or double glass or plastic. Some of the smaller units are hinged so they can be opened.

If prefabricated skylights are not to your liking, you can have special designs and sizes made for you—preferably out of insulating glass or perhaps glass blocks.

The worst problem with all skylights is that they admit too much light and glare when the sun is at its zenith. This is most easily solved by buying a skylight with a translucent plastic or glass. But this obliterates the view. So the next best thing is to install under a transparent skylight a cloth roller shade that can be pulled across the ceiling opening. You can also install shutters that can be opened at various angles.

All skylights and the surrounding roof should be checked regularly for possible leaks. The inner surfaces of kitchen skylights should be washed every six to twelve months with detergent solution to remove accumulated grease.

Sleeve Arms. These are slip-on covers for the arms on upholstered chairs and sofas. Their purpose: To protect the upholstery against soil and wear.

Sleeve arms are made to match the upholstery fabric exactly so that you can hardly tell they are in use. Depending on the fabric, they can be laundered or dry-cleaned.

Some homemakers make headrests for high-backed chairs in the same way.

Slipcovers. There are many reasons for slip-covering furniture: (1) To make an old worn-out piece presentable at low cost. (2) To conceal the bad features of a piece. (3) To change the appearance of a room in different seasons of the year. (4) To protect fine upholstery when there is no need for it to be on display. (5) To cover upholstery that is unpleasantly hot-feeling and hot-looking in summer. (6) To save money on a piece of furniture you need but can't immediately afford to upholster permanently.

Whatever your exact reasons for buying or making slipcovers, don't economize unwisely on the fabric. Money spent on a good grade of cotton, linen, sailcloth, barkcloth, glazed chintz—whatever you use—is in the long run money saved, because there is no reason why slipcovers shouldn't last for many years.

Of course, you must take reasonably good care of them. But this is easy since you can take them off in a minute or two for washing or dry-cleaning, or to remove stains or make minor repairs.

For how to wash and iron slipcovers, see *Laundering.* Follow stain-removal directions for treatment of stains; but before going to work on the stain, test the removal agent on the back of the slipcover.

Sofas. See *Furniture, Upholstered.*

Soil-Release Finishes. See *Fabric Finishes.*

Soil-Retardant Finishes. See *Fabric Finishes.*

Soldering. When you need to make a quick, easy, and permanent repair in metal or when you must join two pieces of metal, soldering is the answer.

All metals commonly found in the home can be soldered. Aluminum, stainless steel, and pewter, however, are difficult to work with; and you should avoid soldering silver because of its value.

Soldering is done with three different tools: (1) A soldering gun is a very fast, trigger-actuated tool used primarily for electrical work and other very small jobs. (2) A soldering iron is the nearest thing to a general-purpose soldering tool because it can be used on jobs ranging from very small to medium size. (3) A propane torch is used for plumbing work and other big jobs.

Solder itself is available as a paste and as a solid wire (you can also buy bars, but most people don't). The paste is brushed or squeezed on the metal before it is heated. It cleans and fluxes the metal as well as soldering it.

Wire solder—the kind usually used—may be a solid wire or may incorporate a core of flux (a material that is needed to remove oxides from metal before it can be soldered). Acid-core solder is used for general work; rosin-core solder for electrical work. If you use solid solder instead, you must first brush a rosin paste or liquid acid flux on the metal.

Special kinds of solder are needed for aluminum and stainless steel.

Two important points should be borne in mind about solder: (1) It will stick to metal only when the metal is heated hot enough. (2) It will come off metal any time the metal is again heated hot enough. In other words, you can easily close a cracked joint in the bottom of a teakettle with solder; but the joint will reopen if you put an empty kettle on a hot burner.

When you do any soldering, make sure you have a hot mat of some sort on which to rest your soldering iron. Make sure also that you will be able to use your torch without setting fire to anything. (Fires caused by plumbers soldering pipes in walls are not unknown.)

If you are soldering water pipes, drain them down below the point at which you are working. Don't under any circumstances try to solder anything containing gas.

Clean the metal thoroughly with steel wool or emery cloth. It should shine brightly. If you are joining two or more pieces of metal, both must be cleaned.

If you use a soldering iron, clean the tip, too. Rub it over sandpaper while it is warming up. If it isn't smooth, go over it with a file. When the tip is hot, hold wire solder against it until it melts and covers the entire tip. This is called "tinning."

Test the flame on a torch. It should be strong, steady, and mainly blue. If it isn't, clean the orifice according to the maker's directions.

Brush flux on the metal to be soldered if you are using solid-wire solder.

The secret of successful soldering is to get the metal (or metals) hot enough so that when you touch it with the solder, the solder will melt instantly, flow evenly, and harden to a smooth, bright finish. Note that the solder should be melted by the metal, not by the heat source.

Generally, when joining two pieces of metal, such as two wires or two strips, you should tin each of them separately. This is done simply by heating each piece and melting solder on it. After both pieces are tinned, put them together, tinned surface to tinned surface, and apply heat. Additional solder should not be necessary.

Plumbing work is an exception to the tinning rule. The main reason for this, obviously, is that if a pipe and a fitting are tinned, the tin will be too thick to allow you to assemble the pieces before they are heated; consequently, you may make an imperfect joint. It follows that when you join a pipe and a fitting, you must fit them together first. Then when you apply heat and solder, the solder will be drawn back into the joint by capillarity.

Once solder is applied, allow it to cool undisturbed for about a minute. This gives it ample time to harden. The metal can then be plunged into water or splashed with water to make it cool enough to handle.

Always clean with a wet rag metal to which acid has been applied.

Solvents. A solvent is a liquid substance which will dissolve another substance and thus permit its ready removal. The following solvents are effective for removal of the substances named after them:

Acetone—fingernail polish, airplane glue (don't use on acetates or rayons).

Alcohol—shellac, carbon paper stains, iodine, mercurochrome, grass stains.

Ammonia—greasy films, general soil.

Carbon tetrachloride—grease, oil, tar, candle wax, rubber cement, adhesive tape, chewing gum (extremely dangerous to use).

Cleaning fluids—grease, oil, tar, wax, adhesive tape.

Detergent solution—general soil.

Fingernail polish remover—fingernail polish (don't use on acetates or rayons).

Gasoline—grease, oil.

Glycerin—cod liver oil, lipstick, ink.

Kerosene—grease, oil, wax.

Lacquer thinner—lacquer, nail polish.

Muriatic acid (hydrochloric acid)—efflorescence, general soil.

Naphtha (benzine)—grease, oil, wax. Also oil and alkyd paint, varnish, floor seal (but works well only on a wet finish).

Paint thinner—same as naphtha but a little less potent.

Prepared paint remover—all types of paint and clear, nonpenetrating finishes.

Prepared wax remover—floor wax.

Rust remover—rust.

Turpentine—oil and alkyd paint, varnish, floor seal (but works only on a wet finish).

Vinegar—hard-water marks. Also many other things when used with a detergent.

Water—latex paint, water paint, and innumerable other things.

White appliance wax—grease, tar, soot, lipstick, heel marks, shoe polish, crayon.

For how to use solvents, see *Stain Removal*.

Source. Allied Chemical Corporation's name for an unusual carpet fiber made of nylon and polyester. The fibrils within it refract light much like a gem, thus giving a soft glow to carpets. The fiber also has excellent crush and abrasion resistance. It is cleaned like other synthetic carpet fibers. See *Rugs*.

Spackle. Spackle is a white filler used for

filling small holes, scratches, dents, and rough areas in almost any surface that is to be painted. (But use patching plaster in large, deep holes.) It is available as a dry powder and a paste.

The powder is mixed in small batches with water. When it begins to set in the mixing pan, it should be discarded. Clean the pan well before mixing new spackle—old and new material should never be mixed. A dry tint can be added to spackle during the mixing process.

Spackling paste is more expensive than dry spackle but more convenient because you don't have to mix it. It also dries more slowly. Keep the can covered tightly when not in use.

Spackle can be applied directly to plaster and interior masonry; but it should not be applied to wood, gypsum board, fiberboard, hardboard, or metal until they have been given a priming coat of paint. The surface in all cases should be clean and dry. It is not necessary to smooth the spackle too carefully with your putty knife, because it sands easily when dry.

Ordinary spackle should not be used outdoors because it is not waterproof. Use an interior-exterior spackle instead.

Spandex. A common stretch fiber widely used in making foundation and support garments. It can be washed and dried like cotton but should not be bleached with chlorine since this causes yellowing and breakdown of the fibers.

Spiders. See *Pest Control.*

Spode. Famous English china originally made by Josiah Spode and now made by W. T. Copeland & Sons. The first English bone china was turned out by the firm. Spode earthenware and stoneware are also produced. See *China.*

Sponges. A good grade of natural sponge is without equal for sopping up water, and it is very strong to boot. But most sponges used around the home are made of cellulose. They are cheap and expendable but do their job well.

A special kind of thin sponge, called a sponge cloth, somewhat resembles a large hot-mat. Made of cellulose reinforced with nylon, it can be used dry for dusting as well as damp for washing.

All sponges should be rinsed well after use. Wash them out frequently in detergent solution; otherwise they become rank and dirty.

Spot Removal. See *Stain Removal.*

Squeegees. The squeegee is a simple T-shaped tool which is indispensable for window-cleaning. The crossbar is edged with a strip of rubber which removes water from a pane of glass in one quick stroke and leaves it spotless. For how to use a squeegee, see *Windows.*

Squeegees are available in a range of sizes to fit virtually all small, standard-size panes exactly. You will save work and wash your windows better if you measure the width of your windowpanes and get a squeegee to fit each size. If your hardware store cannot supply the sizes you need, a window-cleaning equipment and supplies service can. Or you can buy what is available at the hardware store and trim them to size with a hacksaw and knife.

For picture windows and other large-paned windows, use a 12-inch squeegee. Larger sizes are available but are difficult to handle.

Squeegees should be used only on smooth, sound windowpanes. If a pane is cracked, the broken edges are likely to take a nick out of the rubber blades, thus rendering them useless because they will always leave a streak of water at the cut point.

A damaged blade can, however, be reversed or replaced. If making a replacement, it is best to buy ready-made blades, because they are cut precisely. But you can in an emergency make a blade out of a tire tube or rubber gasket material.

Dry squeeges after use. Don't toss them into a drawer with other articles that might damage the rubber. (Professional window cleaners keep their squeegees in special fitted cases.)

Squirrels. See *Pest Control.*

Staffordshire. A fine earthenware made in Staffordshire, England. See *Earthenware.*

Stainless Steel. This is a wonderfully tough, durable material, but it is difficult for fastidious people to live with because it shows water spots, looks blotched even after thorough washing, and gets covered with tiny scratches.

About the only thing you can do to keep it looking decent is to wash it with detergent solution and dry thoroughly. But you could also use a special stainless-steel cleaner.

Stain Removal. This section covers the treatment of stains on all fabrics except rugs and upholstery. For treatment of stains on these and other materials and articles, see *Rugs; Floors, Resilient; Brick; Wood,* etc.

Stain removal requires a small arsenal of removal agents, many of which are needed only a few times a year. While treatment methods vary, several rules apply universally:

1. Take action just as soon as you make or find a stain. All stains are harder to remove when old.

2. Before doing the laundry, always look for stains that you have missed. Pretreatment before putting the article in the washer simplifies removal. Furthermore, you should remember that some stains are set by hot water.

3. On colored fabrics, test liquid removal agents as well as bleach on a hidden corner before tackling the stain itself.

4. If a fabric is dry-cleaned rather than laundered, don't touch it with anything other than a cleaning fluid or absorbent powder.

5. If the stain is caused by something that is a combination of greasy and nongreasy substances (coffee with cream in it, for example), treat the fabric first for the nongreasy substance.

6. Never scrub too hard to remove a stain. For one thing, it won't get better results. For another thing, it may spread the stain and damage the fabric.

7. Keep stain-removal agents together in a handy place—usually the cleaning closet. If a spill occurs when you are not home, other members of the family are more likely to find the proper removal agent in a centralized collection than if they have to look all over the house for this and that.

·8. If you don't know what caused a stain, take the article to a cleaning establishment and let them worry about the problem. They can probably identify the stain and cope with it fairly easily.

Using solvents. Common solvents include water, detergent solution, naphtha, turpentine, ammonia, cleaning fluid, and fingernail polish. When using them, turn the fabric upside down—if possible—if the stain was caused by a greasy substance. Work on the fabric right side up otherwise. Place a pad of clean white cloth underneath to soak up the stain and the cleaning agent. Don't soak unless so directed; just moisten a clean cloth with the cleaning agent and rub the spot from the edges in. Use straight strokes. Blot the area frequently with a dry cloth to see what progress you are making and to soak up dirt. To prevent formation of a ring around the stain, finish the job by very, very lightly applying the cleaning agent to the area around the stain. Then blot the entire dampened area repeatedly and let it dry.

Using an absorbent powder. Powders are particularly useful in coping with fresh greasy stains on light- to medium-colored fabrics. On dark fabrics, they are equally effective but you cannot get rid of the powder mark. Some powders are applied by sprinkling; others by aerosol spray. The latter must be allowed to dry before you remove them. After the powder has had a chance to soak up the stain for a couple of minutes, blow off what you can and brush off the rest. Brush as much as possible from the edges of the spot in.

How to remove specific stains from washable fabrics. Adhesive tape. Pick off excess. Sponge with cleaning fluid.

Alcoholic beverages. White washable fabrics: Sponge with cold water; launder in hot. If stain persists or an old stain turns brown, treat it with bleach.

Colored washable fabrics: Sponge with cold water, then glycerin mixed with a little water. Let stand for a while. Rinse with 1 part white vinegar and 1 part water. Then rinse with water.

Blood. Soak in cold water for half an hour, then wash in warm water. Soak old stains in solution of 1 gallon lukewarm water and 3 tablespoons ammonia, then wash in warm water. If stains persist, use bleach. Or soak in enzyme presoaker.

Butter and margarine. See "Grease and oil, butter and margarine."

Candle wax. Scrape off excess with a spoon. Sponge with cleaning fluid. If any color remains, apply a bleach.

Catsup and chili sauce. Scrape off excess. Sponge with cold water or soak for 30 minutes. Rub laundry detergent into stain. Launder.

Cellophane tape. Scrape off excess and sponge with cleaning fluid.

Chewing gum. Chill in refrigerator or with an ice cube, then scrape off. Sponge with cleaning fluid.

Chocolate and cocoa. Sponge with cold water or soak for 30 minutes. Rub laundry detergent into spot, then launder in hot water (if safe for the fabric), using a bleach. If a grease spot remains, sponge with cleaning fluid. If colored stain remains, sponge with hydrogen peroxide. Then launder again.

Cod liver oil. Sponge or briefly soak in cleaning fluid. Then sponge with warm detergent solution and launder with a bleach safe for the fabric. For persistent stains, sponge with bleach, then launder.

Coffee and tea. Sponge or soak in cold water. If it is safe for the fabric, pour boiling water through the spot, stain side down, from a height of 1 to 3 feet. Launder. If boiling water can't be used, soak in a warm enzyme presoaker, then launder. If the coffee or tea contained cream, sponge with cleaning fluid.

Cosmetics. Rub laundry detergent into spot and launder. Then sponge with cleaning fluid if the cosmetics were greasy. Also see "Lipstick."

Crayon. Marks made by some types of children's crayon are washable in detergent solution. Sponge marks made by other crayons with cleaning fluid. Then launder.

Cream, milk, ice cream. Sponge or soak in cold water. Rub laundry detergent into spot, then rinse. If grease spot remains, sponge with cleaning fluid. If color remains, apply bleach. Or soak in enzyme presoaker.

Dye. If the stain is light and resulted from fabric running in the wash load, wash the article again. Then bleach remaining stain by soaking in warm water containing 1 tablespoon bleach per gallon.

Fruit. Sponge with cold water. Soak in enzyme presoaker. Launder.

Grass. Rub laundry detergent into spot and launder with appropriate bleach. Or you can sponge the spot with denatured alcohol and then wash.

Grease and oil, butter and margarine. Rub laundry detergent into the stain and let it stand for a half hour. Wash in warm water with ample detergent. If stain is still visible, sponge with cleaning fluid. (Note: Grease stains are difficult to remove from some permanent-press and synthetic fabrics, and may not be removable at all if set by heat or age.)

Ice cream. See "Cream, milk, ice cream."

Ink and ballpoint-pen ink. Sponge with cleaning fluid. Make a paste of laundry detergent and ammonia and rub on the stain. Rinse. Then apply bleach appropriate for the fabric.

Iodine. Sponge with alcohol. Wash in detergent solution. Bleach in the sun.

Lipstick. Sponge with cleaning fluid. Rub spot with laundry detergent until outline is removed. Then launder in hottest water and bleach safe for the fabric.

Meat juice and gravy. Scrape off excess and sponge with cold water. Soak in enzyme presoaker, then launder. If grease spot remains, sponge with cleaning fluid.

Mercurochrome. Act fast. Place in cold water at once and then mix 1 part alcohol and 2 parts water. Transfer fabric to this and soak for a while. Then launder. Apply bleach appropriate for the fabric.

Mildew. Rub detergent into spot and then launder. Then mix onion juice with salt (not iodized), moisten the spot, and allow it to bleach in the sun. For old stains, use hydrogen peroxide instead.

Milk. See "Cream, milk, ice cream."

Mud. Brush off when dry. Launder.

Mustard. Soak in cold water. Rub laundry detergent into stain, then rinse. If stain is still visible, soak in warm detergent solution for several hours. Launder, using a bleach safe for the fabric.

Nail polish. If the fabric is acetate or rayon and has not already been dissolved by the polish, sponge it with cleaning fluid—but not nail polish remover. Other fabrics may be sponged with nail polish remover. Then launder and apply bleach if any color remains.

Paint. Act fast. Blot up as much as possible with a dry cloth or paper towel. Then sponge with naphtha, turpentine, or paint thinner if paint has an oil or alkyd base; use water if it is latex or other water-based paint. Launder. Hardened paint may be impossible to remove. Try softening it with paint remover; then scrape it off and apply naphtha, etc.

Pencil. Remove what you can with a soft eraser. Then rub with detergent and launder. However, if the mark was made by an indelible pencil, sponge the stain first with cleaning fluid or alcohol.

Perspiration. Soak in an enzyme presoaker and then launder. If stain persists, dampen fabric and sprinkle pepsin on it; let stand for an hour. Then brush off and launder again.

Rubber cement. Let it harden; if you try to remove it while it is wet, you will just spread it further. Brush rubber cement from a jar on a sheet of paper, and when it is dry, roll it all up into a ball with your finger. Rub the ball on the spot on the fabric to take up as much as possible. Then sponge with cleaning fluid.

Rust. Sponge with 5 percent solution of oxalic acid or a mixture of lemon juice and noniodized salt. Dry in the sun. Then rinse very well and launder.

Salad dressing. Sponge with cold water. Work laundry detergent into the stain, then rinse. If grease remains, sponge with cleaning fluid. Launder again.

Scorch. This may be removable if the fibers are not seriously damaged. Wash in washing machine in the usual fashion, then apply appropriate bleach.

Shellac. Sponge with alcohol. Then launder.

Shoe polish. Scrape off excess. Work laundry detergent into the stain and then launder. If stain persists, sponge with turpentine, cleaning fluid, or alcohol.

Skin oils, hair dressings. Soak in enzyme presoaker and launder.

Soft drinks. Sponge with cold water. Rub laundry detergent into stain; then launder.

Tar. If the tar is fresh, pick off excess and sponge with cleaning fluid. If tar has hardened, rub it with petroleum jelly and let it stand for a while. Then use cleaning fluid.

Tea. See "Coffee and tea."

Tomato juice. See "Catsup and chili sauce."

Urine. Laundering generally does the trick. If not, sponge with 1 part white vinegar and 1 part water. Then wash.

Varnish. See "Paint."

Wine. Sponge with cold water. Soak in enzyme presoaker. Then launder.

Stains, Wood. Stains are used to change the color of wood without concealing the grain and texture. They are applied to furniture, floors, wall paneling, woodwork, and, in recent years, they have been widely used on house walls and other exterior surfaces.

The easiest stains to work with have an oil base. Some are clear; others, which contain a considerable amount of insoluble pigment, are opaque. The latter are often used on wood siding in preference to paint. They have good hiding power and penetrate rough wood especially well; but they do not completely conceal the grain. Two coats are needed on new wood. Application is made with a brush and no further work is necessary.

Clear oil stains used on wood siding color the wood but do not conceal its grain or texture. They last much longer than opaque stains and paint, especially on rough wood. Application is made with a brush. On rough wood, apply two coats, the second within thirty minutes of the first, if possible. On smooth wood, apply only one coat to start and let it weather for two years before applying a second coat.

Clear oil stains which are used on furniture and interior house surfaces are usually applied with a brush and allowed to soak into the wood for a few minutes. You then go over the surface with clean, dry rags to even out the finish and remove the excess stain. After the stain dries for 48 hours, you can apply a transparent finish such as varnish, shellac, or penetrating seal. If you want to achieve a deeper color, you must make a second application of stain before applying the final finish.

Another way to get a deeper color is to let the first coat of stain soak in longer. This is dangerous, however, unless you have prior experience with the stain on the same kind of wood and know to the minute how long it takes to produce a certain effect.

To get the same depth of color on end grain as on flat surfaces is difficult because the end grain soaks up stain thirstily. But you can slow this action by applying turpentine to the end grain before applying stain. This has the effect of diluting the stain.

Clear oil stains are also applied with a rag. Since you get less stain on the wood this way than with a brush, the soft wood fibers soak up less and match the hard fibers more closely.

Water stains are inexpensive, clear stains made by dissolving aniline dye in warm water. They are applied with a brush and then immediately wiped with rags. Even so, care must be taken to brush them on evenly so that laps do not show. When the surface has dried for at least 12 hours, it must be sanded to smooth down the grain, which is raised by the water.

Spirit stains are generally made with alcohol. They are like water stains except that they do not raise the grain. However, they are the hardest of all to apply because they dry in a few minutes; consequently, you must work on small sections at a time and brush the stain on fast and rub it off fast. Alcohol stains are used mainly under lacquer.

Stain Wax. Stain wax is a penetrating stain containing wax and available in various colors. With it you can give woodwork, wood paneling, and wood furniture an attractive natural finish in one step. On such surfaces, the material is adequately durable and easy to maintain. But despite manufacturers' claims, it is not durable enough for use on floors.

The finish must be applied to wood that is dry, clean, and smooth. Flow it on lightly and evenly with a brush. If it looks uneven, after 15 or 20 minutes, rub it with clean rags to remove and spread around excess finish.

To protect the finish or give it a higher luster, you may apply paste wax or liquid floor wax after the stain wax has dried for 24 hours. This is not necessary on surfaces that receive little wear, however.

Stairs. See *Steps.*

Staplers. See *Tools, Workshop.*

Staples. See *Wood Fasteners.*

Static Electricity. Static electricity is an annoyance in cold, dry weather. After washing, synthetic fibers cling tenaciously to one another and to the body. And if you touch a doorknob or another person after walking across a wool or nylon carpet, you get a small shock.

To prevent static in laundered articles, add a fabric softener or anti-static agent to the rinse water (see *Laundering*).

Static in carpets can be minimized by raising the humidity of the house in winter. If this does not solve the problem satisfactorily, apply an anti-static spray such as Statikil (J. E. Doyle Co., 124 West Sixth Street, Cleveland, Ohio) or State Eze 5 (Fine Organics, Inc., 205 Main Street, Lodi, New Jersey) to the carpets.

Steam/Press Valet. A hand-size, book-like electrical appliance for steam-creasing trousers and pleated skirts, pressing ties, and touching up other articles. No ironing board is required. After filling a reservoir with water, steam is applied at the push of a button. Two pressing plates automatically provide correct ironing pressure.

Steel. If you are going to prevent steel from rusting, you must keep it dry. Even galvanized steel will rust if it is exposed to moisture after the zinc that originally protected it begins to wear thin.

The only way to protect raw steel, as used in workshop and garden tools, is to dry it thoroughly as soon as possible after it gets wet. Thereafter, if it is stored in a humid atmosphere, you should rub it with an oily cloth or apply a thin, even spray of light oil.

Steel that is constantly exposed to moisture should be protected with paint. First clean it to remove all signs of rust, grease, etc. Then apply a rust-inhibiting primer and one or two coats of interior or exterior enamel.

Galvanized steel should be allowed to weather for six months before it is given two coats of zinc dust paint. Galvanized steel screen wire should weather in the same way. It then needs one coat of zinc dust paint. This should last for several years.

Once steel is painted, take a look at it now and then to make sure the paint film is intact. If broken, and rusting has started, remove the rust by scraping and sanding; then rub with a liquid or jellied rust remover. Finally apply a primer and finish coat of paint.

Steel surfaces that are badly pitted and thin steel sheets with small holes can be mended satisfactorily with plastic steel after thorough cleaning. Repair breaks in steel with acid-core solder.

If a semi-flexible steel tool, such as the blade of a shovel or head of a rake, is bent, put it in a vise and do what you can to bend it back by hand. Hammering may help.

Steel Wool. See *Abrasives.*

Stemware. Glasses mounted on stems are called stemware. They should be handled with unusual care because the bowl easily breaks off from the stem where they are joined. When this happens, it is possible to rejoin the sections with epoxy glue, but despite the strength of the glue, the glass is likely to break again. For how to care for stemware, see *Glassware.*

Steps.

How to build. Unless you are an experienced carpenter, don't attempt to build a finished flight of stairs. It's a major job. Most repairs are also difficult to make. There is no reason, however, why you shouldn't build simple, straight flights of stairs in the garden, for example, or to get up into unused attic space over the garage.

Wood steps. Wood stairs are supported on stringers cut out of 2-by-12-inch timbers. You need two stringers for fairly narrow steps; three for wide steps. The stringers are notched in the manner illus-

NOTCHED STRINGERS
FOR WOOD STEPS

trated. Precut stringers are sold in many lumber yards.

Generally steps are 7 inches high and 10 inches deep or 8 inches high and 9 inches deep. At the top, the stringers should butt firmly against two 2-inch timbers, called a double header. At the bottom they should rest squarely on poured concrete bases.

The treads are best made of 2-inch-thick lumber, but you can use 1-inch if the stringers are spaced only 15 inches apart.

All flights of more than two steps should, for safety's sake, have a handrail 32 inches high.

Concrete steps. If the steps are up a bank, remove 6 inches of soil from the slope. Lay two oiled boards up the bank to form the side rails of your form. The boards must be wider than the height of the risers. Nail oiled boards between the rails where you want to place the risers. Brace the entire form well to keep the boards from spreading outward. Then pour in concrete and strike the treads off level with the riser boards. After the concrete has set for about 30 minutes, bevel the edges of the treads with a mason's trowel. Do not remove the forms for a week.

If steps are to be built against a vertical surface, such as a wall, dig out a space at the base of the wall 12 inches deep. (If the soil is not well drained, dig deeper and fill partway with gravel.) Pour a rough base of concrete and level it off just below the ground line. Allow this to set for 24 hours. Then build your steps with concrete blocks and mortar. Lay the blocks with hollow core up. When the steps are formed, let the mortar set 12 hours or more. Then fill the hollows with small stones, broken bricks, etc., and trowel a ½-inch layer of mortar over each step to form the tread. Bevel the edges after the mortar has set slightly.

Brick and stone steps. First build concrete steps. Then surface the treads with bricks or flagstones laid in a ½-inch bed of 1:3 Portland cement mortar. The edges of the treads should project about ½ to 1 inch beyond the risers and sides of the steps. Don't bother to cover the risers and sides with brick.

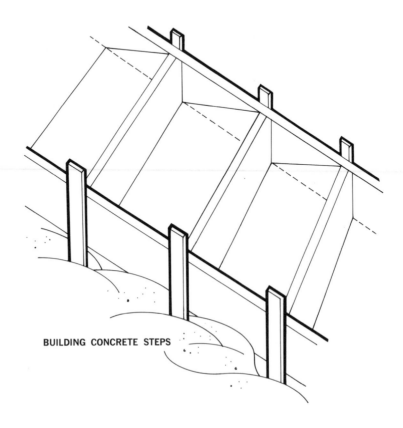

BUILDING CONCRETE STEPS

How to repair steps. If wood treads creak. Drive finishing nails through the treads diagonally into the risers. Countersink the heads and cover with plastic wood.

If edges of concrete steps are broken. Brace a board flat against the riser. The top edge of the board should be level with the tread. Then trowel latex, vinyl, or epoxy cement on to the broken concrete and strike it off level with the board.

If mortar joints in brick and stone steps are weak. Clean them out and fill with latex cement.

If wood balusters are wobbly. If the balusters are dovetailed into the treads, force white wood glue into the joints. If the balusters are toenailed to the treads, secure them with additional nails. To prevent possible splitting of the wood, drill a small hole through the baluster for each nail.

If iron railings come loose from masonry steps. Loosen the post completely by chipping out around it and by wobbling it back and forth. Clean out the hole in the step. Then fill it with epoxy cement and reset the post.

How to protect indoor stairs against unnecessary damage. If you finish the treads in tough urethane varnish and keep them coated with nonskid wax, they will not show excessive damage for several years. Sooner or later, however, you will have to strip off the varnish and apply a new coat. When finishing stair treads, apply the finish to every other tread one day; the alternate treads the next day. This way you will always have dry steps to walk on.

Risers can be protected permanently by gluing laminated plastic sheets to them with contact cement. The plastic will show heel marks, but can be cleaned quickly with a strong detergent solution or cleanser.

Carpeting stairs is a more attractive way to protect them but also more expensive. An alternative is to cover them with a textured vinyl runner.

Individual stair treads of vinyl, rayon, or rubber are also available for use on back stairs and basement stairs.

Cleaning steps. This is a wearisome chore for which there is no simple solution. Vacuum stairs at least once a week with a small dusting tool; and at the same time vacuum the floor or treads around the balusters and the balusters themselves if they are curved.

Clean risers every month or two with a cloth dampened in detergent solution or use a spray-on detergent.

Apply nonskid buffable wax to exposed wood stair treads about every four months, and buff monthly between applications.

Wipe railings and balusters with mild detergent solution once a month. Or use a white cleaning wax.

Stereos. See *Record Players.*

Stone. Stone is fun to build with because it challenges the ingenuity and imagination. And walls and floors and fireplaces built of it can be, if skillfully executed, magnificent.

Working with stone. Cut stones are considerably easier to work with than uncut stones. In a wall, they are laid very much like bricks. In paving, they are simply laid side by side. (If you are paving an area with assorted sizes and shapes of stones, however, you should ask the masonry supplies dealer to give you a carefully worked-out, numbered plan showing where each stone is to go; otherwise you will spend hours developing your own plan and cutting stones to fit.)

Building with natural stones is a study-and-try operation. If you are sticking the stones together with concrete, you can, of course, do things with them that you cannot do with loose stones. Nevertheless, it is always best to fit each stone into its proper niche.

Unlike some masonry materials, stones need not be damp when they are laid because they do not draw moisture out of mortar. They should be cleaned thoroughly, however. Use a mortar of 1 part Portland cement and 3 parts sand. The joints should be no less than ½ inch thick; but they may have to be much more to compensate for any irregularities in the stones. In a wall, if the stones are rectangular or reasonably so, place a bed of mortar on the stones previously laid; butter mortar on one end of the stone being laid; and press it into place. If the stones are irregular, however, just make a bed of mortar and press the stone firmly into this. Then slush mortar around the sides and back.

In paving, stones can be laid on sand or in concrete. In the latter case, after they are pressed into the mortar bed, trowel mortar into the vertical joints and strike it off flush with the tops of the stones.

If you get a skin of mortar on smooth stones, wipe it off with a wet rag at once. On rough stones, remove as much as possible; then after it has dried, scrub it with a wire brush and/or a solution of muriatic acid.

How to repair stone structures. If mortar joints are weak or broken, chip out the mortar and blow out the crumbs. Fill with latex cement or 1 part Portland cement and 3 parts sand.

Hairline cracks in mortar joints can be sealed by brushing on a soupy mixture of cement and water.

If a stone is loose, lift or chip it out of its setting. Scrape down or remove the old mortar that held it. Then coat the stone or the setting with a thin layer of latex cement and replace it. Fill any voids that remain in the joint.

How to repair stone ornaments. If they are broken in two, clean the edges thoroughly; apply silicone rubber adhesive to one of them; and then clamp or weight the two pieces together for 24 hours.

If an ornament is cracked but not broken, leave well enough alone unless it is leaking. In that case, scratch the crack open very slightly and fill it with a slender bead of epoxy glue.

How to clean stone. Follow directions for cleaning bricks (see *Brick*).

Finishing stone. This normally is not done because it conceals the natural beauty of the material. If circumstances are extenuating, however, apply latex or Portland cement paint as in the case of concrete block (which see).

Stone walls that are not completely watertight can be improved by applying a colorless silicone damp-proofing sealer. This must be renewed every year or two, since it loses effectiveness when it ages.

Coating paving stones with a transparent masonry sealer protects them against staining and also makes them easier to clean.

Stoneware. Also called stone china, stoneware is a very hard, non-water-absorptive type of pottery. It was originally used for such things as mugs, jugs, crocks, kitchenware, and other simple articles, and was often not glazed. But today decorative glazed stoneware for the table is made and sold everywhere. It is usually between china and earthenware in cost.

Stoneware can be washed in the dishwasher. If broken, you should mend it with epoxy glue if the piece is used and washed often. Use cellulose cement otherwise.

For a discussion of what stoneware a family should buy, see *Dinnerware*.

Storage Walls. A storage wall is any reasonably large, high wall incorporating a solid bank of storage units such as closets, cabinets, drawers, and shelves. Some storage walls are nothing more than a row of closets or cabinets built along one side of a room. Many others serve as room dividers and have a variety of storage units.

Other differences between storage walls: Some go all the way to the ceiling; others do not. Some are nailed permanently into place; others are movable. Some are built in one complete unit; others are an assembly of cubes—like a lot of boxes stacked together and then nailed. Some open only to one side; others to both sides.

Three similarities between storage walls: They are almost always made of wood or plywood. They rarely serve as bearing walls. And they are always meant to provide a lot of well-organized storage space in relatively small floor space.

Storing. See *Attic Storage; Basement*

Storage; Cleaning Closets; Clothes Closets; Linen Closets. Also see entries for the particular articles you wish to store, such as rugs or screens.

Storm Doors. Most storm doors are combination storm and screen doors made with aluminum or sometimes wood frames. The glass and screen panels set into the frame are interchangeable.

Wood-framed doors with fixed glass panels are also in use but are rarely sold anymore.

In wood-framed doors, glass panes are held in place by wood strips rather than putty. Use care in prying them out because they are not very strong. Broken glass in aluminum doors should be replaced by a dealer.

For how to repair storm doors, see *Doors.*

Clean, paint, and store storm doors like storm windows (which see).

Storm Windows. The most desirable storm windows are invisible. They are ordinary windows with insulating glass. Unfortunately, windows made this way come only with large panes or with large panes covered on the inside by removable mullions. (See *Windows.*)

All other storm windows are separate units which should be installed only on the outside of your regular windows. This means they cannot be used to protect casement, awning, and jalousie windows, all of which open outward. True, it is perfectly possible to install storm sash on the inside of these windows in place of the screens; but if you did this, condensation would form in winter on the windows rather than on the storm sash. (Condensation always forms on the coldest surface.) This, in turn, would ruin the finish on the windows.

Of the separate storm windows, the combinations (combination screens and storm windows) are the best although they are anything but attractive. They are made with aluminum frames that are permanently screwed to the exterior window frame of double-hung windows. The most popular combinations have three tracks—one containing a screen panel covering half the window; the other two containing glass panels equal in size to the two window sash. In winter, the glass panel in the outermost track covers the upper half of the window; the glass panel in the middle track covers the bottom of the window; and the screen panel, which is in the innermost track, is pushed to the top of the window (it may also be removed entirely). In summer, the screen panel is pulled down to the bottom of the frame; and both glass panels are stored in the top of the frame.

Storm windows that are put up in the fall and taken down in the spring are made either with wide wood frames or with very narrow aluminum frames. The former are heavy and unsightly, but sturdy. They are hinged to the top casing so that they can be opened to let in air. Metal adjusting arms hold them secure.

Aluminum-framed storm windows are much more attractive and lighter. They also can be hinged at the top and held open with adjusting arms; but unfortunately, the special hinges used are not very reliable and the windows are often torn off by strong winds. Because of this, many people simply screw the windows into the window frames so they cannot be opened. On casement windows, the storm sash are screwed to the window sash itself.

All storm windows should be washed like regular windows. It is easiest to do the job in the fall. Take the glass panels out of combinations.

Wood frames should be painted with exterior trim enamel every three or four years. The best aluminum frames have a baked-on factory finish which rarely needs repainting. Frames with natural aluminum finish can be left as is, but look better if painted or covered with clear lacquer. See *Aluminum.*

For how to replace broken glass in a wood-framed storm sash, see *Windows.* If the storm sash is made of aluminum, let a dealer handle the job.

Reinforce weak joints in wood frames with steel mending plates.

Keep adjusting arms clean and free of rust and paint. Oil them in the fall.

Store storm windows like screens (which see).

Straw. Straw of several kinds is woven into rugs, table mats, pocketbooks, hats, and many other articles. To clean it, sponge with mild detergent solution and dry in the sun or in a very airy place.

Straw rugs should be vacuumed frequently (use suction only) to remove dirt and grit that settles in the interstices. Lift the rugs every couple of months and vacuum underneath.

If pieces of straw are broken, glue the ends together or patch them with a small piece of straw. Use white wood glue. Or you can cut out the piece entirely: you will probably not notice that it is missing.

Stretch Fabrics. Elasticity is imparted to yarn in several ways, and when such yarns are woven into fabric, the fabric itself becomes elastic.

It might be thought that such fabrics would be damaged by laundering, but this is rarely the case. They can be machine-washed—usually in warm water—and dried in a dryer at low heat. Chlorine bleach should not be used with articles made of spandex, however, because it causes yellowing and degradation.

String. See *Twine.*

Stucco. See *Walls, Stucco.*

Studs. Devices for attaching things to masonry walls (see *Wall Anchors*). The vertical timbers—usually 2-by-4s—in walls are also called studs.

Styrene. Also known as polystyrene, this is a rigid plastic which is used to make a great variety of articles ranging from toys and food containers to wall tiles and small radio cabinets. It has many desirable characteristics but it can be broken fairly easily and is damaged by cleaning fluids, gasoline, and nail polish.

Clean with a sponge dipped in detergent solution. Do not use abrasives. Mend broken articles with plastic-mending adhesive.

Suede. Suede is a soft, velvety-feeling leather that has not been dressed. It soils in a flash and is very difficult to clean. Send it to a dry-cleaning establishment.

Suede that is treated with a soil-retardant finish resists dirt and stains better than ordinary suede. The finish must, however, be applied by the manufacturer of the suede article.

Sun Control. Few things are more delightful than a house bright with sunshine. But the heat and ultraviolet rays that stream through the windows with the sunbeams often raise indoor temperatures to unbearable heights and fade furnishings and floors.

Fortunately, control is not difficult although it is not always attractive.

The windows that most need protection are those facing south and west. Sunshine enters south windows from a low angle in winter and from a high angle in summer; but it enters west windows from a low angle the year round. It follows that the best way to shade west windows is to erect a vertical screen between them and the sun. Similar screening can be used for south windows—and is especially desirable in winter. However, since we usually welcome sunlight in the house in winter, the normal practice is to shield south windows with some sort of horizontal shield projecting out over them.

Various ways of shielding windows are described below. One thing you should note about all of them is that they are designed to turn back the sun at the windowpanes. If the sun rays pass through the glass, they raise the indoor temperature even though the windows are covered on the inside with blinds, shades, or draperies made of metallized fabric.

Trees are the prettiest and best sunshades of all. If they grow large, they can be planted some distance from the house and still give excellent protection for most of the year. Evergreens are effective in all months; but many people prefer deciduous trees because they let in the sun in winter.

Vines are more troublesome to care for than trees but do much the same kind of shading job. They can be grown vertically, horizontally, or both ways. One problem, of course, is that you must erect something for them to grow on.

Shutters are a nuisance because you must close and open them daily unless you like living in a cave. But there is no question about their effectiveness. Those with adjustable louvers are most desirable because they permit you to let in air and light.

Blinds that roll down over windows are also a nuisance. Made with wood or vinyl slats or slender canes of bamboo, they are less durable than shutters and have a tendency to get out of adjustment. They are useful, however, for protecting porches against the sun.

Sliding panels are sometimes used on modern houses to cover large glass walls. The panels may be made of expanded aluminum or pierced wood. They are designed to filter the sun rather than shut it out completely.

Awnings are especially desirable for southern windows because they screen out the high summer sun completely and they screen out most of the low winter sun. Canvas awnings are preferable to permanent metal or vinyl units because they are more attractive and can be adjusted. They are expensive and perishable, however.

Eyebrows are horizontal projections that are a permanent part of the house. They are installed over southern windows only, and are almost always made of wood. Expanded aluminum may be used, however. There is almost no limit to how they can be designed—with lath-like strips parallel to the house walls; wide board louvers parallel to the walls; three-dimensional eggcrates; etc.

Heat-absorbing glass also reduces glare and minimizes fading of materials inside the house. Because the glass is usually ¼-inch plate glass, its use is limited mainly to large picture windows. It is tinted several colors which, of course, distort the view from outside and inside.

Plastic-coated glass does the same job as heat-absorbing glass. The plastic can, however, be applied to windows of all types and sizes, including existing windows. One kind of plastic coating is a liquid that is flowed on the glass. The other coating is an aluminized film that is bonded to the inside of the glass. Both must be applied by trained servicemen. Once they are dry, they can be washed by normal methods.

Sweeping. Save your broom for sweeping the kitchen, basement, garage, terrace, porch, and front walks; it is of little value on rugs and in rooms full of furniture.

Sweeping is also of little value—even on smooth, hard floors—if you wield the broom so violently that you scatter the dirt instead of collecting it. Use short, slow, sweeping strokes, always bringing the dirt to one or more central points. Then pick it up in a dustpan and drop it into a wastebasket. Working outdoors on a breezy day or when the ground is littered with leaves, you will find you save work if you carry a wastebasket with you and empty into it frequently as you go along. See *Brooms.*

Sweeping Compound. A sticky, sawdust-like material used to help pick up dust and dirt from floors. It is scattered on the floor, then swept up. It can be reused until it becomes so dirty that it no longer holds dirt.

Table Linens. It's true, as some casual homemakers contend, that table linens are unnecessary, a nuisance. You can get along perfectly well with paper napkins and mats. But who doesn't want to dress up the dining table for an occasion? Actually, most women never have too many table linens. They look at them in the same way they look at handkerchiefs and dresses: they are always delighted to be given more.

Tablecloths. Colorful informal cloths have almost completely replaced the formal white cloths of the past; but the best tablecloth material is still damask linen. For durability and beauty it is unbeatable; but you must work to keep it looking its best. So it is hardly surprising that most tablecloths now sold are of easy-to-launder permanent-press fabrics or vinyl, which wipes clean with a damp sponge.

Tablecloths are square, rectangular, round, or oval. Sizes vary widely.

Mats. Mats are made of linen, vinyl, rayon, vegetable fiber—just about anything. Although sizes and shapes vary, rectangular mats measuring 12 by 18 inches are usually large enough to protect the table under a table setting incorporating a dinner plate, side plate, cup or glass, knife, fork, and spoon.

For everyday use, mats that can be wiped clean with a sponge are obviously the most practical.

Table pads. You don't need a table pad if you use hot mats to protect your table against hot dishes. But without mats, a pad is essential. It also protects the table against scratches and spills.

You can cut out your own pad from white plastic with urethane backing. Since the pads are flexible, they can be folded any which way when they are stored. Much better pads are thin, stiff boards that fold into rather large sections. These are made of felt, usually have a wood-grained vinyl top and a cotton backing, and may contain a layer of aluminum foil as further insulation. A few standard sizes are available. Others are made to order by large stores.

Note that a silence cloth of cotton felt is not a complete substitute for a table pad because it gives no protection against heat or liquid. It does, however, prevent nicks.

Napkins. Napkins are made of the same materials as tablecloths, except they do not come in vinyl. Dinner napkins range from 17 to 22 inches square. Luncheon napkins are smaller and more variable.

Napkins are generally sold in sets of four, six, eight, or twelve.

Tables. For the general care of tables and how to refinish them, see the various entries under *Furniture.* Some additional dos and don'ts about table care follow:

When a leaf is raised on a drop-leaf table, make sure that it is fully supported underneath. Similarly, on a table with folding legs, make sure the legs are locked securely when opened.

If using a table to write on, put some sort of cushioning material on the table top. Ballpoint pens and hard pencils often leave impressions in a wood table top.

Don't wrap packages, cut fabric, build models, or do any work that might damage the surface, on a fine table without covering it. An old mattress pad makes a good topping.

If a table top is covered with plate glass, be sure that liquids do not seep underneath. Trapped under the glass, they are often hard to see; and if not detected and wiped up quickly, they damage the finish.

Do not clamp anything to a table top, such as an old meat grinder, without protecting the wood on both sides with pieces of hardboard or thin plywood.

In a nest of tables, if the tables do not slide in and out easily, don't try to force them: the wood is swollen and you will end up damaging the tables. Let them dry out near the furnace.

Table sizes. These are extremely variable. The best way to decide what size table you need is to allow 24 inches of space along the rim of a round or oval table for each person. (To measure the circumference of a round table, multiply the diameter by 3.14.)

Provide the same amount of space for each person at a square or rectangular table. However, if you intend to seat people all the way to the end on the long sides of a table, you must allow extra space at both ends on the short sides of the table for comfort.

How to repair tables. If a top is loose on a central pedestal, remove the pedestal and reglue the pieces. You may have to reinforce the joint with angle irons.

If a table leg wobbles, cut a triangle out of a thick piece of hardwood. Notch it to fit around the leg and screw it to the frame. This same repair is made on certain kinds of chairs.

For repairs to damaged veneer, see *Veneer.*

If the top of a card table is torn or burned, remove the top from the frame in which it is set. (This is done in various

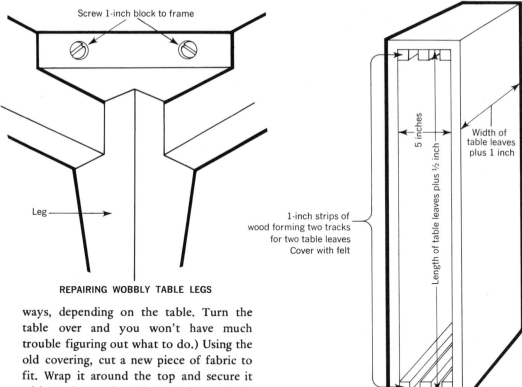

Screw 1-inch block to frame

Leg

REPAIRING WOBBLY TABLE LEGS

5 inches

Length of table leaves plus ½ inch

Width of
table leaves
plus 1 inch

1-inch strips of
wood forming two tracks
for two table leaves
Cover with felt

STORING DINING TABLE LEAVES

ways, depending on the table. Turn the table over and you won't have much trouble figuring out what to do.) Using the old covering, cut a new piece of fabric to fit. Wrap it around the top and secure it with staples or glue. Then set the top back in the frame.

How to store dining table leaves. To protect leaves from scratches and warping, store them in an upright box made of ¼-inch plywood. The box should be about ½ inch longer than the leaves, about 1 inch deeper, and about 5 inches wide. Cut six 1-inch-square strips of wood equal in length to the depth of the box. In the bottom end, nail one strip in each corner and a third in the middle. You thus form two tracks, or grooves. Nail the other strips in the top end of the box in the same way. Mold a piece of felt into the grooves in each end and secure it with white wood glue. To store the table leaves, simply slide one into each opposing top and bottom track.

Tableware. This is what you eat with and serve with. Depending on your taste and pocketbook, you may buy sterling silver, silverplate, or stainless steel.

No one can say exactly what pieces you need or how many. That depends on what you can afford, on what you like to eat, and on the way you entertain. You should

also consider how careful or careless you are with your belongings. If you have a habit of losing things, you should make allowance for that when you are buying tableware because filling in later on may be difficult: many patterns have a rather short life.

Certainly you should try to acquire the following pieces. The figures are simply a suggestion of how many it would be nice to have.

Dinner forks	12
Salad forks	12
Dinner knives	12
Butter knives	12
Teaspoons	24
Coffee spoons	12
Cream soup spoons	12
Tablespoons	3
Salad servers	2
Pie server	1
Gravy ladle	1
Sugar spoon	1

For how to take care of tableware, see

Silver or *Stainless Steel.* For how to repair tableware, see *Flatware.*

Tacks. See *Wood Fasteners.*

Taffeta. A fine, lustrous fabric that makes a rustling sound. Some fabrics have a slight ribbed effect. Taffeta is used in clothing, curtains, and bedspreads; is made of silk, rayon, nylon, and wool. It is usually best dry-cleaned.

Tape-Recording Equipment. The magnetic tape used for recording is very hardy. It doesn't warp, it doesn't become scratched, and there is little deterioration from repeated playing. But it can become distorted if mistreated, and stretch or break under tension and rough handling.

There are three general kinds of tapes. In the reel-to-reel ("open reel") type, used with the larger, more sophisticated recording equipment for the finest sound reproduction, the tape runs from one reel to another on the machine. Cartridge tape is one continuous loop of tape enclosed in a small case or cartridge about 4 by 6 inches. These are used for the most part for playback of prerecorded material, and are often used in automobiles. Cassette tape, the newest, is packaged in a small, flat case, and is threaded on two small reels; the ends of the tape are fastened to the reels for easy rewinding without re-threading. The tape and reels never leave the case. These are used both for recording and playback in some of the new, compact portable recorders for travel and for home and office use.

Open-reel tape should be stored in its own box to protect it from dust or damage to tape edges. The boxes should stand upright rather than in a stack. Stacking is safe for just a few reels, but if too many are stacked, the weight can distort the plastic reels or damage their edges. Tape to be stored should be wound at moderate tension. Excessive tension during storage will cause stretching and distortion of sound. If tape has been stored six months or more, rewind it before using to release stress.

Cassettes have their own protective storage boxes. Clips are available to snap over the exposed end of cartridge tape.

Parts of tape equipment that need periodic attention. Recorder heads (the parts that contact the tape when recording, playing back, and erasing), tape guides, and any other part that touches the tape directly must be cleaned periodically. These parts accumulate metallic particles from the coating on the tape, causing a build-up that affects sound quality and may prevent complete erasure of recorded material. It's best to use a product designed specifically for cleaning these parts, rather than carbon tetrachloride or other cleaning fluids. Most of the special cleaning products are liquids applied with a cotton-tipped swab.

The recorder heads also must be de-magnetized occasionally, since they become slightly magnetized from the tape. This magnetic build-up on the heads can add noise and "hiss" to the recorded tape, and can even erase part of a recording as it is being played. There are inexpensive and simple-to-use devices available to demag-netize heads. Check your operating manual for tips on how to demagnetize and how often. Some recorders demagnetize them-selves automatically.

Tape equipment should be covered to protect it from dust when not in use. Take the tension off mechanical parts during storage by being sure the unit is in the "stop" or "off" position.

Tapes. Adhesive-coated tapes are almost as essential to running the house as string and nails. Most are coated with pressure-sensi-tive adhesive. The following are especially useful:

Aluminum-foil tapes made of metal with an adhesive backing seal holes in gutters, flashing, etc.

Carpet tapes are made of cloth covered on both sides with adhesive. They are glued to the bottom edges of a rug and then stuck to the floor to anchor the rug. The adhesive is strong enough to remove the finish from some wood floors.

Cellophane tapes of the clear type are used for miscellaneous packaging and mending jobs. A similar tape made of poly-propylene is even more transparent and will not turn yellow with age. Cellophane tapes with adhesive on both sides are available.

Electrical tapes for insulating bare wires. The original electrical tape was a black cloth material which did not stick too well. Newer tapes are made of smooth black vinyl. Use the all-weather type of vinyl.

First-aid tapes. White cloth tapes used for bandaging wounds. They can also be used for other things if necessary.

Masking tapes are brown paper tapes used by painters to cover surfaces they don't want to paint. The tapes can be applied and pulled off very easily, and leave no residue if removed promptly.

Package-wrapping tapes. The least expensive have an adhesive that is wet with water or the tongue. The newest are coated with pressure-sensitive adhesive.

Tapestry. A heavy fabric in which a strong pattern is woven. It is used in draperies, hangings, and upholstery, and is made of various fibers. It must be dry-cleaned.

Tartan-Clad. Minnesota Mining & Manufacturing Company's name for a vinyl material that is used to surface furniture and other things. See *Vinyl Veneer*.

Teakettles. Teakettles are made of porcelain-enameled steel or aluminum, unpainted aluminum, stainless steel with a copper bottom, solid copper, copper with a stainless-steel lining, or brass. All are relatively indestructible although enameled kettles may in time become chipped or crazed and kettles with a welded-on bottom may leak in the welded joint.

Kettles with a lift-off top are more troublesome to use than whistling teakettles with top attached. On the other hand, they are a great deal easier to clean inside.

Electric teakettles, or water heaters, may look like regular kettles or small coffeepots. They hold up to 2 quarts, whereas regular kettles hold up to 3. Some have only one heat setting; others give a range of heats. You should make sure that the model you buy will turn itself off automatically if it boils dry.

To remove a stubborn white film made by hard water on the inside of a kettle, pour in water to cover the stained area, add about ½ cup of vinegar, and bring to a boil.

Teflon. Teflon is a plastic (fluorocarbon) which is familiar on kitchen utensils, and to a limited extent on saws, pruners, shears, clippers, putty knives, wall scrapers, and snow shovels. From the home owner's standpoint, its most important characteristic is its nonstick property: foods and such substances as sap do not adhere to it. A secondary advantage as far as cookware is concerned is that you can cook without grease.

However advertised, Teflon is Teflon; but on kitchen utensils, anything labeled simply "Teflon-coated" is to be viewed with suspicion. This is because the coating is quite easily scratched. A newer, much tougher type of coating is labeled Teflon II. This is DuPont's certification mark for scratch-resistant top-of-stove cookware and small appliances that meet DuPont standards.

How to care for Teflon-finished cooking utensils. The following material has been prepared by DuPont:

Before using nonstick cookware or bakeware for the first time, wash it in hot, sudsy water, using a soft sponge or dishcloth. Then rinse it thoroughly with hot water and dry it.

It is a good idea to grease or oil the nonstick surface of a pan prior to the first use. Such preconditioning is especially important with bakeware, frying pans, and griddles. An exception is the tubed angel food cake pan, which should not be greased if it is to be used for angel food cakes because this batter must cling to the sides of the pan during baking. The tubed pan may be greased, however, for baking fancy yeast breads or fruitcakes.

It is not necessary to grease the Teflon finish in order to prevent food from sticking. However, most women find that oils, fats, and butter are desirable in frying or baking, because they contribute much to the flavor of foods and also aid in even browning, especially when foods are fried.

When baking fragile foods or cakes that contain fruit or considerable sugar, greasing the Teflon finish is usually necessary to ensure complete release of the baked goods. Pans for cupcakes and butter cakes, for example, should be greased before every use. Cake pans also may be floured.

Like other frying pans, nonstick frying pans and griddles should be preheated before use.

With aluminum frying pans, best results are obtained at medium to medium-high heat settings. With porcelain-enameled frying pans, low to medium heat settings work best. Avoid extremely high temperatures. At temperatures above 450 degrees, which might be attained readily on high-heat settings, the Teflon finish may discolor or lose its nonstick property.

After new pans are preconditioned, it is usually not necessary to grease saucepans, casseroles, and most bakeware before cooking. Cookie pans seldom require greasing, and neither do muffin pans when plain muffins are baked. However, cupcakes, blueberry muffins, and other muffins with a high sugar content will come from the pans more easily if the cups have been lightly greased. Greasing a cake pan also will aid the removal of a fragile cake. Remember, too, that a cake should cool for about 10 minutes before it is turned out of the pan.

What to do about scratches. Scratches on the Teflon finish seldom affect the nonstick property. Hairline scratches do not widen with use of the pan; nor will the finish peel, if it has been applied properly. Scratches, therefore, really affect only appearance, not performance.

Either the selection of special tools or the careful handling of regular tools for lifting and turning food will contribute to the maintenance of a neat finish without deep scratches or gouges. Some women prefer to use plastic, rubber, Teflon-coated, or wooden spatulas, spoons, forks, and other utensils while working with Teflon-finished pans. Others find that, with experience, they have no trouble using metal tools as long as they avoid digging into the finish. The newer Teflon II certified wares are more scratch-resistant, thus allowing the housewife greater flexibility in the use of tools.

Do not use tools with sharp edges or burrs. Cutting foods with a sharp knife in a Teflon-finished pan should be avoided as much as possible. When cutting is necessary, a dull-edged table knife or plastic knife should be used.

To clean nonstick pans. Always wash the pan with hot, sudsy water after cooking. Although water from the faucet might rinse away most visible residues, a thin layer of food or grease will cling to the surface and eventually build up, causing the finish to stain or even to lose some of its release property. So, periodically scrub the nonstick finish with a plastic mesh pad. Never use steel wool, a metal scouring pad, or a coarse scouring powder.

Teflon-finished utensils may be washed in dishwashers. Certain materials on the outside of some pans, however, may become dull or discolored when exposed to the hot water and detergent.

Preventing and removing stains. With continued use, Teflon finishes may stain. Minor stains are considered normal and do not affect the performance of the pan. On the other hand, dark and widespread staining, which usually results from improper cleaning or overheating, may lessen the effectiveness of the nonstick property. Two important practices that will prevent or reduce stain problems are: (1) avoiding extremely high temperatures when cooking and (2) always using a detergent when washing pans.

While it may be impossible to remove some stains from the Teflon-coated interior of pans, considerable success has been obtained with commercial stain removers such as Stain-Aid or Dip-It. Sometimes the following home remedy also lightens or removes a stain: Mix 2 tablespoons baking soda and ½ cup liquid chlorine bleach with 1 cup water. Simmer this solution for 5 minutes in the stained pan. Remove from heat and check the pan surface. If the stain still remains, repeat the treatment. Caution: This solution is a strong oxidizing agent and may affect pigments in Teflon finishes, causing dark colors to become lighter, but this bleaching effect does not reduce the non-stick performance of the finish. If the cleaning solution is allowed to boil over, it may stain the outside of the pan.

Telephone Receivers. Do not dial with a pencil or any other instrument that goes through the finger holes: you will scratch the face.

Clean telephones as necessary with detergent solution. Wring the cloth out well because water that gets into the handset or base can cause trouble. To clean under the dial, use a cotton swab.

If you want to polish a telephone, use Angel Skin.

The mouthpiece can be disinfected with an aerosol disinfectant or a cloth wrung out in liquid disinfectant solution.

Television Sets. Television sets should be located away from direct heat. Do not allow the vents, which are usually in the back and bottom of the receiver, to be obstructed by draperies or anything else. If a television set is built into a wall or larger piece of furniture, you must provide ample space around it and also excellent ventilation.

Dust and polish a wood cabinet like a piece of fine furniture. If it is made of plastic, wash it off periodically with mild detergent solution; rinse and dry. The face of the screen is also cleaned with detergent solution after it has been allowed to cool.

If problems occur with the picture or sound, you can often correct them by adjusting the controls on the front and back of the set. If the receiver is dead, press the re-set button on the back. Make sure also that the electric cord is plugged in and in good repair, and that the antenna lead-in has not been broken. If you find a break, splice the wires like an electric cord.

Check periodically to see that the antenna is securely fastened to the house, upright, undamaged, and correctly aimed.

Although television sets require considerable expensive service, do not try to make repairs yourself.

Termites. See *Pest Control.*

Terraces. There are four rules that should be followed when you build a paved terrace:

1. Slope the paving away from the house at the rate of 1 inch to 12 feet.

2. If you have a very large terrace, install a storm drain in it to keep the runoff during bad storms from eroding the surrounding lawn and garden.

3. Unless a terrace is on the leeward side of the house and pretty well covered by a roof, do not build it at the same level as the room to which it is connected by a door. Water might leak in under the door.

4. If the terrace is fully exposed to the sun, use a paving material of neutral color. A light color is glary; a dark one becomes uncomfortably warm.

Here are brief directions for using several common paving materials.

How to build terraces. Poured concrete. Build like a walk. Make lengthwise and crosswise expansion joints every 4 to 6 feet. An extremely attractive concrete terrace can be achieved by dividing the area into large squares with 2-inch-thick redwood or cypress boards. Fill the squares with exposed aggregate concrete.

Brick. Build like a brick walk. One problem with brick is that areas that are heavily shaded often become extremely slippery when damp. Use rough-textured bricks to minimize this problem.

Stone. Construct a terrace dry or with mortar as you would a walk.

Concrete block. Use so-called patio blocks, which are actually concrete tiles in several sizes, colors, and textures. Handle as you would flagstone in a walk.

Wood blocks. Use square blocks of redwood or cypress, and lay them tight together as you would brick in a brick terrace. The end grain should face up. Unfortunately, while a terrace of this kind is resilient and handsome, it is often slippery when wet.

Quarry tile. Should be handled like flagstones set in mortar.

For more about building terraces, see *Walks.*

Terra-Cotta. Terra-cotta is an orange-brown earthenware which is often glazed with different colors. It is used to make tiles, ornaments, and various other things.

Terra-cotta that is unglazed stains easily and often permanently, and it must be scrubbed hard with detergent solution and a brush just to take off ordinary dirt. Glazed terra-cotta, however, is quite resistant to staining and is easily cleaned with a damp cloth.

If a piece breaks, coat the edges with epoxy glue and bind them together for 24 hours. Cellulose cement can also be used if you apply a thin coat to both broken edges; let it dry; then apply a second coat to one edge.

Terry Cloth. An absorbent, fuzzy, cotton fabric covered on one or both sides with tiny loops. It is used mainly for towels and bathrobes. Wash and dry like cotton, but do not iron.

Textolite. Brand name for the laminated plastic made by General Electric.

Thermometers. One of the least considered but most important measuring devices in your life is the thermometer. You may need several types.

Weather thermometer is used indoors as well as out to tell the temperature of the surrounding air. For accuracy, install an outdoor thermometer in a place that is protected from the sun and cold winds, and where it will not be affected by heat escaping from the house (next to a chimney, for example). Indoors, the ideal location is next to your thermostat (see *Heating Systems*).

Two weather thermometers of especial interest are (1) an indoor-outdoor unit that gives both temperatures while hanging on an inside wall and (2) a maximum-minimum thermometer that gives the present temperature plus the high and low readings since the last setting.

Clinical thermometer tells your body temperature, and determines whether a person is running a fever. Oral and rectal instruments are used.

Freezer thermometer hangs inside your freezer or refrigerator. Special instruments are made for this purpose, but you can also use a weather thermometer.

Candy thermometer is the key to success in making candy, frostings, jams, etc. The precise temperature control necessary for good results is almost impossible to achieve without such an instrument.

Some candy thermometers are of paddle-like shape with a central mercury tube and markings on each side. Some are tubular. Some have a long stem with a circular dial on top. Reliable units are marked in 2-degree graduations and are readable to 1 degree. All should have a heat-resistant handle and an adjustable clip to hook over the side of a pot.

Deep-frying thermometer looks much like a candy thermometer, but the two are not interchangeable because the latter does not register high-enough temperatures. Furthermore, the temperature gauge of a deep-frying thermometer need not be quite so precise as that on a candy thermometer. Most have 5-degree graduations.

Meat thermometer is pushed deep into a roast. It has a temperature gauge on the top end. On the best models, the stem is sheathed with metal so it can be inserted in the roast without breaking. Other features found on some meat thermometers are an extra-thin stem, a sharp tip designed to pierce the meat easily without the aid of a skewer, and watertight construction so the thermometer can be washed in the dishwasher.

Meat probes, included on some range models, measure roast temperature in the same way as a thermometer. However, they are connected into the electrical system of the range. When the probe finds that the roast has reached the desired temperature, it sounds a buzzer or automatically turns the oven to a low keep-warm temperature.

Oven thermometer. Although ovens have a thermostat that permits you to select any desired temperature, the calibration, even on new ovens, can be off and the temperature can vary. An oven thermometer provides a safeguard and ensures the best baking results.

Thresholds. A threshold is the flat, horizontal strip under a door and parallel with its bottom edge. All exterior doors have thresholds; but they are rarely used today under interior doors, although you still see them in older houses.

Exterior thresholds are made of heavy

oak, as a rule, and are quite durable. But because they are exposed to moisture, sun, and heavy wear, the finish applied to them does not last very long.

The most durable clear finish is urethane varnish; the most durable colored finish, epoxy floor paint. But even these will probably have to be renewed about once a year.

If cracks develop in an exterior threshold, fill them promptly with plastic wood.

Because they project above the floor, interior thresholds also receive heavy wear—sometimes to the point where they must be replaced. To remove an old strip, first remove the stops on the doorjambs. The threshold can then be pried out and a new one fitted in.

Thresholds made of aluminum with flexible vinyl insets are especially useful for stopping drafts under interior and exterior doors. If the strips are not thick enough to close a space completely, install them on top of a wood strip of the appropriate thickness. Also see *Weatherstripping.*

Ticks. See *Pest Control.*

Tile, Ceramic. Ceramic tile, also called glazed tile, has a glass-like finish that will not absorb stains or change color. The finish may be bright, semi-matte, or matte. The material is often used on bathroom walls and floors, but is also used on counters and table tops.

Two types of tile are common: 4¼-inch squares that are installed individually; and mosaic tiles, which are very small tiles of various shapes mounted on wire mesh in 12-inch squares.

How to install tile. Since the advent of organic adhesives resembling those used to install resilient flooring materials, the installation of ceramic tile has become a relatively easy and popular do-it-yourself project. But use of these adhesives is not recommended for installation of tile in shower enclosures and over tubs, because water may get through them into the wall spaces. Here you should use Portland cement.

The tools needed to install ceramic tile are a notched trowel to spread the adhesive, a glass cutter, a sharpening stone, tile-cutting pliers, a level, and a sponge.

If using 4¼-inch tiles, you will need a carton of forty tiles to cover 5 square feet. The tiles used should have spacers on the edges.

The base for the tile must be sound, firm, level, smooth, and free of surface coatings that may flake off or deteriorate. If a floor is made of boards, it must be covered with an underlayment of exterior-grade plywood.

When tiling a wall with 4¼-inch tiles, you should first strike a vertical chalk line. But if you are using mosaic tiles, it's easier to start from a door frame provided the frame is vertical or nearly so (if it is slightly off, the lines of tiles will also be slightly off, but you probably won't notice it). When tiling a floor, start in the most conspicuous corner and proceed in both directions across the room. On a counter, work from front to back. The base for a table top should be sized so that no tiles need to be cut.

Spread the adhesive thinly so the valleys formed by the teeth of the spreader are almost bare. The ridges should be the height of the notches. The adhesive sets fairly slowly but it is best not to spread too much at one time.

Set tiles, whether individual or mosaics in sheets, into the adhesive exactly where you want them. Don't slide them. Once the first tile is in place, the rest are added easily.

To cut a tile on a straight line, score the glazed surface with your glass cutter; lay a large finishing nail on the floor; place the tile over this, with the scored line directly over the nail; then press down on the edges of the tile. If the tile does not break cleanly, you can pinch off the points with your pliers. To make a smooth cut, sand the edge with your sharpening stone.

When making a cutout for a pipe, scratch a line with the glass cutter; then with your pliers gradually nibble away the area to be removed.

When all the tiles are set and the adhesive has had a day to dry, fill the joints with grout mixed according to the directions on the package. Spread this on the tiles and work it into the joints with a window squeegee, or wear rubber gloves and do it with your hands. Before the grout dries, scrape off the excess. Tool the joints between 4¼-inch tiles with the end of an old toothbrush. Joints between mosaic tiles are not tooled. Then clean the surface with warm water and a sponge. Shape the joints further, if necessary. Finally, polish with a dry cloth.

To cure the grout, spray a tiled wall lightly with water about four times in the next 24 hours. Cover horizontal surfaces with damp building felt.

How to repair ceramic tile. Joints cracked or eroded. Scrape them clean and fill with the grout used to make the original installation. If the crack has opened up between wall tiles and a tub rim, you can try grouting it in the same way; but if it opens up again (as it probably will), clean it well, dry thoroughly, and fill it with silicone caulking compound.

Loose tile. Lift it out and remove the old grout and mortar. Apply silicone rubber adhesive to the back of the tile, reset it, and keep it weighted down for 24 hours. Then fill the joints with grout.

Broken tile. If the tile is used for a hot mat or for some similar purpose, clean the broken edges and reglue them with cellulose cement. If the tile is in a wall, floor, or counter, it is very difficult to replace without damaging adjacent tiles. But if you want to try, scrape out the grout around the sides completely. Use an ice-pick or awl. Now, working from the crack in the center, chip the tile out in small pieces with a cold chisel and hammer. Clean out the mortar or adhesive underneath. Then butter the back of a new tile with silicone rubber adhesive; set it into the gap; and after letting the adhesive set for 24 hours, grout the joints.

How to clean ceramic tile. A damp cloth will remove most soil. For grease and stubborn dirt, use a mild detergent. If neces-

sary, use an abrasive cleanser or a strong solution of washing soda. After washing, dry well to make the tiles shine.

In many installations, the grout in the joints becomes badly stained. This may be caused by grease, dirt, mildew, or water impurities. If washing with mild detergent and occasionally with abrasive cleanser makes little impression, scrub the joints frequently with one of the liquid cleaners made especially for the purpose.

Note that if you ever build a house or remodel or add a bathroom, you should specify that the tilesetter grout the tiles with epoxy.

How to remove difficult stains. Rust. Scrub with naval jelly or any other commercial rust remover. Rinse.

Efflorescence. Wash with 1 part muriatic acid in 20 parts water. Rinse immediately and thoroughly.

Paint and nail polish. Scrape with a razor blade. Follow as necessary with paint remover or nail polish remover.

Coffee, mustard, ink, blood. Wash with a chlorine bleach and rinse.

Tile, Quarry. Quarry tile is an unglazed ceramic material in which the same ingredients that appear on the surface are used throughout. In the home, the tiles are used primarily for flooring in halls, sun rooms, family rooms, and in outdoor paving. They are available in several sizes, shapes, and colors.

For how to lay and care for quarry tile, see *Floors, Quarry-Tile.*

Timers. Timers of several types are useful in the home.

For cooking, a minute timer is so essential that most modern ranges incorporate one. This is operated by electricity. Small, separate spring-actuated timers are also sold and are about equally good except for very short operations, in which case they are sometimes extremely inaccurate. Their short-time use can often be improved, however, if you first turn the timer 5 or 10 minutes beyond the right point and then immediately turn it back to the right point.

Three-minute egg timers, of the hour-glass type, are useful for timing both eggs and telephone calls.

Deluxe ranges offer automatic oven timers and timed appliance outlets. These are very useful gadgets provided you operate them in exact accordance with the manufacturer's directions. If these are not printed on the range control panel, tear them out of the use-and-care manual that comes with the range and paste them inside a cabinet door near the range.

Plug-in timers designed to turn the lights on and off in the house while you are away from home will control up to about 300 watts of lighting. Similar timers are sold to control lights and/or small appliances, such as radios and coffee-makers, up to a total of 1875 watts. These are either plugged into a wall outlet or may be installed permanently in a wall outlet. Once set, all these timers will automatically turn the lights or appliances on and off every day at the same time.

Still another permanently installed, day-in-day-out timer will control motors up to 1 horsepower and air conditioners up to 4200 watts. It is designed mainly for farm use.

A different type of timer used strictly to control a single light of up to 300 watts is actuated by a photoelectric eye. One model screws into a standard light socket; another is installed below the light socket in an outdoor lantern post.

Tin Snips. See *Tools, Workshop.*

Tinting. Tinting differs from dyeing in two respects: tinting is done with hot water, dyeing with boiling water, and tinted fabrics are not completely colorfast. Nevertheless, tinting is a good, easy way to change the color of fabrics of all kinds, including threadbare areas in carpets. It is possible to achieve almost any hue you like except black, navy, and dark reds. For these colors, send the article out to be fast-dyed.

All articles to be tinted must first be washed to remove spots and stains.

Small articles can be tinted in a bowl with the hottest water available. Add the tint in the amount specified by the maker.

Then immerse the unfolded article in the color bath for 20 to 30 minutes. Stir it often. Keep the bath hot by placing it over a slowly steaming pot.

When the article is a shade deeper than you desire, remove it and rinse in cold water repeatedly until the water is clear. Then squeeze dry—do not wring—and hang the article up to drip-dry.

Large articles or a quantity of articles can be tinted in your washing machine. Fill the tub with hot water and pour dissolved tint into it through several layers of cheesecloth when agitation starts. Add articles to be colored. Cover lid opening with a sheet of plastic or foil to keep tint from staining the lid. Put the washer through its longest wash cycle, and if necessary reset it and put it through again.

When articles are a little darker than desired, proceed to the rinse cycle. Use cold water. Rinse a second time. Then remove articles and dry on a line or in a dryer at the appropriate fabric setting.

Clean washer thoroughly by putting it through a complete cycle with a 5-minute wash. Use hot water, ½ cup detergent, and ½ cup bleach.

To tint carpets. When a solid-colored carpet becomes threadbare in one or two spots, you can rejuvenate it temporarily by tinting the spots. Simply make a warm solution of tint to match the color of the carpet and apply it with a paintbrush. Be sure to place a waterproof mat of plastic or rubber underneath so you don't damage the floor.

Tinware. Baking utensils made of tin-plated sheet steel. The metal loses its shine and turns dark brown after it has been cooked in; but this actually improves its baking characteristics because foods brown better.

Tinware dents and warps easily, but can be pressed back into shape with your fingers or by holding it over a piece of wood and rapping lightly with a mallet.

Wash utensils in the dishwasher. To prevent rusting, do not cut on the metal or clean with abrasives.

Toasters. Toasters and toaster combinations are as varied as the foods you can toast in them—bread, muffins, rolls, and bagels, to name a few.

Standard toasters come in two- or four-slice models. In the newly popular slim types, the slices fit end to end rather than side by side. In all toasters, the crumb tray should be easy to remove and clean.

A common feature of all toasters is a toast-color control. The type of control varies, however, and can make a difference in the uniformity of results. On some models, the shade setting is controlled by a timer. You may have to adjust this if the bread is dry or if you're toasting several slices one after another. Other controls, usually more expensive, measure the temperature or humidity of the bread. This kind of control compensates for such factors as the staleness or coldness of the bread. One toaster gives very accurate toast-color results by using electronic sensors to measure moisture removed from the bread. It also toasts very quickly—two slices in less than a minute.

Most toasters raise the bread automatically when toasting is completed, but most also have a manual release which allows you to lift and remove bread whenever you like. Some also lower bread automatically.

If you would like to use your toaster for foods wider or smaller than a standard bread slice, look for toasters with a wider toast slot (on some the width of the opening can be changed) and a higher toast lift (so you can take out small items easily).

On some two- or four-slice toasters, the entire unit operates whether you're toasting one slice or four. Others have separate controls for heating only the wells being used or for producing both light and dark slices at the same time. Some models have settings for reheating cold toast.

Toaster-broilers generally have one heating element that is horizontal rather than vertical and that will toast or broil only on one side at a time. Some have a variety of heat settings and a choice of tray positions at different distances from the element. Size varies, but some can broil two average-size steaks at once.

A **toaster-oven** can toast, bake, or top-brown foods. It toasts both sides at once and can toast all bread sizes, including large rolls. For baking, it has heat settings much like those on your regular oven, and it can bake such things as rolls, pies, potatoes, and convenience foods. It is handy for browning such foods as cheese dishes and meringues.

How to care for a toaster. Clean the shell as necessary with a damp cloth or cloth dipped in detergent solution. Open the crumb tray every month or so and clean it out. If food particles stick, wash the tray at the sink.

Never poke around inside a toaster with a knife or other metal object. It is a good way to wreck the heating elements and other parts. If the toaster is plugged in, you may also give yourself a jolt.

Toggle Bolts. See *Wall Anchors.*

Toilets. Three types of toilet are used in homes: (1) The wash-down is the simplest and cheapest, but noisy when flushed. And it does not always flush clean. (2) The reverse-trap costs more but is quieter and cleans more efficiently. (3) The siphon-jet is best of all—and, of course, the costliest.

Most toilets have pedestal bases and are bolted to the floor, but some models are wall-hung, which simplifies floor cleaning greatly.

The best toilet seats are made of solid plastic.

How to repair toilets. Water runs into toilet. When this happens, check whether the stopper ball is falling correctly into the seat of the outlet. The rod on the ball may be bent or the guides attached to the overflow pipe may have gotten out of line. It is more likely, however, that the ball itself has become worn and should be replaced with a new one of the same size. Clean the edges of the outlet at the same time.

Various types of stopper devices are made for replacement purposes on old toilets. They are no more reliable than the ball-on-rod stopper most generally used, although there are times when they are useful.

Many new toilets, however, have a

cylindrical type of stopper which is made of plastic and slides up and down on a small pipe. This is very efficient but in time it, too, may leak. To stop this, swing the refill tube to one side and unscrew the cap above the stopper. Lift out the stopper. Clean the edges of the outlet. If the rubber ring at the bottom of the stopper cylinder is worn, replace it.

Water spills into overflow pipe. Raise the copper float ball as far as possible. If the overflow stops, bend the rod to which the float is attached downward. This lowers the float and should make the water stop running before it reaches the top of the overflow pipe. If it doesn't, unscrew the float ball. If it contains water, it has sprung a leak. Replace it with a new copper or foam-plastic ball.

If the overflow still continues, the washer on the valve plunger needs to be replaced. Release the screws that hold the float arm in place and lift out the valve plunger in the top of the inlet pipe. Unscrew the metal collar on the bottom of the plunger, take out the flat washer, and install a new one of the same size.

Tank does not fill sufficiently. Bend the rod attached to the float ball upward. The tank should fill to within ¾ inch of the top of the overflow pipe.

Drain clogged. Place a plumber's friend over the outlet in the bottom of the bowl and pump the handle up and down. This creates a suction in the drain line and may loosen the stoppage. If it doesn't, crank a coiled spring auger down the drain until it bores through the stoppage or pulls it back out.

Overflow pipe broken. You may be able to unscrew it from the outlet base, but the odds are against you. So turn off the water below the tank and empty the tank completely. Then unscrew the large nut under the tank, remove the outlet, and buy a new one including an overflow pipe.

Leak between the tank and toilet bowl. This doesn't happen in one-piece toilets; and it is relatively rare in toilets made in two pieces. But you never can tell.

How you stop the leak depends on the design of the toilet and exactly where the leak is. But if you examine the situation, you will quickly see what needs to be done. The first step in all cases is to shut off the water and empty the tank. Then remove the tank by unscrewing the screws driven into the wall or the bolts attached to the toilet bowl. If the tank and bowl are connected by a gooseneck pipe, the nuts holding this must be loosened also.

If the large washer under the outlet in the bottom of the tank leaks or if the equally large washer at the back or top of the toilet bowl leaks, you can probably correct matters by wrapping cotton string under the washer and screwing it tight. But this should be considered only a temporary repair. It is easier and far better to buy a new washer.

If the leak is in the pipe between the tank and bowl, it can be slowed and perhaps stopped temporarily by overwrapping with friction tape. But again it is better to replace the pipe.

Crack in toilet tank or bowl. Shut off the water. Empty out the water and clean the crack well with a cleanser. Rinse and dry. Then spread silicone caulking compound over the crack and allow it to dry 24 hours before turning on the water.

Tank top broken. Clean the edges and mend with epoxy glue.

Tank sweats. Install a toilet tank liner made of plastic insulating sheets.

Seat stained or cracked. You can paint it, of course, but the new finish won't last. Buy a new seat. Note that different toilets require seats of slightly different size and shape; so you should try to figure out what company made the toilet in question and then order the proper seat from the firm's nearest distributor or dealer.

Note: toilets without tanks, which are often installed in apartment houses, should be repaired by an expert.

How to clean toilets. See *Bathroom Cleaning.*

Tools, Workshop. Few experienced handymen would ever agree about what tools should be in the workshop. That is because each man works in his own way and has his own favorite tools. But it is hard to imagine a household that does not need the following very, very basic tools:

Pocketknife
6-foot rule
Screwdriver
Crosscut saw
Block plane
¼-inch electric drill
Claw hammer
Pliers
Putty knife
Brad awl

For the jack-of-all-trades of average ability and interest, a much better tool kit would consist of many of the following items. Note that tools needed for special projects such as wallpapering and soldering are not included.

Ax. In the long run, a 2¼-pound ax with a 28-inch handle will probably be of most value because you can use it as a hand ax and also for major cutting jobs.

Brace and bits. For boring holes from 3/16-inch diameter up. The bits, of course, do the cutting, and you need a different bit for each size hole up to 7/8 inch. From that point up to 3 inches, you can use what is known as an expansive bit—one with an adjustable cutter.

The best brace to buy has a ratchet which permits you to bore holes even when you do not have room to turn the sweep handle all the way around.

When using a brace and bit, first make certain the bit is centered squarely in the jaws of the brace. Hold the round, flat head of the brace rigid; grasp the sweep handle in the other hand, and turn it clockwise. The piece to be bored must be held securely; otherwise it will revolve with the bit. If you can put it in a vise, do so. Do not bore all the way through wood from one side, because it will splinter on the back side when the cutting edge of the bit bursts through. The correct procedure is to drill from the starting side until the point of the bit comes through the back side. Then withdraw the bit and complete drilling from the back side.

Braces have a number of moving parts,

all of which should be oiled regularly so that they move easily.

Try not to store bits all jumbled together in a drawer, because they will get nicked and dull. Keep them in slots in a cloth or plastic case. If the cutting edges at the tip of a bit are dull or damaged, touch them up with a small, fine file.

Brad awl. This is like an icepick but with a sharp steel blade only about 1½ inches long. It is extremely useful for making starting holes for brads, screws, cuphooks, etc.

Carpenter's chisel. You can get many sizes, but until you start doing a lot of door-hanging and cabinet work, you probably can get by with a single chisel with a ¾-inch blade.

Work with a chisel with the beveled edge up. When using it as a paring tool, hold and push it with one hand and guide the blade with the other. When making deep cuts to gouge out a lot of wood, hold the chisel at an angle of about 60 degrees and rap the end of the handle sharply but not heavily with a mallet or block of wood. Don't try to cut very deep, because that compresses and twists the wood fibers; and you can't get very far anyway. Just cut about 1/8 inch deep; chip out or pare out the wood to that depth; and then make another 1/8-inch cut.

A chisel is useless unless it is razor sharp. Never use it for prying open cans. You can keep the blade sharp for a long time if you hone it frequently on a sharpening stone. Place the bevel flat on the stone and move the tool back and forth parallel to the stone. Then turn it over, lay it flat on the stone and give the back edge several side-wise strokes. The edge on this side should be perfectly flat; not beveled in the slightest.

If a chisel is nicked or becomes extremely dull, you will have to sharpen it on a grinding wheel. First check the blade with a try square. If it is not square, hold it directly to the wheel until it is. Then hold the beveled edge at a 30-degree angle to the wheel and move it from side to side until you have a sharp edge and even,

30-degree bevel. There will be a burr on the flat side. Don't let the blade get overheated during this operation; dip it in cold water now and then. Finish sharpening the chisel by honing in the way described.

C clamp. So called because it is C-shaped, this is the standard tool for clamping together boards, etc. You need several, preferably in different sizes: 3, 4, and 5 inches.

Unless you are clamping material, such as steel, that cannot be damaged or dented by the clamps, always insert some sort of cushion—usually pieces of wood—between the jaws of the clamp and the material you are working on. By using big, flat, rigid cushions, you can also spread the pressure exerted by the clamp over an area much larger than the clamp jaws themselves.

Claw hammer. A 13- or 16-ounce hammer is about the right size. Test it for feel when buying. It is immaterial whether the handle is of wood, steel, or fiberglass. You can have either a straight or curved claw. The latter is better for pulling nails and is therefore the more useful.

When using a hammer to drive nails, grip the handle at the end in a firm handshake. Swing from the wrist in a series of hard taps, not a few heavy blows. At the striking point, the hammer head should be level with the hand. When pulling nails, place a piece of wood under the head to form a fulcrum and also to prevent damage to the wood from which the nail is being extracted.

When a hammer head comes loose, just drive in the wedges in the end of the handle. If the looseness persists, better get a new handle.

Cold chisel. This is a very hard, heavy tool used for a variety of odd jobs such as cutting bricks and rivets, cleaning mortar off stone, chipping rust from ironwork. A 6-inch chisel with a ½-inch blade is all you need, although there are many other sizes. When the cutting edge dulls, sharpen it with a file. A grindstone would spoil the temper. The edge should be shaped like a tent with walls, not a pup tent.

Electric drill. You will be surprised how much you use this for drilling small holes and also for rough sanding and buffing. A one-speed, ¼-inch drill is adequate. Drills with ¼-inch shanks that bore holes up to 1-inch diameter are available. You can get high-speed drill bits that cut both wood and metal. Carbide-tipped drill bits cut into masonry.

Lubricate the drill according to the instructions that come with it. Keep it clean. Replace the carbon brushes if the drill stops working.

File. Files used in the home workshop are usually flat, half-round, round, or triangular. The teeth range from fine to coarse.

Files are used primarily for shaping and smoothing metal; but a wood rasp with coarse teeth is very handy for cutting down and shaping wood—especially end grain. For the metal work you are likely to do around the home, a flat, medium-coarse mill file and a small triangular file should be enough.

You will protect your hands if you put wood handles on your files. Just slip the tang into the handle and rap the round end of the handle on the floor. When working, it is usually best to grasp the handle in one hand and the tip of the file in the other. Don't press down too hard. Since files cut only on the forward stroke, lift them slightly off the work on the back stroke. This helps to preserve the teeth. File with the whole length of the file; don't just saw back and forth in short strokes.

Don't let files get rusty or clogged with paint: they are useless. If the teeth are clogged with metal or wood, run over them with a wire brush. Special file-cleaning brushes are available. You can also pick the teeth individually with a sharp nail.

Grinding wheel. An electric wheel is preferred. If you have a hand-cranked wheel, you need someone to turn it for you because you should hold tools you are sharpening in both hands.

The wheel should turn toward the tool. Hold the tool steady and squarely to the stone; if the tool slants sideways, the stone will soon become lower on one side than the other.

To keep the tool being sharpened from overheating and losing its temper, dip it frequently in cold water.

Oil the grinding wheel now and then.

Level. This tool is used to determine whether things are perfectly horizontal or perfectly vertical. You need it, for instance, to make sure that doorways are straight or that counter tops are flat.

The tool incorporates two small plastic tubes which are partially filled with liquid. When the level is laid on its long edge, the bubble in the tube paralleling the long edge should be exactly centered in the tube. If it is, the thing on which the level is resting is horizontal. The other tube is used in the same way to find a vertical.

A 2-foot level is a good size.

Miter box. A miter box is needed when you cut lumber accurately to various angles. Ready-built boxes with saw guides that are adjustable to any angle are on the market; but these are more elaborate than you need for most work around the house.

To make your own miter box, cut a 4-inch board into a 2-foot length; and cut two 2-foot lengths out of a 3-inch board. Nail the 3-inch boards to the edges of the 4-inch board to form a long trough. At the center of the trough, saw vertical slots directly opposite each other in the sides of the trough. The slots should be made just to the bottom of the trough. Measure 4 inches from both ends of the right side. Working from both of these marks with an adjustable square, draw 45-degree angles across the two sides of the trough. The angles should slant toward the center of the trough. Then cut vertical slots through the sides from A to A′ and B to B′.

You will now be able to cut small pieces of wood accurately to a 90-degree angle and also to 45-degree angles so that you can fit the pieces together neatly in a corner.

As a rule, a backsaw is used when cutting wood in a miter box; but a crosscut saw can be used just as well.

Nailset. A small, steel, pencil-like tool about 6 inches long. It is used to drive nailheads beneath the surface of wood

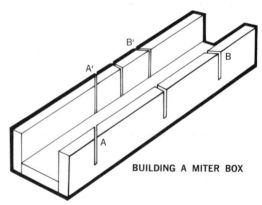

BUILDING A MITER BOX

without damaging the surface. The nail is hammered into the wood with your hammer until it sticks out only about 1/8 inch or less. Place the tip of the set on the nail head and point the set in the same direction as the nail. Then hit the blunt end of the set with your hammer until the nailhead is about 1/16 inch below the surface.

Nailsets are available with tips of several diameters. This makes it easier to set nails with heads of different size.

Plane. A 6-inch-long block plane is a good general-purpose plane because it cuts with and across wood grain and can be used in tight, awkward places. It is held in one hand. For removing a lot of wood quickly, use a jack plane, which is held in two hands. It cuts efficiently only with the grain.

To learn how to handle a plane well takes time and practice. Here are just a few preliminary tips: (1) Don't let the blade project too far below the sole. The purpose of a plane is to remove thin shavings, not thick ones. Make sure the blade is straight; otherwise it will cut deeper on one side than on the other. (2) Work with the grain. When going against the grain, you break off the wood and produce a rough surface. (3) The plane should not parallel the board you are smoothing precisely. Slide it forward at a slight angle. (4) To plane the edges of a board square, hold a short board under the plane and against the side of the board you are cutting and slide it along with the plane. Hold the board with your front hand, hooking your fingers under it and placing your thumb on top of the handle at the front of the plane. (5) When smoothing the end of a board (going across the grain), work from the edges toward the center.

Sharpen the blade of a plane like the blade of a carpenter's chisel. Store a plane on its side with the blade retracted.

Pliers. There are several dozen different designs and sizes. Three that are particularly useful are 6-inch pliers with a slip joint that permits the jaws to open extra wide; long-nose pliers for grasping small articles in hard-to-get-at places; and lineman's pliers for cutting large-diameter wires.

Another tool which does not take the place of any of the above but is good to have available is a locking plier-wrench.

Pocketknife. A sturdy, 3½-inch knife with two or three blades can handle big jobs and little. Dry it thoroughly when it gets wet. Use a blotter to dry inside. Apply a few drops of oil to protect the blades and keep them opening easily.

To sharpen a knife, lay it almost flat on a stone and move it in a rather tight, circular motion. Whet both sides equally. For more about sharpening knives, see *Knives, Kitchen.*

Putty knife. Get one with a blade about 1 inch wide. You need it for filling holes, setting windowpanes, and light scraping. It makes no difference whether the blade has a square or rounded edge; but if the corners become rounded, square the blade on a grinding wheel.

Saw. As a starter, get a 26-inch, coarse (eight teeth per inch) crosscut saw. This is a good general-purpose saw. Later you may also want a fine-cut (ten teeth per inch) saw.

Ripsaws have coarser teeth and are used for cutting with the grain. You don't need one if you have an electric circular saw; but lacking a circular saw, you should have a ripsaw if you are doing extensive carpentry.

A backsaw is a crosscut saw with small teeth. The blade is rectangular, 16 inches long, and reinforced with a steel ridge along the upper edge. It is used for fine, accurate work.

A coping saw has a U-shaped steel frame attached to a handle. The very narrow, fine-toothed blades are interchangeable. The saw is used for intricate work—especially with thin wood—such as cutting circles and scallops.

A keyhole saw has a long, narrow, tapered blade. It is most often used for cutting holes in the middle of a plank or plywood panel. To use it in this way, you first bore a hole through the wood, then insert the saw blade. Use short strokes to avoid twisting or bending the blade.

A hacksaw also has interchangeable blades. It is used for cutting metal. The teeth point away from the handle. Use coarse-toothed blades for thick metals; fine-toothed blades for thin.

When starting to saw with a big saw or hacksaw, use short strokes and guide the blade with the thumb of your other hand. Hold the thumb a bit off the work so that the saw teeth won't cut it.

Remove rust from saw blades with rust remover and steel wool. Rub the blades occasionally with an oily rag, but don't forget to remove the oil film before starting work on wood that must be kept clean.

Let a professional sharpen your saws.

Sawhorse. You need a pair for supporting long lengths of lumber, doors, etc., and for building a wallpaper table. Make them with prefabricated metal sawhorse brackets that tie the legs and rail together. For lumber, use 2-by-4s. Cut the legs so that the distance from the top of the rail to the floor is about 30 inches. The rail is usually 36 inches long but may be a little longer.

Scraper. This simple tool is used for scraping paint, floors, etc. Most people allow it to become dirty and dull, then decide it isn't worth anything (in that state it isn't), and get a new one. But the tool is easy to sharpen with a file run the length of the blade. The edge should be square.

If you use a scraper with two hands—one to pull and the other to put a little pressure on the cutting head—it will cut much better than if you use it in one hand only.

Screwdriver. You need a couple of screwdrivers with blades of different size for driving large and small screws. A screwdriver with an extra-long blade and narrow tip and a close-quarter screwdriver with very short blade and handle are also useful. A tool with three small screwdrivers concealed in the metal handle of a large screwdriver is also useful, for although the big tool is fiendish to use, the small tools come in very handy.

If the blade tip of a screwdriver becomes rounded or is broken, the tool is difficult to work with and also damages screw heads. To sharpen a blade, put it tip up in a vise and square it off with a metal file.

A Phillips screwdriver is also necessary because many of the screws used in appliances, for example, have heads with cross-shaped slots. The tip of the Phillips blade is pointed and star-shaped to fit these slots. For most purposes, a No. 1 size is adequate.

Sharpening stone. The most useful size measures 6 by 2 by 1 inch. It has coarse grit on one side; fine on the other.

6-foot rule. Some people like folding wood rules; others, flexible steel rules. The latter are a bit more compact, unbreakable, and can be used to make fast, accurate inside measurements (the width of a door opening, for example). On the other hand, a folding rule is more rigid and does not need to be supported, as a flexible rule does, when you are making many measurements.

Square. This is an L-shaped tool used for marking and measuring lumber that is to be cut at right angles. A particularly useful type of square has a 12-inch blade and an adjustable handle.

For major carpentry work, you also need a large steel framing square with one arm 24 inches long and the other 16 inches.

Take care to keep your square free of rust and paint spatters. It loses considerable value when you can't see the inch marks. But don't protect it with oil, because this would be transferred to the lumber.

Stapler. Workshop staplers are a wonderful convenience when you are fixing window screens, covering dining room chairs, installing insulation, etc. Ordinarily you would have to use tacks and a hammer—a slow job. But with a stapler, you can fasten things bing, bing, bing. It handles staples up to 9/16 inch in length.

Tin snips. These look like an odd type of scissors, and are used for cutting sheet metal, such as flashing strips and gutters. If you buy duckbill snips, you can make straight, curved, and irregular cuts.

Hold the handles of the snips a little above the metal being cut. Cut in short strokes. Close the blades part way before making a cut. Don't twist snips to pry material apart. And don't cut wire, because you may nick the blades.

Keep snips oiled at the joint, and adjust the joint so that the blades are neither too tight nor so loose that they chew metal rather than cutting it.

Workbench. You can buy one or make one. Making it yourself saves money and gives you complete control of the dimensions. Follow the plan in the illustration. Install a vise at one end of the bench. The best type is a woodworking vise which is permanently installed under the bench so that the top edges of the jaws are level with the top of the bench. The jaws open to a maximum of 12 inches. Less desirable, because it gets in the way, is a clamp- or bolt-on vise which is secured to the top of the bench. The jaws open to only 6 inches maximum.

Wrench. A monkey wrench is an adjustable smooth-jawed tool with jaws forming a rectangular C. If you have one that opens to 4 inches, you can take your plumbing system apart with ease. And you can do many other smaller jobs besides.

A pipe wrench is similarly shaped but has adjustable, toothed jaws. It is used to grasp round pipes and hold them in a vise-like grip.

Open-end wrenches are fairly small tools with no moving parts. Each tool has two U-shaped heads of slightly different size. With a six-piece set you can handle nuts ranging from 3/8 to 1 inch in size.

Hex, or setscrew, wrenches are very small L-shaped tools needed to remove and replace tiny screws with hex-shaped

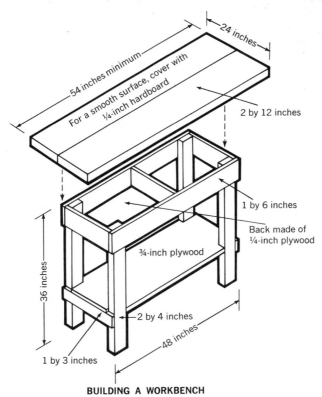

24 inches

54 inches minimum

For a smooth surface, cover with ¼-inch hardboard

2 by 12 inches

1 by 6 inches

Back made of ¼-inch plywood

¾-inch plywood

36 inches

2 by 4 inches

48 inches

1 by 3 inches

BUILDING A WORKBENCH

"slots" in the end. You don't need these wrenches often, but when you do, you need them desperately. There is no substitute for them. Get a set. It costs less than a dollar.

There's no secret about using wrenches. Just remember that when you are tightening a nut or bolt, work clockwise—to the right. When loosening the same nut or bolt, work counterclockwise. (But every once in a while you will encounter a nut and bolt that work the other way.)

Note also that it is better to pull on the handle of a wrench than to push, because if a nut suddenly comes loose when you are pushing, you may injure your hand.

How to store tools. If you keep your workshop tools in sight on a wall, you will save time when using them and you will be more likely to put them away safely after use.

Pegboard, made of hardboard in which holes are punched at 1-inch intervals, is very popular for wall storage of tools, because it is easily hung and neat looking and because it comes with an assortment of metal hangers that allow you to hang many different tools in any way you like. Be warned, however, that the hangers have an annoying tendency to fall out.

A good substitute for pegboard is ¾-inch fir plywood into which you drive nails to hold hammers, saws, wrenches, etc.

An excellent way to store many small tools such as screwdrivers, pliers, wrenches, and chisels is to screw a screen-door spring flat against a wall in a horizontal position. Drive screws through the loops in the ends of the spring. Then drive large staples over the spring more or less at equal intervals. They should hold the spring snug but not tight. Your tools fit between the wall and the spring.

Store hacksaw blades, bits, nailsets, files, and other very small tools in divided trays or drawers.

Planes, electric drills, and power saws should be kept in the boxes in which they come or on divided shelves.

Before storing any tool, dry and clean it well. If the workshop is damp, spray or rub the tool lightly with oil to keep it from rusting. (But do not oil a square.)

HOW TO HANG TOOLS

How to remove rust from tools. If the tools are small enough, the easiest and most thorough way to clean them is to put them into an ultrasonic cleaner (which see) with a rust remover.

Large tools, such as saws, should be cleaned with naval jelly or any other good rust remover. Use steel wool or emery cloth to get rid of stubborn encrustations.

Towels. See *Bath Linens.*

Triacetate. An acetate fiber with greater heat resistance than most acetates. It is woven into a variety of fabrics. Wash in warm water; dry at low heat; iron at low heat.

Tricot. A knitted fabric used in clothing, tricot is made of numerous fibers. This permits some variation in the method of laundering; but as a rule you should handle it like permanent press.

Trisodium Phosphate. A strong cleaning agent sold under such trade names as Oakite, Soilax, and Spic and Span. It is used on walls, ceilings, appliances, kitchen cabinets, etc. It leaves no film and manufacturers say no rinsing is necessary (it is, however, advisable).

Tulipware. A type of stoneware, decorated with tulips, first made by the Pennsylvania-Dutch. See *Stoneware.*

Tupperware. Tupperware is the trade name for a line of kitchen containers made out of polyethylene. The lids are designed to seal very tightly but easily.

Turpentine. Gum spirits of turpentine may be used for thinning oil and alkyd paints and varnishes; for cleaning brushes used in these finishes; and for removing splatters of finish from fabrics, etc. Because of its pungent odor and relatively high cost, however, paint thinner is generally substituted for it. Turpentine is flammable.

Tweed. A rough-textured, coarse, heavy, sturdy fabric used in clothing. It is normally made of wool but may be made of cotton or rayon. Have it dry-cleaned when soiled.

Twill. Twill is a basic type of textile weave distinguished by diagonal lines. Gabardine and whipcord are examples of twill fabrics. The way a twill is cleaned depends on the fiber it is made of.

Twine. Types and weights of twine vary enormously, and it is impossible for the home owner to have the perfect twine for every purpose. If you understand the differences between the twines most useful in the home, however, you will be able to select them better.

Corn-beef twine is a thick, soft, white cotton twine used for kitchen wrapping and light package wrapping. It lacks the strength of jute or sisal. Knots can be very hard to untie.

Jute twine is usually a medium-brown color (although garden twine is green) and feels quite smooth. It ranges in size from the thickness of sewing yarn to that of small rope. It is strong (until frayed) and is used for general wrapping purposes, but particularly when a package is to be mailed.

Seine twine is a white cotton twine, hard and twisted like rope. Because of its strength, it is widely used in construction work for snapping chalk lines and building masonry walls to a straight line, for example. And because it is smooth, it can be rolled onto a stick and unrolled time and again without knotting.

Nylon seine twine is even stronger than cotton.

Sisal twine is inexpensive, straw-colored, coarse, about as strong as jute and used for the same purposes. Because some of the strands stick out from the twine, however, it is sometimes difficult to tie into tight knots.

Although many kinds of store carry twine, it is best to do your shopping at a good hardware store, where the proprietor is likely to know the differences among twines.

Ultrasonic Cleaner. This is an amazing new kind of cleaner that removes dirt, grease, oil, tarnish, stains, rust, and loose coatings from small articles with any kind of hard or semi-hard surface. It does not clean fabrics.

The cleaner is a small portable electrical appliance with a tank containing a general-purpose detergent solution or special liquid cleaner. When the electricity is turned on, high-intensity ultrasonic energy produced by a transducer causes the liquid to bubble violently. The bubbles, which are so small that you cannot see them, act like tiny scrubbing brushes, removing dirt and other soil from the immersed objects. The action makes no sound. The only movement is a slight shimmering of the liquid's surface. If you put your hand into the liquid, you feel only a slight smarting sensation.

Ultrasonic cleaners have three advantages: (1) They can do in a few minutes what it might take you a half hour or more to do by hand. They will, for instance, take rust off badly encrusted tools in about 120 seconds. (2) Because the object being cleaned does not move, there is no danger of breakage. You can clean the most fragile glass and china safely. (3) The cleaners have the unique ability to blast dirt and other soil out of cracks and crevices you cannot get into in any other way. This means they will clean such intricate things as jewelry, repoussé silver, fishing reels, and locks.

The only things that should not be cleaned ultrasonically are worn silverplated items and articles held together with glue or cement. And ultrasonic cleaners cannot clean away contaminants, such as paint, which require special solvents.

Urea. A plastic used to make appliance housings, handles, knobs, electrical devices, etc. It is available in a wide range of colors and has a glossy surface that resists scratching, cleaning fluids, alcohol, oil, and detergents. It retains its shape under normal usage, but will become deformed if exposed to a continuous temperature of 170 degrees.

Clean with detergent solution or cleaning fluid. Mend broken parts with plastic-mending adhesive.

Urethane. Properly called polyurethane. This is one of the most amazing plastics yet developed. You probably first encountered it in mattresses, cushions, and thin-wall insulation in refrigerators and freezers. Now it is also being used for rug cushions, shoe soles and uppers, boat hulls, automobile dashboards, false ceiling beams, exterior doors, window trim, varnish, seamless flooring, house insulation, roofing, furniture, blankets, bedspreads, and clothing.

Urethane is most commonly used as a foam. Depending on its density, this may be soft, resilient, and buoyant, or hard, rigid, and tough, or anywhere in between. In a new development, the plastic is poured in one step to produce an article with a porous core and an integral, decorative skin. The core may be soft or hard; the skin may resemble wood, leather, velvet—almost anything.

In blankets, a very thin, very flexible layer of urethane foam is flocked on both sides with nylon. In fabrics, the urethane is applied to a cloth backing to produce a material resembling vinyl fabrics but considerably softer. When used in fabrics, varnish, and floors, urethane gives unusual resistance to abrasion and tearing.

Articles made of urethane are cleaned with detergent solution; mended with plastic-mending adhesive or epoxy. If a piece of rigid urethane that is used in furniture is scratched or gouged, fill the wound with water putty and sand smooth. Then apply a finish to match the surrounding area.

For how to launder urethane blankets, see *Vellux.* (Also see *Foam; Insulation;* and *Roofs, Urethane.*)

Vacuum Cleaners. There are three types of general-purpose vacuum cleaner and three types of special-purpose cleaner. Most families don't really need the latter, although they find them useful. But you can hardly get along without the general-purpose type if you want to keep your house clean.

General-purpose vacuum cleaners.

Uprights. The upright vacuum cleaner is a one-piece machine with a long handle to which a large suction head and dust bag are connected. It is easier to store and less awkward to handle than other types. And it is outstanding for cleaning rugs because a revolving brush in the suction head beats dust and dirt out of the pile. On the other hand, if the pile is very deep, the cleaner may become choked with fuzz. This is particularly a problem on new rugs.

When equipped with cleaning tools, uprights can also be used to clean bare floors, walls, furniture, etc. This cleaning is done by suction alone. But when the hose and cleaning tools are attached, the cleaner loses its easy maneuverability.

Tanks and canisters are alike although they differ in appearance. A tank cleaner is a long, horizontal cylinder; a canister is a more compact unit of many shapes. The motor and dirt bag are enclosed in this container (whatever its shape), and the container rolls around on wheels or glides at the end of a flexible hose to which the cleaning tools are attached.

The ordinary tank or canister cleaner cleans by suction alone. It is unequaled for cleaning bare floors, walls, and furniture but is much less efficient on rugs. For this reason, many cleaners are now sold with a special attachment that looks something like a small upright cleaner and contains a revolving brush. This does an excellent rug-cleaning job.

Central vacuum-cleaning systems. You have probably seen these in hotels. Small systems are also made for the home. They consist of a large motor and dirt receptacle, which is usually installed in the basement, utility room, or garage; a network of tubes running through the walls, floors, and ceilings; and a long, flexible hose with various cleaning tools. In operation, the hose is plugged into cleaning outlets in the walls; and when the motor is turned on, dirt is picked up by the cleaning tool and sucked back through the hose and hidden pipes into the dirt receptacle. Cleaning is done mainly by suction, but some systems offer an attachment with a revolving brush.

The high cost of the central system is its chief disadvantage. On the other hand, the system doesn't make noise in the living areas of the house. Any fine dust that escapes from the dirt receptacle is confined to that area. And because of the dirt receptacle's size, it takes a long time to fill up and does not lose efficiency as quickly as smaller vacuums. (The dirt receptacle usually needs to be emptied only a few times a year; and in some systems, it doesn't need to be emptied at all because the accumulated dirt is flushed down a plumbing drain.)

Central vacuum-cleaning systems can be installed in any house, new or old, although the work is obviously easier in new houses. Because the hose is about 25 feet long, you don't need many outlets to plug into. In a small house, three or four are usually enough.

Special-purpose vacuum cleaners.

Lightweight uprights. These are sometimes called stick-type uprights or electric brooms. They consist of a long handle with a plastic case containing the motor and dirt bag. The pick-up head usually swivels. Most makes clean by suction alone; a few have revolving brushes. Some have attachments for above-the-floor cleaning.

Lightweight uprights are by no means as powerful as the general-purpose cleaners and for that reason should be used only for quick tidying up.

Hand vacuums are small lightweight units for cleaning automobiles, furniture, stairs, etc. Some have attachments. They usually clean by suction, but some have revolving brushes.

Shop vacuums are large barrel-shaped canister cleaners that are mounted on casters and pulled around at the end of a flexible hose to which the cleaning tools are attached. Cleaning is by suction.

The claim is made that shop vacuums are in a class by themselves when it comes to picking up dirt—especially big, heavy particles. We have not found this to be the case.

Vacuum-cleaning attachments. Don't take these for granted when you buy a new vacuum cleaner. They get hard wear, and if they are not well made of durable materials, they will cause a lot of aggravation and will need to be replaced.

Attachments that are usually included with vacuum cleaners are the following:

Flexible hose. This is 6 to 8 feet long, except in central systems. Some manufacturers guarantee their hoses for up to five years.

Wands. These are two lightweight aluminum tubes which are used individually or together to form a handle for the tools. They should be easy to connnect and disconnect; but the connections should be airtight. Wands are usually the first attachments to break down.

Carpet tool is about a foot wide and made of metal. It should have a swivel arrangement so that you can slide it under low pieces of furniture. Some carpet tools have brushes; some don't.

Floor brush is also about a foot wide, but is made of plastic and has stiff bristles. Some manufacturers make combination floor and carpet tools.

Upholstery brush is about 6 inches wide and has short bristles. It does a better job than an upholstery tool, which lacks bristles.

Dusting brush is about 3 inches across and has long, soft bristles. It is usually round or square.

Crevice tool is a flattened plastic tube used to clean between the seat and back of an upholstered chair, between radiator sections, etc. It is a good gadget, though one you don't use as often as some.

Dirt bags. Almost all vacuum cleaners now use throwaway paper bags. They are far neater than the old cloth bags, but of course they add to the expense of owning a vacuum cleaner.

It is a very good idea to check whether the dirt bags for the vacuum cleaner you are interested in are sold only by the manufacturer and his dealers. Such bags are often overpriced. On the other hand, bags not made by the manufacturer may be of an inferior quality and burst readily.

Useful vacuum-cleaner features. Retractable cords. But unfortunately, when the reel wears out—as it usually does—it is quite costly to repair.

Adjustable cleaning action on upright cleaners. This enables you to adjust the vacuum to the carpet pile and texture.

Adjustable suction control on tank and canister cleaners. Without it, you are likely to pick lightweight rugs right up off the floor.

Swivel top on canister cleaners. The hose is connected into this. It permits you to put the vacuum in the center of the room and clean in all corners without moving it.

Canister cleaners that stand on end (as well as lie flat) take less space in the cleaning closet. They are also easy to use on stairs because they stand firmly on a tread.

Lightweight upright vacuum cleaners that can be converted into hand vacuums.

Bumper guard on uprights, canisters, and tanks protects furniture.

Handle on upright easily adjusts to horizontal so you can get under furniture.

How to use a vacuum cleaner. Central systems should be installed on their own 120-volt, 15-amp circuit. All other vacuum cleaners can be plugged into any 15-amp or 20-amp circuit.

Pick up pins, nails, and other sharp metal objects before vacuuming. If you dislike stooping, attach a magnet to the end of a stick.

If an upright vacuum moves sluggishly on a rug, it should be adjusted upward so that there is less wear on the rug and the revolving brush.

Reduce suction on tank or canister cleaners when cleaning lightweight throw rugs and draperies. You may have to hold draperies taut to keep them from being sucked into the cleaning tool. If you cannot reduce suction enough to keep from picking up a throw rug, stand on one edge of the rug and move the cleaning nozzle away from you.

Do not use a carpet tool on bare floors unless it has bristles. Even though they seem smooth, metal tools can make scratches.

Don't use the end of a wand or the metal end of the flexible hose as a cleaning tool. It is easy to bend these out of shape, and once bent, they are difficult to straighten.

Before cleaning walls, clean the vacuum-cleaner brush thoroughly by vacuuming the bristles. It is then a good idea to wash the brush in detergent solution. Rinse and dry completely.

Throw away a paper dirt bag before it becomes so clogged with dirt that the vacuum no longer picks up. Clean a cloth bag occasionally by brushing it well inside and out.

Do not run a revolving brush over the power cord: it may cut the insulation. And make a habit of pulling the cord plug out of all outlets by hand; don't yank on the cord.

Regularly remove threads and strings that wrap around the revolving brush.

If something goes wrong. Make sure the vacuum-cleaner cord is not broken. Check whether the house fuse has blown.

If the cleaner runs but doesn't pick up, it is probably clogged with fuzz and dirt. On a tank or canister cleaner, shift the hose to the blower end and try to blow the stoppage out of the hose. If this doesn't work, make a tight U-bend in the end of a stiff wire, poke the wire through the hose and into the stoppage, and pull it out.

On a central system, use a plumber's snake to clean the tubes in the wall. On an upright cleaner, remove the bag. Fuzz has probably accumulated in the metal throat to which the bag is attached. Clean it out with a stiff wire.

If the vacuum still does not work or works badly, have it serviced.

If the cloth bag of an upright is torn, patch it with vinyl or fabric, depending on what it is made of. Use plastic-mending adhesive to stick down a vinyl patch; fabric-mending adhesive on fabric.

If a hose is punctured, overwrap it tightly with plastic electrical tape.

If the joint between two wands is loose, either replace the wands or join the two permanently by overwrapping with plastic electrical tape.

Valances. Strictly speaking, valances are short draperies hung from rods over the tops of windows or under the edges of beds. But decorators also make valances out of wood, like cornices, and then cover them with fabric. And the electrical industry uses the word to describe a fluorescent fixture made of wood (not necessarily covered with fabric) and mounted over a window or even on a blank wall. See *Lighting* and *Cornices.* In any case, window valances usually do not have tops; and if hung on rods, they don't even have sides.

Vanity. This is either a dressing table or a built-in cabinet with a sink recessed in the counter top. You can build your own bathroom vanity out of plywood. Excellent stock units are also available. Generally, vanities are 31 inches high (to the top of the counter) and 21 inches deep. The length is variable. For how to take care of a dressing table, see *Furniture, Wood.*

Varnish. This transparent wood finish, which can also be applied to other materials, is formulated in many ways; may have a gloss or flat effect; and may be more or less colorless or contain a stain.

The more common types of varnish include the following: (1) all-purpose varnish for general interior use; (2) interior paneling and trim varnish; (3) floor varnish with high resistance to yellowing and abrasion; (4) bar varnish made especially for counters and tables exposed to alcohol; (5) furniture varnish; (6) spar varnish—a very tough formulation for exterior use; (7) urethane varnish, with the best abrasion resistance of all varnishes.

The most favorable temperature for varnishing is 70 degrees, and the varnish should be fairly warm, too. If it is cold, heat it in a pot of warm water. Never shake the can or stir it violently lest you form bubbles which are hard to brush out.

You should apply varnish in an atmosphere that is as free of dust as possible. If working indoors, vacuum the surface to be covered as well as the room.

If more than one coat of varnish is to be applied, the first is generally thinned by adding ¼ pint turpentine to 1 quart varnish. Read the directions on the can, however.

Apply varnish with a full brush, covering a small area fairly heavily, then spreading the varnish out evenly by brushing across the grain and then with the grain.

The high gloss of most varnishes can be—and for the best effect, should be—reduced by going over them carefully with very fine sandpaper or steel wool. For a superlative luster, rub the surface with pumice stone or rottenstone. (See *Abrasives.*)

While varnish is the toughest and most widely used transparent finish, it has one serious drawback: if damaged, you cannot patch it without showing obvious marks where the new finish overlaps the old.

Varnish is soluble in turpentine and naphtha before it dries; but after drying, it can be easily removed only with paint remover.

Vases.

How to clean. Put small ones in the dishwasher when you are through with them. Wash large ones with detergent solution or, if necessary, scrub with a general-purpose cleanser. If dried scum in a vase resists all normal attempts to remove it, fill the vase with a strong solution of baking soda or household ammonia and let it stand for a day or two.

How to repair small cracks and holes. If a clear glass vase is cracked but not broken, run a ribbon of cellulose cement along the crack on the inside. On a translucent glass or pottery vase, cover the crack with silicone caulking compound. Caulking compound can also be used to seal holes in metal vases. The alternative is plastic metal.

Vellux. Trade name for an unusual fabric developed by West Point-Pepperell, Inc. In essence, it consists of a layer of very thin urethane foam covered on both sides with nylon flocking or on one side with flocking and on the other with tricot or some similar fabric. The material is used in blankets, bedspreads, and clothing.

Vellux is normally washed in warm water for just a few minutes, but if heavily soiled it can be washed in hottest possible water for a longer time without damage to the fabric. Dry at high heat.

Velour. A heavy, soft fabric with a nap or pile—quite similar to velvet. Cotton velour is used in draperies and clothing; wool velour in clothing. Both types need to be dry-cleaned.

Velvet. A soft, lustrous, low-pile fabric with a plain back, velvet varies in weight and in the way it is designed. It is used in clothing, draperies, upholstery, and bedspreads.

Velvet is woven from silk, rayon, nylon, wool, and cotton. It must be dry-cleaned.

Velvet is also the name for a type of woven rug. See *Rugs.*

Velveteen. A cotton or rayon fabric resembling velvet but constructed in a different way. It is used in draperies and clothing and should be dry-cleaned.

Veneer. When we speak of veneer, we generally think of wood veneer—a very thin sheet of wood (usually a fine wood) that is glued to a base of wood, plywood, or particle board.

Because of the great improvements that have been made in glues, wood veneers today rarely crack or come loose from the base. But this was not the case in days gone by. So if you own any old veneered furniture, you will probably have to repair it occasionally.

If veneer is loose, pry it up slightly and scrape the glue from its back and the base. Blow out the crumbs. Then spread a thin layer of white wood glue on either of the surfaces (base or veneer); press the veneer down and wipe off any glue that squeezes out. Clamp or weight for 24 hours.

If a piece of veneer has broken away from the base and become lost, you can usually buy a sheet of new veneer from a woodworking shop or a shop specializing in the sale of fine woods. From this cut a piece somewhat larger than the hole in the furniture. Match grains between the new piece and old as well as possible. Then hold the scrap firmly over the hole and with a very sharp knife cut a square or rectangular or triangular patch slightly larger than the hole. You should simultaneously cut through the old veneer. Remove the old veneer inside the margins of the cut you have made. Scrape the glue from the base, apply white glue, set in the patch, and clamp it down for 24 hours.

The patch must then be sanded level with the surrounding wood. Use medium followed by very fine sandpaper. Then stain and finish the patch.

Dents and scratches in veneer are repaired like those in solid wood. See *Wood*.

If you refinish veneered furniture, be careful when you are sanding not to thin or bevel the veneer around the edges. This is easy to do because there is a natural tendency to drop the hand as you slide the sandpaper off the furniture. You can avoid this if you wrap the paper around a fairly long block of wood and if you keep the block flat on the veneered surface when you come to the edges.

Venetian Blinds. Standard venetian blinds are made with 2-inch metal slats held in wide tapes. So-called mini-blinds have 1-inch slats and no tapes—just two slender cords.

The two types of blind are equally effective in keeping out the sun and providing privacy. But the mini-blind is more attractive because when the slats are open, the blind almost disappears. On the other hand, standard blinds are available in many more sizes and cost considerably less.

If a venetian blind is to be installed inside the window casing, there must be at least 1 inch of flat surface inside the casing to permit mounting of the brackets. Lacking this 1 inch flat surface, you must install the blind outside the casing. In this instance, you should order a blind that is 3 inches wider than the window opening.

The fastest way to dust or wash standard venetian blinds is to drop them to the sill or below, and slant the slats downward. Then go over them with a dust cloth or sponge. Then slant the slats upward and repeat the process. When washing blinds, take care not to dirty the tapes and cords. Mini-blinds are dusted in the same way, but when they need washing, they can be taken down and dunked in a tub filled with detergent solution.

When tapes and cords become too grimy to bear, take down the blinds, remove the cords and then the tapes, and replace them with new soil-resistant vinyl tapes and nylon cords. The alternative is to let a venetian blind cleaning service do the work for you.

If you want to change the color of a blind, take it apart and lay the slats close together but not quite touching on a couple of narrow boards and spray them with an aerosol paint. Cloth tapes can be dyed to match the slats, vinyl tapes cannot be dyed.

Vermeil (vur-*male*). A metal—usually silver—plated with gold. It is not common; but plates, knives, forks, spoons, etc., of vermeil are sometimes given to couples on their fiftieth wedding anniversary. Vermeil should be washed and polished like silver.

Vicuna. Vicuna is the hair of a wild Peruvian llama of the same name. It is extremely soft, beautiful hair which is made into a clothing fabric. But since the animal is protected by law, the supply of hair is limited. (Imitations are now being made from other fibers.) Vicuna garments, whether genuine or fake, should be dry-cleaned.

Vinyl. A versatile plastic used in upholstery, floor and wall coverings, shower curtains, hoses, and many other familiar items. It is strong, abrasion-resistant, and attractive, and is not affected by most household chemicals. On the other hand, it is damaged by nail polish and remover, moth repellents, and heat.

Clean vinyl with detergent and warm water or a special vinyl cleaner. Tears and breaks can be fixed with plastic-mending adhesive. For holes, make patches of vinyl fabric and stick them down with plastic-mending adhesive.

Vinyl Cement. See *Concrete*.

Vinyl Veneer. Vinyl veneer is a tough, thin, flexible vinyl sheet that is permanently bonded to furniture, cabinets, lamps, etc. It can be made to look exactly like wood, leather, and many other materials and finishes, and has exceptional resistance to stains, heat, fading, peeling, and chipping. Clean it with a damp sponge or sponge dipped in detergent solution.

If the veneer is dented but not broken, rubbing it with a smooth piece of metal compresses it and conceals the dent to a considerable extent. The same treatment helps to conceal a cut. But if the veneer is gouged, the hole must be filled with fillers used to repair wood furniture. It is also possible to set in a patch, but the veneer manufacturers recommend against this because of difficulties in working with the adhesive required and in securing a piece of veneer that exactly matches the old.

Voile. A sheer, transparent, soft fabric used in clothing and curtains. It was originally made of cotton but is now made of other fibers as well. Laundering depends on the fiber used.

Waffle Irons. Waffle irons, or bakers, are available as separate appliances, but the waffle iron-grill combination is more popular. The shape is square, rectangular, or, in waffle irons only, round; and the size of the baking or grilling area varies. Many models have nonstick cooking surfaces.

Some combination units have two separate sets of grids—one for waffles and one for grilling. Others have a set of reversible grids: there are no extra pieces to be stored.

Waffle irons have signal lights to indicate when the appliance is at the right temperature to start cooking. On some models, the light also signals when the waffle is done. The grids should have an overflow rim to catch excess batter.

Grilling on nearly all models can be done either with the lid closed so that both sides cook at once or with the lid opened back flat so that both the lid and bottom can be used for open grilling. If both sides are used, be sure the lid is well supported. For closed grilling, the appliance should be able to grill evenly and not turn out lopsided sandwiches. The grill grid should have a spout to drain off grease.

Wash nonstick waffle grids in detergent solution; but don't wash other waffle grids once they are seasoned because that destroys the grease film that keeps waffles from sticking. Smooth grids should be washed.

Wipe off the body of the waffle iron with detergent solution. If food becomes cooked on, clean like chromium plate (which see).

Walks.

How to build poured concrete walks. The concrete for walks is 4 inches thick and should project no more than ½ inch above the adjacent ground level. If the soil is well drained, dig it out to a depth of 3½ inches. Be sure to remove all sod and other organic matter. Then tamp well. If the soil is not well drained, dig deep enough to allow for a 4- to 6-inch base of compacted gravel.

Walks should slope at least 1/8 inch to every 1 foot. (That is, if a walk is 8 feet long, it should incline 1 inch from one end to the other. Or if a walk is 4 feet wide and is laid on flat land, it might incline from one side to the other ½ inch.)

Make forms of 2-by-4s and set them at the height of the finished walk. Stake them firmly in place. If thinner lumber is used, you will need more stakes to prevent the wood from bulging outward when the concrete is poured. Oil the frames well.

To provide for expansion of the concrete, expansion joints should be made at right angles to the walk every 4 to 6 feet. You can make joints with ½-inch boards faced on both sides with tarpaper, or with premolded material carried by masonry supply dealers. (This same type of joint should be used between walks and curbs or other fixed objects, such as house walls, that abut the walks.) You can also make joints by cutting 3/8-inch grooves across the concrete to a depth of 1 inch with your trowel or other piece of metal. Finish the grooves with a T-shaped edging tool, which you can buy or perhaps rent from a masonry supply dealer, held against a straight board.

For how to work with poured concrete, see *Concrete.*

How to make concrete flagstones. These

can be made in any shape by building wood forms 1½ to 2 inches deep; coating them with oil; placing them on a flat piece of tarpaper; and pouring in concrete. After the stones have cured for about 48 hours, construct the walk in the way described below under "How to build flagstone and slate walks." Concrete flagstones of irregular shape can also be poured directly into holes dug in the ground. Since there is no base to prevent heaving by frost, make them about 3 inches thick.

How to build brick walks. The surface of the walk should be level with the ground or just slightly higher. Provide a base 4 inches thick. The bottom 3 inches can be of gravel or crushed stone tamped well. On top of this place a 1-inch layer of sand or stone dust.

The walk should slope 1/8 inch for each foot lengthwise or crosswise. Stretch strings tightly to mark the edges. The strings also serve as your elevation lines.

Bricks laid flat along the edges of a walk or terrace tend to twist downward and outward under pressure. To prevent this, dig narrow trenches 8 inches deep along the sides of the walk and at the ends and set bricks in vertically. Pack soil around them to hold them upright.

Now cut a 4-inch board to a length equal to the width of the walk. Then cut the board into a T-shape by notching both ends to fit over the edge bricks. Between the edge bricks the board should project downward 2 inches—slightly less than the thickness of a brick.

Dampen the sand cushion slightly so the sand will pack. Level it and tamp roughly with a tamper. Then place your T-shaped board over the edge bricks and pull it along the walk to level the sand precisely. Do not try to level too much at one time because the sand is bound to be churned up and will need to be raked and leveled again. You may need to add sand and tamp it further to bring it up to the bottom of the board.

Set the first row of bricks on the sand end to end or side to side according to the pattern you are using. In the past, it was customary to leave a ¼-inch space on all sides of each brick; but the accepted practice today is to set the bricks as close together as possible. Lay a 2-by-4 across the top of the first row of bricks and tap it

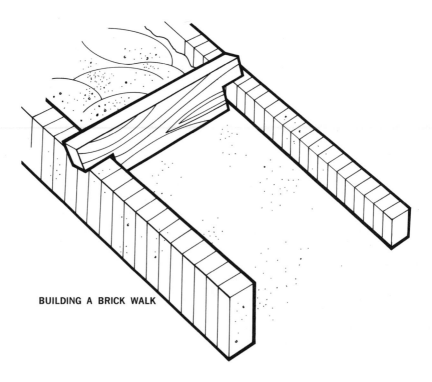

BUILDING A BRICK WALK

down until it rests on the edge bricks on both sides. The center bricks should now be well firmed on the sand cushion; but if they are not, lift them out, rake in more sand, and start again.

Set the second row of bricks snug against the first, and settle them with the 2-by-4 in the same way. Continue thus, leveling the sand, setting the bricks, and firming them in place. Check about every sixth row with a carpenter's square to make sure it is at right angles to the edges of the walk.

When the walk is completed, sweep sand into the joints and spray with water to settle it. The sand helps to lock the bricks together. But since you do not want a gritty surface, sweep up the excess when dry.

If a brick walk is constructed in this way, it is rarely necessary to consider building one on a concrete base. In fact, one well-known Midwestern landscape architect builds driveways of bricks and other small paving blocks in exactly this way except for doubling the thickness of the gravel base.

How to build flagstone and slate walks. If you use rectangular stones of the same size, you can lay out a walk yourself. If you use rectangular stones of different sizes, however, let the masonry supply dealer give you a plan for placing the stones. This raises your cost but saves you the trouble of making your own jigsaw puzzle. (Without a carefully worked out plan, you must cut stones, and inevitably wind up with a great deal of waste stone.)

Whoever plans the walk, lay it on 3 inches of gravel covered with 1 inch of sand. Extend this base about 3 inches to both sides of the walk in order to keep the stones from tilting into soft ground. Slope the walk like other walks. Set the stones 1/8 to ¼ inch apart, and fill the joints with dry sand to which a few handfuls of dry Portland cement have been added.

A second way to make a flagstone or slate walk is simply to scoop out holes for the stones and set them in without worrying about a gravel or sand base. But frost may heave the stones if they are only 1 inch thick, and in time there may be some breakage. So it is wise to use 1½-inch stones.

To lay a walk of irregular flagstones or slates, you can follow the procedure for laying rectangular stones on a sand-gravel base provided that you take the time to fit the stones closely enough to eliminate wide cracks. If you do not feel like doing this, excavate to a depth of 4 to 4½ inches and pour in a 2½- to 3-inch base of concrete, as for a poured concrete walk. Let this set for 24 hours. Then, just before setting the stones, brush the concrete with a grout made of ½ sack Portland cement in 3 gallons water. Immediately spread on this a level ½-inch layer of mortar in the proportion of 1 part Portland cement to 3 parts sand. Embed the stones in this, and trowel more mortar into the joints.

How to build walks with granite blocks. Granite blocks include cobblestones with somewhat rounded corners and cut rectangles of granite with squared corners. They are laid like bricks on a bed of sand.

How to build walks with fieldstone. Fieldstones are rough, uncut stones that are more or less flat on one side. They can be used to make a rather uneven but handsome walk.

Provide a well-tamped 3- to 4-inch base of gravel. Set the stones on this and level them. Then trowel a mortar of 1 part Portland cement and 3 parts sand into the joints. Pack it well and smooth it off even with the edges of the stones.

How to repair walks. If a section of a poured concrete walk settles, the obvious way to fix it is to pry it up with a crowbar and spread additional sand or gravel underneath. Bricks and stones that settle are handled in the same way: just pry them out of the walk and build up the base on which they rest. For other repairs, see *Concrete; Brick;* or *Stone.*

Wall Anchors. A wall anchor is a special device used to install or hang things on walls. It is substituted for nails, screws, thumbtacks, and picture hooks when those devices would, for one reason or another, be inadequate.

The following wall anchors are particularly useful:

Lead anchors are small cylinders of lead used to anchor screws or bolts into masonry and ceramic-tile walls and sometimes into plaster. To use them, you must first drill a hole with a carbide-tipped drill (power driven) or a star drill (a hand tool). The anchor is then tapped into the hole. When a screw or bolt is inserted, it forces the sides of the anchor to expand and grip tight against the surrounding wall.

Lead anchors are most useful when you need to drive only a few screws or bolts into a wall—as in hanging a gate or tying a vine to a brick wall.

Plastic anchors are similar to lead anchors but are not so strong. They are used only for fairly small screws.

Split-wing toggle bolts are long, slender bolts with two-piece, wing-shaped nuts. They are used to hang bathroom fixtures, mirrors, valances, and other heavy articles or articles subject to strain to hollow walls in which ordinary nails or screws would not hold. The walls might be of plaster, gypsum board, fiberboard, or thin hardboard or plywood. For example, if you want a curtain rod to extend well beyond the sides of a window frame, you may find that the wall at the ends of the rod is hollow: if you were to drive in an ordinary screw, there would be nothing it could bite into. So you would use a split-wing toggle bolt instead.

To install a toggle bolt, you must drill through the wall a hole big enough to receive the nut. Then remove the nut from the bolt; slip the bolt through the article to be hung; replace the nut on the bolt; push the nut and bolt through the wall; and screw the bolt tight. This pulls the nut up against the back of the wall and spreads the wings tight against it.

If you ever have occasion to remove the toggle bolt, the nut drops off inside the wall and is lost.

Hollow-wall screw anchors are something like toggle bolts and are used for the same purpose. But since they are shorter than toggle bolts, they cannot be used in walls of such great thickness. On the other hand, the holes you drill for them are smaller.

The nut on a hollow-wall anchor is a cylinder as long as the bolt. When you screw the bolt tight, the nut splits and draws up like a lot of bent knees against the back of the wall. If you remove the bolt at a later date, the nut stays in place. You can reset the bolt in it.

Studs are a type of nail, made of specially hardened steel, used to anchor things to solid masonry. Because they can be installed very rapidly without drilling, they are particularly useful for securing wood furring strips to basement walls.

To use studs, you must have a stud driver. All you do is put the stud into the driver, hold the front end of the driver against the wall, and tap the trigger on the back end with a hammer. A piston inside the driver concentrates the force of light hammer blows to the extent that the stud drives into solid concrete as if it were so much cheese.

Wall Coverings. Wallpaper is by far the most popular wall covering because it is extremely decorative, reasonably durable (more so today than in the past), and relatively inexpensive. The basic types available are discussed under *Wallpapering.* But a number of other coverings are also used:

Vinyl. This versatile plastic covering is second in popularity, and gaining. It is decorative and amazingly durable; widely used in hospitals, schools, commercial buildings.

Vinyl wall coverings are sometimes made of solid vinyl but are usually made of vinyl backed with fabric or paper. The plastic is applied to the backing as a built-up coating or as a thin film that is laminated to the backing. The latter construction is more abrasion-resistant but less common.

Types A, B, and C vinyl wall coverings are sold. The last are very heavy and made for commercial use. Type B is medium-weight and also used mainly in commercial buildings and the like; you might, however, install it in a family room, basement playroom, or other area that carries heavy traffic and gets very rough usage.

Type A vinyl is the kind usually used in homes. It weighs only about 8 ounces a square yard; comes usually in 24- and 27-inch widths and in single rolls 18 feet long or a little less. These coverings are more abrasion-resistant, stain-resistant, and scrubbable than the best wallpapers.

Vinyl is hung like wallpaper. There are, however, several special points to be noted:

1. Hang vinyl wall covering only when the indoor temperature is above 60 degrees.

2. Clean the walls thoroughly, making certain to remove crayon and ballpoint-pen marks. Other wall coverings such as paper must be scraped off completely.

3. Size cement plaster, cement block, asbestos-cement boards, and other alkaline surfaces with acrylic latex paint. It is not essential to size other surfaces but it facilitates installation of vinyl. Use a thinned mixture of the adhesive with which vinyl is hung.

4. Always use the adhesive recommended by the manufacturer of the wall covering. It should not be thinned; can be applied with a paint roller or a wallpaper paste brush. Take care to cover all surfaces. Fold each strip paste surface to paste surface. Then let the paste set for a few minutes. You should usually paste at least two strips ahead of your work.

5. Hang like wallpaper. However, because of the greater thickness of the vinyl, you should lap it around corners 2 or 3 inches.

6. Because vinyl does not breathe, you must take extra pains to paste it down tight. The bristles on a wallpaper smoothing brush should be trimmed to 1 inch in length. Go up and down and sideways time and again over each strip to eliminate blisters. If you are not satisfied that the brush is doing a good job, use a broad knife (a very wide wall scraper).

Should blisters persist, puncture them with a large needle to let out the air and smooth them down. If blisters appear several days after your project is completed, puncture them and squirt a little water underneath with an oil can. Or use a hypodermic needle. Then smooth down.

7. Joints must be butted. If because of unevenness in the wall you cannot avoid lapping the edges, cut lengthwise through the center of the lap with a razor blade. The blade should go through both layers of vinyl. Be sure to hold it straight up and down, lest you bevel the edges of the wall covering. Remove the strips that are cut off and press the edges of the vinyl strips down. They should now butt perfectly.

8. Clean each strip after it is hung with a sponge wrung out in warm water. Then dry.

Laminated papers. These are also called laminated textured papers, although many of them do not have texture. They are wall coverings made with a paper back to which a wide variety of flexible materials are laminated: grasscloth, felt, silk, hemp, burlap, cork, paper-thin wood veneer, metal foil, woven paper.

Laminated papers are usually expensive, and many are imported. Lengths and widths vary. They are hung like ordinary wallpaper, but the job is a fussy one.

The walls to be papered must first be covered with lining paper. Use wheat paste on all laminated papers except silks and other fine fabrics and light-colored papers. For these, use cellulose paste which will not stain or be visible on the surface. Whichever the paste, it must be mixed to a rather heavy consistency.

Paste one strip at a time and hang it immediately. However, if the paper is heavy or stiff, you should allow the paste to soak in for about 10 minutes and then apply a second coat. This softens the paper.

Although the edges of laminated papers are usually trimmed by the maker, you may have to trim them again because they are frequently uneven. The professional way to trim all kinds of wallpaper is to paste the strip first. Then you fold the top and bottom toward the center. Align the edges carefully. Then lay a straightedge along each edge of the strip, or selvage, and cut through the two layers of paper with a razor blade. Another way to trim the edges of wallpaper, which may be easier for you, is to do it before pasting. Just lay the strip pattern side up on your paste table. Do not fold it. Trim each edge with a razor blade, using a straightedge as your guide.

Do not roll the seams of heavily textured laminated papers; and use very little pressure on others.

Silks and other fine fabrics are cleaned— if you get paste on the surface—with a barely damp sponge. Don't rub hard. Other materials can be rubbed a bit more vigorously and can withstand more moisture.

Laminated wood veneers. These are made by laminating very thin veneers of choice woods to a fabric backing. The strips are 10 to 24 inches wide and up to 12 feet long. You can buy matched veneers if you want an overall, continuous wood pattern. You can also buy unmatched veneers to produce a plank-like effect.

Wood veneers are hung like wallpaper, but with some variations:

1. Veneers can be applied to any clean, smooth surface from which other wall coverings have been removed. Porous surfaces should be primed with shellac. To assure adhesion, solid exterior masonry walls must first be covered with gypsum board nailed to wood furring strips.

2. Use the adhesive recommended by the manufacturer of the veneer. It should be heated in warm water to a temperature of 75 to 85 degrees (or to the consistency of heavy cream). The room should be 70 degrees or above.

A priming coat of the adhesive should first be applied to the wall with a stiff paintbrush and allowed to dry. A second coat of adhesive is then brushed on the back of the veneer strips and allowed to become slightly tacky (partially dry) before the strip is hung.

3. Matched veneers are hung in one direction only in the exact sequence printed on the back of the strips. Since the first strip will not match the last, work from an inconspicuous corner all the way around the room.

Unmatched veneers can be hung in any sequence.

4. Before pasting the strips, trim them at top and bottom so they are slightly longer than the wall height. Then, when hanging, allow the top and bottom to overlap the ceiling and baseboard slightly; crease the veneer into the corners; and trim with a razor blade.

5. To smooth veneers on a wall, use a broad knife made of fiber. Always smooth with the grain; never across. Use plenty of pressure. If there are any blisters, slice through them with a razor blade.

Twenty-four hours after veneers are hung, check again for blisters by throwing a flashlight beam across the wall. If you find a blister, wet a scrap of veneer with water and place it over the blister wood side down. Then press down with an electric iron heated to the linen setting.

6. Butt all joints. If laps are unavoidable, slice through them with a razor blade as for vinyl wall covering.

7. Do not try to hang veneer around a lighting fixture. Take the fixture down and make a small hole in the veneer for the wires. After the veneer is hung, cut a larger hole to expose the entire electrical box. Then reconnect the light.

8. Radiators must be removed if veneers are to be hung behind them.

9. Remove adhesive from the face of the veneer at once with a cloth dipped in water or alcohol. If adhesive does dry on the veneer, it can be removed with very fine steel wool.

10. The veneered walls should be given a protective finish 48 hours after the strips are hung (allow more time if the weather is humid). First sand the entire surface with very fine sandpaper. Then apply any finish you might use on other fine wood paneling. Lacquer is preferred, however, because if blisters should appear later, you can heat-treat them as above without damaging the lacquer.

Oil finishes may seep through veneers and weaken the adhesive. Fillers may do the same thing, so you should first seal the veneers with lacquer or shellac.

Fabrics. Almost any fabric can be used as a wall covering, but burlap and felt are the only decorative materials that are pasted up. The others are stretched on a frame.

Burlap is hung like wallpaper with butt joints. Use cellulose paste and give it time to soak into the fabric before hanging. Smooth the fabric carefully, working from the center toward the edges. Be careful not to pull or push hard on the edges because they are easily distorted. Burlap may also ravel.

Felt used for covering walls has a specially treated impervious backing. Hang it like burlap, but with wheat paste. Some decorators and paperhangers use a lining paper under felt, but this is not necessary.

Cork and resilient flooring. Apply these to a wall as you would to a floor. See *Floors, Resilient.*

Wallpapering. Once considered a job that only professionals should undertake, wall-papering is now one of the most common do-it-yourself projects. True, the uninitiated are still a bit fearful of undertaking it. But once someone tries it, he is usually a paperhanger for life.

In short, wallpapering is easy. This is not to say, however, that the work goes fast or that you can achieve a satisfactory effect without paying close attention to what you are doing. It is a rare room that can be papered well in a single day.

Types of wallpaper. Most wallpaper made today is of the conventional un-pasted kind; but as every novice quickly finds out, there is also prepasted paper. If you have never hung wallpaper, you will probably decide to use the latter (assuming you find a pattern you like) because all you have to do is cut it into strips, roll it through a container of water, and smooth it on the wall. This sounds very easy—and is.

Actually, however, if you have ever hung unpasted paper, you will discover that, despite the extra work involved, *it* is easier to hang. Reason: It doesn't come down around your ears as you are trying to smooth it on the wall. And it is easier to position, because once it is on the wall, you can slide it slightly from side to side and up and down. In other words, you don't have to hit it right the first time as you do with prepasted paper.

Experienced paperhangers have been known to start out with prepasted paper because they liked the pattern, but found the work so exasperating that they wound up hanging the paper with a very thin paste in the usual way. There is no problem about doing this.

All wallpaper made today in the United States is washable to some degree. The least washable is made with a protein size. An in-between grade is known as a plastic-bonded paper and is made with a protein size to which plastic is added. The most washable paper is plastic-coated. This is impervious to most stains and can, in some cases, be scrubbed with a mild powdered cleanser.

Unfortunately, the only way anyone—including a wallpaper dealer—can distinguish between the two plastic-covered papers is to drop water on them. This is absorbed by a plastic-bonded paper (and also by paper made simply with protein size) but not by a plastic-coated paper.

One other difference between wallpapers is in the paper stock. Until a few years ago, the stock used was not strong enough to resist tearing when someone tried to rip a strip off the wall. Now some wallpapers are made with a peelable stock. This is so strong that you can pull it off the wall without wetting it.

If peelable wallpaper is available in a pattern you like, use it. True, you may never have occasion to repaper the room in which you hang it. But if you do, it will save you a lot of work.

A not so minor point worth noting about all wallpaper is that manufacturers today discard patterns within a year or two. Very few are kept in production for many years. So if you find a pattern that you are sure you will want to use forever, it's a good idea to buy a double supply at the start. Sooner or later the first paper hung will become shabby enough to be replaced.

Estimating wallpaper needs. Wallpaper is sold by the single roll but is actually made up in bolts containing one, two, or three single rolls. Although roll widths vary from about 18 to 28 inches after trimming, each single roll contains roughly 35 square feet. Part of this is lost, however, when you match patterns and trim the paper, so you should not figure on getting more than 30-square-foot coverage out of a single roll.

Whether you or the wallpaper dealer figures how many rolls of paper you will need, you will probably be the one who determines the size of the wall space to be papered. In a room with windows and doors of more or less conventional size, measure the length of all walls and the height of the walls from the top of the baseboards to the ceiling. Multiply the total wall length in feet by the wall height in feet to get the square feet of wall area. Divide by 30 to determine the number of single rolls required. Then subtract one single roll for every two wall openings or fraction thereof.

In a room with doors and windows of unusual size, figure the total square feet of wall space. Then measure the actual size of each wall opening, including the trim, and subtract from the wall figure before dividing by 30.

In a room in which a wall follows the roof line, the slanting wall and the walls adjacent to it must be measured separately.

Whatever the size and shape of the room you paper, there is one good rule to follow in ordering paper: Don't figure your needs too closely. Err slightly on the high side. It is better to have an unused roll of paper when the job is done than to discover you must order an extra roll. This is because you may not be able to buy an extra roll with the same "run number" as the original rolls, and as a result there may be a slight difference in the color of the roll.

Tools and equipment. Paperhanger's kits are on the market, but the equipment they include is usually cheap and undersized. It is better to buy each item separately. Since the cost is modest, don't skimp on quality. You will need the following things:

8-inch paste brush.

8-inch calcimine brush.

12-inch smoothing brush.

1-inch seam roller.

Pair of large shears (12-inch is excellent).

6-foot folding rule.

Some type of 6-foot straightedge for cutting and tearing wallpaper strips (a regular paperhanger's straightedge is best, but you can do very well with a straight pine board about 2 or 3 inches wide).

A large box of single-edge razor blades (they are cheaper from a wallpaper store than a drugstore).

8 feet of strong cotton string with a plumb bob tied to one end and a nail to the other; also a piece of blue chalk.

Pencils.

Two pails—one for water and the other for paste.

Large sponge.

Clean rags.

Three smooth 12-inch pine boards 6 feet long and two sawhorses to make a paste table.

Stepladder.

Canvas drop cloths to protect floors (old mattress pads are just as good).

The above items are used strictly for the paper hanging. In addition, you will probably need a screwdriver to remove electric switch plates and a pair of pliers to loosen lighting fixtures. You may also need a second stepladder and several 2-inch-thick planks to make a trestle to stand on. And if you are repapering a room, you will also need a patented tool called a Strip Zum to remove the old wallpaper.

How to prepare walls for papering. This is tedious work but essential, because unless a wall is smooth and clean, the wallpaper you apply will never look well. Here are the steps you may have to take.

Knock or scrape out loose and broken

plaster or other material and fill holes and cracks with spackle or patching plaster. Sand smooth.

If bare plaster walls are less than six months old, test them for hot spots with a mixture (made up by your druggist) of 1 gram phenolphthalein powder in 15 cc alcohol. Dab this on the wall here and there. If the plaster turns pink or red, you must swab the walls with a solution of 4 pounds zinc sulfate in 1 gallon hot water. (You can assume that plaster walls over six months old are safe to paper without testing.)

Nail down loose and buckling gypsum board panels and reset nails that have popped through the surface. Cover nail heads with spackle.

If walls are covered with unfinished gypsum board or fiberboard, paint them with a primer sealer; otherwise you will not be able to remove wallpaper at a later date without damaging the boards.

If walls are lightly stippled or have a sand finish, remove the roughness with an electric sander. Walls with a stronger texture or walls that have been badly pitted and scarred should be sanded as smooth as possible. Fill depressions with spackle. Then cover the walls with lining paper (a cheap, rather coarse white wallpaper). This is applied with paste—and always with butt joints—like patterned wallpaper. Extremely rough, uneven walls are covered first with the lining felt used under resilient floor materials and then with lining paper.

Dull high-gloss paint and varnish by washing walls with washing soda. Rinse well.

Remove old calcimine with warm water and steel wool.

Wash all walls that are dirty with detergent solution. Remove crayon and other wax deposits with cleaning fluid. Remove mildew with chlorine bleach.

Removing wallpaper. If close examination of a wall shows the old paper is smooth and tight, the chances are that you can paper directly over it without unhappy results. But before you start hanging new paper, smooth down lapped joints in the old paper by sanding.

As a rule, however, it is best never to hang new paper over old because the paste on the new paper softens the old and may cause blisters which will not disappear.

On a sound plaster wall, you can usually scrape off one or two layers of paper while they are dry with a Strip Zum. Spots that resist should be saturated with water to weaken the old paste. On any other kind of wall, you should always wet the paper before attacking it with your Strip Zum; otherwise the tool may gouge through the paper into the wall itself.

If simple wetting and scraping have little effect on old wallpaper, rent a wallpaper steamer. This consists of a boiler which supplies steam through a hose to a perforated steam plate which is held against the wall. The steam softens the paste and enables you to strip off most papers in large pieces. However, if a paper is plastic-coated or has been painted or varnished, you will probably have to scratch the surface with coarse sandpaper or a nutmeg grater before the steam will penetrate.

Burlap, canvas, and muslin can sometimes be ripped off a wall dry. If not, soak them with water. Whatever you do, work slowly because you may pull part of the wall down with the fabric.

First steps in hanging wallpaper. 1. Unscrew heating grilles, switch and outlet plates. But leave lighting fixtures in place till you are ready to paper around them.

2. Size all surfaces except old wallpaper and lining paper. Size is a powdered glue that makes wallpaper stick better, allows you to slide it around on the wall, and indicates hot spots in plaster by turning pink.

Size is usually made by mixing 1 pound of the powder with 4 pints of warm water and then adding 5 to 7 pints of cold water. Apply with a calcimine brush and give it several hours to dry.

A less common kind of size comes mixed with wheat paste and is applied to wallpaper with the paste.

3. Mix the paste—either a white wheat paste or a cellulose paste which dries clear. One is as good as the other. Follow the mixing directions on the package. The paste should be about the consistency of a thick pea soup. It must be free of lumps.

Always use a clean bucket for paste and always mix a new batch each day. It is, however, permissible to thin the current day's batch with water. In fact, this may be necessary because paste made in the morning becomes quite thick by the afternoon.

4. Make sure the wallpaper is colorfast by sponging water on a scrap. Generally, modern papers will not run; but occasionally they do, and in that case you must take extra pains not to get paste or fingerprints on the printed side.

5. Clear the room so you can work.

6. Look the room over carefully to see whether you will run into any odd problems when you start papering. Are corners straight? Are door and window frames straight? Is the ceiling the same height all the way around?

7. Decide at what point on the walls you will hang your first strip. This will depend on the wallpaper pattern and also on the design of the room. If the paper has a kind of all-over pattern, you can start papering anywhere—probably next to a door. But if the paper has a few scattered, bold spots, you should make sure they are positioned in the places where they will contribute most to the beauty of the room.

The other matter to be considered is whether the room has a dominant feature that automatically attracts the eye as one enters the room. (The dominant feature in a living room, for instance, may be a fireplace and the chimney breast above it.) If the answer is yes, then you should make certain that the wallpaper is correctly positioned at that point. (This usually means that the main design in the wallpaper pattern should be in the exact center of the most prominent wall.)

8. If you are papering the four walls of a room, decide at what point you will finish the job. This is because your last two strips of paper will not meet together perfectly. So it is best to conceal this mismatch as best you can by making the final joint in a corner or perhaps over a door or window—wherever it will be inconspicuous.

There is no law that says you must always paper in one direction from your starting point. On the contrary, depending on your starting point, you may paper to the right, to the left, or to both right and left. For example, if you hang your first strip in the corner where you also expect to hang your last strip, you must work in one direction all the way around the room. However, if you hang your first strip in the middle of the wall opposite the entrance to the room and if you plan to finish the job in the corner to one side of the entrance, then you must work away from the starting strip in both directions.

9. Decide where the wallpaper pattern should meet the ceiling line. This is most important when your pattern has strong design elements. Unfortunately, there are no real rules to guide you except one: Don't position the paper so that a person or animal pictured must be beheaded at the ceiling line. All you can do otherwise is to hold the paper up against the wall and try it this way and that until you hit on the effect that is best.

Establishing a vertical. Wallpaper must hang straight, and the only way you can be certain that it does is to get your first strip straight. A plumb line rubbed with blue chalk is used. (You can also use a 4-foot carpenter's level; but unless you do a great deal of carpentry, this is a more expensive tool than a few amateur wallpapering projects can justify.)

First measure the width of the wallpaper. Then, if your first strip is to be hung next to a door or window frame, measure out from the top of the door frame the width of the paper minus ¾ inch. Mark with a pencil. Hang your plumb line squarely over this mark and drive the nail at the top of the line into the wall. When the bob at the bottom of the line stops swinging, press it against the wall with one hand, pinch the middle of the line between the fingers of your other hand, pull it straight out a few inches and let it snap against the wall. The blue chalk line thus made is your vertical line to which your first strip of paper is hung. (If the chalk line is not vertical—because you pulled the plumb line crooked—erase it and make a second line. In any case, if the chalk line is very intense and powdery, blur it with a dry finger so the chalk won't rub off on the wallpaper.)

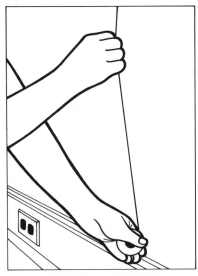

SNAPPING A CHALK LINE

If the starting point for your paperhanging is a corner, the procedure is much the same. In this case, however, you should first hold your plumb line in the corner to determine whether it is straight. Mark the point that is farthest off vertical; measure out from this the width of the wallpaper plus ¾ inch; and make your vertical chalk line at that point.

If you start in the middle of a wall, find the midpoint and measure one-half the width of the wallpaper to either side. Snap your chalk line there.

Hanging wallpaper. Checking run numbers. A run number is the number given to a roll of wallpaper to indicate when it was printed. If a roll of a wallpaper pattern named Springtime is stamped Run No. 3, it was printed the third time that pattern was put on the

presses. If another roll of Springtime carries another run number—say, 6, 10, or 17—this means it was printed during another production run. More important, it means that there may be some slight differences in the colors of Springtime rolls produced in Run No. 3 and Springtime rolls produced in any other run.

As a rule, when you buy a given number of rolls of a certain wallpaper pattern, all the rolls shipped to you are taken from the same production run. But every once in a while there is a slip-up.

To guard against this annoying eventuality, the first step you should take before actually hanging wallpaper is to make sure that all the rolls you have received are stamped on the back with the same run number. If they are not or if for some reason one of the rolls doesn't carry a run number, you should unroll all the rolls a few feet and compare colors. If there are any differences, ask your dealer to replace the odd rolls.

Uncurling wallpaper. If you want to keep your sanity, it is necessary to uncurl wallpaper—especially as the wallpaper roll grows smaller. Hold the paper pattern side up, unroll it several feet, and let the end drop below the top of your paste table. Then, holding the roll in one hand and the end of the paper in the other, bend it back slightly around the table edge and saw it up and down several times.

Tearing the paper into strips. Until you are experienced, tear only two or three strips at a time. The strips need to be only 6 inches longer than the distance from the top of the baseboard to the ceiling. But because of the design of the wallpaper you are hanging, many of the strips you tear may have to be a great deal longer than this. This obviously wastes paper but there is nothing you can do about it short of switching to another pattern.

To start the strip-tearing job, unroll the paper pattern side up on your table. Locate the point at which it will touch the ceiling and measure down from this the height of the wall. Note the point at which the paper will touch the baseboard. Lay your straightedge at right angles across the paper 3 inches below the baseboard line and tear the paper across (or you can cut it with a razor blade). Then tear the strip at the top—3 inches above the ceiling line.

The way in which you match the next strip depends on whether you are going to hang it to the right or to the left of the starter strip. Whichever the answer, push the starter strip to the front or back of the table and unroll the roll alongside. Match the pattern carefully and tear your second strip. Then unroll the roll beside this and tear your third strip. And so on.

If any of the strips greatly exceed the wall height plus 6 inches, tear off the excess paper at the bottom or top or at both ends. Leaving the excess on a strip makes for minor but unnecessary complications in the hanging process.

Pasting the paper. Holding the two or three strips you have torn together, turn them pattern side down on the table along the front edge. Your first strip is now at the top of the pile. Push the bottom strips back a couple of inches. Then starting at the top end of the first strip, spread a thin, even coating of paste over every inch of the back surface. Don't hurry.

To keep from getting paste on the face of the strip and on the table, let the front edge and ends overhang the table edges about ¼ inch. When you paste along the back edge of the strip, raise it slightly with your fingers. To make certain that the side

edges of a strip are well pasted and will adhere securely to the wall, don't just run your paste brush up and down them. Also draw it at right angles across them in light, short strokes.

When you have applied paste to the upper 6 feet of the strip, fold it top to bottom. Align the edges roughly. You can smooth down the fold but don't crease it hard. Now slide the entire strip along the table so that the unpasted bottom portion lies flat; paste it in the same way; and fold the pasted surface in on itself. The top and bottom edges of the strip should meet or overlap slightly.

You can now proceed to hang the strip or you can paste a second strip. But never paste more than two strips at once.

Hanging the first strip. Carry pasted strips from the paste table to the wall over one arm, like a coat.

At the wall, pull the top end of the strip partly open; then grasp the corners in two hands and allow the strip to unfold of its own weight. Check to make sure the top is really the top: some patterns are confusing and easy to hang upside down. Press the paper to the wall at the right height and alongside the vertical chalk line and smooth it down a bit with your hand. Then smooth it down tight with long up and down strokes of your smoothing brush.

If the strip is not positioned properly at the ceiling line or along your chalk line,

APPLYING PASTE TO WALLPAPER

correct the situation now. Sometimes all you have to do is slide the paper slightly to one side or the other. But it is more likely that you will have to pull it partly or completely from the wall and start over again.

When you are satisfied with the placement of the upper part of the strip, unfold the bottom part and smooth it down. Then smooth the entire strip. Make sure there are no blisters. If there are, loosen the strip and start over again.

To trim the strip at top and bottom, brush it firmly into the corners between the wall and ceiling and wall and baseboard. Then crease it lightly with the point of your shears. You can now cut along the crease with a razor blade or you can pull the strip from the wall slightly and trim along the creased line with shears. The latter procedure results in a neater line and better fit, especially if the corner line is bumpy or wavy or if there is an open crack between the baseboard and the wall. Cutting with a razor blade is faster, however; and if you don't try to cut more than two or three strips with one blade, you won't have trouble with a dull blade that tears the paper.

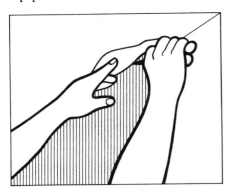

TRIMMING THE FIRST STRIP

With a damp sponge or cloth, wipe off paste that has gotten on the ceiling and baseboard. Also remove any paste that has been smeared on the wallpaper.

Hanging subsequent strips. The procedure is the same as that described; but you must do several additional things.

Match the pattern on adjacent strips carefully. If you don't get a perfect match at all points, don't be surprised. Such mistakes do occur and there is nothing much you can do about them. Just remember that a good pattern match near the top of the wall is more important than one at the bottom simply because it is more visible.

Butt the edges of adjoining strips. A butt joint is flat and less noticeable than a lapped joint. It is also easier to make because you just hang the new strip as close as possible to the preceding strip and then slide it into place. (To slide a wallpaper strip, work from the center and slide the entire strip. If you just push the edges, you may tear the paper; and as the paste dries, the edges may draw back into their original positions.)

Even though you try to butt all joints, however, you probably will have to lap a few of them slightly to compensate for unevenness or crookedness in the walls or to correct for loss of vertical. (You should make a practice of checking every third or fourth strip with your plumb line to make sure you are still hanging the strips straight.) When lapping becomes necessary, try to lap the strips toward a window or lamp so the shadowlines are eliminated.

Roll the joints from top to bottom with your seam roller after the paste has set for 15 to 20 minutes. Use just enough pressure to flatten the seams; not enough to squeeze out paste.

Hanging paper around doors. Doors present two problems for the paperhanger: the frame around them stands out from the wall, and it may not be absolutely vertical. The first problem means that you cannot allow a full-width wallpaper strip that you are hanging to overlap a door a great deal because you will have trouble positioning and smoothing it on the wall and trimming it neatly above the door. On the other hand, the second problem means that you should lap a wallpaper strip slightly over a door; otherwise there may be a gap between the vertical trim and the wallpaper.

To make sense out of this confusion, let's assume you are hanging a paper that is 20 inches wide.

If you are papering to your left toward a door and if the door frame is 7 inches from the edge of the last wallpaper strip you have hung, you must slit the new strip from top to bottom into two narrow pieces. The right piece should be 8 inches wide so it will overlap the door frame an inch. The left piece is 12 inches wide, and you should cut off the bottom portion since you need only a short strip at the top to fit between the ceiling and the top of the door.

When hanging the right piece, butt it to the edge of the last strip you have hung; then smooth it tight into the corner between the door frame and the wall. At the top of the frame, make a slight horizontal cut in the edge of the paper; and smooth the flap above the frame to the wall. Trim off the excess paper along the vertical part of the frame with a razor blade.

Hang the 12-inch strip above the door next to the 8-incher; and next to it, hang a short full-width strip. The space between the latter strip and the left side of the door frame is 3 inches wide.

Since a 3-inch overlap is about as large as you can easily handle when papering around a door (or window), it is not necessary to cut the next full width strip into two narrow pieces. But to make sure you hang the strip straight, measure 20 inches to the left of the last strip and make a vertical chalk line on the wall. Hang the new wallpaper strip to this line and smooth it to the wall up to the door frame. Make a horizontal cut at the top of the door frame and smooth down the flap. It should butt or slightly lap the previous strip. Finally, trim the strip along the left side of the door frame.

Three rules for hanging wallpaper around a door can be digested from this example:

1. If a wallpaper strip will overlap a door frame 3 inches or less, hang the strip in the usual way and then trim it to the frame.

2. If a wallpaper strip will overlap a door frame more than 3 inches, cut it in two long narrow pieces and hang them separately. The piece that butts against the side of the frame should overlap the frame ½ to 1 inch.

3. When hanging paper away from a

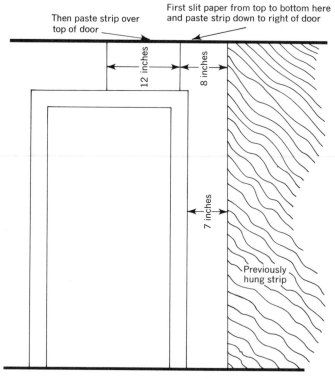

WALLPAPERING AROUND A DOOR

door frame, the strip extending beyond the frame should be hung to a chalk line.

Hanging paper around windows. The procedure is the same as for doors. But the work is slightly more difficult because you must hang short strips both above and below the window.

Hanging paper around corners. Because corners are almost never straight or square, you cannot wrap a full-width strip of wallpaper around them very far without getting puckers. So here again it is usually necessary to cut the strip into two narrow pieces.

Measure from the last strip hung to the corner. Make the measurement at both the top and bottom of the wall. Add ½ inch to the wider measurement. Then cut the new strip to this width and hang it. It will extend ½ inch around the corner. The remaining part of the strip is hung alongside; but don't try to butt the joint because the strip probably won't hang straight. You should, instead, measure the width of the second strip—say, 5 inches.

Then measure 5 inches along the wall from the corner strip. Strike a vertical line at this point, and hang the strip to this line.

Hang paper around an outside corner in the same way.

Hanging paper on a slanting wall. This project is tricky because you are dealing with unusually long strips of paper which persist in falling off the wall and because you cannot easily establish a vertical line on a slant wall.

The solution to the second problem is to snap a vertical line on the knee wall below the slant wall. Then, instead of hanging the strip from the top down, hang it from the bottom up. Smooth it to the knee wall parallel to the chalk line; then unfold the top portion and paste it to the slant wall, working from the bend upward.

If the strip on the slant wall appears to be at an angle rather than straight up and down, the bend in the wall is not horizontal. To correct for this, brush the paper firmly into the bend and cut along the bend with a razor blade. Then straighten

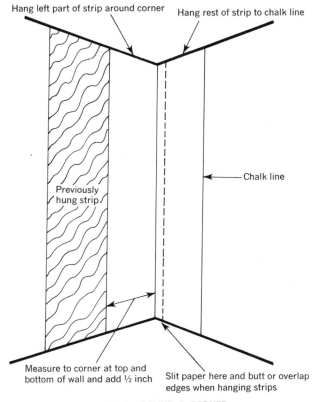

Hang left part of strip around corner   Hang rest of strip to chalk line

Chalk line

Previously hung strip

Measure to corner at top and bottom of wall and add ½ inch   Slit paper here and butt or overlap edges when hanging strips

WALLPAPERING AROUND A CORNER

the strip on the slant wall by eye, and butt or lap the joint in the bend.

Hanging paper in a dormer. This is a difficult task because, depending on the design of the dormer, there are several points where you cannot achieve a pattern match between adjoining strips. For this reason, it is best to use a wallpaper without a pronounced pattern or with a small, overall pattern or a confused pattern: the mismatching is then less obvious.

The actual method of papering a dormer is no different from the method followed in hanging paper elsewhere. The step-by-step procedure varies with the design of the dormer.

If the front wall of the dormer is in the same plane as the knee wall, continue papering along the wall and come back later to fill in the two high triangular walls in the dormer. The drawing shows the easiest way to handle the wallpaper strip that is partly in the dormer and partly out.

If the dormer is a deep, walk-in design, don't try to continue the paper from the main part of the room into it and out again. Paper the dormer separately and forget the mismatch at the corners.

Hanging paper in an open stairway. Start with the longest strip, if possible, and drop it straight from the second-floor ceiling down into the first floor. To facilitate handling of this and other long strips, fold them accordion fashion in short sections. It's a good idea to have a helper to support or catch long stairway strips to keep them from tearing.

Hanging paper around a lighting fixture. Turn off the light and let it cool; then unscrew it from the wall. It can hang by its wire leads unless it is very heavy, in which case someone should hold it for you.

Hang the strip on the wall above the fixture in the usual way and smooth it down almost to the fixture. Then with your shears cut the paper in from one side to the wires. Snip out a hole 2 or 3 inches wide around the wires. Slip the cut edges around the wires, butt them, and smooth down the remainder of the strip. Replace the fixture. If the wallpaper happens to touch the wires, no harm is done because the wires are insulated.

Hanging paper around an electric switch or outlet. Remove the cover plates. Then smooth the paper right over the switch (or outlet). Make a slight cut so the switch toggle can come through.

After the entire strip is smoothed to the wall, go back to the switch and cut a hole

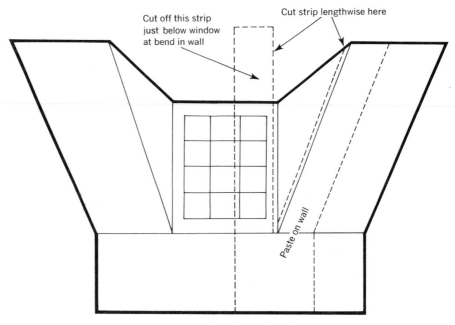

WALLPAPERING A DORMER

around it—preferably with a sharp knife with a wood or plastic handle so you won't get a shock if the blade touches one of the terminals. The hole should not be as large as the box in which the switch is mounted, but should be large enough to expose the entire switch.

Hanging paper behind radiators and toilet tanks. If possible, take out radiators so that you can paper behind them in the normal way. Otherwise, smooth the wallpaper down behind the radiator as far as possible. Then work it down gently the rest of the way with a yardstick. The yardstick is held horizontal and flat against the wall. Don't poke the paper with the end.

Hanging paper around bathroom cabinets. This looks like the same sort of job as papering around windows; but don't do it that way, because it requires too much careful fitting. Simply remove the cabinet from the wall by taking out the screws that fasten it to the studs. Then paper right over the opening. When the paper is dry, cut out around the opening with a razor blade and replace the cabinet.

Hanging paper on ceilings. This is easier than you probably think. The only problem is that you may well need to work on some kind of scaffold because you will work better if your head is within a foot of the ceiling.

Ceilings are always papered before walls, and the paper is allowed to extend down the walls about 1 inch.

The paper should run across the ceiling—not lengthwise. This gives you shorter strips to handle. The strips should be cut to equal the width of the ceiling plus 2 inches.

Before hanging the first strip, strike a chalk line with a string tied to nails driven into the ceiling at opposite sides of the room. The line should parallel the wall that marks your starting point, and should be out from the wall the width of the paper minus 1 inch.

Paste and fold ceiling paper like wall strips. To hang the paper, face the starting wall. If you are right-handed, work from right to left; if left-handed, from left to right. Support the pasted paper on a roll of paper held in your left hand (if you are right-handed). With your right hand, open out one end of the paper and press it to the ceiling along the chalk line; then smooth it down with your smoothing brush. The end of the paper should overlap the wall at your right 1 inch; the back edge of the paper should overlap the starting wall 1 inch.

When the first pasted section is in place, go on to the next. Continue in this way across the room. Then hang the second strip. The edges should be butted.

Hanging scenic papers. Let a professional do this. The papers are expensive and must be handled very carefully. Very costly scenics are often hung on muslin so they can be removed from the wall intact.

How to take care of wallpaper. If plastic-coated or plastic-bonded wallpapers are soiled, they can usually be sponged clean with a little water or mild detergent solution. Most stains can be removed from plastic-coated papers in the same way. If necessary, scrub with a mild cleanser. But stains that have penetrated plastic-bonded and ordinary wallpapers are a lost cause.

Ordinary wallpapers (the least washable kind) are cleaned with a special dough available from wallpaper and paint stores. Knead this in your hand until it is pliable; then rub it on the paper. Overlap strokes and clean thoroughly from top to bottom; otherwise the cleaned areas will stand out more prominently than the dirt you wanted to remove.

To remove grease stains from nonwashable paper, use a spray-on cleaner and dust off the residue.

Nonwashable paper can be made more soil- and stain-resistant by spraying it with wallpaper lacquer or a nonglossy spray used by artists to protect their watercolors. But test these coatings on a scrap of wallpaper before applying them.

If wallpaper of any type comes loose along the edges, lift the paper a fraction of an inch and spread wallpaper paste underneath with a table knife or artist's paintbrush. You can also use a prepared paste that comes in a squeeze tube with a long nozzle. Wipe excess paste from the surface of the paper with a damp cloth.

If an unsightly blister develops in wallpaper, cut through it with a razor blade, apply paste underneath, and press down. Paper that feels stiff and somewhat brittle should be wet with water before you handle it.

Should paper need to be patched, tear the patch from a leftover scrap of the paper; do not cut it. A torn patch blends into the background better than a cut one. Apply the patch with wallpaper paste. (Note: When you finish papering a room, keep some of the scraps that are left. You never can tell when you will need them.)

Walls, Asbestos-Cement. Exterior walls are normally covered with asbestos-cement shingles striated to resemble wood shingles but they are occasionally covered with large, smooth panels. Broken shingles are repaired like asbestos-cement roof shingles. (See *Roofs, Asbestos-Cement.*) Panels must be replaced in toto.

Hose down both types of wall when dirty and scrub with a bristle brush and cleanser if necessary. Paint with any good exterior paint.

Walls, Bearing. A bearing wall is one that supports the structure of the house. All exterior walls are bearing walls; but only a few interior walls are bearing walls.

If you are undertaking a major remodeling project that calls for the removal of an existing interior wall, you must determine beforehand whether it is a bearing wall. To do this, bore a hole through the ceiling close to the wall. Poke a semi-stiff wire up through this in the direction of the wall. If the wire strikes an obstruction within a few inches, the wall is not bearing a load. But if the wire does not strike an obstruction, the wall *may* be bearing a load.

Note the uncertainty. To make an accurate determination of whether a wall is a bearing wall, you should call in an experienced carpenter or contractor.

A bearing wall can be removed only if you replace it with something that will continue to bear the load. The usual procedure is to install a steel girder.

Nonbearing walls, however, can be knocked out without any worries about the structure overhead.

Walls, Brick. Brick garden walls are 4 inches thick (one tier); 8 inches thick (two tiers); or 12 inches thick (three tiers). Two-tier construction is recommended for all garden walls up to 6 feet in height that are not subjected to unusual wind pressure. They need no reinforcement. Above 6 feet (or above 4 feet if there is wind pressure) you should either use three-tier construction or reinforce the two-tier wall with 16-by-16-inch piers spaced no more than 15 feet apart.

One-tier construction should not be used unless the wall is laid out like Thomas Jefferson's famed serpentine wall at the University of Virginia or unless it is reinforced at 15-foot intervals with 12-by-12-inch piers. Even then, one-tier walls should not be over 4 feet high.

All brick walls should be built up from poured concrete footings not less than 18 inches below ground level (deeper in cold climates). The depth of the footing should equal the width of the wall; its width should equal twice the width of the wall.

Build walls from the ends toward the middle, one course at a time (except at the corners) and one tier at a time. After laying up the two tiers in a course, tie them together by troweling mortar into the joint between them. A better way to tie the tiers together is to lay occasional bricks at right angles to the wall. These are used in most bonds and are called headers.

For full instructions on laying bricks, see *Brick.*

How to waterproof house walls. First make sure that all mortar joints are sound. Then clean the wall thoroughly and while the surface is still damp apply Portland cement paint with a scrubbing brush. After the paint has set for several hours, spray it lightly with water and keep it damp for 24 hours. Then apply a second coat of paint and keep it damp for 48 hours.

Transparent, colorless silicone waterproofers do not actually waterproof brick walls. They are only dampproofers. Nevertheless, they are useful for keeping walls reasonably dry. They need to be renewed every five or six years.

How to repair and clean brick walls. See *Brick.*

How to paint brick walls. See *Concrete.*

Walls, Ceramic-Tile. Most people consider tile walls the mark of a superior bathroom. Actually, they may be a nuisance if your water contains minerals that stain the grouted joints brown. But it is difficult to predict whether this will happen unless you are already familiar with the action of your water.

Behind toilets and sinks and on other bathroom walls, tile is generally applied to a height of 4 feet. In tub recesses, it may be applied from the tub rim to the ceiling, but usually rises only 5 feet.

For how to install, repair, and clean ceramic-tile walls, see *Tile, Ceramic.*

To hang things on ceramic tile, drill holes with a carbide-tipped drill and drive screws into plastic anchors. See *Wall Anchors.*

Walls, Concrete-Block. Whether you are building a garden wall or a partition in the basement, concrete block is an ideal material to use.

The mortar used in laying concrete block consists of 1 part masonry cement and 2½ to 3 parts sand. Add enough water to make a workable mix. Trowel strips of the mortar on the top edges of the blocks previously laid. Apply strips of mortar to one end of the block being laid. Then press the block squarely into position and level it. The finished mortar joints should be ½ inch thick. Scrape off the excess mortar at once and allow the rest to set somewhat. Then smooth it with a grooving tool or piece of pipe drawn the long way of the joint. If for any reason you must remove a block once it has been tapped into position, reset it in fresh mortar.

Blocks are usually laid up in a running bond so that all "stretcher" blocks (those running lengthwise of the wall) overlap each other by half a block, and so that the vertical joints in every other course are in line.

To build a straight wall of blocks, set the end blocks first and lay those between to a string attached to the ends. Keep raising the string as you lay up new courses. To make sure a wall is straight up and down, check each new course with a spirit level or plumb bob.

To lay out two walls that come together at a 90-degree angle, build a right-angle triangle of straight boards. One side of the triangle should be exactly 6 feet long; the other side, 8 feet; the hypotenuse, 10 feet. Lay this on the ground where you plan to build the walls and extend strings out from the apex and parallel with the sides.

A garden wall made of concrete block should not exceed 6 feet in height. It must be built up from a poured concrete footing 16 inches wide and 8 inches high. The base of the footing should be a minimum of 18 inches below ground level; and in cold areas, it must be below the frost line. If the wall is more than 4 feet high, the bottom portion up to 2 feet above ground level is reinforced with ½-inch steel bars spaced 4 feet apart. These are embedded in the footing; and the core spaces around them in the concrete blocks are filled with

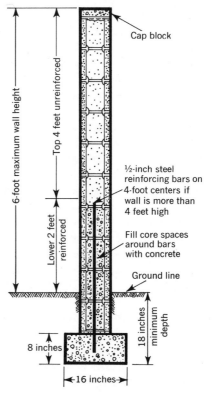

REINFORCING A CONCRETE-BLOCK WALL

poured concrete. The top of the wall is covered with solid cap blocks.

How to repair concrete-block walls. If mortar joints are loose or crumbly, scrape them clean and blow out crumbs; then pack in latex cement and strike it off smooth with a mason's trowel or a short length of ½-inch pipe. If you use masonry cement rather than latex, mix 1 part cement with 3 parts sand. Dampen the joints with water before applying the mortar.

Holes in concrete blocks are filled in the same way.

For how to clean and paint concrete-block walls, see *Concrete.*

Walls, Fiberboard. Fiberboard, also called insulation board, is a semi-soft sheet material made of various kinds of vegetable fibers. The boards come in 4-by-8-foot panels about ½ inch thick or more. They have some insulating value, but not as much as other materials.

Fiberboard panels for interior walls come finished on one side with paint or with a layer of vinyl, burlap, or cork. Although the layered panels are an improvement over the others, no fiberboard can be considered a first-rate building material because it is easily damaged and satisfactory repairs are almost impossible. Furthermore, there is no way to conceal the joints between panels except with moldings.

Fiberboard panels for exterior walls are impregnated with asphalt. The simplest panels are used for sheathing under exterior siding. Other panels are covered with mineral granules on the weather side and may be textured to resemble shingles, bricks, etc. The latter do not need to be painted but look better if they are. Use either a paint designed specifically for fiberboard siding or an exterior latex paint made for use on masonry. Two coats are required.

Walls, Gypsum-Board. Gypsum board has largely replaced plaster as the standard wall finish. It is not as strong or dense as plaster. Neither does it provide such a firm base for nails and screws. But it is a great deal cheaper; does not crack; and since no water is used in its installation, it does not contribute to the warping of wood parts of a house.

Gypsum board is sold in panels 4 feet wide and 8, 10, or 12 feet long. There are three thicknesses: 3/8, ½, and 5/8 inch. The standard panels have a creamy white paper surface which serves as a good base for paint or wallpaper. Panels with special finishes are also available.

Although developers frequently use 3/8-inch gypsum board for walls and ceilings, this thickness should be used only on ceilings and to cover old wall finishes, such as badly cracked plaster. By itself, a 3/8-inch panel is a very poor sound barrier. It also cannot withstand hard punishment.

One-half-inch panels are stronger and stop sound better. Most home owners consider them suitable for installation in most parts of the house. But in places where you want to reduce sound transmission to a minimum, you should use two thicknesses of ½-inch boards.

Gypsum boards of 5/8-inch thickness are used in garages and utility rooms as fire barriers. But they weigh so much that they are difficult to work with and are rarely used elsewhere.

How to install gypsum board. If you are applying gypsum board directly to studs and joists, use either ½-inch boards or two 3/8-inch boards. To re-cover walls, use one layer of 3/8-inch boards.

In order to minimize the number of joints between panels, professionals use 10- and 12-foot panels wherever possible and apply them horizontally. If you feel up to doing the same thing, you should. But note that gypsum boards are heavy and awkward to maneuver. So you will make work much easier for yourself, if you use 8-foot panels and install them vertically.

Use 4d nails for 3/8-inch boards; 5d for ½-inch boards. The nails should be ring-grooved rather than the cement-coated type normally used, because they will not pull out of wood. This eliminates the common gypsum-board ailment known as "nail-popping."

If you are constructing an entirely new

wall, space the studs 16 inches on center. The vertical edges of each gypsum panel must bear on a stud.

After tilting a panel up to the wall, but before placing it flat against the studs, mark the location of the center studs on the face of the panel. Then press the panel into place and secure it with a few nails. The first of these should be driven through the center of the panel; then drive a few at the corners.

Draw lines down the panel to mark the center studs. This will save useless nailing. Space nails 6 to 8 inches apart. An alternative is to drive nails in pairs which are 12 inches apart on center. The nails in each pair are 2 inches apart. Never nail less than 3/8 inch from the edges of a panel. Nail heads should be driven just below the surface of the board. Don't break the paper covering with your hammer.

Gypsum-board panels are cut by scoring on the front side. Use a sharp knife and a straightedge. Bend the panel on either side of the cut sharply backward. Then cut through the paper covering on the back side. The cut edge can be smoothed with a knife or coarse sandpaper.

Cutouts for wall switches, outlets, and lights are made by drilling 1-inch holes and sawing through the board with a keyhole saw.

After the panels are on the wall, the joints are sealed with gypsum-board cement and paper tape. Mix the cement with water as directed on the bag and let it stand for 30 minutes. Spread a thin ribbon over each joint with a 3-inch wall scraper. Then immediately embed a strip of paper in the cement squarely over the joint; smooth it down; and cover it with another thin layer of cement. Take pains to smooth out all ripples and ridges.

After the cement has dried overnight, sand lightly to remove roughness. Then apply another thin coat of cement, feathering the edges an inch or two beyond the previous coat. Allow this to dry, and apply a final coat of cement. This should be still wider than the previous coat and very thin. If possible, in order to make the cement perfectly smooth, use a 6- or 8-inch dry-wall knife, a concrete finishing knife, or a plasterer's trowel. When dry, sand lightly.

Tape is also used to seal inside corners. After applying the first coat of cement, fold the tape down the center and smooth it into place. Proceed from there as on a flat wall.

Outside corners can also be taped, but the preferred procedure is to nail a metal corner bead over the edges of the boards. Apply cement directly over this.

All nail heads are covered with two coats of cement. No tape is needed.

After taping is completed, the wall is ready for painting or papering. Some people prefer to apply a textured paint, since this helps to hide imperfections in the taped joints. But if you have done a careful taping job, any paint will conceal the slight difference between the joints and flat panels.

If you intend to apply wallpaper, the gypsum board must first be primed with paint; otherwise, when you someday try to remove the wallpaper, you will peel the paper covering on the gypsum boards off with it.

A two-thickness installation of gypsum board is made in similar fashion. The first boards should be applied vertically; the second, horizontally. The top layer is cemented to the bottom with a special adhesive and secured with nails spaced 16 to 24 inches apart along the studs.

If 3/8-inch gypsum board is installed over an existing wall, you should first level the wall by removing bulges, excrescences, etc. Then nail the boards directly to the wall. If the wall is anything other than wood, plywood, or sound plaster, the nails must be driven through it into the studs.

How to repair gypsum-board walls. Nail-popping is the worst problem. It is caused by twisting and contraction of the studs. If the nails in the gypsum board are not secure, they pull loose from the wood and blister or pop right through the cement covering the heads. The cure is simple, however. Just drive the nail back in and drive a second nail of the ring-grooved type close by. Cover the heads with spackle.

Small holes and gouges in gypsum board are filled with spackle or gypsum-board cement. If you have a large hole, cut out of a scrap of gypsum board a square or rectangle that is 2 inches wider and higher than the hole. Turn the square upside down and cut through the paper and plaster 1 inch from each side. Remove all the plaster around the edges of the square but be careful not to cut through the paper face of the gypsum board.

Now hold the patch paper-face-forward over the hole in the wall and draw a line around the square of plaster. Cut through the wall along the line with a small saw. Spread an inch-wide strip of gypsum board cement around the edges of the hole. Then press the patch into the hole and smooth the paper flanges into the cement. When the cement sets, cover the flanges with one or two thin layers of cement.

How to hang things on gypsum board. If the wall is double thick, it will usually hold nails and screws as well as plaster does. But if it is only ½ inch thick, nails and screws must be driven through the board into the studs if they are to bear any weight. If nails and screws are not driven into studs, use them for small pictures or lightweight articles only.

Heavy articles such as large mirrors, pictures, and valance boards and articles that may be pulled or leaned on (towel bars and toilet-paper holders, for instance) must either be anchored into the studs with conventional screws or hung with toggle bolts or hollow-wall screw anchors. (See *Wall Anchors.*)

Walls, Hardboard. Hardboard wall panels are strong, dense, durable, easy-to-clean materials which may be installed on all walls in a house, including those around tubs. Unfinished panels are dark brown, and can be painted or given a clear finish like wood. Factory-finished panels come in a variety of attractive finishes and textures, including a tough, waterproof, baked-on finish. The panels most often used are 1/8 or ¼ inch thick and measure 4 by 8 feet. Narrower panels and blocks are also available.

Large panels can be applied directly to studs spaced 16 inches on center. Use special annular-thread hardboard nails which come in colors matching the panels. Space the nails 4 inches apart around the edges of the panel; 8 inches apart at intermediate studs. If possible, nail into the grooves of the panels.

You can also apply panels with contact adhesive applied to the front surfaces of the stud wall and to the back of the panels. Apply two coats of adhesive on both the studs and the panel, and let them dry completely. Then position the panel and hammer it tightly against the studs over their entire length. Use a mallet wrapped in cloth to protect the panel surface.

Panels can be applied to existing walls that are smooth and sound. Use contact adhesive as above and apply two coats to the back of the panels and the wall. It is not necessary to cover either the panels or the wall completely. You need adhesive only around the edges of the panel and in two in-between vertical strips (as if you were applying the panels directly to studs).

Over existing walls, you can use hardboard panels only 1/8 inch thick.

At outside corners, panels may be butted and covered with wood molding strips; or they may be mitered and left uncovered. When used to cover walls in tub recesses, the edges of the panels must be inserted into special metal moldings to guard against leakage.

Following installation, the panels are finished in accordance with the manufacturer's directions. In some cases, of course, no finish is required.

How to repair hardboard walls. If panels that have been installed with adhesive come loose, refasten them with color-matching nails with annular threads.

Scratches and small holes are filled with spackle.

How to hang things on hardboard walls. Unless nails or screws can be driven into the studs, use toggle bolts or hollow-wall anchors. See *Wall Anchors.*

Walls, Interior.

How to clean. Walls in most rooms of

REPAIRING A GYPSUM-BOARD WALL

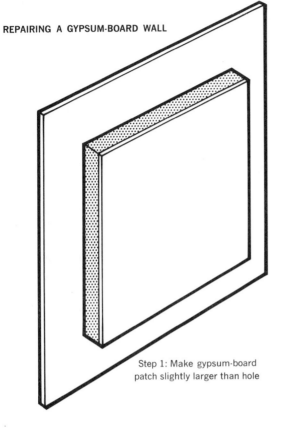

Step 1: Make gypsum-board patch slightly larger than hole

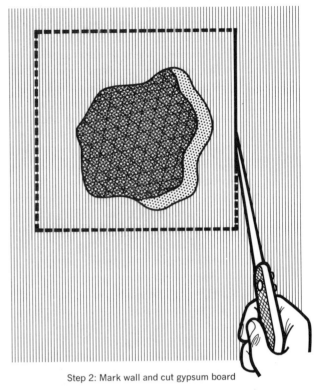

Step 2: Mark wall and cut gypsum board

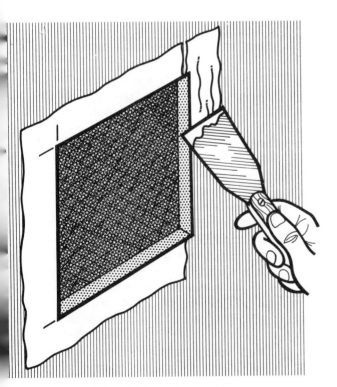

Step 3: Apply joint cement around opening

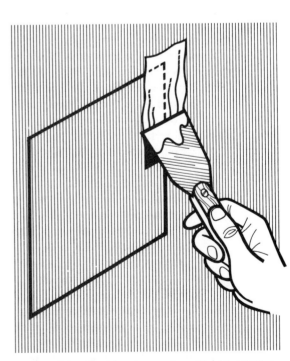

Step 4: Install patch and cover edges with joint cement

the house do not get very dirty and therefore need only to be dusted or, better, vacuumed occasionally. Spot-cleaning to remove smudges and stains is done with a household detergent solution if the walls are painted, tiled, or covered with washable wallpaper or vinyl. Use a dough-cleaner on nonwashable wallpaper.

Kitchen and bathroom walls are cleaned in the same way, but also need to be washed now and then to remove grease and heavy grime. Use a household detergent solution or a cleanser containing trisodium phosphate. Apply this with a large sponge, using up and down strokes. On a textured wall, use a soft brush. Work on a small section of the wall at a time.

Wash walls from the bottom up: if you work from the top down, water dripping down over the dirty wall will make streaks which are likely to remain even after that section of the wall is washed. For the same reason, you should wash the walls before washing the ceiling.

Change the cleaning solution whenever it becomes dirty. Rinsing with clear water following washing is always advisable even though manufacturers of some cleansers say this is not necessary.

Walls, Laminated-Plastic. The plastic is the same as that used on kitchen counters. As made for installation on walls, it usually comes bonded to a special backing which compensates for any slight roughness or unevenness in the wall being covered. The panels are available in several sizes up to 4 by 8 feet.

Laminated-plastic wall panels are especially suitable for use on walls that get hard wear, require frequent cleaning, or are exposed to moisture. They are highly recommended for installation in tub recesses because there are only a few joints which may leak and because they are not stained by minerals and impurities in the water. In short, they require little maintainance or cleaning.

The panels are glued to any smooth, firm base, such as gypsum board. The joints are covered with matching metal molding strips to prevent leaks. Although manu-

facturers imply that anyone can install the panels, it's better to make professional carpenters responsible for the job. Even they get into trouble now and then.

Walls, Metal-Tile. In the past, metal tiles with baked-on enamel finish were sold for installation in bathrooms and kitchens. Although easy to install, they were, like plastic tiles, a poor substitute for ceramic tile.

Today metal tiles with a metallic finish are sometimes used to cover walls behind ranges and counters in the kitchen. The tiles measure 4¼ inches square and are very thin. They are made of stainless steel and of aluminum with a natural or copper finish. Since they come with adhesive applied to the back, you just stick them to any existing wall that is smooth, level, and free of grease, flaking paint, or any other substance that might interfere with the bond.

To install the tiles, draw a true vertical or horizontal line on the wall and lay the first tiles to this. Succeeding tiles are simply butted tight to the first. The joints are not grouted.

When cleaning metal tiles, use a barely damp sponge and detergent solution. Do not use abrasives of any kind.

Walls, Plaster. Plaster walls have declined in popularity because they are expensive, they crack, and the water with which they are made often causes serious warping of the wood parts of a house. Nevertheless, a plaster wall has many virtues. It is, for instance, a much better sound barrier than other types of interior wall finish. It is thick, dense, and strong enough to hold nails and screws; special anchors are rarely necessary to hang things. The surface is smooth, easy to finish and to refinish: it is much easier to strip wallpaper off plaster than other walls, for example.

In short, if you have plaster walls that are in reasonably good condition, you are lucky. You won't have much trouble restoring them to excellent condition.

How to repair plaster walls. Map and shrinkage cracks are tiny cracks that crisscross the wall. They are unsightly, but it is not likely they indicate or will lead to serious trouble. Scrape them open with a beer can opener and smear spackle into them. When dry, sand lightly and refinish.

Structural cracks are large, jagged cracks usually indicating that the house is settling. If the house has stopped settling, the cracks will get no worse than they are; so once you repair them, you can probably forget them. However, if the house continues to settle after the cracks are repaired, you will probably have to do the job over again at some future date.

Cut the cracks open all the way down to the brown coat. Use an old knife and chisel. If possible, undercut the edges so that the cracks are shaped like an inverted V. Blow out the crumbs and wet the edges of the plaster thoroughly with water.

You can fill the cracks with prepared patching plaster or plaster of paris. The former is better because it sets more slowly, giving you time to complete the job carefully. Whichever material you use, press it into the cracks and strike it off flush with the old surface. When dry, sand lightly.

Holes can be filled with spackle if small or shallow. For larger holes, use patching plaster. First chip out all loose and cracked plaster; undercut the edges; wet exposed plaster; then spread the patching plaster into the hole. If the hole is deep, fill it in two stages. The top layer can be applied as soon as the bottom layer is firm but still damp.

If a hole is extremely large and deep, make the same preparations as for a small hole and apply the plaster in two stages. For the first coat, use a coarse wood-fiber plaster. Before it hardens, scratch shallow crisscross lines in the surface so that the patching plaster, which follows, will key into it.

If the plaster lath behind a large hole is rusted and broken, cut it out with tin snips and fill the gap with gypsum lath or gypsum board nailed to the studs. Then fill in with plaster.

If plaster lath is missing behind a small hole, cut a piece of cardboard a little larger than the hole, punch a hole in the center, thread a string through this, and knot it at the back. Holding the other end of the string, push the cardboard through the hole in the plaster, pull it up against the back of the plaster, and hold tight. Then smear patching plaster into the hole over the cardboard. When this is firm, cut the string off close and fill the hole the rest of the way with plaster.

If a plaster wall starts to crumble and scatter dust, the chances are that water is leaking somewhere above it. There is no sense in repairing the plaster until you find the leak and stop it. When you have done this, let the plaster dry for about a month. Then scrape and sand the eroded area well to remove remaining soft plaster. Apply spackle.

Bulges in plaster are also commonly the result of leaks. After stopping the leak, cut the bulge out completely and fill the hole in the way previously described.

How to finish plaster. You can apply a latex paint to plaster as soon as it is hard and dry; but if you intend to use alkyd paint, you must wait six months. You must also wait six months if applying wallpaper or other wall covering. Even then, you should check the walls for hot spots. For how to do this, see *Wallpapering.*

When plaster is patched, the patches must be covered with at least two coats of paint to conceal them.

Walls, Plywood. If you want something unusual in wood paneling, use plywood. You can have fir plywood in a number of interesting textures, or if you are willing to pay the price, you can have hardwood plywoods (though they are not always made of hardwood) ranging from simple birch to exotic rosewood.

Plywood panels measure 4 by 8 feet and are ¼ inch thick. Because of their size, they are particularly easy to install on large, unbroken wall areas. If a room has many windows and doors, fitting the plywood around them demands considerable work.

How to install plywood. Plywood panels can be nailed directly to studs spaced 16 inches on center. Short lengths of 2-by-4s should be nailed between each pair of studs 4 feet above the floor.

To install the panels over an old wall of plaster or other nailable material, nail 2-inch-wide furring strips made of ½-inch fir plywood to the wall. Horizontal strips are needed at the top and bottom of the wall and at 16-inch intervals between. Vertical strips are also needed under the vertical edges of the plywood panels.

On waterproof masonry walls, apply horizontal furring strips cut from 1-by-2-inch boards. Plywood panels nailed to these should be primed on the back with aluminum paint.

Install the panels with 4d finishing nails spaced 6 inches apart at the edges and 12 inches apart through the center. Countersink the heads and cover them with stick putty colored to match the wood if it has a transparent finish. Use spackle or ordinary putty if you are painting fir plywood.

Before installing panels, shift them around to get the best possible match of grain. Start paneling from a corner. To make sure the panel is vertical, measure 4 feet out from the corner and drop a plumb line. Lightly nail the panel along this line; then, if the opposite edge is not parallel with the corner, draw on the surface a line that is parallel to the corner. This is called scribing. The job is best done with a pair of dividers, which are opened just a fraction of an inch more than the widest part of the gap. Hold the dividers steady with one leg against the wall and the pencil leg on the plywood. Then run them from the top of the wall to the bottom. When you saw the panel along this line, it should fit tight into the corner. See illustration, *Kitchen Cabinets.*

The panel may also have to be scribed to the ceiling. This is done in the same way.

Cut plywood with a fine-toothed crosscut saw or a circular saw with a crosscut blade. Support it well on 2-by-4s or sturdy planks laid between sawhorses, and saw it with the good face up.

To allow for expansion, space adjacent panels a fraction of an inch apart. If the

joints are left open, it is advisable to bevel them slightly with sandpaper. If you bevel them deeply with a plane, the core woods will be exposed and must be finished in some way. Joints can also be covered with wood or metal moldings.

When paneling around doors and windows, it is usually easier to remove the trim and extend the panels under it than to cut the panels to fit around the trim. Before replacing the trim, you must nail ¼-inch strips of wood under the edges inside the door opening.

Baseboards and cornices are also nailed over plywood paneling.

How to finish plywood paneling. Fir paneling that is to be painted is treated like solid wood paneling. Apply a primer and one or two final coats of alkyd paint.

Decorative hardwood plywoods are available—in many cases, with a factory finish—and all such plywoods are available unfinished. Finished panels are more expensive; but the finish is more durable and uniform than the average home handyman can apply. On the other hand, when you install finished panels, you must take extra pains not to mar the surface.

If you finish plywood paneling yourself, sand it lightly with the grain. You can then apply a stain-wax if you want to change the color. Floor seal also changes the color, although very slightly.

If you don't want to change the color of the wood one iota, brush on several coats of thinned white shellac. Or apply a water-white lacquer. Finish with a white appliance wax.

How to maintain plywood walls. For how to make repairs, see *Plywood.* For how to remove stains, see *Wood.*

To remove soil marks, rub with a white appliance wax or with a cloth dampened slightly in detergent solution. Never use abrasives. Apply furniture polish or paste floor wax to the entire wall surface every year or two.

Walls, Plastic-Tile. Plastic wall tiles are thin, lightweight, 4¼-inch squares made in imitation of ceramic tiles. They are sold for application to all sound, smooth bathroom and kitchen walls with a special adhesive.

Unfortunately, many people who have used them—especially in tub recesses—have found them unsatisfactory: a poor substitute for the real thing.

How to install plastic-tile walls. Follow instructions given for *Walls, Metal-Tile.*

How to repair walls. If a tile comes loose or pops off, scrape the old adhesive from the wall and the back of the tile; apply new adhesive to the tile; and press into place for several hours. Then spread adhesive into the joints with a pencil or knife point, and remove any excess from the face of the tile.

Note, however, that if the tile has been loosened by moisture, the chances are that the wall base has been damaged. In these circumstances, don't bother to replace the tile: you need an entirely new wall.

If grout between tiles is cracked, scrape it out; smooth in new adhesive with a small spatula or knife; and shape it with a pencil point after it has set up.

Walls, Stone. It takes time to build a garden wall of stone, but when it is finished, nothing is handsomer.

Because stones vary so much in size, a stone masonry wall is rarely less than 1 foot thick and often a great deal thicker. The depth of the footings must equal the width of the wall; their width should equal twice the width of the wall. Footings should be no less than 18 inches below ground level, and should be below the frost line in cold climates.

As in building other masonry walls, work from the ends of the wall toward the middle. Use parallel strings on either side to keep the wall straight. Lay stones in the positions to which they are best suited. Some run lengthwise of the wall; some crosswise; some may even run up and down. If attractive stones are scarce, you can make them go further by using them to face the wall on both sides and filling in between with rubble and mortar.

Dry stone walls should not be less than 18 inches thick; and for any wall more than 2 feet high, a 2-foot thickness is bet-

ter. (The thickness is determined in large part by the size and shape of the available stones. You obviously can build a thinner wall with cut stones than with field stones.) Footings are needed for high, rather thin walls (use the formula given above for masonry walls). But other walls can be built up on a 6-inch base of gravel.

If you are working with assorted rough field stones, it is generally best to build the front and back of the wall with the largest stones and to fill in between them with small stuff. Lay the face stones at right angles to the wall and slant them slightly down toward the center of the wall. If you use flat stones, however, you can lay them up like bricks.

For how to repair and clean stone walls, see *Stone.*

Walls, Stucco. Stucco is a plaster made of Portland cement and used on building exteriors. It is applied in a ¾-inch thickness directly to masonry or steel lath nailed over wood or fiberboard sheathing. The wall thus produced is smooth and seamless but likely to crack as the building settles.

To repair shallow cracks and holes in stucco, simply scrape them open and blow out the crumbs. (Ideally, the hole should be made wider at the back than in front so the new stucco will hold more securely.) Dampen the surface with water. Then trowel in a prepared stucco mixture, which can be purchased at a masonry supplies outlet.

If a hole or crack extends all the way through the stucco, remove all the defective material and dampen the edges of the hole. Then fill the hole to one-third its depth with a mixture of 1 part Portland cement, 3 parts sand and water. Make crisscross lines across the surface of the patch so the next layer will adhere tightly. After the patch has hardened and begins to dry, sprinkle it with water and cover it with damp burlap. Keep it damp for 48 hours.

Then apply a second coat of concrete in the same way. This should come to within ¼ inch of the surface. Keep it damp for another 48 hours. Then fill the hole to the top with prepared stucco mixture.

Stucco does not need to be painted. If you want to color it, it is better to mix a masonry pigment into the stucco mixture. Paint can be applied, however, to any stucco that is completely dry and clean. Use an exterior latex paint designed for masonry.

Walls, Wood-Paneled. You might wonder why anyone today would panel a room with solid boards when so many beautiful plywood panels which are installed in large sheets are available. There are two answers: (1) Solid wood is even more beautiful than plywood, for even though the wood itself may be inferior, it has a texture and warmth that plywood lacks. Furthermore, it has imperfections which make for interest. (2) In a room that is broken up by a lot of doors and windows, individual boards go up faster than big plywood panels.

Any wood that is sawed into boards can be used for paneling; but pine is the most widely available. Pick out the boards yourself at the lumber yard to make sure you don't wind up with a number that are split, warped, or have loose knots or knots ringed in black bark.

Unless you intend to paint the paneling, use the same kind of wood throughout a room. Using knotty pine panels and clear pine trim produces an oddly disturbing look, for example.

How to build a wall. Store the boards indoors when they are delivered. They must be kept dry. Lay them flat and cover them with paper.

Before installation, sand each board lightly with the grain. Then apply the first coat of finish, whether paint or stain. Take pains to cover the edges; then, when the boards shrink, you will not see any unfinished edges.

If the boards contain knots, the knots should be primed before any paint is applied to keep them from bleeding through. Use WP-578 knot sealer.

If the panels are to be installed in a basement, make sure the walls are water-tight. And for good measure, apply shellac or aluminum paint to the backs of the boards.

When paneling a masonry wall or an old plaster, gypsum-board, fiberboard, or hardboard wall, nail 1-by-2 or 1-by-3-inch wood furring strips to the wall. On the average 8-foot wall, you need four horizontal strips—one at the top, one at the bottom, and two evenly spaced between.

You may also apply furring strips to a stud wall; but you will not reduce the room size so much if you nail short lengths of 2-by-4s between the studs and flush with them. You need two rows evenly spaced between the top and bottom plates.

Check the first board you install with a plumb line or spirit level to make sure it is straight up and down. If you then fit all succeeding boards together tightly, they should be straight, too. Nevertheless, it is a smart idea to check every third or fourth board.

At inside corners, install one board all the way into the corner, and butt the adjacent board on the other wall to it. Since most corners are crooked, the boards must first be scribed, as described under *Walls, Plywood.* At outside corners, you can either miter the boards or butt one to the other.

Secure the boards with finishing nails driven diagonally through the edges so they won't show on the surface. If nails must be driven through the board faces, countersink them and cover with beeswax, if using a clear finish, or spackle, if using paint.

Inasmuch as paneling boards generally have beveled or specially milled edges, you cannot nail a baseboard or cornice over them without creating little black pockets that fill up with dust and hair. To avoid this, you can omit the cornice and baseboard. But a better procedure is to install the cornice and baseboard first. They should be slightly furred out from the wall so they project beyond the boards. Then butt the ends of the boards to them.

Sand the boards again lightly before finishing them. For an easy clear finish, use stain-wax or gym seal. Finish with a coat of paste wax and buff well.

For an opaque finish, use flat or semi-gloss alkyd paint.

How to maintain wood paneling. If repairs are necessary, or stains must be removed, see *Wood*.

Wash finger marks and other soil from paneling with a cloth wrung out well in detergent solution. Or apply a white appliance wax. To bring out the warmth and luster of natural paneling, go over the entire wall about once every year or two with furniture polish. For a more durable finish, use paste floor wax.

Wardrobe. A portable clothes closet which is sometimes called an armoire. In the past, when houses generally had few closets, wardrobes were handsome pieces of furniture. Modern wardrobes are more utilitarian; are made of wood, metal, or fiberboard.

Treat wood wardrobes like other pieces of wood furniture. Dust the tops and bottoms of metal and fiberboard wardrobes regularly, and clean all surfaces as necessary with a damp cloth or a cloth dipped in detergent solution.

When moving metal and fiberboard wardrobes, be careful not to rack them. If the floor slants, insert wood shims underneath so they stand straight. To keep them from falling forward if top-heavy, drill two small holes in the back, loop strong picture wire through them and twist the ends together outside the wardrobe. Then hook the wire to an open screw eye driven into the wall in back. In metal wardrobes, the holes for the wire can be close together; but in fiberboard units, they should be much farther apart.

Wash-and-Wear. Wash-and-wear was a name applied to garments made of fabrics containing natural and synthetic fibers and given a mild resin treatment before the fabrics were cut. The garments presumably did not need to be ironed after they were laundered. In actual fact, however, wash-and-wear articles usually required a little touching up with an iron. They were also difficult to get clean.

Today, wash-and-wear has given way to permanent press. But many wash-and-wear garments are still in use. If you have any, launder them as you do permanent press. Soaking in an enzyme presoaker helps to get out dirt.

Washbasins. See *Lavatories*.

Washing Machines. Four types of washing machine are in use.

Wringer washer. This is the oldest type. It has a large tub with an agitator that rotates back and forth and a power-driven wringer with closely spaced rollers that squeeze water from the articles passing through. The washer rolls on casters; is filled by a hose at the laundry tub; and is either emptied by gravity or by pumping back into the laundry tub. Although the wringer washer does an excellent washing job and extracts a great deal of water from fabrics, you must attend it rather closely. For this reason it has been largely superseded by the automatic washer. Nevertheless, wringer washers are still sold because they are inexpensive, economical to operate, save water, and last for many years with relatively little service.

Spinner washer. This washer is also a roll-around machine that must be attended closely. Clothes are washed in a large tub and are then lifted into an adjacent smaller tub where they are rinsed and spun damp-dry. Most spinner washers now sold are compact machines occupying a floor space 27 inches wide and 15 inches deep and holding only 5 pounds of clothes. They are used mainly by very small families and families with small accommodations.

Automatic washer. A square machine that is usually permanently installed, it automatically fills with water, then washes, rinses, and spins the clothes damp-dry, and shuts itself off. It requires no attention once you put the clothes and cleaning agents into it and set the controls. Almost all automatic washers are loaded through a door in the top and have an agitator that rotates or works up and down. But one manufacturer also produces front-opening washers in which clothes are washed in a revolving drum. The latter do not wash as clean as top-opening washers, but they can be installed in places where top-opening washers cannot be used (under and on top of counters, for instance).

Combination washer-dryer. As the name suggests, it washes clothes and completely dries them, too. One kind of combination is a front-opening machine that washes a family-size load and then automatically goes on to dry it. The advantage of this appliance is that it occupies no more floor space than a conventional automatic washer and does the entire washing, rinsing, and drying job without attention. On the other hand, it can handle only one load at a time whereas you can wash one load while you are drying another with a washer and a separate dryer.

In another kind of combination machine, the dryer is stacked on top of the washer (in other words, the appliances are separate though they are built into one cabinet). The resulting unit saves floor space and permits you to wash one load of clothes and dry another at the same time. However, you lose wall space; and in operation you must shift clothes from the washer to the dryer by hand.

Automatic washer features. The most common washer in use today is the automatic. Many makes and models are on the market. Basically, these are all alike, but there is considerable difference in the number of special features offered by the lowest-priced models and the high-priced ones.

These features are not essential to washing clothes clean. You can do just as well with an inexpensive washer as a top-of-the-line model. And a point in favor of the inexpensive washer is that it is less complicated and therefore has fewer breakdowns. On the other hand, the features found in higher-priced washers do save work and simplify the washing of new fabrics, such as permanent press and knitted polyesters.

The following features are especially desirable or worthy of comment:

Washer flexibility. Since they were first introduced, the flexibility of automatic washers has been increased steadily to allow homemakers to wash all washable fabrics completely automatically. Today, all high-priced washers and many in the medium-price range offer maximum flexibility of operation.

You have a choice of several cycles to wash any kind of load. You can set the wash water temperature at hot, warm, or cold; the rinse water temperature at warm or cold. You can adjust the water level. You can select different agitator speeds and different spin speeds. And you can adjust the agitator itself to provide different wash actions.

By contrast, the cheapest washer provides one cycle, one speed, one water temperature, and one water level.

Programmed washers. To operate most automatic washers, you must turn a few knobs and push a few buttons to start the washers and make them perform in the way you desire. This obviously does not require much work, but it means that you must decide how each load of clothes should be handled.

A programmed washer—usually the most expensive model in a manufacturer's line—makes these decisions for you. All you have to do is push a single button—the button that best describes the load to be washed (permanent press or heavy-duty fabrics, for example). The washer then automatically sets the proper water temperature, speeds, and cycle sequence and turns itself on.

Permanent-press cycle. Although this cycle is designed to facilitate washing of permanent-press fabrics, it is also needed for knitted polyester garments and laminated fabrics. Most washers now incorporate it. The cycle is actually nothing more than a normal wash cycle with a final rinse in cool water. This helps to protect against wrinkling of the fabrics. Some washers also sound a signal to tell you when the load is ready to be removed from the wash tub. (Another feature that simplifies washing of permanent-press fabrics is a slow spin speed.)

Soak cycle. Many homemakers have long found it easier and less messy to presoak extra-dirty clothing in the washer than in a laundry tub. But since the advent of enzyme presoakers, washing-machine soak cycles have become even more popular.

If you are buying a new washing machine, however, you should remember that enzyme presoakers are not fully effective unless fabrics are soaked in them for at least 30 minutes. You should make sure, therefore, that the soak cycle in the washer you are considering lasts this long. Many do not.

Rinse action. This varies between makes of washer; but in all cases, the action is thorough enough to remove detergent and dirt particles from most fabrics. However, a second rinse cycle, which is provided by some washers, is desirable if you own washable rainwear, which must be thoroughly rinsed of all detergent to retain water repellency.

Automatic dispensers. These automatically inject detergent, bleach, and fabric softener into the wash load at the proper time. Detergent and bleach dispensers have been common for a good many years; fabric-softener dispensers are becoming increasingly available.

Washer capacity. Washer capacities are measured by most manufacturers in pounds of dry clothes. But some manufacturers refuse to follow this practice because, they say (quite correctly), no one agrees on what goes into the average load of clothes. This makes it impossible for you to compare the size of one washer with that of another. Don't let this worry you.

Washer capacity has been increasing steadily for years. In 1970, the largest washers advertised by companies measuring capacity in pounds held 18 pounds of clothes. Washers sold by companies not measuring capacity in this way were equally large.

Actually, the size of a washer has little bearing on its performance despite manufacturers' insinuations to the contrary. True, you can wash more clothes in an 18-pound washer than in a 12-pounder, but you cannot wash them any better. If you overload either tub, the results are the same. In other words, it is not the size of the tub that makes for clean clothes free of wrinkles, it is the way you load the tub.

Operating an automatic washer. The washer should be connected to its own 20-amp, 120-volt, grounded circuit. If the water supply hoses are permanently connected to faucets (as is usually the case), turn off the faucets when the washer is not in use. Drain the washer either into a laundry tub or a 30-inch standpipe connected into the house drain. In the latter case, the hose should be shortened so that it does not sag; otherwise it may rise up out of the pipe when the washer is emptying.

The washer must be leveled carefully so it will not "walk" across the floor if a load becomes unbalanced. Leveling is done originally by the installation serviceman by adjusting the leveling screws under the four corners of the machine. If at any time after this the washer gets out of level, you should turn the screws in or out as necessary. A carpenter's level laid across the top of the washer will guide you.

When using the washer, follow the manufacturer's operating instructions, which are usually printed inside the lid. Weigh loads you are in doubt about. Place largest pieces in the bottom of the wash tub. Pour detergent, bleach, and fabric softener into the dispensers. Open water inlet faucets. Set water level, temperatures, agitator and spin speeds, and cycle. Start washer.

Washers can be stopped at any time during a cycle by closing the start button. The cycle resumes when you reset the button. Newer models are also stopped while spinning if the lid is raised. This is a safety feature.

When your wash is completed, turn off the faucets and raise the washer lid until the tub is dry. Since the tub is cleaned during the wash cycle, it almost never needs attention; but the inside of the top should be washed with water occasionally. Clean the lint filter after each use and wash it under a faucet frequently so it does not become clogged. To clean the exterior of the machine, wipe it off with a sponge dipped in detergent solution, or apply a white appliance wax.

Scratches through the enamel finish of the washer should be painted immediately, before the metal starts to rust, with appliance touch-up enamel.

If something goes wrong. Don't try to fix a washing machine yourself. Call a serviceman. Before doing so, however, be certain of the following:

The washer is plugged in.

The house fuse has not blown.

The faucets are open.

The washer inlet hoses have not been connected to the wrong faucets.

The inlet hoses and drain hose are not kinked.

You have not run out of hot water.

You used the right amount of detergent.

The washer is level.

Wasps. See *Pest Control—Bees, hornets, wasps.*

Water. As found in nature, water is almost never pure. It contains invisible organic growths and chemicals as well as visible particles of various kinds. These all affect the water's usability and have a direct bearing on the construction and components of a plumbing system.

If you build a new house, you should definitely find out what undesirable elements your water contains before your plumbing system is installed. Even if you have lived for some time in an old house, it is a good idea to understand your water because it may help to explain why certain problems occur.

If you have access to a public water supply, you can be sure the water is safe to drink and you can assume that your plumber is familiar with its chemical analysis. If he isn't, you can get this information from the water company.

If you have a well, it is imperative that you have the water analyzed before you use it; and there may be occasions when you should have it analyzed again. The bacterial analysis can be made by any local medical laboratory. The water for the analysis is collected in a clean pint bottle which should be tightly stoppered until you deliver it to the lab.

A chemical analysis can be made by a manufacturer of water-conditioning equipment or by a private laboratory. The nearest water company will advise you where to send the water samples if you do not know.

Chemicals in water. Calcium and *magnesium* make water hard. In about 85 percent of the contiguous United States, they are present in the water in sufficient amounts to cause trouble for the home owner.

Water hardness is measured in grains per gallon. Water of less than 3.5 grains is soft. Water of 7 grains or more is hard.

Hard water deposits a rock-like scale on the inside of pipes, water heaters, and boilers. This forms in cold water, but builds up rapidly in hot water. The thicker the scale becomes, the more it reduces the flow of water through pipes. In heaters, it acts as an insulator which cuts heating efficiency while raising fuel costs.

Hard water also destroys soap and makes it difficult to wash clothes, cooking utensils, and your own hands.

Iron occurs naturally in many waters; it is also produced by the corrosion of iron and steel pipes. In either case, it may build up deposits in pipes, it stains almost everything it touches, and it gives an unpleasant taste to the water.

Manganese causes the same problems as iron, but is much rarer. The U.S. Public Health Service Drinking Standards for public water supplies recommends that the total content of iron and manganese should not exceed 0.3 parts per million.

Oxygen, carbon dioxide, and *hydrogen sulfide* corrode metals. Oxygen attacks iron and steel particularly, and the higher the water temperature, the faster the rate of corrosion. Hydrogen sulfide also makes water smell like rotten eggs.

Fluoride in an amount of 1 part per million or somewhat more helps to prevent dental cavities; but in amounts above 2½ parts per million, it causes mottling of teeth.

Other, undesirable elements in water. Organic growths, such as bacteria and algae, may make water unsafe to drink, give it a bad taste or odor, or cause slimy or clogging deposits.

Suspended particles, called sediment or turbidity, rarely do any harm but are nonetheless objectionable. The U.S. Public Health Service puts a limit of 10 parts per million on turbidity for public water supplies.

Acidity, which is measured on a pH scale, contributes to the corrosion of metals. Water with a pH of less than 7 is acid; and the lower the pH, the greater the acidity. Raising the pH value by adding soda ash to water or by passing the water through crushed limestone or marble helps to retard the rate of corrosion.

Water Coolers. See *Ice-Water Dispensers.*

Water Conditioners. Also see *Water Softeners.* The nationwide concern about pollution has brought with it a host of new products for removing or counteracting the many undesirable elements that may be found in water, whether it comes from a public supply or from your own well. Some of these are single-purpose devices; many are multi-purpose.

Which if any type of conditioner you need depends, obviously, on what is wrong with your water. For instance, if the water is very soft and corrosive, you should probably pass every drop that you use through a tank of limestone in order to protect your pipes, water tanks, and plumbing fixtures. On the other hand, if you simply want to get rid of an objectionable taste in water, you probably need nothing more than a so-called purifier which produces a few gallons of potable water per day.

Various people can advise you about the water conditioners you need. Foremost among these are water softener dealers representing manufacturers who have progressed from water softeners into all types of water conditioners. Unfortunately, while these men are competent, they may also be objectionably aggressive, and they usually carry only a single line of products. Other people who may be less biased and equally competent are water specialists who install complete water systems.

How to purify water on an emergency basis. If for some reason your water supply becomes contaminated, there are two quick and easy ways you can kill the bacteria and make it safe to drink: (1) Boil it for several minutes if you need only a small amount of water. (2) Chlorinate it if you have a shallow well. To do this, you must first figure how many gallons of water the well contains. (Square the radius of the well and multiply it by 3.14 and then by the water depth. This tells you how many cubic feet of water are in the well. To find the gallonage, multiply the cubage by 7.5.) Then all you have to do is drop into the well ¼ teaspoonful chlorine crystals for each 100 gallons water.

For long-term treatment of a contaminated water supply, you should install a chlorinator that automatically feeds the right amount of chlorine into the water.

Note that many water conditioners are called purifiers but do not actually kill bacteria. Most are designed simply to remove odors, bad taste, and turbidity.

Waterford. Famous Irish crystal that is made into tumblers, bowls, vases, chandeliers, etc. See *Glass.*

Water Heaters. Unless you move continually from new house to new house, there will come a time when you must buy a new water heater. It will not be an exciting purchase, but it will be an important one. No modern family can get along without hot water.

What size do you need? This depends on how many people are in your family, your bathing habits, whether you have a dishwasher and an automatic clothes washer, and how often you use them. It also depends on how rapidly the water heater you are interested in heats water.

Gas and oil heaters are generally fast-recovery heaters. That is to say, they can heat cold water to the desired temperature very rapidly. For this reason, the heaters installed are generally rather small.

This is also true of indirect, or instantaneous, heaters.

Electric heaters, on the other hand, have a rather slow recovery rate; so in order to make up for this, they generally have a somewhat larger capacity.

All water-heater dealers and plumbers have tables which enable them to determine what size heater any family will probably need. For example, if two people occupy a one-bathroom house containing a dishwasher and automatic washer, broad experience indicates they can probably get by very well with a 30-gallon fast-recovery gas or oil heater or a 52-gallon slower-recovery electric heater. Four people in a two-bathroom house should have a 50-gallon gas or oil heater or an 82-gallon electric heater.

In a one-bathroom house, you would need an indirect heater capable of delivering 2.75 gallons per minute; in a two-bathroom house, a 3.25 GPM heater.

Fuel. Although the foregoing discussion seems to indicate that the fuel used in a water heater determines its performance, this is not the case. One fuel heats water about as well as another. The difference in water-heater performance stems mainly from differences in the way the heaters are designed.

Your choice of fuel depends to some extent on your personal preferences but mostly on the comparative cost of the different fuels. Since all water heaters consume lots of fuel, it makes sense to buy the one that is going to cost least to operate either because the basic price of the fuel is lowest or because you already happen to use large quantities of it to heat your home and cook your food.

Types of water heater. Most water heaters are storage units—insulated round tanks in which water is heated and stored until a faucet is opened. They operate on gas, LP gas, oil, or electricity. The first three must be vented into a flue; consequently, they are generally installed in the basement or utility room near the furnace. Electric heaters are not vented and can be installed anywhere.

The material of which the water-heater tank is made is of critical importance because of the corrosive effect of hot water. In areas where the water is exceptionally corrosive, the best tanks are of solid copper or copper on steel. Theoretically, plastic tanks should also be excellent but they are so new that little is known about their durability.

Glass-lined steel tanks cost much less and are today the most widely used. Although they are not quite as corrosion-resistant as copper, they are very good. Most are guaranteed for five years, and the best are guaranteed for ten.

Galvanized steel tanks, once common, have virtually dropped out of existence because there are only a few areas in the United States where they can survive for any length of time.

The other type of water heater in use is the tankless indirect heater. This is a small heater which can be connected to any oil- or gas-fired automatic hot-water or steam boiler used to heat the house. It cannot be used with manually fired boilers or warm-air furnaces.

The heater is said to be indirect because it does not heat water by direct flame. Instead, the water is circulated through a copper coil which is surrounded by hot water from the boiler.

In winter, indirect heaters are very economical to operate because the water used to heat the house also heats the water in the hot-water faucets. In summer, however, the heaters consume somewhat more fuel than storage water heaters. Nevertheless, most people who have indirect heaters consider them quite economical.

They are also quite free of problems except in areas where the water is hard. There the coils may become so clogged with chemicals that they must be periodically flushed out with acid. This is a job to be done by professionals.

Water temperatures. Because very hot water is needed to run a dishwasher and clothes washer properly, your water-heater thermostat should be set at about 160 degrees. This will allow for some loss of heat as the water goes through the pipes; but unless the water heater is far removed from the dishwasher or clothes washer, the temperature of the water entering the appliances should be about 150 degrees or a little less.

To prevent excessive heat loss from pipes, it is advisable to insulate the pipes leading to the dishwasher, washer, and kitchen sink. There is no harm in insulating the pipes to the bathrooms also; but inasmuch as you don't run hot water in the bathrooms many times during the day, the water standing in the pipes is bound to cool off despite the insulation.

A better—and more expensive—way to assure that you get hot water at an outlet the instant you turn it on is to install a small circulating pump which circulates hot water constantly between the water heater and the outlet. This, of course, requires a return pipe as well as a supply pipe. Both are insulated.

How to keep from scalding oneself when the water heater is set at 160 degrees is a problem that worries many people. But there are several solutions: One is to install mixing faucets or valves in lavatories, tubs, and sinks. Thermostatically controlled valves are also available. Another is to equip the water heater with a special device which delivers water at two different temperatures. A third solution, which is particularly suited to a large, rambling house, is to install two small water heaters—one near the kitchen and laundry and the other in the sleeping area.

Operating a water heater. To get rid of the sediment that slowly accumulates in storage water heaters, open the drain valve at the bottom every two or three months and draw off a pail of water.

Have an oil burner serviced annually. Gas and electric heaters do not require service except in an emergency.

Drain the water heater if you close up the house in winter.

If something goes wrong. Call a plumber.

Water Pumps. In most homes that are not served by a public water supply, water is pumped from a well into a closed tank partly filled with air under pressure. When you open a faucet, the air forces water through the supply pipes to the faucet.

Three types of pumps are commonly used today: a submersible pump, which is installed deep in the well itself; a jet pump, which is installed in a pump house or basement; and a piston pump, which, like the jet pump, is installed above ground.

Obviously there is nothing you can do about a submersible pump. You cannot oil it; and if anything goes wrong with it, you must get the well driller or pump installer to haul it up and repair it.

Jet and piston pumps should be lubricated in accordance with the manufacturer's instructions. You can also make simple repairs described in the instruction manual.

How to correct an air cushion in the pressure tank. Regardless of the type of pump you own, this is sometimes necessary. As pointed out above, water flows from a pressure tank because of the cushion of compressed air in the tank above the water. This cushion occupies about one-third to one-half of the tank, and it is presumably maintained by an air valve—very similar to a tire valve—which admits air when the pump is operating. On modern systems, the air valves are automatic; on old systems, they are controlled by hand.

Unfortunately, despite these air valves, the air cushion often becomes too small and the water level too high. The tank is then said to be water-logged, and the effect is to make the pump turn on and off more frequently than normal. You can tell when this happens by the way the water flows from a faucet. First it flows hard, then it slows down rapidly, then it flows hard again, and so on.

If you have an automatic air control, you can restore the right amount of air to the tank (and thus lower the water level in the tank) by doing the following things: (1) Replace the valve core in the valve body. Do not use an automobile tire valve core. Use only the valve made especially for your water system. If this doesn't correct the problem, (2) drain the system entirely (be sure a valve or pipe on the outlet side of the tank is open so that air can be admitted to the tank). Then refill the tank. (3) An alternative is to pump air through the valve into the tank with a tire pump. If trouble still continues, call a pump serviceman.

If your pressure system is not equipped with an automatic air control, you will find what looks like an ordinary tire valve on the pump. Normally this is capped. To admit more air, remove the cap. You should be able to hear the valve sucking in air as the pump operates. If you don't, loosen the valve slightly. If it still doesn't suck, replace it with a new valve core. If this still doesn't work, empty the system (as above) and refill it.

One thing to watch out for if you have a manual air control is that you do not leave the cap off the valve too long. If the valve is working properly, it will within a few hours or a day (depending on how much water you are using) admit too much air to the tank. Then water will flow from your faucets in violent bursts accompanied by violent bursts of air and you will have to drain the system entirely. Ordinarily, when the pressure tank has an adequate air cushion, the cap is kept on the valve.

Note also that when you empty a pressure system and then refill it (regardless of the way the air is controlled), you may find that water flows spasmodically—sometimes in spurts—from faucets. This may continue for an hour or even for a day or so. Do not worry unless it continues for several days. It is caused by air bubbles in the system and will disappear as these are forced out of the lines.

If water is turbid. When a new well is drilled, the water may run cloudy and brown for several days before the sediment causing the problem settles or is pumped out. Turbidity after that is rare, but sometimes occurs if you pump the well very hard for several days (to fill a swimming pool, for example). Generally, this should cause you no anxiety. The water should gradually clear. If it doesn't, consult your well driller.

If you run out of water. There may be something wrong with the pump; or you may actually have drawn the water level down below the intake.

If you have a submersible pump, the well driller can probably drop it farther down into the well. Unlike the intake pipe of other pumps, submersible pumps are quite commonly suspended rather high up in the well.

But if your well actually has gone dry, you will have to bring in water in tank trucks and pour it into the well. Call your fire department. If it cannot help you, it will tell you who can.

Water Repellents. One type of water repellent is applied to fabrics to minimize staining and to waterproof rainwear. See *Fabric Finishes.*

A second type of repellent is a colorless, transparent liquid containing silicone that is sometimes applied to masonry walls to keep water from seeping through the pores. Although these are often called waterproofers, they actually are effective only against dampness—not active leaks. They must be renewed every five or six years.

A third type of water repellent is a colorless liquid that is applied to wood—especially the wood siding and trim on houses—in order to make it retain its natural color more or less. It also retards splintering and cracking of wood and stops mildew if it contains a mildewcide. Two coats of repellent are usually applied to new wood. Thereafter an additional coat is applied only when the wood begins to darken slightly. This occurs more rapidly in wet climates than in dry.

Water Softeners. The hardness of a water supply is proportional to its content of calcium and magnesium salts and is expressed in grains per gallon. Water with less than 3.5 grains per gallon is considered soft. Between 3.5 and 7 grains, it is moderately hard; from 7 to 10.5 grains, it is hard; and above 10.5 grains, it is very hard.

Water with more than 3.5 grains hardness occurs in 85 percent of the area covered by the first forty eight states. Anyone who has lived with such water is familiar with the problems it creates: Soap dissolves slowly and doesn't make suds. Dishes and glasses are streaky after washing. Laundered clothes are gray. Scummy rings encircle bathtubs. Scale forming in hot water pipes and water heaters reduces heating efficiency, wastes fuel, and often leads to premature failure of the system.

Detergents used for washing clothes and dishes counteract the effects of water containing less than 15 grains hardness. But they are, of course, powerless against the rest of the water that courses through your pipes and is used for other purposes. Hence the need for mechanical water softeners.

A water softener is a large tank installed on the main water supply line and containing a mineral called zeolite. As water flows through the tank, hardness in it is removed by the zeolite. After a few weeks, however, the zeolite becomes so clogged with calcium and magnesium salts that it loses its effectiveness and must be put through a rather complicated process known as regeneration. This involves flushing a strong current of water through the zeolite, then adding salt and finally rinsing well.

Most home owners who buy water softeners outright take care of regenerating the units themselves. The work is much simpler if they own an automatic rather than a manual softener.

Many families, however, prefer to rent water softeners from a local water-softening service firm which installs the equipment for a modest fee and thereafter replaces the tired tank of zeolite with a new one every month. In the long run, this is the most expensive plan but it relieves the home owner of all work and worry.

The size water softener required depends on the hardness of the water and the size of the family. Installation should be made so that the only water treated is that which is used in the house. Water for the garden, car-washing, and pool-filling should be bypassed.

Waxes.

Floor waxes. Floor waxes are either water-based or solvent-based. For any type of resilient flooring—*except* vinyl cork or cork tile—you should use a water-based wax. Water-based wax is easy to apply and is less apt to yellow the floor; most impor-

tant—a solvent-based wax will soften the binder and actually damage asphalt tile and noncolorfast rubber tile.

Water is harmful to cork or wood flooring, so for these types of flooring you should use solvent-based waxes. They are available in both paste and liquid form. Besides being identified on their containers, solvent-based waxes are also easily recognized by their naphtha, or "dry-cleaning fluid," odor. Their containers are marked "flammable."

Water-based waxes for resilient floors. The kind of wax that will work best for you depends on your personal preference and on what kind of wear the floor gets. Water-based waxes fall into three different categories, each with special qualities:

Self-polishing waxes are easy to use, and they dry to a tough, hard film with a bright shine. They are a practical choice if you want a hard shine and do not have an electric polisher. They are scuff-resistant, and because they are, they do not respond well to buffing. When a traffic area becomes worn, the entire floor must be rewaxed. Some self-polishing waxes do not lose their shine when washed with detergent solutions between waxings. Before applying this kind of wax, the floor must be washed, rinsed, and allowed to dry.

Buffable waxes have a slight shine when they dry, but as they need buffing to bring out the full gloss, they are most practical only if you have an electric polisher. These waxes also can be applied with the wax dispenser of a polishing machine. The kind of wax that responds to buffing is also soft enough to show scuff marks; but the shine can be restored between waxings by machine-buffing, worn spots can be touched up with additional wax, and the whole floor can be buffed to an even gloss. Before applying a buffable wax, the floor should be washed, rinsed, and allowed to dry thoroughly. Between waxings, dry-mop, sweep, or vacuum the floor before buffing.

Clean-and-polish waxes are designed to be a one-step operation. Self-polishing, they also contain a detergent that cleans the floor as the wax is being applied. They are time savers because they eliminate the washing, rinsing, and drying operations. You pick up the dirt on an applicator and then rinse the applicator in clear water. Before applying, it is best to sweep or vacuum the floor. As you apply the wax, rinse the applicator (cloth or sponge) frequently to remove the dirt, or refold the cloth to a clean section as you move from one spot to another. These waxes are practical for use in areas that do not get heavy traffic, and they are handy for touching up worn areas between regular waxings.

Solvent-based waxes for wood and cork floors. Here, also, there are three kinds of wax:

Paste wax is the most durable but also the most difficult to apply since you must get down on hands and knees and rub it on the floor with a damp cloth. Then, after it has dried for about 20 minutes, you must buff it by hand, or preferably, with an electric floor polisher. Thereafter you need to buff it only when it begins to look dull or dirty. Except in heavy-traffic areas, you should not have to apply new wax more than once every six months.

Buffable liquid wax is applied like other liquid waxes, with a wool applicator. It must then be buffed by hand or with a floor polisher. Although not as durable as paste wax, it nevertheless lasts a long time and maintains a pleasant luster if you rebuff it from time to time.

Clean-and-polish waxes, despite their name, are not unique in the cleaning department: both kinds of buffable waxes contain cleaning agents, too. The essential difference is that solvent-based clean-and-polish waxes—like those with a water base—are self-polishing. You just apply them to the floor, and that's that. Unfortunately, their durability is fairly low.

Furniture waxes. These are made in liquid and paste form, and can be applied to wood paneling and kitchen cabinets as well as furniture. The paste waxes give best protection to the surface and last longest but are most troublesome. Waxes used on wood floors can also be applied to furniture.

Appliance waxes. These are white liquids that clean as well as polish. They are very effective in removing many stains and simultaneously applying a protective finish to appliances, cabinets, woodwork, counter tops, metals, tile, leather, and vinyl.

Waxing. The way you wax depends on what you're working on and the kind of wax you're using. Always read the directions on the label. But the following rules apply in all cases:

1. Whatever the applicator used, it should be reasonably clean, free of grit, and flexible.

2. Apply wax sparingly. A thin film gives about as much protection as a thick one, looks better, and doesn't scratch as badly or collect as much dust.

3. If buffing is called for, use as much weight and apply as much friction as possible. An electric polisher is best for use on floors. A buffing wheel on an electric drill does a good job on furniture, paneling, etc.

4. If the applicator gets very dirty during application of wax, change it: there is a limit to how much dirt it can absorb.

5. Don't be in too much of a hurry to apply a new coat of wax. The sooner you build up a heavy film, the sooner you will have to strip it all off.

The procedure for applying any self-polishing floor wax is as follows:

Make sure the floor is swept or vacuumed clean. Then pour enough wax on the floor to do an area about 4 feet square at a time. Spread it evenly over the floor using enough pressure to loosen the dirt (but you should not have to scrub). Then finish evening out the wax with long strokes in the same direction. Allow the wax to dry about 30 minutes before walking on the floor. Wash the applicator out in detergent solution and rinse well.

Wax Paper. A roll of wax paper is almost a household necessity. At one time, it was the only wrap available to protect foods stored in the refrigerator; but it is no longer used so widely for this purpose because aluminum foil and plastic bags and wraps are better.

However, wax paper still serves the cook in many ways—from lining cake pans to catching sifted flour.

You can use it also for the following purposes:

If the soleplate of an iron is scratched, smooth it with emery cloth; then heat it slightly and run it over a piece of wax paper to make it slide easily.

Place a sheet of wax paper under freshly glued articles to keep them from sticking to the surface on which they are standing. The wax paper will not stick to them as other materials do.

Weatherstripping. Weatherstripping is used around doors and windows to keep out cold and moisture and to stop drafts. Almost all windows made today have efficient built-in weatherstripping. Exterior doors, however, must still be weatherstripped when they are installed. If the best interlocking weatherstripping is used (as it should be), installation is an elaborate task and should be left to a professional.

Weatherstripping of several types is easily applied to existing doors and windows. The best, because it is hidden, is a thin, corrugated, spring-metal strip 1¼ inches wide. It comes in long rolls from which you can cut any length with tin snips.

Around doors, the metal strips are tacked to the side and top jambs with small brads. The nailing flange faces the door. The rest of the strip is bent slightly outward so that it presses against the edges of the door.

Metal strips are also used in wood-framed casements and single wood-framed hopper and awning windows in the same way. They can also be tacked to the pulley stiles in double-hung windows provided the sash fit loosely in the stiles.

Most other types of weatherstripping keep out weather by pressing tight against the face of doors and windows. The strips are fastened to the stops. The least expensive are made of foam plastic or of felt bound along one edge with aluminum. The former comes with an adhesive on one edge and is simply smoothed down on the stops. Better strips are made of vinyl or rubber. They look neater and will last for years. They are installed with tacks, brads, or staples.

For weatherstripping metal casement windows, you need special U-shaped strips—usually of vinyl—which are fitted over the edges of the casement frames.

An easy way to stop drafts under doors is to install an aluminum threshold which contains an oval vinyl insert that presses against the bottom of the door. The metal threshold is either ½ or 7/8 inch high; the insert projects a bit above it. If it is necessary to increase the height of the threshold, it can be nailed to a board, which is in turn nailed to the floor.

Other bottom-of-the-door weatherstrips are attached to the outside face of the door. The simplest is an aluminum strip with a vinyl flap that projects below the door bottom. A more elaborate but excellent weatherstrip looks rather similar but incorporates a spring that flips the vinyl flap outward and upward when the door is opened. When the door is closed, the flap automatically seals against the threshold. This strip is particularly useful when the door must clear a deep rug.

Weatherstrips for use under garage doors are nailed to the bottom of the doors. There are special strips, but you can also use rubber strips like those for windows.

If you have a window air conditioner that makes no provision for weatherstripping the joint between the conditioner and the double-hung window, you can wedge a large, square polyester foam strip between them.

How to repair weatherstripping. Weatherstrips that are tacked to door and window stops often become torn, worn, and hardened with paint. They are so inexpensive that it is silly to try to repair them. Replace them with new weatherstrips.

If a door or window weatherstripped with metal binds, rub the strips with paraffin or spray them with silicone lubricant. You'll save further trouble if you do this about once a year.

If a door or casement window with interlocking metal weatherstripping is difficult to close, check whether the U-bend in one-half of the strip has become clogged with dirt and clean it with a thin screwdriver. (Make a habit of cleaning the strips under doors and windows with a vacuum cleaner.) If the problem is not caused by dirt, the chances are that the two halves of the strip do not mesh because they are bent. They can be straightened with a screwdriver and/or hammer. Don't be too violent. If the door or window still does not close, it may be that it is hanging on a slant because the screws in the hinges are loose. Try tightening.

If a spring-metal strip vibrates in the wind, bend the free end toward the door or window edge.

Wedgwood. A famous brand of English china first made by Josiah Wedgwood. The firm also makes other types of dinnerware. (See *China.*)

Weights and Measures.

What you need. Several measuring devices are almost essential around the home: a yardstick, seamstress's tape, 6-foot folding rule or flexible steel rule, several measuring cups and a couple of sets of measuring spoons, and assorted thermometers (see *Thermometers*). Kitchen and bathroom scales are also desirable.

Measuring spoons in a set hold ¼ teaspoon, ½ teaspoon, 1 teaspoon, and 1 tablespoon.

Cups used for measuring liquids should have rims slightly higher than the 1-cup line so you won't spill what you are measuring. For measuring dry materials, use a cup with the 1-cup line at the rim. Then you can fill the cup higher than the rim and level off the excess with a knife.

Tables of Weights and Measures

Linear measure

12 inches = 1 foot
3 feet = 1 yard
5280 feet = 1760 yards = 1 mile

Area measure

144 square inches = 1 square foot
9 square feet = 1 square yard
43,560 square feet = 4840 square yards = 1 acre
A square 208.71 feet on all sides = 1 acre

Cubic measure

1728 cubic inches = 1 cubic foot
27 cubic feet = 1 cubic yard
1 cubic yard of gravel, sand, concrete, soil, etc., covers:
    54 square feet if spread 6 inches deep
    81 square feet if spread 4 inches deep
    108 square feet if spread 3 inches deep
    162 square feet if spread 2 inches deep
    324 square feet if spread 1 inch deep

Dry measure

1 cup = ½ pint
2 pints = 1 quart
8 quarts = 1 peck
4 pecks = 1 bushel

Liquid measure

16 fluid ounces = 4 gills = 1 pint
2 pints = 1 quart
4 quarts = 1 gallon

Avoirdupois weight

16 drams = 1 ounce
16 ounces = 1 pound
100 pounds = 1 hundredweight
2000 pounds = 1 short ton

Kitchen measure

3 teaspoons = 1 tablespoon
2 tablespoons = 1 ounce
16 tablespoons = 1 cup
1 cup = 8 ounces = ½ pint
2 cups = 16 ounces = 1 pint
4 cups = 32 ounces = 1 quart

Electrical units

1000 watts = 1 kilowatt
746 watts = 1 horsepower
1 kilowatt = 1 1/3 horsepower
1 kilowatt-hour = 1000 watts for 1 hour*

*If an electrical utility charges 3 cents per kilowatt-hour for current consumed, you can operate ten 100-watt bulbs for 1 hour for a cost of 3 cents.

Useful equivalents

1 gallon = 231 cubic inches
1 cubic foot = 7.48 gallons
1 gallon water = 8.33 pounds
¼ pound butter = ½ cup
1 average coffee cup = 6 ounces
1 fifth liquor = 25.6 ounces
1 sack cement = 1 cubic foot
1 cup inorganic fertilizer such as 5-10-5 = approximately ½ pound
1 square shingles = 100 square feet
1 board foot = a 1-inch-thick board with an area of 144 square inches

---

Whipcream. A light, soft polyester fabric resembling crepe but with a less decidedly crinkled texture. It is used for clothing and blanket covers. Launder like polyester.

Wicker. A name applied to furniture and other articles made of willow. See *Willow.*

Wiggle Nails. See *Wood Fasteners.*

Willow. The long, slender twigs of certain species of willow are often woven into baskets and furniture pieces. The best and most durable of these articles are made of entire twigs; cheaper articles are made of twigs split in half.

Willow articles should be finished; otherwise the wood will soon become stained and dirty, and will probably turn gray. Use paint; or for a clear finish, apply lacquer, shellac, or varnish with a spray gun or brush. Once finished, willow pieces can be cleaned by washing with mild detergent solution. You'll need a brush to get into the crevices.

If strips of willow are cracked, coat both edges with cellulose cement and hold them together until the cement sets. (White wood glue is just as good, but since the strips are usually difficult to clamp and since the glue takes hours to set, its use is not very practical.)

Broken strips can sometimes be glued in the same way, but it is a good deal easier to cut them back to the nearest joint: you probably will never know they are missing. If there is any chance that the cut ends remaining will come loose, anchor them with a dab of cellulose cement.

Wilton. A beautiful type of carpet originated in Wilton, England. See *Rugs.*

Windows. If you sealed the windows in your house and put in a central air-conditioning system, you would undoubtedly save yourself a great deal of housework and repair work. Windows, in short, are work-makers. But they are necessary; they have many virtues; and there are few families that could bring themselves to give them up.

Types of window. Double-hung. This is the most familiar window. It has two sash which slide up and down in parallel tracks known as pulley stiles. Modern windows have reliable spring balances; but old ones were balanced by a weight and pulley; and very old ones had no balances at all. Double-hung windows with sash that lift out or tilt so that you can wash both sides from indoors are desirable.

Single-hung windows are almost never used today but are still found in old houses. They are like double-hung windows except that the top sash is fixed.

Sliding windows are, in effect, double-hung windows turned on their side: the two sash slide back and forth horizontally in parallel tracks. But since the sash need not be balanced, there is less that can go wrong with them. In some cases, the sash are removable for washing.

Casements are hinged at the side and swing outward. They are installed as single sash or in pairs that meet together in the middle of the window opening. Some windows are designed so you can slip your arm between the sash and the hinge jamb; thus you can wash both sides from indoors. But other casements, especially older units, do not have this convenience. In all instances, screens are installed inside the window and are therefore very easy to put up and take down.

Awning windows are horizontal units, usually not very high. They are hinged at the top and open outward. There may be one or more sash in an opening. So-called projecting units can be washed completely from indoors. Screens are installed inside.

Hopper windows are narrow, horizontal windows—the reverse of awning windows. They are hinged at the bottom and open in. They are single windows used mainly in basements or in clerestories. You can wash both sides from indoors.

Jalousies consist of a number of very narrow horizontal strips of glass that swing out and upward when opened, and overlap when closed. The glass strips are not framed, which means that there is a certain amount of air and water leakage between them. For this reason, jalousies should never be used in cold climates in rooms that are occupied in winter because you will freeze to death. In mild, dry climates, however, jalousies are delightful. They are washed from indoors and screened on the inside.

Fixed windows are just that—windows that do not open. Picture windows are generally fixed; but all fixed windows are not picture windows.

Windowpanes. The basic difference in windowpanes is their size: they are either fairly small and used in multiples or they are large single panes.

Small panes are made of sheet glass. Rather large panes, such as those in the average sliding window, are also made of sheet glass, or of insulating glass, which consists of two sheets of glass with a sealed air space between. Very large panes are made of plate glass or insulating glass; but they should be made of tempered safety glass in floor-to-ceiling windows flanking glass doors. The panes in jalousies are also made of plate glass.

Multi-paned windows—those with small panes—take more time to wash and paint than large single-paned windows. And if you require double-glazing to keep out the cold, you must install storm windows, because insulating glass is not made in small sizes. For these reasons, some windows are now produced with large panes that are divided into small panes by snap-in mullions. In other words, when the mullions are in place, the windows look from a distance like conventional multi-paned windows. When you want to wash the windows, however, you can take out the mullions, which are made of flexible vinyl, to expose the single, large, easy-to-wash sheet of glass (it may be insulating glass).

But large-paned windows are not without problems. For one thing, their size makes you more conscious of the fact that they are dirty; consequently, you tend to wash them more often. While washing goes quickly, it is fairly difficult to eliminate streaks. If you break a large pane, it is more difficult and costly to replace than a small pane (people living in modern glass houses often carry special plate-glass insurance). Finally, birds are often confused by large panes of glass and crash into them.

How to wash windows. Advertised window-washing products do not hold a candle to a simple, cheap, home-made water solution. Don't bother with them.

Into 1 gallon water mix any one of the following: 2 or 3 tablespoons vinegar; 2 or 3 tablespoons household ammonia; 1 tablespoon powdered cleanser. The water need not be warm; but change it when it gets dirty.

You will need one or more squeegees. If you have small-paned windows, you should ideally have a squeegee that exactly fits each different pane size. If your windows have large panes, use a 12-inch squeegee. (See *Squeegees.*) You will also need a chamois.

Wet a sponge in the washing solution, wring it partly dry, and wipe it over the entire surface of the pane. Then hold the rubber blade of the squeegee against the pane at the top and draw it downward across the glass to the bottom. You don't need to exert any pressure. Lift it off and wipe the blade with your chamois. Then wipe the excess moisture from the bottom mullion or window frame.

On large panes, it is necessary to draw the squeegee down across the glass repeatedly. The strokes should overlap slightly. Always dry the squeegee after each stroke.

That's all there is to it. The job is quick, easy, and with reasonable care produces a spotless window. Professionals never wash windows in any other way.

Note: Squeegees are of little value on jalousies. Simply sponge the glass strips with cleaning solution and dry with a chamois. Then polish with a dry cloth.

How to replace a windowpane. This is a very easy job on modern windows in which the panes are held in place, not by putty, but by snap-in vinyl strips. All you do is pull out the strips, set in the new pane, and push the strips back into their grooves.

Conventional windowpanes should be set in putty only when the temperature is above 40 degrees and will stay there for several days. Take out loose pieces of glass; then with a wood chisel, cut and scrape out the putty in the mullions. Remove this down to the bare wood, but be careful not to gouge the wood. Then lift out the rest of the glass, pull out the tiny metal glazier's points, and scrape out any putty remaining.

Buy or cut a new pane of glass just a shade smaller than the rabbeted opening. You can reset the pane either with oil-based putty or with latex putty, more commonly known as elastic glazing compound. (See *Putty.*) If using the former, brush linseed oil on the exposed edges of the rabbets. The putty can be applied immediately. If using latex putty, the bare wood is primed with oil paint which must be allowed to dry before the putty is applied. This means that in order to keep out cold, insects, etc., you must cover the window with a board or cardboard until the pane is put in.

Whichever putty is used should be spread in a thin layer on both rabbet surfaces. Then set in the glass and press it firmly on all sides so that it is embedded in the putty.

Drive in the glazier's points on all four sides of the pane. The points can be tapped in with the edge of a screwdriver or pushed in with the blade. You need only one point per side on small panes; two or three on large panes.

Spread putty into the joints against the edges of the glass. One way to do this is to roll the putty into pencil-size rolls which are pressed into the joints. Another way is to spread the putty into the joints with a putty knife almost as if you were spreading butter thickly on bread.

Hold your putty knife more or less parallel with one edge of the glass and smooth the putty from corner to corner. The knife

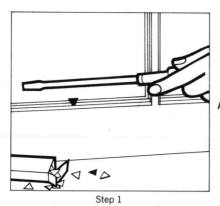

REPLACING
A WINDOW PANE

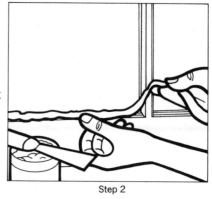

Step 1   Step 2

should be held at an angle to form a sharp bevel from the outer edge of the mullion to the glass. Do not spread the putty so far out on the glass that you can see it from inside the window. The putty must, of course, stick tight to both the wood and the glass. If you don't make the bevel right the first time, add more putty or remove it and reapply.

Carefully scrape up excess putty. After the beveled strips have set (it takes about two weeks), apply oil paint or varnish if the frame is to have a natural finish.

Panes in metal windows are replaced in essentially the same way. The metal must be free of rust but is not primed. Panes are held in place with special metal clips rather than glazier's points. Don't lose these. Special metal-sash putty must be used.

Window frames. Frames are made of wood, aluminum, steel, or wood encased in a vinyl sheath.

Wood frames are the most attractive and have the best insulating value; and if you live in a corrosive atmosphere, you can be pretty sure nothing very serious is going to happen to them. On the other hand, they may rot (modern wood frames should, however, be treated with wood preservative). Unsupported windows such as casements and awning windows may warp and sag. All windows may swell and stick or contract and admit cold air. And all must be painted.

Paint windows inside with interior oil or alkyd paint; on the outside, with house paint or, better, trim enamel. The best clear finish is urethane or spar varnish.

The frequency with which wood windows must be painted depends almost entirely on how much moisture they are exposed to. If you get heavy condensation in the house, you will find that any interior finish on horizontal mullions and the bottom rail wears out very rapidly—often in less than a year. Outside finish usually lasts three or four years, but should be renewed when the siding is painted.

Windows must be scraped well before new paint is applied. There is no easy way to do this. Use any tool that seems to work—a knife, putty knife, scraper, beer-can opener—and don't let it slip and gouge the wood. Finish with sandpaper and be careful not to scratch the edges of the glass.

If the mullions and frame on the inside are soggy because of standing condensation, let them dry thoroughly before scraping, sanding, and painting. A heat lamp or electric heater is helpful.

Window mullions are best painted with a sash brush. One type is oval; the other is like a conventional paintbrush but the end is cut on a slant. Use whichever you find easier to handle. A very thin line of paint should extend onto the glass on the outside.

Paint mullions first, then the sash frame, then the casing (the framework around the entire window).

Aluminum frames retain their shape well and work easily and reliably. But they transmit cold. And although manufacturers claim they never need finishing, they very often do—they may corrode and disintegrate near the seacoast and in polluted atmospheres, and they often turn rough and gray elsewhere.

If you wish to retain the natural aluminum finish, apply two coats of methacrylate lacquer to the outer surfaces of the frames; apply wax indoors. If you paint the frames, prime them with zinc chromate. Then apply trim enamel outdoors; any good oil or alkyd paint indoors.

For how to clean aluminum frames, see *Aluminum*.

Steel frames are the strongest of all and retain their shape best. They work easily unless rust has been allowed to build up. But they transmit cold and must be painted just as often as wood.

After cleaning the steel thoroughly to remove every possible vestige of rust, prime it with a rust-inhibiting primer and follow with one or two coats of trim enamel or interior oil or alkyd paint.

Windows with a sound finish can be washed like wood with detergent solution. Or you can clean inner surfaces with white appliance wax.

Vinyl-clad wood frames are quite new and are used on only a few types of window. They have not been in use long enough to determine whether they are really as good as they seem. What is known is that they have the virtues of wood and very few of the disadvantages (although there is a limited choice of finish). They do not need any finishing. The vinyl should, however, be washed regularly with detergent solution or cleaned indoors with white appliance wax.

Weatherstripping windows. Most modern windows are internally weatherstripped at the factory and need no further attention. For how to weatherstrip old windows, see *Weatherstripping*.

Stopping water problems. If water leaks in around the edges of the sash, see *Weatherstripping* for what to do. If water enters between the top of the casing and the house wall, see *Flashing*.

If water dripping off the sill curls back under the sill and then drips down the house wall, tack a strip of ¼-inch quarter-round under the sill along the front edge. One of the flat sides of the quarter-round should face forward. This will serve as a drip edge, forcing water to fall straight to the ground.

Many sills have a built-in drip edge consisting simply of a slight channel cut in the bottom of the sills.

How to make other window repairs. Double-hung windows. If the lower sash rattles in the wind, run a sharp knife up and down the joints between the stops and the sash to break the paint seal. Then pry off the stops, working as much as possible from the back side so you don't spoil the appearance of the wood. Hold the sash firmly against the parting strips; move the stops a fraction of an inch closer to it; and renail them in this position. Work the sash all the way up and down to make sure it slides easily.

If the upper sash rattles (rather unusual), remove the stops as above and lift the lower sash out of the frame. Then with a knife, loosen the paint along the edges of one of the parting strips and pry the strip out. Take out the upper sash. Stick one or more strips of plastic electrical tape to the side of each parting strip that bears against the upper sash. Then replace the sash, parting strips, lower sash, and stops. This is not a perfect repair, because the tape may in time come loose, but it's about the only easy solution.

If a sash is painted shut, run the point of a sharp knife around the edges. This sounds like an easy job, and is; but if you work too fast or carelessly, the knife will slip and gouge the paint on the window or casing. If paint has sunk deep into the joint, force the thin blade of a putty knife through it.

If a sash binds, rub paraffin on the pulley stiles or spray them with silicone lubricant. If this doesn't do the trick, it's probably because the sash is binding against the stops. In the case of a bottom sash, simply pry up the stops and move them away from the sash a fraction of an inch. If the upper sash is binding, remove the lower sash entirely, pry out the parting strips, and scrape down the sides slightly.

If the cord for a bottom sash is broken, remove one of the stops and pull out the sash. Unscrew the sash pocket cover from the pulley stile, lift out the weight, and remove the old cord. Buy a new cotton or wire-reinforced cotton sash cord of the same size and cut it to the same length. Thread it over the pulley and down to the bottom of the pocket. Tie it to the weight with a pair of half hitches (see *Knots*). Pull the weight up to the pulley; place the sash in the bottom of the frame; stretch the cord down tight to the cord hole in the side of the sash; tie a large knot in the end and cram it into the hole. Make sure that it fits tight. Replace the sash in the frame and move it up and down a couple of times to make certain it works properly; then replace the pocket cover and stop.

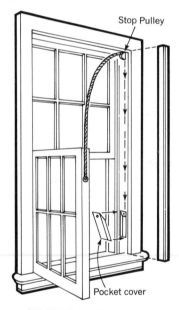

Stop Pulley

Pocket cover

REPAIRING WINDOW CORD ON DOUBLE-HUNG WINDOWS

The cord for an upper sash is replaced in the same way after you remove the lower sash.

If a window lock doesn't latch, it is usually because the hook on the upper sash is too low or is not in alignment with the lock. If out of alignment, unscrew it, fill the holes in the sash with plastic wood,

and set the hook in its proper position. If the hook is too low, insert a small wood shim under it.

Sliding windows. If a window rattles, binds, or is stuck, fix it like a double-hung window. Clean the bottom track regularly with a vacuum cleaner and, if necessary, detergent solution and fine steel wool. Rub paraffin or floor paste wax on the track a couple of times a year.

Casement windows. Keep the adjusting arm free of dirt, rust, and paint and oil it two or three times a year so that it operates smoothly. Oil hinges also.

If a wood casement sags badly at the free side, remove it, push it back into square, and reinforce the corners with steel mending plates. These can be recessed to make them less noticeable. If this fails to correct matters, you had better buy a new sash. (For how to correct other casement problems, see *Doors.*)

Awning windows and jalousies. If these work stiffly or do not close tight, the operating mechanism is probably clogged with dirt, paint, or corrosion. Clean the entire mechanism about every three months and keep it lubricated. (For how to correct other problems in single awning windows, see *Doors.*)

Hopper windows. If a window has a wood frame, repair it like a door. If it is a basement window, the frame is undoubtedly made of steel, and the main problem is to keep it free of rust. Paint and lubricate it regularly.

Windowshades.

Roller shades. The only difference among roller shades is in the fabric. Solid vinyl is least expensive; then comes vinyl-treated cotton; then fiberglass laminated with vinyl. Most shades admit some light; but some are treated to give total darkness. Shades treated on the back with milium reflect the sun's rays and help somewhat to keep rooms cooler.

Roller shades are also made of narrow bamboo or wood strips woven together. When rolled up, these form a much larger roll than a fabric shade; and in some cases, they are too large to install inside the window casing. (If installed outside the casing, they would stick out too far.)

How to clean shades. Most new shades are washable; older ones may not be. Clean washable shades with mild detergent solution; nonwashable shades with wallpaper dough cleaner.

You can spot-clean shades while hanging, but for overall cleaning, take them down and unroll them on a flat surface. Wash, rinse, and dry a section at a time. Use as little water as possible. When both sides are clean, hang the shade open until it is thoroughly dry; then roll it up all the way and leave it overnight to "iron" out all wrinkles.

How to repair shades. If a shade is a bit too wide to hang inside a window casing, it can often be made to fit by filing the ends of the pins down slightly. You might also recess one or both of the brackets.

If a shade falls out of the brackets because it is too narrow, move brackets mounted on the outside of the casing closer together. If the shade is inside the casing, try pulling the pin in the roller out about ¼ inch. The alternative is to insert a wood shim under one or both brackets.

If the spring is too tight, raise the shade to the top, take it out of the brackets, and unroll it 18 inches. Replace it in the brackets and test the tension. Repeat this process until the tension is right.

If the spring is too loose and the shade is reluctant to roll up, lower it about 18 inches from the top, remove it from the brackets, and roll it up by hand. Replace in the brackets; test the tension; and repeat the process as necessary.

If a shade is torn, it should be replaced. But you can make a temporary repair by applying a patch of cotton or vinyl fabric. Use fabric-mending adhesive for the former; plastic-mending adhesive for the latter.

If a shade is torn from the roller, spread it out flat and refasten the shade with staples or tiny tacks.

Other types of shade. Austrian shades are elegant shades of many materials with shirred panels which are raised and lowered by pulleys and cords inserted between the panels.

Roman shades are similar except that they usually hang flat when down, and fold in even pleats when they are raised.

Accordion shades are stiffer shades with crisp horizontal accordion pleats. These also are raised or lowered by pulleys and cords.

Austrian and Roman shades can be taken down and laundered if made of washable fabric; otherwise they must be dry-cleaned. Accordion shades can be spot-cleaned with cleaning fluid or a cloth moistened in detergent solution; but complete cleaning is impossible.

Windowsills. Few parts of the home get dirtier faster than windowsills. They are spotted by rain and condensation dripping off the inner surfaces of the windows. And in a community with polluted air, after one day they are covered with soot and grit.

The only sure way to stop this is to close and seal all windows and air condition the house. Otherwise you must bow to the inevitable, and wipe a damp cloth across the sills frequently. Unfortunately, this treatment combined with the subtly corrosive effect of water and dirt will in time wear out any paint or clear finish that has been applied to the sills.

What to do? The best answer is simply to install windowsills that are more resistant to wear. Marble is a favorite in some areas. Or you can cover wood sills with ceramic tile, laminated plastic, or a flexible vinyl or polyester.

To protect exterior windowsills from cracking and decay, paint them every two or three years with a couple of coats of good exterior trim enamel. Fill cracks as soon as they develop with polysulfide rubber caulking compound or a paintable silicone caulk.

If an exterior sill is beyond repair, cover it as boats are covered with fiberglass fabric. Clean the sill thoroughly. Cut a piece of fiberglass to cover all surfaces of the sill and work polyester resin into it well. Then brush additional resin on the sill and smooth the fiberglass carefully into this. Sand when dry. Then brush on one or two additional coats of resin. You can apply paint, if you wish, after the resin has had several days to dry.

Wok. Woks are shallow, round-bottomed pans originated in the Orient for fast-cooking of meats and vegetables, usually in a small amount of oil. The best pans are made of heavy, rolled steel which should be seasoned in the oven with salad oil before they are put into regular use. The 14-inch size is generally the most useful.

Electric woks are also available.

Wood.

Types of wood. There are hardwoods and softwoods. The former include oak, maple, birch, mahogany; the latter, pine, fir, spruce, and woods from other evergreen trees.

The best hardwood lumber of board thickness is classified A Finish (virtually free of defects) and B Finish (with a few defects). Both grades are suitable for transparent finishes; other grades, as a rule, are not.

Although there are many differences between hardwoods, making one especially suitable for this and another especially suitable for that, the chances are that these do not concern you greatly. If you are like most home owners, your main reason for using a hardwood is because you like its color and texture, and you will select it accordingly.

With some exceptions, however, all softwoods have pretty much the same appearance, and they are more likely to be painted than stained. Consequently, when buying lumber, you should think first about the attributes of the various woods.

White pine is almost universally the first choice for interior work. It is attractive, light, strong, very resistant to splitting, and easy to work with.

For general outdoor work, there is little difference between spruce, hemlock, and white fir. All are reasonably easy to work with and take finishes well. Douglas fir is also excellent although it is a little harder and heavier and more difficult to work with.

Cypress and redwood are outstanding if you need a wood with maximum resistance to decay. Cypress is heavier and less attractive but has greater resistance to splitting. Redwood is such a beautiful wood that it is widely used indoors and out mainly for its effect. Painting it is almost a criminal act.

A cardinal rule in buying softwoods is never to buy a better grade than the job calls for. To do otherwise is a waste of money.

Softwood lumber starts with No. 1 Clear (sometimes referred to as A Select)—free of defects; No. 2 Clear (or B Select)—just a shade below No. 1; C Select—small imperfections usually on one side; D Select—small imperfections on both sides. These top grades are followed by the utility grades starting with No. 1 Common and grading down to No. 5 Common. No. 1 and No. 2 have knotholes and other defects but they are quite good enough for painted paneling, furniture, and the like and also for knotty pine paneling. You might use No. 3 for rough shelves in the basement, but that's about as far down the list as you're likely to go.

Any lumber you buy should have been air-dried or kiln-dried—it doesn't matter which. Never buy green lumber, especially if it is damp or oozing sap. And watch out for pieces that are warped.

Obviously, the best way to buy lumber once you know which wood and which grade you need is to pick out the boards yourself.

Lumber sizes. One of the confusing things about lumber is the way it is sized.

One inch is the standard thickness for boards (although you can get thinner and thicker boards). So when the amateur handyman asks for a 6-inch board, he expects he will be given a board 1 inch thick and 6 inches wide. Imagine his surprise when he finds the board actually measures only 25/32 inch thick by 5 5/8 inches wide. What's happened, he wonders.

The explanation is simple: The board *was* 1 by 6 inches as it was originally cut from a log, but it was so rough no one would have wanted it. So it was put into a planing mill, where a fraction of an inch was taken off all sides.

The actual size of all finished lumber is less than its nominal size: For example, a 4-inch board is actually 3 5/8 inches; 8-inch, 7½ inches; 12-inch, 11½ inches. A 2-by-4 is 1 5/8 by 3 5/8 inches; a 2-by-8, 1 5/8 by 7½ inches.

Milled lumber. Also called millwork, this is lumber that has been trimmed to a special shape. Tongue-and-groove boards are milled lumber. So are clapboards, half-rounds, quarter-rounds, lattice strips, and many other simple and fancy pieces of wood.

There are a great many standard mill-work patterns that lumber yards stock or which they may be able to secure for you. But although patterns are kept in the pattern books, many have been allowed to lapse. As a result, if you try to buy a molding or cornice board to match something in an old house, you may not find it in stock. For a price, however, you can have it made for you. You can also have millwork made to new designs.

Wood preservatives. A wood preservative is an oil- or water-based liquid used to make lumber more resistant to decay and termites. The preservative may be applied under pressure at a mill; or you can apply it by brushing, spraying, or dipping at home. The wood most often treated is the common softwood lumber that goes into the structure of the house; but any wood that is in contacct with the ground—fence posts, for example—should also be treated.

Government tests indicate that pressure-treated wood outlasts even redwood and cypress. The life of wood treated in other ways, however, is extended only a few years. It's obvious, then, that if you are constructing anything that seems likely to rot, you would be smart to buy pressure-treated lumber, expensive as it is. If you then cut or drill any of the lumber, you should slather additional preservative on the cut surfaces.

Oil-based creosote and pentachlorophenol are the best preservatives for unfinished wood used outdoors. On wood that is to be painted or stained or that is used indoors, use a water-based preservative.

How to work with wood. Sawing. Always saw wood with the good face up. Support the wood well and hold it tight. Use clamps if necessary or even nail it down: the holes are easy to fill. To keep from splintering the wood badly, hold the piece to be cut off when you have cut almost all the way through.

Smoothing. For how to plane, see *Tools, Workshop.* For how to sand, see *Abrasives.* End cuts of softwood are often very rough and require a great deal of sanding. If you get tired of the work, smear water putty on the end to fill all pores. Then sand smooth when this dries.

Nailing. Many woods split readily when boards are nailed near the end. They include yellow pine, hemlock, oak, maple, hickory, and cherry. But individual boards of other kinds of wood may split easily, too. One way you can sometimes prevent splitting is to blunt the ends of nails with your hammer before driving them in. A much more reliable way is to drill holes slightly smaller than the nails almost through the boards.

If a board is slightly twisted or bent, driving nails through it at different angles will help to prevent it from springing loose.

There are three named nailing methods: (1) face-nailing, in which the nail is driven through the face, or surface, of a board; (2) toenailing, in which the nail is driven through one board into another at an angle; (3) clinch-nailing, in which a nail is driven all the way through two pieces of wood and the point is then bent over to keep the nail from loosening.

On rough work and on lumber that is hidden from view, drive nails all the way in with your hammer. If you dimple the surface, no matter. On exposed wood, however, drive the nail heads to within about 1/8 inch of the surface; then use a nailset to drive them the rest of the way. On most work, the nail heads should be countersunk—driven about 1/16 to 1/8 inch beneath the surface—and covered with spackle or putty.

Screwing. Use wood screws. If the wood is very soft and the screw is short, punch a small starting hole with an awl, icepick, or a nail; then sink the screw with a screwdriver. But in hardwoods or if the screw is long, you will make the work much easier for yourself by drilling a hole slightly smaller and shallower than the screw.

As a rule, screw heads can be countersunk in very soft wood simply by putting a little extra weight on your screwdriver. If this proves difficult, put a countersink bit in a hand brace and drill a hole slightly wider than the screw head.

Screws, of course, hold better in wood than nails—even nails with ring-grooved shanks. But don't count too heavily on them when driven into the end grain.

Bolting. Bolts are used when you want to make certain that two overlapping pieces of wood do not come apart. Just drill a hole the size of the bolt through both pieces, insert the bolt, and attach the nut. In softwood, if you screw the nut and bolt tight enough, the heads will sink into the wood and stay put. If you want to protect the wood, however, or if the wood is very hard, insert a flat metal washer under the head of the bolt and another under the nut. A lock washer should be inserted between the nut and flat washer.

Gluing. If you don't need the great strength of epoxy, use white wood glue for wood not exposed to moisture; waterproof resorcinol glue for wood that is. (For how to glue, see *Gluing.*)

Glue alone makes a strong joint; and the strength of the joint increases with the size of the glued surfaces and the smoothness of the surfaces. (If wood is rough or porous, glue sinks into the voids so it cannot make contact with the opposing surface.) But in some situations, a nailed or screwed joint is stronger.

The ideal joint is made with glue plus nails or screws.

Simple ways to join wood. Butt joints. These are very easy to make by butting the end of one piece of wood against the side of another. The end must be cut square. You can then fasten the pieces together by driving nails or screws through the side piece into the end of the other piece. Or you can secure the pieces by toenailing. Or you can drive wiggle nails across the outside edges of the joint.

Unfortunately, butt joints made in these ways are not very strong. They can, however, be reinforced by nailing, screwing, or gluing a block of wood into the corner between the two joined pieces. Or you can screw on mending plates in the ways pictured.

It is rarely advisable to try butting two pieces of wood end to end. The joint simply is not strong enough. True, it can be strengthened with steel mending plates or cleats as shown; but it still leaves much to be desired.

Miter joints. These are usually corner joints made by beveling the ends of two pieces of wood in a miter box. (See *Tools, Workshop.*) The pieces are then held together by nails or screws driven from one into the other or by wiggle nails driven across the joint. Adding glue is an excellent idea.

You can reinforce a miter joint with an iron corner brace or angle iron.

Dado joint. This is stronger than a butt joint and requires no reinforcement. It can be used to form a corner joint, but is mainly used to join the end of one piece of wood to the middle of another.

The dado itself is a notch cut in the side piece of wood with a saw and chisel. The end piece that is fitted into this is called the housed member. It is held tight with glue, or with nails or screws driven through the back of the dado.

Lapped joint. If you lap one piece of wood over another and nail the two together, you form a lapped joint. It isn't pretty, and it isn't strong unless you use bolts, so it is not a joint you will use very often.

But if you cut some of the wood away from both pieces so they are parallel and the joint is flat, you improve both the appearance and the strength of the joint. Several kinds of lapped joints are illustrated.

365

MAKING JOINTS

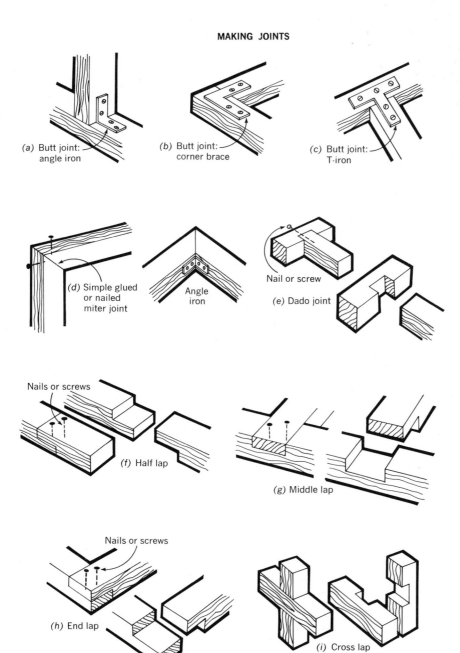

(a) Butt joint: angle iron

(b) Butt joint: corner brace

(c) Butt joint: T-iron

(d) Simple glued or nailed miter joint

Angle iron

Nail or screw

(e) Dado joint

Nails or screws

(f) Half lap

(g) Middle lap

Nails or screws

(h) End lap

(i) Cross lap

How to finish wood. For how to apply a transparent finish, see *Furniture, Wood.* If painting, smooth the wood with sandpaper. Prime knots in softwood with WP-578 knot sealer. Then apply a primer and one or two coats of finish paint. Use oil or alkyd paint. Latex paint can be used, however, if an oil-based primer is applied first.

How to repair damage and defects. Loose knots. Tap them all the way out, coat with glue, and replace. When the glue dries, fill the crack around the knot with plastic wood.

Board bent. Suspend it between sawhorses bent side up. Place a concrete block in the middle of the board. Check the board daily to see how the repair is progressing. Don't weight it so heavily or for so long that it bends the other way.

Unfortunately, once a board is bent, it is likely to bend again. But if it is fastened down securely along its length, you should have no further trouble.

Board cupped. A cupped board is bent longitudinally. Wet the concave side and cover it with damp rags for 24 hours in a warm room. If this doesn't do the trick, make ½-inch-deep cuts on the concave side from one end of the board to the other. They should be spaced about an inch apart. When installing the board, the convex side should be exposed. Don't try to nail the board flat all at once, because it is likely to split along one or more of the saw cuts. But if you drive the nails in deeper and deeper over a period of several weeks, the bend should disappear.

Board split. If a board has been split for a long time, you may not be able to bring the broken edges together without causing it to split further. Test for this possibility by seeing how difficult it is to push the two pieces together. If they are reluctant to give, you had better not try to make the repair.

If the split board is a loose piece of lumber, spread wax paper on a piece of plywood laid flat on the floor and lay the split section of the board on top. Nail a second board to the plywood along one side of the split board. Coat the split edges with glue. Then nail a third board along the other side of the split board, and drive thin wedges between the two. This forces the split edges together and holds them firmly while the glue dries. (Of course, if you have C clamps large enough to span the split board, you don't have to go through all this trouble of wedging.)

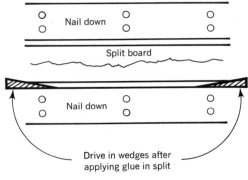

REPAIRING SPLIT BOARDS

If the split board is a panel in a wall, making it impossible to put any pressure on the sides, there is nothing you can do about the split short of filling it. However, if you can get at one edge—for example, the bottom edge of a clapboard—you can glue the split edges, nail a board along the open edge, and drive wedges between the two.

Wood rotten. Chisel out the decayed area, preferably in rectangular shape. Then shape a piece of sound wood to fit, glue in place, and fill the cracks around it with water putty or plastic wood. The alternative is to fill the hole gradually with water putty.

Holes, gouges, checks, etc. If the wood is bare, fill the holes with water putty or plastic wood. If the wood is painted, apply spackle (the other fillers are just as good but spackle is easier to handle). If the wood has a transparent finish, you'll probably be smart to leave minor holes alone except for touching up with a little stain and finish. But if it is a large hole, use plastic wood that is stained to match the finish.

An alternative to plastic wood is a shellac stick that matches the finish. Heat a little spatula or an old steel knife blade on an electric range element or over an alcohol flame, hold it against the shellac stick, and drip the melting shellac into the hole. Keep smoothing it down with the heated spatula until it is level with the surrounding surface. Finish with fine sandpaper or steel wool.

Break in an ornamental molding. Fill with water putty and shape with your fingers. When it begins to stiffen, shape and smooth it further with a small spatula, screwdriver, or other tool. Sand when dry.

Dents. In painted wood, just fill the dent with spackle. If wood has a transparent finish, cover the dent with a damp cloth. Turn a bottle cap upside down on top and heat it with a laundry iron. If the dent does not come out after several tries, sand off the finish and try again.

Burns. Scratch out the worst of the charred wood with a knife; remove the rest by sanding. Wash with naphtha. Then apply stain and finish.

Burns in painted wood are filled with spackle.

Scratches. If in bare wood, sand with the grain. If in shellac, rub with alcohol; then if a slight scratch remains, brush on fresh shellac mixed 50-50 with alcohol.

If scratches are in a gym-seal finish, remove wax from the surface and brush on fresh gym seal. When dry, remove the high gloss with fine steel wool.

Scratches in lacquer can usually be obliterated by rubbing with lacquer thinner. Those in varnish are almost hopeless because the only solvent for hardened varnish is varnish remover and because you can't patch varnish so that the patch is invisible. About all you can do is to try to make the scratch as inconspicuous as possible by rubbing it with the meat of an oily nut, a little paste wax, or a furniture wax stick.

Varnished surface cracked. This is a fairly common problem on old furniture and woodwork. The finish looks something like smooth alligator skin. Chances are that it can be fixed only by removing it completely. But before going to that trouble, test the following possible cure on a small area:

Mix a little light-duty laundry soap in 1 quart warm water and add 1 tablespoon turpentine and 3 tablespoons linseed oil. Scrub the surface thoroughly with this; rinse it off and allow it to dry. Then dip a rag in linseed oil or motor oil, dip it lightly in powdered pumice stone, and rub the surface without too much pressure. Clean with naphtha and apply paste wax.

How to take care of wood. Don't do anything to bare wood until it becomes dirty. Some dirt can then be removed with an eraser or wallpaper dough cleaner. Stubborn soil must be removed by light sanding or steel-wooling.

Unfinished wood siding that is allowed to weather gradually turns a silvery gray, but the color is usually not uniform. Hosing down the sides of the house once or twice a year hastens the weathering process and contributes to uniformity. It is also necessary to remove accumulated dirt.

Painted wood and wood with a hard transparent finish can be cleaned with a cloth dampened in detergent solution if the paint film is sound. Rinse well and dry. Note, however, that water is not good for wood because it raises the grain and may make stains. So don't use it on any wood, such as a floor, that is likely to have a scratched finish. Clean with white appliance wax instead. Naphtha and turpentine can also be used.

Wood with a natural finish should be polished or waxed to protect it and to give it a warm glow. How often this should be done depends on how much wear the wood gets. Table tops might need a new application of wax every month; paneled walls probably need to be waxed or polished only once every year or two.

How to remove stains. If the stains are in the wood itself, you are probably out of luck. Try rubbing with a little naphtha. Then try sanding lightly. If you are desperate, you can then try bleaching. But don't count on anything.

If wood is painted, you can remove some stains with detergent solution; others with white appliance wax. Try both: they are easy. Except for the stains noted below, all stains that remain should be sanded. Then apply a new coat of paint.

If stains are caused by knots bleeding through the paint, cover them with shellac or aluminum paint. Then repaint. If stains continue to appear, you must remove all the finish down to the wood and prime the knots with WP-578 knot sealer.

For how to handle mildew stains, see *Mildew.*

Stains on wood with transparent finishes are handled in the following manner:

White water stains. Rub with cigarette ashes and vegetable oil.

Heat marks. In order, try rubbing with camphorated oil; fine steel wool; a rag dipped in vegetable oil and then in rotten-stone. Don't go further than the method that works.

Alcohol spots. Rub with a rag dipped in vegetable oil and then in rottenstone.

Heel marks, crayon, grease, tar, shoe polish, food stains. Rub with white appliance wax.

Paint and nail polish. Scrape off very carefully with a knife or razor blade. Clean lightly with fine steel wool. Then apply wax.

Candle wax. Scrape off with a knife and clean with naphtha or cleaning fluid.

Woodenware. Bowls, spoons, and other pieces made of wood should never be put into the dishwasher because the harsh detergent and high heat will combine to bleach and roughen the wood. Always wash such pieces by hand.

Salad bowls that have not been given a finish may simply be wiped out with paper towels after use—thus the bowls will retain the flavor left by salad dressing. But since this flavor will in time become rank, it is a better idea to rinse the bowls with clear water after wiping them.

Bad scars in woodenware can be filled with plastic wood. Small scratches are removed with sandpaper.

If woodenware is broken, repair it with epoxy glue. This withstands hard usage and water better than the white wood glue that is normally used to repair wood.

Wood Fasteners. Nails are the most common type of wood fastener; screws, the next. (See entries for both.) Others follow:

Nuts and bolts. See *Metal Fasteners.*

Brads. Small finishing nails.

Tacks. Different types are known by different names, but there is nothing to be gained by belaboring the point. For most purposes, you can use one kind of tack interchangeably with another.

Tacks are available in steel, copper, and aluminum. They range from 3/16 inch in length (No. 1 size) to 7/8 inch (No. 18 size). Half-inch tacks—a good average—are No. 6 size.

Staples. The largest staples are made of galvanized steel and are used for anchoring fence wire. In the household tool kit, the staples most often found are small insulated staples used for anchoring extension cords. Medium-size staples driven by staple guns are extremely useful for tacking down upholstery fabric, screen wire, posters, etc.

Wiggle nails. More properly called corrugated fasteners, these look like a miniature piece of corrugated roofing that has been beveled at one side to form sharp teeth. They come in various sizes up to about an inch wide and are used primarily in mitered joints and for joining boards side to side.

Skotch fasteners are also used mainly in mitered joints. They are rather wide, flat metal strips with sharp teeth pointing down at the corners.

Chevron fasteners, also used in mitered joints, are L-shaped strips, smooth on the top edge and with teeth along the bottom edge.

Wood Fillers. The only material commonly known as a wood filler is a semi-thick paste that is brushed on wood like paint. It is used to fill the pores in open-pored woods such as oak. It is also occasionally used to fill and smooth the edges and ends of boards. For how to use it, see *Furniture, Wood.*

Various other materials are used to fill large holes, cracks, and dents in wood. See *Putty; Plastic Wood;* and *Spackle.*

Shellac sticks are also used to fill large

holes in furniture and woodwork with a transparent finish. See *Wood*.

Wood Preservatives. See *Wood*.

Woodwork. Woodwork is a broad word encompassing most of the wood surfaces inside the house—paneled walls, doors, windows, mantels, baseboards, trim, cornices, balusters, etc. Flooring, ceilings, and cabinets are the most important wood surfaces that do not count as woodwork.

Woodwork receives heavy wear and considerable abuse in homes because in many cases it projects out from the walls and thus is in the line of traffic. Consequently, it generally needs a tough, washable finish such as semi-gloss or gloss paint or urethane varnish. Wall paneling, however, is often coated with nothing more than stain-wax.

Like all interior surfaces, woodwork needs occasional dusting; but mainly it needs to be sponged to remove soil, grease, wax, and fingermarks. For this, use water, detergent solution, or white appliance wax.

Floor wax that has been slopped on baseboards should be removed at once with a damp cloth if the wax is water-based or with naphtha or turpentine if it is solvent-based. Wax that has been allowed to harden requires hard scrubbing with naphtha.

Wool. Next to cotton, wool is our most important natural clothing fiber and—despite the advent of new synthetics—is still one of the most important carpet fibers. It has beauty, durability, resilience; great warmth and good resistance to fire. But from the homemaker's standpoint, it also has several annoying weaknesses. For one thing, it picks up soil quite easily. It loses strength when wet and must therefore be handled carefully when laundered. It shrinks badly. And it is attacked by moths.

Dry-cleaning wool is less troublesome than laundering; but many woolen articles may be laundered. Use tepid water—not over 100 degrees—and a light-duty or cold-water detergent. Wash for only a few minutes with gentle agitator action. If

bleaching is necessary, use only hydrogen peroxide or sodium perborate.

Many coarse woolens can be dried in a dryer at low heat but should be removed while damp and blocked to original shape. It is safer to dry these articles in the air, however; and all fine woolens must be dried this way. If the articles have been hand-washed, just squeeze the water out of them; don't wring. Then put the articles on stretchers or lay them on a towel and carefully pull them into shape.

To press woolens, set your iron at medium heat. A steam iron gives faster and better results than a dry iron. Press on the wrong side or cover with an ironing cloth.

For how to clean wool rugs, see *Rugs*.

Workbench. See *Tools, Workshop*.

Worsted. A hard, durable wool fabric used in clothing. It should be dry-cleaned.

Wrenches. See *Tools, Workshop*.

Wrought Iron. Wrought iron is an almost pure form of iron. It is tough and malleable and is used—though not so much today—in such things as ornamental ironwork, chains, bolts, and pipe.

Unlike cast iron, wrought iron is very resistant to rusting. If protection seems indicated, apply a rust-inhibiting primer and any good exterior paint.

If a wrought-iron article is broken, take it to a welder for repair. You can fill pitted areas with plastic steel.

Yardsticks. A yardstick is a more or less essential household tool for measuring rather large objects such as rooms, rugs, and draperies. It is, however, less useful than a 6-foot rule simply because it is only half as long.

In days gone by, yardsticks were made of maple and other hardwoods, frequently edged with brass, and they could be expected to last for years. But today, they are generally made of cheap softwood which readily snaps in two. This is a small loss, because yardsticks are very inexpensive. Nevertheless, it is a good idea to drill a hole in one end, loop a string through this, and hang the stick in a closet when it is not in use.

Yellowing. Many materials in time turn yellow because of exposure to sun, lack of sun, exposure to soil, wear, and for various inexplicable reasons. Unfortunately, the problem is frequently difficult, if not impossible, to correct.

For example, when ivory turns yellow with age, the only thing you can do about it is to wash it with alcohol and expose it to the sun; but even then, the ivory may not return to its original color.

Many paints and clear finishes (especially varnish) also turn yellow; and in this case, there is nothing whatever to be done. This is one of the principal reasons why you should not use a hard finish, such as lacquer, on resilient floors: when it yellows, the only way to restore the color of the floor is to remove the lacquer completely; and this can't be done without damaging the flooring. Many floor waxes also turn yellow; but they can be removed fairly easily with a prepared floor cleaner or strong ammonia solution.

Happily, the situation in regard to fabrics is somewhat better. True, you cannot as a rule bleach fabrics that have been scorched or stored for many years. But other yellowing problems can usually be solved by following the directions at *Laundering* under "Reconditioning clothes."

Yellow Jackets. Another name for several kinds of wasp. See *Pest Control—Bees, hornets, wasps.*

Zinc. A hard, bluish-white metal which can be rolled into sheets that were once used to cover kitchen counters. The material can be cleaned with detergent solution. If tarnished, scrub it with vinegar and water.

Zinc is most commonly used today as a coating on steel to protect it from rusting. The material is called galvanized iron or galvanized steel. See *Steel.*

Zinc is also used as a pigment in certain paints. Zinc chromate primer is the best paint for use as a base coat on aluminum. Zinc dust primer is used on galvanized steel.

Zippers. Most zippers are metal; some are made of plastic. When washing and ironing garments including either type, close the zipper. When putting garments through a wringer, flatten the zipper and put it through straight. A metal zipper should be covered on both sides so it won't damage the wringer rolls. Do not touch a hot, dry iron to a plastic zipper. Use a pressing cloth and steam.

To improve the operation of a metal zipper that works sluggishly, rub a cake of paraffin lightly over the teeth.

If a garment is caught in a metal zipper, be gentle and patient. You can free it only by careful, gradual pulling and twisting. A plastic zipper is much easier to handle. Fold it lengthwise and pull the teeth apart at the garment. Then open the zipper all the way and zip it up again.

If a metal zipper becomes jammed, you may be able to fix it with a special zipper-repair kit from a variety store; but don't count on it. You would be better off having a zipper-repair service take over.

If a metal zipper won't work because the teeth are missing or bent, replace it.